MODERN STUDIES IN PROPERTY LAW: VOLUME 8

This book contains a collection of peer-reviewed papers presented at the Tenth Biennial Modern Studies in Property Law Conference held at the University of Liverpool in April 2014. It is the eighth volume to be published under the name of the Conference. The Conference and its published proceedings have become an established forum for property lawyers from around the world to showcase current research in the discipline. This collection reflects the diversity and contemporary relevance of modern research in property law. Incorporating a keynote address by Sir John Mummery, retired Lord Justice of Appeal, on 'Property in the Information Age', a number of chapters consider the contribution of property law to issues central to the human condition; the home, health and death. Other papers illustrate an enduring need to question and explore fundamental concepts of the subject as well as to consider the challenges of reforming the law. Collectively the chapters demonstrate the vibrancy and importance of property law in dealing with modern concerns across the common law world.

Previous volumes in this series:

Modern Studies in Property Law: Volume 1
Edited by Elizabeth Cooke

Modern Studies in Property Law: Volume 2
Edited by Elizabeth Cooke

Modern Studies in Property Law: Volume 3
Edited by Elizabeth Cooke

Modern Studies in Property Law: Volume 4
Edited by Elizabeth Cooke

Modern Studies in Property Law: Volume 5
Edited by Martin Dixon

Modern Studies in Property Law: Volume 5
Edited by Susan Bright

Modern Studies in Property Law: Volume 6
Edited by Susan Bright

Modern Studies in Property Law: Volume 7
Edited by Nicholas Hopkins

Modern Studies in Property Law

Volume 8

Edited by

WARREN BARR

·HART·
PUBLISHING
OXFORD AND PORTLAND, OREGON
2015

Published in the United Kingdom by Hart Publishing Ltd
16C Worcester Place, Oxford, OX1 2JW
Telephone: +44 (0)1865 517530
Fax: +44 (0)1865 510710
E-mail: mail@hartpub.co.uk
Website: http://www.hartpub.co.uk

Published in North America (US and Canada) by
Hart Publishing
c/o International Specialized Book Services
920 NE 58th Avenue, Suite 300
Portland, OR 97213-3786
USA
Tel: +1 503 287 3093 or toll-free: (1) 800 944 6190
Fax: +1 503 280 8832
E-mail: orders@isbs.com
Website: http://www.isbs.com

Hart Publishing is an imprint of Bloomsbury Publishing plc.

British Library Cataloguing in Publication Data
Data Available

ISBN: 978-1-84946-622-6

Typeset by Compuscript Ltd, Shannon
Printed and bound in Great Britain by
CPI Group (UK) Ltd, Croydon CR0 4YY

Preface

In April 2014, the Tenth Biennial Conference on Property Law was held at the University of Liverpool; the first time the Conference has been hosted in the North of England. I would like to thank the members of the Conference Editorial Board for entrusting the Conference to me, and to Liverpool. Sited at the Mersey Maritime Museum on the scenic Albert Dock, the Conference proceedings retained their international flavour and the unique mix of conviviality, scholarly rigour and fascinating academic debate that has been a hallmark of every Conference since its origins at the University of Reading in 1996.

The Conference saw a welcome return of the Postgraduate Research Stream, inaugurated at the Ninth Conference at the University of Southampton, which took place on the final day and demonstrated that the future of the property law research is in very safe hands. New this year was the introduction of 'Work in Progress' sessions for academics to discuss and work through new ideas, short of presenting a full paper. These sessions were very well attended and received, and it is hoped will become a permanent feature of the Conference going forward.

This volume, the eighth such edited collection, presents a wide spectrum of topics across the length and breadth of property law discourse. No theme for the Conference was suggested, but the papers have usefully grouped themselves into several topics with numerous, interlinking themes. Every paper in this volume has been subject to peer review, and a very real debt of gratitude is owed to those anonymous referees who have given freely of their time and attention, and have enhanced the quality of the volume in consequence. To introduce these papers, I can do no better than deliberately 'borrow' words from the editor of the previous volume, Professor Nicolas Hopkins, who put is so well: 'Collectively, the contributions to this volume demonstrate the breadth, depth and variety of modern property law scholarship'. Each chapter deserves to be read in its entirety, and what follows is not a complete description of the contents of this volume, but instead just enough to whet the academic appetite as to the coverage of topics by the various authors.

This volume opens with the text of the keynote address, given by Sir John Mummery. This fascinating speech, reproduced here with only minor amendments and additions for publication, explores the concept of property in information; a key driver of modern commerce and communications. It suggests a cautious approach to recognising property in information, and sets the tone for the other two contributions in this section, which deal with reform and legal process. Andrew Stevens reflects broadly on the impact of the Scottish Law Commission on Property Law, while John Mee draws out cautionary tales for would-be reformers in the narrower, but very important, reforms of the law of prescription in Ireland.

Part II contains essays relating to the planning law in England and Wales. Charles Mynors calls for a (much needed) simplification of the planning processes and presents an important overview of the difficulties with the current systems.

Barbara Boguz considers the balance between societal and economic interests in land regulation, and suggests that the state (and law) is more concerned with the former, not the latter, as issues such as regulating open spaces tend to fall primarily to private citizens. Finally in this section, Adam Barker considers whether there is any sound reason to allow some licensees not in actual possession of land to bring actions for recovery of land, re-investigating the decision in *Manchester Airport v Dutton* [2000] 1 QB 133 and its impact for developers of land who are often contractual licensees themselves.

Adding an international flavour, Part III considers property law and provision of property on death. Heather Conway's paper introduces this section, and investigates claims made by financially independent children to contest distribution of property by will or intestacy in England and Wales and Northern Ireland. Fiona Burns considers the use of statutory wills in England and Australia in dealing with the property of the mentally incapacitated, who otherwise would be unable to make wills for themselves. Siôn Hudson and Brian Sloan explore the limits of mutual wills in England and Wales in informal care situations and the fetters on testamentary freedom involved. Caryl Yzenbard brings this section to a close with a consideration of the distribution of property on intestacy in the United States.

Part IV, loosely termed property and ownership, draws together discourse across some baseline issues of property law from different perspectives. Chris Bevan considers the role of the 'home' in modern property law, particularly after the two key decisions of the English Supreme Court in *Stack v Dowden* [2007] 2 AC 432 and *Jones v Kernott* [2012] 1 AC 776. Alison Clarke considers how communal land and resource rights should be accommodated within systems which record land rights on a register; a truly international exploration, but with a particular emphasis on sub-Saharan Africa. Jill Morgan conducts a comparative study of the US and UK approaches to recognising property ownership in mineral rights such as carbon capture and storage; essential developments for environmental storage of dangerous substances and gases. Chris Willmore investigates whether leasehold structures, particularly discontinuous leases, can be repurposed to enable voluntary sector partnerships and collaboration. Refreshing perspectives on the norm continue as Graham Ferris reflects on formalities through the lens of 'speech acts', which it is agued may add clarity to analysis of some legal problems while Junita Roche conducts an exploration of the issues of deemed tenancies for life raised by the UK Supreme Court in *Mexfield v Berrisford* [2012] 1 AC 955 by an historical analysis of what the author terms 'constitutional land law' and looks to the very roots of the foundation of our system in so doing.

Last by but no means least, the final part of this volume considers specific issues relating to title. In turn, Simon Cooper considers the important issue of reliability of registered title, thought to be a cornerstone of the English system; while Lu Xu builds on research into the English version of commonhold, a system that has failed to gain much traction in the years since its introduction. Hanri Mostert and Leon Verstappen close this section, and the book, with an international dimension, suggesting that two apparently divergent law systems seem to be converging in their approaches to dealing with problems imposed by adherence to the *'numerus clausus'* principle; namely rigidity and uncertainty.

I would like to extend my thanks to all contributors, both to the Conference and this volume. The Biennial Conferences continue to go from strength to strength, thanks to the energy and hard work of all those involved. I would like to thank Richard Hart and his team at Bloomsbury Publishing, for their continued support through the publication of this edited collection.

On a personal note, I would like to thank Sir John Mummery for agreeing to give the keynote speech at the Conference, and for his continued support of the work of the Charity Law and Policy Unit. At Liverpool Law School, I would like to thank Rachel Barrett, Management Services Team and Charlotte Hood-Fredriksen, one of my current PhD students, for handling the administrative burden of the organisation and smooth running of the whole Conference with the utmost efficiency and good humour. I am extremely grateful to Dr John Picton, Lecturer in Law for his stewardship of the PGR Stream of the Conference. Special thanks go to my friend and colleague, Professor Debra Morris, for her invaluable help and support throughout this and other academic endeavours. Liverpool played host to an International Charity Law Symposium under Professor Morris' leadership, directly after the Property Conference, the outputs of which can be found in a special issue of the *Charity Law and Practice Review*. Thanks also to Dr Karen Atkinson, Research Associate to the Charity Law and Policy Unit for her invaluable assistance in the production of this manuscript.

I am sure you, the reader, will agree that the contents of this volume collectively demonstrate that property law research is in an extremely rude state of health and I am already looking forward to the Eleventh Modern Studies in Property Law Conference, which will take place at the Queen's University of Belfast in 2016.

Warren Barr
Professor of Law, Charity Law and Policy Unit, University of Liverpool
January 2015

Table of Contents

Part I

Law Reform and Property Law

1

Property in the Information Age

SIR JOHN MUMMERY*

I. INTRODUCTION

Does property exist in the content of an email? If it does, who owns it?

In *Fairstar Heavy Transport NV v Adkins*[1] the parties asked the High Court to rule on whether Fairstar had a proprietary claim to the content of business-related emails. The emails were held on a personal computer belonging to their chief executive, Mr Adkins. As he refused access, Fairstar applied to the court for orders compelling him to give access and allow inspection.

The judge concluded that Fairstar had no proprietary interest as claimed by them. Their application for access failed, as the content was information and there is no property in information. Fairstar did not claim confidentiality or copyright or any other intellectual property right in the content.

On Fairstar's appeal the ground of debate shifted. The Court of Appeal concluded that the parties had not formulated the relevant issue for decision by the judge. The judgments on the appeal side-stepped the novel property claim as a point on which it was unnecessary for the court to reach a decision. Instead the appeal was allowed on the basis of well-established agency principles entitling Fairstar to orders for preservation, access and inspection of the emails held by Mr Adkins in his capacity as their agent.

Silence on the property claim is disappointing for legal 'completists', who like a decision from the court on every point. The true function of the courts is to decide the outcome of proceedings for valid reasons set out in a judgment. It is not good judicial practice to volunteer legal opinions on every point raised in a case, certainly not if a decision on the merits can be reached without deciding every point canvassed.

Technology has transformed the communications world. There is pressure on the courts to keep pace with the changes. This is not always possible without legislation. Decisions by courts on novel claims, such as the assertion of property in the content of emails, must be made in a principled way. The difficulty with Fairstar's common law claim to ownership of information is in squaring it with orthodox principles of property law. If information is not property and cannot be owned at common law, only Parliament can provide that kind of protection in legislation, as it has done over the centuries in the case of intellectual property.

---

* Retired Lord Justice of the Court of Appeal.
[1] *Fairstar Heavy Transport NV v Adkins* [2013] EWCA Civ 886.

The interesting questions raised by Fairstar's proprietary claim are these. What is the rationale for treating intangible creations of the human mind as property? What are the essential legal characteristics of property and ownership?

In this chapter I will outline the key factors and basic principles involved in the classification of property and the particular problems presented in attempting to classify information as property.

II. PROPERTY CLAIM

Facts, data, news, ideas and other kinds of information certainly have commercial, as well as educational and intellectual, value. In the expanding knowledge economy 'information assets', as they are sometimes called, can secure business investment in developing global markets for products and services. An income stream from the territorial licensing of data of all kinds can be substantial. The collection, storage, analysis, sharing and licensing of data of every description is big business: transactional data, customer and client records, personal details, medical records (NHS Care Data), credit information and so on. The data is often in a continuous state of flux. That differentiates it from most other creations of the human mind currently protected as property: patent law, which protects inventions, and copyright law, which protects works, covers material identified in a form that is fixed and falls within the statutory criteria for that protection.

As in the case of intellectual property, money, skill and time are invested in the collection, storage, analysis, licensing and sharing of information. The aim is to reap reward from improving existing services, developing new products and services and targeting marketing opportunities more effectively. Property protection for information would give it security and the certainties of title, duration and enforceability that help to attract investment.

The advances in communicating, storing, retrieving and processing information efficiently, world-wide and in an instant are rapidly overtaking traditional forms of communication. But cyberspace communications give rise to practical problems in devising effective legal protection. National legal systems have territorial limits. Similar problems were encountered in the development of intellectual property. Hence the long drawn-out process of negotiating international treaties and conventions and working towards progressive harmonisation of intellectual property laws.

A similar process would be involved in attempting to provide greater legal protection for information than that available under existing law. One thing is certain: the calls for information protection are unlikely to diminish. The virtual world is inhabited by many for part of every day. Its effects are universal. The courts and Parliament must do the best they can to provide satisfactory solutions where there is a consensus that more legal protection for certain sorts of information is justified.

III. PROPERTY IN COMMUNICATIONS

The application of property law principles to traditional channels of communicating information are clear. They are a starting point for dealing with the problems of the new information technology.

The physical sheets of paper used in writing a letter are initially the property of the person who purchased the paper. When a letter is sent the sheets of paper on which it is written become the property of the addressee who receives the letter.

Property in the written composition contained in the letter is treated differently. That property is owned by the person who composes the letter. Its author selects and arranges the order of the words used to communicate information, facts, feelings, ideas and so on.

Thus, in property terms, there is a divide: the addressee receiving a letter becomes the owner of the paper, but not of the copyright in the written work, which is retained by the author of the letter.

Turning from the physical and literary form of the letter to the substance of the information communicated in it (ie ideas, facts, thoughts, knowledge and so on) that is not normally regarded as property or as something owned at all, either by the sender or by the recipient of the letter. That does not mean that the information in the letter can be used or disclosed as the recipient wishes. The information conveyed is subject to the law of obligations that is obligations enforceable against another party as a personal or relational matter rather than on the basis of proprietary rights enforceable against everyone.

Thus, if the exchange of letters is in the context of a binding contract, such as employment or agency, or evidences a legally recognised relationship of some kind, such as would arise from a reasonable expectation of confidentiality, there may exist an express or an implied obligation protecting the confidentiality of the information passing between them from being either disclosed or used for a purpose that departs from the purpose for which the information was communicated.

Even in the absence of a binding contract, information can be protected by an equitable duty of confidentiality arising from the relationship between the parties, the nature of the information imparted and the particular circumstances in which and the purpose for which the information was communicated. Equity has developed the law of confidential information in a similar fashion to its development of the law of trusts, that is by reference to considerations affecting the conscience of the recipient entrusted with it. That obligation can be enforced against the initial recipient of the information and also by injunction against a third party receiving the information with notice of its confidential nature and the circumstances in which it was communicated.

Is the personal obligation approach to the legal protection of contractual and confidential information adequate for the knowledge economy? If not, does the 'property' label fit information, as conveyed in the content of an email?

The systematic analysis of legal concepts involves addressing the nature of the rights claimed, such as whether they are proprietary or personal.

'Property' rights relate to the ownership and control of different kinds of resources. In distinguishing between 'what's mine' and 'what's not mine' property has the quality of exclusivity that defeats the rival claims of any other person to access, use and enjoyment of that resource.

On a personal note, as a farmer's eldest son, I was brought up having an easy familiarity with property and its classification. I feel most at home with the solid security of the immovable: the farm is still there, as it has been for hundreds of years, but ownership has changed and it is farmed by one of my tenanted brothers. There were also cows and sheep, as less permanent forms of movable property, and the even more temporary annual crops of wheat, barley and oats and the fleeces shorn every summer from the backs of the Romney Marsh sheep.

Leaving the farm for legal practice I met with intangible property, as the chambers that would have me specialised in copyright, trade marks, trade secrets and confidential information. The claim to property in intangible resources is different from traditional experience on a farm of the relationship between people and things. The claim to property in information per se is different again from property in the range of carefully drafted statutory protections for patents, copyrights, trade marks and designs, which were developed in legislation designed to keep up with the rise of commerce and industry.

Lawyers usually turn to the law of obligations to find ways of protecting information assets: contracts, the equitable doctrine of trust and confidence and now the recent legal developments in the right to respect to private and family life as a way of protecting or exploiting personal information. Extensive claims are being made by celebrities, who make a living from being publicised, to ownership of themselves and of information about their personal lives, their appearance and so on. It may all have gone too far. Claims for 'informational autonomy' and 'personal space' inevitably lead to clashes with contrary claims for freedom of expression. But that is a topic for another occasion.

The claim for acceptance of property in information assets is often based on arguments that a valuable resource has been produced by the investment of work, skill, and money in its creation; and that the resulting resource can be commercially exploited like property by being licensed or sold. Information is disclosed, licensed and used under the terms of Consultancy Agreements, Know-How Licenses, Technology Assistance Agreements and Joint Venture Agreements which are similar in content to dealings familiar in the world of Intellectual property.

Why, some ask, is there not a bundle of rights in information adding up to something that is more like property than a purely personal obligation arising either from a consensual relationship or from breach of a general duty imposed by the law not to inflict unjustified loss and damage on other people?

What part, if any, does property play in the protection of information rights from infringement by wrongful disclosure and unauthorised use? The cases show that, as a general rule, property plays little or no part. Property at common law is about rights with respect to things and resources that are analogous to things. That is supplemented by the limited scope of statutory protections awarded to intangible property in the intellectual creations of the human mind, such as inventions, literature, art and music and so on.

IV. A FEW RECENT CASES

Over the years attempts have been made to persuade the courts to extend property protection to information. I am grateful to Professor David Vaver for references to a few recent cases showing how the courts continue to respond to arguments for recognition of information as property.

In *Your Response Ltd v Datateam Business Media Ltd*[2] sums were due under a contract for the management of an electronic database. The relief sought by the manager included a common law lien over the electronic database pending payment of the outstanding fees. Such a lien would entitle the manager/creditor to withhold access to the data until payment was made.

The district judge held that there could be such a lien over intangible electronic data. He said that the law needed to keep abreast of technological developments. The appeal was allowed by the Court of Appeal on the ground that a lien right was *in rem*, not *in personam* and that the data was not a *res*. I note the following points from the judgments.

In the first place, the right to withhold access to the data would not give the manager property in the data. The rights in respect of the data were contract-based. There could be no claim for conversion of intangible property, such as data.

Next, electronic data was not a kind of property that was capable of possession and of being subject to a lien. There were intellectual property rights, such as copyright and data base rights, but there was no case for treating the electronically-held information itself as property. There was a distinction between property in the physical form in which the data was recorded and rights of access to the information, which were not property.

Thirdly, to accede to a property claim in the data as information would have unintended and unjust consequences impacting on rights of priority and the claims of other creditors in an insolvency situation.

In the next case *Nautical Data International v C-Map USA Inc*[3] the Federal Court of Appeal in Canada also dealt with a claim to ownership of data. The allegations were ambiguous. The court observed that generally speaking data in the sense of mere information could not be owned as if it were property, though its confidentiality could be protected by an obligation imposed by contract. There was no principle of property law that would preclude anyone from making use of information displayed in a publicly available form.

Tucows v Renner[4] before the Court of Appeal for Ontario was a different case. It was alleged that the plaintiff made use of a domain name 'renner.com' in bad faith. The plaintiff started an action for a declaration that it had not registered the name in bad faith. The name could be used to access a web page relating to the plaintiff.

A point taken on jurisdiction turned on whether the case was 'a proceeding in respect of personal property' in Ontario. On appeal it was held that the courts in Ontario had jurisdiction, as, for the purposes of this provision, the domain name was personal property located in, and having a real and substantial connection with, Ontario. It was part of the intangible property of Tucow's business, but it was more like ordinary goodwill, which is part of the bundle of rights to assets used in a business, than mere information.

---

[2] *Your Response Ltd v Datateam Business Media Ltd* [2014] EWCA Civ 281.
[3] *Nautical Data International v C-Map USA Inc* [2013] FCA 63 [14].
[4] *Tucows v Renner* 2011 ONCA 548, (2011) 106 OR (3d) 561.

With those cases in mind I return to *Fairstar*. As already explained, the dispute was about access rights, rather than about exploitation, use or disclosure of information. The novelty was that Fairstar characterised their access rights as proprietary in nature. The parties put to the court an agreed form of question as to whether the claimants had a proprietary interest in the content of the business-related emails received and sent by Mr Adkins on his personal computer. It was unfortunate for Fairstar that their computer system was set up in such a way that those emails could not be accessed on any equipment owned by them when they formed suspicions about some of the business communications of Mr Adkins with third parties. Fairstar obtained interim ex parte orders for the safekeeping of the computer, which was within the jurisdiction, in order to preserve the emails pending a decision on their proprietary claim for access to them.

The Court of Appeal allowed the appeal on the basis that the parties had irrelevantly characterised the dispute as one that turned on the existence of property rights in the emails when it was the case that, in his capacity as agent for Fairstar, Mr Adkins was under an obligation to allow them, as his principals, to have access to emails relating to the business conducted by him while their chief executive.

V. INSTITUTION OF PROPERTY

In dealing with a novel property claim, such as that made by Fairstar, a return to first principles is advisable. What is the rationale for the institution of property? What are the characteristics of property? What kinds of resource fall within the rationale and have the defining characteristics of property?

The institution of property is very big question involving political, economic and social arrangements between people individually and collectively. They are outside the scope of this chapter, which will touch on just a few very general points about the workings of the institution of property.

First, the world is full of resources of different kinds. It is also full of human beings, who use, control, conserve and manage resources by sharing some together and by enclosing some in order to exclude other people from them. In communities resources are therefore a source of both community and individual wealth and power. Property in individuals is linked to the freedom of the individual, but, at the same time, the institution of property limits the freedom of other people to acquire and use resources owned by others.

To keep order in society by preventing and settling quarrels and disputes there must be clear, certain and enforceable rules for determining the legal allocation of resources, ownership, transfer, succession, the regulation of use and so on.

The institution of property usually recognises the relevance of deserts, the need to incentivise and reward work, skill and ingenuity and their benefits for the individual and for the community. There is commonly a connection between work and the expectations of ownership of property derived directly or indirectly from work. The natural expectation is that the activity of working on resources, such as things, involves control and management of them and entitles a person to rights in respect of that work and to be able to say 'That's mine, not yours'.

Over time the domain of property does not remain permanently fixed in structure or scope. It evolves and changes, just as the conditions of the world and the people living in it constantly change. It has become increasingly complex, in particular in the restrictions placed on the use of property, such as environmental restrictions affecting land. There is also complexity in the development of intellectual property law in balancing the claims of the individual with those of the public by limiting duration of ownership and by providing defences and making exceptions.

An obvious requirement for the enclosure of property and the exclusion of others from it is that it should be possible to define it with reasonable precision, so that the individual knows and others know what is and what is not the property of that person.

Finally, there are detailed rules that differ according to the kind of resource. So there is a difference between, on the one hand, real property and things which may be exhaustible by use or consumption and consequently affected by scarcity value and, on the other hand, the world of intellectual property in which large numbers of people can use the resource without exhausting it. Another factor is duration: for example, in the use of digital technology there may be processes which have only very temporary duration and property rights might cause considerable inconvenience.

VI. SOME PROPERTY CHARACTERISTICS

The rationale for property links in to certain basic property characteristics.

In brief, property and ownership of it are essentially about the legal relations between people and things. The legal content of the relationship is a collection of rights generally binding on and enforceable against everybody at the instance of the person recognised as owner, not just against people in a particular relationship with the owner.

The essential rights are those of enclosure, restriction of access, exclusion of others from use and management and rights of alienation. An owner thus enjoys a position over property akin to a monopoly. The political, economic and social consequences of monopoly power may make it necessary, in the interest of the public good and of owners of other property, to place limits on the exercise of rights of ownership of property, so that they are hardly ever absolute.

VII. INFORMATION AS PROPERTY

How far does information fall within the rationale and satisfy the characteristics of property?

Information is a creation of the human mind. It involves work in the form of ingenuity, skill, time effort and so on, perspiration, as well as inspiration. In many cases, however, information is not solely and exclusively attributable to creation by one person or organisation. Information has been passed down from earlier times, and is passed on by other people in other places. The information created by different people can take different forms, but also be derived from the same source and information can itself be a source for the creation of other information by others.

The effect of giving property rights to information itself may, by excluding others, impair the creation of further information. The creator of information cannot reasonably expect to have absolute and perpetual rights in the information against the rest of the world.

All this points to a general principle that, in general, the content, as distinct from the particular form in expression of information, is a resource that should be free for all to use. The person controlling access to unpublished information can determine by contract rather than by reliance on property whether it is disclosed or used and, if so, on what terms. The enforceable rights are against those who have agreed to be bound by the terms of disclosure and use.

When legislation privatises information by giving it the status of property, as in the case of patents for inventions and copyright in works of various description, it has done so in carefully defined terms, for set periods of time and subject to worked out exceptions and defences that achieve a balance between recognition of the contribution of the creator and the public interest in dissemination and use. The same problems do not arise where information is governed by an express or implied agreement.

Let us look again briefly at the content of emails. The claim to the content of the emails in order to gain access to them was understandable so far as the emails related to Fairstar's business in which Mr Adkins occupied a position of trust as their agent. The denial of the claim by Mr Adkins was understandable so far as the emails were on his personal computer and related to his personal affairs. He was also able to point to Fairstar's failure to install a system for ensuring that they were able to control information relating to their business.

The legal puzzle was created by labelling the issue as one that turned on property in and ownership of the emails. That was an unnecessary route to gaining access to the emails. It sowed the seeds of confusion and spawned unnecessary difficulty. The correct route was the agency route under which Mr Adkins, as agent, had personal obligations to Fairstar by virtue of his particular relationship with them.

VIII. NO PROPERTY IN INFORMATION

There are three main reasons for not recognising property in information.

The first is public policy. Some creations of the human mind, such as inventions, literature, music and art, are protected by legislation, which aims to balance the claims of creators to exclusivity, enclosure and credit, the interests of entrepreneurs in investment; and the common good in the dissemination and availability of the blessings of creation to the public for their use and enjoyment.

As a general rule, where there is a legislative policy, as there obviously is in the careful compromises of competing interests in the area of creations of the human intellect, the common law should follow that policy. It would be contrary to the policy of the law evident in legislation for the courts to develop greater rights in creations of the human mind than that allowed by legislation in the case of property of that nature.

Take the limits of copyright as an example. It has always been a fundamental principle of the Copyright Acts that, while enacting that copyright in specific works is property, that there is no copyright in information as such. Copyright subsists only in the particular forms in which the information is expressed. It would be contrary to that policy for the common law to undermine that legislative principle by generally treating information as property.

Next, information presents definitional difficulties. Even if the common law set off down the property path to the protection of information, it would soon come a cropper, because of the difficulty in practice of formulating a satisfactory and sufficiently certain definition of the informational subject matter. That would make it difficult to enforce property rights in information. The boundaries of property must be clear. Uncertainty and vagueness would place the public in an unacceptable position, on the one hand, as to who was the owner of what property, which could not be used without first obtaining permission from and making agreed payment to the owner, and, on the other hand, what was information freely available for use by all. Members of the public need to know, in advance of use, where they stand before embarking on a project that makes use of the information.

The third point is that there are available alternatives. Denial of property rights does not create a vacuum leaving the creator of the information exposed with no rights at all.

In many cases the person having control of information is, despite having no property rights in it, in a position to negotiate contractual terms for access to, for the disclosure and for the use of the information, sometimes in more stringent terms than might be allowed in any legislation for the protection of the information. The contract cannot, however, be made to bind a non-party simply by describing the subject matter of the contract as property. That classification is for the general law to make. It is not a matter for the parties to determine.

IX. CLOSING COMMENTS

It would be rash to conclude that the law will never develop the concept of property to cover new sorts of information. Never say 'never' is one lesson of experience. The time may arrive when the public interest plainly requires legislation defining property rights in specified sorts of information, along with defences and exceptions worked out to reflect other aspects of the public interest.

In the meantime all that the courts can do is to continue to draw the boundaries according to established property law principles. The enclosure of information further than currently allowed by intellectual property legislation would exclude the rest of the world from knowledge, which Parliament has not yet seen necessary to enclose as property. It would not be wise for the courts to extend the scope of a body of case law that is traditionally wary of monopolies and restraints on competition and protective of freedom of communication.

The judge of the public interest in this area is Parliament, which, far better than the courts, can work out through the processes of consultation and full debate the complex checks and balances always required to curb monopolies and prevent abuses of them.

A cautious approach by the courts to property claims would not leave information without any legal protection. Contract and equivalent relationships recognised as generating legal obligations can be used to protect 'information assets' without having to hold that there is property in them. The flexibility of contract, the established doctrines of confidentiality and the developing right to respect for privacy are all available for the protection of information. The courts should stick to their constitutional role: developing the case law principles as clearly and simply as possible and adapting them in a common sense and cautious way to concrete situations, one case at a time. That is far preferable to attempting to achieve too much by ambitious judicial activism and probably failing in the process.

2

A Golden Era? The Impact of the Scottish Law Commission on Property Law

ANDREW JM STEVEN*

I. INTRODUCTION

[I]t is hard to overestimate the influence that the SLC has had on the evolution of Scots law. Consider, for example, property law, or family law, or criminal law, or the law of diligence, or the law of bankruptcy, to mention just some fields. Without the SLC, we would today be looking out on a different legal landscape.[1]

SO WROTE MY predecessor, Professor George Gretton, in an article published in 2013. My aim is to measure in more detail the impact of the Scottish Law Commission (SLC) on property law. Both the SLC and the Law Commission for England and Wales (LC) were established by the Law Commissions Act 1965 and thus celebrate their golden anniversaries in 2015. But has the result of property law reform by the SLC been to create a golden era?

The first thing is to delineate what is meant by 'property law' for present purposes. The chapter will cover immoveable property (which in Scots law traditionally comes under the heading of 'heritable property') and moveable property (personal property). Subordinate property rights such as lease and security are included. But, for reasons of space, trusts and succession are excluded.[2] In passing it can be mentioned that the SLC has carried out substantial reviews of both trust law and succession law. A final report in the long-running trusts project was published in 2014.[3] Two reports have been published on succession law but neither has been implemented.[4]

* I am grateful to George Gretton, Shona Wilson Stark and Susan Sutherland for their assistance.

[1] GL Gretton, 'Of Law Commissioning' (2013) 17 *Edinburgh Law Review* 119, 130.

[2] Albeit, in Scots law, property law and trusts and succession can be treated together. See, eg GL Gretton and AJM Steven, *Property, Trusts and Succession*, 2nd edn (Haywards Heath, Bloomsbury Professional, 2013). On the inter-relationship between the trust and property law, see also G Gretton, 'Up there in the *Begriffshimmel*?' in L Smith (ed), *The Worlds of the Trust* (Cambridge, Cambridge University Press, 2013) 524 especially 527–29.

[3] Scottish Law Commission, *Report on Trust Law* (Scot Law Com No 239, 2014).

[4] Scottish Law Commission, *Report on Succession* (Scot Law Com No 124, 1990); Scottish Law Commission, *Report on Succession* (Scot Law Com No 215, 2009). For discussion see the symposium on succession law published at (2010) 14 *Edinburgh Law Review* 308. On the non-implementation, see DJ Cusine, 'Legal Rights: A Little Discretion Required?' 2014 *Scots Law Times (News)* 13.

The chapter will be structured as follows. Following this introduction, Section II will consider the setting-up of the SLC and the then expectations of it. Section III will then look at the human resourcing of its work on property law. Section IV will look at the SLC's Programmes of Law Reform and the place of property law within them. Section V will consider the SLC's property law projects. Section VI considers the future. Section VII is the conclusion.

II. THE CREATION OF THE SLC

The idea of law reform bodies began before 1965. Examples from abroad include the Louisiana State Law Institute, which was set up in 1938. There were also several *ad hoc* committees at home including the Law Reform Committee for Scotland, which was established in 1954.[5] But it was the publication of *Law Reform Now*, edited by Gerald Gardiner QC and Andrew Martin in 1963 that was the catalyst for the creation of the LC and the SLC. Gardiner went on to become Lord Chancellor in 1964 under Harold Wilson and took what became the Law Commissions Act 1965 through Parliament.[6] *Law Reform Now* is a collection of essays, mainly on particular areas of English law. Thus there is a wide-ranging chapter on land law by Gerald Dworkin calling for reform of land registration, covenants and easements amongst others.[7] The first essay in the book, by Gardiner and Martin, entitled 'The Machinery of Law Reform'[8] is a manifesto for the setting up of the LC. It is interesting to compare the first and final sentences:

> We think that we are justified in treating as axiomatic the proposition that much of our English law is out of date, and some of it shockingly so ... In our opinion *all* of the immediate reforms urged in this section are necessary if the law is to fulfil its function in contemporary Britain. (Author's underlining)

But despite the seamless shift from England to Britain, *Law Reform Now* is very much an English book. So why was the SLC set up under the 1965 Act as well as the LC? Recent research by Shona Wilson Stark has revealed that the then Secretary of State for Scotland (William Ross) and Lord Advocate (Gordon Stott) were pivotal figures.[9] Gardiner's original intention was that a Law Commission should be created in England and then expanded to Scotland if it was successful, either by establishing a separate body or by having a 'Commission for Great Britain'.[10] The second of these suggestions was peremptorily dismissed by the Secretary of State on the basis that England and Scotland already had separate Law Reform Committees. He and

---

[5] See Gretton, 'Of Law Commissioning' (n 1) 121–22.
[6] See Lord Gardiner, 'The Role of the Lord Chancellor in the Field of Law Reform' (1971) 87 *LQR* 326.
[7] G Dworkin, 'Land Law' in G Gardiner and A Martin (eds), *Law Reform Now* (London, Gollancz, 1963) 79–121. The LC has been active in a number of the areas which he mentions.
[8] Ibid, 1–14.
[9] See S Wilson Stark, 'The Longer You Can Look Back, The Further You Can Look Forward: The Origins of the Scottish Law Commission' (2014) 18 *Edinburgh Law Review* 59, 68–72. See also Lord Hope of Craighead, 'Do We Still Need a Scottish Law Commission?' (2006) 10 *Edinburgh Law Review* 10, 12–16 and Gretton, 'Of Law Commissioning' (n 1) 123.
[10] Wilson Stark, 'The Longer You Can Look Back' (n 9) 69.

the Lord Advocate then lobbied the Lord Chancellor for a separate Scottish body to be established immediately.[11]

Agreement was then subsequently reached in government that such a body would be set up, although on a smaller scale than that for England. The 1965 Act provided for the two Commissions, the SLC having the purpose of 'promoting the reform of the law of Scotland'[12] whereas the LC had the rather wider purpose of 'promoting the reform of the law'.[13] Both Commissions are required by the 1965 Act to:

> [T]ake and keep under review all the law with which they are respectively concerned with a view to its systematic development and reform, including in particular the codification of such law, the elimination of anomalies, the repeal of obsolete and unnecessary enactments, the reduction of the number of separate enactments and generally the simplification and modernisation of the law.[14]

III. HUMAN RESOURCING

The SLC and the LC each have five Commissioners. The LC Commissioners are all appointed on a full-time basis. At the SLC it is possible to be appointed on a full-time or part-time basis. Both Commissions are chaired by a judge, currently by Lord Pentland at the SLC and Lord Justice Lloyd Jones at the LC.[15] But the LC is considerably bigger and is divided into four teams, each headed by a Commissioner: Commercial Law and Common Law, currently led by David Hertzell; Criminal Law, currently led by Professor David Ormerod QC; Property, Family and Trust Law, currently led by Professor Elizabeth Cooke; and Public Law, currently led by Nicholas Paines QC. Each team has a manager (a lawyer) and several lawyers and research assistants.

In contrast the SLC has teams for each project, normally[16] comprising only three people: a Commissioner, a project manager (a Scottish Government lawyer) and a legal assistant. The four Scottish Commissioners other than the Chairman have never had fixed areas of expertise, but there are noticeable trends. There has invariably been a practising QC, who is a part-time Commissioner.[17] Currently this is Laura Dunlop QC, the first female Scottish Commissioner, who was appointed in 2009, and who leads the Adults with Incapacity Project.[18] One of her predecessors

---

[11] Ibid, 70.

[12] Law Commissions Act 1965, s 2(1).

[13] Ibid, s 1(1). This has now been restricted to the law of England and Wales by an amendment made by the Justice (Northern Ireland) Act 2002, Sch 12 para 8.

[14] Law Commissions Act 1965, s 3(1). For discussion see Lord Hunter, 'Law Reform: The Scottish Law Commission' 1988 *Juridical Review* 158, 162–64; Gretton, 'Of Law Commissioning' (n 1) 125–35 and Wilson Stark, 'The Longer You Can Look Back' (n 9) 75–83.

[15] Lloyd Jones LJ sits in the Court of Appeal and Lord Pentland in the Outer House of the Court of Session.

[16] An exception is the current compulsory purchase project which has two Commissioners: Patrick Layden QC, handling public law aspects and myself handling property law aspects.

[17] Every one of these has subsequently become a Court of Session judge. Patrick Hodge (1997–2003) now sits in the UK Supreme Court as Lord Hodge, along with Lady Hale, Lord Carnwath and Lord Toulson, former Commissioners at the LC.

[18] See Scottish Law Commission, *Report on Adults with Incapacity* (Scot Law Com No 240, 2014).

in the 1970s was JPH Mackay QC, who later became Lord Mackay of Clashfern and Lord Chancellor. There has also always been a professor or two with expertise in private law, beginning with the long-serving Professor Sir Thomas B Smith QC (1965–80)[19] and Professor Alexander (Sandy) Anton CBE (1966–82).[20] They were followed by the longest-serving Scottish Commissioner of them all, Professor Eric Clive CBE (1981–99)[21] who was the principal author of the significant reforms to Scottish family law in the 1980s and 1990s. He was succeeded by Professor Joe Thomson (2000–09)[22] and Professor Hector MacQueen (2009–present).[23]

But what about property law? The SLC story mirrors the more general history in Scotland. In the nineteenth century property law got lost. Some of it was taught under 'Scots law', for example, moveable property and servitudes.[24] The rest, was taught under 'conveyancing', for example the transfer of land and real burdens (covenants).[25] The result in the twentieth century was a significant lack of doctrinal coherence. This led to poor property law legislation, the nadir being the Land Registration (Scotland) Act 1979.[26] The blame for this state of affairs primarily lay in the universities having separate professors of Scots law and professors of conveyancing who were responsible for their own courses. Professors of Scots law, latterly, were full-time academics whereas professors of conveyancing were part-time, because they continued to work in legal practice. Scots law primarily means Scottish private law and the appointments of Professors Smith,[27] Anton and Clive[28] gave the SLC experts in this field in its first 30 years. But in the same period the Commission had

---

[19] See DL Carey Miller and DW Meyers (eds), *Comparative and Historical Essays in Scots Law* (Edinburgh, Butterworths/The Law Society of Scotland, 1992) and E Reid and DL Carey Miller (eds), *A Mixed Legal System in Transition: TB Smith and the Progress of Scots Law* (Edinburgh, Edinburgh University Press, 2005).

[20] Professor of Jurisprudence at the University of Glasgow from 1959–73. See PR Beaumont, 'The Contribution of Alexander (Sandy) Anton to the Development of Private International Law' 2006 *Juridical Review* 1.

[21] See EE Sutherland (ed), *The Future of Child and Family Law: International Predictions* (New York, Cambridge University Press, 2012) Preface. He went on to achieve further distinction by editing with Christian von Bar, *Principles, Definitions and Model Rules on European Private Law: Draft Common Frame of Reference* (Oxford, Oxford University Press, 2010).

[22] Regius Professor of Law at the University of Glasgow from 1991–2005. See J Chalmers, 'Resorting to Crime' in RG Anderson, J Chalmers and J MacLeod (eds), *Glasgow Tercentenary Essays: 300 Years of the School of Law* (Edinburgh, Avizandum Publishing, 2014) 70 at 88.

[23] Professor of Private Law at the University of Edinburgh since 1994.

[24] See, eg WM Gloag and RC Henderson, *Introduction to the Law of Scotland* (Edinburgh, W Green & Son, 1927) Preface: 'We have confined our work to those branches of the law which are usually dealt with in classes of Scots and of Mercantile Law. Conveyancing [and certain other areas] are therefore, only incidentally referred to'.

[25] See, eg J Burns, *Conveyancing Practice According to the Law of Scotland*, 4th edn (by F MacRitchie, Edinburgh, W Green & Son, 1957).

[26] See below, at V.C.v. The property law aspects of the Matrimonial Homes (Family Protection) (Scotland) Act 1981 are another example of deficient legislation, although subsequent amendments have somewhat improved the position.

[27] Smith was Professor of Scots Law at the University of Edinburgh from 1968–72. He resigned on becoming a full-time Commissioner.

[28] Clive was Professor of Scots Law at the University of Edinburgh from 1977–81, resigning on his appointment as a full-time Commissioner.

two long-serving part-time Commissioners who were professors of conveyancing: John (Jack) Halliday CBE (1965–74)[29] and Philip Love CBE (1986–95).[30]

In the 1980s work commenced on the 25 volume *The Laws of Scotland: Stair Memorial Encyclopaedia*. The General Editor was Professor Smith. He conceived that property law should be treated once again in a unified way[31] and commissioned a young lecturer in the Law Faculty at the University of Edinburgh to write the title on it. That lecturer was Kenneth Reid and in 1993 the title appeared in volume 18 of the Encyclopaedia.[32] What Smith conceived Reid delivered. Few works in modern Scottish law have had as great an influence.[33] Property law became re-established as a coherent subject because of the work of Reid and also his close colleague George Gretton. As Niall Whitty[34] put it: 'Before vol 18, property law had been the hand-maiden of conveyancing; after vol 18 the roles were very properly reversed'.[35] The professor of conveyancing then became an endangered and, as of June 2014, extinct species.[36] Reid was appointed to a Personal Chair in Property Law at the University of Edinburgh in 1994.[37] A year later he joined the SLC where he directed a series of major projects on land law discussed below. He was a Commissioner for 10 years until 2005 and was awarded the CBE for his contribution to law reform.[38]

Reid was succeeded by Gretton,[39] who served from 2006–11 and was responsible for completing a large project on land registration,[40] as well as starting two

---

[29] Halliday was Professor of Conveyancing at the University of Glasgow from 1955–79. See DJ Cusine (ed), *A Scots Conveyancing Miscellany: Essays in Honour of Professor JM Halliday* (Edinburgh, W Green & Son, 1987).

[30] Love was Professor of Conveyancing and Professional Practice of Law in the University of Aberdeen from 1974–92 and subsequently Principal and Vice-Chancellor of the University of Liverpool from 1992–2002.

[31] KGC Reid, *The Law of Property in Scotland* (Edinburgh, Butterworths/The Law Society of Scotland, 1996) (hereinafter 'Reid, *Property*') para 1.

[32] A revised version was published three years later as Reid, *Property*.

[33] See, eg R Paisley, *Land Law* (Edinburgh, W Green & Son, 2000) 1, fn 1; Gretton and Steven, *Property, Trusts and Succession* (n 2) Preface. In a book review published at 1996 *Juridical Review* 74, Lord Hope of Craighead wrote: 'I do not think that one can speak too highly of this work'. But he also mistakenly said that Reid was now 'Professor of Scots Law at the University of Edinburgh'. In fact this was prescient as Reid assumed that chair 12 years later.

[34] Whitty was a long-serving member of the legal staff at the SLC, who, in an unprecedented move then became a Commissioner from 1995–2000.

[35] NR Whitty, 'The *Stair Memorial Encyclopaedia* and the Institutional Tradition' in S Hetherington (ed), *Halsbury's Laws of England: Centenary Essays 2007* (London, LexisNexis, 2007) 203, 223, fn 133. Thus 'Conveyancing' still appeared as a title in the Encyclopaedia.

[36] On the retirement of Professor Robert Rennie from the University of Glasgow. The Chair of Conveyancing at Edinburgh has been vacant since 1991 when Professor Iain Noble retired. At Aberdeen it has been vacant since Professor Douglas Cusine resigned in 2000 to become a sheriff. Cusine's natural successor was Roderick Paisley who had been appointed to a Personal Chair in Commercial Property Law in 1999. In a move remarkably similar to what happened with Kenneth Reid at Edinburgh in 2008, Paisley was translated to the Chair of Scots Law in 2013.

[37] He subsequently became Professor of Scots Law in 2008. For his inaugural lecture, see KGC Reid, 'Smoothing the Rugged Parts of the Passage: Scots Law and its Edinburgh Chair' (2014) 18 *Edinburgh Law Review* 315.

[38] On his achievements it has been said: 'No man has left so large a footprint on the Scottish law of property'. See R Rennie (ed), *The Promised Land: Property Law Reform* (Edinburgh, W Green, 2008) Preface.

[39] Lord President Reid Professor of Law at the University of Edinburgh since 1994.

[40] See below, at V.C.v.

important projects on moveable property: one on moveable transactions;[41] the other on positive prescription and corporeal moveables.[42] I succeeded Gretton in 2011[43] and at the time of writing am half way through my five-year appointment. The prescription project was completed in 2012,[44] the moveable transactions project is ongoing and there is a project on heritable securities (mortgages) to be started.

IV. PROGRAMMES OF LAW REFORM

The main way in which the SLC initiates projects is to have them included in the programmes of law reform agreed with government. Since devolution in 1999 programmes are agreed with the Scottish Ministers. In recent years these have been for a five-year period and prior to finalisation there has been wide-ranging consultation as to what should be included. The First Programme appeared in 1965 and contained five items. These were: (1) evidence; (2) obligations; (3) prescription and the limitation of actions; (4) judicial precedent; and (5) interpretation of statutes.[45] The Second Programme, published in 1968, added nine new areas, including succession, criminal procedure and family law, but no property law.[46] The Third Programme, published in 1973, added only international private law.[47]

There was then a 17-year gap until 1990 and the publication of the Fourth Programme.[48] It added two topics: property law; and judicial factors, powers of attorney, and guardianship of the incapable. The reason for the addition of property law is given as follows:

> In a number of our previous exercises (such as matrimonial homes) we have, to some extent, impinged incidentally on property questions. We take the view, however, that a programme on this topic would enable us to take on directly subjects falling under this head and in this connection our first objective is the consideration of land tenure law reform with a view to the completion in due course of statutory reform of feudal tenure. We would also propose in due course to examine other matters and in particular aspects of leasehold property law.[49]

This signalled the start of the SLC's work towards feudal abolition. By this time the SLC had accumulated a total of 17 areas for reform. Work on these was at varying stages from complete to just started. In the Fifth Programme, published in 1997 under the new chairmanship of Lord Gill[50] a fresh approach was taken.[51] All the

---

[41] See Scottish Law Commission, *Discussion Paper on Moveable Transactions* (DP No 151, 2011).
[42] See below, at V.B.ii.
[43] I am the first Commissioner who is younger than the SLC.
[44] *Report on Prescription and Title to Moveable Property* (Scot Law Com No 228, 2012).
[45] Law Commissions Act 1965: First Programme of the Scottish Law Commission (1965).
[46] Scottish Law Commission, *Second Programme of Law Reform* (Scot Law Com No 8, 1968).
[47] Scottish Law Commission, *Third Programme of Law Reform* (Scot Law Com No 29, 1973).
[48] Scottish Law Commission, *Fourth Programme of Law Reform* (Scot Law Com No 126, 1990).
[49] Scottish Law Commission, *Fourth Programme of Law Reform* (Scot Law Com No 126, 1990) 1. See also the letter from the Chairman of the SLC, Lord Maxwell to the Lord Advocate, Lord Cameron of Lochbroom dated 21 August 1987 and the reply from the Lord Advocate dated 14 December 1987 agreeing that land tenure reform would be the main objective. Source: SLC internal Fourth Programme of Law Reform file.
[50] Since 2012 Scotland's most senior judge, the Lord President of the Court of Session.
[51] Scottish Law Commission, *Fifth Programme of Law Reform* (Scot Law Com No 159, 1997).

previous programmes were superseded and the areas in which the SLC would be working in the next three to five years set out. The seven areas given can only be described as broad: (1) civil remedies: diligence; (2) codification; (3) general principles of private law; (4) obligations; (5) persons; (6) property; and (7) trusts.[52] Property was then further divided into: (a) feudal tenure; (b) leasehold tenure; (c) mutual boundary walls; and (d) tenement property.[53] What had been described as 'reform of feudal tenure' in the previous programme had now become explicitly abolition of the feudal system.[54]

The Sixth Programme, published in 2000, carried over a number of the same items from the previous programme.[55] But this time the sub-topics under the heading 'property' were leasehold tenure and land registration. In the Seventh Programme, published in 2005, 'property' disappeared, with leasehold tenure and land registration promoted to items in their own right.[56] They were joined in the property law field by assignation of, and security over, incorporeal moveables. In the Eighth Programme, which will be completed at the end of 2014, there are four projects involving property law.[57] The project on incorporeal moveables is extended to include security over corporeal moveables. It is joined by projects on compulsory purchase; heritable securities; and prescription and corporeal moveable property.[58]

The other principal way in which the SLC receives work is by references from Ministers. These may have to take priority over projects within the current programme. For example, the judicial factors[59] project, which dates back to the Fourth Programme in 1990, was not completed until 2013 because resources had to be deployed elsewhere, in particular on criminal law references.[60] In the area of property law a notable reference was 'to consider the implications of the decision of the House of Lords in *Sharp v Thomson* 1997 SC (HL) 66 and to make recommendations as to possible reform of the law'.[61] *Sharp* was the most controversial Scottish property law decision in modern times as it cast doubt on registration being needed for the transfer of landownership. The academic literature on it is immense.[62] However, by the time that the SLC came to report the House of Lords had already drawn back from *Sharp* in the subsequent case of *Burnett's Trustee v Grainger*.[63] The report only had to make a very limited set of recommendations relating to corporate insolvency law.[64]

---

[52] Ibid, para 2.2.
[53] Ibid, para 2.32.
[54] Ibid, para 2.33–2.35.
[55] Scottish Law Commission, *Sixth Programme of Law Reform* (Scot Law Com No 176, 2000).
[56] Scottish Law Commission, *Seventh Programme of Law Reform* (Scot Law Com No 198, 2005).
[57] Scottish Law Commission, *Eighth Programme of Law Reform* (Scot Law Com No 220, 2010).
[58] See below, at V.B.ii and VI.
[59] A judicial factor is a person whom a court appoints to manage property where there is a need for this, eg in common property where the co-owners are in dispute.
[60] Scottish Law Commission, *Report on Judicial Factors* (Scot Law Com No 233, 2013) para 1.2.
[61] Scottish Law Commission, *Report on Sharp v Thomson* (Scot Law Com No 208, 2007) para 1.1.
[62] See ibid, App B. See also DL Carey Miller, 'Scots and South African Property: Problem Transplants' in E Cooke (ed), *Modern Studies in Property Law: Property 2000*, vol 1 (Oxford, Hart Publishing, 2001) 293–308.
[63] *Burnett's Trustee v Grainger* 2004 SC (HL) 19. See further Gretton and Steven, *Property, Trusts and Succession* (n 2) paras 4.22–4.27.
[64] While these have regrettably not (yet) been implemented, recommendations relating to personal insolvency law made in the earlier *Discussion Paper on Sharp v Thomson* (DP No 114, 2001) were made law by the Bankruptcy and Diligence etc (Scotland) Act 2007, s 17.

It can be seen that during its first 25 years property law did not appear within the SLC's programmes of law reform. But since 1990 it has been a constant feature. This is not to say that property law was completely ignored in those early years. Three important examples are the work carried out on prescription (under the item on this in the First Programme),[65] on matrimonial property (under the family law item in the Second Programme)[66] and on execution of deeds (under the evidence item in the First Programme and the obligations item in the Second Programme).[67] But it was only in the second half of the SLC's near-50 year history that property law became a specific subject on which reform was to be carried out.

V. PROPERTY LAW PROJECTS

A. Introduction

In this section the main projects which the SLC has carried out on property law since its establishment in 1965 will be considered. Projects which are currently ongoing are excluded but will be mentioned later. We will look at moveable property first and then immoveable property. Normally projects result in a report with a draft Bill[68] attached to it which the Government[69] must decide whether or not to implement.

B. Moveable Property

i. The 1970s Memoranda

In 1976, under the principal authorship of Professor TB Smith the SLC published no less than eight consultative memoranda on corporeal moveables. The subjects were: (a) general introduction and summary of provisional proposals;[70] (b) passing of risk and of ownership;[71] (c) some problems of classification;[72] (d) protection of the onerous bona fide acquirer of another's property;[73] (e) mixing, union and creation;[74] (f) lost and abandoned property;[75] (g) usucapion or acquisitive prescription;[76] and (h) remedies.[77]

---

[65] See below, at V.B.i.

[66] Scottish Law Commission, *Report on Matrimonial Property* (Scot Law Com No 86, 1984) which was implemented by the Family Law (Scotland) Act 1985, ss 24–26.

[67] Scottish Law Commission, *Report on Requirements of Writing* (Scot Law Com No 112, 1988) which was implemented by the Requirements of Writing (Scotland) Act 1995.

[68] The *Report on Boundary Walls* (Scot Law Com No 163, 1998) is a notable exception as the SLC concluded that no legislation was needed.

[69] Nowadays in devolved matters, the Scottish Government and in reserved matters, the Westminster Government.

[70] Scot Law Com Memorandum No 24.

[71] Scot Law Com Memorandum No 25.

[72] Scot Law Com Memorandum No 26.

[73] Scot Law Com Memorandum No 27.

[74] Scot Law Com Memorandum No 28.

[75] Scot Law Com Memorandum No 29.

[76] Scot Law Com Memorandum No 30.

[77] Scot Law Com Memorandum No 31.

The question which immediately arises is how this is compatible with the fact that property law only became a programme item in 1990. Was there a reference from the Government? There was not. Only one of the memoranda can immediately be justified, namely that on usucapion or positive prescription, because prescription was the third item on the First Programme of Law Reform.[78] The general introduction memorandum states:

> In the course of our examination of the law of prescription, it was suggested to us that the law on that subject, insofar as it affects corporeal moveables, should be clarified. Prescription is the ultimate determinant of the right of ownership curing all defects of acquisition on onerous or gratuitous title. Accordingly we came to the conclusion that problems relating to the acquisition of title to corporeal moveables merited a comprehensive separate study.[79]

The study was further justified by the fact that in 'the context of transfer of rights in moveables the rules of property law and the law of obligations often intersect'[80] and that obligations was also one of the items in the First Programme. These arguments do not persuade as the scope of the memoranda clearly go beyond obligations and prescription law. It is difficult to resist the conclusion that this work cannot clearly be justified within the 1965 Act.[81]

The memoranda, taken together, contain proposals relating to diverse areas of the law of corporeal moveables. There is no attempt at codification of the subject. It is no surprise given their principal author that the approach is strongly civilian and English law is generally eschewed.[82] The only memorandum followed up by a report was that on lost and abandoned property.[83] This was then implemented in a modified form by the Civic Government (Scotland) Act 1982, Part VI.[84] Thus this work of the SLC on corporeal moveables has had very little impact. The lack of implementation is perhaps not surprising given the unclear foundation on which the work proceeded and there is to some extent less commercial importance in the topics covered than in other areas of property law such as land registration. The proposals touching on sale of goods would have also required approval by Whitehall and Scottish-specific proposals in the field of commercial law have had limited success over the years.[85]

---

[78] See above, at IV.

[79] Scot Law Com Memorandum No 24, para 2.

[80] Ibid.

[81] Such a conclusion is supported by the SLC internal Fourth Programme of Law Reform file which contains a memorandum from the Chairman, Lord Hunter to Commissioners dated 26 October 1973 proposing that 'Property in Corporeal Moveables' be expressly included in the Fourth Programme in order to make the work on this 'fully legitimate'. This view was accepted by TB Smith in a reply dated 30 October 1973. The Fourth Programme did not actually appear until 1990 where as we have seen it included the item 'Property Law'.

[82] See DL Carey Miller, 'TB Smith's Property' in Reid and Carey Miller (eds), *A Mixed Legal System in Transition* (n 19) 173–98.

[83] *Report on Lost and Abandoned Property* (Scot Law Com No 57, 1980).

[84] See further Reid, *Property* (n 31) para 548 (WM Gordon).

[85] See further, CK Davidson, 'The Scottish Law Commission, 1965–95' (1995) 1 *Scottish Law & Practice Quarterly* 18, 21–22; Gretton, 'Of Law Commissioning' (n 1) 149–51.

ii. Prescription and Title to Moveable Property

In its Eighth Programme the SLC returned again to the subject matter of the one 1970s memorandum which was clearly justified by the First Programme: prescription. Most countries have a rule that when someone has had possession (in good faith or sometimes not) of a corporeal moveable (chattel) for a certain period then that possession can no longer be challenged. In England this is achieved by limitation with challenges generally being excluded after six years.[86] Civilian systems such as France and Germany tend to vest ownership in the possessor by means of acquisitive prescription.[87] In Scotland, however, there is no clear rule, certainly under statute.[88] This uncertainty could be somewhat of an embarrassment if a case were to come before the courts in relation to a valuable artwork or the like. In a report published in 2012 the SLC proposed a 20-year rule which would require both good faith and an absence of negligence on the part of the possessor.[89] The period is a comparatively long one but this was dictated by the need to protect cultural assets and the near-impossibility of trying to define 'cultural' in order to take an alternative approach of having a shorter period for 'ordinary' property and a longer period for 'cultural property'.[90]

The SLC also recommended a 50-year rule allowing holders of property to acquire ownership after that period if they were unable to contact the owner. This recommendation is aimed at helping the museums and galleries sector dispose of assets where the owner cannot be traced. The Scottish Government's response to the report has been positive, with recognition that 'legislation in this area would bring clarity and economic benefit'.[91] But it wishes to carry out its own consultation on the area and for the moment is unable to allocate resources due to other priorities.

C. Immoveable Property

i. Prescription

As has been seen prescription and the limitation of actions was an item in the First Programme.[92] The law on prescription under which rights can be created

---

[86] Limitation Act 1980, s 2. But the possessor must be in good faith under s 4(2) of the same Act. See *De Preval v Adrian Alan Ltd* (QBD, 24 Jan 1997), discussed in J Ulph and I Smith, *The Illicit Trade in Arts and Antiquities: International Recovery and Criminal and Civil Liability* (Oxford, Hart Publishing, 2012) para 5.43.

[87] See Scottish Law Commission, *Discussion Paper on Prescription and Title to Moveable Property* (DP No 144, 2011) pt 5.

[88] The elderly decision in *Parishioners of Aberscherder v Parish of Gemrie* (1633) Mor 10972 concerning a church bell suggests a common law period of 40 years, but the better view is that this is a case about negative prescription. See ARC Simpson, 'Positive Prescription of Moveables in Scots Law' (2009) 13 *Edinburgh Law Review* 445.

[89] Scottish Law Commission, *Report on Prescription and Title to Moveable Property* (Scot Law Com No 228, 2012).

[90] See AJM Steven, A Smith and N Campbell, 'Prescription and Title to Moveable Property' 2012 *Scots Law Times (News)* 139 and CM Campbell, 'Prescription and Title to Moveable Property' (2012) 16 *Edinburgh Law Review* 426.

[91] Letter from Roseanna Cunningham MSP, Minister for Community Safety and Legal Affairs to Lady Clark of Calton, Chairman of the SLC dated 30 July 2013, available at www.scotlawcom.gov.uk/law-reform-projects/completed-projects/prescription-and-title-to-moveable-property/.

[92] See above, at IV.

or extinguished by the passage of time was in a dusty state in the 1960s, being dependent on a number of old statutes dating back to the Prescription Act 1469. In its report on the subject published in 1970, the SLC recommended that these be repealed and replaced by a modern code.[93] Important substantive reforms were also recommended including reducing the period of possession required for prescriptive acquisition of servitudes from 20 years to 10 years.[94] One thing deliberately missing from the code, however, was corporeal moveables[95] and as described in the previous section that gap has yet to be filled. The report was implemented by the Prescription and Limitation (Scotland) Act 1973. It has been a largely successful piece of legislation,[96] but in more recent years has become complicated by amendments. The time may be coming for another review.

ii. Feudal Abolition and Title Conditions

The feudal system of landholding, whereby land is not held outright but rather as a 'vassal' of someone else (a 'superior') and then ultimately of the Crown was widespread in Europe in the Middle Ages.[97] By the 1990s it had been abolished just about everywhere apart from Scotland.[98] Of course it only remained in a diluted form. Vassals were no longer expected to fight battles for their superiors.[99] But land could still be sold by means of subinfeudation, something which was banned in England by the statute *Quia Emptores* of 1290. This was commonly done to enable real burdens[100] to be imposed without the need to retain neighbouring land. Thus builders would generally sell plots in a housing development by means of subinfeudation and impose real burdens requiring maintenance or preventing trade, etc. The builders would have title to enforce the burdens because they were superiors. But the law was also regularly abused. The householder wanting to make a modest alteration, such as adding a conservatory to his property, would have to pay the superior for permission to do this if there was a burden against alteration. The house could be in Kilmarnock but the superior could be living in Kent.

The conundrum of what to do about real burdens was one of the main reasons why the feudal system survived for so long. The picture was complicated by the fact

---

[93] Scottish Law Commission, *Report on Reform of the Law Relating to Prescription and Limitation of Actions* (Scot Law Com No 15, 1970).

[94] Thus making proof of possession less difficult. See DJ Cusine and RRM Paisley, *Servitudes and Rights of Way* (Edinburgh, W Green & Son, 1998) para 10.12.

[95] *Report on Reform of the Law Relating to Prescription and Limitation of Actions*, para 3.

[96] For an example of an important property law case, see *Bowers v Kennedy* 2000 SC 555, on the meaning of '*res merae facultatis*', one of the imprescriptible rights in Sch 3 to the 1973 Act. The case held that the right of a proprietor of landlocked land to reach that land was such a right.

[97] See, eg FL Ganshof, *Feudalism*, 3rd edn ((P Grierson tr, London, Longmans, 1964); Reid, *Property* (n 31) paras 43–46 (GL Gretton) and HL MacQueen, 'Tears of a Legal Historian: Scottish Feudalism and the Ius Commune' 2003 *Juridical Review* 1.

[98] KGC Reid, *The Abolition of Feudal Tenure in Scotland* (Edinburgh, Butterworths, 2003) para 1.6. In England and Northern Ireland land law is feudal only to the extent that land is formally held of the Crown. In the Republic of Ireland the last vestiges of feudalism were abolished by the Land and Conveyancing Law Reform Act 2009.

[99] Tenures Abolition Act 1746, which was passed after the Jacobite Rebellion.

[100] The nearest English equivalents are covenants.

that real burdens were not purely feudal. They could be imposed in ordinary transfers as well as feudal grants.[101]

When property law was added to the work of the SLC by the Fourth Programme, reform and ultimately abolition of the feudal system was what the Government had in mind. The project was commenced by Philip Love[102] and taken over by Kenneth Reid.[103] Reid realised that for feudal abolition to work there needed to be a separate but related project on real burdens.[104] A discussion paper on the latter was published in 1998.[105] This was followed by a final report on feudal abolition in 1999[106] and on real burdens in 2000.[107] These both contained draft Bills, which substantially formed the bases of the Abolition of Feudal Tenure etc (Scotland) Act 2000 and the Title Conditions (Scotland) Act 2003. There was strong political will to abolish the feudal system, not least from Scotland's first First Minister following devolution, Donald Dewar.[108]

What followed, when coupled with the implementation of the Tenements (Scotland) Act 2004,[109] was nothing short of a revolution.[110] Section 1 of the 2000 Act provides:

> The feudal system of land tenure, that is to say the entire system whereby land is held by a vassal on perpetual tenure from a superior is, on the appointed day, abolished.

The day appointed was 28 November 2004. On that day vassals[111] became absolute owners, superiorities were abolished and future subinfeudation was forbidden.[112] A right to claim compensation was given to former superiors for loss of feu duty.[113]

In the run-up to the appointed day superiors were given limited rights to preserve enforcement rights in relation to real burdens.[114] The most important case was the

---

[101] Indeed the leading case of *Tailors of Aberdeen v Coutts* (1840) 1 Rob 296 involved non-feudal deeds. See further DJ Cusine, '*Tailors of Aberdeen v Coutts*: A Look Behind the Scenes' in HL MacQueen (ed), *Miscellany Five* (Edinburgh, Stair Society vol 52, 2006) 145–68.

[102] Love was the Commissioner responsible for Scottish Law Commission, *Discussion Paper on Property Law—Abolition of the Feudal System* (DP No 93, 1991).

[103] See KGC Reid, '700 Years at One Blow: The Abolition of Feudal Land Tenure in Scotland' in P Jackson and DC Wilde (eds), *The Reform of Property Law* (Aldershot, Ashgate, 1997) 299–310 and KGC Reid, 'Vassals No More: Feudalism and Post-Feudalism in Scotland' (2003) 11 *European Review of Private Law* 282.

[104] See K Reid, 'Modernising Land Burdens: The New Law in Scotland' in S van Erp and B Akkermans (eds), *Towards a Unified System of Land Burdens* (Antwerp, Intersentia, 2006) 63, 67 and S Wortley and AJM Steven, 'The Modernisation of Real Burdens and Servitudes: Some Observations on the Title Conditions (Scotland) Bill Consultation Paper' (2001) 6 *Scottish Law & Practice Quarterly* 261, 262–63.

[105] Scottish Law Commission, *Discussion Paper on Real Burdens* (DP No 106, 1998).

[106] Scottish Law Commission, *Report on Abolition of the Feudal System* (Scot Law Com No 168, 1999).

[107] Scottish Law Commission, *Report on Real Burdens* (Scot Law Com No 181, 2000).

[108] See his 1998 McEwen Lecture available at www.caledonia.org.uk/land/dewar.htm. He was then Secretary of State for Scotland.

[109] See below, at V.C.iii.

[110] AJM Steven, 'Revolution in Scottish Land Law' (2004) 8.3 *Electronic Journal of Comparative Law*, www.ejcl.org/83/art83-5.html.

[111] Or more accurately the vassal who held the *dominium utile*, ie was lowest in the feudal chain.

[112] Abolition of Feudal Tenure etc (Scotland) Act 2000, s 2.

[113] Ibid, ss 7–16.

[114] See generally Reid, *The Abolition of Feudal Tenure in Scotland* (n 103) chs 3–4; DA Brand, AJM Steven and S Wortley, *Professor McDonald's Conveyancing Manual*, 7th edn (Edinburgh, Butterworths, 2004) ch 19 and S Wortley, 'Preserving Feudal Burdens as Praedial Real Burdens: Reallotment under the Abolition of Feudal Tenure etc (Scotland) Act 2000' (2003) 71 *Scottish Law Gazette* 73.

'100m rule' where the enforcement right could be reallotted to neighbouring land held by the superior provided normally that there was a permanent building on it within 100m of the burdened property.[115] The building had to be in use wholly or mainly as a place of human habitation or resort. The policy was that open land did not merit protection from real burdens. On the other hand if the superior lived in a house on the neighbouring property that was within 100m of the burdened property then the right to enforce could be transferred to the property where the house was located. In very restricted circumstances burdens could also be preserved as 'personal real burdens', a new type of real burden without a benefited property. Thus, for example, superiors which were designated as 'conservation bodies' could preserve burdens relating to conservation as 'conservation burdens'.[116]

The 2003 Act also came into force on 28 November 2004 and effectively codified the law of real burdens, but its remit stretched wider to other 'title conditions', in other words conditions affecting land which the Lands Tribunal for Scotland can vary or extinguish.[117] The legislation overhauled the Tribunal's jurisdiction.[118] It also tidied up the overlap between servitudes and real burdens. In general, following the appointed day, limited rights to use another's land had to be constituted as servitudes whereas positive and negative obligations such as duties to maintain and prohibitions on trading had to be constituted as real burdens.[119] In contrast to the common law where real burdens only had to be registered against the title to the burdened property, the legislation promoted transparency by also requiring new burdens to be registered against the benefited property.[120] Burdened proprietors can therefore see exactly who can enforce their burdens. Provision was made for a limited number of personal real burdens (with no benefited property) as mentioned above in the context of superiors preserving rights.[121]

In taking what became the 2003 Act through the Scottish Parliament the Scottish Executive[122] largely followed the SLC's script. The Justice Minister (Jim Wallace)[123] said:

> It is a classic piece of law reform. It has examined the common law with a cool eye. Where the law was sensible and useful, it has been reproduced in the codes that are set out in the bill's opening sections. Where the law was uncertain, it has been clarified. Where the law was poor, it is being replaced.[124]

But one place where there was deviation was in relation to real burdens affecting building developments, typically housing schemes. Where, as was often the case, the builder had reserved the right to vary the burdens the common law said that the

---

[115] Abolition of Feudal Tenure etc (Scotland) Act 2000, s 18.

[116] Ibid, s 27.

[117] Title Conditions (Scotland) Act 2003, s 122.

[118] Ibid, ss 90–104. See J Wright, 'The Lands Tribunal: The New Jurisdiction' in Rennie, *The Promised Land* (n 38) 173–94 and A Todd and R Wishart, *The Lands Tribunal for Scotland: Law and Practice* (Edinburgh, W Green, 2012).

[119] Title Conditions (Scotland) Act 2003, ss 2 and 79–81.

[120] Ibid, s 4.

[121] Ibid, ss 38–48.

[122] As it was then called. It is now the Scottish Government.

[123] Now Lord Wallace of Tankerness, the Advocate General for Scotland.

[124] Scottish Parliament, Official Report 26 February 2003 col 18741.

individual plot-holders could not enforce against each other.[125] The SLC proposed no change here. But the Scottish Executive felt that the abolition of superiors would leave housing schemes under-regulated and promoted a provision, which became section 53 of the 2003 Act, which over-rode the rule. This was a mistake. The provision is opaque and over-generous and has caused significant problems in practice in relation to obtaining minutes of waiver.[126] Ten years on, following a report by the Justice Committee of the Scottish Parliament, the matter has been referred back to the SLC.[127]

The abolition of the feudal system and reform of title conditions was a quiet triumph for the SLC. No challenge was made on the basis of the European Convention on Human Rights (ECHR). It was accepted that Scottish land law needed to be modernised. As Lord Rodger of Earlsferry noted, albeit provocatively, the feudal system was 'unceremoniously binned by the Scottish Parliament—unmourned even by its supposed acolytes, the Professors of Conveyancing'.[128]

iii. Tenements

The appointed day of 28 November 2004 was also important for a third piece of legislation coming into force: the Tenements (Scotland) Act 2004. Once again this was based on the work of the SLC. The law of the tenement (or apartment ownership or condominium ownership as it might be known elsewhere) had previously been non-statutory, in effect governed by case law and the work of the institutional writers.[129] The result was uncertainty (for example, as to ownership of parts of the building used by more than one proprietor), unfairness (in the absence of real burdens to the contrary, the top floor proprietor had sole responsibility for roof repairs) and the lack of a system of management (unless there were appropriate real burdens, recourse had often to be made to the rules of common property where unanimity was required for decisions).[130]

In a discussion paper published in 1990 the SLC took the approach that many of the problems under the common law could be solved by the greater use of common property.[131] The roof would thus be made common and all the flat owners would have to share in its repairs. Following Kenneth Reid's arrival in 1995 this approach was departed from. Reforming the law of the tenement would have modest benefit if the reform only applied to new buildings. If, as was clearly sensible, the reform

---

[125] Reid, *Property* (n 31) para 399.

[126] For criticism, see K Reid, 'New Enforcers for Old Burdens: Sections 52 and 53 Revisited' in Rennie, *The Promised Land* (n 38) 71–90 and S Wortley, 'Love Thy Neighbour: The Development of the Scottish Law of Implied Third-Party Rights of Enforcement of Real Burdens' 2005 *Juridical Review* 345.

[127] See Scottish Parliament, Official Report 9 Jan 2014 col 26398 (Roseanna Cunningham MSP, Minister for Community Safety and Legal Affairs). The Committee's report is available at www.scottish.parliament.uk/parliamentarybusiness/CurrentCommittees/64203.aspx.

[128] Lord Rodger of Earlsferry, *The Courts, the Church and the Constitution: Aspects of the Disruption of 1843* (Edinburgh, Edinburgh University Press, 2008) 95.

[129] Eg Stair, *Institutions of the Laws of Scotland* (Edinburgh, 1681) II.7.6.

[130] Scottish Law Commission, *Report on the Law of the Tenement* (Scot Law Com No 162, 1998) paras 2.13–2.22. As early as 1965 the Society of Solicitors in the Supreme Courts of Scotland had called on the SLC to codify this area. Source: SLC internal Fourth Programme of Law Reform file.

[131] Scottish Law Commission, *Discussion Paper on the Law of the Tenement* (DP No 91, 1990).

should apply to all tenements redistributing ownership would engage article 1 Protocol 1 of the ECHR as a deprivation. No compensation scheme was workable. The new approach was therefore to separate ownership and management. For the most part the common law rules on ownership would be codified with some uncertainties tidied up. But there would be a default management scheme which would apply in all tenements, subject to the terms of any real burdens. Majority rather than unanimity would be required for decisions on maintenance, whether to employ a property manager or install an entryphone system and the like. The SLC published a report to this effect in 1998.[132]

The new approach found favour with the Scottish Government and the draft Bill formed the basis of what is now the Tenements (Scotland) Act 2004. While there have been a series of cases where the legislation has not been properly interpreted by the lower courts,[133] the 2004 Act can also be regarded as a success. Some would have preferred a more expansive approach involving compulsory residents associations, such as under the English commonhold legislation.[134] But the very limited take-up of that legislation rather vindicates the policy of the SLC.

iv. Leasehold Reform

When the feudal system was abolished a risk was that it could simply be recreated by the back door through the use of ultra-long leases. Thus the 2000 Act, following a recommendation of the SLC, bans the creation of any new lease over 175 years in length from 9 June 2000.[135] But there are many existing ultra-long leases in certain parts of Scotland. In effect they were quasi-feudal grants. In parallel with its work on feudal abolition the SLC considered what should be done about these. A discussion paper was published in 2001[136] followed by a report in 2006.[137] The report was implemented by the Long Leases (Scotland) Act 2012. The approach taken mirrors that taken in feudal abolition. There will be an appointed day, 28 November 2015, on which the rights of landlords in ultra-long leases[138] will be abolished and the tenant will become owner of the land.[139] The former landlord will then be entitled to claim compensation in respect of lost rent.[140] In the run-up to the appointed day certain lease conditions can be converted into real burdens, for example in favour

---

[132] *Report on the Law of the Tenement* (n 130).

[133] Eg *Hunter v Tindale* 2012 SLT (Sh Ct) 2, discussed in KGC Reid and GL Gretton, *Conveyancing 2011* (Edinburgh, Avizandum Publishing, 2012) 129–32.

[134] Commonhold and Leasehold Reform Act 2002. See CG van der Merwe, 'The Tenements (Scotland) Act 2004: A Brief Evaluation' 2004 *Scots Law Times (News)* 211; Lu Xu, 'The Impact of Apartment-Ownership Law: Reforming English and Scots Law' in H Mostert and M J de Waal (eds), *Essays in Honour of CG van der Merwe* (Durban, LexisNexis, 2011) 257–74 and Lu Xu, 'The Law of the Tenement and Real Burdens: On the Brink of Recidivation' 2013 *Juridical Review* 157.

[135] Abolition of Feudal Tenure etc (Scotland) Act 2000, s 67.

[136] Scottish Law Commission, *Discussion Paper on Conversion of Long Leases* (DP No 112, 2001).

[137] Scottish Law Commission, *Report on Conversion of Long Leases* (Scot Law Com No 204, 2006).

[138] An ultra-long lease (subject to some exceptions) is a registered lease granted for more than 175 years and with an unexpired duration, immediately before the appointed day, of more than 175 years (or 100 years in the case of houses).

[139] Long Leases (Scotland) Act 2012, s 4.

[140] Ibid, ss 45–61.

of neighbouring land owned by the landlord.[141] The implementation of this legislation brings to a conclusion the work on land tenure reform identified in the Fourth Programme.

v. Land Registration

Scotland introduced land registration very early in 1617 by establishing the Register of Sasines, a register of deeds.[142] But after 300 years the drawbacks of that register were increasingly recognised. In particular, there was no national map on which all titles were plotted and conveyancing was complicated. This resulted in the passing of the Land Registration (Scotland) Act 1979 which introduced a new register known as the Land Register of Scotland, a register of title.[143] Properties transferred from the old register to the new when they were sold.

It soon became clear that the 1979 Act was defective for various reasons. It was far too short, extending to only 30 sections some of which were on other subjects. 'Nobody could accuse the Act of being well drafted' said a judge in the highest court in the land.[144] Moreover, the 1979 Act lacked solid conceptual foundations. '[It] has all the intellectual sharpness of a mashed potato'[145] wrote George Gretton. The 1979 Act created a system later labelled by the SLC as 'bijuralism'[146] whereby it did not obey the underlying rules of Scottish property law. In particular it provided for what is immediate indefeasibility.[147] No matter what problems there might be with a deed of transfer provided that it was given effect in the Register it did not matter.[148] The Keeper of Registers of Scotland,[149] had in the words of the SLC, a 'Midas touch'.[150] Inappropriate emphasis was given to possession by a proprietor in preventing rectification of the register. Even at a practical level the 1979 Act was not working. Since transfers onto the new register were generally only induced by sale, as of 2012 only 56 per cent of titles and 23 per cent of the Scottish land mass was on the new register.[151]

As a result of all these problems the Keeper asked the SLC to review the 1979 Act. Land registration appeared in the Sixth Programme in 2000. The SLC produced

---

[141] Ibid, ss 10–36.

[142] Registration Act 1617.

[143] The 1979 Act was based on two reports, neither the work of the SLC: Scottish Home and Health Department, *Registration of Title to Land in Scotland* (1963, Cmnd 2032) and Scottish Home and Health Department, *Scheme for the Introduction and Operation of Registration of Title to Land in Scotland* (1969, Cmnd 4137).

[144] *Short's Tr v Keeper of the Registers of Scotland* 1996 SC (HL) 14, 26 per Lord Jauncey of Tullichettle. But the blame should not be heaped on the draftsman. The underlying policy was not sufficiently thought through. See *MRS Hamilton Ltd v Keeper of the Registers of Scotland* 2000 SC 271, 275 per Lord President Rodger.

[145] In his case comment on the case of *Kaur v Singh*: see 1997 SCLR 1075, 1085.

[146] Scottish Law Commission, *Discussion Paper on Land Registration: Void and Voidable Titles* (DP No 125, 2004) para 1.11.

[147] Ibid, para 3.25. This term now has had impact beyond Scotland. See, eg M Harding and R Hickey, 'Bijural Ambiguity and Values in Land Registration Systems' in S Bright (ed), *Modern Studies in Property Law*, vol 6 (Oxford, Hart Publishing, 2011) 285–307.

[148] Land Registration (Scotland) Act 1979, s 3(1)(a).

[149] The equivalent of the English Chief Registrar.

[150] *Discussion Paper on Land Registration: Void and Voidable Titles* (n 146) para 5.34.

[151] See www.ros.gov.uk/pdfs/landmasscoveragereport2012.pdf.

three discussion papers[152] principally authored by Kenneth Reid and then a report[153]—perhaps the lengthiest that it has published on any topic—under the leadership of his successor George Gretton. Members of staff from Registers of Scotland were seconded to the SLC to help. The report appeared in 2010 and was swiftly implemented by the Land Registration etc (Scotland) Act 2012. It is expected to come fully into force later in 2014.

If the 1979 Act is a mashed potato then the 2012 Act is a chip off the Gretton and Reid block. Incoherence is replaced with coherence and brevity with appropriate depth.[154] A framework to speed up the move of properties from the old register to the new is provided.[155] The various parts of the register such as the national (cadastral) map are put onto a statutory footing.[156] Land registration law is reformed to bring it into line with the general rules of property law.[157] Immediate indefeasibility is replaced with deferred indefeasibility. Thus a defective deed of transfer is not cured by registration but a subsequent acquirer can rely on the entry in the register, subject to some qualifications.[158] The Midas touch is thus abolished. Electronic conveyancing is facilitated.[159] A new system of 'advance notices', influenced by comparable institutions in England and Germany, is introduced which allows prospective grantees of rights in land to make a registration which will protect them against certain events happening prior to them registering their deed, for example the owner fraudulently transferring the land to someone else.[160] The overall result is to produce a sophisticated system which meets the needs of Scotland in the twenty-first century.[161]

VI. THE FUTURE

At present there is much property law work ongoing at the SLC. There are two major projects on compulsory purchase and moveable transactions. The SLC will then undertake a project on heritable securities (mortgages) and the review of section 53 of the Title Conditions (Scotland) Act 2003 mentioned above.[162] Other property law

---

[152] Scottish Law Commission, *Discussion Paper on Land Registration: Void and Voidable Titles* (DP No 125, 2004); Scottish Law Commission, *Discussion Paper on Land Registration: Registration, Rectification and Indemnity* (DP No 128, 2005) and Scottish Law Commission, *Discussion Paper on Land Registration: Miscellaneous Issues* (DP No 130, 2005).

[153] Scottish Law Commission, *Report on Land Registration* (Scot Law Com No 222, 210) (2 vols).

[154] For an overview of the new law, see Gretton and Steven, *Property, Trusts and Succession* (n 2) ch 6.

[155] Land Registration etc (Scotland) Act 2012, s 48.

[156] Ibid, ss 2–15.

[157] 'By bringing registration law more closely into line with general property law, the bill addresses legal tensions that have caused confusion and uncertainty for property owners since the introduction of the land register. The changes will ensure that the land register continues to underpin the Scottish economy'. Scottish Parliament, Official Report, 31 May 2012 col 9596 (Fergus Ewing MSP, Minister for Energy, Enterprise and Tourism).

[158] Land Registration etc (Scotland) Act 2012, s 86.

[159] Ibid, ss 99–100.

[160] Ibid, ss 56–64.

[161] Scottish Parliament, Official Report 31 May 2012 col 9595 (Fergus Ewing MSP, Minister for Energy, Enterprise and Tourism).

[162] See above, at V.C.ii.

topics may be chosen as part of the SLC's Ninth Programme. As the then Chairman of the SLC, Lord Drummond Young, said to me when I became a Commissioner, reform of property law is rather like painting the Forth Bridge.[163] More generally, the introduction of a new streamlined procedure in the Scottish Parliament for SLC draft Bills which can be regarded as technical law reform may also offer opportunity for speedier implementation.[164]

VII. CONCLUSION

The question suggested by the title of this chapter is whether the work done by the SLC on property law in its near-50 year existence has created a golden era. In the field of land law, this is certainly true. The projects on feudal abolition, title conditions, ultra-long leases, tenements and land registration, which were carried out over many years, have revolutionised our law. No other body could have achieved this. Government departments have neither the time nor resources, given other priorities, and the systematic reform achieved could have never been done by the courts.[165] Even although the Midas touch will disappear from land registration, in terms of modernising Scottish land law, my view is that the SLC's work has been worth its weight in gold. In relation to moveable property less work has been carried out and less achieved. But it is to be hoped that the projects on prescription and moveable property, and moveable transactions will in due course also lead to much needed reform.

---

[163] The metaphor is not quite as accurate as it once was, due to developments in paint. See news.bbc.co.uk/1/hi/magazine/7252561.stm.

[164] See E Cooke and H MacQueen, 'Law Reform in a Political Environment: The Work of the Law Commissions' in D Feldman (ed), *Law in Politics, Politics in Law* (Oxford, Hart Publishing, 2013) 141 at 147–48. For a critical analysis of the equivalent English procedure using the House of Lords, see S Wilson, 'Reforming the Law (Commission): A Crisis of Identity?' [2013] PL 20.

[165] This prompted Kenneth Reid to comment in his inaugural lecture as Professor of Scots Law at the University of Edinburgh that 'the new rulers of the universe are the members of the Scottish Law Commission'. See Reid, 'Smoothing the Rugged Parts of the Passage' (n 37) at 339.

3

Reforming the Law of Prescription: A Cautionary Tale from Ireland

PROFESSOR JOHN MEE[*]

THE LAW ON the prescriptive acquisition of easements and profits,[1] as it evolved in England and Wales and was inherited by other common law jurisdictions, has long been considered unsatisfactory. 'Clouds and darkness [had] settled down over the whole subject' even before the 'fitting addition to the chaos' represented by the Prescription Act 1832.[2] It is not surprising, therefore, that reform is under consideration in a number of jurisdictions. The Law Commission of England and Wales put forward a set of proposals in its 2011 Report on *Making Land Work: Easements, Covenants and Profits à Prendre*,[3] and other law reform bodies have also made recent recommendations on the matter in, for example Northern Ireland,[4] Tasmania[5] and Victoria.[6]

As part of a wide-ranging reform of land law in the Republic of Ireland, the law of prescription was radically recast by Part 8 of the Land and Conveyancing Law Reform Act 2009 (the LCLRA). The three existing forms of prescription—common law prescription, prescription under the doctrine of lost modern grant, and statutory prescription under the Prescription Act 1832—were abolished and replaced by a new form of statutory prescription. The period for the acquisition by prescription was reduced to 12 years, creating what one commentator has described as 'The most liberal system of prescription ever proposed'.[7] The new regime was due to come into

---

[*] Law Faculty, University College Cork.

[1] That is, acquisition on the basis of long enjoyment of the relevant right.

[2] J Salmond, *Essays in Jurisprudence and Legal History* (London, Stevens and Haynes, 1891) 120.

[3] *Making Land Work: Easements, Covenants and Profits à Prendre* (Law Com No 327, 2011); henceforth 'Law Commission Report'. See generally M Dixon, 'Editor's Notebook' [2012] *Conveyancer and Property Lawyer* 1; B Bogusz, 'The Doctrine of Lost Modern Grant: Back to the Future or Time to Move On?' [2013] *Conveyancer and Property Lawyer* 198.

[4] *Report [on] Land Law* (NILC 8, 2010) 21–24; 150–56; 253–57. See also *Consultation Paper [on] Land Law* (NILC 2, 2009) 80–90.

[5] Tasmanian Law Reform Institute, *Law of Easements in Tasmania* (Final Report No 12, 2010) 7–9, 22–32, 48–52.

[6] Victoria Law Reform Commission, *Easements and Profits: Final Report 22* (2011) 50–57, 61–62. See also Victoria Law Reform Commission, *Easements and Profits: Consultation Paper* (2010) 59–69.

[7] P Bland, 'A "Hopeless Jumble": The Cursed Reform of the Law of Prescription' (2011) 16 (Irish) *Conveyancing and Property Law Journal* 54, 59 (henceforth 'A Hopeless Jumble'). Strictly speaking, this claim goes too far given that in California, eg, the period for prescription is five years (and five years of non-user will extinguish a prescriptively acquired easement): WH Pivar and R Bruss, *California Real Estate Law*, 5th edn (Chicago, Dearborn, 2002) 384.

effect after a three-year transition period but, before this period had elapsed, the scheme was modified by the Civil Law (Miscellaneous Provisions) Act 2011. Unfortunately, even after the 2011 amendments, there appear to be significant difficulties with the new Irish scheme. This chapter analyses the problems that have arisen in Ireland in relation to the reform of the law of prescription and considers the possible lessons for reformers in other jurisdictions, giving special attention to comparisons with the proposals made by the Law Commission for England and Wales in 2011.

The first section of the chapter briefly sets the recent Irish reforms in the context of the major overhaul of Irish land law in the LCLRA. Having discussed the decision in Ireland to reform rather than abolish the prescriptive acquisition of easements and profits, the chapter then analyses the main features of the new legislative scheme. The chapter next considers the difficulties that have arisen in relation to the transitional issues arising from a move from the old position, where a number of forms of prescription are recognised, to a situation where a claim can only succeed under one form of statutory prescription. Finally, the chapter assesses the extent to which the 2011 reforms have succeeded in addressing the problems with the original scheme in the LCLRA.

I. LAND LAW REFORM AND THE LAW OF PRESCRIPTION IN IRELAND

Ireland did not have an equivalent of England and Wales' Law of Property Act 1925 and important aspects of Irish land law remained substantially unreformed up to 2009. One comparatively modern aspect of the law was the system of land registration, governed by the Registration of Title Act 1964. This system is broadly similar to that which existed in England and Wales prior to the reforms (eg in relation to the scope of adverse possession) in the Land Registration Act 2002. Ireland also has a long-established system of registration of deeds,[8] relevant to land not yet covered by the registration of title system, which continues to serve a function somewhat similar to the Land Charges scheme in England and Wales.[9]

The Law Reform Commission (LRC) played a major role in the development of the LCLRA. As part of an ongoing project in the land law and conveyancing area, the LRC published a number of reports on specific points, including one in 2002 in relation to the prescriptive acquisition of easements.[10] Not long afterwards, in the context of a governmental project to prepare for the introduction in Ireland of a system of electronic conveyancing,[11] the LRC published a more general report on *Reform and Modernisation of Land Law and Conveyancing Law* in 2005.[12] In 2006, a Bill was introduced based on the draft Bill appended to

---

[8] See Registration of Deeds and Title Act 2006, Pt 3, replacing the Registration of Deeds Act 1707.
[9] Under the Land Charges Act 1972.
[10] *Report on the Acquisition of Easements and Profits à Prendre by Prescription* (LRC 66-2002), henceforth 'the LRC Report'. Irish Law Reform Commission Reports are available at www.lawreform.ie. See also P Bland, 'Clothing Fact with Right[:] Proposed Changes to Prescription and Adverse Possession' (2003) 8 (Irish) *Conveyancing and Property Law Journal* 86.
[11] For a detailed account of this project, see Law Reform Commission, *eConveyancing: Modelling of the Irish Conveyancing System* (LRC 79-2006) ch 1.
[12] Report on *Reform and Modernisation of Land Law and Conveyancing Law* (LRC 74-2005).

that report.[13] The Land and Conveyancing Law Reform Act was ultimately passed in 2009 and virtually all its provisions came into force on 1 December 2009.

In the area with which the current chapter is concerned, the position in Ireland before 2009 was broadly similar to that in England and Wales. The old law was very complicated, in that three separate forms of prescription could be relied upon by a claimant. A common thread running through these three types of prescription was the need to show 'user as of right', that is enjoyment of the right claimed without force, secrecy or permission. The three types of prescription are: (1) common law prescription; (2) prescription under the doctrine of lost modern grant; and (3) statutory prescription. Common law prescription requires the claimant to show user as of right from time immemorial (ie since 1189), thus allowing the court to conclude that there must have been a grant of the right before that date. The courts were willing to accept proof of 20 years' enjoyment as raising a presumption that the enjoyment went back to 1189. Unfortunately, this presumption gave way to evidence showing the more recent origins of the enjoyment in question. It has been suggested in England that, in light of the development of the doctrine of lost modern grant (discussed below), 'common law prescription may be considered, for practical purposes, almost, if not entirely, obsolete'.[14] Under the doctrine of lost modern grant, developed by the courts around the end of the eighteenth century, proof of 20 years' user as of right allows the court to presume that a grant was made in modern times but that this grant has been lost and so cannot be produced in court. Despite complaints about the fictional nature of the doctrine, it has kept its importance into modern times.

As a result of the deficiencies in common law prescription and the unsatisfactory element of fiction in the doctrine of lost modern grant, an attempt was made by the legislature to reform the law in this area. Unfortunately, the resulting legislation, the Prescription Act 1832 (extended to Ireland by the Prescription (Ireland) Act 1858) is 'one of the worst drafted Acts on the Statute Book'.[15] It left the situation even more confused than before, since it did not succeed in replacing the two existing forms of prescription. A further source of complexity is that the statute provides for two distinct prescriptive periods: a short period of 20 years for easements and 30 years for profits and a long period of 40 years for easements and 60 years for profits. The short period aimed to fulfil the function of the doctrine of lost modern grant by reforming common law prescription, while the long period has independent significance largely because, in calculating it, it is not necessary to subtract periods when the servient owner was under a legal disability. A key limitation on prescription under the 1832 Act is that the period of user as of right must come 'next before some suit or action', that is the right must have been enjoyed up until the taking of legal proceedings.[16] Thus, the right under the Act remains inchoate and does

---

[13] See generally, J Mee, 'The Land and Conveyancing Law Reform Bill 2006: Observations on the Law Reform Process and a Critique of Selected Provisions' (2006) 11 (Irish) *Conveyancing and Property Law Journal* 67 and 91.

[14] Law Commission for England and Wales, *Easements, Covenants and Profits à Prendre: A Consultation Paper* (CP 186, 2008) 67 (henceforth 'Law Commission CP').

[15] English Law Reform Committee, *Fourteenth Report, Acquisition of Easements and Profits by Prescription* (London, HMSO, 1966) 14.

[16] s 4.

not crystallise until adjudicated upon by the court.[17] This limitation, in particular, meant that the doctrine of lost modern grant retained its importance, since it has the key advantage over statutory prescription that the period of user does not have to come immediately before the action is brought. Thus, for example, in the Irish case of *Orwell Park Management Ltd v Henihan*,[18] a claim under the doctrine of lost modern grant, based on user as of right from 1937 to 1972, was not defeated by the fact that the right had not been used from 1972 to 1989.

This last point creates a problem for potential purchasers of land, which the English Law Commission described as a 'conveyancing trap of some magnitude'.[19] This problem was explained by the Irish Law Reform Commission as follows:

> An easement which has been legally established at some point in the past, but which has not been used for a considerable period of time, may not be readily discoverable upon an inspection of the land. Notwithstanding this, the purchaser will be bound by that easement.[20]

Crucially, the purchaser will be bound even if title to the land is registered.[21] It is provided in Ireland's Registration of Title Act 1964, section 72(1)(h) that the burdens which affect land without registration include

> easements and profits à prendre, unless they are respectively created by express grant or reservation after the first registration of the land.

Thus, although an easement or profit obtained by prescription will not (under the old law of prescription) show on the register, it will nonetheless bind the land since it has not been created expressly. The desire to address this problem helped to shape the new Irish legislation on prescription.

II. REFORM OR ABOLITION?

Prescription has long been recognised by the law but in modern times its status has become less secure. It was suggested by Lord Hoffmann in *R v Oxfordshire County Council*[22] that 'Any legal system must have rules of prescription which prevent the disturbance of long-established de facto enjoyment'.[23] However, in the context of a system of land registration that aspires to be 'not a system of registration of title but

---

[17] However, it is not necessary to wait until a dispute arises and it is possible to go to court to seek a declaration as soon as the requirements of the statute have been satisfied.

[18] *Orwell Park Management Ltd v Henihan* [2004] IEHC 87 (Irish High Court; available on BAILII (www.bailii.org)).

[19] *Land Registration for the Twenty-First Century: A Consultative Document* (Law Com No 254, 1998) 75.

[20] LRC Report (n 10) 13.

[21] If title to the land is unregistered, at common law the easement or profit will be binding on the purchaser because it is a legal (rather than an equitable) interest which, when compared to the purchaser's interest, comes 'first in time': see JCW Wylie, *Irish Land Law*, 5th edn (Haywards Heath, Bloomsbury Professional, 2013) 139. Given that there is no deed capable of registration associated with the easement or profit obtained by prescription, the registration of deeds system in the Registration of Deeds and Title Act 2006 is not applicable to the relevant situation (ibid, 141–42).

[22] *R v Oxfordshire County Council* [2000] 1 AC 335.

[23] Ibid, 349. See generally, A Goymour, 'The Acquisition of Rights in Property through the Effluxion of Time' in E Cooke (ed), *Modern Studies in Property Law*, vol 4 (Oxford, Hart Publishing, 2007).

a system of title by registration',[24] it is not obvious that it is necessary to permit the acquisition of easements and profits by prescription.[25] While prescription does not excite the same controversy as the broadly analogous doctrine of adverse possession (the scope of which has been radically curtailed in England and Wales),[26] it does allow 'the acquisition of rights which were neither intended by the servient owner nor for which he was paid or compensated'.[27] As long ago as 1966, the majority of the English Law Reform Committee decided to recommend abolition.[28] However, notwithstanding the legal 'climate change' that has made it possible to question the need to permit the prescriptive acquisition of easements and profits,[29] the Irish legislation involves reform, rather than abolition, of prescription.[30]

The possibility of abolition was discussed briefly in the Law Reform Commission's Report in 2002.[31] However, the LRC concluded that 'legal recognition should be given to a situation where a right has been enjoyed openly over a long period of time', arguing that 'there is no less moral justification for the acquisition of easements by prescription than there is for obtaining a title to land by adverse possession'.[32] The discussion was not particularly rigorous and, strangely, no mention was made of the relationship between prescription and land registration.[33] Thus, while there is a fair case for the abolition of prescription, this case was not fully ventilated in the course of the law reform process in Ireland. Arguably, the difficulties that have arisen from the attempt to modify the law of prescription in Ireland add a modest degree of further weight to the argument in favour of outright abolition (on a prospective basis) in other jurisdictions.

III. THE NEW IRISH LEGISLATIVE SCHEME

The new Irish scheme[34] differs from the older forms of prescription in a number of ways. The 1832 Act had merely attempted to build on the common law, providing that a common law prescription claim would not be defeated only by the fact that the period of user did not go all the way back to 1189. The LCLRA, by contrast,

---

[24] Law Commission, *Land Registration for the Twentyfirst Century: A Consultative Document* (Law Com No 254, 1998) 220–21, quoting *Breskvar v Wall* (1971) 126 CLR 376, 385 per Barwick CJ.

[25] See generally, S Bridge, 'Prescriptive Acquisition of Easements: Abolition or Reform?' in E Cooke (ed), *Modern Studies in Property Law*, vol 3 (Oxford, Hart Publishing, 2005); F Burns, 'Easements and Servitudes Created by Implied Grant, Implied Reservation or Prescription and Title-by-Registration Systems' in M Dixon (ed), *Modern Studies in Property Law*, vol 5 (Oxford, Hart Publishing, 2009). See also C Sara, 'Prescription—What is it For?' [2004] *Conveyancer and Property Lawyer* 13.

[26] Land Registration Act 2002, Pt 9 and Sch 6.

[27] F Burns, 'Prescriptive Acquisition of Easements in England and Legal "Climate Change"' [2007] *Conveyancer and Property Lawyer* 133, 140.

[28] Law Reform Committee, *Fourteenth Report* (n 15) 11–12.

[29] See generally Burns (n 27).

[30] The LCLRA even retains the possibility of prescriptive acquisition of profits, in contrast to the approach proposed by the English Law Commission. Note the discussion in LRC Report (n 10) 21–22 and contrast Law Commission Report (n 3) 28.

[31] LRC Report (n 10) 20–22.

[32] Ibid, 21.

[33] See further, J Mee, 'Reform of the Law on the Acquisition of Easements and Profits à Prendre by Prescription' (2005) 27 *Dublin University Law Journal* 86, 94–98.

[34] See generally, Wylie, *Irish Land Law* (n 21) 408–20.

gives a comprehensive statement of the new rules (relying only on the old law in an implicit way, by borrowing existing concepts). Although the drafting of the relevant provisions is rather unclear, the intention of the drafters was that, after the expiry of a transition period, claims could only be made on the basis of the new rules, with the old rules forming the basis for any possible claim during the transition period. However, as will be discussed in a later Part of the chapter, various difficulties arose in connection with the intended transition to the new rules. Before these problems are considered, the current Part will look in turn at the key features of the new scheme.

A. The Length of the Prescription Period

The standard period for a successful prescription claim is set by the LCLRA at 12 years user as of right, with a more stringent requirement of 30 years for state land and 60 years where the state land is foreshore.[35] It is provided in section 33 of the LCLRA that '"user as of right" means use or enjoyment without force, without secrecy and without the oral or written consent of the servient owner'. The reference to 'oral or written consent' is intended to clarify that, unlike in one respect under the Prescription Act 1832,[36] oral consent is effective to destroy a claim to 'user as of right'.

The decision to shorten the period from 20 years to 12 years arose from a view on the part of the Law Reform Commission that 'In this somewhat technical area of the law, there is particular merit, from the point of view of both accessibility and consistency, in bringing together, so far as policy will allow, the law of limitations with the law on prescription'.[37] In its 1966 Report, the English Law Reform Committee had similarly favoured (if prescription were not to be abolished) reducing the period to 12 years in order to ensure consistency with the law on adverse possession as it then stood in England and Wales.[38] The Law Reform Committee pointed out that the limitation period in respect of adverse possession had been 20 years at the time of the Prescription Act 1832, so that the periods for adverse possession and prescription had been aligned in the past.[39]

More recently, however, the Law Commission was not convinced by the argument in favour of aligning the period applicable in the prescription context with the 10-year period now applicable in relation to adverse possession under the Land Registration Act 2002. The view to this effect put forward in the Law Commission's 2008 Consultation Paper[40] was supported by a majority of those responding to the consultation.[41] In its 2011 Report, the Law Commission acknowledged that under

---

[35] s 33.

[36] A claim under the longer period set down by the 1832 Act is not defeated by proof that oral, rather than written, consent had been given at the start of the period (although the giving of oral consent during the period would set the clock back to zero): see C Harpum, S Bridge and M Dixon, *Megarry and Wade: The Law of Real Property*, 8th edn (London, Sweet and Maxwell, 2012) 1316.

[37] LRC Report (n 10) 19. In Ireland, the standard limitation period for adverse possession remains at 12 years for both registered and unregistered land.

[38] *Fourteenth Report* (n 15) 14.

[39] Ibid.

[40] Law Commission CP (n 14) 80–84.

[41] *Easements, Covenants and Profits à Prendre Consultation Analysis* (Consultation Paper 186 (Consultation Analysis), 2011) 57–58.

its proposed 'entirely new scheme of prescription, the qualifying minimum period of long use could have been of any length' but explained its recommendation in favour of a 20-year period on the basis that 'the general feeling' of consultees supported the choice of this period which had 'the benefit of familiarity from the current law'.[42]

On the whole, the decision in Ireland to reduce the prescription period to 12 years appears to have been misguided. As Peter Bland points out, the fact that 'it will be easier for students to remember the general prescriptive period if it is the same as the limitation period for the recovery of land ... is a facile justification for the policy aim of assimilating adverse possession and prescription'.[43] Any benefit accruing from 'alignment' and 'consistency' seems rather abstract and limited by the fact that there are many differences between prescription and adverse possession unrelated to the length of the limitation period. On the other hand, decreasing the prescription period to 12 years has the concrete effect of making it considerably easy to succeed in a prescription claim. This does not seem to make sense in light of the fact, mentioned above, that there are serious arguments in favour of abolishing prescription altogether. Indeed, it may be that the English Law Commission also over-estimated the value of retaining the familiar 20-year prescription period. It is arguable that a simple method of reducing potential litigation in relation to prescription and filtering out comparatively unmeritorious claims would be to increase the prescriptive period, say to 30 or 40 years.

B. Absence of Interruption

Section 33 of the LCLRA provides that there must be no 'interruption', which is defined as 'interference with, or cessation of, the use or enjoyment of an easement or profit a prendre for a continuous period of at least one year'.[44] Apparently inadvertently, this provision appears to conflate two separate requirements under the old law—the requirement in the relevant sections of the 1832 Act[45] that there be no interruption in the enjoyment of the right (meaning no 'hostile obstruction')[46] and the requirement, not expressly set out in the 1832 Act but implicit in the requirement to establish user as of right for a particular period, that the enjoyment of the right be sufficiently continuous.

Under the old law, user must be continuous but not incessant,[47] so that 'a non-user for more than a year ... may be so explained as to warrant a jury in finding an actual enjoyment for the statutory period'.[48] Thus, for example, in *Carr v Foster*,[49]

---

[42] Law Commission Report (n 3) 53.
[43] Bland, 'A Hopeless Jumble' (n 7) 55.
[44] s 33.
[45] ss 1, 2 and 3.
[46] *Megarry and Wade* (n 36) 1314. Wylie suggests that the interruption could be 'due to natural causes' rather than be the result of the acts of the servient owner or a stranger: *Irish Land Law* (n 21) 403. However, this suggestion is not supported by the authority cited, *Hall v Swift* (1838) 4 Bing NC 381, and cannot be reconciled with the wording of s 4 of the 1832 Act which makes a requirement in relation to the time when the claimant had notice 'of the person making or authorizing the [interruption] to be made'.
[47] *Hollins v Verney* (1884) 13 QBD 304, 315 per Lindley LJ.
[48] Ibid, 314.
[49] *Carr v Foster* (1842) 3 QB 581.

a claim to a common of pasturage was not defeated by the fact that there had been a two-year gap in the use of the right because this was explained by the fact that the claimant's predecessor in title did not have any commonable beasts at the time. The new Irish legislation's definition of 'interruption' has the potential to defeat a claim (probably in comparatively unusual circumstances) where there has been a cessation of a year or more in the enjoyment of the right and, under the old law, this cessation could have been explained away on the basis of the circumstances.

C. Retention of 'Next before Some Suit or Action' Requirement[50]

Section 4 of the 1832 Act stipulated that the prescription periods in that Act

> shall be deemed and taken to be the period next before some suit or action wherein the claim or matter to which such period may relate shall have been or shall be brought into question.

The effect of this provision is that an easement or profit is not established simply upon the completion of the requisite period of enjoyment of the right claimed; the enjoyment must continue up to the time that the matter is contested in a 'suit or action'. The inclusion of this requirement in the 1832 Act was described by Holdsworth as 'absurd'[51] and by Simpson as 'the fatal flaw in the scheme of the statute'.[52] Claimants who did not satisfy the 'next before some suit or action' requirement could choose to rely instead on the doctrine of lost modern grant, meaning that the law became more, rather than less, complex after the introduction of the 1832 Act.

Possibly, however, the 'fatal flaw' in the 1832 Act can more accurately be identified as the introduction of the 'next before some suit or action' requirement *combined with* the failure to abolish the doctrine of lost modern grant. Citing the view of Lord Blackburn in *Dalton v Angus*,[53] Simpson argued that

> the lost modern grant fiction had to be preserved, for otherwise great injustice would have been done in cases where a claimant could show twenty years' user, but could not show twenty years' user immediately before he brought his action.[54]

Lord Blackburn had spoken of the fact that 'old rights even from time immemorial' would have been liable to be defeated if the old forms of prescription had been abolished.[55] Clearly, however, it could have been stipulated in the 1832 Act that the abolition of the old doctrines would be prospective in nature. This would have ensured the survival of any rights that could, at the time that the 1832 Act came into force, have successfully been claimed under the old doctrines.

Thus, the experience with the 1832 Act does not, of itself, demonstrate that the 'next before some suit or action' requirement is unsuitable to be included in a

---

[50] The LCLRA dispenses with the old phrasing of 'next before some suit or action' and this phrase is used in the current chapter only as a convenient shorthand.

[51] W Holdsworth, *A History of English Law*, vol VII (London, Methuen & Co, 1937) 351.

[52] AWB Simpson, *A History of the Land Law*, 2nd edn (Oxford, Oxford University Press, 1986) 268.

[53] *Dalton v Angus* (1881) 6 App Cas 740, 814.

[54] Simpson, *A History of the Land Law* (n 52) 269.

[55] (1881) 6 App Cas 740, 814.

modern system of prescription. Although the precise reasons for inclusion in the 1832 Act are not clear,[56] the requirement is not without some attractions in practical terms. The initial approach of the Law Commission for England and Wales, in its 2008 Consultation Paper on *Easements, Covenants and Profits à Prendre*, was to recommend its retention.[57] The advantage identified at the time by the Law Commission was that 'In the event of litigation the court is required to confine its review to a relatively recent period of time, when the evidence will be easier to obtain and to evaluate'.[58] However, the responses to the Law Commission's Consultation Paper showed that the relevant rule 'is exceptionally unpopular'.[59] In one sense, of course, it is not surprising that the rule would be the subject of 'clearly evident and widespread dislike'[60] since, in light of the 1832 Act's failure to abolish the doctrine of lost modern grant, the rule serves no coherent function in the current law. However, consultees felt that, even under a new scheme, the relevant requirement could cause injustice, for example 'in cases where use stopped because of advancing age or illness'.[61] The Law Commission accepted this argument and did not include the requirement under discussion in its final proposals.[62]

In contrast, the new Irish scheme does include the 'next before some suit or action' requirement.[63] The main justification identified for this approach was that it would facilitate conveyancing by eliminating the 'conveyancing trap'[64] of prescriptive easements capable of binding a purchaser even though they could not easily be discovered because they had not been exercised for a long time before the conveyance.[65] Overall, however, it seems that it would have been preferable for the Irish reformers to have discarded the requirement. A key difficulty with making prescriptive acquisition subject to a 'next before some suit or action' requirement is that it encourages litigation, since delay in crystallising the right could lead to its being lost due to

---

[56] The explanation offered by Holdsworth, *A History of English Law* (n 51) 350–52 is that 'both the framers of the Act, and the Real Property Commissioners [whose *First Report* (1829) preceded the 1832 Act], were guilty of confusing the mode of the operation of a statute of limitation, and the mode of the operation of prescription': ibid, 351. This position is supported, on the basis of a somewhat different argument, by Simpson, *A History of the Land Law* (n 52) 268–69. However, notwithstanding the eminence of the relevant commentators, their arguments in this instance seem artificial and unconvincing (although the point cannot be pursued here). An alternative explanation suggested by the *First Report of the Real Property Commissioners* (1829) is that the reformers saw themselves as improving the law of common law prescription by reducing the length of 'legal memory', ie the 'time whereof the memory of man runneth not to the contrary': ibid, 51. Their proposal was that, instead of lasting all the way back to 1189, legal memory would last for a specified period of years measured back from the present. In order to establish a prescriptive right, the claimant would have to show enjoyment throughout that truncated period of 'legal memory', ie right up to the time of the claim.

[57] Law Commission CP (n 14) 80–81.

[58] Ibid, 81.

[59] Law Commission Report (n 3) 54.

[60] *Easements, Covenants and Profits à Prendre Consultation Analysis* (Consultation Paper 186 (Consultation Analysis), 2011) 62.

[61] Ibid, 61.

[62] Law Commission Report (n 3) 54–55.

[63] See LCLRA, s 35(2) which requires there to have been 'a relevant user period immediately before the commencement of the action'.

[64] See text to nn 19–21 above.

[65] Note the discussion in LRC Report (n 10) 25–27, also referring to the advantage that claims would have to be based on comparatively fresh evidence which would make it easier to ascertain the facts.

future events. As is illustrated by the manner in which English law has developed, the conveyancing problem presented by prescriptive easements and profits can be addressed from a different angle.[66]

In fact, the LCLRA adds an element of flexibility to the 'next before some suit or action' requirement. Section 35(3) of the LCLRA provides that the court has discretion to waive the requirement if it 'is satisfied that it is just and equitable to do so in all the circumstances of the case'. This provision was introduced at the last moment,[67] in light of concerns that had earlier been raised in the Oireachtas (the Irish Parliament) that the requirement might operate in a harsh manner in individual cases. Unfortunately, this attempt to improve matters appears—very much in the spirit of past legislative reform in relation to prescription—to have achieved the worst of all worlds.

In the first instance, it is clearly unsatisfactory that the court is given discretion to disapply the 'next before some suit or action' requirement but no attempt is made to identify any factors to guide the exercise of that discretion. There are, unfortunately, other instances in the LCLRA where a similarly untramelled discretion is given to the court, apparently on the basis of a belief that it is important to keep the law 'simple' and that this can be achieved by leaving it up to the court to make the rules on a particular point. This is clearly a questionable approach, particularly in a small jurisdiction where there may not be a sufficient volume of cases to allow the courts, within a reasonable time, to develop a body of jurisprudence which would clarify the points left entirely open by the wording of the legislation.[68]

Secondly, allowing the court discretion to disapply the requirement does not take away the incentive to litigate because the unpredictability of the discretion means that a claimant cannot safely be advised to refrain from litigation to crystallise his or her right on the basis that the requirement might possibly be disapplied if a problem were to arise in the future. On the other hand, the existence of the discretion creates an incentive for those who fail to satisfy the 'next before some suit or action' requirement to litigate in the hope of establishing that it would be 'just and equitable' for the court to disapply that requirement. Thus, the insistence upon a 'next before some suit or action' requirement, combined with a vaguely worded discretion to waive that requirement, seems to maximise the potential to generate contentious litigation.

---

[66] Under the (English) Land Registration Act 2002, Sch 3, para 3, an unregistered legal easement or profit will not override a registered disposition unless: (i) it is within the actual knowledge of the purchaser; or (ii) it would have been obvious upon a reasonably careful inspection of the land; or (iii) it has been used within the previous year. See generally, PH Kenny, 'Vanishing Easements in Registered Land' [2003] *Conveyancer and Property Lawyer* 304; J Gaunt and P Morgan, *Gale on Easements*, 19th edn(London, Sweet and Maxwell, 2012) ch 5.

[67] The provision was inserted at Report Stage, eight days before the Bill was finally passed. See *Dáil Debates* vol 686, No 3, cols 712–14.

[68] Note the comments by the Finnegan J, speaking for the Irish Supreme Court in *Mahon v Lawlor* [2011] 1 IR 311, 323, on the absence of guidance in s 31 of the LCLRA which gives the court discretion to make orders (eg for sale or physical partition) on the application of a person with an interest in land subject to co-ownership.

D. Suspension in Cases of Disability

Under the LCLRA, the user period is suspended for any period where mental incapacity makes the servient owner 'incapable ... of managing his or her affairs', although such a suspension can only extend the period up to a maximum of 30 years.[69] The suspension does not apply where

> [t]he court considers that it is reasonable, in the circumstances of the case, to have expected some other person, whether as trustee, committee of a ward of court, an attorney under an enduring power of attorney or otherwise, to have acted on behalf of the servient owner during the relevant user period.[70]

This latter provision has the disadvantage that the court is required to make a judgment in each case, which might not be predictable in advance, as to whether it would have been reasonable to expect someone to have acted on behalf of a person lacking mental capacity. The outside limit of 30 years provided for in the legislation already appears to serve as a generalised legislative assessment of the period within which it is reasonable to expect someone to act on behalf of the person who lacks capacity. Thus, arguably it would have been better to omit the complication of requiring the court to make an individualised assessment in every case as to whether someone could reasonably have been expected to have acted on behalf of the servient owner who lacks capacity.

E. Prescription by and against Tenants

The Irish legislative scheme contains simplified rules on prescription by and against tenants.[71] This reflects the fact that, prior to the recent Irish reforms, there was a greater willingness on the part of the Irish courts, as compared to those in England and Wales, to allow prescription in this context.[72] Section 36 of the LCLRA provides that, if the tenant is the claimant, the right acquired attaches to the land and it will benefit the landlord at the end of the tenancy. Where the claim is against a tenant,

---

[69] LCLRA, s 37. Compare the English Law Commission proposals under which 'Use is not qualifying use ... if it takes place at a time when the person in whom the fee simple in the servient tenement is vested is not competent to grant an easement in relation to that use for an interest equivalent to a fee simple absolute in possession'. See cl 17.3 of the Law Commission's Draft Bill: Law Commission Report (n 3) 195.

[70] s 37(2)(a). The wording of this provision appears to be defective in that it requires the court to make an all or nothing judgment as to whether a suspension should apply 'until the incapacity ceases'. It is possible to envisage a case where no one had been in a position to act on behalf of the servient owner for some of the period of user but, then, at a later point, such a person was appointed. Logically, in this kind of situation, the period of user should be suspended only for the period in which there was no one who could reasonably have been expected to act on behalf of the servient owner. See RA Pearce and J Mee, *Land Law*, 3rd edn (Dublin, Round Hall, 2011) 284.

[71] LCLRA, s 36.

[72] See VTH Delany, 'Lessees and the Doctrine of Lost Grant' (1958) 74 *LQR* 82; M Merry, 'Rights of Way and Long User: The English Restriction and the Irish Rule' (2008) 38 *Hong Kong Law Journal* 51; M Merry, 'A Matter of Authority but not of Principle—Acquisition by Lessees of Easements by Long Enjoyment' [2010] *Conveyancer and Property Lawyer* 176; KFK Low, 'The Lost Modern Grant: Untwisting Tangled Tales in a Former Colony' (2011) 127 *LQR* 200; PG Turner, 'Prescription by and against Lessees' [2012] *Conveyancer and Property Lawyer* 19. The Law Commission did not favour moving English law in the direction of the Irish position: Law Commission Report (n 3) 57–58.

the right acquired ends when the tenancy ends unless the tenant obtains a renewal or extension and in this case it attaches to the land for the period of that renewal/extension. Also, if the tenant acquires a superior interest, it attaches to that superior interest.

F. Registration

It is provided in section 35(1) of the LCLRA that an easement or profit can only be acquired under the statutory scheme upon the registration of a court order under section 35. Where the court is satisfied that the statutory requirements have been satisfied, it is required to make an order declaring the existence of the easement or profit claimed and this must then be registered in the Land Registry or in the Registry of Deeds as appropriate. The registration requirement is designed 'to facilitate conveyancing by ensuring that future purchasers will become aware of the easement's or profit's existence'.[73] However, the scheme in the LCLRA had the disadvantage that it was not possible for an easement to be acquired by prescription without the need for a court action. The further reform in the Civil Law (Miscellaneous Provisions) Act 2011 inserted a new section 49A into the Registration of Title Act 1964,[74] which allowed the Property Registration Authority to register an easement or profit acquired on the basis of prescription, with no need for an application to court, in uncontentious cases. This provides a convenient method, broadly analogous to a long-established procedure in relation to adverse possession,[75] whereby a prescriptive easement or profit can be recognised and registered without the need for litigation.[76]

IV. TRANSITIONAL ISSUES

Significant difficulties have arisen in relation to transitional issues in respect of the introduction of the new scheme. The handling of such issues is a recurring, if not particularly glamorous, aspect of the work of law reformers. The experience in the present context in Ireland provides a reminder of how badly things can go awry. The original intention was that the LCLRA would introduce a new, improved and simplified prescription regime which would, after a short transition period, replace the old forms of prescription. The transition period was set at three years.[77] However, for reasons that are explained below, serious concerns were expressed by practitioners

---

[73] LRC, *Report on Land and Conveyancing Law* (74-2005) 124. See J Mee, 'Reform of the Law on the Acquisition of Easements and Profits à Prendre by Prescription' (2005) 27 *Dublin University Law Journal* 86, 102–103 suggesting this idea.

[74] See s 41 of the Civil Law (Miscellaneous Provisions Act) 2011.

[75] See s 49 of the Registration of Title Act 1964.

[76] The procedure is only available where title to the dominant land is already registered or where the application for the registration of the prescriptive easement or profit is made in the context of an application for first registration of the dominant land: see s 49A(2) of the Registration of Title Act 1964, as inserted by s 11 of the Civil Law (Miscellaneous Provisions) Act 2011. This restriction reflects the policy of encouraging the extension of the scope of the land register.

[77] s 38.

about the scheme and, as a result, the relevant provisions of the LCLRA were amended by the Civil Law (Miscellaneous Provisions) Act 2011. The effect of this was to extend the transition period to 12 years, the same length of time as the basic prescription period under the new regime set out in the LCLRA.

A. The Problem

The difficulty raised by the LCLRA, in its original form, was as follows. Unlike the Prescription Act 1832, the LCLRA abolishes the other methods of prescription, although preserving their operation for the duration of the transition period.[78] The LCLRA states that the acquisition of easements and profits under the old law 'is abolished' (section 34) and that this abolition does not apply where a claim is made under the old law during the transition period (section 38). According to Professor John Wylie, who was centrally involved in the shaping of the 2009 reforms, once the transition period was over, a claimant would no longer be able to rely on common law prescription or the doctrine of lost modern grant even if, before the LCLRA came into force or during the transition period, he or she had satisfied the requirements of the relevant doctrine.[79] The purpose of adopting this strict approach was to ensure that a simplification of the law would be achieved quickly, since the complicated old rules would cease to be of any relevance after the expiry of a short transition period.

It will be necessary at a later point to look more closely at the plausibility of this interpretation of the legislation but, assuming that it is correct, the result is that there would be a nine-year interval, described caustically by Bland as 'the Wylie window',[80] where no prescription claim could succeed. There could be no successful claim under the new regime until a claimant had accumulated 12 years of user after 1 December 2009 (ie until 1 December 2021) and there could be no claim under the old forms of prescription once the three-year transition period ended on 30 November 2012. Therefore, someone who had a claim under the doctrine of lost modern grant, having accumulated (say) 50 years of user as of right, would be in a very precarious position after the end of the transition period on 30 November 2012. He or she would have no recourse if, before 1 December 2021, the servient

---

[78] At least this was the intention of the drafters. However, although the operation of common law prescription and the doctrine of lost modern grant is expressly preserved for the duration of the transition period (by the combination of ss 34 and 38), the repeal of the Prescription Act 1832 is not subject to any qualification: see LCLRA, s 8(1) and Sch 2. The assumption seems to have been that the protection in s 27 of the Interpretation Act 2005 for 'acquired' and 'accrued' rights in the context of a repeal would somehow save ripening claims under the Act: see Wylie, *Irish Land Law* (n 21) 409. Unfortunately, this argument is very weak and, therefore, it seems that the Prescription Act 1832 is not available to claimants, even during the transition period, leading to some practical consequences in terms of prescription involving tenants and possibly in relation to easements of light. Note that a similarly optimistic view of the scope of the Interpretation Act 2005 led the drafters of the LCLRA into serious difficulties in the context of the repeal (without a saver) of important legislation related to the enforcement of mortgages: see *Start Mortgages v Gunn* [2011] IEHC 275 (on BAILII) and the eventual legislative response, the Land and the Conveyancing Law Reform Act 2013.

[79] See JCW Wylie, *The Land and Conveyancing Law Reform Act 2009: Annotations and Commentary* (Haywards Heath, Bloomsbury Professional, 2009) 144.

[80] Bland, 'A Hopeless Jumble' (n 7) 56.

owner physically interfered with the exercise of the right or took legal action to prevent its exercise. The claimant would only be able to claim under the new form of statutory prescription if he or she could maintain his or her user until 1 December 2021 and there would be no guarantee that this could be achieved. Thus, all prescriptive entitlements, unless they had been vindicated in court prior to the expiry of the transition period, would become precarious.

The result of this would be that a dominant owner who had satisfied the requirements of the doctrine of lost modern grant would have to be advised to take steps to establish the right before the end of the transition period. Bland argued that the consequences of this would not be appetising:

> The owner of the property accessed by an inchoate right of way over a boreen[81] will have to sue every owner of the land over which the boreen passes … If his land has historically drained into a ditch or other artificial watercourse, he may be faced with any number of potential defendants in a claim for an easement of watercourse. There must be few Irish properties which are not benefited by inchoate rights, such as rights of support, light or conduit. [Litigation would be] necessary unless the servient owner can be persuaded to grant an express right[82] … The result is the creation of discord and enmity between neighbours, the waste of costs, and the bloating of the Circuit Court lists, all for no social purpose.[83]

These comments point towards a key flaw in the approach taken in the LCLRA.[84] In practice, numerous prescriptive entitlements exist that are never the subject of dispute between neighbours. Insisting that such rights must be crystallised by a certain deadline seems likely to lead to a fair deal of unnecessary litigation and the loss of rights held by those who do not realise the need for action.

It will be seen shortly that fears of an avalanche of claims prior to the expiry of the transition period led the Irish legislature to intervene to extend the transition period from 3 years to 12 years. Before this reform is discussed, it is necessary to consider whether the wording of the relevant provisions of the LCLRA does indeed ensure (as the drafters intended) that claims under the old law will be destroyed upon the expiry of the transition period, a question which retains its relevance notwithstanding the extension in 2011 of the length of the transition period. This enquiry raises interesting questions as to the manner in which the doctrine of lost modern grant operates to create easements and profits.

---

[81] A small lane or (probably unpaved) road in the country.

[82] Bland was writing before the 2011 reforms which allow for the possibility of establishing a right without litigation by means of an application to the Property Registration Authority, although only where the servient owner raises no objection sufficient to raise a doubt as to the claimant's entitlement.

[83] Bland, 'A Hopeless Jumble' (n 7) 56.

[84] The original scheme was also capable of generating odd results in the case of claimants whose period of user began before the commencement of the legislation but who could not satisfy the requirements of the old law before the end of the transition period. Consider, eg a claimant whose period of user began in 1994. At the end of the transition period in 2012, the claimant would have clocked up only 18 years of user and so could not succeed under the old law. However, she could not succeed under the new law until she had clocked up 12 years of user after the commencement of the scheme in 2009—ie not until 2021, when she would have accumulated a total of 27 years of user. In the context of a change in the law that reduced the prescription period from 20 years to 12 years, it is difficult to justify this kind of result—notwithstanding Professor Wylie's suggestion (*Irish Land Law* (n 21) 412) that 'Arguably, any scheme of such transitional provisions was bound to have "winners" and "losers"'. See generally Professor Wylie's discussion of the issues ibid, 409–12, where he is not inclined to concede that the original scheme in the LCLRA 'drew a disproportionate balance beween the interests of dominant and servient owners' (ibid, 412).

B. Does the LCLRA Destroy Claims Under the Old Law after the Transition Period?

There is an important difference between a claim under the doctrine of lost modern grant and under the Prescription Act 1832. In relation to the Prescription Act 1832, even after the required statutory period of user has been clocked up, the claimant's entitlement is still inchoate and can be lost if no court action is taken to crystallise the right. On the other hand, a right claimed under the doctrine of lost modern grant is safe as soon as the 20-years user as of right has been clocked up and it is not liable to be lost if the user stops at a later stage. On this basis, it is possible to argue that the right has been established at this point and would not be affected by the subsequent legislative abolition of the doctrine of lost modern grant.[85]

Although it seems clear that this was not the intention of the drafters, there is some support in the LCLRA for this understanding of the implications of the LCLRA's abolition of the doctrine of lost modern grant. In stating the position that will prevail after the expiry of the transition period, section 35 merely states that

> an easement or profit shall be acquired at law by prescription only on registration of a court order under this section.

This provision is phrased in the future tense and would not appear to affect the position of a person who, prior to the commencement of the section, had already 'acquired' an easement on the basis of the doctrine of lost modern grant. Also consistent with this view is the phrasing of section 34, which states (subject to section 38) that acquisition under the old law

> is abolished and after the commencement of this Chapter acquisition by prescription shall be in accordance with section 35.

There is no express indication that the abolition of the old law is to be retrospective. Even if acquisition under the old law 'is abolished' from now on, that would not affect acquisition which has already occurred, and the same argument applies to the statement that, once the abolition of the old law takes place, acquisition 'shall be' (seeming to mean 'shall in future be') in accordance with the new law.

The counter-argument to the above interpretation of the LCLRA is that, even though a claim under the doctrine of lost modern grant can be said to be 'in the bag' after 20 years of user as of right, the effect of the LCLRA is to take away the bag. Even if a person has the necessary elements for a successful claim under the doctrine of lost modern grant, he or she needs the doctrine to survive to allow that claim to be made. This is not altered by the fact that, while the doctrine survived, he or she could have—but did not—make a claim under the doctrine.[86] It could,

---

[85] See Pearce and Mee, *Land Law* (n 70) 286. Note that the reform proposed in England would ensure that 'if an easement has actually been acquired under the old law at the point of reform then any dispute about it will be determined according to the old law': Law Commission Report (n 3) 64. The Law Commission simply assumed that, if a claimant 'has already met the demands of common law prescription or, far more likely, lost modern grant, at the date of reform then an easement has already arisen by prescription and there is no transitional issue at all': ibid.

[86] If the doctrine of lost modern grant had been contained in a statutory provision, it might have been argued that, on the repeal of the relevant statute, s 27 of the Interpretation Act 2005 would have preserved rights which had been acquired or accrued prior to the repeal. However, the doctrine is not statutory and so the effect of its abolition is not governed by s 27.

of course, be argued that this result is unfair, and potentially in conflict with the protections for property rights in the Irish Constitution of 1937[87] and/or with the European Convention on Human Rights.[88] The provision of a transition period, however, makes this argument somewhat more difficult and the drafters of the LCLRA clearly did not see any problems in this respect. While the point seems to be unclear, the following discussion proceeds on the basis that the effect of the LCLRA 2009 is indeed that an easement or profit 'acquired' under the old law prior to 1 December 2009 is liable to be lost if no action is taken to vindicate it before the end of the transition period.

C. Extension of the Transition Period

In response to the concerns that were expressed about the original scheme in the LCLRA, the Civil Law (Miscellaneous Provisions) Act 2011 extended the transition period to 12 years.[89] This was intended to eliminate the nine-year window during which no prescriptive acquisition would have been possible. The key question is whether the simple tactic of extending the transition period to 12 years is sufficient to address the problems that were identified with the original scheme. Assuming once more that the drafters' interpretation is correct, the revised law is still capable of depriving people of rights already 'acquired' under the old methods of prescription merely because they fail to take action to vindicate them during a transition period.

The problem was admittedly much more acute when the transition period was three years. As has been seen, prior to the extension of the transition period, a claimant who had satisfied the requirements of the doctrine of lost modern grant would, unless he or she took steps to crystallise the right during the transition period, become vulnerable to losing the right during a nine-year window. During this window, there would be no possibility of making a successful claim even if the claimant's user continued right up to the time of the dispute—this is because the old law would no longer apply but the claimant could not yet satisfy the requirements of the new law by showing 12 years of user after the new scheme came into force. After the 2011 reforms, however, if a dispute arises after the expiry of the extended transition period of 12 years, it will normally be possible for the claimant to crystallise his or her right by claiming under the new 12-year prescriptive period, provided that he or she takes action within one year of the right ceasing to be enjoyed. However, a difficulty would arise if, at any point after the expiry of the transition period, the claimant ceases to use the right for a year or more. This could easily happen, for example if the then owner of the dominant land is an older person who has lost his or her ability to exercise the right due to infirmity. The benefit of all the previous

---

[87]   Bunreacht na hÉireann, art 43 and art 40.3.2.

[88]   See art 1 of Protocol 1 of the European Convention and the European Convention on Human Rights Act 2003 (Ireland).

[89]   See s 38 of the 2011 Act, amending s 38 of the LCLRA. The relevant changes to the law followed upon a submission made to the Department of Justice by the Law Society of Ireland, the professional body representing solicitors in Ireland.

years of user would be lost in this event and the right could only be claimed successfully if a further period of 12 years of user had elapsed by the time any dispute arises. Also, if the claim happens to relate to state-owned land, in respect of which the prescription period is much longer, the dominant owner will not be able to make a successful claim under the new law until long after the 12-year transition period has expired.[90]

There would also be a problem if the running of the 12-year period had been suspended due to the mental incapacity of the servient owner in circumstances where it was not reasonable to expect someone else to act on his or her behalf.[91] The effect of a suspension triggered by mental incapacity would be to ensure that, even though the 12-year transition period had expired, the claimant could not satisfy the requirements of the new law by showing 12 years of user after the new scheme came into effect. This in turn would mean that the claimant's right could be defeated even if his or her enjoyment continued to the end of the transition period and right up to the time that a dispute arose (after the servient owner's land came into the hands of someone with mental capacity). A dominant owner might not be in a position to judge whether one of his or her neighbours was, for example, beginning to suffer from dementia and so lacked mental capacity in a way that would trigger a suspension of the prescription period. Therefore, it seems that the general advice to land owners would have to be that there was a risk that a prescriptive right could no longer be protected if it did not crystallise during the transition period. In principle, it would be prudent for all land owners to consult their solicitors and obtain advice as to whether, in their individual circumstances, they might be at risk of losing important rights if they did not take steps to vindicate them. Thus, when the 2021 deadline draws closer, there could again be concerns about an avalanche of claims or at least about the creation of widespread uncertainty on the part of landowners as to whether legal action needs to be taken. It may be, therefore, that the Irish scheme is, even after the reforms of 2011, still unsatisfactory and needs to be reformed (again) prior to the end of the extended transition period in 2021.

V. CONCLUSION

The new Irish scheme in relation to the acquisition of easements by prescription is an ambitious one. It has run into difficulties because of its aggressive approach to the destruction of claims based on the old law. At a theoretical level, there is an appeal to the idea of tidying up the position in relation to prescriptive rights, by requiring those with claims under the old law to advance them within a transition period and imposing a requirement that thereafter any claims must be made within a year of the right ceasing to be used. However, in practice, this approach has the disadvantage of encouraging litigation in relation to matters that otherwise might never have become

---

[90] This problem is pointed out by Bland, 'A Hopeless Jumble' (n 7) 57. A claimant could not reach 30 years user as of right (or 60 years in the case of foreshore), so as to be able to rely on the new statutory scheme, until 2039 (or 2069).

[91] See s 37 dealing with mental incapacity on the part of the servient owner.

the subject of dispute. There is much to be said for the Law Commission for England and Wales's view that the avoidance of litigation should be one of the principles guiding the reform of the law of prescription.[92] Modifications to the Irish scheme in 2011 have improved the situation somewhat but do not seem to have eliminated all the problems. Therefore, although some of the choices made by the Irish legislators are worthy of consideration by legislators in other jurisdictions, in some respects the story of the Irish reforms constitutes the cautionary tale promised in the title of this chapter.

---

[92] Law Commission Report (n 3) 54–55.

Part II

Property and Planning

4

Simplifying Planning Law: A More Radical Approach

CHARLES MYNORS*

I. INTRODUCTION

MANY OF THOSE who try to navigate their way around what is laughably called the 'statute book' would probably share the feelings of King Edward VI:

> I would wish that the superfluous and tedious statutes were brought into one sum together, and made more plain and short, to the intent that men might better understand them; which thing shall most help to advance the health of the Commonwealth.[1]

That was in 1550, and the problem has grown more than a little since then.

One area of public life that has seen a particular growth in Government activity over the last century—with a corresponding increase in both legislation and guidance—is the management and control of the use and development of land. This is usually considered to be outside the scope of mainstream property law, but it obviously has very significant consequences for all those engaged in land transactions. Unfortunately, however, there is a broad measure of agreement within the professional community that the planning system is now far too elaborate, and that it significantly prevents the provision of much needed housing, infrastructure and other new development.[2]

After a period of languishing in obscurity, planning issues also seem to have recently attained greater prominence with the public and the media; and the resulting political enthusiasm for change has resulted in a system that is as misunderstood as it is criticised.

---

* PhD, FRTPI, FRICS, IHBC. The author is in practice as a barrister at Francis Taylor Building, Temple, London EC4 7BY (www.ftb.eu.com). This paper was to have been written jointly by him and Professor Patrick McAuslan; sadly Patrick McAuslan died in January 2014; see www.theguardian.com/law/2014/feb/13/patrick-mcauslan.
[1] Cited at the start of Office of the Parliamentary Counsel, Cabinet Office, *When Laws Become Too Complex: A Review into the Causes of Complex Legislation* (March 2013).
[2] See, eg 'A New Vision for Planning—there Must be a Better Way', a paper by Leonora Rozee, the former Deputy Chief Executive of the Planning Inspectorate, in *Planning Theory and Research* (March 2014); *The Planning System: The Need for a Real Overhaul*, Martin Goodall's Planning Law Blog (21 August 2014); 'Let's Rebuild our Rambling System', Angus Walker, in *Planning* (12 September 2014).

Thus, lay commentators habitually refer to 'the need to reform planning law' when what they actually mean is 'the desirability of reforming planning policy and procedure' (national and local). But policy and law are inextricably linked, and a well-structured and conceptually coherent legal framework is likely to facilitate the emergence of a system of land use management that is both usable by professionals and generally acceptable to the public. The 'planning manifesto' recently produced by a firm of city solicitors suggested that the first of four themes underpinning further reform was simplification—defined as 'making the existing system, guidance, regulation and advice simpler; to save time, reduce waste, and avoid a culture where legally challenging everything is the norm'.[3]

The Government is at least to some extent aware of this problem. In recent years, it has started the process of structural reform by vigorously pruning the policy guidance issued by various relevant central Government departments[4] over many years and still in force. In March 2012, it introduced the National Planning Policy Framework (NPPF), a single document to replace a raft of 21 planning policy guidance notes and statements (PPGs and PPSs) and 23 other pieces of Government guidance.[5] Two years later, on 6 March 2014, a further 155 Circulars, Good Practice Guides, and other Government policy documents were scrapped, following the appearance of the on-line Planning Practice Guidance (PPG), which in turn resulted from the review of guidance by Lord Taylor.[6] And, significantly, the Labour Party made it plain that it intended to retain the NPPF if it wins the election in 2015.[7] However, simply cancelling guidance is relatively straightforward.

The slightly more complex, and politically less exciting, task of simplifying secondary legislation has also begun to be tackled. The first move was the appearance of the Town and Country Planning (Development Management Procedure) (England) Order 2010—which replaced 16 statutory instruments (SIs), but which was itself amended five times before being replaced just before the General Election in 2015.[8] At the same the, the Town and Country Planning (General Permitted Development) Order 1995 and the 22 Orders amending it were finally consolidated into one order.[9] And the Government has also undertaken, in response to the recent Red Tape Challenge, to consolidate a further 74 SIs into a more manageable 20; and to cancel altogether another 35, without replacement.[10] This too is a major step in the right direction—although it remains to be seen whether the remaining elements of that package will actually be implemented.

But all that, whilst extremely commendable, still leaves untouched the jungle of primary legislation. There are currently in force around 44 Acts that deal with land

---

[3] Addleshaw Goddard, *A Forward Looking Planning Manifesto* (August 2014).

[4] The DOE, the DETR, the DCMS, the DTLR, the ODPM, the DCLG.

[5] planningguidance.planningportal.gov.uk/blog/policy/achieving-sustainable-development/annex-3-documents-replaced-by-this-framework/.

[6] http://www.planningportal.gov.uk/uploads/cancelled-guidance_06032014.pdf.

[7] Roberta Blackman-Woods MP, Shadow Planning Minister, at the Housing and Planning Conference, 16 September 2014.

[8] See now SI 2015/595; and TCP (Development Management Procedure) (Wales) Order 2012 (SI 2012/801).

[9] See now TCP (General Permitted Development) (England) Order 2015 (SI 2015/596); the 1995 Order remains in force in Wales.

[10] www.redtapechallenge.cabinetoffice.gov.uk/themehome/planning-administration/.

use and planning (including access and rights of way), and significant parts of a further 16 or so. Of those 60 Acts, about a third are relatively insignificant remnants of provisions that are now wholly or largely redundant. However, many of the remaining 40 or so are still substantial pieces of legislation, and the overall pattern of what topics are dealt with in which statutes, and in what level of depth, is completely unclear. They also omit many of the principles that have emerged in the courts over the last 70 years, by way of clarifying the statutory text. It would seem to be desirable to draw them together into a clearly structured and consistently drafted legislative code, that can be readily understood and easily used by professionals, the public and the politicians.

The statutes regulating the development and use of land and related topics are thus arguably as 'superfluous and tedious' as any, and certainly need to be brought together, and made more plain and short, so that men and women might better understand them.

This chapter explores how that might be achieved. It might be considered by some that its title is inaccurate, in that what is being advocated is in essence simply a programme of consolidation, with a measure of codification—which is not particularly 'radical'. However, the scope of the proposed exercise is ambitious, in that it seeks to cover not just planning but also cognate topics such as the built heritage, access to land, and compulsory purchase. It is also more radical than is likely to be immediately attractive to politicians, who tend to be more concerned with 'improving' the system of land-use control, rather than enabling the existing system to operate more effectively and to be generally understood.

II. THE LAW REGULATING THE USE AND DEVELOPMENT OF LAND

A. The Emergence of Primary Legislation

The increasing population and resulting development pressures in the period between the two World Wars saw the appearance of various pieces of town planning legislation, albeit in a somewhat embryonic form—culminating in the Town and Country Planning Act (TCPA) 1932 and the Town and Country Planning (Interim Development) Act 1943. That period also saw the emergence of the Rights of Way Act 1932, which would now be regarded as being at the border between planning law and highways law.

However, the modern planning system, as a universal mechanism to control the use and development of land, started with the passage of the New Towns Act 1946, the TCPA 1947, and the National Parks and Access to the Countryside Act 1949, which together set up the system that still exists, more or less, today. As will be clear from their titles, these were concerned with more than simply the regulation of development, and also started to facilitate the promotion of public development, and access to private land. Indeed, from today's perspective, it is perhaps surprising that the New Towns Act came first; but that emphasises the expectation at the time that the emerging system would be spearheaded by proactive involvement by the public sector to create a brave new world, whereas today it is to a large extent reactive.

The 1946 Act has been replaced by the New Towns Act 1981, and the programme of new towns has since been largely wound up. The statutory scheme under the 1981 Act still exists, at least on paper; but the emphasis is now more on special development bodies of one kind or another, such as development corporations; and even they have been to some extent superseded. Essentially it has been realised that, not surprisingly, the shortage of public finance has limited the extent to which public authorities can on their own achieve major regeneration of existing urban areas; and the increasing encouragement given to public participation has led to major opposition to development on new sites outside built-up areas.

The 1949 Act is still at least partially in force, albeit supplemented by much subsequent legislation (notably the Countryside Act 1968, the Wildlife and Countryside Act 1981 and the Countryside and Rights of Way Act 2000). These together provide for the regulation of access to land, rights of way, and wildlife protection. The Law Commission is currently considering the reform of wildlife law; but the other elements of that package are still in existence, albeit in a somewhat unclear pattern. And the most recent development has been the unexpected growth in significance of commons and village green legislation, to the point where the Government is now seeking to rein it in as far as is politically acceptable.

The 1947 Act—as it turned out, much the most significant of the three original pieces of legislation—was substantially amended (in particular by the Town and Country Planning Act (TCPA) 1954, which largely repealed the financial provisions that had lain at the heart of the original post-war scheme), before being replaced by the TCPA 1962. That was a consolidating Act, and was in turn amended by the TCPA 1968 and other Acts, which were all, in turn, replaced by the next consolidating Act, the TCPA 1971. The 1971 Act lasted slightly longer than its predecessors, but was amended by (amongst others) the Town and Country Planning (Amendment) Act 1972, the Town and Country Amenities Act 1974, the Local Government, Planning and Land Act 1980 and the Housing and Planning Act 1986.

B. The 1990 Acts

In due course, the 1971 Act and the various Acts that had amended it were all swept away by four new Acts:

— the Town and Country Planning Act 1990 (dealing with mainstream planning control);
— the Planning (Listed Buildings and Conservation Areas) Act 1990 (P(LBCA)A);
— the Planning (Hazardous Substances) Act 1990; and
— the Planning (Consequential Provisions) Act 1990.

But the resulting clarity did not last. Since 1990, the pace of new legislation being enacted has, if anything, increased. Thus, immediately after the 1990 consolidation, the Planning and Compensation Act 1991 made significant changes to enforcement procedures. The Transport and Works Act 1992 introduced a new mechanism for gaining approval for transport projects. The Planning and Compulsory Purchase Act (PCPA) 2004 changed the system of development plans; and removed Crown immunity. The Planning Act 2008 introduced a system of 'development consent' for nationally significant projects. Further changes, not always particularly carefully considered, have been made by the Localism Act 2011, the Growth and Infrastructure Act 2013 and the Enterprise and Regulatory Reform Act 2013. And a variety of other amendments have been made to the detailed provisions of the 1990 Acts.

Further, whereas in the past there was at any time only one Town and Country Planning Act, which was from time to time amended, there are now a plethora of Acts of Parliament, with somewhat similar provisions; and many are freestanding pieces of legislation. There is thus no overall coherent scheme of statute law governing this whole area of activity; there are in fact, as noted at the outset, some 60 general Acts currently in force that deal in whole or in part with these issues, as listed in Table 1—as well as some local legislation, especially in London. No doubt others could be added.

Table 1: Planning and development law as it is...

1.	Green Belt (London and Home Counties) Act 1938 (the whole Act)
2.	National Parks and Access to the Countryside Act 1949 (the whole Act)
3.	Mineral Workings Act 1951 (the whole Act)
4.	Town Development Act 1952 (the whole Act)
5.	Agricultural Land (Removal of Surface Soil) Act 1953 (the whole Act)
6.	Historic Buildings and Ancient Monuments Act 1953 (the whole Act)
7.	Town and Country Planning Act 1954 (the whole Act)
8.	Opencast Coal Act 1958 (the whole Act)
9.	Town and Country Planning Act 1959 (the whole Act)
10.	Caravan Sites and Control of Development Act 1960 (the whole Act)
11.	Land Compensation Act 1961 (the whole Act)
12.	Town and Country Planning Act 1962 (the whole Act)
13.	Town and Country Planning Act 1963 (the whole Act)
14.	Compulsory Purchase Act 1965 (the whole Act)
15.	Civic Amenities Act 1967 (the whole Act)
16.	Agriculture Act 1967 (Part III, Schedule 5 (rural development boards))
17.	Forestry Act 1967 (Part II)
18.	Caravan Sites Act 1968 (the whole Act)
19.	Countryside Act 1968 (the whole Act)
20.	Protection of Wrecks Act 1973 (the whole Act)
21.	Mobile Homes Act 1975 (the whole Act)
22.	Development of Rural Wales Act 1976 (the whole Act)
23.	Inner Urban Areas Act 1978 (the whole Act)
24.	Ancient Monuments and Archaeological Areas Act 1979 (the whole Act)
25.	Local Government, Planning and Land Act 1980 (Parts XV, XVI, XVII, XVIII)

(continued)

Table 1: *(Continued)*

26.	New Towns Act 1981 (the whole Act)
27.	Wildlife and Countryside Act 1981 (Parts II, III; Schedules 10A–17)
28.	Compulsory Purchase (Vesting Declarations) Act 1981 (the whole Act)
29.	Acquisition of Land Act 1981 (the whole Act)
30.	Derelict Land Act 1982 (the whole Act)
31.	National Heritage Act 1983 (sections 32–38)
32.	Wildlife and Countryside (Amendment) Act 1985 (the whole Act)
33.	Wildlife and Countryside (Service of Notices) Act 1985 (the whole Act)
34.	New Towns And Urban Development Corporations Act 1985 (the whole Act)
35.	Mineral Workings Act 1985 (the whole Act)
36.	Housing and Planning Act 1986 (the whole Act)
37.	Environmental Protection Act 1990 (Part VII)
38.	Town and Country Planning Act 1990 (the whole Act)
39.	Planning (Listed Buildings and Conservation Areas) Act 1990 (the whole Act)
40.	Planning (Hazardous Substances) Act 1990 (the whole Act)
41.	Planning (Consequential Provisions) Act 1990 (the whole Act)
42.	Planning and Compensation Act 1991 (the whole Act)
43.	Transport and Works Act 1992 (Part I)
44.	Leasehold Reform, Housing and Urban Development Act 1993 (Part III)
45.	Environment Act 1995 (Part III, Schedules 7–10 (national parks); section 96, Schedule 13, 14 (mineral planning permissions); section 97 (hedgerows))
46.	Regional Development Agencies Act 1998 (the whole Act)
47.	Countryside and Rights of Way Act 2000 (the whole Act)
48.	National Heritage Act 2002 (the whole Act)
49.	Planning and Compulsory Purchase Act 2004 (the whole Act)
50.	Natural Environment and Rural Communities Act 2006 (Parts 1, 5, 6)
51.	Commons Act 2006 (provisions relating to village greens)
52.	Sustainable Communities Act 2007 (the whole Act)
53.	Planning Act 2008 (the whole Act)
54.	Planning and Energy Act 2008 (the whole Act)
55.	Marine and Coastal Access Act 2009 (Part 9)
56.	Localism Act 2011 (Part 5, Chapter 3; Part 6; Part 8, Chapter 2)
57.	Growth and Infrastructure Act 2013 (first part)
58.	Mobile Homes Act 2013
59.	Enterprise and Regulatory Reform Act 2013 (sections 60, 61, 63, Schedules 16, 17: heritage planning)
60.	Criminal Justice and Courts Act 2015 (sections 91, 92, Schedule 16).

And it is not just the number of statutes; they are getting longer. Thus the 1946, 1947 and 1949 Acts together contained 161 sections and 18 Schedules. By contrast, the four 1990 Planning Acts alone—as they first appeared—contained 479 sections and 26 Schedules. But they have now been significantly lengthened, to around 550 sections, as a result of numerous amendments over the last 24 years; and they have been supplemented by separate provisions in other Acts (notably the PCPA 2004 and the Planning Act 2008) introducing a further 300 or so sections and numerous Schedules. Alongside all this, the separate Acts dealing with new towns, access, and countryside matters, amongst others, still remain.

The number of Acts would not of itself necessarily be a problem; but the way in which the legislation has emerged has led to the law on different topics being spread, apparently randomly, over a number of different Acts, which makes it difficult for those seeking to use and apply it—and indeed for Parliament when it seeks to introduce amendments. Law that is not clear is not helpful even to professionals working regularly in the field, who find it difficult to work with—and it is incomprehensible to ordinary citizens or to those, such as CABs, advising them—as is recognised by the Good Law Project currently being promoted by the Cabinet Office. It is noticeable, for example, that the principal reference work in this particular field, the *Encyclopaedia of Planning Law*, has expanded from three to nine volumes over the last 30 years; and that its editors still find it difficult to keep up with the numerous changes.

In the words of one seasoned professional, 'the planning system is a mess'.[11]

C. The Resulting Problem

There is periodically some enthusiasm on the part of Parliament for changing and 'improving' the system—although the experience of history is that such changes are not always for the better. But there has hitherto been little appetite within the political establishment (of any party) for simplifying the legislation that already exists, so as to have a clearer framework to guide present decisions, and to act as a stimulus for future change. Nor has there been much impetus on the part of the relevant central Government department to address this problem.

In the past, mainstream planning legislation has been consolidated every so often—generally by the Law Commission (as in 1971 and 1990)—although that has not dealt with the legislation in related fields. More recently, the Commission has produced a substantial review of the law of compulsory purchase and compensation, yet to be implemented, and it is currently reviewing the law on the protection of wildlife. But it has no plans at present to tackle the 1990 planning legislation itself, far less the other related statutes.

It was suggested that, as part of its twelfth programme, starting in 2014, the Commission might wish to tackle a major exercise of simplifying this body of statutory law, along the lines indicated here; it declined, on the grounds that doing so would involve substantial resources of professional time and, more significantly, that these

---

[11] Rozee (n 2).

days it only tackles a project if there is an undertaking from the relevant Government department that indicates a serious intention to take forward law reform in that area. It commented:

> Our discussions with the Department for Communities and Local Government strongly suggest that they would not give us such an undertaking at present. The Department's view is that, given the significant amount of substantive law reform of planning law that has taken place in recent years, these changes should be allowed to become established before any further law reform takes place.[12]

That seems unfortunate, since it is precisely because there has been so much substantive law reform that there is the need for simplification. And simplification, as opposed to substantive change, fits in with the oft-repeated desire of Governments—of all parties—that the processes of central and local government, and the legislation regulating them, should be effective, efficient and proportionate, and that the planning system should be straightforward. More recently, therefore, Government officials have indicated that there may be a greater willingness to contemplate a more wide-ranging simplification exercise of the kind contemplated here, possibly in association with the Good Law Project.

What is needed is a major programme of consolidation and rationalisation, which would on any analysis take several years—during which, as the recent changes become established, it may indeed emerge that minor adjustments are needed to avoid resulting problems. More recently, as noted above, a number of commentators have started to press for a more substantial reform of the legislation.[13] And support has been forthcoming from the Planning Officers' Society, whose members would have the responsibility for implementing any changes.[14] It is hoped that, now the election is out of the way, ministers will be in a position to supply the necessary political backing for reform.

And, of course, this problem will get gradually worse; and so some measure of simplification will have to take place sooner or later. The legislation will not sort itself.

III. WHAT COULD BE ACHIEVED

A. General Approach

What is now required is thus a major programme of simplification. That would be primarily consolidation, but also some rationalisation, since it is inevitable that such an exercise would throw up a number of areas where there is scope for technical improvement, to remove redundant or overlapping provisions, and to clarify those that are obscure or inconsistent.

It would be good to ensure that, as far as possible, all the relevant legislation is adjusted on a consistent basis to ensure that broad principles are set out in primary

---

[12] Letter to the author, 14 March 2014.
[13] See n 2 above.
[14] 'This has considerable merit'; email to author, 23 July 2014.

legislation whereas detailed procedural provisions should in future all be in secondary legislation—in line with the approach that has been increasingly followed in recent years. That would facilitate the making of future changes to detailed procedures without the waste of parliamentary time. Similarly the detailed arrangements as to the operation of the various public bodies should be in secondary legislation—so that each body can look to a single set of regulations that provides for its day-to-day requirements.

It is noteworthy that there are certain statutory controls that are largely the subject of freestanding sets of regulations—such as those governing hedgerows, protected trees, and outdoor advertising.[15] Doing this simplifies the relevant Act itself, and also helps users as they can find all the law they need in one place. It would be sensible to see whether there are any other codes that could similarly be taken out of primary legislation.

It would also be helpful to include some of the principles established by the courts by way of interpreting the text of the statutes. For example, the concept of planning permission being required for a change in the use of a parcel of land begs the question of which parcel should be considered; but the doctrine of the 'planning unit'—the device invented by the courts to deal with this issue[16]—is nowhere mentioned on the face of the statute. And the extent of the curtilage of a building is to be considered at different dates for different purposes.[17] The common feature of such points is that they came before the courts as a result of uncertainty or confusion as to the interpretation of existing legislation, which were (to a greater or lesser extent) resolved by the resulting judicial rulings. It would be good if the resulting definitions and concepts were to be incorporated into the body of the relevant statute.

The same is true of certain principles that have, entirely non-controversially, been incorporated for many years within Government guidance but which have, in effect, acquired the status of legal principles—such as the tests to be applied to determine the validity of planning obligations and conditions.[18]

Finally, it would obviously be good to examine how other countries have dealt with the legislation relating to these topics—the underlying problems are, after all, the same, even if the political and legislative arrangements are different. France, for instance, revised its planning laws in 2007 because of their complexity and the consequent over-involvement of judicial bodies in planning matters. And Ireland has a system that is similar to the UK, but somewhat less elaborate. There may well be lessons that can be learnt.

If an exercise of consolidation also includes an element of codification, or indeed other forms of change, they would require Parliamentary approval, which would open up the possibility of the whole exercise becoming procedurally over-complex, resulting in nothing being achieved. However, it would be sensible at least to consider

---

[15] Hedgerows Regulations 1997, TCP (Control of Advertisements Regulations) 2007 (SI 2007/783), and TCP (Tree Preservation) Regulations 2012 (SI 2012/605).

[16] *Burdle v Secretary of State* [1972] 1 WLR 1207.

[17] Compare *Morris v Wrexham CBC* [2002] 2 P&CR 7 and *Lowe v Secretary of State* [1991] 1 PLR 58.

[18] NPPF, paras 204, 206.

what technical changes would in principle be desirable, and whether they would be politically desirable or otherwise.

In accordance with those principles, the general aim should thus be to consolidate the 60 or so Acts dealing in whole or part with these issues, and to reduce them to a consistently drafted set of new Acts, each dealing with a discrete topic. Clearly there may be a number of ways in which the overall subject area could be divided, but the eight headings below together indicate one possible statutory scheme.

B. Specific Topics

i. *Planning Authorities and Planning Policy*

The starting point should be a clarification of the various public authorities administering the system. There should be a clear rule that 'the planning authority' means the unitary local authority, where there is one, and the district council in areas where there is a two-tier system; save that national parks authorities, the Broads Authority and development corporations would remain the sole planning authority in their respective areas.[19] County councils, where they exist, would then only be planning authorities where specifically provided for in relation to a specific function (as with, for example, minerals and waste planning)—although of course a county council could be appointed as such in a particular case by an agreement under the Local Government Act 1972.

In the past, Parliament has created a variety of other types of authority that have been capable of being planning authorities—including enterprise zone authorities, AONB conservation boards, housing action trusts, and English Partnerships.[20] In practice these authorities have never been made planning authorities. It would of course always be possible in the future for a new body simply to be given the same powers as a development corporation—as was effectively done with the Olympic Delivery Authority.[21]

The Planning Inspectorate is also a key player; but is nowhere regulated—as it is in Ireland.[22] That may be satisfactory, but it should at least be considered.

Secondly, there needs to be a clear statement of what is the policy basis for the planning system. There is a hierarchy of policies, which in England includes the following:

— the National Planning Policy Framework, and Planning Practice Guidance;
— national policy statements relating to specific topics (introduced by the Planning Act 2008);
— the spatial development strategy, development plan documents, and the sustainable community strategy (now regulated under Parts 2 and 3 of the PCPA 2004, and the Sustainable Communities Act 2007);
— neighbourhood plans (introduced by the Localism Act 2011); and
— supplementary planning documents.

---

[19] TCPA 1990, Pt 1, Sch 1.
[20] TCPA 1990, s 6; Housing Act 1988; Countryside and Rights of Way Act 2000, s 86.
[21] London Olympic Games and Paralympic Games Act 2006, s 5.
[22] Planning and Development Act 2000 (An Bord Pleanala), Pt VI.

This all needs to be given a logical statutory basis. For example, central Government policy (the first item on the list) is hugely influential in practice, but is nowhere mentioned on the face of the statute. And the much-vaunted primacy of the development plan is to be found not in the TCPA 1990, but in section 38(6) of the PCPA 2004, which has itself been much altered. Indeed, curiously, the 1990 Act now contains nothing at all about planning—as opposed to development control.

The procedural details as to the actual production of each type of policy should be governed by secondary legislation. But thought should be given as to the extent to which primary legislation should influence the topics that may or should be the subject of policies—why, for example, is there a specific Act allowing the inclusion in the development plan of policies encouraging energy efficiency?[23] The emergence of a statement of central Government policy is a good time for this to be reviewed.

ii. Countryside

The next step logically is to provide for the protection of the natural environment, including but not limited to the countryside. This is largely the subject of a plethora of statutes going back over many years: Parts I, II and III of the National Parks and Access to the Countryside Act 1949, Part II of the Forestry Act 1967, the Countryside Act 1968, Part II of the Wildlife and Countryside Act 1981, the Wildlife and Countryside (Amendment) Act 1985, the Wildlife and Countryside (Service of Notices) Act 1985, Part VII of the Environmental Protection Act 1990, Chapter I of Part VIII of the TCPA 1990, Part III and section 97 of the Environment Act 1995, Parts III and IV of the Countryside and Rights of Way Act 2000, and Parts 1 and 5 of the Natural Environment and Rural Communities Act 2006.

The administration of Government policy in this area has suffered numerous changes, with the arrival and departure of the Countryside Commission, the Countryside Agency, the Commission for Rural Communities, and English Nature. The starting point here should be to make plain the structure and role of Natural England, the national parks authorities, and (possibly) the Broads Authority.

There is then a hierarchy of different types of designation—including national parks, areas of outstanding natural beauty (AONBs), and nature reserves, as well as special protection areas under European legislation. These need to be clarified, along with the need for consent to be obtained for operations affecting them. Also relevant is the law relating to works to trees, recently simplified in the Planning Act 2008, and hedgerows.

The legal framework for wildlife management—described recently by the Law Commission as 'overly complicated, frequently contradictory and unduly prescriptive'—is clearly related to this topic. However, it may be more appropriate for this to be the subject of a separate statute, in the light of any conclusions emerging from the Commission's review.[24] And thought should be given as to whether forestry legislation

---

[23] Planning and Energy Act 2008.
[24] http://lawcommission.justice.gov.uk/areas/wildlife.htm.

should remain separate, or be brought within the general scope of the present simplification exercise, especially following the creation of Natural Resources Wales, which
has taken over the Forestry Commission's functions in Wales.

iii. Built Heritage

There is then the relatively limited topic of identifying those elements of the built
heritage which are to be afforded special protection—referred to in recent Government policy as 'designated heritage assets'.[25] They include world heritage sites
(governed by the Unesco World Heritage Convention, but hardly mentioned in UK
legislation), scheduled monuments (under the Ancient Monuments and Archaeological Areas Act 1979), listed buildings and conservation areas (under the Planning (Listed Buildings and Conservation Areas) Act 1990, amended by Part 5 of
the Enterprise and Regulatory Reform Act 2013), protected wrecks (under the
Protection of Wrecks Act 1973, and registered parks and gardens (largely outside
legislation).

The relevant statutory provisions simply need to be brought together. The powers
as to the carrying out of repairs and the giving of grants (in the Historic Buildings and
Ancient Monuments Act 1953 and the 1990 Act) could also be simplified. It would
also be sensible to give statutory force to the new structure of English Heritage and
Historic England, introduced in April 2015[26]—replacing the provisions currently in
the National Heritage Acts of 1983 and 2002.

Areas of archaeological importance (under the 1979 Act) have not been much
used, and the Government agreed twenty years ago to abandon that system at the
first appropriate legislative opportunity.[27] That could be done as part of this exercise.

iv. Promotion of Development

As noted already, the original core of the planning and development legislation
was the encouragement and facilitation of development by public bodies, principally through the programme of new towns. It is perhaps not surprising that
there have been periodically calls for the reinstatement of such a programme, as
reliance on private sector development alone has not been sufficient to generate
the required level of new building activity. The Government has also started to
promote the idea of new garden cities.[28] Latterly, the preferred vehicle for public-
sector urban regeneration has been the urban development corporation, usually
created for a specific period and, more recently, mayoral development corporations in London.[29]

---

[25] NPPF, Glossary.
[26] www.gov.uk/government/uploads/system/uploads/attachment_data/file/263943/1291-B_English_
Heritage_Accessible__1_.pdf.
[27] *Protecting the Heritage* (May 1996).
[28] Budget 2014, paras 1.145, 1.146.
[29] Local Government, Planning and Land Act 1980, Pt XVI; Localism Act 2011, Pt 8, Ch 2.

It would be sensible to consolidate and update the relevant legislation, which can then be harnessed to support any future development initiative by the government of the day. This is to be found in the Inner Urban Areas Act 1978, Parts XV, XVI and XVIII of the Local Government, Planning and Land Act 1908, the New Towns Act 1981, the New Towns and Urban Development Corporations Act 1985, Part III of the Leasehold Reform, Housing and Urban Development Act 1993, and Chapter 2 of Part 8 of the Localism Act 2011.

The reduction of the burden of planning controls through the creation of simplified planning zones and enterprise zones, on the other hand, has generally not been a success, in that it has been hardly taken up in practice. It is noteworthy that the current guidance from central Government makes almost no reference at all to either. Simplified planning zones could therefore be simply abandoned, along with references to enterprise zone authorities as planning authorities.

Arguably this might be the place to include the provisions relating to the improvement of waste land, in Chapter II of Part VIII of the TCPA 1990—a rarely used but potentially effective form of intervention to achieve the improvement of land in the public interest.

v. Regulation of Development

This is probably the most significant in practice of the various topic areas. There are in fact a variety of consent mechanisms within the overall ambit of the 'planning system'. The principal one is planning permission, under Parts III to VII of the TCPA 1990. This has been the subject of numerous amendments over the years—notably by the Planning and Compensation Act 1991 and the Localism Act 2011 (in relation to enforcement), and the Planning and Compulsory Purchase Act 2004—and badly needs to be clarified.

In particular, the Government now seems to envisage several types of consent mechanism:

— outline permission in response to an application, followed by approval of reserved matters;
— detailed permission, followed approval of matters reserved by condition;
— permission granted by development order, subject to approval of details in response to application;
— permission granted by development order, with no need for any further approval.[30]

As noted, the Government has at last consolidated the permitted development order, but the primary legislation also needs to be clarified.

It is also noticeable that there are a variety of duties—under a wide variety of statutes and regulations—laid on those determining applications for planning permission, including the following:

— to make the decision in accordance with the development plan, so far as material;[31]

---

[30] Budget 2014, para 1.147.
[31] TCPA 1990, s 70; TCPA 2004, s 38(6).

— to have special regard to the desirability of preserving any listed buildings affected, and pay special attention to desirability of preserving or enhancing the character of any conservation area;[32]
— to have due regard to the need to eliminate unlawful discrimination against disabled people;[33]
— to take into account representations made by owners of land or in response to publicity for application;[34]
— to have regard to desirability of conserving the natural beauty and amenity of the countryside;[35] and
— to have regard to any other material considerations.[36]

This list is the result of past political battles, but should be rationalised—or at the very least made explicit in one place. Should other matters be included?

In addition, alongside planning permission, there are a variety of other codes, controlling:

— certain types of mining (under Part I of the Opencast Coal Act 1958 and section 96 of the Environment Act 1995);
— caravan sites (under the Caravan Sites and Control of Development Act 1960, the Caravan Sites Act 1968, the Mobile Homes Act 1975, Part XVII of the Local Government, Planning and Land Act 1980);
— works to scheduled monuments and listed buildings (under the Ancient Monuments and Archaeological Areas Act 1979 and Part I of the Planning (Listed Buildings and Conservation Areas) Act 1990);
— the storage of hazardous substances (under the Planning (Hazardous Substances) Act 1990); and
— the display of outdoor advertising (under the TCP (Control of Advertisements) Regulations 2007).

These have to some extent been the subject of consideration by the Penfold Review on non-planning consents—and that has resulted in changes being made including, for example, the merging of conservation area consent into planning permission (by the Enterprise and Regulatory Reform Act 2011). But there is no reason why the same approach could not easily be adopted in relation to scheduled monument consent and listed building consent—the latter, in particular, is now very closely aligned to planning permission, after changes made by the 2011 Act, and there is little purpose served by the existence of the two systems operating in parallel.

It might be possible to integrate some of these other controls into the mainstream planning permission system; or it may be appropriate to separate them out into regulations. Advertising, for example, is classified as 'development' in the Republic of Ireland, and accordingly largely dealt with under normal planning legislation;[37]

---

[32] P(LBCA)A 1990, ss 66, 72.
[33] Equality Act 2010, s 149.
[34] TCP (Development Management Procedure) (England) Order 2015 (SI 2015/595), art 33; TCP (Development Managements Procedure) (Wales) Order 2012 (SI 2012/801), art 21.
[35] Countryside Act 1968, s 11.
[36] TCPA 1990, s 70(2).
[37] Planning and Development Act 2000, ss 2(1), 3(2)(a); Planning and Development Regulations 2001 (SI 2001/600), Sch 2, Pt 2.

but in the UK it has always been dealt with by means of a freestanding code in secondary legislation.

Another system of control operating alongside the normal planning system is the new procedure to obtain 'development consent' under the Planning Act 2008 (as amended by the Localism Act 2011) for major infrastructure projects. This was initially dealt with by the Infrastructure Planning Commission, but has recently been brought under the auspices of the Inspectorate. Now that system is starting to bed down, it will soon be possible to see whether it is helpful for it to remain separate, or whether it should be incorporated into mainstream planning control—and how it should relate to the system of authorisation by orders under the Transport and Works Act 1992.

Planning inquiry commissions, on the other hand, have never been used since the idea was first introduced, and could now be abandoned.

'Development consent' is also the term used in European legislation to refer to the authorisation of proposals requiring an environmental impact assessment. Generally that will be planning permission, and the assessment will be carried out under a procedure provided for in a freestanding set of regulations, which transpose the requirements of the relevant EU directives, which have now been codified as Directive 2011/92/EU.[38] The applicability of that procedure, and its application in practice, have been the subject of a large number of court challenges. However, in principle, the purpose of the Directive is the same as that of the UK planning system—to assess the impact of proposed development, and to see whether that impact (if harmful) is outweighed by the resulting benefit—and it is arguably unsatisfactory to have the two systems operating in parallel. It would therefore seem to be desirable to explore whether they can be brought together into a single regime that complies with the Directive but also fits seamlessly into the mainstream planning system. Here, too, thought will need to be given as to how much should be in primary legislation and how much in secondary regulations.

Indeed, the term 'development consent' is in many ways preferable to 'planning permission'—it is after all the proposed development that is to be authorised, not the plan. But that may be a step too far, as the term 'planning permission', however illogical, is well entrenched.

vi. Infrastructure Funding

There have been various attempts to introduce a financial or fiscal element into the control of development, from betterment levy through to development land tax. The most recent attempt, the community infrastructure levy (CIL), is largely the subject of regulations, but the relevant primary legislation—in Part 11 of the Planning Act 2008, as amended by the Localism Act 2011—could usefully be the subject of a separate statute.

Alternatively it might be preferable for a new Infrastructure Act to incorporate both the CIL provisions and the development consent procedure under the 2008 Act.

---

[38] TCP (Environmental Impact Assessment) Regulations 2011 (SI 2011/1824).

vii. Access and Rights of Way

One strand of the legislation in this area has always been to achieve a degree of public access to some land—initially by means of access orders to open country under Part V of the National Parks and Access to the Countryside Act 1949, and more recently by the introduction of the 'right to roam' (access land) provisions in Part I of the Countryside and Rights of Way Act 2000.

More recently, the law relating to town and village greens (now in the Commons Act 2006, recently amended by the Growth and Infrastructure Act 2013) has in effect provided another form of access land—albeit as a probably unintended by-product of commons legislation and customary rights law. It would be sensible to recognise this by introducing village greens as a further category of access land under the 2000 Act.

Related to this is the creation of rights of way over land. The law on this is spread across several statutes—Part IV of the 1949 Act, Part III of the Wildlife and Countryside Act 1981, Part II of the 2000 Act, and Part 6 of the Natural Environment and Rural Communities Act 2006—and is the subject of further changes proposed in the Deregulation Bill currently before Parliament.[39] These have together created a procedure that would benefit from being consolidated and updated.

It would be helpful to draw together all this legislation, and also to link it to the main planning system. Compared to other provisions considered in this chapter, these are not urgently in need of reform, and may well need little if any updating; but since they are linked to others that are in need of simplifying, it would be sensible not to leave them unconsolidated.

viii. Land Acquisition and Compensation

The legislation governing the powers of public authorities to acquire land under compulsory purchase powers or by agreement is notoriously complex.

Acquisition procedure is governed principally by the Compulsory Purchase Act 1965, the Acquisition of Land Act 1981, the Compulsory Purchase (Vesting Declarations) Act 1981, and Part IX of the TCPA 1990, with a few additional provisions to be found (still) in the TCPA 1959. The assessment of compensation is the subject of the Land Compensation Acts of 1961 and 1973, with additional provisions in Part II of the Opencast Coal Act 1958 and Part III of the Planning and Compensation Act 1991. Additional provisions have been inserted into many of the above Acts, under both headings, by Part 8 of the PCPA 2004 and Part 9 of the Localism Act 2011; and further changes made by the Growth and Infrastructure Act 2013.

This has been the subject of two major Law Commission reports, relating to acquisition procedure and a compensation code.[40] These have not been progressed by the Government, which is unfortunate. It would be possible simply to consolidate the statutes referred to above as part of the general simplification exercise envisaged by this chapter, but clearly such an exercise would be a golden opportunity to enact

---

[39] Deregulation Bill, councils 21–27 and Sch 7.
[40] http://lawcommission.justice.gov.uk/areas/towards-a-compulsory-purchase-code-1-compensation-a%20consultative-report.htm.

the recommendations of the Commission, along with other changes being considered by the Government in consultation with key players such as the Compulsory Purchase Association.[41]

It might well be that the consolidation of the legislation relating to the acquisition of land should be a separate exercise, following on immediately after the other simplification proposals described in this chapter. This is an area of law fraught with technicalities, and it would be essential, more than with any of the other topics considered here, to ensure that any draft Bill was the subject of extensive consultation with all major stakeholders.

C. Miscellaneous Provisions

It would be helpful for users of the legislation if all of the supplementary provisions relating to the above topics were to be gathered together in one place. This would include their application to the Crown, local authorities, statutory undertakers, and in other special cases (which can be referred to regularly by those to whom they are relevant, but ignored by others). Certain other matters could also be usefully dealt with on a generic basis, to ensure consistency—such as entry onto land, injunctions, and some financial provisions.

One of those more general issues is the specific statutory provisions allowing for court challenges to decisions. It would be worth considering whether, following the changes recently made to these provisions,[42] which bring them largely into line with those relating to general judicial review challenges under Part 54 of the Civil Procedure Rules (CPR), they are in fact still needed at all.

And all of the relevant definitions should be in one place (or at least referred to in one place), so that they can then be used on a consistent basis in all of the other Acts. Indeed there may be scope for issuing an online version of the new legislation with automatic hyperlinks to definitions (and relevant secondary legislation).

Finally, as well as the 40 or so statutes referred to above in relation to specific topics, there is a further, relatively small, group of statutes (or parts of statutes) that have been largely repealed, or whose remaining provisions are now more or less redundant. These need to be finally dispatched; although there may need to be a very small amount of consequential tinkering with other Acts to ensure that there is no resulting loss of effective control. That could be left to a future Statute Law Reform exercise to be carried out by the Law Commission, but it would seem to be more logical to do it as part of the present simplification exercise.

Acts that could be repealed in their entirety thus include the Green Belt (London and Home Counties) Act 1938, the Mineral Workings Act 1951, the Agricultural Land (Removal of Surface Soil) Act 1953, the Town and Country Planning Acts of 1954, 1962 and 1963, the Civic Amenities Act 1967, the Mobile Homes Act 1975, the Development of Rural Wales Act 1976, the Derelict Land Act 1982, the Mineral

---

[41] See Hansard, Written Answers, 25 April 2013, col 1120W.
[42] Criminal Justice and Courts Act 2015, s 91 and Sch 16, para 3.

Workings Act 1985, the Housing and Planning Act 1986, and the Regional Development Agencies Act 1998. Part III of the Agriculture Act 1967 (hill land) and sections 18–23 of the Forestry Act 1967 (felling directions) are also redundant, and could be repealed at the same time.

It has also been noted above that the provisions relating to simplified planning zones and areas of archaeological importance could be abolished without any loss. Those relating to scheduled monument consent, listed building consent and village greens are not required in their present form, and could more satisfactorily be included in other statutory codes.

Part II of the TCPA 1990 (development plans) has already been repealed, as has Part V (compensation for restrictions on new development in limited cases). And of course, once the whole exercise has been completed, the Planning (Consequential Provisions) Act 1990 would be redundant, and would be repealed.

D. Wales

A further consideration is that, at present, nearly all of the 60 Acts listed in Table 1 apply to England and Wales. However, the details, particularly as to the administration of the various control regimes, are starting to diverge on either side of the border. The role of the Secretary of State is taken by the Welsh Ministers; local authorities in Wales are all unitary; the development plan regime is different; and some of the 'national' bodies—such as Historic England, Natural England, and Natural Resources Wales—operate either in England or in Wales, but not both.

And almost all secondary legislation, including many commencement orders bringing into effect new primary legislation—now applies only in one or other jurisdiction.

This is likely to continue, as the Assembly exercises its recently acquired powers to legislate in this area. The Planning (Wales) Bill is thus on course to obtain Royal assent later in 2015; although this contains only relatively modest technical amendments.[43] But it is noticeable that it is in the form of amendments to the TCPA 1990 and the PCPA 2004; and the very fact that it includes a number of new provisions to be inserted into the TCPA 1990 with numbers such as 'section 71ZB' indicates that something needs to be done. And the Historic Environment (Wales) Bill is likely to obtain Royal assent early in 2016; but this too is likely to be largely technical.

A major simplification exercise of the kind envisaged in this chapter would be an ideal time to produce for England and for Wales separate versions of each of the nine or so new replacement statutes for the topics listed above. Initially the two versions would be similar, although by no means identical—somewhat in the same way as, for example, the Town and Country Planning Act 1947 was, at least initially, very similar to the Town and Country Planning (Scotland) Act 1947—although in due course they would no doubt start to diverge. But it would be much easier to do

---

[43] http://wales.gov.uk/docs/desh/consultation/131204draft-planning-bill-wales-en.pdf.

the exercise of creating a statutory code for Wales at the same time as doing it for England, rather than creating a Welsh code on a piecemeal basis.

This would fit in well with the current project by the Law Commission to consider the law relating to planning and development control in Wales;[44] although it would go further than just planning. And clearly it will have implications for the Government of Wales Acts of 1998 and 2006.

IV. RELATED LEGISLATION OUTSIDE THE SCOPE OF THE SIMPLIFICATION PROJECT

Of course any area of law is only one part of the overall body of legal rules and principles in force at any one time. And clearly there has to be a limit to the extent of any simplification exercise, however ambitious in scope. There will therefore be some legislation that will be relevant to and affected by such an exercise, but which will be outside its immediate focus.

A. Legislation Governing Specific Activities, with Land Use Implications

There are a variety of statutes relating to specific activities and industries that have major land use implications. These include amongst many others the Forestry Act 1967, the Housing Act 1988, the Water Act 1989, the Electricity Act 1989, the New Roads and Street Works Act 1991, the Water Industry Act 1991, and the Housing and Regeneration Act 2008. These would generally fall outside the scope of the presently envisaged simplification exercise, but it would be appropriate at least to consider including some provisions in them. They would in any event need to be amended to reflect the outcome of the simplification project.

Part I of the Transport and Works Act 1992 is somewhat similar, in that it relates to the authorisation of various categories of public works, particularly in relation to railways and harbours. This too might prove to be outside the scope of the simplification exercise, but it would be worth exploring whether it should be incorporated into the new provisions for the approval of major infrastructure projects, currently in the Planning Act 2008, as there is some degree of overlap.

One other category of special legislation is the group of Measures of the Church England (which have a status equivalent to that of Acts) governing works to churches and cathedrals—notably the Care of Churches and Ecclesiastical Jurisdiction Measure 1991 (recently amended) and the Care of Places of Worship Measure 1999. It is to be hoped that the General Synod will soon be consolidating these and other related provisions into a new Care of Churches Measure; but that will obviously be outside the scope of the present exercise—as is the Care of Cathedrals Measure 2011, itself the result of a consolidation.

---

[44] http://lawcommission.justice.gov.uk/areas/planning-in-Wales.htm.

B. Other Parts of the United Kingdom

The corresponding law in Scotland would in general be outside this exercise—notwithstanding the result of the recent referendum. However, the statutes relating to ancient monuments apply to the whole of Great Britain, even though the Historic Environment (Amendment) (Scotland) Act 2011 has resulted in them applying somewhat differently north of the border. It would therefore be necessary to make appropriate provision for the continuing application of the relevant law to Scotland, so that there were no loose ends. And the same approach may need to be applied in relation to other GB-wide legislation, such as the Forestry Act 1967 and the Transport and Works Act 1992.

Northern Ireland too would be outside this exercise. However, it is noticeable that the legislation there, covering broadly the same topics, is significantly more concise; and it would be good to explore how this is achieved, and whether there are lessons to be learned.

V. THE WAY FORWARD

A. The Timing

There is never an ideal time for legislative reform. However, there has been a considerable amount of legislation dealing with planning and related subjects in the last decade, culminating in the Acts of 2004, 2008, 2011 and 2013 noted above. Not only has this lead to the statute law in this field being unduly complicated, but it also means that the Government may have limited enthusiasm for further substantive change over the next five years. And the Conservative Manifesto in the run-up to the 2015 general election and the Queen's speech immediately after it both indicate a wish to pause before making major changes.

This is therefore a good time to consolidate the mass of existing legislation, before the iterative process of change starts all over again.

B. The Process

One apparent objection to such a programme, however desirable it might seem to be in principle, is that there would not be enough (or any) Parliamentary time. However, this problem can be lessened if the process is carefully managed.

There has been hitherto a practice, spearheaded by the Law Commission, whereby the major statutes were periodically consolidated; and the Commission has been responsible for some 200 consolidation Bills in the 50 years since its creation. The availability of electronic databases means that it is no longer necessary to consolidate legislation solely to produce a reliable up-to-date version of an Act, as amended, but there is still a need for a consolidation process to draw together different enactments on a topic, or series of related topics, into a single Act or set of Acts. The Commission notes that 'The need is particularly acute following repeated legislative activity on a subject over several years that has not resulted in a single statutory text'.[45] That clearly applies in the case of the statutory code considered in this chapter.

However, the Commission's consolidation programme has been significantly curtailed in recent years. That is no doubt particularly due to shortage of resources. A major consolidation exercise is very time-consuming, and in practice the Commission normally expects a financial contribution to be made by the relevant Government department towards its costs. Just as importantly, there also needs to be a commitment by the department to provide sufficient practical support to see the project through to completion and enactment. And that is likely to include new secondary legislation and guidance, along with training for all the principal stakeholders in the field.

Amendments to legislation, found to be necessary in the course of the consolidation exercise (or already known to be desirable), cannot be directly incorporated in consolidation Acts. However, they could be the subject of a legislative reform order (LRO), made under the Legislative and Regulatory Reform Act 2006. That enables an LRO, which can amend primary legislation, to be made where a Minister is satisfied that the order would remove or reduce any burden resulting from the legislation in question. A 'burden' is defined as 'a financial cost, an administrative inconvenience, an obstacle to efficiency, productivity or profitability; or a sanction, criminal or otherwise, which affects the carrying on of any lawful activity'; and may be 'financial cost or administrative inconvenience resulting from the form of any legislation (for example, where the legislation is hard to understand)'.[46]

An LRO must be the subject of extensive consultation, including with all relevant organisations likely to be affected by the proposals in it.[47] It is then considered by the Regulatory Reform Committee of Parliament, again in accordance with an expedited procedure.[48]

That might seem to be an attractive method of dealing with any necessary changes; but experience suggests that there can be considerable uncertainty as to what may properly be included within an LRO. The alternative approach would be to have a more conventional amending Bill, incorporating all the necessary technical changes, major and minor, drafted by reference to the relevant statutes as they stand. Such a Bill would hopefully be relatively uncontroversial. It would of course take up some Parliamentary time, but the reward would be that the amending provisions (along with any others made by Parliament during the passage of the Bill) could be incorporated into the emerging consolidated package, timed to come into force on the same date. The result would thus be to bring all the new law into force at once, including the changes—with the possible exception of those relating to acquisition of land.

---

[45] http://lawcommission.justice.gov.uk/areas/consolidation.htm.
[46] Legislative and Regulatory Reform Act 2006, s 1(3), (5).
[47] Legislative and Regulatory Reform Act 2006, s 13.
[48] Standing Orders of the House of Commons, SOs 18, 141.

C. The Next Steps

It would seem that the best way forward is for a dedicated group to be set up to handle the project on a full-time basis, under the direct supervision of the Under Secretary of State for Planning. The devil is in the detail; so the group should be led by an experienced practitioner, with drafting support from the Office of the Parliamentary Counsel (OPC), and professional and secretarial support from the Department for Communities and Local Government (DCLG). It would probably be most appropriate for the group to work within the DCLG. And it would be expedient for the work of the group to be overseen by a review panel or representatives of the organisations and professions likely to be affected by the outcome of the exercise.

The first step would presumably be the production of a full report setting out the broad pattern of the legislation likely to result from the exercise, with an indication of which provisions seem to be redundant. That could be along the lines of this chapter, but much expanded to include full details as to how all of the existing law could best be dealt with, and what changes would be necessary or desirable. As part of this, it would also be essential to consider carefully what other legislation should be included or excluded in such a review. Such a report would need to be produced in conjunction with the Law Commission (as far as it wishes to be involved) and all the key stakeholders in the area—and of course liaising with the relevant authorities in Wales and Scotland. That would be necessary to ensure that all practitioners and others in the field were aware of the forthcoming changes—although it would also assist in complying with the requirements of the LRO procedure if that were eventually to seem the appropriate route to deal with amendments. And the ongoing exercise would no doubt be the subject of appropriate presentations to professional and academic conferences and to Government bodies.

Once the relevant Government departments are committed to going along with the exercise in principle, it would then be possible to prepare a series of new Bills in draft, incorporating all of the existing law, corrections and minor improvements (as defined above). In parallel, either an LRO or, more likely, an amending Bill would need to be prepared, presumably by the OPC, incorporating any more substantial changes. Not the least problematic part of the exercise would be to check all of the references to and from other legislation, to ensure that the consequential effects of the simplification exercise were properly thought through.

It would also be helpful to produce in parallel as much as possible of the accompanying secondary legislation, as that would probably take on an increased role by way of providing more of the detailed provisions, some of which are currently in primary legislation. Happily, that process would be greatly assisted by following on from the current Red Tape Challenge, which is hugely reducing the amount of secondary legislation.

And finally the LRO or the amending Bill, and the consolidating Bills thereafter, would need to be steered through the relevant Parliamentary process. Bearing in mind that the amending Bill would probably be a relatively uncontroversial measure largely containing technical amendments—such as transferring items from primary to secondary legislation, abolishing redundant provisions, and incorporating principles from established case law—its passage should not be unduly difficult. It would probably not be necessary to introduce a new standing order, as was necessary for the Tax Law Rewrite (TLR) Programme in the period 2000–10.[49]

Consolidation Bills—that is, Bills that consolidate existing Acts with no substantive changes other than corrections and minor improvements—can go through Parliament by means of an expedited procedure, involving consideration by a special joint committee, without taking up scarce parliamentary time.[50] Such legislation is generally prepared by the Law Commission; but there is no requirement that it must be.

D. Timescale

It is difficult to be precise about the length of time that would be required to complete the exercise. However, bearing in mind the experience of those involved with the TLR programme—the nearest comparable exercise carried out recently—an initial estimate might be that it would occupy a full-time group of three or four people for around three or four years.

If therefore, for example, the exercise were to start in early 2016, that would enable the recently elected Government to incorporate into the process (via the amending Bill) any changes it might wish to introduce. With or without any such changes, the resulting package of Bills might be complete in 2018–19.

There would then need to be a run-in period during which guidance could be updated, and websites and printed publications amended. Hopefully, although the form of the new legislation would be much more straightforward than that of the existing legislation, in substance it should be not too dissimilar, so the exercise of rewriting guidance would be not too onerous. That process would also be greatly assisted if the draft Bills were made available at an early stage.

It would of course be possible to introduce the new Bills in several stages, as was done with the TLR programme. That has the disadvantage of necessitating much more complex transitional provisions, although the advantage of resulting in a more extended period in which to update guidance. As noted above, that might be appropriate in relation to the statutory code relating to the acquisition of land, leading to the programme being conducted in two phases. Otherwise, however, it would seem to be preferable to do it in one operation as far as possible.

VI. THE OUTCOME

As an indication of one possible pattern that might emerge from such an exercise, it would seem that 43 statutes could be repealed in whole, and a further 14 in part—as listed in Table 1—and in their place could be enacted nine new statutes, as set out in Table 2.

---

[49] Standing Orders of the House of Commons, SO 60.
[50] Consolidation of Enactments (Procedure) Act 1949, s 2; Standing Orders of the House of Commons, SOs 58, 140.

Table 2: Planning and development law as it could be

1. *The Town and Country Planning Act 2019*

   National and local planning authorities; national policy statements; development plans; neighbourhood plans.

2. *Natural Environment Act 2019*

   Natural England; national parks; areas of outstanding natural beauty; nature reserves; trees; hedgerows.

3. *Heritage Protection Act 2019*

   Historic England; world heritage sites; ancient monuments; listed buildings; conservation areas.

4. *Promotion of Development Act 2019*

   New towns; development corporations; enterprise zones.

5. *Regulation of Development Act 2019*

   Definition of development; seeking development consent (planning permission/listed building consent); remedies (appeals, purchase notices); major infrastructure projects; enforcement; special controls (minerals, advertisements, caravans).

6. *Infrastructure Funding Act 2019*

   Community infrastructure levy.

7. *Rights of Way and Access to Land Act 2019*

   Rights of way; access to open land; village greens.

8. *Acquisition of Land Act 2019*

   Acquisition of land by agreement; compulsory purchase; blight; minerals; compensation.

9. *Planning and Development (Miscellaneous Provisions) Act 2019*

   Definitions; application to the Crown, statutory undertakers, local authorities; court challenges; repeals; transitional provisions.

The result of an exercise along these lines would be a huge simplification and clarification of an important area of statute law, which would yield significant savings in time and money on the part of professionals, public authorities and members of the general public.

5

Land: Balancing Competing Economic and Social Interests

BARBARA BOGUSZ*

I. INTRODUCTION

THE RECOGNITION OF land as an economic resource has never been in doubt, but land regulation and usage should not be confined to a functional examination through the narrow prism of economic benefit. Land use policy also embraces wider social ideals which both statute and courts have recognised, for example, through the protection afforded to town and village greens (TVGs).[1] In the case of TVGs, they have been protected primarily for customary or, more recently, for ecological/environmental purposes rather than for some explicit economic justification.[2] Yet the assertion that land used primarily for social purposes is devoid of *any* economic value is an oversimplification which may be challenged and, economic value and social benefit should not be considered as mutually exclusive ideals. Though the economic value of land designated for social usage may be a secondary consideration by contrast with land intended for strictly commercial or developmental purposes, it may be implied from the policy objectives of the Growth and Infrastructure Act 2013 (GIA 2013), as well as regulatory and judicial principles, that land utilised for social purposes may also derive economic benefits to a local community.[3] For example, recreational access for the benefit of all users to England's coast line through the creation of a national coastal path provides ancillary benefits of an economic nature through tourism to the local community the paths serve.[4]

The social construct of land, such as that recognised through the law of easements, freehold covenants and TVGs, by which the activities of property owners are restricted, can be said to have derivative socio-economic benefits to third parties.

---

* Lecturer in Law, School of Law, University of Leicester. The author would like to gratefully acknowledge and thank the anonymous reviewer for the comments and observations about this chapter.
[1] See, eg Commons Act 2006 and *Oxfordshire CC v Oxford City Council* [2006] UKHL 25, [2006] 2 AC 674 (HL) and *R (on the application of Lewis) v Redcar and Cleveland BC* [2010] UKSC 11, [2010] 2 AC 70 (SC).
[2] *R v Oxfordshire CC, Ex p Sunningwell Parish Council* [2000] 1 AC 335 (HL).
[3] This is evident in relation to large-scale projects such as the Olympic Park and Legacy project which capitalise on the promotion of the social and cultural aspects of sporting events as well as the economic regeneration of East London.
[4] John Vidal, 'Nick Clegg pledges to complete England's coastal path by 2020', *Guardian*, 3 September 2014 http://theguardian.com/environment/2014/sep/03/nick-clegg-england-coastal-path.

Put bluntly, easements and covenants help to protect and maintain the character of a neighbourhood and may be said to promote its social utility. More controversially TVGs, whose social justification at the expense of economic development has been used speculatively, have recently been the subject of increased litigation in which the primary aim has been the maintenance of the environmental characteristics of a neighbourhood and bring into focus sharply the tension that exists when the public seeks to influence the use of private land.[5] Thus the clamour to protect TVGs may be said to be rooted in a culture of 'NIMBYism' where conservation of the heritage or character of a neighbourhood by restricting commercial development has, ironically, potentially a simultaneous effect of preserving the economic value of land within the locality. TVGs provide a prime example of how communities or neighbourhoods perceive social and economic land use, and how the neighbourhood or community can act as drivers to determine the status of land through, in particular, customary use.

Modern land use policy reflects a more transformative approach to land whereby the social dimension is considered and given more prominence alongside economic policy objectives. This is particularly the case where the state engages in legacy projects and in the creation of recreational assets, but has also occurred in providing collective participation for local communities and neighbourhoods in determining and shaping their local amenities thereby spawning a new form of local democracy. The underlying rational for the GIA 2013 is one of fostering economic growth and increasing competitiveness at a global level, and part of fulfilling this aspiration is through building developments in compliance with the National Planning Policy Framework (NPPF).[6] One consequence of this is that this raises the prospect of tensions between competing public and private interests. This chapter will examine whether more recent legislation, for example, the Growth and Infrastructure Act 2013 together with the recent government's planning policy following the publication of the NPPF has resulted in a coherent framework for a regulatory strategy through which two potentially competing aims of land usage may be secured. In particular, this chapter will consider the policy implications of the current regulatory framework and whether it provides a mechanism through which to reconcile the competing social and economic interests that vie with each other within land use policy.

II. BALANCING POTENTIAL COMPETING INTERESTS IN LAND

Conflicting interests over the use of land is an inherent tension within economic and urban development. Within this context, striking a regulatory balance between exploiting land as a finite economic resource whilst simultaneously recognising the wider social value of land is a complex conundrum. The collision between planning

---

[5] Eg in *Oxfordshire CC v Oxford City Council* (n 1) the House of Lords allowed the registration of trap grounds in North Oxford which included an area submerged in reeds and scrubland to be protected as a TVG. More recent examples include fields once owned by the Curtis family in *Betterment Properties (Weymouth) Ltd v Dorset CC* [2012] EWCA Civ 250, [2012] 2 P & C R 3 (CA), and a beach in *R (on the application of Newhaven Port and Properties Ltd) v Secretary of State for the Environment, Food and Rural Affairs* [2013] EWCA Civ 673, [2014] QB 282 (CA). See further, B Bogusz, 'Regulating Public/Private Interests in Town and Village Greens' [2013] *International Journal of Law in the Built Environment* 21.

[6] Department for Communities and Local Government, *National Planning Policy Framework* (London, DCLG, 2012) (NPPF).

law and policy, environmental considerations and social uses of land, as seen in disputes involving TVGs, has created a tension within the public sphere which the legislator has, thus far, proved unable to reconcile satisfactorily and meet the concerns of these competing interests. English law and policy relating to the regulation of land is often characterised by the presence of winners and losers, and arguably does not provide a coherent regulatory framework within which these competing interests are sufficiently protected.

Historically, the communal and social institutions fostered prior to the enclosure of land in England made way for a change in land usage. In this context, following enclosure, not only was land arguably being used more efficiently in comparison to the communal open field system, but it was the shift away from the field system to that of individual property ownership of land which undoubtedly changed the perception of land usage.[7] The movement towards enclosure of land in many parts of England was limited to an extent from the mid to late 1800s onwards where land was secured, not simply for purposes of enclosure but also for the protection of commons and significantly for public use and enjoyment.[8] The latter encompassed not only the social recreational dimension to land but also took into account free public access to common land.[9] It was this philanthropic concern which considerably slowed down the progress of enclosure,[10] and also had a broader economic impact upon the construction of national infrastructure, for example new railways, whose construction regularly threatened the picturesque landscape. In a policy concession to these social objectives such developments were curtailed or compromises made to prevent intrusion of the railways on to common land.[11]

It is the mutation from the rural landscape to increasing urbanisation which has necessitated the recognition of a multifaceted understanding of land usage where access and preservation are equally important values. Preservation would enshroud not only the rights associated with common land, but also the recreational customary rights that are associated with TVGs, which are more recently manifesting themselves as environmental concerns. Public access over land from the nineteenth century was not restricted to customary rights, the wider social, economic and environment benefits of public parks and open spaces as a public amenity were also realised.[12] Parks were created through various means such as acquisition by funding initiatives from people in a local area[13] and gifts,[14] and through statute.[15]

---

[7] J Yelling, *Common Field and Enclosure in England 1450–1850* (London, Macmillan Press, 1977) 7.

[8] Lord Eversley, *Commons, Forests and Footpaths* (London, Cassell, 1910) 324–25.

[9] Public access for the purposes of 'rights of access for air and exercise' was extended as a general right over metropolitan commons, borough and urban district commons: Law of Property Act 1925, s 193. See also, Law of Property Act 1925, s 194 which prevents the erection of fences or construction of buildings which may impede or prevent access to land.

[10] See further, Royal Commission, *Report of the Royal Commission on Common Land, 1955–58* (Cmnd 462, 1958) paras 80–83.

[11] See further, P Readman, 'Preserving the English Landscape, *c*1870–1914' (2008) 5 *Cultural and Social History* 197.

[12] *Report from the Select Committee on Public Walks with the Minutes of the Evidence Taken Before Them* (Parliament, House of Commons, 1833).

[13] In Manchester, both Philips Park and Queens Park were purchased with the aid of public subscriptions and opened in 1846. Birkenhead Park in Wirral was the first publicly funded park and opened in 1847.

[14] Joseph Strutt, a textile manufacturer, gave Derby Arboretum as a gift to the people of Derby in 1840.

[15] Eg Open Spaces Act 1906.

In the post-war era of reconstruction and rebuilding Britain, conservation of the countryside, the promotion of recreational areas as well the protection of areas of amenity were embraced and safeguarded by the state against both private and public developments through the enactment of legislation such as the National Parks and Access to the Countryside Act 1949 (NPACA 1949). This policy may have seemed somewhat incongruous by taking into account open spaces and their protection for recreational purposes in the light of the post-war pressures for urban and town planning, housing and restoring basic amenities which were priorities of the Atlee Government in the post-World War II era. As the decades passed and urban living became the reality the social value of access to land for purposes of recreation and enjoyment was never in doubt. The NPACA 1949 was itself proclaimed as the 'people's charter' which was aimed at 'everyone who loves to get out into the open air and enjoy the countryside'.[16]

The difficult question of how to strike an appropriate balance between the economic justifications for using land more efficiently with the wider social communal use of land cannot be addressed easily. This becomes more problematic as modern urban development spreads and competes with the preservation of the landscape in its rural context or for public use and enjoyment. In recent years this has become a paramount consideration with regards to TVGs where there is increasing tension between landowners seeking to utilise their land for building developments and that of the public who have exercised their customary rights over land. The increase of urbanisation from the nineteenth century and the accompanying population shift made the preservation of open spaces a matter of increased public concern.[17] In the twenty-first century the transformation of property regulation to encompass environmental and ecological concerns has had the supplementary effect of informing and empowering citizens to assume a greater interest in and responsibility over their local communities and its environment. This empowerment of citizens can be attributed to the changes in political ideology, notably in the 1980s, which centred on restructuring the state and where the focus was on empowering the individual, active citizenship and engagement with business knowledge.[18] The overall result of these socio-economic changes has been the progressive development of a wider participatory and horizontal model of rural governance involving working in public/private partnerships and including a range of stakeholders, communities and citizens as opposed to paternal vertical governance of state regulation of urban development and rural land usage.[19]

---

[16] J Blunden and N Curry (eds), *A People's Charter?* (London, HMSO, 1989) 62–64. The NPACA 1949 did not necessarily fulfil its true potential and was subsequently superseded by the Countryside Act 1968, which sought to deal with the increasing numbers of visitors to the countryside and coastal areas.

[17] In the 20th century Milton Keynes is a good example where a new town was designed with village greens as an integral utility for citizens inhabiting a built-up environment and which incidentally was built around the village of Milton Keynes (now known as Middleton) which already had a village green.

[18] M Woods, *Rural Geography: Processes, Responses and Experiences in Rural Restructuring* (London, Sage, 2005) 165.

[19] This inclusionary model of rural governance finds its nexus in the 1995 White Paper on Rural England (Department of the Environment, *Rural England: A Nation Committed to a Living Countryside* (Cm 3016, 1995)) and this approach continues through to the White Paper published in 2000 on protecting the countryside: Department of the Environment, Transport and the Regions, *Our Countryside: The Future: A fair Deal for Rural England* (Cm 4909, 2000).

III. PUBLIC/PRIVATE: DIVISION OR COEXISTENCE?

Property ownership in the modern era is not simply constructed on the basis of economic freedoms but envelopes the broader social or community orientated interests associated with land usage.[20] Together with the public regulatory mechanisms, for example planning control, any notion of absolutism of property ownership or non-interference is dissipated, and the overriding objective is to strike a balance between the rights of property owners and the community at large. At the micro level this can manifest itself between property owners who engage in private bargains, for example in the form of easements permitting or restricting use or access to land. Easements historically have been upheld where a right over servient land provides a clear benefit to the dominant land.[21] Often such rights of access promote utility of the land thereby seeking to ensure that the use of land which remains a scarce resource is maximised. Similarly, freehold covenants may be used to protect the character of a property, and these covenants are not limited to just the appearance of individual properties, but also how this contributes to the appearance of the broader geographical area. These types of privately bargained rights have never been subject to wider controls or planning regulation.[22]

The creation of such covenants not only creates interests over land, in a narrow property law sense, but more broadly such covenants may give rise to an impression that land in a specific geographical area possesses characteristics, be they social or environmental, which are worth protecting, moreover they create future obligations of what is acceptable.[23] Thus, even those 'mundane' third party property rights which many viewed as being a functional conveyancing requirement may possess or create effects which go beyond the one dimensional aspect of land usage. On this analysis easements and covenants are mechanisms which are upheld by the law as valuable property rights which not only have an economic dimension but also regulate and sustain the broader social characteristics of the land. This formula permeates across all aspects of land usage leaving significant scope to create tensions between landowners who wish to exploit their land for economic purposes and the

---

[20] Mitchell perceptively describes property ownership as 'a web of relations' and the public as stakeholders have a role in the decisions made over property, see J Mitchell, 'What Public Presence? Access, Commons and Property Rights' [2008] *Social and Legal Studies* 351, 353.

[21] This type of privately bargained right, together with freehold covenants, have never been subject to wider controls or planning regulation.

[22] In the case of freehold covenants these have been viewed as a form of localised private legislation to protect and maintain the character of a local area or neighbourhood. Specifically, these types of covenants, ie 'schemes of development' or 'building schemes', regulate obligations at a local level. See K Gray and S Gray, 'The Idea of Property in Land' in S Bright and Dewar (eds), *Land Law: Themes and Perspectives* (Oxford, Oxford University Press, 1998) 42.

[23] Under s 84(1) Law of Property Act 1925 the Upper Tribunal has a discretionary power to modify or discharge restrictive covenants which are no longer desirable due to changes in the socio-economic make-up of the environment in which they exist. Reasons for modification or discharge are broad and include changes in the character of the neighbourhood or other material circumstances which are deemed significant to the Tribunal (s 84(1)(a)). Examples include: *Re Wards Construction (Medway) Ltd's Application* (1994) 67 P & C R 379 where a covenant was modified to permit redevelopment of land due to the change in the character of the neighbourhood from building developments which had taken place over time. In *Re Quaffers Ltd Application* (1988) 56 P & C R 142 the covenant was discharged because the surrounding motorway network had made a fundamental change in the character of the neighbourhood for which the restriction was intended to protect.

wider community who opposed development or change of use of land because it may have a potential impact on their own recreational/social or even economic interests.

Notwithstanding the restrictions on land usage that may exist it is irrefutable that the period since the 1980s is characterised by a shift towards development and an increased rate of urbanisation. Whereas the imposition of easements and covenants may be considered in a micro context, urbanisation is a macro policy trend which is apparent across the country. Pressure for housing, economic and industrial development and shifting populations have all necessitated that long cherished notions of a 'green and pleasant land' are no longer as relevant in the twenty-first century. Urbanisation, together with a variation in land usage has brought about a change in the socio-economic relationship between individuals and land. In many respects the relationship is more polarised. For example, the environmental lobby and pro-development groups are regularly at loggerheads with respect to whether, how and to what extent land may be developed. This conflict is perhaps most clearly evident when one considers the law, policy and practice relating to TVGs. Town and village greens have become a 'flash point' in which developers and environmentalists regularly collide.[24] Yet the state, through the legislative process together with the judiciary has failed to provide a satisfactory mechanism through which disputes concerning public and private rights may be resolved.[25]

More significantly, in the broader perspective of communal relations and living, the social dimension inherent in land usage is becoming more important as an antidote to what could be described as 'urbanisation creep'. This creep arises where the edge of the town gradually advances into the rural domain due to the increasing use of land on peripheral locations of towns for commercial purposes, such as warehouses, retail parks, superstores and rubbish tips. The established network of transport links of roads and motorways, and perhaps now to a lesser extent the railway, has facilitated the growth in the developments of such commercial enterprises. In large part, the increasing number of TVG disputes can be viewed as a more proactive measure on the part of citizens to protect areas of land for recreational purposes where there has been long-established use, and they have, in a number of instances, proved to be an effective vehicle through which urbanisation may be challenged.

A. Public Access over Private Land

Public access over private land is both multifarious and organic with each form raising distinct regulatory challenges.[26] From a regulatory standpoint, of the more

---

[24] See *Redcar* (n 1) and *Sunningwell* (n 2).

[25] The Supreme Court in *Paddico (267) Ltd v Kirklees Metropolitan Council* [2014] UKSC 7, [2014] 2 WLR 300 (SC) found in favour of the landowners on the issue of whether it was 'just' to rectify the register after a lapse of time where land was registered as a TVG when it should not have been *ab initio*. This case focuses solely on the formalities regulating rectification of the register and does not represent a major shift in judicial policy towards town or village greens. For an alternative view, see further N Pratt, 'The Application of the Equitable Doctrine of Laches to the Rectification of the Town and Village Green Register' [2014] *Journal of Planning and Environment Law* 588.

[26] The various forms of access include, inter alia, public rights of way, open access land and National Parks. A more recent development in this area is providing coastal access for the public around the English coast.

complex forms of access to private land are TVGs and common land.[27] TVGs and common land are often referred to in the same breath; indeed TVGs are often mistakenly considered to be common land, but from a regulatory standpoint they are undoubtedly different beasts.

Historically, in the case of common land, the existence of common land is rooted in the economic development of England whereby a Lord of the Manor would permit *specific* smallholders to utilise unused parts of the manorial land for rearing livestock.[28] In the nineteenth century, the Inclosure Acts maintained this existing common land and enabled it to be fenced off. This development, intended to promote better management of common land is by stark contrast to the regulatory framework of TVGs where the enduring and defining regulatory principle, which the courts have consistently upheld, requires access to the land to be 'as of right' and uninhibited.[29] However, though in regulatory and substantive terms TVGs and common land are different, neither TVGs or common land create *any* form of general public right of usage; on the contrary, in both instances the statute provides the parameters within which a strictly defined and limited class of the general public may exercise certain customary rights over the land.

Through the creation of TVGs and common land public law and the courts have imposed limitations upon private landowners in favour of third parties. But, unlike easements which constitute proprietary rights for the dominant owner, neither designation as a TVG or common land constitutes the granting of any form of proprietary interest in favour of the user and in this they differ in form and substance from easements and covenants. However, while there remains no change of entitlement, the public law may have a particularly adverse impact upon a landowner's rights which are far in excess of the constraints that exist upon the granting of an easement. In particular, by granting customary rights this may lead to a disproportionate influence or control over the land, for example, through users seeking to restrict the commercial development of the land.

Land that is subject to registration as a TVG or a right of common remains private land and statute does not alter ownership rights. It is for this reason that neither right is deemed incompatible with article 1 of the First Protocol to the European

---

[27] The use of the nomenclature of 'common land' does not necessarily imply either ownership by a public body which generates a specific public right of way or usage (though much common land is, today, in local authority ownership), or that the land is available for use by the public at large. For a comprehensive overview of the historical development of common land, see N Ubhi and B Denyer-Green, *Law of Commons and of Town and Village Greens* (Bristol, Jordans, 2006) Ch 5.

[28] This 11th century practice was consolidated through the Inclosure Acts of the 19th century by which time much of the manorial ownership had ceased and the land had been transferred into private ownership, and where manorial rights existed they continued to do so unaffected by these changes. Under the Inclosure Acts common land was maintained and fenced off to enable its continued use and for better management.

[29] The question of 'as of right' was discussed in *Redcar* (n 1) where the Supreme Court reviewed the case law and discussed what type of restrictions with regard to accessing the land are required before the users are no longer entering as of right (see paras 17–20). See further R Austen Baker and B Mayfield, 'Uncommon Confusion: Parallel Jurisprudence in Town and Village Green Applications' (2012) 76 *Conveyancer and Property Lawyer* 55, 60, and L Blohm, 'The "By Right" Doctrine and Village Green Applications—a Response' [2014] *Conveyancer and Property Lawyer* 40. Moreover, s 29 of the Commons Act 1876 makes encroachment or inclosure of a green and interference with or occupation of the land illegal unless it is with the aim of improving the enjoyment of the green.

Convention on Human Rights (ECHR).[30] However, it would be inaccurate to suggest that the statutory regime is absolute and that registration as a TVG generates no spill over effect or other material impact upon the property. On the contrary, in the case of TVGs, the statutory provisions, though concisely drafted have been on a number of occasions been subject to broad judicial interpretation. The judiciary has employed significant discretion in their application of the criteria, which has, in turn, encouraged opportunistic litigants to use TVG applications in order to secure environmental or conservation objectives.[31] The liberal interpretation of the criteria has encouraged the 'village greens industry'[32] to push at an already open door and to exploit the judicial liberalism to thwart planning applications more effectively than via the planning process. For this reason, a TVG application must be every land developer's worst nightmare because, not only can the inquiry process be lengthy, the effect of a successful application is to prevent *any* further development on the land.

B. Regulating the Relationship between Public and Private

The principle of entitlement, or what Gray describes as the 'quantum of property' has remained a constant principle of English land law and expresses the bundle of rights owned by an estate owner.[33] The concept of 'private property' is one which has always emphasised the individual freedom of landowners to control their land without interference from the state, but this idea of property absolutism has, in Gray's view, been replaced by a property relativism that pursues peaceful coexistence between landowners and which suggest that landowners cannot exploit their land regardless of the common good.[34] For example, registration of TVGs in accordance with the statutory regime grants recreational users rights over privately owned land, and these rights form part of a welter of other forms of third-party right or statutory control that can exist over land, and which may limit the quantum of property which an individual may claim.

Within Locke's understanding of property ownership, which contended that property ownership was inextricably linked to labour, he isolated the ownership of private property from a notion of property for the 'common good'.[35] Locke's interpretation would therefore suggest that customary rights have no place in privately owned land, and by doing so he draws a sharp distinction between society as a whole and the property rights of the individual. This 'dualistic' understanding therefore discounted the possibility for forms of property to exist that do not fall exclusively into public or private ownership and usage.

Yet, in the twenty-first century, this monochrome assumption that land is either exclusively in public or private control, and used exclusively for either public or

---

[30] See *Oxfordshire CC v Oxford City Council* (n 1) paras 86–90.
[31] Ibid. In this case the land at issue consisted of scrubland which was not suitable for recreational purposes.
[32] See R Meager, 'The "Village Green Industry": Back in Business' [2010] *CLJ* 238.
[33] See K Gray and S Gray, *Elements of Land Law*, 5th edn (Oxford, Oxford University Press, 2009) 1.5.11–1.5.16.
[34] Ibid, 1.5.54.
[35] J Locke, *Two Treatises of Government* (Hamilton, Ontario, McMaster University, 2000).

private purposes can be criticised for being one dimensional, and encapsulates an outmoded view of property ownership and regulation. Furthermore, it is debateable if English land law ever adhered to this rigid Lockean distinction because an element of reciprocity has always existed between landowners. It would not be incorrect to conclude that the rights of one landowner are necessarily constrained by the rights of neighbouring third parties. To continue with the example of TVGs, the enduring purpose of their existence has been to permit an identifiable group of the public, residing in a particular locality, to exercise recreational rights over another's land. By protecting this right, public law and the courts have consistently recognised a right the primary purpose of which is to promote the social use of land.

In addition to rights created by TVGs and common land, the need for planning control and environmental considerations have increasingly become important public policy requirements which influence the regulation of land, and which can divide landowners and the public. Thus, in the twenty-first century, land use has diverged significantly from the Lockean understanding of private property rights as natural rights, and the view that landowners can exercise their rights in isolation from others is wholly unrealistic. The rejection of this notion of property ownership has, since the latter part of the twentieth century, been largely moulded through socio-economic and environmental values which the public law encompasses, and which increasingly reflects the pervasive ecological demands of the social citizen.

The increased prominence of environmental concerns within land use policy has created tensions in the regulation of what have become competing socio-economic values. This has led to significant debate about the precise scope to which non-economic factors can and should be determinants of land use policy. For example, in the context of environmental regulation Rodgers[36] has criticised two classic functional property typologies, which categorise legal rules used to protect property rights, previously posited by Calabresi and Melamed,[37] and Harris,[38] as not fully appreciating the 'legacy effect' of environmental factors which may influence future land usage. Rodgers' critique of these functional typologies, and their emphasis upon project delivery, is that they come at the expense of land use policy not sufficiently encompassing the long-term benefits nor the positive forward-looking land management obligations which environmental objectives can input into the land use matrix.[39] However, while environmental factors are useful, it may be argued that simply determining land usage through this single prism, does not fully meet the expectations of the various relationships that individuals have with land.

To this extent it may be argued that, when regulating public/private relationships within the context of land, environmental policy is a highly important factor, but one which should not necessarily be considered as *primus inter pares*. A more preferable paradigm to Rodger's property management typology, which focuses on the interaction between land use and property rights in the application of environmental

---

[36] C Rodgers, 'Nature's Place? Property Rights, Property Rules and Environmental Stewardship' [2009] *CLJ* 550.

[37] G Calabresi and AD Melamed, 'Property Rules, Liability Rules, and Inalienability: One View of the Cathedral' (1972) 85 *Harvard Law Review* 1089.

[38] JW Harris, *Property and Justice* (Oxford, Oxford University Press, 1966) 22ff.

[39] Rodgers (n 36) 556–58, 569–74.

law in land use policy, arises from a broader view point which focuses on the balancing various strands of land based utility which combine to form the constituent elements of any land interest.[40] This latter regulatory model advocated by Gray and Gray embodies the various relationships with land. Specifically this is whether public or private, or a hybrid of these two, which Gray and Gray conveniently define as 'quasi-public',[41] offers a more inclusive mechanism through which to regulate the balance of relationships. It is this latter quasi-public use of land which reflects more broadly the various push and pull factors which interact with property rights, and includes, inter alia, environmental public policy objectives as well as social purposes which shape and impact upon the way which land is and will be used in the future. Whilst it may be incorrect to surmise that one consequence of the increased state regulation has led to the creation of some new form of 'hybrid' public/private property right per se, from a regulatory perspective it can be concluded that the modern state, through its use of the public law, has emerged as the primary source of this change which grants the public greater powers to influence how private property is used.[42]

The dynamic behind this change can be attributed in part to what Gray and Gray describe as 'meta principles' in law. These reflect normative drifts that shape modern English land law, namely: rationality when dealing with one-off transactions, and in particular on the exchange value of dealings at a micro level. These also embrace social cooperation in dealings between neighbours which are infused with reasonableness, and finally, in a wider context of citizens' interactions on community oriented issues these interactions are based on reciprocity.[43] Of the three swathes of tendencies influencing norms relating to land the latter two demonstrate more accurately the drivers behind the more environmentally aware citizen and society, and this has increasingly imbued land usage discourse with what Gray and Gray term as 'community value'. In this context the notion of civic equity provides a justification for the sacrifice of land for compulsory purchase for an overriding public necessity. Taken together with the second meta principle, of where neighbourliness reflects social cooperation under which reasonableness finds its nexus, TVGs sit between these two areas and cannot be readily classified in Gray and Gray's taxonomy of meta principles. By contrast, easements and rights of access, such as the right to roam or vehicular access over common land, more readily reflect reasonable access and neighbourhood in the context of social well-being. In contrast TVGs reflect neighbourliness through long use and the broader social gains of access for recreational purposes to land, but their protection is justified on wider values of citizenship and community, for example, as exemplified by Lord Hoffmann in *R v Oxfordshire County Council, Ex p Sunningwell Parish Council*.[44]

---

[40] See Gray and Gray (n 22) 39ff.

[41] Rodgers (n 36) 558. K Gray and S Gray, 'Private Property and Public Property' in J Maclean (ed), *Property and the Constitution* (Oxford, Hart Publishing, 1999) 18–20.

[42] See T Murphy, S Roberts and T Flessas, *Understanding Property Law* (London, Sweet & Maxwell, 1987) 180–82, where the authors identify that increasingly since 1945 'an owner of land in modern society ... is potentially subject to a plurality of restrictions and controls on his freedom to enjoy the property as he wishes'.

[43] See generally, K Gray and S Gray, 'The Rhetoric of Realty' in J Getzler (ed), *Rationalizing Property, Equity and Trusts: Essays in Honour of Edward Burn* (London, Lexis Nexis, 2003) 204–80.

[44] *R v Oxfordshire CC, Ex p Sunningwell Parish Council* [2000] 1 AC 335 (HL), 347–48.

More generally, public disapproval of greenfield development, which is considered as lying at the outer reaches of urbanisation creep, is reflected in an array of planning and environmental policies both at national and EU level which may restrict development. These policies are supported by an enhanced robust planning enforcement regime.[45] The closer public affinity towards their immediate environment has been characterised as a 'return to the land' where increased use of land for more traditional agricultural and/or social activities by the general public, together with the protection of the local environment by local people has become an integral part of land policy and usage.[46] To this end, the public law agenda, together with greater awareness amongst citizens, has helped to fashion what can be defined as the 'environmental citizen' who uses the legislation proactively, usually at the expense of the landowner who seeks to develop their land. The environmental citizen is interested in the cultural heritage and legacy of land and such citizens are aware of their rights and are able to coordinate their interests through potent civil society organisations to create a semi-formal national political movement which expresses an anti-development platform. Moreover, environmental citizens in their pursuit of their aims pursue an environmental agenda[47] which addresses *their* immediate socio-economic and environmental needs, and the courts have proved amenable to their concerns, through, inter alia, permitting the registration of a large number of TVGs. The patchwork nature of the disputes around the country, when considered in its entirety such that it includes not just TVGs but also tree preservation orders, and re-routing footpaths and bridleways, reinforces the argument that local action has the capacity to resonate with citizens everywhere.

IV. MODERNISATION:[48] LAND POLICY FIT FOR THE TWENTY-FIRST CENTURY?

In 2010, with the inception of a new Coalition Government came a move towards empowering citizens collectively, and more specifically, communities. Though the jury is still out on the question of how much power the Localism Act 2011 has *really* transferred to local communities from central government, the general principle of a greater commitment to localism cannot be disputed. The Localism Act 2011 endeavours to promote greater local democracy and community engagement, and

---

[45] On the changing nature of land and how land usage is influenced by public law regulation and citizen attitudes, see R Home, 'Land Ownership in the United Kingdom: Trends Preferences and Future Challenges' [2009] *Land Use Policy* 103, 107; P Bibby, 'Land Use Change in Britain' [2009] *Land Use Policy* 2, 8–9. See also, D Adams and A Scott, 'In Search of Positive Planning' [2013] *Town and Country Planning* 88, 89.

[46] This arises from an observation made by Professor Sue Farran in her paper: S Farran, 'Earth under the Nails: The Extraordinary Return to Land' in N Hopkins (ed), *Modern Studies in Property Law* (Oxford, Hart Publishing, 2013).

[47] Citizens are aided in doing this, eg by EU legislation such as the consolidated Directive 2011/92/EU of the European Parliament and of the Council of 13 December 2011 on the assessment of the effects of certain public and private projects on the environment Text with EEA relevance [2011] OJ L26/1.

[48] Modernisation is an agenda that been applied to a broad range of policies since the mid-1990s with a focus upon creating a state and its institutions as a monolith that is fit to meet the expectations of the people in the 21st century. Land has not been immune from this: see, eg Law Com 271 which led to the Land Registration Act 2002.

this includes participation in the decision-making process when land usage and land use policy is at issue.[49] For example, under the Act, a community organisation will be able to purchase assets of community value and, engage and contribute to neighbourhood planning in a more proactive manner with the potential to build new homes, businesses, playgrounds or community centres.[50] In this way the local people within their neighbourhood can 'shape the place', and within this paradigm the local community can also envision '*their*' local public spaces.[51]

The new localism agenda, in which communities assume greater control over land use policy, may be identified as the third and most recent incarnation of a policy by which the general public is granted some form of stakeholder rights over private land. One significant period, which may be identified as enabling controlled and limited use of private land, arose in Victorian times when wealthy industrialists took the initiative to make their land available to the community in the form of a recreational park.[52] Interestingly, this initiative shares some of the principles of the modern day localism agenda because it occurred without the direct intervention of the state and essentially could be categorised, in today's language, as a 'bottom up' scheme which was designed to improve the lives of the local community. By contrast, the second identifiable period, started in the twentieth century, was an age in which the state gradually assumed increased regulatory control over broad-range national assets. The state's influence hit its apex in the post-war period through nationalisation and which led, for example, to the creation of National Parks.[53] The private became public and land was considered a national asset and the state could determine the purposes for which it was used.

The identifiable departure in regulatory principles within modern day localism is that it has brought about a clear move away from the state assuming overall responsibility for creating land use policy. The core principle of localism is that in order to determine land use a principle of self-determination, from the bottom up, is actively encouraged by which local groups organise themselves, through the use of local referenda, in order to determine the most appropriate use of land in their community. This may be explained as the creation of a new form of local democracy in which land use policy has journeyed from a period of individual paternalism, through an age in which the state dominated, to one where the individual is empowered and encouraged to take decisions.

The opportunity for community asset transfer benefits the community and provides the necessary continued support for community based activities. Though there are potentially negative effects that could arise from this form of participatory engagement with the local community. On the one hand, it could also be used as

---

[49] Localism Bill: Explanatory notes. Available at www.publications.parliament.uk/pa/bills/lbill/2010-2012/0071/en/2012071en.pdf.

[50] http://mycommunityrights.org.uk/community-right-to-build/.

[51] A Layard, 'Property Paradigms and Place-making: Right to the City; a Right to the Street?' [2012] *Journal of Human Rights and the Environment* 254, 262. See also C Allen and L Crookes, 'Fables of the Reconstruction: A Phenomenology of "Place Shaping" in the North of England' (2009) 80 *Town Planning Review* 455, 458.

[52] This included the Public Health Act 1875, Open Spaces Act 1906, and the Public Amendment Act 1907, and signalled a transfer from private initiative to state policy.

[53] See, eg the discussion above regarding National Parks.

a mechanism by which a community may seek to prevent developers from buying property with a view to building on the land, and on the other, there could be exclusionary effects that stem from the community engagement process as well as the final decision. Whilst this process provides the community with means to determine their place, that power of 'place shaping' also contains a 'symbolic power to exclude'.[54] This power to exclude, according to Walsh,[55] is evident in situations involving compulsory purchase programmes and which can have a negative impact on local communities.[56] The power to exclude, which may not have been envisaged by the decision-markers, is a potential negative consequence of shaping the place through collective participation of neighbourhood planning.[57] This then raises questions relating to representativeness of these 'already-engaged actors' or groups participating in neighbourhood planning.[58] Such parties may be pursuing a narrow agenda which could affect a decision(s) on land use.[59]

Despite the potential negative consequences of this process the development of community and neighbourhood engagement has the potential to create a new form of socio-environmental governance that functions by bottom-up citizen participation. In particular, this form of socio-environmental governance is premised upon land in a neighbourhood or community as being considered as a shared resource that the local community have control over and by using the community asset transfer this enables local people to achieve their objectives of shaping the place. This devolved approach is intended to reflect the connection which citizens have with their local community or neighbourhood, and they are considered to be stakeholders whose voice should be heard within their neighbourhood and community when planning decisions are taken, whether for social or commercial reasons. Such direct participation may be viewed as an expedient formula through which social and commercial priorities may be brought together and the need for a lengthy and potentially divisive planning dispute may be avoided.

More recently, the Coalition Government has sought to encourage economic growth and to compete more effectively at a 'global stage' by undertaking a number of practical reforms to eliminate barriers which delay or inhibit decision-making in relation to business investment, new infrastructures and job creation.[60] This policy objective is encapsulated within the GIA 2013, and though the aim of competing on a global stage appears to be somewhat aspirational, the underlying theme centres on promoting economic development, job creation and social cohesion through amongst other things, the building of new affordable homes. Together with the

---

[54] Allen and Crookes (n 51) 469.

[55] R Walsh, 'The Evolving Relationship between Property and Participation' in N Hopkins (ed), *Modern Studies in Property Law* (Oxford, Hart Publishing, 2013) 285.

[56] These could include a disparity between the compensation and the cost of buying an alternative property which could impact upon the possibility of buying another property, communities or neighbourhoods being destroyed and for some may also include mental health issues.

[57] Walsh (n 55) 285.

[58] A Layard, 'The Localism Act 2011: What is 'Local' and how do we (Legally) Construct it?' [2012] *Environmental Law Review* 134, 139–40.

[59] Walsh (n 55) 286. See also, P Brest, 'Constitutional Citizenship' (1986) 34 *Cleveland State Law Review* 175, 196.

[60] http://www.gov.uk/government/news/bill-to-boost-growth-and-infrastructure-goes-before-parliament.

National Planning Policy Framework (NPPF) 2012[61] this policy circle is squared (at least in theory) through the Coalition Government's 'help to buy scheme' which offers state guarantees for mortgages taken to purchase properties where there is a housing need. The help to buy scheme is particularly generous for new build houses, often located in urban areas where affordable housing may be in short supply, and has been extended to 2020 in the March 2014 budget.[62]

The GIA 2013 seeks to remove the obstacles that often hinder the progress of housing developments. For example, an amendment to section 106 of the Town and Country Planning Act 1990 enables developers to renegotiate their planning agreements with the Local Planning Authority where the development scheme has stalled because it is no longer economically viable to go ahead.[63] This could arise where the original obligations on providing a set number of affordable housing negotiated during better economic times would have been economically viable, but the change in the economic climate has meant the building programme(s) stalled because they were no longer economically feasible. Where such a situation has arisen then under section 106BA of the GIA 2013 the planning authority is required to review those planning obligations where the affordable housing requirement makes the project non-viable with a view to making those development projects viable.[64]

This review may impact upon the number of affordable houses to be built, but the desire to proceed with economically viable projects to promote economic growth appears to potentially outstrip the wider social mix of the community within that development. This is evidenced by the announcement in the 2014 budget of the creation of a new 'garden city' in Ebsfleet on the fringes of London.[65] This proposed development illustrates the government's dualist approach to land policy in which it simultaneously seeks both social and economic objectives. To that extent, the GIA 2013 and the announcement of a new garden city has at least partial echoes of the policy of the NPACA 1949 which provided that development in the nation's infrastructure and social enjoyment of land should go hand in hand. This development is also a nod to the Ebenezer Howard's vision from the 1890s of a garden city.[66] The city would be surrounded by green belt and provide a balanced combination of the social and economic benefits and opportunities that are present in both towns and the countryside. The reference to 'garden city' is intended to conjure up the notion of a pleasant urban environment for local inhabitants, but it also suggests that land use policy in the twenty-first century has more than just a passing reference to a utilitarian objective of promoting 'happiness' amongst the population.

---

[61] The planning policy document promotes and reinforces the presumption of sustainable development from an inclusionary and pro-active development perspective, focusing on three elements for sustainable development, namely economic, environmental and social: see paras 7–22.

[62] Originally it was supposed to end in December 2015.

[63] GIA 2013, s 106BA.

[64] GIA 2013, s 106 BA(5). See generally, M White, 'Renegotiating Planning Obligations: An Overview of the Law' [2013] *Journal of Planning and Environment Law* 1232.

[65] Deirdre Hipwell, 'Garden City and Stamp Duty Hike aim to increase Housing Supply' *The Times*, 19 March 2014 www.thetimes.co.uk/tto/business/budget2014/article4038397.ece. Two notable garden cities built in the early 1900s include: Welwyn Garden City and Letchworth.

[66] Howard's model of a garden city has been incorporated within the National Planning Policy Framework as a basis for planning large scale developments. See further, NPPF (n 6).

The tension that exists in local communities, where planning issues are at stake, usually surrounds the divergent views that may arise from planning applications and such tensions can often only be resolved through lengthy and costly planning inquiries. The Penfold Review in 2010[67] considered the issue of whether non-planning consents could be streamlined to promote efficiency and effectiveness of the planning process so as to fit within the government's policy of deregulation and supporting sustainable growth. One area identified for review was that of the registration of TVGs where this could have a negative impact on building development. The Penfold Review found that where building developments had already obtained planning approval, the development had often stalled because of an application which had been made to register a TVG. Where such a situation had arisen, Penfold identified that the motivation behind this was, in some cases, a means by which building developments were frustrated. Though this is not strictly speaking an issue of non-planning consent, it was seen as being high on the agenda for reform since it posed a commercial risk to developers and consequently it would impact negatively upon economic growth.[68] Penfold recommended that any potential application for a TVG should be presented at an earlier stage at the point where consideration is given to 'if' or whether the development should go ahead leading to more expediency.[69] Furthermore, as part of the streamlining proposition Penfold further suggested that improvements be made where planning and non-planning consents were concerned in specific areas and to avoid duplication. To this end, where there is a conflict between overlapping consent with respect to the same piece of land, for example in circumstances of the registration of a TVG and where planning consent has already been obtained, the application to register a TVG will have the effect of placing a moratorium on the development whilst the local authority determines whether or not to register the TVG application.[70] If TVG status is granted the land is then subject to two conflicting permissions which traditionally have meant that the development, notwithstanding the completion of the planning process, is stopped.

Section 15C of the Commons Act 2006 effectively prevents the operation of the right to register a TVG except only in circumstances where one of the triggering events has arisen, for example, where a draft development plan document has been published which identifies the land for potential development.[71] If the document is subsequently withdrawn at a later stage then this will amount to a terminating event and the right to register the TVG becomes exercisable again. Taking on board the spirit of Penfold's streamlining measures, the 2013 Act reduces the grace period for applying for registration after the requisite 20 years of recreational use 'as of right' has ceased from two years to one year.[72] Finally, landowners have been given the power to effectively stop the clock from ticking to prevent any claim for a TVG where land has been used for recreational purposes for a period of time. This involves the

---

[67] A Penfold, *Penfold: Review of Non-Planning Consents* 2010, available at www.bis.gov.uk/penfold.

[68] In a study commissioned by Defra in 2009 it was found that just under half of the applications for a town or village were connected to a potential threat of building development. See http://randd.defra.gov.uk/Default.aspx?Menu=Menu&Module=More&Location=None&ProjectID=16581.

[69] Penfold (n 67) para 4.25.

[70] GIA 2013, s 16 inserting s 15C in the Commons Act 2006.

[71] See Sch 1A of the Commons Act 2006 as inserted by Sch 4 GIA 2013.

[72] s 14 GIA 2013 inserts s 15(3A) into the Commons Act 2006.

landowner simply depositing a statement with an accompanying map to the commons registration authority.[73] In the GIA 2013 the government generally adopts Penfold's rational approach to resolving disputes concerning non-planning consents and in particular his recommendation concerning the future registration of TVGs. Though pragmatic and rational, the solution within the GIA 2013 is undoubtedly value laden with a presumption that, on balance, growth and economic development are considered to be more worthy objectives than permitting the potential registration of a TVG.

Although this legislative change will make it more difficult for those parties who have an interest in protecting a long-established recreational activity on a landowner's property, the harshness of this is to some extent mitigated by providing for Local Green Space designation.[74] This scheme does not attempt to replace customary rights such as TVGs but provides an alternative additional conduit by which local communities can protect green areas of significance which are local in character, in close proximity to the community it serves and is demonstrably special to the local community. The type of land envisaged as potentially coming within the scope of such a designation could include areas of outstanding natural beauty, historic significance and urban areas of tranquillity and recreational value.[75]

According to the NPPF where development issues arise within Local Green Space, it must be consistent with the policy protecting green belt land which aims to prevent urban sprawl by keeping land permanently open.[76] Green belt boundaries have in the past been fluid and moved in to fulfil building development requirements. However, that does not necessarily lead to a loss in protected green belt land rather another piece of land located elsewhere is designated as green belt.[77] Where this sort of situation may arise, alteration according to the NPPF is only permitted in 'exceptional circumstances' through the Local Plan which covers the future development plans of a local area.[78] This approach of relocating a Local Green Space could potentially become a reality given the policy direction of sustainable development in the NPPF which could be viewed as being pro-developer rather than protecting green belt land from the urban sprawl. The potential redesignation of Local Green Space may arise irrespective of the local characteristics of the green space, and at a distance away from the local community which sought the designation of the Local Green Space initially. This lack of permanent affixing to the land of the Local Green Space is in some sense similar to the policy of deregistration of TVGs which are more than $200m^2$ in area. Section 16 of the Commons Act 2006 provides that where an application for deregistration is made for land which is more than $200m^2$ in area it must be accompanied with a proposal for replacement land to be registered as a substitute to the released land. In contrast, where the land is less than $200m^2$ in area, deregistration is possible subject to compliance with certain conditions, and without

---

[73] s 15 GIA 2013 inserts s 15A into the Commons Act 2006.
[74] NPPF (n 6) paras 73–78.
[75] Ibid, para 77.
[76] Ibid, paras 79–92.
[77] See R Gant, G Robinson and S Fazal, 'Land-Use Change in the 'Edgelands': Policies and Pressures in London's Rural-Urban Fringe' [2011] *Land Use Policy* 266.
[78] NPPF (n 6) para 82.

the obligatory proposal for replacement land.[79] It is apparent that neither the Local Green Space nor the TVG (over 200m^2) are protected in absolute terms to remain in the same designated area forever though their permanency is ensured to a certain extent albeit the designated area may be subject to change.

The paradigm used by the government to reconcile, on the one hand, limiting the ability of those who have a vested interest in protecting a TVG and that of providing an alternative to creating a 'modern green' in the form of a Local Green Space is similar to the observations made by Gray in relation to compulsory purchase of land for commercial recreational purposes, for example to build a golf course or football stadium.[80] Gray in the context of recreational property considered 'at what point did a purported exercise of eminent domain cross the borderline between beneficial state intervention and impermissible preferment of another's private commercial advantage?'[81] Gray's question identifies the tension between the public and private interests, and encapsulates the government's policy that economic regeneration and public utility must go hand in hand. However, in the various examples Gray considered, in relation to recreational property,[82] he questions the justification posited for urban regeneration that there exists some dual benefit that offers both economic and social gains. Significantly Gray dissects the economic and social benefits of these regeneration ventures to identify projects which can be characterised for exhibiting a measurable economic benefit with some definitive social gains.[83] Thus, to return to Local Green Spaces, if viewed through Gray's analysis, then their designation may be questionable especially where the economic objective significantly outweighs the utility that the Local Green Space can deliver to the community. In particular, Gray's matrix may lead to scepticism that Local Green Spaces are insufficient because they do not offer the rights that were associated with a TVG. Put bluntly the designation of a Local Green Space can be viewed as a functional trade-off in order to permit a development to proceed in circumstances where a TVG may have previously existed.

The socially motivated doctrines of being for the 'greater public good' or social utility provide the nexus for the justification for state intervention. The case for state intervention in the case of TVGs is couched in the terms of promoting sustainable economic growth through building developments, which include affordable housing, and at the same time fostering private commercial enterprise. The social benefits cannot be ignored, but they appear in the GIA 2013 to be ancillary to the primary aim of the securing economic growth objective. On this analysis, though the creation of Local Green Spaces to some extent may mitigate against the curtailment of the ability to register a TVG and may offset commercial development, it is questionable whether the character or potentially lack of enduring nature of a Local Green Space will pacify opponents of a development and may provide a basis for further flashpoints.

---

[79] Commons Act 2006, s 16(6)–(9).

[80] See generally, K Gray, 'Recreational Property' in S Bright (ed), *Modern Studies in Property Law* (Oxford, Hart Publishing, 2011).

[81] Ibid, 13.

[82] Ibid, 20–27.

[83] In the case of the Olympic and Legal project the regeneration of East London encompassed the concept of some form of 'national prestige and importance' as the prime purpose, with economic rejuvenation being enveloped within that. The Olympics with its social and cultural, public interest dimension provided the vehicle for justifying urban regeneration and economic development (see Gray (n 80) 20–21).

V. THE SOCIAL DIMENSION OF LAND

The regulation of land usage has always encompassed an economic and social dimension, but it is the extent to which the emphasis is placed on either or both of those elements that is at issue. In the previous section it was noted that contemporary planning policy focuses predominantly on the economic benefits to be gained from the development of land and this has been achieved at the expense of fully integrating into land use policy a defined and universal understanding of what constitutes a social need for land. It is true that the social dimension of land has a dynamic and protean character which reflects the changing nature of our society, our perceptions and community dynamics, but there remain some underlying core and universal features which are associated with social usage such as for recreational purposes and health benefits. It is these features which have remained a constant and are justifications for the social usage of land.

Historically, land has not been solely used for agriculture and pasture, but it has also provided local communities with a meeting place and acted as a venue for social and recreational activities, notably in this context TVGs existed for recreational purposes even though their exact origin is unclear. To this extent the land can be said to embody the social and customary nature of a place within the community which it serves. In referring to TVGs in the present day connotations of nostalgia and heritage usually prevail over these areas of land and perhaps provide some form of justification for their protection.[84] This nostalgic view of village greens is exemplified in the *Report of the Royal Commission on Common Land 1955–58*[85] where it states '"Village green"—the very words are evocative of great age and tranquillity, of turf as rich in hue as it is trim in a setting untouched by time'. Lord Hoffmann in *R v Oxfordshire CC, Ex p Sunningwell Parish Council*[86] reinforced the nostalgic imagery of a village green by describing the town or village green under section 22(1) of the Commons Act 1965 as 'the traditional village green with its memories of maypole dancing, cricket and warm beer'.

This poetic view of a town or village green is far removed from what has recently been recognised and registered as a green, for example, a beach.[87] In identifying the traditional connotations of a village green and long usage, Lord Hoffmann recognises the importance of balancing interests of the landowner and the public interest in the preservation of open spaces where usage for recreational purposes has occurred over a long period of time. His Lordship's reasoning encapsulates the social dimension of TVGs, which is representative of the altruistic spirit of the legislation which seeks to protect and preserve TVGs and elucidate Parliament's intention.[88] By protecting this right, public law and the courts have consistently recognised a

---

[84] See further, Lord Denning MR in *New Windsor Corporation v Mellor* [1975] Ch 380 (CA), 386–87.

[85] Royal Commission, *Report of the Royal Commission on Common Land, 1955–58* (n 10) para 18.

[86] *Sunningwell* (n 2) 347F.

[87] *R (on the application of Newhaven Port and Properties Ltd) v Secretary of State for the Environment, Food and Rural Affairs* [2013] EWCA Civ 673, [2014] QB 282. The High Court is currently considering whether a skateboarding park in the Southbank Undercroft can be registered as a TVG: see N Richmond and L Rachel, 'A Village Green on the South Bank?' (2013) 1323 *Estates Gazette* 73.

[88] See Lord Hoffmann's judgment in *Oxfordshire CC v Oxford City Council* (n 1) for an historical outline of the development of the law in this area, in particular paras 2–27.

right whose purpose is to promote the social use of land and also acts as a means to promote retrospective heritage protection of a nostalgic perception of TVGs. Lord Hoffman further underscores this point by referring to TVGs as an 'important national resource'[89] suggesting that they deserve to be protected because they constitute part of a *shared* social heritage, irrespective of whether a person actually physically makes use of them.

In the previous section it was noted that the designation of a Local Green Space provides a mechanism by which green space can be protected for use by the local community and is not dependent upon long usage 'as of right' for registration purposes as in the case of TVGs. This provision of Local Green Space within the NPPF can be viewed as a means offsetting the economic objectives of promoting economic growth with sustainable development. Specifically, government objectives of increasing the housing stock are offset by providing local communities with a stakeholder status giving them the means by which land can be divested to the community through asset transfer or by the designation of a communal Local Green Space. This latter development is an antidote to streamlining the registration process for TVGs which had the effect of making it more difficult to register a TVG.

Though in more recent history, it is becoming apparent that in a broader perspective of communal relations and living, the social and recreational dimension inherent in land usage is becoming more important as a counter-balance to urbanisation. In this context from the late 1800s to the mid-1900s it is clear that although there was a huge pressure to build housing, protection for green spaces for public use and enjoyment was given equal importance to stem the flow of urbanisation. The protection of National Parks, as areas of outstanding natural beauty is an enduring example of the protection of the broader social facets of land and this form of national policy is as relevant today as it was in the immediate post-war era. In more recent times, the government's response to demands from the environmental citizen for increased access to rural land[90] and the coastal areas[91] have resulted in a more managed approach with the state regulating access.[92] The 'right to roam' and having access to coastal paths can be viewed as civic rights and which promote social equity, inclusion and utility,[93] but they also provide a formal means by which they implement a 'mediated sense of place for rural sites'.[94] This management of rural land by the state in part enables the state to directly ensure that such designated spaces do not interfere with economic development. The planned creation of an integrated coastal path network is part of the social matrix of land and through this project has gained national significance which is perhaps on a par with the legacy of the NPACA 1949. In that

---

[89] See the judgment of Lord Hoffmann in *Bettison v Langton* [2001] UKHL 24, [2002] 1 AC 27, 31.

[90] Countryside and Rights of Way Act 2000.

[91] Marine and Coastal Access Act 2009.

[92] The environmental citizen can no longer be simply perceived as an urban socialist but one who is more representative of a wider 'class' of citizen who has an increased interest in recreation and the environment: see B Mayfield, 'Access to Land: Social Class, Activism and the Genealogy of the Country and Rights of Way Act' [2010] *Statute Law Review* 63.

[93] See S Pascoe, 'Social Obligation Norm and the Erosion of Land Ownership?' [2012] *Conveyancer and Property Lawyer* 474, and K Gray, 'Pedestrian Democracy and the Geography of Hope' [2010] *Journal of Human Rights and the Environment* 45.

[94] A Layard, 'Shopping in the Public Realm: A Law of Place' [2010] *Journal of Law and Society* 412, 435.

context the coastal paths project will form a part of our national heritage,[95] it will enhance the experience of open air recreation and boost tourism.[96]

The justifications for state intervention are based on perceived utility to the public on the one hand in relation to the social benefits, but also coupled together with the potential economic benefits. This approach adopted by the government reflects Rodgers' view of how environmental regulation is no longer simply focusing on protection, but should also adopt a forward-looking approach.[97] Such a methodology will undoubtedly impact upon how property rights are exercised. Property rights within the framework of environmental regulation are characterised as limiting or restricting the exercise of rights, but it is also apparent that a net effect of this policy involves a redistribution of rights. This redistribution of rights is rooted in utilitarian arguments of voluminous social benefit that may be achieved through the fulfilment of public policy objectives and such an interpretation may also be applied to current state intervention in the case of creating a network of coastal paths. Though economic benefits may not be necessarily the prime motivation where coastal paths are concerned, the perceived greater public benefit and preservation of national heritage offered a justification for intervention redistribution, and possibly the restriction, of landowner's property rights that this entails.

It is without question that preservation of coastal paths carries a degree of social utility. Yet, the rationale behind this is not without difficulty, especially when the geographical location of coastal paths is considered and the ability of coastal paths to be used by a significant part of the population. It may be argued that for many citizens the preservation of land for social utility purposes lies 'closer to home' and is encapsulated through a culture of NIMBYism and that challenges raised from loss of green belt land, or the restriction to register TVGs potentially outweighs the benefits of creating coastal paths. State intervention in land distribution projects tends to focus on 'grandstand' projects where economic regeneration and protecting national heritage go hand in hand, for example the post-war rebuilding and nationalisation of industry was accompanied by the 1949 legislation. A similar interpretation may be applied to modern times where economic growth through land development have been accompanied by roaming rights in the Countryside and Rights of Way Act 2000 and now the creation of coastal paths. However, irrespective of the government's ambitions the significant litigation to protect TVGS in recent years demonstrates that the environmental citizen remains primarily concerned about local issues and how they affect their own neighbourhood.

VI. CONCLUDING REMARKS

The current policy trend within land regulation appears to broadly maintain the approach adopted since the industrial revolution. Land continues to be viewed

---

[95] This is a legacy from the Labour Government. In their 1997 manifesto the Labour Party was committed to providing 'greater freedom for people to explore our open countryside', and they regarded the countryside as a 'natural asset' and a 'part of our heritage which calls for careful stewardship': www.labour-party.org.uk/manifestos/1997/1997-labour-manifesto.shtml.

[96] In June 2012 the first coastal path running along Weymouth Bay had been completed and the Minister at the time had expressed the economic benefits from such a path being made accessible to the public: see www.naturalengland.org.uk/about_us/news/2012/290612.aspx.

[97] Rodgers (n 36) 557–58.

as primarily an economic facility whereby urbanisation is promoted to the extent of fulfilling the demand for housing. This has been tempered, only marginally, by incorporating social utility into land use policy but such social objectives are largely secondary, and policy changes have reflected a public desire to use land for social purposes, as seen in the right to roam which is guaranteed by the Countryside and Rights of Way Act 2000.

Today, the GIA 2013 and NPPF have shifted the emphasis and focus more directly on the economic benefits that can be extracted from land usage rather than creating an equal balance with social benefits. The NPPF is directed towards fostering a competitive environment on a global stage with the vision of achieving this through a presumption of sustainable economic growth. Economic policy, therefore, takes primacy while social and recreational considerations are relegated to an ancillary consideration. Where local recreational spaces are concerned their protection has generally been left in the hands of citizens who form part of an informal 'bottom up' movement that relies upon socio-environmental direct action. This empowerment of the local citizen is to be welcomed and can be said to promote local democracy and stakeholder involvement in the local community, but such sporadic participation lacks a coherent strategy through which clear socio-environmental policies may be achieved more generally and land protected for social purposes. Land use policy, continues to emerge in a piecemeal fashion and the state may suggest a consensus around the need for economic development but protection of the land for social purposes is left primarily in the hands of the citizen to determine the extent of their access to open spaces and rural areas.

6

Developers versus Protestors: Contractual Licensees and Possession Claims Post Dutton

ADAM BAKER[*]

C AMPAIGNS AGAINST PLANNED development or user of land have become prominent in recent decades. Since the 1960s many demonstrations have taken the form of 'sit-ins', in which activists seek to prevent access to the property in issue. For developers given contractual licences to perform work on the land,[1] such opposition can be problematic. If assistance from other quarters is not forthcoming, they may wish to seek possession of the land in their own right.

The leading authority on such actions is *Manchester Airport plc v Dutton*.[2] In that case the plaintiff airport company had been licensed by the National Trust (the landowner) to enter and occupy land for the purpose of lopping and felling trees in connection with the construction of a runway. The actions of protestors encamped on the land made the work effectively impossible. In a decision that has attracted much academic scrutiny,[3] and in a victory for the airport company, Laws LJ held that 'a licensee not in occupation may claim possession against a trespasser if that is a necessary remedy to vindicate and give effect to such rights of occupation as by contract with his licensor he enjoys'.[4] Yet many writers regard this as a flawed decision.

This chapter investigates whether there is any sound reason for allowing some licensees, who are not in actual possession, to bring actions for the recovery of land. Having contextualised such claims and overviewed *Dutton*, two possible options are identified. The first is to interpret the legislation governing possession claims in conformity with that decision. This would mean taking a broad view of Parliament's intention, seeing it as being to provide a swift remedy for those entitled to take possession of land. That would support an 'updating construction' of the modern

---

[*] University of Leeds. Many thanks to Michael Cardwell and the anonymous reviewers for their comments on earlier drafts of this chapter. Any errors remain my own.

[1] Developers are typically licensees: *Surrey Heath BC v Lovell Construction Ltd and Haden Young Ltd* (1988) 42 BLR 25 (QB) 51.

[2] *Manchester Airport plc v Dutton* [2000] QB 133 (CA).

[3] See G Seabourne and E Paton, 'Unchained Remedy: Recovery of Land by Licensees' [1999] *Conveyancer and Property Lawyer* 535; W Swadling, 'Opening the Numerus Clausus' (2000) 116 *LQR* 354; J Hill, 'The Proprietary Character of Possession' in E Cooke (ed), *Modern Studies in Property Law*, vol 1 (Oxford, Hart Publishing, 2001).

[4] *Dutton* (n 2) 150.

action, reflecting the fact that one can now have a right to take possession that is not title-based. But this approach is controversial. Failing its acceptance, one is left with only the second option. It is speculated that, in some extreme cases, a failure to make a possession order in favour of a *Dutton* licensee would infringe their rights under article 1 of the First Protocol to the European Convention on Human Rights. This could justify providing a remedy in such cases.

I. BACKGROUND TO *DUTTON*

A. Modern Environmental Protest

The nature of environmental protest has changed over time. In the nineteenth and early-twentieth centuries, campaigners focussed on issues such as customary rights of access to land.[5] It was only in the 1960s that local protests against unwanted development became numerous.[6] Since then, unauthorised occupation of premises has become a feature of the political landscape.[7] It is a tactic often used by so-called 'militant environmental activists'.[8]

The 1990s were a particularly active period for protest camps,[9] which were commonly a reaction to proposed transport developments.[10] The case of Manchester Airport's second runway is a good example of this.[11] The saga began in 1994 with the lodging of an application for the construction of the runway, the intended site consisting entirely of green belt land, including within it an Area of Special Country Value and part of a Conservation Area. Following an inquiry the Secretaries of State accepted the case for the new runway. Yet this was far from the end of the matter. Protestors quickly set up camps on the land affected, some including tunnels dug as deep as 70ft. Following a protracted but successful battle to evict the campaigners from these areas, some of them then moved to nearby Cedar's Wood and Arthur's Wood in 1999.[12] The latter of these areas became the subject of the *Dutton* litigation.[13]

---

[5] C Rootes, *Environmental Protest in Western Europe* (Oxford, Oxford University Press, 2003) 21.

[6] W Rüdig, 'Between Moderation and Marginalization: Environmental Radicalism in Britain' in B Taylor (ed), *Ecological Resistance Movements* (Albany, University of New York Press, 1995) 222–25.

[7] N Cobb, 'Property's Outlaws: Squatting, Land Use and Criminal Trespass' [2012] *Crim LR* 114, 123; D Mead, 'A Chill through the Back Door? The Privatised Regulation of Peaceful Protest' [2013] *PL* 100, 100.

[8] M Button, T John and N Brearley, 'New Challenges in Public Order Policing: the Professionalisation of Environmental Protest and the Emergence of the Militant Environmental Activist' (2002) 30 *International Journal of the Sociology of Law* 17, 23.

[9] D Wall, 'Snowballs, Elves and Skimmongtons?: Genealogies of Environmental Direct Action Tactics' in B Seel, M Paterson and B Doherty, *Direct Action in British Environmentalism* (London, Routledge, 2000) 81–82.

[10] Rootes (n 5) 36–37.

[11] The following account is chiefly drawn from L Butcher, *Aviation: Manchester's Second Runway, 1993–2001* (HC Library Standard Note SN/BT/101) www.parliament.uk/briefing-papers/SN00101.pdf.

[12] PR Taylor, 'Treetop Protest saves Giant from the Axe, for now' *Manchester Evening News*, 31 July 1997, 20.

[13] The encampment on Arthur's Wood took the form of tree-houses connected by ropewalks and included a tunnel.

As the 1990s came to a close, protests of this sort became less frequent.[14] Nevertheless, the potential for a return to the methods of that time cannot be discounted. The decline in protest camp activity owed in part to a shift in the policy of the then Government against new road building;[15] and the prospect of future decisions that raise new tensions is very real. Today a number of controversial issues loom large, from HS2[16] to fracking,[17] the development of the green belt[18] to further airport expansion.[19]

B. Alternatives to Developer Actions

For developers given a licence to carry out work on land, such opposition may present real difficulties. In some rare instances they may wish to bring civil proceedings in their own right. This is because assistance from the police[20] and/or the site owner may not be forthcoming. With the former, considerations of both cost and reputation may act as a deterrent to action.[21] Even if they are minded to step in, moreover, officers may face practical challenges. Protest camp tactics have evolved in favour of methods, such as occupying trees, that frustrate attempts at arrest.[22] Chief constables may thus elect to take a back-seat role, making arrests only when the occupants are removed by other means.

This then leaves only the prospect of intervention by the licensor. Assuming that they enjoy legal title to the land, they will have standing to bring a possession claim. Sometimes their contract may include an express or an implied duty to intervene; that is, to take reasonable steps to ensure the availability of the land.[23] But it seems that such obligations are atypical in construction contracts.[24]

The greatest difficulties for the licensee will arise if the site owner is unable or unwilling to act, even if only in the short to medium-term. This was the problem

---

[14] S Farrell, 'Crop Crusaders are Latest in Protest Chic' *The Times*, 5 September 1998.

[15] On which see Department of the Environment, Transport and the Regions, *A New Deal for Transport: Better for Everyone* (Cm 3950, 1998).

[16] 'High Speed 2' (HS2) is a proposed high-speed railway, presently intended to stretch from London to Leeds and to Manchester via the Midlands.

[17] This process has already been the subject of local direct action protests: T Webb, 'Protesters bring Halt to Fracking in West Sussex' *The Times*, 27 July 2013, 2.

[18] J Aldred, 'Planning: Trust Survey highlights Threat to Greenbelt Land' *The Guardian*, 19 December 2013, 19.

[19] Airports Commission, *Airports Commission: Interim Report* (London, HMSO, 2013); G Topham and A Vaughan, 'Heathrow Protesters on Alert for Fresh Runway Battle' *The Guardian*, 16 December 2013, 8.

[20] Most obviously, because the protestors are committing the offence of 'aggravated trespass': Criminal Justice and Public Order Act 1994, s 68.

[21] C Barnard and I Hare, 'The Right to Protest and the Right to Export: Police Discretion and the Free Movement of Goods' (1997) 60 *MLR* 394, 409; B Doherty, M Paterson and B Seel, 'Direct Action in British Environmentalism' in B Seel, M Paterson and B Doherty, *Direct Action in British Environmentalism* (London, Routledge, 2000) 19.

[22] B Doherty, 'Manufactured Vulnerability: Protest Camp Tactics' in B Seel, M Paterson and B Doherty, *Direct Action in British Environmentalism* (Routledge, London 2000) 67–68.

[23] *Cartwright v Merthyr Tydfil CBC* (CA, 22 May 2000). See J Sharples, *Land Licences* (Bristol, Jordans, 2011) 8.16 and 8.30–8.31.

[24] *LRE Engineering Services Ltd v Otto Simon Carves Ltd* (1981) 24 BLR 127 (QB). Cf *Rapid Building Group Ltd v Ealing Family Housing Association Ltd* (1984) 29 BLR 5 (CA).

faced by the airport company in *Dutton*, whose licensor was the National Trust. Even if it had decided to litigate, procedural hurdles would have probably slowed down the claim.[25] Seabourne and Paton have also speculated that its trustees may have considered that to bring possession proceedings would have been outside of their powers.[26] The statutory purpose of the National Trust is to:

> [P]romot[e] the permanent preservation for the benefit of the nation of lands and tenements (including buildings) of beauty or historic interest and as regards lands [to preserve] (so far as practicable) … their natural aspect features and animal and plant life.[27]

Such concerns may have been in the minds of the trustees. But it is also likely that they wished to avoid the reputational consequences of proceeding themselves.[28] Even the conferral of a licence on the airport company by the National Trust had led campaigners to accuse it of 'selling out',[29] having been 'bribed' off with a package that included 100 acres of local land.[30]

C. Actions for the Recovery of Land by the Developer

In sum, therefore, there will be instances, howsoever rare, in which the developer wishes to bring civil proceedings against the activists. If the protestors are in adverse possession of at least some part of the affected area, this means bringing an action for the recovery of land.[31]

It is worth explaining something of the history of this action. Originally it was one of ejectment, which claim was abolished by the Common Law Procedure Act 1852. This Act directed that, instead of proceedings by ejectment, a writ should be issued, which was shorn of the fictions that had surrounded ejectment.[32] A new action was thus created.[33] It was then re-named one 'for the recovery of land' post the Judicature Acts 1872–75. In 1970 it was consolidated in Order 113 of the Rules of the Supreme Court, which added provisions for the obtaining of summary possession and for claiming against 'persons unknown'.

Today the action for the recovery of land is governed by Part 55 of the Civil Procedure Rules (CPR). Part 55.1(b) defines a 'possession claim against trespassers' as one

---

[25] The trustees would almost certainly have sought an indemnity for their costs: *Re Beddoe* [1893] 1 Ch 547 (CA). Such an application would in turn have required the consent of the Charity Commission: Charities Act 1993, s 33 (now Charities Act 2011, s 115).

[26] Seabourne and Paton (n 3) 541–42.

[27] National Trust Act 1907, s 4(1).

[28] Although they swore an affidavit concerning their view of the licence arrangement, this may show only a desire to avoid proceedings at their own behest if possible. *Cf* Seabourne and Paton (n 3) 541.

[29] D Ward, 'Sell-out Claim as Trust agrees to fell Trees' *The Guardian*, 8 February 1999, 9.

[30] D Ward, 'Trust denies Land Bribe' *The Guardian*, 11 February 1997, 8.

[31] In theory an injunction may be sought if the licensor has warranted the availability of the land and the protestors commit the tort of inducing a breach of this term (on which tort, see *OBG Ltd v Allan* [2007] UKHL 21, [2008] 1 AC 1 (HL)). Such provisions are however not likely to be common, and practitioners emphasise the advantages of a possession order over an injunction: A Phillips and T Storm, 'Prepare for the Worst' (2007) 748 *Estates Gazette* 156. See also *Dutton* (n 2) 140 (Chadwick LJ).

[32] Common Law Procedure Act 1852, s 168.

[33] *Gledhill v Hunter* (1880) 14 Ch D 492 (Ch) 498: 'It is no longer ejectment: it is a different kind of action'.

'for the recovery of land which the claimant alleges is occupied only by a person or persons who entered or remained on the land without the consent of a person entitled to possession of that land'. What then does it mean to be 'entitled to possession' of land? In ejectment, the plaintiff required a legal interest, giving a present right to possession. This was widely assumed to be true also with the modern action.[34] On this view, the only concession to licensees is that, if they are in actual possession of the land, they can claim against mere wrongdoers.[35] In this respect, a licensee may be able to show possession even if they cannot exclude their licensor under their contract: one must always consider the position on the ground.[36] Had it been on the land before the protest began, the licensee in *Dutton* may well have succeeded on this basis.[37]

II. THE DECISION IN *DUTTON*

A. The Judgments

The problem for the airport company, of course, was that it had not gone onto the land. The actions of the protestors made this impracticable. On an orthodox view of the law, as was favoured by Chadwick LJ, *locus standi* could hence not be shown. But matters were viewed differently by Laws and Kennedy LJJ. The former thought that the case law on ejectment did not prove how one should approach the issue today.[38] It was incorrect to treat the modern action as governed by the same rules.[39] The 'true principle' is that 'a licensee not in occupation may claim possession against a trespasser if that is a necessary remedy to vindicate and give effect to such rights of occupation as by contract with his licensor he enjoys'.[40]

Kennedy LJ concurred with Laws LJ, but also offered some additional reasons for the outcome. In his view, the plaintiff was within the words of RSC Order 113, as was then applicable. His Lordship regarded this provision as having altered the law:

> The plaintiff does have a right to possession of the land granted to it by the licence. It is entitled 'to enter *and occupy*' (my emphasis) the land in question ... If it is said that such an approach blurs the distinction between different types of right and different types of remedy it seems to me that is the effect of the wording of Order 113.[41]

Despite Chadwick LJ's dissent, the protestors' appeal was thus dismissed.

---

[34] M Wonnacott, *Possession of Land* (Cambridge, Cambridge University Press, 2006) 22, 26–27, 69–70 and 96.

[35] *Dutton* (n 2) 143–44 (Chadwick LJ), 147 (Laws LJ). See A Baker, 'Bruton, Licensees in Possession and a Fiction of Title' [2014] *Conveyancer and Property Lawyer* 495.

[36] *Hounslow LBC v Twickenham Garden Developments Ltd* [1971] Ch 233 (Ch) 257.

[37] *Dutton* (n 2) 143–44 (Chadwick LJ), 147 (Laws LJ).

[38] Ibid, 149.

[39] Ibid.

[40] Ibid, 150.

[41] Ibid, 151.

B. The Claimants Afforded Standing

Having reviewed the decision in *Dutton*, the next matter to assess is that of which licensees it protects. Perhaps the first thing to consider in this regard is the title of the licensor. Although this is not stated explicitly by either Laws or Kennedy LJJ, one assumes that a claim would fail if the licensor has either no title at all or a weaker one than that of the defendants. If that is true, it also implies the proper approach to be taken to limitation in this area. When the licensor's estate is unregistered,[42] the licensee's position would be governed by section 15(1) of the Limitation Act 1980.[43] This may also be so if the licensor's estate was registered:[44] section 96(1) of the Land Registration Act 2002 disapplies section 15, but only 'in relation to' a registered estate.

The next thing to consider is the type of licence protected. On this issue there is some ambiguity. A first point is that Laws LJ spoke of a possession order being granted only if it is 'a necessary remedy',[45] which may imply that no other course should be reasonably available to the licensee. Laws LJ indeed seemed to rely on the fact that a possession order was 'the only practical remedy' in that case.[46] Nevertheless, this consideration has not been picked up in later cases.

Even if this point is overlooked, there are other matters to grapple with. Textbook writers have distinguished between occupational and non-occupational licences,[47] which approach is consistent with Kennedy LJ's judgment in particular. Subsequent cases, however, also employ the language of 'effective control'. Thus in *Countryside Residential (North Thames) Ltd v T*,[48] Waller LJ explained that 'there is a clear difference between a licence granted for the purpose of access, which does not provide effective control over the land, and a licence to occupy which does'. On this basis the court refused to make a possession order in favour of a licensee entitled to carry out investigatory work before development. In *Mayor of London v Hall*,[49] similarly, Lord Neuberger MR said that *Dutton* helps those licensees 'entitled to use and control, effectively amounting to possession'.

The decision in *Dutton* itself contains just one reference to 'effective control'; but perhaps it is a significant one. This occurred in the context of Laws LJ's statement that 'the airport company could have obtained an order for possession; at least if it was in effective control of the land'.[50] The words 'effective control' must be a reference to de facto possession. In making this point, Laws LJ was drawing attention to what he saw as an anomalous distinction between the treatment of such licensees

---

[42] In the case of a sub-licence, one would look to the estate of the head licensor.

[43] The licensor would have to be treated as 'some person through whom' the licensee claims: Limitation Act 1980, s 15(1).

[44] Law Commission, *Land Registration for the Twenty-First Century: A Conveyancing Revolution* (Law Com No 271, 2001) 14.10.

[45] *Dutton* (n 2) 150.

[46] Ibid, 151.

[47] C Harpum, S Bridge and M Dixon, *Megarry & Wade: The Law of Real Property*, 8th edn (London, Sweet & Maxwell, 2012) 4–026.

[48] *Countryside Residential (North Thames) Ltd v T* (2001) 81 P & CR 2 (CA) [13].

[49] *Mayor of London v Hall* [2010] EWCA Civ 817 [27].

[50] *Dutton* (n 2) 147.

who are in and out of possession.[51] From this fact we may perhaps infer the required threshold. What suffices is a theoretical scope for showing de facto possession while exercising one's rights under the agreement.[52] Certainly, it would be dubious to give possession to a licensee who could never show it by enjoying their licence.

If this is correct, the use of an 'occupational right' test has the potential to mislead. It will often point to the correct conclusion, but it need not always do so. First, there are contractual privileges that, though 'occupational' in nature, may not satisfy a threshold of 'effective control'. A possible example is a licence of storage.[53] Even the quite extensive storage of goods on land can be compatible with the landowner being in possession of it.[54] Secondly, there are rights of 'effective control' that may not be 'occupational'. In one case, for instance, the use of marsh land for shooting was held to constitute adverse possession of it.[55] Had a licence for shooting been granted over such land, the licensee could therefore have had a right of 'effective control'. But it is not clear that the entitlement would be 'occupational'.

An 'effective control' test is thus the one that best captures the reasoning in *Dutton*. On balance, it can probably be squared with the recent decision in *Vehicle Control Services Ltd v Revenue and Customs Commissioners*.[56] In this case Lewison LJ took the two principles emerging from *Dutton* to be that:

(i)　[T]he court has power to grant a remedy to a licensee which will protect but not exceed his legal rights granted by the licence; and

(ii)　in every case the question must be, what is the reach of the right, and whether it is shown that the defendant's acts violate its enjoyment.[57]

The first of these observations causes us little difficulty. If the licensee claimant has no rights, the exercise of which could establish de facto possession, the court could hardly grant a possession order in their favour. To do that would be to exceed the legal rights under the licence. As to the second point, it is difficult to countenance that *Dutton* has affected the tort of inducing a breach of contract.[58] It may be that Lewison LJ's second principle merely amplifies his first one.

The actual dispute in *Vehicle Control Services* concerned a licensee engaged to run (but not to occupy) a car park. Its rights included ones of issuing permits and towing away improperly parked vehicles. In purporting to apply *Dutton*, the Court of Appeal held that the parking charges imposed by the licensee under its agreements with the vehicle owners were treatable as damages for trespass to land.[59] Lewison LJ reasoned that since the agreement between the licensee and the landowner gave it the right to eject trespassers, and as the licensee's contracts with the motorists gave it the

---

[51]　Ibid.

[52]　The relevant right can be one that is implied for a limited purpose. In one case its implication was necessary to allow a claimant, whose leasehold estate had ended, to fulfil a covenant to yield up the properties with vacant possession: *Alamo Housing Cooperative Ltd v Meredith* [2003] EWCA Civ 495, [2003] HLR 62.

[53]　Such rights can be 'occupational': see *Kling v Keston Properties Ltd* (1983) 49 P & CR 212 (Ch).

[54]　See, eg *Kettel v Bloomfold Ltd* [2012] EWHC 1422 (Ch).

[55]　*Red House Farms (Thorndon) Ltd v Catchpole* [1977] 2 EGLR 125 (CA).

[56]　*Vehicle Control Services Ltd v Revenue and Customs Commissioners* [2013] EWCA Civ 186.

[57]　Ibid, [34].

[58]　On which see *Allan* (n 31).

[59]　For this reason the payments were not subject to Value Added Tax.

same right, it was necessary for it to have standing to sue in trespass. Crucially, no right to occupation or possession was necessary for this to be so.[60]

Precisely what should be made of this decision is unclear. The Supreme Court has affirmed that one must show actual possession to be able to sue in trespass.[61] Perhaps the licensee in this case was allowed to assume possession for the limited purpose of towing away or immobilising vehicles (and issuing charges in the alternative), this being implicit given the rights afforded to it by the licensor to take such action against vehicle owners. This right, in turn, would then have to justify our treating the licensee as being in constructive possession for the purpose in question. Perhaps this is a logical extension of *Dutton*. It would be odd if a licensee, who could bring a possession claim if the defendants took possession of some or part of the land, had no remedy if their conduct fell just short of that.

As this overview suggests, the outer limits of *Dutton* are somewhat hazy. There is also room for dispute about the proper interpretation of a given claimant's licence. Yet the reading offered here does allow one to borrow from the case law on adverse possession. This provides at least some measure of certainty in its application.

C. Analysis of *Dutton*

Many writers view *Dutton* as a flawed decision. Their objections are ostensibly compelling. First, they dismiss any attempt to rely on the wording of the modern form of the action. Parliament's intention was to make only procedural changes, not to alter the substance of the claim.[62] This conclusion then throws one back onto the common law position regarding *locus standi*. Plainly a contractual licence, as a mere personal right, is not a title for this purpose. In addition, one cannot develop the law otherwise because section 1 of the Law of Property Act 1925 enacts a *numerus clausus* of legal interests in land. *Dutton* thus veers onto impermissible territory.

These arguments notwithstanding, the courts have shown little desire to depart from *Dutton*. Baroness Hale has supported the outcome;[63] Lord Rodger has referred to it uncritically;[64] and we have seen that the Court of Appeal applied it in *Vehicle Control Services*.[65] Even Lord Neuberger MR, who once expressed views more supportive of a contrary analysis,[66] appeared to modify his stance in *Mayor of London v Hall*.[67] As his Lordship stated in that case:

> [T]here is obvious force in the point that the modern law relating to possession claims ... should develop and adapt to accommodate a claim by anyone entitled to use and control, effectively amounting to possession, of the land in question—along the lines of the views expressed by Laws LJ in Dutton's case.[68]

---

[60] *Vehicle Control Services* (n 56) [35].
[61] *Bocardo SA v Star Energy UK Onshore Ltd* [2010] UKSC 35, [2011] 1 AC 380.
[62] Swadling (n 3) 356–57.
[63] *Secretary of State for the Environment, Food and Rural Affairs v Meier* [2009] UKSC 11, [2009] 1 WLR 2780 [35].
[64] Ibid, [6].
[65] *Vehicle Control Services* (n 56).
[66] *Meier* (n 63) [60]–[69].
[67] *Hall* (n 49).
[68] Ibid, [27].

It is possible to share this view. As we have seen, *Dutton* helps those licensees who, had they been on the land, could potentially have brought a possession claim. A lack of equivalence between the two cases has little to recommend it in policy terms. This can be seen by analysing the reasons behind section 1 of the Law of Property Act 1925, which prevents the creation of new legal property rights. First, and in terms of protecting purchasers, *Dutton* is not problematic, as disponees of the licensor seem to be unaffected.[69] As regards other third parties, it is true that the possession of a *Dutton* licensee on the land is outwardly manifested, whereas the right of the same licensee yet to enter onto the land is not. Yet this is not a significant point. The interim period should be a short one, and occurs equally with other possessory rights that can exist without registration.[70] The squatter, indeed, should know that someone has a better right to the land than them. But perhaps most importantly of all, this uncertainty is not a risk to third parties in terms of financial liability. They cannot be sued for pure economic losses, whether in an action for trespass or one for the recovery of land.[71] Any liability that they do incur would also have been payable in any event to the landowner, had they brought the claim.

In light of this, a court may strain to find a justification for *Dutton*. Arguments based on statutory interpretation may be advanced in this regard. Both Baroness Hale[72] and Griffith Williams J[73] have opined that the language of the CPR countenances claims by some licensees. *Dutton*'s critics aver that Parliament intended only procedural reform, but one could ask whether this view neglects the bigger picture. Perhaps the policy of the Common Law Procedure Act 1852 was to offer a swift remedy to those with the right to possession of land. When the new action was introduced, the procedural changes made were felt to be sufficient to achieve that. There was no reason to reform the law on standing, for there was no issue with it. The Act must be set in its historical context. At the time, a person with a 'right to possession' had title to land: the idea of their being a licensee 'would have caused merriment'.[74] Unsurprisingly, therefore, the 1852 Act is drafted with allusions to the plaintiff's 'title'.[75] Subsequent developments were then merely reactive, dealing with such threats to this policy as had come to Parliament's attention. Thus when, in *Dutton*, it was forcibly brought home that one could have a right to possession that was not a 'title', reference to that term was dropped from the CPR.

A court minded to uphold *Dutton* could adopt such reasoning. Whatever a 'right to possession' meant in 1852, the policy identified here would go against construing that expression from a Victorian perspective. This accords with how, ordinarily,

---

[69] Squatters, moreover, are not 'purchasers' whom the register is designed to assist: E Cooke, *The New Law of Land Registration* (Oxford, Hart Publishing, 2003) 90. In theory, at least, squatters could confer privileges over or out of their possessory estate, but the reality is that protestors will have no wish to grant interests and third parties no desire to take them.

[70] Eg with many legal leases granted for seven years or less.

[71] K Gray and SF Gray, *Elements of Land Law*, 5th edn (Oxford, Oxford University Press, 2009) 10.1.35–10.1.37.

[72] *Meier* (n 63) [35].

[73] *Mayor of London v Hall* [2010] EWHC 1613 (QB) [96].

[74] AWB Simpson, *A History of the Land Law*, 2nd edn (Oxford, Clarendon Press, 1986) 265.

[75] For the same reason, the courts in the late 1800s naturally interpreted the 'action for the recovery of land' as ejectment by another name: *Gledhill v Hunter* (1880) 14 Ch D 492 (Ch).

statutes are interpreted in light of modern conditions:[76] a so-called 'updating construction' rather than an 'historical' one.[77] The general rule may apply here as well. A useful consequence of this approach is that it would not offend section 1 of the Law of Property Act 1925: one is dealing with a mere statutory entitlement. A contractual licence would be no more an 'interest in land' than a 'matrimonial home right' is.[78]

Nevertheless, there is much academic opinion against any such view. As Lord Neuberger MR has observed, the contrary argument enjoys 'real force'.[79] Should it prevail, one is faced by section 1 of the 1925 Act, and there the matter ends. The *Dutton* privilege would almost certainly be a new 'interest in land'. True, there are statements that only rights that can bind the grantor's successors in title are so describable,[80] and this entitlement would lack that capacity. Yet the danger is that these definitions would be revised to reflect *Dutton*. In jurisprudential terms, indeed, the right would also be proprietary: it is exigible not against a single person or group of persons, but against a very large and indefinite class.[81]

III. HUMAN RIGHTS AND CLAIMS BY LICENSEES

Thus far, we have seen that any statutory interpretation-based defence of *Dutton* is contentious. Should it not be accepted, the case is vulnerable to being overruled. If that occurred, one would have to ask whether any other ground exists for allowing possession claims by licensees.

One possibility in this regard is to rely on human rights principles. Inevitably this takes us beyond the actual reasoning in *Dutton*. Although the facts of that case will be used to illuminate the discussion, our assessment hence proceeds in more general terms. For this purpose we will focus specifically on article 1 to the First Protocol of the European Convention on Human Rights. Relying on article 8 of the Convention may be a better option for those who enjoy the land in question as their 'home',[82] but this is of no real relevance to claims by developers.[83]

---

[76] See generally *R (ZYN) v Walsall MBC* [2014] EWHC 1918 (Admin) [39]–[48].

[77] O Jones, *Bennion on Statutory Interpretation*, 6th edn (London, LexisNexis Butterworths, 2013) 797.

[78] On matrimonial home rights, see *Wroth v Tyler* [1974] Ch 30 (Ch) 46.

[79] *Hall* (n 49) [26].

[80] '[T]he quality of being capable of enduring through different ownerships of the land' is an essential feature of an 'interest in land': *National Provincial Bank Ltd v Hastings Car Mart Ltd* [1964] Ch 665 (CA) 696 (Russell LJ). See also *National Provincial Bank Ltd v Ainsworth* [1965] AC 1175 (HL) 1260–61 (Lord Wilberforce); *Pritchard v Briggs* [1980] Ch 338 (CA) 396 (Goff LJ).

[81] WN Hohfeld, *Fundamental Legal Conceptions as Applied in Judicial Reasoning: And other Legal Essays* (New Haven, Yale University Press, 1923) 65–114.

[82] This possibility has also been mooted in the context of private nuisance: *McKenna v British Aluminium Ltd* [2002] Env LR 30 (Ch) [52].

[83] A development site is not the place where a developer 'lives and to which [it] returns and which forms the centre of [it's] existence': *Uratemp Ventures Ltd v Collins* [2001] UKHL 43, [2002] 1 AC 301 [31] (Lord Millett).

A. Article 1

As is well-known, article 1 enacts that

every natural or legal person is entitled to the peaceful enjoyment of his possessions.

If this provision is to be relevant to claims by licensees, three matters must be shown: first, that the licensee enjoys a 'possession' within the meaning of the provision; second, that there has been an 'interference' with its enjoyment; and, third, that the interference is disproportionate.

B. The Meaning of 'Possessions'

Our discussion begins with the first of these hurdles. Although some maintain doubt on this point,[84] it is far from clear that a contractual licence can never be a 'possession' for the purposes of article 1.[85] Certainly, article 1 can extend to contractual rights[86] and licences to conduct economic activity on land.[87] What matters is whether the privilege in issue is an 'asset'.[88] In deciding this question, the courts will ask whether the right is marketable and transmissible and whether it has present economic value.[89] By keeping these factors in mind, we may explain away the one case in which a contractual licence was held not to be a 'possession'.[90] This concerned a temporary licence given to a soldier to occupy a military lodging at a rent much below the market rate. This privilege was not viewed as being equivalent to an agreement under private law.

In contrast to the view taken in that case, many contractual licences could qualify under the 'asset' test. Even if the licence is not assignable—which is a 'highly relevant factor'[91]—it may still be a 'possession' if a 'market price' has been paid for it.[92] There is indeed good sense in such an approach. The appropriate justification for interferences with such rights ought to be the proportionality of them; one should not avoid the issue by using an unduly narrow definition of 'possessions' to begin with.

---

[84] E Lees, 'Actions for Possession in the Context of Political Protest: The Role of Article 1, Protocol 1 and Horizontal Effect' [2013] *Conveyancer and Property Lawyer* 211, 216; J Howell, 'Land and Human Rights' [1999] *Conveyancer and Property Lawyer* 287, 295.

[85] The concept is not defined in the same way as it is under domestic law: *Tre Traktorer Aktiebolag v Sweden* Series A no 159 (1989) 13 EHRR 309, para 53.

[86] *Bäck v Finland* (2005) 40 EHRR 48; *Wilson v First County Trust* [2003] UKHL 40, [2004] 1 AC 816 [30] (Lord Nicholls).

[87] *JLS v Netherlands* (1995) 20 EHRR CD41 (milk quotas).

[88] *Murungaru v Secretary of State for the Home Department* [2008] EWCA Civ 1015 [30] (Sedley LJ), [58] (Lewison J).

[89] Ibid [58] (Lewison J); *R (on the application of New London College Ltd) v Secretary of State for the Home Department* [2012] EWCA Civ 51 [94] (Richards LJ).

[90] *JLS v Spain* App no 41917/98 (ECtHR, 27 April 1999). See RCA White and C Ovey, *The European Convention on Human Rights*, 6th edn (Oxford, Oxford University Press, 2014) 498.

[91] *Murungaru* (n 88) [56] (Lewison J).

[92] *R (New London College Ltd)* (n 89) [94] (Richards LJ); *R (Nicholds) v Security Industry Authority* [2006] EWHC 1792 (Admin), [2007] 1 WLR 2067 [74].

Dutton itself is something of an awkward case to which to apply these criteria. As no assignment of the licence was permitted, one must ask whether a 'market value' had been paid for it. But this is a difficult question to answer. It is unclear what a 'market value' is for an entitlement granted in conditions not resembling an open market. This is especially so when the privilege is not given to be exploited commercially, howsoever important it may be to the licensee's business. It is also not plain from the case report what consideration was given. Insofar as the licence agreement is disclosed, it recites that it was in consideration of certain agreements on behalf of the airport company. There is no statement of what these actually were. One national newspaper, however, reported claims that the National Trust's cooperation was bought with a package valued at some £750,000.[93]

The value of the licence to the airport company is also tolerably clear. Its importance can be seen by looking at the then existing timetable for the second runway. Although completion was later pushed back for other unforeseen reasons,[94] at the time of *Dutton* (in February 1999) the second runway was intended to open in March 2000. This is a limited time frame, made even smaller by the prospect of the protestors seeking leave to appeal, a process which could have been expected to take a few more months. By the time of the *Dutton* litigation, therefore, the need to enjoy the licence must have been pressing. Some idea of this may be gleaned by considering the airport company's agreement with a contractor to develop the runway area itself. Under this contract the latter agreed to pay liquidated damages of £250,000 per week in the event of its failure to complete the work on time.[95]

C. Interference with Possessions

If the licensee claimant does have a possession within the meaning of article 1, the next question to ask is whether there has been an 'interference' with its enjoyment. This can take the form of a 'deprivation' of the possession or a 'control' of its use; but the concept is not limited to these categories.[96]

There is an argument that any claim would fail at this stage. Article 1 is engaged when rules interfere with property rights as between private parties,[97] but the domestic cases go no further.[98] This is shown by *Horsham Properties Ltd v Clark*.[99] In that case Briggs J described the reach of article 1 in terms of 'state intervention into private rights through overriding legislation'.[100] This is not the problem in the present context.

---

[93] D Ward (n 30).

[94] Bad weather during the construction phase was a factor in this regard: see D Hayward, 'Runway Finally Takes Off' *New Civil Engineer*, 25 January 2001.

[95] D Hayward, 'Manchester Runway 11 Months Late' *New Civil Engineer*, 7 December 2000.

[96] *Sporrong & Lonnroth v Sweden* Series A no 52 (1983) 5 EHRR 35.

[97] *M v Secretary of State for Work and Pensions* [2006] UKHL 11, [2006] 2 AC 91 [89] (Lord Walker).

[98] A Goymour, 'Proprietary Claims and Human Rights—a "Reservoir of Entitlement"?' (2006) 65 CLJ 696, 710–16.

[99] *Horsham Properties Ltd v Clark* [2008] EWHC 2327 (Ch).

[100] Ibid [36].

This cannot however be seen as the full picture. It is in fact clear that 'interferences' can be committed by private parties.[101] The real issue is *how* this is dealt with. In order to explain why this is so, one notes first that the state may be liable for the failure of its law to offer sufficient protection from such 'interference'. This emerges in the context of article 1 from *OBG Ltd v United Kingdom*.[102] That case, the sequel to *OBG Ltd v Allan*,[103] arose after the House of Lords refused to develop the law, and particularly the torts of conversion and inducing a breach of contract, to provide a remedy to the applicants, whose intangible property had been interfered with. In giving its judgment, the European Court of Human Rights explained that:

> [T]he only issue in the present case is whether the House of Lords' refusal to develop the law of tort to allow for an award of damages to the applicants in respect of their intangible assets was compatible with the United Kingdom's positive obligations under Article 1 of Protocol No. 1. In determining that issue, the Court must examine first, whether the House of Lords' judgment pursued a legitimate aim in the general interest and, if so, whether a fair balance was struck between that general interest and the interest of the applicants.

Although the Court found against the applicants on the facts, its very willingness to consider the complaint shows that a failure by the courts to develop the law can place the state in breach of article 1.[104] This point brings us to the crux of the matter at hand. If the 'interference' is caused by a private party, the state can be liable; so does this imply that the courts should seek to address such issues at the domestic level? When there is a statute that could be widely construed to prevent the interference, this issue turns on the proper approach to section 3(1) of the Human Rights Act 1998: this requires that,

> so far as it is possible to do so, primary legislation and subordinate legislation must be read and given effect in a way which is compatible with the Convention rights.

In other cases it is a question of 'horizontal effect' under section 6.[105]

Given the role of statute in actions for the recovery of land, here one may consider section 3. As respects other legislative entitlements, the courts have used that provision to justify interpreting the qualifying criteria in a way that expands their reach.[106] Ought not the same approach to be taken under article 1? Nothing in the wording of that provision confines it to direct interferences by the state. It could be argued that, once the European Court of Human Rights developed the doctrine of 'positive obligations' in this area, any view of section 3 that treats article 1 as merely a negative protection is too narrow. The process of 'giving effect' to Convention rights should be approached accordingly.[107] Any contrary stance would force

---

[101] *Blumberga v Latvia* [2008] ECHR 1075, para 67.
[102] [2011] ECHR 2087.
[103] Above (n 31).
[104] See also *Blumberga* (n 101) para 67; *Broniowski v Poland* [2004] ECHR 274, para 143.
[105] See, eg J Wright, 'A Damp Squib? The Impact of Section 6 HRA on the Common Law: Horizontal Effect and Beyond' [2014] *PL* 289.
[106] Eg *Ghaidan v Godin-Mendoza* [2004] UKHL 30, [2004] 2 AC 557.
[107] s 3 should not be used 'to make decisions for which [the courts] are not equipped' (*Ghaidan* (n 106) [33] (Lord Nicholls)), but this is not the sort of highly contentious social issue at which this qualification is aimed.

litigants to go to Strasbourg, a mode of proceeding that is hard to square with the intention of 'bringing rights home'.[108]

Should this argument have merit, the potent effect of section 3 could be brought to bear in the present context. That provision is 'a powerful tool'.[109] The construction adopted in light of it may come as a surprise to those who enacted the relevant law.[110] Thus in the present context, rule 55.1(b) would be read as widening the action, countenancing claims by licensees when not making a possession order in their favour would infringe their article 1 rights. Such persons would be 'entitled to possession' within the meaning of the rule. If this happened, section 1 of the Law of Property Act 1925 would again be irrelevant: the remedy would be statutory, and so not affect the quality of the licensee's right. All other statutory references to 'interests in land' or such like would then be treated similarly.

Even if this view of section 3 is not accepted, that is not the end of the matter. There would still be the option of proceeding to the European Court of Human Rights. As *OBG Ltd v United Kingdom*[111] shows, the state can be found liable if its law does not ensure that 'possessions' are protected in the way required by article 1.

D. Proportionality

The final issue to be considered is that of proportionality. It must be asked 'whether a fair balance [has been] struck between the demands of the general interest of the community and the requirements of the protection of the individual's fundamental rights'.[112] In this regard the state enjoys a 'wide margin of appreciation'.[113] To adopt Gardner's account, a breach arises only when the interference is positively disproportionate.[114]

We have already seen that the policy of section 1 of the Law of Property Act 1925 is not materially undermined by granting possession orders to *Dutton* licensees.[115] This is an important starting point: it avoids the problem that befell the claim in *OBG Ltd v United Kingdom*.[116] In that case, as was noted above, the European Court of Human Rights considered a claim arising out of an interference with intangible property. It was held that the failure of the courts to extend the torts of conversion and interference with contract to address this was not disproportionate. The House of Lords had 'pursued a legitimate aim in the general interest', this being 'to maintain reasonable limits' on the relevant torts.[117] The tort of conversion is one of

---

[108] This being the policy of the 1998 Act: Home Office, *Rights Brought Home* (Cm 3782, 1997) para 1.19.

[109] *Re S (Care Order: Implementation of Care Plan)* [2002] UKHL 10, [2002] 2 AC 291 [37] (Lord Nicholls).

[110] *R (Wilkinson) v IRC* [2005] UKHL 30, [2005] 1 WLR 1718 [18] (Lord Hoffmann).

[111] Above (n 101).

[112] *Sporrong* (n 96) para 69.

[113] *JA Pye (Oxford) Ltd v United Kingdom* (2008) 46 EHRR 45, para 75.

[114] S Gardner and E MacKenzie, *An Introduction to Land Law*, 3rd edn (Oxford, Hart Publishing, 2012) 39.

[115] See the text accompanying nn 67–70 above.

[116] Above (n 102).

[117] Ibid, para 89.

strict liability; to expand it would be to allow claims for pure economic loss; and other torts already apply in cases when the defendant has acted with intent. The present context is however different. Third parties would not be materially affected by giving possession to some licensees. As has been observed already, there is no question of recovering pure economic losses; and the remedy of possession cannot be obtained by pleading other causes of action with a suitably higher standard of fault. Such an order is only possible under a possession claim.

Even if these points get us past the problem in *OBG Ltd*, it does not however seem 'positively disproportionate' to deny all *Dutton* licensees the remedy of a possession order. In fact, one submits that an article 1 based challenge could be sustained only in the most exceptional instances. Such cases combine three key features. The first is the absence of any other practical remedy on the facts. The second is that the licensee could not reasonably have arranged their bargain differently, or indeed not contracted at all. Finally, the granting of a possession order would have to not unduly interference with the defendants' Convention rights.

We begin then with the practical remedy point. Even if a possession order cannot be obtained save under Part 55 of the CPR, it may be that the licensee's predicament can be solved in another way. When this is the case it does not seem 'positively disproportionate' to refuse them a possession order. Such instances, indeed, are likely to be common. Possible alternative ways forward include action by the landowner or the police, and the potential application of the tort of inducing a breach of contract. There may also be remedies under the contract, such as for damages or specific performance.[118] Indeed even if the licensor has not promised to take reasonable steps to ensure the land's availability, it may be reasonable to bargain for such action when the problem arises. An indemnity for costs could be offered as part of this.

The second of our three points concerns the assumption of risk. In *Horsham Properties Ltd v Clark*,[119] Briggs J stated that any deprivation of a mortgagor's equity of redemption, consequent upon the exercise by a mortgagee of its power of sale, was not disproportionate for the purposes of article 1. One reason for this was that the loss flowed from the parties' own bargain.[120] Although the present context is slightly different, in that the interference is not caused by the other contracting party, a comparable view could be advanced nonetheless. If a party chooses to take a licence rather than, say, a lease, and then fails to contract for any protection by the licensor, this is their choice. No one has forced them to take this risk; it is one to which they have exposed themselves. In economic terms, the allocation of risk as between the licensor and the licensee is a matter for private bargaining. The price paid for the licence should reflect this. If the potential costs for the licensee are too high, they can simply elect not to contract at all.

We pause briefly at this juncture. If one views these two factors cumulatively, there is virtually no prospect of a case in which a failure to make a possession order is positively disproportionate. Doing so is not especially problematic in terms of its consequences, but nor is there a compelling case *for* that result. There will often be another way forward; and if there is not, it may be said that the licensee could have

---

[118] It would not appear to matter that the licensor is not worth suing: *OBG Ltd* (n 102) [95].
[119] Above (n 99).
[120] Ibid, [44].

avoided the problem. The matter can thus be reasonably approached either way. The denial of a possession order in these cases does not seem to satisfy the high threshold of positive disproportionality.

Yet 'virtually never' is not the same thing as 'never'. It may be that facts like those in *Dutton* illustrate this. If we begin by looking at the issue of other practical remedies, Laws LJ seemed to think that no such alternative existed in this case.[121] The reasons for this are relatively clear. Police intervention was not forthcoming; the failure to seek an injunction against the defendants in tort was 'understandable in the circumstances';[122] and there was no contractual term, pursuant to which damages or specific performance could have been ordered against the licensor.[123] This leaves us only with the possibility of (eventual) action by the National Trust. Even if its trustees would have been prepared to act without being forced to do so—and one may entertain doubt on this point—the proceedings would have moved slowly.[124] This would have held up a project deemed to be of national importance. At the same time, the ensuing publicity would cause reputational damage to a charity 'of exceptional importance' to the country.[125]

In line with the view of Laws LJ, it hence seems that there was no other 'practical remedy' in *Dutton*. This leads us onto the second hurdle suggested above. As will be recalled, this relates to the idea that a licensee voluntarily assumes the risk that they take on. Ordinarily this is a potent objection. Again, however, it melts away on facts like those in *Dutton*. The airport company, in undertaking a project deemed to be in the national interest, had no other choice but to bargain as it did. It could not have bought the land or leased it, for such a transaction would have been beyond the powers of the licensor.[126] There seems to have been no prospect of bargaining for action by the National Trust, given the doubts as to its ability to act against the protestors. Finally, the airport company could not have taken its business elsewhere, as the use of the runway depended on the lopping and felling of trees on the land. In sum, it had to get a right to perform this work; and that right had to take the form it did.

For these reasons, it is felt that the facts in *Dutton* illustrate those in which an article 1 based argument could get past these first two conditions. At the same time, the sheer unusualness of those facts is important. Confining article 1 to the margins helps to ensure legal certainty. If Part 55.1(b) of the CPR exists to provide a remedy without undue delay, nuanced arguments about proportionality could undermine that.

If there is a case in which these first two hurdles could be surmounted, the final point to assess would be whether making a possession order unduly interferes with the defendants' Convention rights. There are two matters to consider in this regard. The first is the consequent interference with the property of defendants, whose act of taking adverse possession generates a title in their favour. One should not overplay this point. The Supreme Court has acknowledged that human rights considerations

---

[121] *Dutton* (n 2) 150.
[122] Ibid, 140 (Chadwick LJ).
[123] An award of damages would also have resulted in a significant loss to the charitable sector.
[124] See the text accompanying nn 25–27 above.
[125] As it was described in *Scott v National Trust for Places of Historic Interest or Natural Beauty* [1998] 2 All ER 705 (Ch) 716.
[126] National Trust Act 1907, s 21(2) and National Trust Act 1939, s 12.

may override rules based on strict property rights.[127] That this could only ever occur exceptionally is consistent with the view taken here about how rarely article 1 would be of aid to licensees. In the present context, indeed, any property held by the demonstrators may be less relevant than it is in other ones. They are present on the land to publicise their cause and impede development, and any right acquired by them in the course of their doing so is incidental.

Two further Convention rights on which defendants may rely, at least in seeking a postponement of a possession order,[128] are articles 10 and 11. The former concerns 'the right to freedom of expression', while the latter guarantees the right 'to freedom of peaceful assembly'. These provisions extend to both the manner and the place in which the defendants wish to express their views.[129] In addition to their applicability when a possession claim is brought by a public body,[130] the current trend is to assume that they will also be relevant when the claimant is a private individual;[131] though this has yet to be clearly settled. For now we will assume that this view prevails. In this event, the potential factors to consider include:

> [T]he extent to which the continuation of the protest would breach domestic law, the importance of the precise location to the protesters, the duration of the protest, the degree to which the protesters occupy the land, and the extent of the actual interference the protest causes to the rights of others, including the property rights of the owners of the land, and the rights of any members of the public.[132]

Recent cases suggest that arguments based on articles 10 and 11 are unlikely to prevail. Only in 'exceptional circumstances' would a possession order be postponed, at least when it concerns private land.[133] In particular, the defence will only succeed if otherwise the defendants would be prevented from '*any* effective exercise of their freedom to express their views', to the extent that 'the essence of their freedom would be destroyed'.[134] A postponement of the order is also unlikely if the protest has been ongoing for some time, such as the 70 days in *Hall*.[135]

It is unclear whether the approach would be the same in the present context. Insofar as the balance adopted in these cases reflects the fact of the claimant having a property right, a *Dutton*-type licensee may be treated less generously. There is a lack of authority on this point. It is, however, suggested that any such difference would be very slim, assuming that article 1 aided licensees in only the most exceptional cases.

What is plainer is that such a defence would not have succeeded on facts like those in *Dutton*. The outcome in that case was not a lamentable siding with monied

---

[127] *Manchester City Council v Pinnock* [2010] UKSC 45, [2011] 2 AC 104.

[128] These articles do not give a right to continue a protest on another's land indefinitely: *University of Sussex v Persons Unknown* [2013] EWHC 862 (Ch) [30].

[129] *Hall* (n 49) [37] (Lord Neuberger MR).

[130] *Pinnock* (n 127).

[131] *Malik v Fassenfelt* [2013] EWCA Civ 798 [26] (Sir Alan Ward). Lord Toulson and Lloyd LJ reserved their opinions on this matter. See also *Sun Street Property Ltd v Persons Unknown* [2011] EWHC 3432 (Ch) [28]; *Manchester Ship Canal Developments Ltd v Persons Unknown* [2014] EWHC 645 (Ch) [46].

[132] *City of London Corp v Samede* [2012] EWCA Civ 160 [39] (Lord Neuberger MR).

[133] *Manchester Ship Canal Developments Ltd* (n 131) [34]; *SOAS v Persons Unknown* [2010] PLSCS 303.

[134] *Sun Street Property Ltd* (n 131) [32] (judge's emphasis); *Manchester Ship Canal Developments Ltd* (n 131) [34]. See also *University of Sussex* (n 128).

[135] *Hall* (n 49) [49] (Lord Neuberger MR).

interests.[136] On considering the relevant factors noted above,[137] we see that the protest was in breach of domestic law, that it had been ongoing for months, and that it threatened to impede the completion of works deemed to be of national importance. It is also not clear that the protest could not have continued nearby. Insofar as their goals were publicity[138] and hitting the developers in their pockets,[139] the protestors were plainly successful.[140] They cannot reasonably have expected much more than they achieved.

IV. CONCLUSION

The decision in *Dutton* has received a lukewarm assessment from legal scholars. Given however that the courts have shown little wish to return to the view favoured by its critics, this article has explored whether there is any basis for allowing some licensees to bring possession claims. Consistently with *Dutton*, the relevant licensees are those whose licensor has a better title than the defendant(s), and who have a right of 'effective control'.

There are perhaps two routes to allowing such claims, whether by all such licensees or merely some of them. The first is to take an expansive view of Parliament's intention in creating the action for the recovery of land. Many authors have regarded this as a hopeless idea, but it does find some judicial support. Its success depends on treating Parliament's intention as being to provide a swift procedure for the recovery of possession. The law now accepts that one can enjoy consensual possession without a proprietary right to do so, and so the interpretation of the modern action could reflect that.

The second option for permitting claims by some licensees is to rely on human rights law. In a very small class of cases this may have a prospect of success. Given how relatively exacting the test of proportionality is under article 1, however, this route would not be widely available. Many licensees protected under *Dutton* could not succeed on this basis. It may indeed be that facts like those in *Dutton* itself, being of a most unusual nature, are illustrative of those that could raise an article 1 argument.

It is only by confining this second route to the most extreme cases that it would be palatable. A lower threshold would create uncertainty, making outcomes hard to predict. This would be contrary to the purpose of Part 55 of the CPR. If the courts feel that *Dutton* licensees deserve a remedy more generally, they may seek to justify this with a statutory interpretation argument. It cannot be discounted that this is what they will do.

---

[136] *Cf* A Grear, 'A Tale of the Land, the Insider, the Outsider and Human Rights' (2003) 23 *Legal Studies* 33, 52.

[137] See the quotation accompanying n 132 above.

[138] See L Holmwood, 'On Campus: The Mud Pack' *Guardian*, London, 6 May 1997, Higher Education 4.

[139] As was claimed by one Manchester airport protest coordinator: M Streeter, 'Final Eviction ends Runway Protest' *Independent*, London, 17 June 1997, 3.

[140] The 1997 protests that preceded the *Dutton* dispute are alone said to have cost the airport and the contractors some £6 million: S Griggs, D Howart and B Jacobs, 'Second Runway at Manchester' [1998] *Parliamentary Affairs* 358, 366.

Part III

Property and Death

7

Do Parents Always Know Best? Posthumous Provision and Adult Children

HEATHER CONWAY*

I. INTRODUCTION

IN ENGLAND AND Wales, the Inheritance (Provision for Family and Dependants) Act 1975 allows specific individuals to claim against a deceased person's estate, if dissatisfied with an intestacy or wills distribution.[1] Almost 40 years after its inception, claims by 'independent' adult children are still one of the most contentious aspects of the legislation[2]—in other words, those brought by an adult child who is economically self-sufficient[3] or who was not financially dependent on the deceased before death (even if in financial need). The lack of guidance in the 1975 Act itself is partly to blame, given that the statute simply limits such claims to 'maintenance'[4] and specifically directs the court to look at the 'manner in which the applicant was being, or ... might expect to be, educated or trained'[5]

* Senior Lecturer, Queen's University Belfast. The paper draws on an unpublished report written by the author and Lisa Glennon (formerly Queen's University Belfast): Report for the Changing Ageing Partnership, Institute of Governance, '"To Give or Not To Give?": The Transmission of Wealth On Death by Older Persons' (Queen's University Belfast, October 2010).

[1] Known as the family provision jurisdiction in England and Wales (and in Northern Ireland where identical legislation is in force), and see G Douglas, 'Family Provision and Family Practices—The Discretionary Regime of the Inheritance Act of England and Wales' (2014) 4 *Oñati Socio-Legal Series* for a recent overview. Similar mechanisms exist in other common law jurisdictions: see L Englefiend, *Australian Family Provision Law* (Australia, Lawbook Company, 2011), and C Harvey and L Vincent, *The Law of Dependants' Relief in Canada*, 2nd edn (Toronto, Carswell, 2006).

[2] s 1(1) of the 1975 Act lists the eligible categories of claimant, and includes 'a child of the deceased' (s 1(1)(c)).

[3] Or deemed capable of such self-reliance.

[4] The basis of all claims under the 1975 Act is whether 'reasonable financial provision' has been made for the claimant (s 1(1)). While a surviving spouse or civil partner is entitled to such provision as is 'reasonable in the circumstances' (s 1(2)(a)), a maintenance threshold restricts all other claimants (s 1(2)(b)). The concept of 'maintenance' is not defined in the statute. However, the dictum of Goff LJ in the Court of Appeal decision in *Re Coventry* [1980] Ch 461, 485 is still regarded as authoritative: 'What is proper maintenance must ... depend on all the facts and circumstances of the particular case ... it is not just enough to enable a person to get by, [but] on the other hand, it does not mean anything which may be regarded as reasonably desirable for [an applicant's] general benefit or welfare'.

[5] 1975 Act, s 3(3).

alongside the general factors which apply in all family provision claims.[6] These include the financial resources and future needs of the applicant and any beneficiaries of the estate, the size of the estate, and 'any obligations and responsibilities which the deceased had towards any applicant ... or towards any beneficiary'.[7] Beyond the legislation, other issues have created additional confusion: the absence of a pre-existing financial tie between the parties; the notion that an independent adult child must establish some sort of 'moral obligation' to claim against a dead parent's estate, despite this additional legal threshold having no legislative basis; and tensions between the deceased's testamentary freedom and the claimant's financial circumstances where the claim arose through exclusion from, or inadequate provision under, a will.[8]

Against this backdrop, the Court of Appeal decision in *Ilot v Mitson*[9] (where a daughter was awarded a significant portion of her mother's estate, despite a lengthy period of estrangement) may be seen as encouraging claims by independent (if, albeit, 'needy') adult children, undermining testamentary freedom even further and questioning the reasonableness of the parent's actions. This chapter critically analyses the existing legal framework and questions whether English courts may be tempted to shift to an increasingly 'child friendly' stance post-*Mitson*—something which has always been apparent in Northern Ireland.

II. THE POST-1975 LEGAL LANDSCAPE

While claims by independent adult children were initially treated quite favourably by English courts,[10] the decision in *Re Coventry*[11] (still regarded as the leading authority) signalled a much more cautious approach. In this case a 46-year-old son, and the deceased's only child, claimed from his father's modest estate. The son, who was in good health and earning, had lived rent-free with his father for the last 20 years of the father's life but was not financially dependent on him. The deceased's estranged wife inherited the entire estate and the son claimed under the 1975 Act that reasonable financial provision had not been made for him.[12] However, neither the existence of the parent–child relationship nor the fact that the son had a relatively small income and no home of his own was enough to persuade the court

---

[6] In contrast to general factors, specific factors apply to each category of applicant and are directly referable to the relationship in question (1975 Act, ss 3(2)–(4)).

[7] 1975 Act, s 3(1).

[8] While family provision claims by independent adult children (as with all other categories of applicant) can occur where the parent has died testate or intestate, the focus here is on the former and the extent to which the testator's intent can be overridden by the courts.

[9] *Ilot v Mitson* [2011] EWCA Civ 346, [2012] 2 FLR 170.

[10] Eg in *Re Christie* [1979] Ch 168 where an adult son's request for additional provision from his mother's estate (essentially to match the value of property he expected to inherit under an earlier version of her will) was granted even though the son was not in financial need and did not require additional provision for maintenance purposes.

[11] *Re Coventry* [1979] 2 WLR 853, [1980] Ch 461.

[12] While the deceased died intestate in *Re Coventry*, it is implicit in the judgments that the outcome and applicable legal principles would have been the same had the deceased made a valid will.

that he should receive a portion of his father's wealth. In reaching this conclusion, Oliver J appeared to introduce a concept of 'moral obligation' when determining claims by independent adult children. According to the judge:

> It cannot be enough to say 'here is a son of the deceased; he is in necessitous circumstances; there is property of the deceased which could be made available to assist him …' there must, as it seems to me be established some sort of moral claim by the applicant to be maintained by the deceased or at the expense of his estate beyond the mere fact of the blood relationship.[13]

The Court of Appeal upheld the decision, though Goff LJ rejected any suggestion that establishing a moral obligation was a prerequisite in all adult child cases.[14]

Despite this attempt to curb the role played by moral obligations, subsequent decisions interpreted Oliver J's comments in *Re Coventry* as being of general application while maintaining a fairly strict approach towards adult children. From these cases it was clear that merely being a child of the deceased did not generate any entitlement to an (increased) inheritance; an applicant had to establish some sort of 'moral claim' or 'special circumstance(s)' over and above the filial tie.[15] However, some cases attempted to retreat from this stance, though with varying degrees of success. In *Re Hancock*[16] the applicant (one of seven children) was 69 at the time of the hearing, had no earning capacity and was not financially well-off. She received nothing under her father's will which left a valuable plot of land to five of his children and the residue to his wife (the applicant's mother). However, the deceased's will had asked his wife to make some provision for the applicant, if resources permitted. When the deceased died the land was valued at £100,000; by the time of the hearing, the land had been purchased by a large supermarket chain for £663,000. The applicant's mother died after the sale but before the family provision hearing, leaving the applicant £1,000 in her will. Looking at claims by adult children generally, Butler-Sloss LJ (as she then was) began by clarifying the role which 'moral obligation' plays in such cases:

> [I]t is clear to me that the 1975 Act does not require … that an adult child … has in all cases to show moral obligation or other special circumstance. But on facts similar to those in *Re Coventry* … if … the adult child is in employment, with an earning capacity for the foreseeable future, it is unlikely he will succeed in his application without some special circumstance such as moral obligation.[17]

---

[13] [1979] 2 WLR 853, 865.
[14] [1980] Ch 461, 487.
[15] See, eg *Re Jennings* [1994] Ch 286 and *Re Abram (Deceased)* [1996] 2 FLR 379. A number of suggestions as to what constitutes 'special circumstance(s)' were put forward by Oliver J in *Re Coventry*, including the provision of care (at a personal cost) by the applicant to the deceased. Others (albeit connoting some element of dependency) were situations in which the applicant was actually dependent on the deceased; if the applicant was incapable of earning a living due to physical or mental disability; or if the applicant was still in vocational training. It is not clear whether there is any conceptual distinction between 'moral obligation' and 'special circumstance(s)'. While some cases suggest that they are separate concepts (*Re Coventry*), others regard moral obligation as being subsumed into special circumstance(s), or vice versa (*Re Abram (Deceased)* [1996] 2 FLR 379; *Re Hancock* [1998] 2 FLR 346).
[16] *Re Hancock* [1998] 2 FLR 346.
[17] Ibid, 351.

In other words, a moral obligation was not an absolute prerequisite in claims by adult children; however, an independent adult (including someone with earning capacity) was unlikely to succeed without one.[18]

Turning to the outcome, the court awarded the applicant annual periodical payments of £3,000—a small sum in light of the ultimate value of the estate—though the reasons for the court's decision are not entirely clear. The applicant was in financial need but was not dependent on her father, and no moral obligation was found on the facts. Instead, the court appears to have been influenced by two other interrelated factors: the original term in the father's will which requested his wife to make some provision for the applicant, and the windfall generated by the substantial increase in sale value of the land. The former was relevant insofar as there was no apparent animosity between father and daughter, the court taking the view that a 'good reason to exclude a member of the family has to be a relevant consideration'.[19] However, the windfall increase in estate value appeared to tip the scales heavily in the applicant's favour since the estate was now large enough to make some provision which would improve the applicant's financial situation; had the application been heard before this occurred 'failure to provide for the plaintiff out of the estate [would not have been] unreasonable'.[20] *Re Hancock* did re-clarify, to some extent, when a moral obligation may be relevant yet left unanswered the more fundamental question of what actually *constitutes* a moral obligation.[21] This definitional vacuum was, to some extent, addressed by the Court of Appeal the following year in *Espinosa v Bourke*.[22]

In this case, the deceased had lived with his adult daughter and grandson for several years before his death. While the daughter gave up her part-time job to take care of the household, the deceased paid the bills and discharged the mortgage on the property. Relations between father and daughter were strained largely because the father did not approve of her various romantic relationships, culminating in the daughter moving to Spain during the last year of her father's life and marrying an unemployed fisherman. During this time the 87-year-old father was looked after by his grandson and a cleaner. In his will, the deceased left the bulk of his estate to his grandson, making no provision for the daughter on the basis that she had been 'adequately provided for' during his lifetime and had shown 'a degree of irresponsibility'.[23] However, some years earlier, the father had promised his dying wife that he would leave a specific portion of her estate to their daughter. While the deceased was under no legal obligation to fulfil this promise,[24] the court nevertheless awarded the daughter £60,000 out of an estate valued at £196,000. The rationale for making

---

[18] Borkowski has suggested that, rather than establishing any new principle, this dictum merely represents the correct interpretation of Oliver J's comments in *Re Coventry*: A Borkowski, 'Moral Obligation and Family Provision' [1999] *Child and Family Law Quarterly* 305.

[19] [1998] 2 FLR 346, 352, confirming a similar point made by Goff LJ in *Re Coventry* [1980] Ch 461.

[20] [1998] 2 FLR 346, 353.

[21] This omission is not confined to *Re Hancock*, given the lack of meaningful guidance in previous case law. For example, Borkowski has questioned whether 'moral' denoted some sort of 'ethical code and notions of right and wrong', or questions of 'basic fairness', and questioned 'whether a parent [could] ever be said not to have a moral obligation to provide for his child's maintenance, whether adult or not': Borkowski (n 18) 311.

[22] *Espinosa v Bourke* [1999] 1 FLR 747.

[23] Ibid, 749.

[24] The facts did not seem to generate an estoppel claim.

this award is not entirely clear, though the decision tried to clarify some of the more fundamental issues surrounding family provision claims by adult children. Once again the question of 'moral obligation' was central to the daughter's claim, with Butler-Sloss LJ positioning this within section 3(1)(d) of the 1975 Act:[25]

> [This provision] refers to 'any obligations and responsibilities'. Plainly those obligations and responsibilities extend beyond legal obligations and that is why, in my view, the word 'moral' has been used to underline and explain that the deceased's obligations and responsibilities are not to be narrowly construed as legal obligations but to be taken into account in a broad sense of obligation and responsibility.[26]

Following on from this, Butler-Sloss LJ attempted to dispel the myth that the word 'moral' in this context was intended to act as a judicial 'gloss' on section 3(1)(d); the concept of moral obligation was subsumed within this general legislative provision and should not be elevated to a 'threshold requirement'.[27] Moreover, this one factor should not eclipse all the other general factors listed under sections 3(1)(a)–(g) of the 1975 Act; judges should apply a more rounded test. The court reiterated the factual reality that an adult child who was of working age and either in employment or capable of obtaining employment would probably fail in the absence of a moral obligation.[28] Turning to the facts of *Espinosa* itself, while the court found a moral obligation, the content of that obligation is unclear. Although the daughter was financially dependent on her father, the court did not dwell on this point, preferring to focus on the unfulfilled promise which the father had made to the applicant's mother.[29] It also highlighted the value of the estate and the lack of competing financial demands on it from anyone other than the daughter and grandson. However, no reference was made to the father's express wish to omit his daughter from his will.

That these cases contain little continuity in terms of legal principle can be seen most clearly in *Re Garland*[30] where the court did not refer to moral obligation despite the prior judicial emphasis on this construct. In this case the deceased had two adult daughters, but had separated from their mother many years earlier. This caused a rift between the father and younger daughter (the claimant) as the father believed that she had taken her mother's side following the separation; when the mother committed suicide she left her entire estate (£33,000) to the claimant who used this to purchase a house mortgage free. From 1986 to 2001 (when he died) the father and claimant never saw or spoke to each other despite occasional correspondence. The elder sister was much closer to the father and he helped her out financially; the father made it clear that she would inherit his entire estate, and that he would not benefit the younger sister as she had made no effort to stay in touch with him. At the time of the father's death the claimant was 43 and living in 'very difficult

---

[25] This refers to 'any obligations and responsibilities which the deceased had towards any applicant ... or towards any beneficiary of the estate'.
[26] [1999] 1 FLR 747, 755. It was stressed that any interpretation of 'moral' as distinguishing between 'right and wrong' would fall under s 3(1)(g) which refers, inter alia, to the parties' conduct.
[27] Ibid.
[28] According to Sir John Knox in *Re Hancock*, this would typically be the 'weightiest factor' in the applicant's favour: [1998] 2 FLR 346, 357.
[29] See also, *Re Pearce* [1998] 2 FLR 705 where an application by an adult son was successful, the court holding that his father owed him a moral obligation because the son had worked on the family farm without pay after being repeatedly told (by his father) that he would inherit the farm on his death.
[30] *Re Garland* [2007] EWHC 2 (Ch).

financial circumstances';[31] her house required major renovations, and she was living on state benefits, receiving no financial support from the father of her two younger children, and had credit card debts of around £5,000. Shortly before his death, the father asked the elder sister not to let the claimant 'starve'. The elder sister received some £284,000 from her father's estate; she gave £6,000 to her younger sister who subsequently claimed under the 1975 Act.

The court systematically reviewed the general factors listed in section 3(1) of the 1975 Act but focused its attention on the financial circumstances of the claimant and her elder sister, as well the parties' conduct. In relation to the former, the court noted that the claimant was living in 'very low income and sub-standard housing',[32] but suggested that she was largely responsible for the state of the property. It acknowledged that the other daughter, whose relationship with her father was much closer than the claimant's, was better-off financially but 'still in genuine need of the benefit which she was given under [her father's] will'.[33] Turning to the parties' conduct and other relevant circumstances, the court emphasised the fact that the claimant had not spoken with her father for 15 years before his death, and that she had received all of her mother's estate. While the court accepted that the claimant's financial need was a 'powerful factor' in her favour,[34] it was the estrangement from her father and prior inheritance from her mother which persuaded the court that no award should be made:

> [The] father was reasonably entitled to conclude that the fact that the claimant had not met or spoken to him for so long, and the fact that she had already had a relatively substantial benefit from her mother's estate, meant that she no longer had any claim on his bounty. It may well be that he did not have a full appreciation of the extent of the claimant's financial difficulties ... [However] I do not think that by making no provision for the claimant he was acting unreasonably.[35]

This suggests that an independent adult child would face an uphill struggle to claim successfully under the 1975 Act—even if in dire financial circumstances. However, while the judge applied the correct statutory framework, the rationale is seriously flawed. The court's reference to whether the deceased was acting 'unreasonably' in disinheriting his daughter is clearly the wrong test under the 1975 Act; what should have driven the court's reasoning was whether 'reasonable financial provision' had been made. These are fundamentally different enquiries since the former contemplates a subjective assessment of the correctness or otherwise of the deceased's actions while the latter mandates a qualitative yet largely objective evaluation of whether, on the facts, reasonable financial provision has been made for the applicant. In *Garland*, there appears to have been an overwhelming bias in favour of the 'dutiful' daughter who conformed to idealised notions of being a 'good child' in sharp contrast to the 'irresponsible' daughter who had made bad lifestyle choices and was, to some extent, the author of her own misfortune. Testamentary freedom was also overlooked in the judgment, even though the claimant's exclusion from her father's will could have been explained on this basis.

---

[31] Ibid, [33].
[32] Ibid, [61].
[33] Ibid. The elder daughter also suffered from diabetes which might limit her future earning capacity.
[34] Ibid, [62].
[35] Ibid, [63].

III. 'CHARITY BEGINS AT HOME': THE *MITSON* LITIGATION

The significance (or otherwise) of testamentary freedom, clear evidence of financial need, and years of estrangement between parent and child were also apparent in *Ilot v Mitson*[36] though with fundamentally different outcomes.

The claimant daughter in *Mitson* had been brought up by her mother, but in 1978 and aged 17, left home to live with a man her mother disapproved of. This led to a breakdown in communication between mother and daughter, and the pair were not reconciled before the mother's death in July 2004. In the interim the daughter married her partner (the mother was not informed of the wedding) and had five children with him; she subsequently chose not to work in order to be a stay-at-home mother. Having executed her final will in April 2002 and drafted a statement explaining her decision to exclude her only child, the mother wrote to her daughter informing her of this and alluding to the hurt that the daughter had caused by leaving home at 17. The daughter responded in a letter, accepting that she would inherit nothing from her mother. When the mother died, she left a net estate of £486,000 to various charities with no provision for her only child who was then aged 44, had not worked since the birth of her first child (the husband worked part-time) and was living in a three-bedroom house rented from a Housing Association. The daughter argued under the 1975 Act that her mother had failed to make reasonable financial provision for her, and the district judge awarded her £50,000 from the estate. However, the daughter appealed on the basis that this amount was insufficient; initially, King J reversed the earlier decision with the result that the daughter was awarded nothing.[37]

King J set out the key provisions of the 1975 Act and the approach adopted by courts in previous claims by adult children, before outlining a list of principles (albeit not determinative) for consideration in such cases. According to King J:

i)   It is for the Claimant to prove ... [their] case
ii) Nothing in the 1975 Act undermines the basic proposition that a citizen of England and Wales is at liberty at his death to dispose of his own property in whatever way he pleases
iii) Section 3 of the Act does not 'rank' the matters to be taken into consideration ... That is not to say that in an individual case one or two factors may not have a magnetic or even decisive influence on the outcome ...
iv) The question is not whether the deceased acted unreasonably but whether, looked at objectively, the lack of disposition produces an unreasonable result ...
v)   There is no threshold requirement that an adult child claimant has to establish some form of moral obligation or special circumstance
vi) Necessitous circumstances cannot in themselves be a reason to alter the testator's dispositions
vii) The ability of the claimant to earn a living is a significant factor
viii) An express reason for rejecting an applicant is a relevant consideration.[38]

These principles had to be read in conjunction with the statutory checklist of factors in section 3 of the 1975 Act. However, in the present case, the district judge

---

[36] [2011] EWCA Civ 346, [2012] 2 FLR 170.
[37] [2009] EWHC 3114 (Fam).
[38] Ibid, [49].

had 'erred in law'[39] by asking whether the deceased had acted unreasonably instead of asking whether, on an objective basis, the lack of provision for the daughter was unreasonable taking account of these statutory factors. Having blamed the parties' estrangement on the mother's inability to forgive her daughter for leaving home and marrying against her wishes, the district judge had concluded that the mother's rejection and subsequent exclusion of her only child from her will was unreasonable; according to King J, this was contrary to the statute:

> The District Judge may well have thought, (and indeed may even be right when applying contemporary mores), that the deceased was unreasonable in her inability to forgive her only child for running away all those years ago and further, that she was unreasonable in preferring to leave her estate to a group of charities in which she had shown little or no interest; that is not however the issue that the Act requires the court to resolve. The question is was the *provision* unreasonable.[40]

Taking all this and the section 3 factors into account, King J emphasised that the daughter throughout her adult life had no expectation of inheriting from her mother, a fact which she had appeared to accept; the parties' 26-year estrangement was also 'profound and enduring'.[41] King J accepted that the daughter was in financial need (although not in any way financially dependent on her mother), but held that this was the result of her own 'lifestyle choices'—the daughter had opted to stay at home to look after her children who were aged between 11 and 25 at the date of the hearing, while her husband was in part-time employment.[42] There was nothing on the facts which gave rise to a moral obligation and consequent weighty factor envisaged by *Espinosa v Bourke*[43] where an adult child applicant was of working age and in employment or with some earning capacity, and 'mere' financial need did not suffice. In this respect, the district judge in *Mitson* had come 'perilously close to allowing necessitous circumstances to be determinative',[44] something which runs contrary to established authority.[45] King J was sympathetic towards the daughter, given her family's financial position and the fact that her mother had bequeathed such a 'substantial and life-changing' amount of money to charities in which the mother had shown 'no particular interest in her lifetime'.[46] However, the underlying philosophy of the 1975 Act was clear; the emphasis was on reasonable financial provision, and unreasonable treatment was not enough in itself.

The case went to the Court of Appeal, which upheld the daughter's claim. Reinforcing the idea that the first stage test—whether the deceased's will failed to make reasonable financial provision—was, by its very nature, a 'value judgment' or 'qualitative decision'[47] based around the statutory criteria in section 3 of the 1975 Act, Sir Nicholas Wall P stressed that this was 'very much a matter for the first instance

---

[39] Ibid, [58].
[40] Ibid, [61].
[41] Ibid.
[42] King J was not criticising this decision, describing it as 'one of a range of choices faced by every contemporary family'—ibid.
[43] [1999] 1 FLR 747.
[44] [2009] EWHC 3114 (Fam) [64].
[45] *Re Coventry* [1979] 2 WLR 853.
[46] [2009] EWHC 3114 (Fam) [68].
[47] Citing the comments of Goff LJ in *Re Coventry* [1980] 1 Ch 459, 487.

tribunal'[48] and should not be disturbed unless 'plainly wrong'.[49] The district judge had asked himself the right questions at some point in his judgment and evaluated the section 3 factors as required; having done so he was entitled to conclude that 'no provision did not constitute reasonable provision'.[50] Echoing these sentiments, Arden LJ stressed that 'Cases under the 1975 Act are very fact-specific and, moreover, there are different ways of expressing the exercise of a value judgment'.[51] The district judge had not focused exclusively on the presence of a filial relationship and financial need, but had taken account of all the section 3 factors. Moreover, the 1975 Act clearly contemplated an adult child being able to make a claim even if he/she could subsist without doing so. Looking at the applicant's circumstances in the present case, Arden LJ concluded:

> The applicant has made her career in the home and she is living in straightened circumstances. The applicant and her husband have lived together and brought up their family with little income save for state benefits. The District Judge was clearly correct to consider whether the applicant had any capacity for earning money herself. If she had some plan, say to take a well-paid job when her family commitments enabled her to do so, that would have to be taken into account. But the absence of such a plan was rightly treated as a neutral factor. The fact that she had made the career choice did not mean that the complete absence of provision by the testatrix [*sic*] a reasonable one.[52]

Overall, the Court of Appeal emphasised that any decision on whether the deceased's will failed to make reasonable financial provision rests with the trial judge and if they apply the law correctly, then any exercise of discretion will be difficult to challenge; in the present case King J was wrong to allow the appeal and substitute her own decision. The court also stressed that a 'moral obligation' was not a condition for an award (although it was a factor which judges could take into account), while rejecting any notion that the function of family provision is to consider what the testator 'ought' to have done. As regards the issue of quantum, the claimant's outstanding appeal was remitted to the High Court which upheld the original award of £50,000.[53]

Perhaps we should not read too much into the Court of Appeal decision, since the court was largely concerned with the role of a judge when exercising an appellate jurisdiction.[54] However, the outcome still raises questions, even though the decision itself (as one comment put it) 'says little that is new'.[55] While all claims under the 1975 Act are inherently fact-specific, it is still not really clear why the daughter

---

[48] [2011] EWCA Civ 346 [25].

[49] Ibid, [43].

[50] Ibid, [50].

[51] Ibid, [63].

[52] Ibid, [73].

[53] *Ilot v Mitson* [2014] EWHC 542 (Fam). Parker J held that it had not been wrong for the district judge to limit the award on the basis that, although the claimant and her family lived in straitened circumstances, the fact they had done so for many years and had no expectancy of inheriting from the deceased did not justify an award which improved their circumstances. The claimant had been seeking an award equivalent to half the value of the deceased's estate. At the time of writing, the decision on quantum was being appealed to the Court of Appeal.

[54] Though one might argue that the Court of Appeal does come perilously close, at times, to asking whether the deceased's actions were reasonable: see, eg the final sentence of Arden LJ's comments noted at text to n 52.

[55] A Taylor, 'Wills and Probate: Left Out in the Cold' (2011) 161 *New Law Journal* 1401.

succeeded in *Mitson*—though perhaps this is an unavoidable consequence of the legislation itself because, as long as the statutory checklist seems to have been applied and evaluated in some way, it is possible for any outcome to be justified on the facts and not vulnerable on appeal. The fact that the daughter was in financial need seems to have been an important consideration—and while the 1975 Act directs the court to look at the applicant's financial resources/needs,[56] case law on previous claims by independent adult children makes it clear that necessitous circumstances are not enough in themselves.[57] Perhaps other factors were at play in *Mitson*—for example, the fact that the intended beneficiaries were charities with no lifetime association to the deceased (as opposed to another child or family member) and 'needs-neutral',[58] and the fact that the mother was deemed more culpable for the long-term estrangement from her daughter (something which clearly seems to have influenced the decision of the district judge). However, any suggestion that the decision was merely shifting the 'burden' of maintaining the daughter away from the state was firmly rejected by Sir Nicholas Wall P,[59] though Arden LJ did stress that 'state ... provision for financial hardship does not mean that it is unreasonable for a testatrix to make no provision for an adult child'.[60]

There is little doubt that the Court of Appeal decision strengthens the idea of adult children being able to make a successful financial provision claim despite not having been financially dependent on their parent (even for many years), and raises questions as to what steps a testator can actually take to disinherit an adult child[61]—the mother in *Mitson* had gone to great lengths to exclude her daughter, to no avail, and none of the judgments seemed to attach any significance to the daughter's letter in which she accepted that she would not inherit anything.[62] Concerns have been expressed post-*Mitson* that wills are looking 'increasingly vulnerable'[63] to challenge, and that the decision will encourage more independent adult children to claim under the 1975 Act notwithstanding the deceased's express wishes.[64] The Court of Appeal merely paid lip service to the notion of testamentary freedom in *Mitson*—and while this is not a specific factor which courts are required to evaluate under section 3[65]

---

[56] 1975 Act, s 3(1)(b).

[57] See, eg *Re Coventry* [1979] 2 WLR 853 and *Re Hancock* [1998] 2 FLR 346.

[58] J Holland, '*Ilot v Mitson*: A Lesson for Practitioners?' (2012) 2 *Elder Law Journal* 59.

[59] '[A]lthough the applicant's current income is largely made up of benefits and tax credits, I do not base my decision on the ground that a claim under the Act can properly be used to relieve the State of the obligation to support an applicant': [2011] EWCA Civ 346 [14]. This must be correct; a parent's financial status while alive would not affect a child's ability to claim state benefits, so why should the position be any different on death (beyond the fact the death unlocks the capital value of an estate).

[60] Ibid, [75].

[61] See Holland (n 58).

[62] The case also suggests that charities might lose out to family provision claims when a charitable bequest is challenged, and notwithstanding the deceased's philanthropic intent: see M McGregor-Lowndes and FM Hannah, *Every Player Wins a Prize? Family Provision Applications and Bequests to Charity* (The Australian Centre for Philanthropy and Nonprofit Studies, Brisbane, Queensland, 2008) discussing similar concerns in Australia.

[63] 'Last Rites,' *Private Client Adviser*, 24 May 2011.

[64] Holland (n 58). See also S Evans, 'Testators' Wishes, Dead or Alive: Is there a Difference?' [2013] *Conveyancer and Property Lawyer* 481, 483, the author noting that a 'constant characteristic' of cases such as *Mitson* is 'that once dead, the deceased person's wishes cease to exist as a property right and therefore cease to be anything to which significant attention need be paid'.

[65] In other jurisdictions, courts must consider the deceased's desires or intent: see, eg s 11 of the Family Protection Act 1955 (NZ) (as amended).

it is part of the contextual background to all family provision claims where the estate distribution derives from a valid will. If English courts may now be more willing to override a testator's express wishes when dealing with independent adult children, parallels may be drawn with Northern Ireland where this approach has been apparent for years.

IV. THE NORTHERN IRELAND APPROACH

Case law decided under the equivalent Inheritance (Provision for Family and Dependants) (NI) Order 1979[66] illustrates that Northern Ireland courts have always been much more 'child friendly' when looking at claims by independent adult children who were disinherited by the deceased,[67] ruling in the applicant's favour in each of the three reported cases to date.[68] While it is dangerous to draw conclusions from a limited body of case law, this overwhelming bias towards adult children has led to suggestions that Northern Ireland judges have 'come perilously close to sanctioning exactly what [they] claim they have no authority to do, that is rewrite the deceased's will'.[69]

Re McGarrell[70] is the first of these cases. Here, the deceased's adult daughter did not work and was living in rented social housing with her husband and four children aged from 12 to 20. In his will the deceased made a charitable gift of one-third of his estate, leaving the remainder to the husbands of two of his nieces. The applicant claimed that the will had failed to make reasonable financial provision for her since she had, for many years, carried out housework for her father and his sister-in-law at the old family home. In addition, the father had lived with the applicant and her family for nine months shortly before his death. However, he spent the last year of his life in residential care against his wishes, which may have prompted the father's decision to exclude her from his will.

Hutton J (as he then was) began by acknowledging that the applicant was living in 'difficult financial circumstances',[71] and took this to mean that reasonable financial provision would constitute an award of maintenance. He then asked whether the deceased's will had made reasonable financial provision for the applicant and, in deciding that it had not, found that the applicant had established a moral claim on her father's estate. This was based on two things: the housework carried out over many years[72] and, more importantly, the nine-month period during which the father

---

[66] 1979 No 924 (NI 8).

[67] Somewhat ironic given that both policymakers and the judiciary in Northern Ireland were much more hostile to the inception of a discretionary family provision system: S Grattan, *Succession Law in Northern Ireland* (Belfast, SLS Legal Publications (NI), 1996) 176 referring to the introduction of the Inheritance (Family Provision) Act (NI) 1960 which was the precursor to the 1979 Order.

[68] Even allowing for the fact that Northern Ireland is a small jurisdiction, three such reported claims since 1979 is a low number. Anecdotal evidence suggests that the judicial tendency to rule in favour of an independent adult child (combined with the estate bearing litigation costs) encourages many disputes to settle.

[69] Grattan (n 67) 198.

[70] *Re McGarrell* [1983] 8 NIJB.

[71] See transcript, 5.

[72] It emerged during the trial that the applicant had received state payments for acting as a home help to her father's sister-in-law (who was also residing in the old family home). While the court suggested that these payments also went some way towards remunerating her father's care during the same period, it accepted that the level of the remuneration did not reflect the number of hours involved.

lived with the applicant and her family in cramped living accommodation. According to the court, the moral claim generated by these two factors was not off-set by the father's alleged resentment towards the applicant for spending his last months in residential care.

The following year in *Re Creeny*[73] the applicant was the 57-year-old son of the deceased and was living in England, having been estranged from his father for many years. The applicant had left school, aged 17, to work in his father's business. This entailed long working hours and low pay, and when the applicant married, his wife also worked in the business without remuneration. The son expected that the business would eventually pass to him, and when the father retired in 1964 the applicant took over the business although the father retained ownership of the premises. However, the business did not prosper, and having quarrelled about this and the sale of other family property owned by the father, the son moved to England in 1972. In his will, the deceased left his entire estate to his 56-year-old daughter, prompting the applicant to apply under the 1979 Order. The applicant and his family were not financially well-off; although he and his wife were both in employment (albeit in relatively low-paid jobs), they had eight children of whom five were still living at home. In contrast, the applicant's sister was financially secure—although she had never worked, the sister had married a successful dentist and was living in an affluent area of Belfast. The couple also owned other rental property, and had three children, two of whom still lived at home.

Once again, the court began by outlining the two-stage test of whether reasonable financial provision had been made and, if not, what provision should follow. In addressing questions of need and hardship, Carswell J (as he then was), observed:

> So long as one does not depart from the concept of maintenance as the necessary foundation for an applicant's claim, his own financial need is not the touchstone or sole criterion. The financial provision made under a will ... may accordingly be reasonable in all the circumstances even though an applicant may still remain in some degree of financial hardship; and conversely, it may not be unreasonable even if the applicant is not suffering significant financial hardship if comparisons with other beneficiaries or applicants and such moral factors as the conduct of the persons concerned are imported into the determination.[74]

In other words, while needy circumstances do not justify an award, one might still be made even if an applicant was not suffering financial hardship—apparently on the basis of moral factors and when drawing comparisons with other beneficiaries. It is this latter point which tipped the scales in the applicant's favour in *Creeny*, as the court appeared to be swayed by the respective 'life positions' of the siblings and a perceived need to inject some measure of parity into the distribution of the father's wealth. While Carswell J accepted that 'One has to be careful about drawing conclusions from comparison of the visible standard of living of each family',[75] he concluded:

> It appears undeniable ... that in past years [the sister] and her family were substantially more prosperous than [the applicant] and his family, and that [the sister's] family possess considerably greater capital assets than [the applicant's] family.[76]

---

[73] *Re Creeny* [1984] NI 397.
[74] Ibid, 403–04.
[75] Ibid, 405.
[76] Ibid.

The applicant's case was based upon his financial need (when compared with his sister's financial situation), as well as his alleged reasonable expectation to inherit the business and other family property. In making his determination, Carswell J gave little more than a rhetorical nod to testamentary freedom and the fact that the court's function is not to re-write a will or to substitute what the court deems would have been reasonable.[77] The judge also emphasised the apparent need to consider the terms of the 1979 Order and its various statutory factors—though Carswell J did not actually go through them, and simply concluded that reasonable financial provision had not been made. In awarding the applicant a one-third share of his father's estate, Carswell J accepted that the applicant did 'to a material extent receive his patrimony' and that the making of financial provision could not simply be based on past expectations.[78] This in itself was not enough to establish any moral claim on the estate. Much more important were 'the relative financial resources of [the siblings] … the work done by [the applicant] and his wife for the benefit of the family business, and such intangible factors as the conduct of the parties and their relative merits in the affairs of the family'.[79]

Some 23 years later, the most recent Northern Ireland case concerning adult children suggests that courts are still strongly inclined towards such applicants. In *McKernan v McKernan*[80] the 51-year-old applicant was the third of the deceased's four children. At the time of her mother's death, the applicant (who was unemployed and receiving state benefits) was still living at home along with her two older brothers. The fourth child (the defendant) was married with three young children of his own; as a result of a family row, the applicant and the defendant had not been on speaking terms for several years before their mother's death. The deceased was particularly close to the defendant but regarded the applicant as lazy and a trouble-maker, and when making her will the deceased expressed the view that it was time for the applicant to 'look after herself'.[81] The deceased left the bulk of her estate to the defendant, but also made some provision for her two eldest children; the applicant, who was only given a right to reside in the family home for six months after her mother's death, applied successfully under the 1979 Order.

Deeny J began by erroneously asking whether the deceased's decision to make no financial provision for the applicant 'was reasonable in all the circumstances'[82]—in other words, whether the deceased's actions were reasonable as opposed to whether reasonable financial provision was made for the applicant. It seems that this distinction was lost on Deeny J, who then proceeded to set out the correct test by questioning whether the deceased's will 'did make reasonable financial provision for the applicant'.[83] In deciding that it did not, Deeny J appeared to focus on two inter-related factors. The first was the fact that the applicant had lived with her mother; according to the court 'The provision of a roof over her head [was] … partial

---

[77] Ibid, 406.
[78] Ibid, 407.
[79] Ibid.
[80] *McKernan* v *McKernan* [2007] NICh 6.
[81] Ibid, [10].
[82] Ibid, [26].
[83] Ibid, [27].

maintenance'.[84] The second derived from the judge's interpretation of article 5(1)(d) of the 1979 Order[85] and the requirement to consider 'any obligations and responsibilities which the deceased had towards any applicant'. According to Deeny J, this included 'the fact of being the parent of the applicant'—in other words, the mere existence of the parent–child bond was enough in itself. Deeny J at least attempted to give testamentary freedom a more prominent role, indicating that the deceased's expressed wishes should be considered under article 5(1)(g) which refers to other relevant matters including conduct. However, while accepting that the deceased in this case 'was quite clear in her mind that she did not want to leave a legacy to her only daughter',[86] and accepting the mother's view that her daughter 'was not a dependable provider of care to the mother and was viewed by her … as lazy',[87] this did not justify excluding the daughter from the will. The omission, according to Deeny J, produced an 'unreasonable result'.[88] In deciding what type of order to make, Deeny J outlined several options, but suggested that the most suitable would be to confer a permanent right of residence in the family home on the applicant.

V. LOOKING AHEAD: COMPETING PRINCIPLES AND POLICIES

Since *Re Coventry*,[89] much judicial time and effort has been expended on trying to formulate a workable and coherent set of universal principles to supplement the statutory framework for determining family provision claims by independent adult children. The extent to which courts have succeeded in this objective is questionable—and the Court of Appeal decision in *Ilot v Mitson*[90] does little to alter this perspective. Perhaps the best example is the nebulous concept of 'moral obligation', with judges attempting to explain its origins and where it sits within the rubric of the legislation, as well as a distinct lack of clarity over what the concept actually entails or when it becomes a critical factor.[91] Courts have also been sidetracked by questions of whether or not the deceased acted reasonably instead of focusing on a statutory test of reasonable financial provision, and while claims by independent adult children are fact-specific and thus require some sort of individualised justice, the overall result is doctrinal confusion and a body of case law with little consistent rationale. For example, the deceased's reasons for disinheriting a child or treating them less favourably than their siblings may or may not be a weighty factor,[92] as is

---

[84] Ibid, [28].
[85] The general factors in art 5(1) of the 1979 Order are identical to those listed in s 3(1) of the 1975 Act.
[86] [2007] NICh 6 [28].
[87] Ibid, [36].
[88] Ibid.
[89] [1979] 2 WLR 853, [1980] Ch 461.
[90] [2011] EWCA Civ 346, [2012] 2 FLR 170.
[91] In addressing the first of these issues, Atherton suggests that concepts of 'moral duty' are inherent in the very concept of testamentary freedom itself, the latter being circumscribed by the testator's duty to provide for his/her children as outlined in *Banks v Goodfellow* (1870) 5 LR QB 549, 563–65: R Atherton, 'The Concept of Moral Duty in the Law of Family Provision—A Gloss or Critical Understanding' (2000) 6 *Australian Journal of Legal History* 5.
[92] Eg long-term estrangement and/or behaviour which the parent did not approve of is regarded as 'disentitling conduct' in *Re Garland* [2007] EWHC 2 (Ch) but not in *Espinosa v Bourke* [1999] 1 FLR 747 or *McKernan v McKernan* [2007] NICh 6.

evidence that a child has poor financial prospects or is clearly in financial need[93]—although *Mitson* may result in a more sympathetic attitude towards the claimant where such issues are raised with a corresponding shift in judicial emphasis. More generally, there are no discernible trends in the value of any award relative to the value of the deceased's estate, and few attempts to rationalise the sum given to the claimant by the court.[94]

In light of these observations and the final outcome in *Mitson*, there is little to discourage independent adult children from testing the boundaries of the court's jurisdiction under the 1975 Act,[95] while a 'perfect storm' of socio-economic developments may aggravate the situation further. High levels of personal wealth among the 'baby boom generation' mean that there are larger estates to fight over—even with the fall in property prices and historically low interest rates on savings accounts following the recent economic recession.[96] Changing trends in the intergenerational transfer of wealth between parent and child are also important, something which 'no longer occurs primarily upon the death of the parents, but … during [their] lifetime'.[97] Many parents are providing their children with financial support well into adulthood as fiscal pressures take their toll. University fees are one example; others include helping out with house purchases,[98] as well as unpaid childcare for grandchildren.[99] There is always the possibility of these and other forms of financial assistance being transmuted into some sort of dependency or ongoing 'maintenance' which strengthens the case for a successful family provision claim by an adult child who is otherwise economically self-sufficient. Finally, shrinking social security budgets may encourage more adult children to apply under the 1975 Act (or 1979 Order); perhaps the bigger issue here is whether a dead parent's estate should have to provide for a child in receipt of state benefits rather than the public purse, assuming that sufficient wealth is available. Any debate on the recalibration of Government obligations and parental responsibilities exceeds the scope of the present chapter. Whether judges may be tempted to achieve the same result (albeit indirectly) in family provision claims remains to be seen—though the Court of Appeal in *Mitson*[100] was quick to point out that this was not what it was doing.

---

[93] Compare *Re Garland* [2007] EWHC 2 (Ch) with *Re McGarrell* [1983] 8 NIJB.

[94] Contrast, eg the respective awards in *Re Hancock* [1998] 2 FLR 346 and *Espinosa v Bourke* [1999] 1 FLR 747 (even allowing for factual variances).

[95] There may also be a tendency to reach a settlement to avoid uncertainty of outcome and costs.

[96] Of course, parents are now living longer and may consume more of their capital in maintaining themselves post-retirement and into old age; care home costs may also dissipate an estate significantly, even with government proposals to protect people's saving and homes from unlimited care costs. See Department of Health Press Release, *New Fairer Capped Funding System to Help Everyone Plan for the Cost of Care* (July 18 2013) located at www.gov.uk/government/news/new-fairer-capped-funding-system-to-help-everyone-plan-for-the-cost-of-care.

[97] J Langbein, 'The Twentieth Century Revolution in Family Wealth Transmission' (1988) 86 *Michigan Law Review* 722, 723—a trend which continues today.

[98] Assuming adult children can find an affordable property and secure a mortgage; many are now living at home for much longer because they are unable to buy (or rent) on their own. See 'Three in 10 Parents Have Grown-Up Children Still Living at Home,' *The Guardian*, 6 September 2013. This trend is set to continue—'Half of Young Adults Will Live with Their Parents within a Generation from Now,' *The Independent*, 1 May 2014.

[99] 'Grandparents Save UK £11 billion in Childcare Each Year,' *The Telegraph*, 3 September 2012 referring to a RIAC commissioned report which suggested savings of £1,868 per family.

[100] [2011] EWCA Civ 346 [14] and see text to n 59.

In one sense, family provision claims by independent adult children are just another example of the eternal conflict between family law and property law when the two collide on death through the medium of succession.[101] One of the central questions to emerge in family provision claims is where the 'dividing line' should fall 'between altering the will so far as necessary to provide "proper" provision, which was allowed, and ... making a new will for the testator, which was not'[102]—and those involving independent adult children are just another example.[103] However, such claims raise their own unique problems. One of the main difficulties is that there is no clear sense of the obligations (if any) which exist between parents and independent adult children; unlike infants and minors where there is a clear element of financial dependency which transcends the death of a parent, the same is not true of independent adult children who are (or should be) capable of providing for themselves and were not financially reliant on their parent before the latter's death.[104] Attitudes towards inheritance also come into play, and there is a sense in which disinheriting adult children or treating siblings unequally seems unnatural or instinctively wrong. Studies reveal ingrained social expectations around inheritance and who are the 'natural recipients' of a testator's bounty; adult children are often seen as the automatic beneficiaries of their parents' wealth,[105] and perhaps we should not be surprised if judges (who bring their own emotional instincts and cultural 'baggage' to the cases which come before them) may be tempted to correct parental disinheritance or unequal distribution between children in some way.[106] Yet, another basic social (and legal) assumption comes into play here. While absolute testamentary freedom is something of a legal myth,[107] it remains a core ideal of all common law succession systems that an individual enjoys the 'right to distribute property upon death solely according to the dictates of their own desires, unfettered by the constraints of society's moral code or the claims of others'.[108] Testamentary freedom dictates that parents should be able to exclude or marginalise their children under a valid will,[109] and does not sit easily with what may now be an increasing willingness to uphold family provision claims by independent adult children. Lastly,

---

[101] See MA Glendon, 'Fixed Rules and Discretion in Contemporary Family Law and Succession Law (1986) 60 *Tulane Law Review* 1165 and RF Croucher, 'How Free is Free? Testamentary Freedom and the Battle between "Family" and "Property"' (2012) 37 *Australian Journal of Legal Philosophy* 9.

[102] Atherton (n 91) 12.

[103] Ibid.

[104] In most of the cases discussed throughout, there was no pre-existing financial tie between the deceased and the applicant; the child's financial position was not caused (or exacerbated) by the parent's death.

[105] Empirical studies around inheritance reveal that 'equal treatment of children is seen as the norm' and 'reigns supreme when it comes to the division of major assets': J Finch and J Mason, *Passing On: Kinship and Inheritance in England* (London, Routledge, 2000) 77. Research has also suggested that 63% of people expect to inherit from their parents, with this figure increasing where parents are owner-occupiers of a family home: K Rowlington and S McKay, *Attitudes to Inheritance in Britain* (Joseph Rowntree Foundation, 2005) ch 2.

[106] Though, in the latter scenario, courts have not substituted an equal division between siblings: see, eg *Re Hancock* [1998] 2 FLR 346 and *Re Creeny* [1984] NI 397.

[107] M Leslie, 'The Myth of Testamentary Freedom' (1996) 38 *Arizona Law Review* 235.

[108] Ibid, 235.

[109] The most extreme example occurs in the US where parents can disinherit both infant and adult children (something that has been criticised, especially with minors: see DA Batts, 'I Didn't Ask to Be Born: The American Law of Disinheritance and a Proposal for Change to a System of Protected Inheritance' (1990) 41 *Hastings Law Journal* 1197).

when looking at these claims, other salient factors are at play—for example, the symbolic importance of inherited wealth (especially parental wealth);[110] what a lack of or disparity in provision says about the relationship between parent and child;[111] and notions of fairness and favouritism where there is more than one child.[112] Disinheriting a child (or treating them less favourably than their siblings) is also the ultimate parental sanction—a final and lasting sign of displeasure, disappointment and rejection.[113] As part of the contextual backdrop, these factors may help to explain why claims by independent adult children are especially fraught and equally difficult for courts to deal with.

VI. CONCLUSION

Post-*Mitson*, it would be wrong to suggest that English law is drifting towards a system of forced heirship or that parents have an unassailable posthumous duty to support their independent adult children where the latter challenge an estate distribution. What is emerging, however, is a sense in which such applications may be increasingly successful—as well as the applicant's economic situation and financial needs having a much greater say in the outcome. Wills are also looking increasingly vulnerable, and may be effectively re-written by courts (something which has always been apparent when looking at cases from Northern Ireland), despite clear mental capacity and compliance with will-making formalities on the part of the testator.

The latter point is just one aspect of the courts' approach to family provision claims by independent adult children that could be revisited when the opportunity next arises. Atherton has noted that testamentary freedom must be 'viewed within a context of family responsibilities'.[114] However, there is a sense in which it has become little more than an illusory concept which merits a passing reference in judicial decision-making, despite strong supporting statements in cases such as *Re Coventry*.[115] Perhaps the time has come to re-centralise the notion of testamentary freedom when looking at adult child claims (and family provision claims more generally), or at least give it a more prominent role. Some of the cases discussed here

---

[110] JG McMullan, 'Keeping Peace in the Family When You Are Resting in Peace: Making Sense of and Preventing Will Contests' (2008) 8 *Marquette Elder's Advisor* 61, 82.

[111] There is a basic concept of passing property down through generations; property, as a 'symbol of identity [and] relations' communicates the giver's 'personal preferences, and opinions of the receiver': S Kreiczer-Levy, 'Inheritance Legal Systems and the Intergenerational Bond' (2012) 46 *Real Property, Probate and Trust Law Journal* 495, 504.

[112] 'Brothers and sisters may fight over estate property, but they are really sorting out old issues of sibling rivalry and dominance': J Folberg, 'Mediating Family Property and Estate Conflicts' (2009) 23 *Probate & Property* 8, 8.

[113] 'To be disinherited by a parent is to be disowned—to become an orphan retroactive to birth. Even to receive less than other beneficiaries who are similarly situated is exquisitely painful': PM Accettura, *Blood & Money: Why Families Fight Over Inheritance and What To Do About It* (Michigan, Collinwood Press, 2011) 35.

[114] Atherton (n 91) 8.

[115] Oliver J at first instance stated that: 'Subject to the court's powers under the Act and to fiscal demands, an Englishman still remains at liberty at his death to dispose of his own property in whatever way he pleases or, if he chooses to do so, to leave that disposition to be regulated by the laws of intestate succession': [1979] 2 WLR 853, 864–65 and approved by Buckley LJ on appeal at [1980] Ch 461, 495.

represent a significant encroachment on the deceased's wishes, even where the individual has attempted to explain or defend their actions, and *Mitson* makes it clear that long-term estrangement does not justify a child's exclusion or marginalisation.

Reviewing the Northern Ireland case law on adult children, Grattan has observed that:

> It should be remembered that it was not the objective of the 1979 Order to interfere with the freedom which every testator enjoys to exclude an adult, able-bodied child from his will, any more than it was to prescribe fairness and equality between offspring.[116]

The same comments apply to the 1975 Act; the purpose of the family provision system is not to 'pass judgement' on the parent's actions or to substitute what might be viewed as a more appropriate estate division when dealing with claims by independent adult children. Courts could avoid such subjective rationalisation by focusing on the legislative requirement of 'reasonable financial provision' instead of assessing the reasonableness or otherwise of a particular estate distribution—something which is clearly wrong. Applying and evaluating the various statutory factors in a more precise and consistent manner would also ensure that the decision-making process has a stronger jurisprudential basis. In the author's opinion, the basic principles set out by King J in *Mitson*[117] for determining applications by independent adult children across a diverse range of factual scenarios could help meet this particular objective. While the decision itself was overturned on appeal, these principles could help judges evaluate both the strength of individual claims and the range of competing interests, while bringing some much-needed clarity to the law in this area.

---

[116] Grattan (n 67) 198.
[117] [2009] EWHC 3114 (Fam) [49] and see text to n 38.

8

Property of the Mentally Incapacitated: Statutory Wills in England and Australia

FIONA BURNS[*]

I. INTRODUCTION

IN THE twentieth century it became increasingly clear in England[1] and Australia that when a person lacked testamentary capacity, distributing the assets in accordance with an outdated will or under intestacy could be an imperfect course of action. There were (and are) a trio of testamentary gaps where the insistence on testamentary capacity and/or the operation of the current intestacy scheme could be insensitive to a deceased's particular circumstances, resulting in perverse results far removed from what the deceased would have liked. These gaps occur when: the deceased lacks testamentary capacity from birth; the deceased becomes incapacitated and had never made a will; and the deceased becomes incapacitated after making a will which is no longer current because of changed circumstances. Recourse to family provision is not satisfactory because it does not provide another method for making a will and is only available to provide assets for a relatively small list of proven dependents.[2]

Legislatures in England and Australia have taken steps to develop a framework for creating wills for persons who are unable to make wills for themselves. When a person does not have testamentary capacity, the court may order or authorise the execution of a will on his behalf. However, while these jurisdictions have implemented statutory wills regimes, they have done so differently and from dissimilar perspectives.

After, this introduction, the chapter is divided into four following parts. The second part describes and analyses the development of statutory wills in England prior to the introduction of the Mental Capacity Act 2005 (c 9) (MCA). It is important to appreciate why and how the statutory wills jurisdiction emerged in England because the modern law in England and Australia has linkages (albeit different linkages) to the earlier English law. The third part considers current English law and some

---

[*] Associate Professor, Faculty of Law, University of Sydney.
[1] Reference to England includes reference to Wales.
[2] Eg Inheritance (Provision for Family and Dependents) Act 1975, s 1.

critical problems which have arisen under the MCA. The fourth part describes and analyses the development of statutory wills in Australia which has been influenced, to some small degree, by the English law prior to the introduction of the MCA. This part also highlights some recent important developments. The final part summarises the potential weaknesses in the English and Australian statutory wills regimes and suggests tentatively that in the future both countries may need to consider the impact of the UN Convention on the Rights of Persons with Disabilities in regard to statutory wills.

For the purposes of clarity, and when appropriate, the mentally incapacitated person for whom a will could be authorised will be referred to as 'the testator'.

II. THE DEVELOPMENT OF STATUTORY WILLS IN ENGLAND PRIOR TO THE MCA

Mental disability is neither a new nor uniform condition. England developed a protective jurisdiction to care for mentally incapacitated persons and their property. The Crown had jurisdiction over the property of 'lunatics' under statutes dating from the fourteenth century. The jurisdiction was exercised by the Lord Chancellor together with other judges and legal functionaries.[3]

Until relatively recently, what action could be taken when a person was mentally incapacitated and had not made a valid and current will received little attention. Traditionally, subject to some relics from medieval law,[4] there was no third course of action. A person's assets would be distributed either under a valid will or under the intestacy scheme. There are several possible reasons for this hiatus. First, many of the people under the protective jurisdiction may not have had sufficient assets to warrant any legislative or judicial consideration. Second, in the wealthy classes, family assets were often tied up in complex settlements spanning generations which obviated the need for wills or reliance on intestacy.[5] Third, people had shorter lifespans.[6] Diseases associated with mental incapacity and an ageing population were not prevalent.[7] Fourth, in the nineteenth century, 'freedom of testation' was highly important.[8] A judicial creation of a will would have been seen as usurping a person's property rights. Finally, it was assumed that there was no need for a third course of action—intestacy was a default system that universally applied.[9]

---

[3] HS Theobold, *The Law Relating to Lunacy* (London, Stevens and Sons Ltd, 1924) chs I–VII; WS Holdsworth, *A History of English Law*, 3rd edn (London, Methuen and Co, 1922) 475–76; C Harpum, S Bridge and M Dixon, *The Law of Real Property*, 8th edn (London, Sweet & Maxwell, 2012) para 36-021.

[4] Eg primogeniture: AWB Simpson, *A History of the Land Law*, 2nd edn (Oxford, Oxford University Press, 1986) ch 1.

[5] Holdsworth (n 3) vol 7, 376–81; S Anderson, 'Succession, Inheritance and the Family' in W Cornish et al, *The Oxford History of the Laws of England*, vol XII (Oxford, Oxford University Press, 2010) 8–27.

[6] Eg Office of National Statistics (UK), 'Death Registrations: Deaths Fall below a Million' www.statistics.gov.uk/cc/nugget.asp?id=952.

[7] JR Martyn and N Caddick (eds) *Williams, Mortimer and Sunnucks on Executors, Administrators and Probate* (London, Thomson Reuters, 2013) para 13-09.

[8] Anderson (n 5) vol XII, 6.

[9] CH Sherrin and RC Bonehill, *The Law and Practice of Intestate Succession*, 3rd edn (London, Thomson, 2004) paras 2-00–2-19.

A. Wills, Property and the Mentally Incapacitated at the End of the Nineteenth Century

Notwithstanding the absence of statutory wills before the twentieth century, English law developed two responses to the problem of testamentary incapacity that deserve consideration.

i. The Changing Definition of Testamentary Capacity

In order to make a valid will a testator had to have testamentary capacity. The law was (and remains) weighted in favour of finding a valid will. It was presumed that the testator had capacity. The party propounding the will was not required to provide evidence of testamentary capacity[10] unless the will was formally challenged on the ground of incapacity.[11] However, several authorities had suggested that even the slightest sign of an unsound mind invalidated a will.[12] In *Banks v Goodfellow* (*Banks*)[13] Cockburn J loosened the test for testamentary capacity by presaging a decision-specific or functional approach to incapacity in which medical evidence was helpful but not conclusive. He observed:

> [A] testator shall understand the nature of the act and its effects; shall understand the extent of the property of which he is disposing; shall be able to comprehend and appreciate the claims to which he ought to give effect; and with a view to the latter object, that no disorder of the mind shall poison his affections, pervert his sense of right, or prevent the exercise of his natural faculties that no insane delusion shall influence his will in disposing of his property and bring about a disposal of it which, if the mind had been sound, would not have been made.[14]

It was also recognised that a testator lacking testamentary capacity could have a lucid interval in which he made a valid will.[15] Therefore, a testator could suffer from a mental disability, but still have sufficient testamentary capacity to make a will.

ii. The Emergence of the Substituted Judgment Doctrine

While a court exercising the lunacy jurisdiction in the nineteenth century had no power to authorise a will on behalf of a mentally incapacitated person, it was able to authorise gifts and allowances in favour of third parties who were adversely affected by the person's inability to make decisions about his property.[16] Courts did so reluctantly,[17] taking care not to squander assets and taking into account the person's pre-eminent moral obligations in favour of spouses and children.[18]

---

[10] *Steed v Calley* (1836) 1 Keen 620, 635; 48 ER 44.6, 4.52.

[11] *Smee v Smee* (1879) 5 PD 84, 91.

[12] *Waring v Waring* 6 Moo PC 341; 13 ER 715; *Smith v Tebbitt* (1867) LR.1 P&D 398.

[13] *Banks v Goodfellow* (1870) LR 5 QB 549.

[14] Ibid, 565.

[15] Eg *Nichols and Freeman v Binns* (1858) 1 SW & Tr 239; 164 ER 710; Martyn and Caddick (n 7) para 13-17; RG Martyn, C Ford, A Learmonth, M Oldham, *Theobold on Wills*, 17th edn (London, Thomson Reuters, 2010) para 3-010.

[16] *Ex p Whitbread; Re Hinde, a Lunatic* (1816) 2 Mer 99, 35 ER 878; Theobold (n 3) ch LXV.

[17] L Harmon, 'Falling Off the Vine: Legal Fictions and the Doctrine of Substituted Judgment' (1990) 100 *Yale Law Journal* 1, 20–21, 24.

[18] Theobold (n 3) 464.

In *Ex p Whitbread; Re Hinde, a Lunatic (Ex p Whitbread)*[19] Lord Eldon set a possible foundation for statutory wills:[20] he made an *inter vivos* provision for relatives out of the incapacitated person's assets on the basis of substituted judgment. Lord Eldon considered 'what it is likely the Lunatic himself would do, if he were in a capacity to act' and the manner that 'the Court thinks it would have been wise and prudent in the Lunatic himself to apply it, in case he had been capable'.[21] The approach was superficially attractive. Lord Eldon paid homage to the person's proprietary interest and likely proprietary intention, but simultaneously transferred assets to third parties.

However, the judgment had anomolies. It was not clear whether Lord Eldon created a subjective substituted judgment doctrine or whether, as has been suggested,[22] it evolved into a substituted judgment based on the application of an objective test— what a wise and prudent person in the lunatic's situation might do. Some later cases held that judicial intervention was only available when the person (while sane) had actually expressed a desire that relatives benefit, particularly when no moral obligation was otherwise owed.[23] Moreover, it was difficult to apply the substituted judgment doctrine when the person never had mental capacity, because there was no evidence of the person's earlier wishes.[24] Finally, orders in favour of third parties did not sit well with the overarching demand that courts exercise the protective jurisdiction for the person's benefit[25] (although Lord Eldon suggested that a person would benefit from his relative's elevated maintenance and education).[26]

B. Statutory Wills in the Twentieth Century

Subsequently the shift towards the creation and implementation of statutory wills took place in three stages.

i. Inter vivos *Settlements: Section 171 of the Law of Property Act 1925 c 20 (LPA)*

Under section 171 of the LPA the problem of testamentary incapacity was dealt with via *inter vivos* intervention. The High Court was able to order a receiver (who managed the person's affairs) to execute an *inter vivos* settlement of the person's property in favour of third persons before the incapacitated person's death.[27] The order could be made if the mentally incapacitated person had acquired the property under a settlement, will or intestacy;[28] or there was a change in intestacy law or the

---

[19] *Ex p Whitbread; Re Hinde, a Lunatic* (n 16).
[20] *Re Frost* (1870) 5 Ch App 699; RF Croucher, 'An Interventionist, Paternatlistic Jurisdiction? The Place of Statutory Wills in Australian Succession Law' (2009) 33 *University of New South Wales Law Journal* 674, 676.
[21] *Ex p Whitbread; Re Hinde, a Lunatic* (n 16) 102–103, 879.
[22] Harmon (n 17) 22–23; Croucher (n 20) 677–78.
[23] *Re Evans* (1882) LR 21 Ch D 297; *Re Darling* (1888) LR 39 Ch D 208.
[24] Harmon (n 17) 35.
[25] *Re Pink* (1883) LR 23 Ch D 577, 579.
[26] *Ex p Whitbread; Re Hinde, a Lunatic* (n 16) 102, 879.
[27] LPA, s 171(2); S Barber, 'Re C (A Patient) Revisited: How Strong is the Family's Claim' [1996] *Private Client Bulletin* 34, 35–39.
[28] LPA, s 171(1)(b).

circumstances after which the person had made the will. A court had to be 'satisfied that any person might suffer an injustice' if the property devolved under intestacy or under the will.[29] While courts took into account the fact that the person might recover his mental faculties later,[30] they did not consider what was for the person's benefit (because the *inter vivos* settlement of property was not considered to be for the benefit of mentally incapacitated people).[31] However, courts applied a substituted judgment doctrine, based on what it was likely that the person would have done with her property, if she had been sane.[32]

ii. Mental Health Act 1959 c 72

The Mental Health Act 1959 replaced the Lunacy Act 1890 53 Vic c 5. However, the former Court of Protection (created in 1947)[33] continued to protect and manage the property of mentally incapacitated persons until their death.[34] A person under the court's protection was unable to make any valid *inter vivos* disposition, even during a lucid period, but was still able to make a valid will because it would not take effect until after his death.[35] Initially the court did not have power to authorise a statutory will, but the court was able to order settlements of a person's property[36] taking into account who would inherit his estate.[37] In 1969 the legislation was amended, permitting the court for the first time to order:[38]

> [T]he execution for the patient of a will making any provision (whether by way of disposing of property or exercising a power or otherwise) which could be made by a will executed by the patient if he were not mentally disordered ...

However, the power was unexercisable when the testator was a minor;[39] and in other cases could not be exercised unless the judge had reason to believe that the patient was incapable of making a will.[40] While the latter limitation was superficially logical, it glossed over the interface between the nature of incapacity under the mental health regime (based essentially on a 'black and white' medical diagnosis of incapacity)[41] and the approach in *Banks*.

A court order itself did not have dispositive effect.[42] The order required a person authorised by the court to execute a will on the testator's behalf in accordance with the formal requirements for wills.[43] The will was deemed to be a will for the purposes of the Wills Act 1837[44] except to the extent that the will purported to deal

---

[29] Ibid, s 171(1)(c).
[30] Ibid, s 171(4); *Re CWM* [1951] 2 KB 714.
[31] *Re Freeman* [1927] 1 Ch 479, 489; *Re Greene* [1928] Ch 528, 547.
[32] *Re Freeman* (n 31) 488 (Hanworth MR).
[33] *In the Matter of MB (A Patient)* [2005] EWCA Civ 1293, [2006] 1 WLR 278 [26].
[34] Ibid, [27].
[35] *Re Beaney* [1978] 1 WLR 770, 772.
[36] *Mental Health Act 1959*, s 103(1)(d).
[37] *Re L (WJG)* [1966] 1 Ch 135.
[38] Administration of Justice Act 1969 c 58, s 17 incorporating s 103(1)(dd).
[39] Mental Health Act 1959, s 103(2)(a).
[40] Ibid, s 103(2)(b).
[41] *Re S and S (Protected Persons); C v V* [2008] EWHC B 16 (Fam) [51].
[42] *Re Davey* [1981] 1 WLR 164, 172.
[43] Mental Health Act 1959, s 103A.
[44] Ibid, s 103A(3).

with immovable property outside England or Wales[45] or the testator was not domiciled in England or Wales.[46]

iii. *Mental Health Act 1983 c 20*

The statutory wills provisions outlined above were substantially replicated in the Mental Health Act 1983.[47] The court's power to order the execution of the will under section 96(1)(e) followed the court's general powers enabling it to 'do or secure the doing of all such things as appear necessary or expedient … for making provision for other persons or purposes for whom or which the patient might be expected to provide if he were not mentally disordered'.[48]

In view of the objective nature and expression of the judicial powers, it was arguable that a statutory will could have been authorised by an objective consideration of what, in the court's opinion, was for the benefit of the patient and his family. An objective approach to medical decision-making had already evolved into the 'best interests'[49] test and was preferred by English judges.[50]

However, courts differentiated statutory wills from medical decisions, preferring to apply a substituted judgment doctrine under the 1959 and 1983 Acts. In *Re D(J)*[51] Megarry VC framed the modern substituted judgment test:

> The first of the principles … is that it is to be assumed that the patient is having a brief lucid interval at the time when the will is made. The second is that during the lucid interval the patient has a full knowledge of the past, and a full realisation that as soon as the will is executed he or she will relapse into the actual mental state that previously existed, with the prognosis as it actually is … The third proposition is that it is the actual patient who has to be considered and not a hypothetical patient … Fourth, I think that during the hypothetical lucid interval the patient is to be envisaged as being advised by competent solicitors … Fifth in all normal cases the patient is to be envisaged as taking a broad brush to the claims on his bounty, rather than an accountant's pen.[52]

Jurisprudentially, the decision was superficially appealing because, consistent with *Ex p Whitbread*, it appeared to be anchored in the intentions of the testator. Moreover, it was compatible with the law of wills where courts had held that a mentally incapacitated person could have a lucid moment when making a will.[53]

C. Comment

Although there were obvious differences between section 171 of the LPA and the mental health legislation, there were several similar approaches. The legislative

---

[45] Ibid, s 103A(4)(a).
[46] Ibid, s 103A(4)(b).
[47] *Mental Health Act* 1983, ss 96 and 97.
[48] Ibid, s 95(1)(c).
[49] Eg *Re C (An Adult): Refusal of Treatment* [1994] 3 WLR 290; *Re A (Male Sterilisation* [2000] 1 FLR 560.
[50] *In the Matter of MB (A Patient)* (n 33).
[51] *Re D(J)* [1982] 1 Ch 237.
[52] Ibid, 243–44.
[53] *Ex p Holyland* (1805) 11 Ves 10; 32 ER 990; *Creagh v Blood* (1845) 8 I Eq R 434; 2 Jos & Lat 509.

powers were a response to perceived adverse consequences to third parties when a mentally incapacitated person died without a valid and current will. Consequently, the main concerns of the courts exercising these powers were: the interests of the person's family and third parties for whom he had a moral obligation; and that such parties had an opportunity to put their case.[54]

Second, the courts applied a substituted judgment doctrine. This predilection was understandable. For example, the making of *inter vivos* gifts[55] from the assets of mentally incapacitated persons continued to be influenced by such decisions as *Ex p Whitbread*.

When a statutory will was executed, it was regarded as a will for the purpose of the Wills Act 1837 which assumed that the will evidenced the testator's testamentary scheme for the distribution of *his* assets and was not simply a casual record of possible intentions.[56] Moreover, the legislative language of the mental health legislation could also be read as suggesting substituted judgment[57] (but not necessarily one entirely centred on subjective considerations). The legislation directed the court to create terms 'which the patient might be expected to provide' and 'which could be made by a will executed by the patient if he were not mentally disordered'.

While the substituted judgment doctrine in *Re D(J)*[58] was endorsed for statutory wills by the Court of Appeal,[59] it was rejected[60] in favour of or subsumed under[61] the 'best interests test' for medical decision-making. Foremost, substituted judgment was artificial. When the person never had capacity to make a will, courts effectively substituted what a rational person in the testator's circumstances would do.[62] In *Re C (A Patient)*[63] Hoffmann J tried to bridge the gap between subjective substituted judgment and the court's value judgement, by stating that the court considered what the testator 'might be expected to provide'[64] and assumed that the testator 'would have been a normal decent person, acting in accordance with contemporary standards of morality'.[65] Even when the testator had lost capacity, the court did not replicate the testator's wishes (when they were ascertainable) because the court polished the person's character by discounting antipathies; and assumed that the testator was advised by competent lawyers. In *Re Davey*,[66] Fox J reflected both the substituted judgment doctrine (objectively modified) and concerns for third parties, observing that 'the essential question in the end would have been what if anything would be reasonable provision in all the circumstances for the various contestants'.[67]

---

[54] *Re HMF* [1976] 1 Ch 33; *Re B (Court of Protection: Notice of Proceedings)* [1987] 1 WLR 553, 556–57.
[55] *Re DML* [1965] 1133; *Re L (WJG)* [1966] 1 Ch 135.
[56] Cf *Estate of Knibbs* [1962] 2 All ER 829.
[57] *G v Official Solicitor* [2006] EWCA Civ 816, [2006] WTLR 1201, 1206.
[58] *Re D(J)* (n 51).
[59] *G v Official Solicitor* (n 57) 1206.
[60] *Airedale NHS Trust v Bland* [1993] AC 789, 817 (Butler-Sloss LJ); 894–95 (Lord Mustill).
[61] Ibid, 833 (Lord Hoffmann).
[62] Consider *Re L (WJG)* (n 37).
[63] *Re C (A Patient)* [1991] 3 All ER 866.
[64] Ibid, 869–70.
[65] Ibid, 870.
[66] *Re Davey* (n 42).
[67] Ibid, 171.

Finally, consistent with the history of the protective jurisdiction, the power to authorise wills was contained in mental health statutes rather than in the Wills Act 1837. The signal was clear: the devolution of a mentally incapacitated person's estate was a mental health issue; primarily remediable under the mental health regime, taking into account the law of wills.

III. STATUTORY WILLS AFTER 2005

A. Mental Capacity Act 2005 (c 9) (MCA)

The approach to statutory wills in *Re D(J)* was overtaken by the implementation of the MCA, the foundation for which was an earlier Law Commission Report.[68] From 1 October 2007, Part VII of the Mental Health Act 1983 was repealed and the MCA became effective. It is not possible to discuss the MCA in detail. Rather, it is apposite to highlight features that directly affected the making of statutory wills.

Under the MCA, a new Court of Protection was established.[69] The court is able to make decisions for people who lack the capacity to do so,[70] including decisions about their property.[71] However, the aim of the legislation is to empower mentally disabled people to make decisions for themselves or when this is not possible, to be involved in the decision-making process.[72] While diagnostic determinations of mental disability remain important, the legislation introduced a functional and decision-specific concept of mental incapacity.[73] Therefore, notwithstanding a mental disability, a person is assumed to have capacity in relation to a decision or transaction unless it is established to the contrary.[74] It is important to seek (if possible) the person's wishes, views and preferences.[75] A person is unable to make a decision for himself if he is unable to understand, retain, use or weigh relevant information or communicate his decision.[76] A person who is able to understand information through visual aids,[77] or can understand information for a short time,[78] is not deemed to be unable to make a decision.

The Act requires that any act or decision made for or on behalf of a person must be in that person's 'best interests', an 'umbrella' concept which is the ultimate benchmark for all judicial decisions.[79] Although the Act does not define what this means, it has a checklist of factors to be considered.[80] Medical decision-making cases decided

---

[68] Law Commission, *Mental Incapacity* (Law Com No 231, 1995).
[69] Mental Capacity Act 2005 (MCA), Pt 2.
[70] Ibid, s 16.
[71] Ibid, s 18.
[72] Eg Law Commission (n 68) paras 2.40, 3.29–3.33.
[73] MCA, s 2(1); *Re S and S (Protected Persons)* (n 41) [51]–[53]; *Re RGS* [2012] EWHC 4162 para 4.
[74] MCA, s 1(2).
[75] *C v V* (n 73) [54].
[76] MCA, s 3(1).
[77] Ibid, s 3(2).
[78] Ibid, s 3(3).
[79] Ibid, s 4.
[80] Ibid.

before the MCA, emphasised that 'best interests' not only included medical, but also psychological, emotional and social benefits.[81]

Subject to these fundamental principles,[82] a court may execute[83] or make an order[84] for the execution of a will or codicil[85] by an authorised person on behalf of the testator. However, while the broad thrust of the MCA is innovative, the earlier statutory wills provisions in the 1959 and 1983 Acts are encased in the new framework and are generally replicated in Schedule 2. A court remains empowered to order a will 'which could be made ... by P [the person] if he had capacity to make it'.[86] Accordingly, an issue is to what extent the new framework has influenced how courts handle applications for statutory wills?

B. Reaction Against the Substituted Judgment Doctrine

Notwithstanding the similarity of the language of the MCA to the earlier statutory wills provisions, the new framework has been influential. In *Re P (Statutory Will)*[87] Lewison J held that Megarry VC's substituted judgment doctrine could no longer be directly applied to the making of settlements or wills under the MCA. The legislation did not require the 'counter-factual assumption' of a temporarily lucid testator.[88] The court was required to follow the criteria under the MCA such as (if possible) encouraging the testator to participate in the decision[89] and considering the beliefs and values that would be likely to influence his decision if he had capacity,[90] before forming a value judgement as to what was in the testator's 'best interests'.[91] He also suggested that it was appropriate to apply the 'balance sheet' approach (developed for medical decision-making),[92] listing the factors for and against the exercise of the court's powers.[93]

In subsequent cases, the court has followed the 'best interests' approach[94] (ignoring substituted judgment)[95] and effectively created a three-pronged method for determining whether to order a will or an *inter vivos* settlement. First, the court must consider the checklist and criteria under the MCA. There is no hierachy of factors and their relevance will depend on the circumstances of the case.[96] Second, it has been observed that the court may recognise factors that are of such 'magnetic

---

[81] Eg *Re Y (Mental Patient: Bone Marrow Donations)* [1997] Fam 110, [1997] 556.

[82] MCA, s 16(3).

[83] Ibid, s 18(1)(i).

[84] Ibid, s 16.

[85] Ibid, s 64(1).

[86] Ibid, Sch 2(2).

[87] *Re P (Statutory Will)* [2009] EWHC 163 (Ch), [2010] Ch 33.

[88] Ibid, 44.

[89] MCA, s 4(4).

[90] Ibid, s 4(6)(b).

[91] Ibid.

[92] *Re A (Male Sterilisation)* (n 49) 560; *W v M* [2011] EWHC 2443 [247]–[248].

[93] *Re P (Statutory Will)* (n 87) 44.

[94] *NT v FS* [2010] EWHC 684 (COP); *In the Matter of M* [2009] EWHC 2525 (COP), [2009] WTLR 1791 [28]–[29].

[95] *KGS v JDS* [2012] EWHC 302 (COP); *Re D (Statutory Will)* [2010] EWHC 2159 (COP), [2012] Ch 56.

[96] *In the Matter of M* (n 94) [32].

importance'[97] that they will influence or even determine the case. Third, the court has approved the balance sheet approach, although this is not prescribed in the MCA.[98] Sometimes the court has actually drawn up a balance sheet of factors for and against the will before determining what is in the best interests of the testator.[99]

C. Comment

The MCA has much to recommend it. The application of the new framework and the 'best interests' test in statutory wills cases was a logical step in the coordinated protection of mentally incapacitated persons. In relation to property matters, including the making of statutory wills, the MCA refocuses the court's attention away from the interests of third parties to the mentally incapacitated person, his wishes and best interests. The guidelines have to be applied with care, particularly when the applicant is a prospective beneficiary under the statutory will.[100] In view of the 'mental gymnastics' associated with substituted judgment,[101] it is arguable that the mental process for determining a statutory will has been simplified and streamlined.

Nevertheless, there are some unresolved issues, arising from the fact that statutory wills provisions are contextualised in mental health legislation.

First, the legislation does not provide an explanation of the relationship between the concept of capacity under the MCA and the concept of testamentary capacity, although it has been assumed that both concepts are the same.[102] This is important because Schedule 2 of the MCA refers to the capacity to make a will and the will executed under the MCA is treated as a will under the Wills Act 1837. It has been suggested that the concept of capacity in the MCA is consistent with the common law and does not replace it.[103] Alternatively, it has been contended that there may be less reliance on *Banks*, as professional witnesses may find the criteria under the MCA more straightforward.[104] It is arguable that the concept of capacity under the MCA must be close to or consistent with the concept of testamentary capacity because both are functional, namely fact and decision-specific (although the test in *Banks* is more specifically prescriptive).

Second, so far the testator's incapacity in the cases has been clear cut,[105] but this may not always be the case. The case law concerning testamentary capacity demonstrates that a functional approach to capacity enables people with mental disabilities to make wills. However, the relativity of the functional approach means that a will (or decision) can be open to challenge. In the case of wills, the question is whether the testator who suffered a mental disability exhibited sufficient testamentary characteristics. In the case of a decision to execute or order the execution of a will on

---

[97] *Crossley v Crossley* (2007) EWCA Civ 149, (2008) FLR 1467 [15]; *In the Matter of M* (n 94) [32].
[98] *Re G (TJ)* (2010) EWHC 3005 COP [37].
[99] *KGS v JDS* (n 95) [30]–[32].
[100] B Rich, '*Re P*: Statutory Wills: An Epitaph for the "Lucid Interval"' [2009] *Private Client Bulletin* 210, 216.
[101] *Re P (Statutory Will)* (n 87) 44.
[102] *ITW v Z* [2009] EWHC 2575 (Fam).
[103] *In the Matter of MM (An Adult)* [2007] EWHC 2003 (Fam) [79]–[80].
[104] Martyn et al (n 15) para 3-006; Martyn and Caddick (n 7) para 13-04.
[105] Eg *Re P (Statutory Will)* (n 87); *In the Matter of M* (n 94).

behalf of a testator (or not to do so), the question is whether the court misjudged the testator's capacity in view of the criteria in the MCA.

Third, the MCA does not apply to persons under the age of 16 years.[106] There is no judicial power to order a will on behalf of a young minor who (whether mentally incapacitated or not) owns valuable assets, even though the outcome of the intestacy scheme may have perverse results such as an abusive parent inheriting the child's assets.[107]

Fourth, it is debatable whether the making of a will on behalf of a testator can be considered in his 'best interests'. Wills are ambulatory, do not take effect until after the testator's death[108] and do not relate to the testator's care or financial maintenance. Some applications may be made by the manager of the testator's affairs who has concerns that the testator has been improperly treated by a person who stands to gain under a current will.[109] However applicants may only be concerned that the absence of a valid and current will, may adversely affect their inheritance prospects. Lewison J held that the court could consider how the testator would be remembered after death and that 'for many people it is in their best interests that they be remembered with affection by their family and having done "the right thing" by their will'.[110] This view has been endorsed because 'best interests' is not only a monetary concept and 'best interests' 'do not cease at the moment of death'.[111] Nevertheless, this rationale defies logic (to the extent that it has been disputed in one case)[112] because unless the person has participated in the creation of the will, the will has not been created by the person trying to do 'the right thing', but by a decisionmaker.[113] Moreover, the interests of family members may conflict and some may not consider that the court has done 'the right thing'.[114] However, it has been suggested that it would be in a testator's best interest to avoid the expense of a family provision claim in regard to her estate.[115]

Fifth, there is the question to what extent ought the testator's wishes be a factor to which the court must pay close attention? There is no ready answer. Section 4(6)(a) of the MCA states that the court

> must consider, so far as reasonably ascertainable—the person's past and present wishes and feelings (and in particular, any relevant written statement made by him when he had capacity).

Taken in isolation, this direction could appear to mandate substituted judgment, but it is only part of the checklist.

In *Re S (Protected Patient)*[116] Judge Marshall QC appeared to come close to express favour for an indirect re-introduction of a substituted judgment doctrine. She stressed the importance of implementing rational wishes and feelings (which

---

[106] MCA, s 4(6)(b), (2)(5).
[107] Consider *Application of Fenwick* (2009) 76 NSWLR 22, [2009] NSWSC 530.
[108] *Re Walker* [1905] 1 Ch 160, 172.
[109] *In the Matter of M* (n 94).
[110] *Re P (Statutory Will)* (n 87) 47.
[111] *In the Matter of M* (n 94) [38].
[112] *NT v FS* (n 94) [8].
[113] *Re G (TJ)* (n 98) [53].
[114] Ibid.
[115] Rich (n 100) 219.
[116] *Re S (Protected Patient)* [2009] WTLR 315.

were neither impracticable nor irresponsible), highlighting that one of the chief aims of the MCA was to empower a person to partcipate in decisions about himself and that it was in the best interests of the person to do so.[117] She held that such wishes ought to carry great weight and a presumption in favour of implementation ought to arise.[118]

In view of Marshall QC's opinion, Lewison J downplayed the determinative effect of the testator's wishes and feelings. The main object of the MCA was achieved by the court making a value judgement as to what was in the testator's best interest.[119] The court was required to have regard to section 4(6)(a) and it would form part of (but not entirely) matters for consideration in the balance sheet approach; and he cautioned against the risk of re-introducing a substituted judgment or viewing such wishes as having a presumptive status.[120]

In view of the three-pronged test referred to above, it is likely that the approach of Lewison J will predominate and the issue-specific relevance[121] and rationality of the wishes or feelings would be taken into account, but not be necessarily determinative.

However, additional factors will be whether the person had capacity when the wish or feeling was expressed and how and when the wish or feeling was expressed. In this regard, the extent to which former wills ought to be taken into account may pose a dilemma for the court.[122] The will may have been executed when the testator had testamentary capacity and it is a relevant written statement. Nevertheless, it may be a document which does not or only partially reflects the testator's past and present wishes. Likewise written and (alleged) oral statements of testamentary intention will need to be scrutinised carefully.

Sixth, in *Banks* the court held that a testator 'shall be able to comprehend and appreciate the claims to which he ought to give effect'.[123] A question is whether the court ought to make a will which recognises the testator's moral obligations and the statutory rights of persons under the Inheritance (Provision for Family and Dependants) Act 1975. Section 4(6) appears to require the court to do so because the court must consider 'the beliefs and values that would be likely to influence his decision if he had capacity'[124] and 'the other factors that he would be likely to consider if he were able to do so'.[125] Schedule 2(2) directs that the will may make any provision 'which could be made in a will executed by [the person] if he had capacity'.

In *NT v FS*,[126] the testator had made a will when he had capacity, but in view of changed circumstances, an application for a statutory will was made on his behalf. In framing the will, Judge Behrens recognised that the testator had moral obligations to a party (N) who would have a claim for family provision.[127] Unfortunately, he did not adequately explore the possibility of family provision proceedings which can be

---

[117] Ibid, [56], [58].
[118] Ibid, [57].
[119] *Re P (Statutory Will)* (n 87) 46.
[120] Ibid. Note *Re D (Statutory Will)* (n 95) [16].
[121] *In the Matter of M* (n 94) [35].
[122] Ibid.
[123] *Banks v Goodfellow* (n 13) 565.
[124] MCA, s 4(6)(b).
[125] Ibid, s 4(6)(c).
[126] *NT v FS* (n 94).
[127] Ibid, [85].

expensive and divisive. He held that it was neither helpful to speculate on the extent of such a claim nor frame the statutory will solely with family provision issues in mind[128] because, inter alia, it was unclear what the size of the estate would be after allowing for pre-death expenditures and taxation.

It is arguable that a court ought to take into account that there could be family provision proceedings and authorise a will that attempts to avoid subsequent litigation. The legislative provisions are wide enough to encompass such considerations and the minimisation of litigation costs is in the best interests of the testator.

Finally, statutory wills have been vehicles for purposes unforeseen by law reformers.[129] For example, in *Re D (Statutory Will)*[130] the testator had made a will (while having apparent capacity) which departed from the terms of previous wills and was made in suspicious cirumstances. At an initial hearing, the need for a statutory will was raised and the court held that it did not have the power to adjudicate disputes as to the validity of non-statutory wills. Authorising a statutory will when the earlier will was tainted by disputes about validity could encourage applications for statutory wills as a way of side-stepping the issue of validity.[131] In the main proceedings, Judge Hodge QC decided that while a previous will was a relevant factor, the weight to be given to it would depend upon the circumstances of the case and how it was created.[132] He held that it was in the testator's best interests to be remembered for doing the 'right thing'[133] and ordered the execution of a will in terms similar to that of an earlier indisputably valid will. On the facts, the decision was probably appropriate and it is arguable that it was in the best interests of the testator to have her circumstances reviewed and a statutory will created to avoid litigation after her death. Nevertheless, the danger is that an application for a statutory will could be used to foil the operation of an otherwise valid and current will.

IV. AUSTRALIA

A. Law Reform

The Australian colonies 'received' English law to the extent that it was relevant to Australian conditions.[134] They inherited and adapted the English law in relation to wills[135] and lunacy[136] and many later English developments in these areas.[137] This meant they absorbed the wisdom in such cases as *Banks*, but also some of

---

[128] Ibid.

[129] *LG v DK* [2011] EWHC 2453 (COP).

[130] *Re D (Statutory Will)* (n 95).

[131] Ibid, [5].

[132] Ibid, [16].

[133] Ibid.

[134] Australian Courts Act 1828 (9 Geo IV c 83); AC Castles, *An Australian Legal History* (Law Book, 1982) 9–13.

[135] GE Dal Pont and KF Mackie, *Law of Succession* (LexisNexis, Butterworths, 2013) paras 21.18–21.20.

[136] Eg JM Bennett, *A History of the Supreme Court of New South Wales* (The Law Book Company Ltd, 1974) ch 7; P Powell, *The Origins and Development of the Protective Jurisidiction of the Supreme Court of New South Wales* (Francis Forbes Society for Australian Legal History, 2004) 9–14.

[137] Powell (n 136) 15–21.

the imperfections in English law, like the trio of testamentary gaps referred to earlier. Notwithstanding these gaps, Australia was slow to appreciate the problem. It appears that some states in Australia adopted a provision akin to section 171 of the LPA,[138] but there was little serious deliberation about the implementation of statutory wills (except in South Australia (SA))[139] until the 1980s. Inititally this was undertaken at state level because the individual states have jurisdiction over succession law and mental health in the federal system. Tasmania[140] and SA[141] implemented statutory wills legislation first and other states followed.[142] During the 1990s the question whether there ought to be a statutory wills regime was taken up under the Uniform Sucession Laws project which promotes standardised succession law throughout Australia.[143]

In order to appreciate the Australian response, it is helpful to note briefly several trends in leading law reform reports in the 1980s and 1990s.[144] The law reform bodies were aware of the creation of statutory wills provisions in the Mental Health Act 1983 and the English concept of a statutory will was influential.[145] They recognised the trio of testamentary gaps referred to earlier and the problems and expense caused to relatives and dependents.[146]

Australia departed from the English approach because it was assumed that statutory wills could be best dealt with as a succession issue, responding to a precise factual context: a person's testamentary incapacity[147] (rather than the person's mental incapacity).[148] While organisations other than the state Supreme Courts had some jurisdiction over people who suffered mental incapacity, it was assumed that the Supreme Courts (which had special expertise in succession law) would have carriage of the statutory wills regime.[149] These courts could authorise a statutory will when the testator was unable to meet the specific test for testamentary incapacity in *Banks*.[150] Moreover, in view of the succession context, the law reform bodies recommended that these courts be empowered to authorise a statutory will for minors (whether the minor was mentally incapacitated or not).[151]

The approach of the law reform bodies as a whole to the substituted judgment doctrine in *Re D(J)*[152] appears to have been rather equivocal with only one report

---

[138] Eg Property Law Act 1958 (Vic), s 171; Chief Justice's Law Reform Committee, Parliament of Victoria, *Wills for Mentally Disordered Persons* (1985) paras 36–38.

[139] The Aged and Infirm Property Act 1940 (SA), ss 7 and 29(2).

[140] Wills Legislation Amendment Act 1995 (Tas).

[141] Wills (Wills for Persons Lacking Testamentary Capacity) Amendment Act 1996 (SA).

[142] Croucher (n 20) 479.

[143] Dal Pont and Mackie (n 135) para P.21.

[144] Chief Justice's Law Reform Committee, Parliament of Victoria (n 138); Law Reform Committee, Parliament of Victoria, *Reforming the Law of Wills* (1995); Law Reform Commission of NSW, *Wills for Persons Lacking Will-Making Capacity* (Report 68, 1992); Law Reform Commission of NSW, *Uniform Succession Laws: The Law of Wills* (Report 85, 1998) ch 5.

[145] Eg Chief Justice's Law Reform Committee, Parliament of Victoria (n 138) paras 3–12.

[146] Eg ibid, para 5; Law Reform Committee, Parliament of Victoria (n 144) para 36.

[147] Eg Queensland Law Reform Commission, *Assisted and Substituted Decisions*, vol 1 (Report 49, 1996) 50–51.

[148] Eg Chief Justice's Law Reform Committee (n 138) para 20.

[149] Ibid, para 5A.17.

[150] Eg Law Reform Committee, Parliament of Victoria (n 144) paras 5A.24, 5A.31.

[151] Eg Law Reform Commission of NSW (1992) (n 144) para 2.31.

[152] *Re D(J)* (n 51).

expressing direct support for the substituted judgment and assuming that the process of substituted judgment was straighforward.[153] The law reform bodies, did not question the efficacy and usefulness of the doctrine. They neither discussed whether the doctrine ought to be primarily objective or subjective nor how to deal with cases where the person had always lacked testamentary capacity. Instead, the law reform proposals largely concentrated on evidential issues (such as evidence relevant to the making of an authorisation)[154] and procedural matters (such as the two-tiered application procedure explained below and the registrar's powers).[155] What was in the 'best interests' of the mentally incapacitated person did not prefigure in the recommendations.

B. The Statutory Will Provisions

i. Overview

In view of the multiplicity of jurisdictions in the Australian federation, it is not possible to outline the legislation in each state. Instead, it is apposite in a short paper of this nature to outline some of the main features with reference to the Uniform Succession Law Model[156] (which most states and territories have broadly followed to some degree). However, as will be indicated below, there are some important differences in the state legislation.

On the application of any person, the court may make an order authorising the making, altering or revoking of a will on behalf of a person who lacks testamentary capacity and who is alive at the time the order is made.[157] An application may be made on behalf of a minor.[158] The application process is two-tiered. A person must initially obtain leave of the court to make an application for an order.[159] The legislation sets out a non-exhaustive list of matters which the application must cover including: evidence of the likelihood of the mentally incapacitated person regaining testamentary capacity;[160] a reasonable estimate of the size of the estate;[161] evidence of the person's wishes;[162] evidence of any person who might be reasonably expected to benefit under the intestacy rules;[163] or evidence of any person who would be likely to make a family provision claim.[164] The court must refuse leave unless it is satisfied, inter alia, that there is reason to believe that the testator lacks testamentary capacity;[165] the applicant is an appropriate person to make the application;[166] and adequate steps have been taken to allow the representations of parties who have a

---

[153] Law Reform Commission of NSW (1992) (n 144) para 2.20.
[154] Law Reform Commission of NSW (1998) (n 144) ch 5, paras 5.12–5.21.
[155] Ibid, paras 5.36–5.38.
[156] Ibid, para 5.45.
[157] Ibid, para 5.45 containing model provision s 19.
[158] Ibid, s 19(4).
[159] Ibid, s 20.
[160] Ibid, s 21(a).
[161] Ibid, s 20(2)(b).
[162] Ibid, s 20(2)(d).
[163] Ibid, s 20(2)(g).
[164] Ibid, s 20(2)(h).
[165] Ibid, s 21(a).
[166] Ibid, s 21(d).

legitimate claim to the estate.[167] If the court is satisfied with the information provided, the court may grant leave for the application to proceed and make an order authorising the will. A valid will is created when it is in writing, signed by the registrar and sealed with the seal of the court.[168] The registrar retains the will.[169]

ii. Differences between States

Notwithstanding the model described above, there are some signficant differences between the states, several examples of which deserve mention.

First, unlike the other states, Tasmania has empowered its Guardianship and Administration Board to make a will on behalf of a mentally incapacitated person when there is no existing will.[170]

Second, unlike the other states, Western Australia (WA) does not permit the court to order a will for an incapacitated minor.[171]

Third, the states have adopted dissimilar language creating the test against which the proposed will, alteration or revocation must be measured when the person lacks testamentary capacity. In SA, the court must be satisfied that 'the proposed will, alteration or revocation would accurately reflect the likely intentions of the person'.[172] In Victoria, the court considers whether the will 'reflects what the intentions of the person would be likely to be, or what the intentions of the person might reasonably be expected to be'.[173] In the Australian Capital Territory (ACT),[174] New South Wales (NSW)[175] and Tasmania,[176] the test is whether 'the proposed will, alteration or revocation is, or is reasonably likely to be, one that would have been made by the person'. Queensland requires that the will 'is or may be a will ... that the person would make';[177] the Northern Territory refers to a will that 'is or might be one that would have been made by the proposed testator';[178] and WA obliges the court to authorise a will 'which could be made by the person concerned'.[179]

Fourth, most schemes are based on a two-tiered approach enabling courts to 'weed out' unmeritorious cases.[180] However, in practice it has been possible to combine the two proceedings because the information required for both overlaps. Accordingly, it was suggested that the process should be one stage not two[181] because the prospect of having the costs awarded against a claimant ought to be sufficient to deter an unmeritorious claimant.[182] Victoria has recently amended its legislation to reflect this recommendation, so that there is a single application process in that state.[183]

---

[167] Ibid, s 21(e).
[168] Ibid, s 24.
[169] Ibid, s 25.
[170] Wills Act 2008 (Tas), ss 29–41.
[171] Wills Act 1970 (WA), s 40(2)(b).
[172] Wills Act 1936 (SA), s 7(3)(b).
[173] Wills Act 1997 (Vic), s 21B(b).
[174] Wills Act 1968 (ACT), s16E (b).
[175] Succession Act 2006 (NSW), s 22(b).
[176] Wills Act 2008 (Tas), s 24(e).
[177] Succession Act 1981 (Qld), s 24(d).
[178] Wills Act (NT), s 21(b).
[179] Wills Act 1970 (WA), s 42(1)(b),
[180] Law Reform Committee, Parliament of Victoria (n 144) para 5A.21.
[181] Victorian Law Reform Commission, *Succession Laws Report* (August 2013) recom 4.
[182] Ibid, para 3.34.
[183] Wills Act 1997 (Vic), ss 21-22.

Finally, the extent to which the testator may participate in the proceedings is unclear in some states.[184] In NSW and the ACT the court may order that the testator must be separately represented,[185] ensuring that the testator's wishes and interests are taken into account. Victoria has recently amended its legislation to permit the court to order separate representation of the testator lacking testatmentary capacity.[186] Other states entitle the testator to appear and be heard at the hearings[187] or require the court to ensure that adequate steps have been taken to ensure that *all* persons with an interest in the application have been given representation,[188] so perhaps the representation of the testator is covered.

C. Comment

Generally speaking the most obvious feature in the Australian law of statutory wills is that the schemes are not uniform: they are merely similar. It is theoretically possible that in comparable circumstances a will could be authorised in one state and not authorised in another. In addition to the practical issues highlighted above, two matters have been the subject of judicial scrutiny.

i. A Connection with the Testator's Intention or Likely Intentions

One has been how the courts will determine whether the will is one that the testator would have made. Certainly, the courts have not uncritically adopted the test set out in *ReD(J)*[189] and the differences in statutory language have not been merely semantic. Judicial responses have been varied, complex and contradictory. Commentators have suggested that there are three separate language-based tests: the strict South Australian test, the Victorian test and the rest.[190] However, arguably, there have been five responses which have not necessarily been confined to one state jurisdiction and which have sometimes been overlapping. While it could be contended that these methods suggest fragmentation, it is also arguable that despite the different statutory language, courts are slowly evolving towards a purposive approach grounded in the language of the relevant state statute.

First, some courts[191] have accepted that in view of the statutory language, (and notwithstanding the methods adopted in other state jurisdictions), the court ought to make a substituted judgment in accordance with in *Re D(J)*[192] and in *Re C (A Patient)*.[193]

---

[184] N Crago, 'Reform of the Law of Wills' (1995) 25 WALR 255, 259.
[185] Succession Act 2006 (NSW), s 25; Wills Act 1968 (ACT), s 16H.
[186] Wills Act 1997 (Vic) s 21D.
[187] Wills Act 1935 (SA), s 7(a).
[188] Eg Succession Act 1981 (Qld), s 24(b).
[189] *Re D(J)* (n 51).
[190] Dal Pont and Mackie (n 135) paras 3.7–3.19.
[191] Eg *Re Keane: Mace v Malone (No 2)* [2012] 1 Qd R 319; [2011] QSC 49, [73–74]; *Re Matsis; Charalambous v Charalambous* (2012) 8 ASTLR 361; [2012] QSC 349 [28].
[192] *Re D(J)* (n 51).
[193] *Re C* (n 63).

Second, some courts have taken a literalistic appoach. This has been manifested in two connected ways. One has been that the courts have rejected[194] or ignored[195] the English cases on substituted judgment because the language of the former Mental Health Act 1983 and the local statutory provisions are different. The other is that the courts have carefully scrutinised the nature and extent of the legislative directive. For example, in the Victorian case, *Boulton v Sanders*[196] the court held that it was not sufficient that the testatrix would have probably preferred the will to intestacy or that the will was one of a number of possible wills which might reflect the testatrix's intentions. Rather, 'the requirement of accurate reflection demands a substantial degree of provision and exactitude about the "likely intentions"'.[197] In view of the original narrowness of the test, the legislation was amended to include a broadbrush and objective test of what the person's intentions are reasonably expected to be.[198] Nevertheless, it appears that a strict approach remains strong in Victoria.[199]

Third, some cases have manifested a purposive approach. The court has given priority to the broad thrust of the legislation, avoiding technical interpretations or the rejection of the approaches of other jurisdictions. Some of the cases have involved a person who never had testamentary capacity[200] and some have been decided in SA where a strict 'likely intentions' test applies.[201] Initially interpretative sources were derived from English cases decided under the Mental Health Act 1983,[202] but the net has widened.[203] For example, in *Griffin v Boardman*[204] White J was influenced by the decision of Lewison J in *Re P.*[205] Notwithstanding the difference between the South Australian 'likely intentions' test and the 'best interests' test under the MCA White J held that subjective intentions were not necessarily decisive in determining 'likely intentions'. The court could take into account concerns about how the person would be remembered after her death. On the facts, it was 'reasonable to suppose' that the person would not wish to be hurtful by depriving a caregiver of a share in the estate.[206]

Fourth, Palmer J in *Re Application of Fenwick*[207] established a structured contextual method (which can also be seen as purposive), allocating subjective and objective elements to different broad factual scenarios. He recommended that the court:

> [S]hould start 'with a clean slate': it must interpret the words of the section in the light of the problems and difficulties which the legislation seeks to remedy, bearing in mind that legislation of this kind should receive a benevolent construction.[208]

---

[194] *Re Fletcher; Ex p Papaleo* [2001] VSC 109 [20].
[195] *Re DH: Application by JE and SM* [2011] ACTSC 69.
[196] *Boulton v Sanders* (2004) 9 VLR 495, [2004] VSCA 112.
[197] Ibid, [112].
[198] *State Trustee Ltd v Do & Nguyen* [2011] VSC 45 [11]–[12]
[199] *Saunders v Pedemont* [2012] VSC 574 [88]–[90]; *cf* Rich (n 100) 214.
[200] Eg *Hoffman v Waters* (2007) 98 SASR 500; [2007] SASC 273; *Deecke v Deecke* [2009] QSC 65.
[201] Eg *RAK* [2009] SASC 288.
[202] *Monger v Taylor* [2000] VCA 304; *State Trustees Ltd v Hayden* (2002) 4 VR 229; [2002] VSC 98; *Hoffman v Waters* (n 202).
[203] *RAK* (n 201).
[204] *Griffin v Boardman* [2009] SASC 315 [53].
[205] *Re P* (n 87).
[206] *Griffin* (n 204) [54].
[207] *Re Application of Fenwick* (n 107).
[208] Ibid, [148].

Like judges in Victoria, Palmer J carefully construed the language of the NSW legislation, emphasising that it contained subjective and objective elements: the proposed will 'is or is reasonably likely to be' one made by the testator.[209] However, his recommendation differed from the purposive approach referred to above because he rejected *Re D(J)*[210] and *Re C (A Patient)*,[211] finding these cases artificial, illogical and unworkable.[212] Instead he identified three separate factual categories for which a statutory will could be ordered. Lost capacity was when the testator had had testamentary capacity, but later lost it.[213] The court would be concerned with the actual or reasonably likely subjective intention of the incapacitated person.[214] Nil capacity was where the testator never had testamentary capacity[215] and considerations would be entirely objective: is there a fairly good chance that a reasonable person faced with the circumstances of the testator would make such a will?[216] Pre-empted capacity cases were where a minor lost mental capacity at an age when he had formed relatonships and could have had a fairly good understanding of will-making.[217] To the extent that evidence of subjective intention was available, it would be evaluated; otherwise the matter would be determined objectively.[218] The decision has been highly influential in Australia.[219]

Finally in NSW, several decisions[220] have emphasised that the authorisation of a statutory will is connected to the inherent protective powers of the Supreme Court (as a superior court of record).[221] While the courts still relied on the statutory powers in the Succession Act 2006 (NSW), they added a further judicial principle or gloss to the statutory wills regime (which was not envisaged in the Uniform Succession Laws model).[222] For example, in *Re Will of Jane*,[223] Hallen AsJ held that the judicial power to authorise a statutory will was 'not a power of "substituted judgment"'.[224] Observing that 'Equally important is the overarching principle in relation to any decision made on behalf of an incapable person that it must be made in his, or her, best interests'.[225] It remains unclear whether this additional gloss will affect the interpretation of the judicial powers in the other states. Indeed, a related issue, whether it would be appropriate for a body solely exercising a protective jurisdiction to authorise statutory wills, was considered by the Law Reform Commission in

---

209 Ibid, [150]–[152].
210 *Re D(J)* (n 51).
211 *Re C* (n 63).
212 *Application of Fenwick* (n 107) [48]–[105].
213 Ibid, [154].
214 Ibid, [170].
215 Ibid, [171].
216 Ibid, [176].
217 Ibid, [177].
218 Ibid, [188].
219 Eg *Saunders v Pedemont* (n 199).
220 Eg *Application of Fenwick* (n 107); *AB v CB* [2009] NSWSC 680; *Secretary, Department of Family and Community Services v K* [2014] NSWSC 1065. The Fenwick case combined two otherwise separate and distinct applications in relation to Fenwick (who was a testator who had made a will in the past and had subsequently lost testamentary capacity) and Charles (a minor who had never had testamentary capacity.)
221 Powell (n 136) 75–76.
222 NSW Law Reform Commission (1998) (n 144) paras 5.12–5.45.
223 *Re Will of Jane* [2011] NSWSC 624.
224 Ibid, [98].
225 Ibid, [99].

Victoria.[226] The Commission queried whether the Victorian Civil and Administrative Tribunal (VCAT) which has expertise in dealing with persons with incapacity could have the power to authorise statutory wills.[227] It decided not to recommend juridictional change, inter alia, because the members of the VCAT did not have expertise in succession law.[228] However, the Commission did not appear to consider whether a 'best interests' test ought to be implemented.

ii. Is it Appropriate to Order the Will?

The other issue (which has arisen in recent times) is how to deal with the effect that the proposed will may have on the operation of other rights, proceedings or legislation. In addition to determining whether the will has a nexus with the deceased, the court must also determine whether it is appropriate[229] for the order to be made (for example, from a public policy perspective). However, what is reasonable or appropriate has not been defined in the legislation. In several cases, courts have grappled with the problem that the application for a statutory will has been prompted by considerations other than or in addition to meeting what would have been the mentally incapacitated testator's wishes. For example, a court refused to make an order for a statutory will where the effect and intent of the application for the proposed will was to ensure that the beneficiary would not inherit under the will, thereby defeating the claims of the beneficiary's creditors.[230] However, in another case,[231] the testatrix (when she had testamentary capacity) had made gifts in favour of her son and daughter-in-law under her will. Later, the son and daughter-in-law instituted divorce proceedings. As the testatrix no longer had testamentary capacity, her husband made an application for a codicil amending the will and excluding the daughter-in-law from inheriting under the will on the ground that the testatrix would have wanted her son's share of her estate to be protected from the divorce proceedings. The trial judge held that it was not appropriate to order the codicil because of the intent behind the application was asset protection.[232] However, the Queensland Court of Appeal upheld the appeal noting the primacy of the testatrix's interest in the application for the codicil and that it was highly likely that the testatrix would have rationally made the codicil without pressure.[233] Perhaps the difference in the cases lies in the view that, from a public policy perspective taking steps to avoid the payment of creditors is qualitatively different from merely protecting family assets in view of a future beneficiary's divorce proceedings.

V. CONCLUSION AND FUTURE CONSIDERATIONS

Initially Australia and England had a common heritage in relation to statutory wills because Australian law reformers adopted the idea of the statutory will from

---

[226] Victorian Law Reform Commission (n 181).
[227] Ibid, para 3.38.
[228] Ibid, para 3.39.
[229] Eg Succession Act 2006 (NSW), s 22(b).
[230] *Hausfeld v Hausfeld* [2012] 9 ASTLR 535; [2012] NSWSC 989.
[231] *Gau v Gav* [2014] QCA 308.
[232] Ibid, [35].
[233] Ibid, [57].

English law and were, to some extent, influenced by the English judgments before the implementation of the MCA. However, England and Australia have taken different paths. The English statutory wills provisions are embedded in a broad legislative and judicial scheme protecting people who suffer a mental disability and who are unable to make decisions for themselves. The major problem with the scheme is that there is insufficient consideration of the wills perspective. The legislation does not cover minors (including mentally incapacited minors) and does not provide specific guidance about the significance (if any) of the concept of testamentary capacity, the relevance of family provision claims or the existence of earlier wills.

The Australian statutory wills provisions are largely located in state legislation concerned with the law of succession. The schemes' weaknesses are that there is a lack of uniformity in key criteria. Therefore, the Uniform Succession Laws project's goal of legislative uniformity is undermined with the result that practical decision-making is not necessarily informed by the same framework, criteria and legal reasoning. Cases having similar facts could have different outcomes in various states.

It is anticipated that in addition to these respective weaknesses, both jurisdictions may have to reconsider the statutory wills legislation in view of the UN Convention on the Rights of Persons with Disabilities (the Convention) to which they are both signatories.[234] While the Law Commission evaluated UN documents pre-dating the Convention,[235] the Australian law reformers do not appear to have considered the impact of any international instruments.[236] Although it is probably too early to determine the precise extent of the Convention's effect, the spirit and the text of the Convention are important in three ways. First, the Convention was framed in the context of an increasing awareness of the need for asymmetrical approaches to equality.[237] Therefore, in order to create equality of opportunity for persons with disabilities, it may be necessary to provide additional or different sources of support, including 'reasonable accommodation' to enable the equal exercise of rights.[238] Second, article 12(2) of the Convention requires signatories to 'recognise that persons with disabilities enjoy legal capacity'[239] and accordingly 'take appropriate measures to provide access ... to the support they may require in exercising their legal capacity'.[240] Third, the Convention also states, inter alia, that such 'measures relating to the exercise of legal capacity respect the rights, will and preferences of the person' and 'are proportional and tailored to the person's circumstances'.[241] Although there is little case law about the application of the Convention to succession law, there is one Australian case which suggests that in the future judges may consider the impact of the Convention in succession law. In *Nicholson v Knaggs*,[242]

---

[234] www.un.org/disabilities/countries.asp?navid=12&pid=166. The United Kingdom ratified on 8 June 2009. Australia ratified on 17 July 2008.
[235] Law Commission (n 68) para 2-40.
[236] Eg Victorian Law Reform Commission (n 183); *cf Nicholson v Knaggs* [2009] VSC 64 [58]–[75].
[237] OM Arnardóttir, 'A Future of Multidimensional Disadvantage Equality' in OM Arnardóttir and G Quinn, *The UN Convention on the Rights of Persons with Disabilities* (Leiden, Martinus Nijhoff, 2009) 41, 59–60, 64.
[238] art 2.
[239] art 12(2).
[240] art 12(3).
[241] art 12(4).
[242] *Nicholson v Knaggs* (n 236).

a Victorian case concerned with the doctrine of testamentary undue influence, Vickery J took into account the Convention and pointed out:

> The effect of article 12(2) in the present context is to provide for an obligation on Australia to recognise that persons with disabilities enjoy the exercise of the right to freedom of testamentary disposition on an equal basis with all other persons.[243]

Viewed from the perspective of the Convention and the comment of Vickery J, it is arguable that the statutory wills regimes are a positive start towards an antidiscriminatory law of wills. Prior to the implementation of the statutory wills regimes, a mentally incapacitated person could not be assisted to make, revoke or amend a will. The law was effectively discriminatory because the mentally incapacitated person had no choice; and there was no third course of action available between traditional will-making and intestacy.

The impetus for statutory wills was the interests of third parties (particularly relatives) in a defensible distribution of the mentally incapacitated person's assets. However, it is arguable that the availability of statutory wills has had the largely unintended effect of recognising and reframing the legal capacity of mentally incapacitated persons and providing them with an avenue for the exercise of that legal capacity. The substituted judgment doctrine in *Ex p Whitbread, Re D(J)* and the various subsequent legislative forms reflect a recognition of the testator's proprietary interests and wishes. The 'best interests' test arguably goes further—it places the testator in the centre of deliberations. Judges have sometimes struggled to explain why the making of a will on behalf of a mentally incapacitated testator is in that person's 'best interest', but perhaps in view of the Convention, the answer is clear and profound. It is in that person's interest to have a third course of action available—thereby ensuring that he is not a second class citizen who does not have a tailor-made, current and logical will operative at the date of his death.

---

[243] Ibid, [75].

9

Testamentary Freedom: Mutual Wills Might Let You Down

SIÔN HUDSON AND BRIAN SLOAN*

I. INTRODUCTION

MUTUAL WILLS (GIVING rise to a binding arrangement about testamentary dispositions to which equity might give effect) are rarely made and carry with them considerable doctrinal and practical difficulties.[1] Indeed, Kerridge has said that 'It is rarely sensible for persons to make mutual wills'.[2] Cases involving mutual wills nevertheless continue to be reported, and Griffiths claims that such cases 'almost always raise issues of convoluted law for the academic lawyer and significant financial consequences for the practitioner and his client'.[3] In Harpum's view, they 'create conceptual difficulties that are wholly disproportionate to their practical unimportance',[4] and it seems extraordinarily optimistic for Mitchell to have suggested in 1951 that 'There is ... little dispute about the nature of the rights involved, or about the conditions necessary to the existence of the agreement'.[5]

This chapter considers the potential impact of mutual wills in the increasingly important context of informal care, using Dr Sloan's previous work on informal carers in private law as its backdrop.[6] It begins by outlining the mutual wills doctrine focusing on English Law, before evaluating the limitations that mutual wills might place on a testator's ability to leave property to a carer who has provided essential support to the survivor after one party to a mutual wills arrangement has died. The chapter then goes on to explore the restrictions that the doctrine can place on the carer's ability to bring claims against the survivor's estate, whether framed in proprietary estoppel or under family provision legislation, highlighting the fact that

---

* Partner, Miller Sands Solicitors, Cambridge; College Lecturer and Fellow in Law, Robinson College, Cambridge. We are grateful to the conference attendees and the anonymous referee for their comments on earlier versions of this chapter.

[1] See, eg M Pawlowski and J Brown, 'Problems with Mutual Wills—A Study of Probate Practice' [2012] *Conveyancer and Property Lawyer* 467.

[2] R Kerridge, *Parry and Kerridge: The Law of Succession*, 12th edn (London, Sweet & Maxwell, 2009) para 6–41.

[3] GLlH Griffiths, 'At Best Inconvenient and at Worst Little Short of Disastrous? Recent Considerations on Mutual Wills' [2011] *Conveyancer and Property Lawyer* 511, 514.

[4] C Harpum, 'The Uses and Abuses of Constructive Trusts: The Experience of England and Wales' (1997) 1 *Edinburgh Law Review* 437, 442.

[5] JDB Mitchell, 'Some Aspects of Mutual Wills' (1951) 14 *MLR* 136, 136.

[6] See, generally, B Sloan, *Informal Carers and Private Law* (Oxford, Hart Publishing, 2013).

the mutual wills doctrine cannot be understood solely as a fetter on testamentary or donative freedom and has a strong link to the general normative difficulties surrounding testamentary contracts. In doing so, the chapter compares the effect of the mutual wills doctrine, and the constructive trust that can be generated by it, with the minimum equity-based remedial approach of proprietary estoppel. It highlights the advantages of the minimum equity-style approach as compared to the rigidity of the courts' approach to mutual wills, albeit with an awareness of the perceived disadvantages of judicial discretion in property law.

The chapter argues that the current law on mutual will agreements unjustly prioritises the wishes of the first party to die and the interests of those intended to benefit under the arrangement, prejudicing the testamentary and donative freedom of the second to die (referred to in this chapter as the 'survivor'), and the potential claims of her carers and others. Its thesis is advanced in the light of the fact that carers often suffer significant health and financial disadvantages as a result of the duties they have undertaken and are unlikely to be in the contemplation of the parties when the mutual wills arrangement is drawn up.

II. THE MUTUAL WILLS DOCTRINE

The mutual wills doctrine can apply where two people (often a married couple) agree not to revoke (or not to vary in a particular respect) their wills even after the first death in the relationship. The aim of the arrangement might be to ensure that the parties' children from previous relationships ultimately benefit from their estates after the survivor has taken a benefit from the first to die and then dies herself, without having to rely on the survivor voluntarily making provision for children who are not her own. It has been said that the doctrine aims to 'frustrate' (rather than prevent) the unconscionable revocation of a will by the survivor,[7] thus preventing what has been described as a 'blatant fraud' from being perpetrated.[8] The doctrine was seemingly established in English Law in the eighteenth-century case of *Dufour v Pereira*,[9] a decision influenced by existing concepts in civil law jurisdictions.[10] In the recent case of *Fry v Densham Smith*, Mummery LJ described the doctrine as 'anomalous' because in situations where it applies 'absolute beneficial testamentary dispositions ... do not take effect in accordance with their terms'.[11] Croucher describes it as a 'doctrine of the "older and wiser"',[12] providing 'a kind of insurance against the fickleness of changing affections',[13] though as we hope to make clear it is also a doctrine of undesirable entrenchment.

---

[7] Kerridge, *Parry and Kerridge, The Law of Succession* (n 2) para 6-38.

[8] AJ Oakley, *Parker and Mellows: The Modern Law of Trusts*, 9th edn (London, Sweet & Maxell, 2008) para 10-314.

[9] *Dufour v Pereira* 1 Dick 419; Hargrave, *Juridical Arguments and Collections*, vol 2.

[10] R Croucher, 'Mutual Wills: Contemporary Reflections on an Old Doctrine' (2005) 29 *Melbourne University Law Review* 390; M Lupoi, 'Trust and Confidence' (2009) 125 *LQR* 253, 275–78.

[11] *Fry v Densham-Smith* [2010] EWCA Civ 1410, [2011] WTLR 387 [30]. See also *Re Goodchild (decd)* [1997] 1 WLR 1216 (CA) 1230 (Morritt LJ).

[12] Croucher, 'Mutual Wills: Contemporary Reflections on an Old Doctrine' (n 10) 392. This observation realistically makes sense only if it refers to the age of the mutual wills themselves.

[13] Ibid, 393.

The doctrine requires an arrangement about testamentary dispositions by the parties, an agreement that the arrangement be binding, and an event triggering that binding force. It is clear that there must be two separate agreements: an agreement as to the disposal of at least some of the parties' property on death (pursuant to which a will is made,[14] although Hughes has argued that the survivor need not actually have made the will in order for the doctrine to apply),[15] and an agreement that the survivor should be bound by the first arrangement. This second agreement has been the subject of much analysis. It must amount to a binding contract (with the mutual execution of the wills apparently constituting sufficient consideration)[16] rather than a mere 'honourable engagement'.[17] This requirement apparently persists in England and Wales even if it is thought by some to be contestable,[18] and indeed Rimer J went so far as to say in *Birch v Curtis* that the doctrine was not based on mere inequity or a benefit unmatched by a burden (and indeed a direct benefit for the survivor is unnecessary),[19] but rather it should be understood as a means of enforcing a contract.[20] This is consistent with the leading Australian case of *Birmingham v Renfrew*,[21] which has been influential in English Law.[22] A reason given for requiring a contract is that the doctrine is able to affect all the property of the survivor and not just that derived from the first to die. While the core scenario might be thought to be one where the agreement relates to property so derived and the wills of the two parties are in substantially similar terms, Oakley argued that 'there seems to be no reason in principle why the doctrine ... should not also extend to an agreement that, if A leaves property to B, B will leave that property and other property of his own on to C'.[23]

The second agreement (that the arrangement should bind the survivor) need not be contained in the will itself, but the evidential requirements are relatively strict. The mere fact that the parties simultaneously made substantially identical wills does not mean that they are mutual wills, and in *Birch v Curtis* Rimer J refused to imply into an agreement that wills should be made on particular terms a further agreement that they should not be revoked, which is consistent with the much older decision in *Re Oldham (decd)*.[24] The evidence of the relevant agreements must be 'clear and satisfactory', according to *Re Cleaver (decd)*.[25] The rigorous approach to the evidence of the parties might mitigate the reach of the doctrine. That said, it is striking

---

[14] The making of mutual wills in such circumstances severs a joint tenancy: *Re Heys (decd)* [1914] P 192.

[15] R Hughes, 'Mutual Wills' [2011] *Private Client Business* 131, 132.

[16] *Re Dale (decd)* [1994] Ch 31, 38 (Morritt J).

[17] *Re Goodchild* (n 11) 1225 (Leggatt LJ). See J Stevens, 'Avoiding Disinheritance' (1996) 146 *New Law Journal* 961 for criticism. See also, eg *Baird v Smee* [2000] NSWCA 253; *Pridham v Pridham* [2010] SASC 204, but *cf* Wills Act 2007 (NZ), s 30, referring merely to promises.

[18] P Luxton, '*Walters v Olin [sic]*: Uncertainty of Subject Matter—An Insoluble Problem in Mutual Wills?' [2009] *Conveyancer and Property Lawyer* 498, 502; J Cassidy, *Mutual Wills* (Sydney, Federation Place, 2000), cited in Croucher, 'Mutual Wills: Contemporary Reflections on an Old Doctrine' (n 10) 407.

[19] *Re Dale* (n 16).

[20] *Birch v Curtis* [2002] EWHC 1158 (Ch), [2002] 2 FLR 847 [60]. See also, eg AH Brierly, 'Mutual Wills—Blackpool Illuminations' (1995) 58 *MLR* 95, 97.

[21] *Birmingham v Renfrew* (1937) 57 CLR 666 (HCA).

[22] See, eg *Olins v Walters* [2008] EWCA Civ 782, [2009] 2 WLR 1 [2] (Mummery LJ).

[23] Oakley, Parker and Mellows, *The Modern Law of Trusts* (n 8) para 10-319.

[24] *Re Oldham (decd)* [1925] 1 Ch 75.

[25] *Re Cleaver (decd)* [1981] 1 WLR 399 (Ch) 947 (Nourse J).

that in the Court of Appeal decision in *Fry v Densham-Smith* Mummery LJ held that it was open to the judge to find that the doctrine was applicable even though he admitted 'Direct evidence is not available on the two critical points' of the claim that mutual wills existed, namely the agreement and (perhaps more surprisingly) the actual execution of a mutual will by the survivor.[26] Hughes opines that the law has thus moved on from *Birch v Curtis*.[27]

The final requirement is an event rendering the arrangement binding. It was for some time unclear when mutual wills became binding, but Kerridge suggests that since the survivor need not receive any benefit under the first will to come into effect, 'the binding event *must* be the death of the first party'.[28] In *Carvel Foundation v Carvel*, Lewison J held that the relevant trust generated by the doctrine (discussed further below) 'does not arise under the will of the surviving testator', but 'arises out of the agreement between the two testators not to revoke their wills [and] arises when the first of the two dies without having revoked his will'.[29] This meant that the ultimate beneficiary under the mutual wills arrangement in the case at hand was not technically a beneficiary under the will of the survivor, and indeed it was held in the 1930 case of *Re Hagger (decd)* that there is no lapse when the intended beneficiary dies after the first testator but before the survivor.[30] Logically the beneficiary's interest in the trust property began on the death of the first testator and so would form part of his estate. Analogously, it is clear from *Re Green (decd)* that the mutual wills doctrine would not be defeated by the survivor's re-marriage,[31] despite the fact that a re-marriage[32] (or indeed an entry into a civil partnership)[33] would ordinarily revoke the survivor's *will*.

If the arrangement is not binding until the death of the first party, the wills remain in substance revocable before then. While notice of such revocation is in principle required,[34] in *Stone v Hoskins* it was held that the first to die can effectively give sufficient notice by dying having left a later will that is not consistent with the arrangement,[35] since 'The only object of notice is to enable the other party to the bargain to alter his or her will also, but the survivor … is not in any way prejudiced' by the departure.[36] If this is true, the notice requirement is insubstantial and there may still be difficult issues of contract law to resolve, although Mitchell suggests, following *Stone v Hoskins*, that there would be no contractual claim by the survivor where the first testator dies having revoked the will subject to the arrangement.[37] Luxton describes a mutual wills arrangement as an 'unusual contract' because (inter alia) it

---

[26] *Fry v Densham-Smith* (n 11) [32]. See Griffiths, 'At Best Inconvenient and at Worst Little Short of Disastrous? Recent Considerations on Mutual Wills' (n 3) and Hughes, 'Mutual Wills' (n 15).

[27] Hughes, 'Mutual Wills' (n 15) 134.

[28] Kerridge, *Parry and Kerridge, The Law of Succession* (n 2) para 6-36.

[29] *Carvel Foundation v Carvel* [2007] EWHC 1314 (Ch), [2008] Ch 395 [28].

[30] *Re Hagger (decd)* [1930] Ch 190. *Cf* TG Youdan, 'The Mutual Wills Doctrine' (1979) 29 *University of Toronto Law Journal* 390, 418–19.

[31] *Re Green* [1951] Ch 148.

[32] Wills Act 1837, s 18.

[33] Ibid, s 18B.

[34] *Dufour v Pereira* (n 9).

[35] *Stone v Hoskins* [1905] P 194. See Croucher, 'Mutual Wills: Contemporary Reflections on an Old Doctrine' (n 10) 395–402 for a general discussion of notice.

[36] *Stone* (n 35) 197 (Sir Gorrell Barnes).

[37] Mitchell, 'Some Aspects of Mutual Wills' (n 5) 137.

can be terminated by notice without breach.[38] It is also conceivable that, in a case where the survivor does not take a benefit under the arrangement, he could remain unaware that the first testator had breached the agreement and have no reason (or perhaps opportunity) to alter his own will before he dies. In such circumstances, Oakley contemplated the possibility of a successful claim for damages by the survivor's estate against the estate of the first to die for the value of the property that should have been left pursuant to the agreement.[39]

If the three requirements for the mutual wills doctrine are satisfied, equity imposes a (possibly remedial)[40] constructive trust[41] over the property covered by the mutual wills when the 'binding event', that is the first death, occurs.[42] The trust does not prevent the revocation of the survivor's will, and indeed it has been said that 'English law knows of no such thing as an irrevocable will',[43] but the executors take the survivor's property subject to the trust. The property bound depends upon the construction of the parties' arrangement, though Lowe and Douglas claimed that: 'it is still not settled whether any property acquired by the testator after the first party's death is also subject to the trust or whether this will attach only to the property which he has at that time'.[44]

Mitchell saw a conflict between *Re Hagger* and *Re Oldham* on this point, though preferred the view that where the scope of the trust is not defined by the agreement it does include subsequently acquired property (subject to an ability to deal with income).[45] Martin is particularly critical, however, of any suggestion that all of the survivor's property (including subsequently acquired property) could be subject to the trust in the absence of an express agreement, since then 'the consequences of the doctrine could be draconian for the survivor; for example if he acquires new dependants after the death of the first testator; similarly if the agreed beneficiary acquires a fortune elsewhere or is guilty of misconduct'.[46]

A 'floating trust'[47] or 'floating obligation'[48] analysis has historically been adopted such that the trust crystallises only on the survivor's death. This would allow the survivor to make use of any property left to him by virtue of the arrangement, but not to make *inter vivos* dispositions deliberately designed to defeat the arrangement.[49]

---

[38] Luxton, '*Walters v Olin [sic]*: Uncertainty of Subject Matter—An Insoluble Problem in Mutual Wills?' (n 18) 502.

[39] Oakley, Parker and Mellows, *The Modern Law of Trusts* (n 8) para 10-323.

[40] Croucher, 'Mutual Wills: Contemporary Reflections on an Old Doctrine' (n 10) 405. *Cf* Luxton, '*Walters v Olin [sic]*: Uncertainty of Subject Matter—An Insoluble Problem in Mutual Wills?' (n 18) 498–99.

[41] G Virgo, *The Principles of Equity and Trusts* (Oxford, Oxford University Press, 2012) 307 points out that there could be an express trust depending on the circumstances. *Cf* Oakley, *Parker and Mellows: The Modern Law of Trusts* (n 8) para 10-332.

[42] It is also possible that there could be a claim under the Contracts (Rights of Third Parties) Act 1999.

[43] N Lowe and G Douglas, *Bromley's Family Law*, 10th edn (Oxford, Oxford University Press, 2007) 1091. See, eg *Re Heys* (n 14).

[44] Lowe and Douglas, *Bromley's Family* Law (n 43) 1093.

[45] Mitchell, 'Some Aspects of Mutual Wills' (n 5) 139–40.

[46] J Martin, *Hanbury and Martin: Modern Equity*, 19th edn (London, Sweet & Maxell, 2012) para 12-033.

[47] See *Ottaway v Norman* [1972] Ch 698 in the context of secret trusts.

[48] *Birmingham v Renfrew* (n 21) 689 (Dixon J), approved in Re Cleaver (n 25). For further discussion, see *Fazari as Executrix of the Estate of Domenico Antonio Cosentino (decd) v Cosentino* [2010] WASC 40.

[49] *Birmingham* (n 21) 689. See CJ Davis, 'Floating Rights' [2002] *CLJ* 423, 427–31; 452–53 for discussion.

It has been recognised that this causes severe problems with certainty of subject matter,[50] even if Nourse J in *Re Cleaver* both emphasised that such certainty was essential and denied that the 'floating trust' approach could cause any difficulty with it.[51] In *Healey v Brown*, Deputy Judge David Donaldson considered obiter that 'where the fiduciary duty is breached by such a voluntary disposition *inter vivos* of the property in question, the "crystallisation" of the floating obligation must occur at the moment of that disposition'.[52] He also gave some thought to what might or might not be a permissible dealing with the property, and opined that it would have been permissible had the survivor sold the relevant property to fund nursing home care. On the facts of the case, however, the survivor had transferred the property (a flat) to the joint names of himself and his son as joint tenants, such that the son ultimately prima facie took the whole of the property beneficially by survivorship. This disposition, he held, 'could scarcely run more directly and fully counter to the intention of the mutual will compact that the flat should pass to his deceased … wife['s] niece on his own death'.[53] The mutual wills claim per se ultimately failed due to non-compliance with formality requirements.

Olins v Walters, however, suggests that the trust might crystallise immediately on the first death.[54] While Luxton is of the view that the implications of that suggestion were not properly considered,[55] Mummery LJ specifically opined that:

> [T]he trust is immediately binding on [the survivor] in relation to the deceased's property left to him on the basis of the contract [and] is not postponed to take effect only after the death of [the defendant] when the property, or what may be left of it, comes into the hands of his personal representatives.[56]

Olins was an unusual case in that the survivor was still alive (and disputing the existence of the relevant arrangement, albeit unsuccessfully) at the time of the judgment. Virgo argues that the immediate trust, 'possibly coupled with a power to benefit from the property', is the preferable analysis.[57] Writing with Davies, he notes that the death of the third party beneficiary would not defeat the trust, unlike what they perceived to be the situation with the floating trust analysis.[58] Martin emphasises that any 'duty not to dissipate the assets in the survivor's lifetime will be unenforceable if the beneficiary does not discover his rights until the survivor's death',[59] but that if the obligation is not to make a testamentary disposition, 'the difficulties are all the greater; for the trust property would be indefinite until his death'.[60]

---

[50] See, eg Luxton, '*Walters v Olin [sic]*: Uncertainty of Subject Matter—An Insoluble Problem in Mutual Wills?' (n 18).

[51] *Re Cleaver* (n 25) 947.

[52] *Healey v Brown* [2002] WTLR 849 [13].

[53] Ibid, [14].

[54] *Olins v Walters* (n 22).

[55] Luxton, '*Walters v Olin [sic]*: Uncertainty of Subject Matter—An Insoluble Problem in Mutual Wills?' (n 18) 503–04.

[56] *Olins v Walters* (n 22) [42].

[57] Virgo, *The Principles of Equity and Trusts* (n 41). This appears to have been accepted in *Fry v Densham-Smith* (n 11).

[58] PS Davies and G Virgo, *Equity and Trusts: Text, Cases and Materials* (Oxford, Oxford University Press, 2013) 342.

[59] Martin, *Hanbury and Martin: Modern Equity* (n 46) para 12-031.

[60] Ibid, para 12-032.

Whatever the precise features of the mutual wills doctrine, the basic explanation for its existence seems clear enough. On Gardner's reliance-based analysis (which he applies to constructive trusts in general), where 'X (the first decedent) transfers the property to Y (the survivor) in reliance on Y's undertaking to in turn bequeath the property to Z (the third person)', he justifies the doctrine on the basis that 'X thus loses the opportunity to provide for Z as he intended' and 'The constructive trust over the relevant property in Y's hands corrects that loss'.[61] It could be argued that no unconscionability truly arises until Y purports to act inconsistently with the arrangement, but it seems that equity effectively looks on as done that which ought to be done and recognises the trust at the point where X is unable to adjust his testamentary dispositions. Importantly, Gardner also accounts for cases where Y does not benefit from the will on X's death, which also fall within the doctrine following *Re Dale (decd).*[62] Gardner explains the application of the doctrine in cases where X makes a direct bequest to Z alongside an agreement that Y will also do so on the basis that X 'loses the opportunity to adjust his own bequest so as to arrive at, or at least closer to, the overall position for Z that he intended, or to extract a more effective ... engagement from Y', and the constructive trust corrects that loss even though the property has been in Y's hands all along.[63] As will become clear, however, the existence of the doctrine can prevent a response to other forms of unconscionability, both in a technical and in a broader sense.

III. THE INFORMAL CARE SCENARIO

The world's population is ageing, and in the United Kingdom, 23 per cent of the population is projected to be aged 65 or older by 2035, while only 18 per cent will be under 16 by then.[64] The demand for formal state-provided social care is projected to increase, and while reform is being undertaken to attempt to make the system fit for purpose,[65] social care recipients will have to contribute a significant amount to the cost of their care needs.[66] The mutual wills doctrine has the potential to prejudice their ability to do so, or at least the ability of a local authority to recover care costs after their deaths.[67]

Even in the context of a reformed *formal* social care system, however, it seems inevitable that society will continue to rely on the considerable efforts of the *informal* carer, who provides care in the absence of a contractual or other legal duty to

---

[61] S Gardner, 'Reliance-based Constructive Trusts' in C Mitchell (ed), *Constructive and Resulting Trusts* (Oxford, Hart Publishing, 2010) 71.

[62] *Re Dale* (n 16).

[63] Gardner, 'Reliance-based Constructive Trusts' (n 61) 75.

[64] Office for National Statistics, 'Older People's Day 2011' (2011) 1.

[65] Care Act 2014.

[66] See, eg the discussion in B Sloan, 'Informal Care and Private Law: Governance or a Failure Thereof?' (2015) 1 *Canadian Journal of Comparative and Contemporary Law* 275.

[67] *Cf* the remarks in *Healey v Brown* (n 52) on this issue, discussed above. Mutual wills could be used as a means of attempted avoidance as regards this and other forms of liability (see also the discussion of family provision below), though *cf* Care Act 2014, s 70, which is due effectively to replace Health and Social Services and Social Security Adjudications Act 1983, s 21.

do so.[68] The 2011 census data indicate that there are 5.8 million informal carers in England and Wales,[69] as compared to the 5.2 million recorded by the 2001 census.[70] Meanwhile, the representative organisation Carers UK estimates that 60 per cent of people will become a carer at some point in their lives.[71] Such carers often suffer considerable financial and health-related disadvantages as a result of the responsibilities that they undertake,[72] and Dr Sloan has advocated a rationalisation and an expansion of the role that private law can play in supporting them.[73]

The potentially detrimental impact that the doctrine of mutual wills can have on carers is illustrated by the relatively modern case of *Charles v Fraser*.[74] It concerned the mutual wills of two sisters, Mabel and Ethel, who lived together after the deaths of their respective husbands. Judge Jonathan Gaunt held that there was:

> [A]pparently considerable and consistent evidence from close friends and relatives of the sisters that the [relevant] Wills had been made subject to an agreement between the sisters and that it was part of that agreement that the gifts on the death of the survivor were not to be changed.[75]

The wills were made in 1991 and Mabel died in 1995. In 2003, in an incident that the judge described as 'rather puzzling' in the light of her frequent discussion of the agreement she made with Mabel,[76] Ethel altered her will. Two of the new beneficiaries were neighbours who provided regular assistance to her, particularly after she broke her ankle in an accident. Judge Gaunt considered that 'It was no doubt because of these various kindnesses that Ethel wanted to include both Jill Fraser and John Rose [the neighbours] in her will in 2003'.[77] She then changed her will again in 2006, purporting to leave her entire estate to Jill Fraser, seemingly with the exception of a £10,000 legacy for a member of staff from a caring agency. Ethel died later that year and probate of her 2006 will was granted, though Mrs Fraser's counsel conceded that by the time of that will Ethel 'had become confused and ... her memory was failing her'.[78]

The judge held that 'The weight of the evidence that there had been an agreement and that part of it was that the wills were not to be changed was such that the Court would need strong grounds for rejecting it'.[79] He explained the 2003 will on the

---

[68] See, eg J Herring, *Caring and the Law* (Oxford, Hart Publishing, 2013) ch 2 for a discussion of the difficulties relating to definitions in this context.

[69] Office for National Statistics, 'More than 1 in 10 Providing Unpaid Care as Numbers Rise to 5.8 Million' (2013).

[70] Office for National Statistics, 'Focus on Health' (2004) 10.

[71] Carers UK, 'Facts about Carers 2012' (London, 2012) 2.

[72] See, eg Sloan, *Informal Carers and Private Law* (n 6) 16.

[73] See, generally, ibid.

[74] *Charles v Fraser* [2010] EWHC 2154 (Ch), [2010] WTLR 1489.

[75] Ibid, [27].

[76] Ibid, [38] (Judge Jonathan Gaunt).

[77] Ibid, [47].

[78] Ibid, [62].

[79] Ibid, [68] (Judge Jonathan Gaunt).

basis of Ethel 'having taken the view that it would be alright if she simply changed her gifts and not Mabel's', and that she

> [H]ad either forgotten, or perhaps no longer appreciated, the full force and effect of the agreement which she had made or felt that she was not violating the spirit of the agreement and that it was alright to change 'her part'.[80]

He rejected the suggestion that the agreement had related to only part of the sisters' 1991 wills, and drew his conclusions in spite of 'the inherent improbability of a testator being prepared to give up the possibility of changing his or her will in the future, whatever the change of circumstances'.[81] Jill Fraser and John Rose were thus unable to benefit from Ethel's estate.

It is true that there was very strong evidence of an agreement in *Charles*, that Ethel's neighbours had not done as much for her as other carers have done in other private law cases,[82] and that there was much cause to doubt the validity of her 2006 will. The case nevertheless highlights the general problem that the doctrine can cause in inflexibly preventing a testator from reacting to new circumstances long after the other party to the mutual wills arrangement has died.

We now turn to the interaction between the mutual wills doctrine, and its contractual basis, with a third party carer's apparent entitlement to, or potential claims against, the estate of the surviving party.

A. Testamentary Freedom and Practical Problems

The most basic criticism to be levelled at the inflexibility of the mutual wills doctrine in the context of care, demonstrated by *Charles* itself, is that it thwarts a care recipient who appreciates a form of moral 'obligation' (or who simply has a desire) to reward or compensate a carer by changing her will to include a gift to that carer after the first death in the mutual wills arrangement.[83] It is interesting, however, that in the Australian case of *Barns v Barns* (discussed further below)[84] the mutual wills at issue were given effect by the deceased and his wife precisely in order to (attempt to) *ensure* that their son, who had worked on their farm, should receive their assets. Although Cassidy sets out a number of circumstances where mutual wills may be appropriate,[85] a survivor's circumstances may change so significantly after the first death that the mutual will agreement is no longer appropriate for their wishes and their family.[86]

---

[80] Ibid, [70] (Judge Jonathan Gaunt).

[81] Ibid, [64] (Judge Jonathan Gaunt).

[82] See, eg *Jennings v Rice* [2002] EWCA Civ 159, [2003] 1 FCR 501; *Campbell v Griffin* [2001] EWCA Civ 990, [2001] WTLR 981.

[83] See JC Tate, 'Caregiving and the Case for Testamentary Freedom' (2008) 42 *University of California Davis Law Review* 129 for a defence of freedom of testation precisely on the basis that it enables care recipients to reward caring family members.

[84] *Barns v Barns* [2003] HCA 9, (2003) 214 CLR 169.

[85] J Cassidy, 'Exploring the Benefits and Pitfalls of Using Mutual Wills' (2005) 10 *Deakin Law Review* 121, 123–24.

[86] Pawlowski and Brown, 'Problems with Mutual Wills—A Study of Probate Practice' (n 1) 477 and Martin, *Hanbury and Martin: Modern Equity* (n 46) para 12-033.

As already stated,[87] the fact that the testator had previously entered into a mutual will arrangement does not render her will irrevocable. Consequently, a testator who has not perhaps fully appreciated the impact of the mutual will is not literally prevented from executing a new will contrary to the terms of the mutual will arrangement.

Indeed, on a practical level, it is likely that the will drafter is unaware of the mutual will, which may well have been drawn up and crystallised decades previously on the death of the first to die, such that the testator appears to have the usual measure of testamentary freedom. On the assumption that the new will is validly executed, it is the only will that is capable of being proved. The situation is likely to be further complicated if the mutual will is not discovered until the estate has already been administered and distributed according to the last will, and it may never be discovered if the ultimate beneficiary is not aware of the agreement.[88] In such circumstances, the supposed beneficiary under the later will will hold the property under the constructive trust for the benefit of the beneficiary under the mutual wills arrangement.[89] The comparative rarity of a mutual wills arrangement means that most practitioners would not think to raise the issue with a testator and, in any case, the testator may not understand the significance of the agreement that may have taken place decades earlier. If the same solicitor, or the same firm, were responsible for the original arrangement it is arguable that they should be expected to be aware of it, but in these times of cost- and service-conscious clients, the concept of the family solicitor for life is somewhat unrealistic.[90] In their 2012 study of probate practitioners, Pawlowski and Brown found that the favoured approaches to protecting beneficiaries who might lose out if a survivor changes her will is by using a life interest trust in the will of the first to die, or simply to make direct gifts on the first death.[91]

Where the mutual wills doctrine is applicable, any new will deals only with the testator's property at death which is not already subject to the constructive trust that arose on the death of the first to die. If the gift to a carer falls outside that property, then it will stand, but inevitably if the testator has not appreciated the limited testamentary freedom that she has at the time the new will is drawn up, the gift will adeem.

Because of the strict contractual nature of the mutual wills doctrine, the carer is very probably left with nothing if his apparent entitlement in the estate relates entirely to property subject to the mutual wills arrangement. This is despite the fact that he may have incurred a vast detriment in caring for the deceased. As will become clear, we would advocate a means by which the interests of such a carer can be balanced with those of the mutual will beneficiary.

B. Proprietary Estoppel

Mutual wills also cause problems when a carer brings a claim against the estate if he has not been (adequately) included in the will. With the present form of the mutual

---

[87] Lowe and Douglas, *Bromley's Family Law* (n 43) 1091. See, eg *Re Heys* (n 14).
[88] Pawlowski and Brown, 'Problems with Mutual Wills—A Study of Probate Practice' (n 1) 477.
[89] *Charles v Fraser* (n 74).
[90] Pawlowski and Brown, 'Problems with Mutual Wills—A Study of Probate Practice' (n 1) 481.
[91] Ibid, 469.

wills doctrine, the constructive trust would have already arisen (and may have crystallised if Mummery LJ's view in *Olins v Walters* is followed) at the time of the first death, and it seems that a carer bringing a proprietary estoppel claim (for example) might well have difficulty in arguing that the property subject to the trust is available to satisfy his estoppel equity, regardless of the court's view of how deserving he is of a remedy.

Proprietary estoppel is a property law doctrine of which Gardner has claimed that 'There is no definition ... that is both comprehensive and uncontroversial',[92] though its elements must be outlined before its relationship with the mutual wills doctrine can be considered. The Law Commission has said that an estoppel claim arises where:

> The owner of land, A, in some way leads or allows the claimant, B, to believe that he has or can expect some kind of right or interest over A's land. To A's knowledge, B acts to his detriment in that belief. A then refuses B the anticipated right or interest in circumstances that make that refusal unconscionable.[93]

Lord Walker in *Thorner v Major*,[94] the leading House of Lords authority on proprietary estoppel, distilled the salient features as a representation made with reliance on it by the claimant and consequential detriment suffered by that claimant. The subject matter of an estoppel claim usually concerns some kind of real property, although the doctrine is not in practice so restrictive.[95]

The detail of the types of representations made by a testator in successful estoppel claims is outside the scope of this chapter, but there is an interesting parallel with mutual wills in the case law about the revocability of an estoppel representation. In *Taylor v Dickens*,[96] Judge Weeks decided that a representor was free to change her mind even after the detriment had been incurred, because the testator had not promised not to change her will, and the claimant had merely trusted her not to do so. However, Robert Walker LJ in *Gillett v Holt*[97] was sceptical about this decision, given that the essence of the proprietary estoppel doctrine is to compensate for the refusal of the representor to give effect to the promise. Thus it could step in where the representor fails to make a will or, as in *Gillett* itself, where the representor unconscionably changes his will in the light of a representation and detrimental reliance. This thinking was reflected in the decision in *Cobbe v Yeoman's Row Management* where Lord Walker explained that in successful estoppel claims, 'the claimant believed that the assurance on which he or she relied was binding and irrevocable'.[98]

---

[92] S Gardner with E MacKenzie, *An Introduction to Land Law*, 3rd edn (Oxford, Hart Publishing, 2012) 130.

[93] HM Land Registry and Law Commission, *Land Registration for the Twenty-First Century: A Conveyancing Revolution* (Law Com No 271, 2001) para 5.29. B McFarlane, *The Law of Proprietary Estoppel* (Oxford, Oxford University Press, 2014) seeks to distinguish between acquiescence-, representation- and promise-based strands of the doctrine: see especially ch 1.

[94] *Thorner v Major* [2009] UKHL 18, [2009] 1 WLR 776 [29].

[95] See, eg *Strover v Strover* [2005] EWHC 860 (Ch), [2005] WTLR 1245.

[96] *Taylor v Dickens* [1998] 1 FLR 806 (Ch).

[97] *Gillett v Holt* [2001] Ch 210 (CA) 225, 227–28.

[98] *Cobbe v Yeoman's Row Management Ltd* [2008] UKHL 55, [2008] 1 WLR 1752 [66]. Cf *Thorner v Major* (n 94).

The second element of proprietary estoppel is that the claimant carer must have relied on the representation, and this reliance must be reasonable.[99] The requirement of reliance raises a problem in the case of an entirely altruistic carer, who would gladly continue to care in the absence of a representation. However, cases such as *Wayling v Jones*[100] have established a reverse burden of proof for reliance, in situations where the claimant has proved a representation and detriment. This was followed in *Campbell v Griffin* where a carer acted 'out of friendship and a sense of responsibility'.[101] The fact that the carer suggested that he would have moved out of the property, despite continuing to care, was enough to prevent the reverse burden of proof from being discharged, and so the estoppel claim was successful.

Detriment is the easiest aspect of a proprietary estoppel claim for a carer to prove, because the very act of caring usually means that some detriment has been incurred. Detriment can thus encompass both the conferment of a benefit on the representor, or the carer giving up something valuable,[102] and in most care cases both aspects will be present. However, if the carer has received benefits as part of his caring responsibilities, these must be balanced against the detriment.[103] That said, it is the unconscionability of the representor failing to fulfil the promise that cements the estoppel; indeed, Lord Scott has described unconscionability as the 'key that unlocks the door' to the remedy.[104] Lord Walker acknowledges that unconscionability unifies and confirms the other elements.[105]

Once the proprietary estoppel claim is established, the court must decide how best to give effect to the claimant's 'inchoate equity'[106] and award the appropriate remedy,[107] which may or may not be an interest in the property that was the subject of the representation. The key question is whether this remedy is to satisfy the claimant's expectation, or simply to reverse the detriment suffered. In *Gillett v Holt*, it was clear that the court's role was to 'form a view as to what is the minimum required' to satisfy the equity,[108] and in *Henry v Henry* the Privy Council acknowledged that proportionality between expectation and detriment 'lies at the heart of the doctrine of proprietary estoppel and permeates its every application'.[109] Thus in some cases where a claim is successfully made out, the equity falls short of the amount sought by the claimant.[110] The discretion of the court in satisfying the equity is said to be based once again on unconscionability.[111]

---

[99] See *Murphy v Rayner* [2011] EWHC 1 (Ch), where the dishonesty of the carer prevented her from relying on the representation.

[100] *Wayling v Jones* [1995] 2 FLR 1029 (CA).

[101] *Campbell v Griffin* (n 82) [20].

[102] See, eg *Parker v Parker* [2003] EWHC 1846 (Ch), [2003] NPC 94.

[103] *Henry v Henry* [2010] UKPC 3, [2010] 1 All ER 988 [65] (Sir Jonathan Parker, giving the advice of the Board).

[104] *Blue Haven Enterprises Ltd v Tully* [2006] UKPC 17 [24].

[105] *Cobbe v Yeoman's Row Management Ltd* (n 98) [92].

[106] K Gray and SF Gray, *Elements of Land Law*, 5th edn (Oxford, Oxford University Press, 2009) para 9.2.88.

[107] Compare McFarlane, *The Law of Proprietary Estoppel* (n 93) chs 7 and 9.

[108] *Gillett v Holt* (n 97) 237 (Robert Walker LJ).

[109] *Henry v Henry* (n 103) [65] (Sir Jonathan Parker, giving the advice of the Board). See McFarlane, *The Law of Proprietary Estoppel* (n 93) ch 7 for discussion.

[110] See, eg *Powell v Benney* [2007] EWCA Civ 1283, (2007) 151 SJLB 1598.

[111] N Hopkins, 'Unconscionability, Constructive Trusts and Proprietary Estoppel' in M Bryan (ed), *Private Law in Theory and Practice* (Abingdon, Routledge-Cavendish, 2007) 217.

In *Jennings v Rice*, Robert Walker LJ distinguished between two categories of proprietary estoppel case for the purposes of awarding a remedy.[112] On his analysis, some cases have a relatively clear bargain about the claimant's expectation and the detriment required for the expectation to be fulfilled, such as one with a friend or relative who cares for the testator on the clear understanding between the two that he will inherit the house or perhaps have a home for his life.[113] Other cases fall into the non-bargain category, that is, where the claimant's expectation is 'uncertain, or extravagant, or out of all proportion to the detriment ... suffered'.[114] In the bargain cases,[115] the court might well simply fulfil the expectation by transferring the property promised if the case is 'free from other complications',[116] and equity will be satisfied, though McFarlane has emphasised that it should not be assumed that the expectation will be satisfied even in bargain cases.[117] In the non-bargain cases, the court apparently has a wider discretion and it is open to the court to satisfy the equity in a more limited manner. An example of this is *Powell v Benney*,[118] where in return for performing some household tasks, the testator had promised the claimants his two houses. While the detriment in the case had been established as the amount of expenditure of £8,830 that the claimants had incurred, Judge Levy awarded a sum of £20,000 taking into account the size of the estate and the disappointment the claimant had suffered, and this was upheld on appeal. Gardner has criticised the bargain and non-bargain dichotomy, arguing that many scenarios do not comfortably fall into one camp or the other.[119] But while Lord Walker has suggested extra-judicially that a spectrum might be more realistic,[120] the dichotomy has not apparently been overturned in any subsequent cases and so remains good law.

The rigidity of the mutual wills doctrine can be contrasted with the approach in estoppel cases. The property over which the mutual wills trust crystallises is determined by the agreement rather than a 'minimum equity'-style approach as with estoppel.

Hughes[121] has emphasised the *similarity* of the two doctrines in the light of *Thorner v Major*,[122] even though the only express reference to mutual wills in the House of Lords decision in *Thorner* came from Lord Walker, who described mutual wills as 'arguably a special case' when describing the level of certainty required of the promised proprietary interest for estoppel purposes.[123] Both doctrines can clearly limit the extent to which a testator may go back on a testamentary promise. The existence of estoppel has been key to the argument that a contract should not be required to give effect to a mutual wills arrangement,[124] and indeed in some cases

---

[112] *Jennings v Rice* (n 82) [45]–[56].
[113] Ibid, [45].
[114] Ibid, [50].
[115] This specific terminology is not used by Robert Walker LJ himself in *Jennings*, but *cf* S Gardner, 'The Remedial Discretion in Proprietary Estoppel—Again' (2006) 122 *LQR* 492.
[116] *Jennings v Rice* (n 82) [45].
[117] McFarlane, The Law of Proprietary Estoppel (n 93) para 7.164.
[118] *Powell v Benney* (n 112).
[119] Gardner, 'The Remedial Discretion in Proprietary Estoppel—Again' (n 115).
[120] R Walker, 'Which Side "Ought to Win"?—Discretion and Certainty in Property Law' [2008] *Singapore Journal of Legal Studies* 229, 239.
[121] Hughes, 'Mutual Wills' (n 15) 135.
[122] *Thorner v Major* (n 94).
[123] Ibid, [63].
[124] See, eg Croucher, 'Mutual Wills: Contemporary Reflections on an Old Doctrine' (n 10) 408.

claimants arguing that mutual wills were created use estoppel as an alternative basis of their claim.[125] It is also true that under both doctrines the relevant property might fluctuate over time and the obligations of both the representor (in estoppel) and the survivor (in mutual wills) can ultimately be determined by the court.

Nevertheless, it is surely more significant, as well as being normatively questionable in some circumstances, that the parties are able *conclusively* to decide for themselves what property is subject to a mutual wills arrangement without judicial intervention, while the property forming the subject of an estoppel representation might ultimately be considered a disproportionate remedy when a claim is litigated. For example, it seems possible that a mutual wills arrangement could comprise the survivor's entire estate, even if the actual property matching that definition cannot be known until the survivor's death and even if the terms of the arrangement are the subject of litigation. With estoppel, the exact extent of the claimant's entitlement can never be certain until the 'minimum equity' approach is applied (or the case is settled without resort to litigation), and it might be possible that the equity is extinguished altogether by the time the claim is brought.[126]

While uncertainty itself might be problematic,[127] the court is at least able to balance the various competing interests in the estate where estoppel is at issue, even if that is true to a limited extent (particularly in bargain cases).[128] For example, while McFarlane criticises any suggestion that the claims of a third party should affect the nature and extent of an estoppel promisee's liability (as distinct from the remedy chosen to satisfy it),[129] he accepts that changes in circumstances are relevant and that in practice the satisfaction of an estoppel equity is unlikely to be allowed to exhaust an estate and leave a new spouse (for example)[130] without provision.[131] Under the mutual wills doctrine, no such opportunity to take account of the surrounding circumstances is afforded to the court (at least where the parties to the arrangement have clearly defined the extent of the property to be subject to the arrangement). The Court of Appeal in *Olins v Walters* approved[132] Norris J's statement at first instance that the mutual wills constructive trust is 'shaped by the exact terms of the contract that [the two testators] have made'.[133] Whatever the differences in the level of certainty required by the two doctrines,[134] the fact remains that parties to a mutual wills arrangement are more able to 'lock' the extent of the constructive trust than parties to an estoppel arrangement are able to do so with their equivalent remedy.[135]

---

[125] See, eg *Birch v Curtis* (n 20).

[126] See, eg *Sledmore v Dalby* (1996) 72 P & CR 196 (CA).

[127] See, eg J Mee, 'Proprietary Estoppel and Inheritance: Enough is Enough?' [2013] *Conveyancer and Property Lawyer* 280.

[128] See, eg Sloan, *Informal Carers and Private Law* (n 6) 72.

[129] Cf, eg the Australian case of *Giumelli v Giumelli* [1999] HCA 10, 196 CLR 101.

[130] See, eg *Macdonald v Frost* [2009] EWHC 2276 (Ch), [2009] WTLR 1815.

[131] McFarlane, *The Law of Proprietary Estoppel* (n 93) paras 5.89–5.112, 7.85, 9.52–9.61; 10.05–10.09.

[132] *Olins v Walters* (n 22) [38] (Mummery LJ).

[133] *Olins v Walters* [2007] EWHC 3060 (Ch), [2008] WTLR 339 [9].

[134] For a general discussion of the level of certainty required for estoppel representations, see Sloan, *Informal Carers and Private Law* (n 6) 41–44.

[135] Similarly, while the quantum of a common intention constructive trust is (at least in theory) based upon the common intention of the parties (cf Lord Kerr's admission in *Jones v Kernott* that the permitted process of imputation 'has nothing to do with what the parties intended, or what might be supposed

The potential injustice is particularly highlighted where a mutual wills claim clashes with an estoppel one made by a carer. The carer might be able to argue that since his equity arose during the care recipient's lifetime even if the promise was a testamentary one,[136] an estoppel representation is a permissible means for the care recipient to deal with the property *inter vivos*[137] and therefore his claim can relate to property that would otherwise be subject to the mutual wills constructive trust even if it is brought after the care recipient's death.[138] An inconsistency would arguably exist if bona fide small *inter vivos* gifts were permitted but a putative estoppel equity relating to a bona fide promise of provision were held not to be enforceable as a result of mutual wills. It is not, however, clear that the court would accept such a submission if the focus of the doctrine is to permit 'full enjoyment for the survivor's *own* benefit and advantage' (emphasis added) subject to a specific testamentary obligation,[139] and Mummery LJ's immediate trust analysis could cause particular problems. A court would almost certainly refuse to prioritise a carer's claim where the representation (unbeknownst to the detrimentally relying carer) was deliberately intended to defeat the mutual wills claim.

It is arguable that if some version of a minimum equity approach were open to the court in satisfying a mutual wills claim, then the court could balance (even to a limited extent) the equity required to satisfy both estoppel and mutual wills claims where the relevant litigation occurs simultaneously, and consequently make an award that does not entirely disappoint either party. Such a 'minimum equity' approach could also be useful where estoppel itself is not in issue but (for example) the care recipient has purported to change her will in favour of a carer.

Admittedly, the possible justification for the current dichotomy in the court's approach between the two doctrines is that it is the very absence of a contract and any formalities that justifies the minimum equity approach in estoppel, and thus the court must step in to do only what is necessary to correct the unconscionability where that doctrine applies. This is clearly true of at least Lord Walker's 'non-bargain' cases in relation to estoppel. His 'bargain cases' might have more in common with mutual wills situations, and since the minimum equity is apparently less subject to judicial discretion in such estoppel cases, the absence of discretion in mutual wills is arguably justifiable. That said, we have noted the criticism of the 'bargain'/'non-bargain' dichotomy, and (unlike in mutual wills cases) some discretion still exists even on Robert Walker LJ's original analysis. In any case, the

---

would have been their intention had they addressed that question': [2011] UKSC 53, [2011] 3 WLR 1121 [74]), it is said to be ambulatory in nature (see, in particular, *Jones v Kernott*; see Sloan, *Informal Carers and Private Law* (n 6) 81–88 for a discussion of the common intention constructive trust in the context of care). With mutual wills, the intention cannot change once the first testator dies; the only way of limiting the extent of its constructive trust is seemingly to dispose of the relevant property *inter vivos*, which will invite challenges.

[136] See, eg *Gillett v Holt* (n 97). Cf *Fazari as Executrix of the Estate of Domenico Antonio Cosentino (decd) v Cosentino* (n 48) on the perceived importance in Australia of whether a disposition is of a 'testamentary nature' in this context.

[137] Cf *Healey v Brown* (n 52) on using the property to fund *formal* care.

[138] See, eg McFarlane (n 93) ch 8 on the doctrinal difficulties surrounding the impact of proprietary estoppel on third-party recipients of the relevant property.

[139] *Birmingham* (n 21) 680 (Dixon J).

influence of contract law is keenly felt in mutual wills scenarios, and the objection to the caring estoppel claimant's weaker position may therefore relate not merely to the mutual wills doctrine, but also to the underlying validity of a contract surrendering testamentary freedom. Indeed, a contract to leave property by will,[140] or not to revoke a will,[141] is valid, and it is likely that reform of the mutual wills doctrine cannot realistically be contemplated without reconsideration of that principle and the policy factors surrounding the distinction between *inter vivos* and testamentary dispositions.[142]

Another difficulty with comparing the two 'equities' is that they do not address the same type of unconscionability. However, if anything, the position of the estoppel claimant may be normatively stronger as a result. In the mutual wills context, unlike the core estoppel scenario, the 'victim' of the unconscionability will not benefit directly from the ultimate remedy. The beneficiary himself has not inevitably suffered a direct detriment (although a situation where he may have incurred a detriment on the expectation of inheritance is not implausible), but rather the unconscionability stems from the first to die's drawing up of his will in a particular way because of the agreement and not revoking it before death, and the suggestion that if he knew the wills were not mutual, on Gardner's analysis, he may have adjusted the gifts.[143] Rimer J was anxious to emphasise in *Birch* that the beneficiaries of a mutual wills arrangement may be volunteers,[144] and it has been said that mutual wills represent a situation where the intended beneficiary does not 'rely in any sense on the agreement (he may not even be aware of it)', but nevertheless 'equity will regard it as against conscience for the owner of the property to deny the terms upon which he received it'.[145]

The difficulty with this approach is that the unconscionability is fixed at a point in the past, a point at which the carer was not necessarily even contemplated by any of the parties. To use Gardner's terminology again, the 'loss' suffered by the first to die or his heirs (corrected by the constructive trust) may be objectively smaller than the detriment suffered by the survivor's promisees or intended heirs. The parties to the mutual wills arrangement can never be sure that the burdens of the arrangement were broadly equivalent, as in 'bargain' cases associated with estoppel.[146] There may be a case for imputing onto the first to die a knowledge of the present day facts and adjusting the mutual will accordingly. The ultimate solution may therefore be to subject both estoppel promisees and putative mutual will beneficiaries either to a 'minimum equity'-style approach or to an equivalent statutory regime for the enforcement of testamentary promises.[147]

---

[140] *Parker v Clark* [1960] 1 WLR 286 (Assizes).
[141] *Robinson v Ommanney* (1883) 23 Ch D 285 (CA).
[142] See, eg Sloan, *Informal Carers and Private Law* (n 6) 138–47.
[143] Gardner, 'Reliance-based Constructive Trusts' (n 61) 75.
[144] *Birch v Curtis* (n 20) [60].
[145] *De Bruyne v De Bruyne* [2010] EWCA Civ 519, [2010] 2 FLR 1240 [51] (Patten LJ).
[146] See *Jennings v Rice* (n 82) [45] (Robert Walker LJ).
[147] See, eg Law Reform (Testamentary Promises) Act 1949 (NZ), discussed in Sloan, *Informal Carers and Private Law* (n 6) ch 3.

C. Family Provision Claims

It has been seen that proprietary estoppel may assist a carer where the care recipient has made a representation that the carer will be rewarded for his efforts. That said, there may be situations where such a representation has not been made but it is nevertheless unconscionable (in a broad sense) for the carer not to be compensated. A possible avenue of claim, albeit a limited one, is the Inheritance (Provision for Family and Dependants) Act 1975.[148]

Carers who have a formal familial or a sexual relationship with the deceased are much more likely to be able to bring a claim under the 1975 Act. There are only two categories in the Act under which a non-familial carer can qualify, which are as a dependant[149] or as a cohabitant.[150] To qualify in the dependant category, the claimant must prove to the court that he was maintained by the deceased immediately before the death.[151] A difficulty arises often in a care situation where in fact the care recipient was the one being maintained by the carer, although the courts have adopted a rather generous interpretation of maintenance.[152] To qualify in the cohabitant category, the claimant must show that for two years prior to the death, he lived in the same household as the care recipient as if he were his or her spouse or civil partner.[153] Again, this may be too high a hurdle for a carer to clear, although some cases have interpreted the statute widely and suggested that the absence of a continuing sexual relationship may not be critical.[154]

The relevance of mutual wills to the present discussion is that provision under the 1975 Act is made out of the 'net estate',[155] which includes 'all property of which the deceased had power to dispose by his will (otherwise than by virtue of a special power of appointment) less the amount of', inter alia, his 'debts and liabilities'.[156] There is specific provision for property received by virtue of a *donatio mortis causa* made by the deceased to be treated as part of the net estate,[157] though no such provision is apparently made for mutual wills. A contract by which the deceased avoided the effect of the 1975 Act can in substance be set aside by court order,[158] but only where, inter alia, full valuable consideration was not given by anyone.[159] Indeed, the Law Commission confirmed in 2011 the view that 'property that is the subject of a contract to leave property by will may be brought into the net estate', apparently only 'if the contract was for less than full value'.[160] It is likely that full

---

[148] See, generally, Sloan, *Informal Carers and Private Law* (n 6) ch 5.
[149] Inheritance (Provision for Family and Dependants) Act 1975, s 1(1)(e).
[150] Ibid, ss 1(1)(ba), 1(1A), 1(1B).
[151] Ibid, ss 1(1)(e), 1(3).
[152] See, eg M Cardinal, 'In Practice—Inheritance or Estoppel—How the Cohabitant Succeeded' [2004] *Family Law* 364. See also Inheritance and Trustees' Powers Act 2014, Sch 2, paras 3 and 5(4).
[153] Inheritance (Provision for Family and Dependants) Act 1975, ss 1(1)(ba), 1(1A), 1(1B).
[154] *Re Watson (decd)* [1999] 1 FLR 878 (Ch) 884.
[155] Inheritance (Provision for Family and Dependants) Act 1975, s 2.
[156] Ibid, s 25(1).
[157] Ibid, s 8(2).
[158] Ibid, s 11(2). See also s 10, concerning similar 'dispositions'.
[159] Ibid, s 11(2)(c).
[160] Law Commission, *Intestacy and Family Provision Claims on Death* (Law Com No 331, 2011) para 7.10, though *cf* para 7.46. See also *Schaefer v Schuhmann* [1972] AC 572 (PC); *Thorner v Major* [2008] EWCA Civ 732, [2008] 2 FCR 435 [32] (Lloyd LJ); Law Commission, *Second Report on Family Property: Family Provision on Death* (Law Com No 61, 1974) paras 222–42.

valuable consideration would be found to have been given in a genuine mutual wills arrangement.[161]

The significance of this is that, as Hughes has said, 'a mutual Wills constructive trust will *probably* mean (in the case at least of the second to die) that the second to die's testamentary dispositions are immune from alteration under the Inheritance (Provision for Family and Dependants) Act 1975' (emphasis added).[162] As with estoppel, therefore, a claimant carer's interests are subordinated to those of a potentially undeserving mutual wills beneficiary, and a court is deprived of an effective means of balancing the claims. Conversely, *Re Goodchild (decd)* demonstrates that even if an arrangement is not sufficiently clear to merit application of the mutual wills doctrine, the mistaken belief by one party that mutual wills have in fact been made is relevant to a claim under the 1975 Act by the alleged mutual wills beneficiary.[163] It should be noted that there is a complex relationship between proprietary estoppel and family provision claims[164] and a statutory approach may be preferable,[165] but again there is at least a minimum equity approach in relation to estoppel and the claims can thereby be balanced in principle.[166]

In *Barns v Barns*,[167] in contrast to the relationship between mutual wills and the 1975 Act in England and Wales, a majority of the High Court of Australia held that the mutual wills doctrine did not prevent the application of the Inheritance (Family Provision) Act 1972 (SA) to the relevant property following the first death. At the same time, the full court also held that the making of mutual wills in order to avoid such legislation was not contrary to public policy. Cassidy has criticised the approach of the majority in *Barns* as representing a misunderstanding of the mutual wills doctrine, and she argues that its precedential value is weak.[168] While its result is consistent with the argument of this chapter in the sense that mutual wills are not able to thwart deserving family provision applicants, it seems fundamentally inconsistent with the orthodox constructive trust analysis. If the trust does not arise until the first death, the majority approach in *Barns* might look defensible, but there is still the problem (as Callinan J recognised in dissent) that the arrangement is immediately contractually enforceable and he did not see that it should be treated differently from any other contractual obligation placing property out of the scope of the legislation.

There was a legislative complication in *Barns*, since the 1972 Act specifically provided (and still does) that the family provision order should be given effect as though it were a codicil to the will executed immediately before death.[169] The New South

---

[161] See R Croucher, 'Contracts to Leave Property by Will and Family Provision after *Barns v Barns* (2003) 196 ALR 65—Orthodoxy or Aberration?' (2005) 27 *Sydney Law Review* 263 on the Australian concept of 'notional estate', cited, eg in *Camernik v Reholc* [2012] NSWSC 1537 [125] (Hallen J).

[162] Hughes, 'Mutual Wills' (n 15) 133 fn 10. See also Mitchell, 'Some Aspects of Mutual Wills' (n 5) 141.

[163] *Re Goodchild* (n 11). Cf *Re Styler* [1942] Ch 387.

[164] See Cardinal, 'In Practice—Inheritance or Estoppel—How the Cohabitant Succeeded' (n 152) for discussion.

[165] See, eg Sloan, *Informal Carers and Private Law* (n 6) 72.

[166] See, eg *Jennings v Rice* (n 82) [52] (Robert Walker LJ).

[167] *Barns v Barns* (n 84).

[168] J Cassidy, 'Life (or more so Death) after *Barns v Barns*' (2006) 25 *University of Tasmania Law Review* 61.

[169] Inheritance (Family Provision) Act 1972 (SA), s 10.

Wales Court of Appeal nevertheless recognised in a different statutory context in *Delaforce v Simpson-Cook* that following *Barns* 'A contract not to revoke a will, or to leave specific property by will could be defeated, if there were eligible dependants, by an order for provision under' what is now the Succession Act 2006 (NSW), or 'the designation of the property as notional estate' under the same Act.[170] It was also said that 'A proprietary estoppel by encouragement based on similar promises must be subject to the same contingencies'.[171]

The inconsistency of the Australian approach with the traditional constructive trust analysis arguably furthers the suggestion that a minimum equity approach to mutual wills (or a statutory equivalent), as in proprietary estoppel, could be preferable. Rather than rigidly dismissing the constructive trust and allowing the family provision claim to override it completely (or indeed vice versa), a balancing act between the claims could be undertaken. Such an approach would require legislative amendment in England and Wales, though in light of the existing anti-avoidance provisions in the 1975 Act (which themselves generate an inconsistency) that may prove less controversial than tampering with estoppel.

IV. CONCLUSION

The conclusion of many works on mutual wills is that, from both a practical and a normative perspective, the doctrine should be abolished in its entirety. However, such a broad brush may be too onerous an attack on *contractual* freedom, and indeed unlikely, and a rather more nuanced tweaks to its operation may be preferable.

It has been seen from the above discussion that it is not the mutual wills doctrine itself that necessarily causes a problem for claimant informal carers, but rather the inability of equity to interfere with the rigid contract that governs the mutual will. Indeed, it seems that a mutual wills beneficiary could enforce the relevant arrangement by virtue of the Contracts (Rights of Third Parties) Act 1999,[172] though this is not yet clearly established by the case law.[173]

In an area of law where equity has had much to say, it could be seen as anomalous that a mere contract should have such force. Indeed, a will which is usually executed with a great deal of prior thought, solemnity and formality can easily be disregarded by a court if the circumstances of a claim so dictate. Yet a simple agreement, which

---

[170] *Delaforce v Simpson-Cook* [2010] NSWCA 84, (2010) 78 NSWLR 483 [34] (Handley AJA). See also *Hills v Chalk & Ors (as executors of the estate of Chalk (decd))* [2008] QCA 159, [2009] 1 Qd R 409 [44] (Keane JA).

[171] *Delaforce v Simpson-Cook* (n 162) [35] (Handley AJA).

[172] Kerridge, *Parry and Kerridge: The Law of Succession* (n 2) para 6-06. Cf Pawlowski and Brown, 'Problems with Mutual Wills—A Study of Probate Practice' (n 1) 475. There is also the possibility that the arrangement could be enforced by the beneficiary via the principle in *Beswick v Beswick* [1968] AC 58, though Pawlowski and Brown, 'Problems with Mutual Wills—A Study of Probate Practice' (n 1) 480 claim that this was rejected in *Re Dale* (n 16) 38 (Morritt J).

[173] In *Birch v Curtis* (n 20) in the course of explaining why a mutual wills arrangement was enforceable by third parties, Rimer J simply noted that 'the doctrine of mutual wills pre-dates by centuries the enactment of the Contracts (Rights of Third Parties) Act 1999' ([61]).

need not be in writing,[174] and the implications of which the testators may well not fully appreciate, reigns supreme.[175]

Admittedly, the argument that a contract entered into willingly by testators when drawing up mutual wills should be disregarded is rather inconsistent with the assertion that an estoppel representation is a valid fetter on the testator's written testamentary wishes. However, if a minimum equity approach were adopted in the mutual wills context as well as the estoppel context, the two doctrines would more comfortably coexist. Such an approach would allow the court to have jurisdiction over the entirety of the deceased's estate in deciding the quantification of the awards to both beneficiaries, thereby allowing it to balance the unconscionability in respect of both claims. On the other hand, Martin has described the imposition of a trust as 'a clumsy and inadequate way of dealing with a complicated problem', and advocated a contractual approach.[176]

If a minimum equity approach were incorporated into a statute, this would sit more coherently with family provision claims and allow a court to balance all three heads of claim.[177] Despite this, even in New Zealand where a statutory approach has been adopted to mutual wills via the Wills Act 2007 (in addition to pre-existing statutory approaches to both testamentary promises[178] and family provision)[179] the relationship between the three claims is not spelled out in that Act. Section 30 of the Wills Act in fact enshrines the mutual will beneficiary's full claim by stating that:

> A person who would have received a benefit from [the survivor]'s will if [the survivor] had kept the promise may claim from [the survivor]'s estate *any* part of the benefit that [the survivor]'s estate does not provide.[180] (Emphasis added)

No express attempt is made to balance any alternative claim in the 2007 Act. Although Nicky Richardson has noted that 'With the new legislation it is now unnecessary to resolve doctrinal disputes about the conceptual basis of mutual wills',[181] she would have preferred the legislation to abolish the doctrine altogether.[182]

For the moment,[183] in any case, the contractual rigidity of a mutual wills arrangement in English Law is unsatisfactory. Despite the care recipient's superficial testamentary freedom, a carer who has 'st[u]ck around'[184] with the care recipient through a long illness or old age to his detriment is currently likely to be let down by the effective inability of the court to look behind the contract-based constructive trust.

---

[174] *Cf Healey v Brown* (n 52) [23] (Deputy Judge David Donaldson) for a finding that s 2 of the Law of Property (Miscellaneous Provisions) Act 1989 requires a mutual wills agreement relating entirely to land to be in writing, which has been criticised (Luxton, '*Walters v Olin [sic]*: Uncertainty of Subject Matter— An Insoluble Problem in Mutual Wills?' (n 18) 502).

[175] This might suggest at least that *additional* formalities should be imposed for mutual wills. We are grateful to Professor Alison Clarke for this point.

[176] Martin, *Hanbury and Martin: Modern Equity* (n 46) para 12-034.

[177] See Sloan, *Informal Carers and Private Law* (n 6) 243.

[178] Law Reform (Testamentary Promises) Act 1949 (NZ).

[179] Family Protection Act 1955 (NZ).

[180] Wills Act 2007 (NZ), s 30(2). *Cf Dillon v Public Trustee of New Zealand* [1941] AC 294 (PC).

[181] N Richardson, 'Legislation for Mutual Wills in New Zealand' [2010] *Trust Law International* 99, 108.

[182] Ibid, 109.

[183] The doctrine is within the scope of the Law Commission's forthcoming project on the law of wills: see Law Commission, 'Wills' http://lawcommission.justice.gov.uk/areas/wills.htm (accessed 19 September 2014); E Cooke and L Campbell, 'Under Review' (2014) 164 *New Law Journal* 13.

[184] As George Michael might have said: G Michael, 'Freedom 90' (Columbia Records, 1990).

10

Intestate Property Distribution at Death in the United States

CARYL A YZENBAARD[*]

I. INTRODUCTION

THE DYNAMICS OF the family have changed dramatically over the past half-century. Today, it is common to have serial marriages with related or unrelated children living with a parent; many children are born outside the bonds of wedlock or are being raised by non-parents; partners of the same or opposite sex are cohabiting.[1] When an individual in this new non-nuclear family dies, how will his or her property be distributed?

Timely estate planning can ensure that the property will be distributed according to the decedent's intent.[2] Nonetheless in the United States today, as in the past, at least half of decedents die intestate.[3]

Intestate statutes are designed to provide for the distribution of property at the time of death when an individual dies without a will. The distribution scheme of such legislation is said to reflect the intent of the typical individual.[4] All American

---

[*] Professor of Law, Northern Kentucky University.

[1] Most of the authors cited in this chapter discuss these societal changes. R Brashier, 'Disinheritance and the Modern Family' (1994) 45 *Case Western Law Review* 83, 87. ML Fellows et al, 'Committed Partners and Inheritance: An Empirical Study' (1998) 16 *Law and Inequality* 1, 3. F Foster, 'The Family Paradigm of Inheritance Law' (2001) 80 *North Carolina Law Review* 199, 200. Note: 'Looking for a Family Resemblance: The Limits of the Functional Approach to the Legal Definition of Family' (1991) 104 *Harvard Law Review* 1640, 1640 noting that the traditional nuclear family is becoming an American anachronism.

[2] S Gary, 'The Parent–Child Relationship Under Intestacy Statutes' (Spring 2002) 32 *University of Memphis Law Review* 643, 648 who notes that though one can opt out of the intestate statutes by drafting a will most do not. A Hirsh, 'Incomplete Wills' (2013) 111 *Michigan Law Review* 1423, 1425 who suggests that courts should have greater latitude to effectuate intent with partial intestacy than when presented with complete intestacy. R Weisbord, 'Wills for Everyone: Helping Individuals Opt Out of Intestacy' (May 2012) 53 *Boston College Law Review* 877, 878.

[3] Dukeminier, and Sitkoff, *Wills and Trusts*, 9th edn (USA, Wolters Kluwer, 2013) 64 who notes that roughly half the population dies intestate. Those who have a will tend to be older and wealthier. P Harrington, 'Untying the Knot: Extending Intestacy Benefits to Non-Traditional Families by Severing the Link to Marriage' (2011) 25 *Journal of Civil Rights and Economic Development* 323, 326 noting that over half of adults do not have a will and that another 20% use a will without using a lawyer which may, in turn, then be invalid.

[4] M Higdon, 'When Informal Adoption Meets Intestate Succession: The Cultural Myopia of the Equitable Adoption Doctrine' (Spring 2008) 43 *Wake Forest Law Review* 223, 254 notes the objectives include the presumed intent of the decedent; clarity, simplicity and that it be comprehensive. Ease of administration should also be present. Yet they are over inclusive or concerned solely with legal status and under inclusive with the narrow view of family.

intestacy statutes have the virtue of efficiency and ease of administration. In general there is no room for deviation from the statute regardless of the need or justice of the situation.[5] Thus, are they fair and just? There are a few family protection devices;[6] however, they are limited and may be waived by a marital contract.[7]

The Uniform Probate Code (UPC), initially enacted in 1969 and amended since that time, has been influential in the United States.[8] As initially drafted, it attempted to reflect what the average testator would have wanted. When initially drafted, the traditional family consisted of a mother and a father neither of whom had been married before and the children were the children of both parents (either genetically or by adoption).[9] Amendments were made in 1990[10] and again in 2008[11] to attempt to reflect specific changing social patterns.

Kentucky, in contrast, has had great reverence for the preservation of the bloodlines. To date, Kentucky has resisted calls for changes to its statutes.[12]

It is the position of this chapter, that changes must be made regarding intestate succession to reflect current society. In the past 20 years, many commentators have

---

[5] Gary (n 2) 654 noting that although changes have been made in intestacy statutes regarding who is a family member the changes are based on marriage, biology or adoption and thus inadequately serve many decedents.

[6] The primary family protection is a homestead allowance which either protects the decedent's residence or provides a specific monetary allowance which is typically exempt from creditors. UPC §2-402 provides $22,500 for the surviving spouse, or if none to be shared by minor or dependent children. The family allowance is designed to provide support during the time of estate administration. UPC §§2-404, 2-405 provides for an allowance not to exceed $27,000. The family allowance is for the surviving spouse and minor and dependent children. The third protection is exempt property. UPC §2-403 allows the surviving spouse to receive up to $15,000 in personal property (or children if no such spouse).

[7] See Yzenbaard, *Kentucky Intestacy, Wills and Probate* (USA, Thomson West, 2004) para 4.5.

[8] As noted in Dukeminier (n 3) 67, approximately one-third of the states adopted laws which substantially conformed to major portions of the 1969 Code. J Carroll, 'Avoiding Blacklash: The Exclusion of Domestic Partnership Language in the 2008 Amendments to the Uniform Probate Code and the Future for Same-Sex Intestacy Right' (2013) 85 *Temple Law Review* 623, 623 which notes that the UPC is one of the most influential uniform laws promulgated by the Uniform Law Commission.

[9] See Carroll (n 8) 630.

[10] As noted in the prefatory note to art II of the UPC, changes were made as a result of an ordered study. One of the reasons cited was the advent of the multiple-marriage society resulting in a significant fraction of the population being married more than once and having children by a previous marriage. As a result, the spousal share was revised. L Waggoner, 'The Multiple-Marriage Society and Spousal Rights Under the Revised Uniform Probate Code' (1991) 76 *Iowa Law Review* 223, 224 who notes that the changes in the American family from the later half of the 1970s to the present (ie 1991) were among the great events of the age and that changes will continue as there are more serial marriages.

[11] Changes made in 2008 divided intestacy into two subparts, allowed for a notarised will; and brought in certain provisions of the Uniform Trust Code. A recent suggestion is that the UPC be amended again to provide a share for a family member who provided substantial uncompensated care in a family residence to a decedent. See T Gallanis and J Girtler, 'Family Caregiving and the Law of Succession: A Proposal' (2012) 45 *University of Michigan Journal of Law Reform* 761, 777.

[12] Although most states have a combined statute dealing with all property owned at the time of death, Kentucky does not. KRS §391.010 deals with real estate and KRS §391.030 deals with personal property (hereinafter only §KRS §391.010 will be cited because §391.030 basically follows it). Both must be applied after the dower statute of KRS §392.020 has been applied. Kentucky also has a statute dealing with ancestral property whereby real property given to the decedent who died intestate and without issue is returned to the donor. See KRS §391.020. Most states and the UPC do not have such a statute. Kentucky also stands outside the mainstream of American jurisprudence regarding the ability of an alien to inherit; jointure; and the ability of an heir to transfer an expectancy. See Yzenbaard (n 7) paras 2.11, 2.13 and KRS. §392.120.

called for change.[13] Rather than 'tinkering' with the intestacy statutes to reflect specific societal changes, the intestacy statutes should remain as the rebuttable default statute. The Probate Court, however, should have the opportunity in an exceptional case to modify the statute either because of dependency or justice. This proposal accepts the current American system of intestate statutes but adds a potential modification based loosely on the family maintenance statutes adopted by many of our English-speaking neighbours. It extends to areas not commonly discussed by other reformers such as in the area of half-bloods, representation, and advancements.[14] Various intestate issues are discussed as currently resolved in the more liberal UPC and the more traditional view of Kentucky (though recognising that each state has its own statute).

II. THE FAMILY MAINTENANCE SYSTEM

First introduced in 1900 in New Zealand,[15] the family maintenance system basically gives discretion to the Probate Court to modify a decedent's will to provide for certain individuals who were dependent on the decedent. Currently, eligible dependents

[13] Changes have been called for especially regarding committed but unmarried partners; the disinheritance of descendants; and for grand families. Protection for committed partners include: Carroll (n 8) 652 (suggesting a type of registration system be used); T Gallanis, 'Inheritance Rights for Domestic Partners' (2004) 79 *Tulane Law Review* 55, 90 (statutory solution); Harrington (n 3) 348 (calls for a new statute to be written); J Seidman, 'Functional Families and Dysfunctional Laws: Committed Partners and Intestate Succession' (2004) 75 *University of Colorado Law Review* 211 (suggesting several proposals). L Waggoner, 'Marital Property Rights in Transition' (1994) 59 *Missouri Law Review* 21, 71 proposes a legislative proposal for 'near spouses'. Proposals to protect children include D Batts, 'I Didn't Ask to Be Born: The American Law of Disinheritance and Proposal for Change into a System of Protected Inheritance' (1990) 41 *Hastings Law Journal* 1197, 1253 (protective protection for a minor or dependent child rather than family maintenance or forced heirship); Brashier, (n 1) 182 (suggesting posthumous support for children until majority); Higdon (n 4) (equitable adoption and statutory solution); P Monopoli, 'Toward Equality Nonmarital Children and the Uniform Probate Code' (2012) 45 *University of Michigan Journal of Law Reform* 995; H Shapo, 'A Tale of Two Systems: Anglo-American Problems in the Modernization of Inheritance Legislation' (1993) 60 *Tennessee Law Review* 707; T York, 'Protecting Minor Children from Parental Disinheritance: A Proposal for Awarding a Compulsory Share of the Parental Estate' (1997) 1997 *Detroit College of Law Review* 861, 880. Protection for grandparents and grandchildren are called for by M Harris, 'Why a Limited Family Maintenance System Could Help American Grand Families: A Response to Kristine Knaplund's Article on Intestacy Laws and their Implications for Grandparents Raising Grandchildren' (2007) 2007 *National Association of Elder Law Journal* 239; Higdon (n 4) (equitable adoption and statutory salutation); K Knaplund, 'Grandparents Raising Grandchildren and the Implication for Inheritance' (Spring 2006) 48 *Arizona Law Review* 1 (will for grandchildren); and Note, 'Expanding the Statutory Definition of Child in Intestacy Law: A Just Solution for the Inheritance Difficulties Grandparent Caregivers' Grandchildren Currently Face' (2010) 17 *Elder Law Journal* 401.

[14] S Gray, 'The Probate Definition of Family: A Proposal for Guided Discretion in Intestacy' (2012) 45 *University of Michigan Journal of Law Reform* 787, 819. Her proposal is excellent and calls for limited discretion to allow a court to deviate from the statutes in limited situations (especially with committed couples). See also R Chester, 'Disinheritance and the American Child: An Alternative from British Columbia' (1998) 1998 *Utah Law Review* 1, 5. His proposal calls for a limited maintenance statute based on dependency and justice taken from the system used in British Columbia. The proposal advanced herein resembles these two fine proposals but expands them. It retains traditional intestacy statutes but allows for deviation both for dependency and justice.

[15] The Testator's Family Maintenance Act 1900 (NZ Sta No 20). In 1939 it was modified to apply to intestate inheritance as well. The New Zealand plan as well as the other plans are discussed in J Laufer, 'Flexible Restraints on Testamentary Freedom—A Report on Decedents' Family Maintenance Legislation' (1955) 69 *Harvard Law Review* 277. The conclusion is that the maintenance principal offers an intelligent, forthright and relatively simple solution for the protection of spouses and children.

include the surviving spouse, children, grandchildren, stepchildren, parents, as well as a 'de facto spouse' and others who were at the time either dependent on the decedent or shared a household with the decedent.[16] Similar legislation has been adopted in England for both testate and intestate individuals,[17] as well as in Australia[18] and some Canadian provinces.[19] In general, modifications are made to provide for individuals who were dependent on the decedent at some point in time. Nonetheless, in at least one Canadian provenance, British Columbia, modifications also may be made based on morality or justice.[20]

Such a scheme does give significant discretion to the probate judge.[21] It can affect the testamentary freedom of the decedent.[22] It has the potential for delay and litigation.[23] In point of fact, however, the system seems to have worked well where adopted. Estate planners are aware that changes may be made by the court and thus the will is drafted to hopefully care for all potentially dependent individuals.[24] Litigation has been limited and settlements are encouraged. Although several commentators have suggested that American jurisdictions adopt a family maintenance

[16] The New Zealand Act was amended in 1982 to provide for 'de facto spouses' and others who were at one time either dependent on the decedent or share a household with the decedent. The court will intervene if necessary to provide for the dependent either by a lump sum or payment of periodic payments.

[17] Inheritance (Provision for Family and Dependents) Act 1975. As originally drafted, reasonable financial provision could be given, whether the decedent died testate or intestate, to a spouse; a former spouse who has not remarried; a child; any person who was treated by the decedent as a child; or any person whom immediately before the death of the decedent was maintained in whole or in part by the decedent. Intestacy laws in England, Australia and Singapore are explored in an article by F Burns, 'Intestacy Law in Australia, England and Singapore—Another Aid to Social Sustainability in an Aging Population?' [2012] *Singapore Journal of Legal Studies* 366. English intestacy laws were also discussed and compared with Scottish laws in an article by F Burns, 'Surviving Spouses, Surviving Children and the Reform of Total Intestacy Law in England and Scotland: Past, Present, and Future' (2013) 33(1) *Legal Studies* 85. The prior act was discussed in Note, 'Provision for Dependents: The English Inheritance Act of 1938' (1940) 53 *Harvard Law Review* 465.

[18] The Australian Act is discussed by B Sloan, 'The Concept of Coupledom in Succession Law' (2013) 623 *CLJ* 2011.

[19] Several Canadian provinces also have a family maintenance system as discussed in Harris (n 13) 251. These provinces include British Columbia, Alberta, Manitoba, Nova Scotia, New Brunswick, Saskatchewan and Ontario; however, in general they are more limited as they may apply only to a testate estate and may be limited to spouses and children of the decedent who are dependent, disabled or incompetent.

[20] See discussion by Chester (n 14) 8. A child or a spouse may petition to vary the terms of the will to provide the applicant with a provision that is 'adequate, just and equitable'. Chester then discusses the case of *Tataryn v Tatayr's Estate* (1994) 2 SCR 807 in which case the court determined that it must address the legal obligation to the surviving spouse. Although the English Act does not expressly include the concept of moral duty, Conway noted in her paper given at The Modern Studies in Property Law (Liverpool, April 2014) that courts often consider what is just especially in cases involving independent adult children.

[21] See Chester (n 14) 7.

[22] Ibid.

[23] In fact, in both New Zealand and England a lawsuit is needed to activate the statute. But see Shapo (n 13) 714 who reviewed the American and the English systems. She noted that the 1975 Act has not unleashed a flood of litigation nor imposed crippling uncertainty on English inheritance laws. She notes that under the 1975 Act, a spouse and others can petition the court. The court will first determine if the will or the law of intestacy made reasonable financial provision for the applicant (an objective test). The court then will consider the financial resources and needs of the applicant now and in the foreseeable future. The needs of others are considered as is the size of the estate. If a spouse, the age of the applicant, the duration of the marriage and contributions made by both are reviewed. The court will also consider what would have been received as an award in a divorce proceeding. Several cases are reviewed. The court may order a lump sum or an installment payment.

[24] See Batts (n 13) 1216 and Chester (n 14) 32.

system, it is unlikely that it will be done because of the American love of the freedom of testation and distrust of judicial discretion.[25] Nonetheless, a form of flexibility should be allowed when appropriate and just using existing intestate statutes.

A. The Proposal (Hereinafter 'The Proposal')

This proposal applies only to intestate estates. Thus, any concern with testamentary freedom in general will not apply. One may still draft a will as desired.[26] Discretion, though limited is given to the Probate Court.[27]

The presumption is that the intestate statute shall apply. The presumption, however, is rebuttable by clear and convincing evidence. The Probate Court may modify the application of the intestacy statute for an individual who was, in fact, dependent on the decedent and is not adequately provided for by the statute.[28] In addition, the Probate Court may modify the application of the intestacy statute when it just and moral to so do.[29] An individual may petition the court for relief or the court may, on its own accord, appoint a guardian ad litem to protect an individual. The proof required would be clear and convincing evidence (although even a higher standard such as beyond a reasonable doubt could be used).[30]

Depending on the circumstances, factors to be considered could include: (a) any written expression of intent; (b) the length of any marriage or relationship; (c) the age of the parties; (d) the size of the estate; (e) outside sources available to the parties; and (f) the relationships among the parties.[31]

How would the proposal work in specific situations using the UPC and Kentucky?

B. Surviving Spouse

The surviving spouse is protected by all American intestacy statutes. But who is a spouse? A spouse is one to whom the decedent was married. It can include same sex marriages in those states that have recognised such marriages or have provided

---

[25] See Brashier (n 1) 133 and 182 who finds the amount of discretion makes it infeasible for use in America.

[26] By limiting the proposal to intestate estates, the concern with the freedom of testation is avoided. Of course, the use of the elective or forced share already is a limitation on the freedom of testation. Perhaps at some time, the proposal should be extended to testate estates as well based on either dependency or justice.

[27] Discretion is given. The proposal advocated in this paper gives broader discretion than that advocated by Gray (n 14). It goes beyond most of the family maintenance statutes in that it is not expressly limited to dependency.

[28] See nn 16 and 17.

[29] This proposal expands the discussion from British Columbia discussed by Chester (n 14).

[30] See Bogert and Yzenbaard, *The Law of Trusts and Trustees*, 3rd edn (USA, West, 2009) s 472, fns 14–17 that although most courts require clear and convincing evidence to impose a constructive trust many require more. The same could apply here.

[31] See Waggoner Working Draft attached as an Appendix to Fellows et al (n 1). Proposals for discretion for intestacy statutes are noted in Gary (n 14) starting at 819. The Gary proposal is very good. The proposal advocated in this paper would extend it to other situations and adds the concept of morality and justice. It would use existing intestacy statutes rather than a proposed new statute.

for another form of recognition.[32] It does not include those who cohabit with each other whether of the same or of the opposite sex and regardless of the length of time they have been together. No jurisdiction currently considers the length of time of the marriage when awarding a share to the surviving spouse.[33]

The UPC provides the surviving spouse with the entire estate if all the descendants (whether minor or not) of the decedent are also all the descendants of the surviving spouse or if the decedent had no descendants and no surviving parents.[34] It is only when the decedent had a child by another,[35] or if the surviving spouse had a child by another person,[36] that the surviving spouse will receive 'up front' money and then will share with the decedent's descendants. In like manner, if the decedent left no descendants, but a parent or parents then the surviving spouse again receives 'up front' money and then shares the estate with the parent or parents.[37]

The amendment to give all to the surviving spouse when there are mutual descendants presumes that this spouse will serve as a conduit and pass such property along to the descendants. In point of fact, this may not occur. The surviving spouse may consume much of the property. The spouse may remarry and either leave the property to the new spouse by will, or the new spouse may elect against any will made by the surviving spouse, or the new spouse will receive a share by intestacy.[38]

Kentucky provides the surviving spouse basically with one-half of the estate unless the decedent left no descendants; no parents; and no descendants of parents in which case the survivor receives all.[39] Kentucky does provide, however, that a spouse who

---

[32] The comments to UPC §2-102 notes the Restatement (Third) of Property, Wills and Donative Transfers (1999) regarding the right of a domestic partner to be treated as a spouse in s 2.5, comment g. Therein it is noted that a developing question is the right of the domestic partner of an unmarried intestate decedent to be treated as a surviving spouse for intestacy. A few states, have by statute granted intestacy rights to the surviving domestic partner. See n 13. A multi-factor test was proposed by Waggoner (n 13) 76 who suggests the following as factors: the duration, constancy and exclusivity of the relationship; the degree of pooled financial resources; the procreation or adoption of children; if there was a marriage ceremony and how the parties held themselves out. These factors were carried forward by Gallanis (n 13) 90.

[33] Contrast this with UPC §2-203 where the amount of the surviving spouse's elective share depends on the number of years of marriage.

[34] UPC §2-102(1)(A) and (B). Under the pre-1990 Code the surviving spouse received the entire estate only if there were neither surviving descendants nor parents. If there were descendants, one-half went to the descendants in excess of $50,000. As with all distributions, debts, taxes and other expenses are paid first.

[35] UPC §2-102(4). The surviving spouse receives 'up front' money of $150,000 plus half of the estate. The comments note that in this situation the decedent's descendants are not the natural objects of the bounty of the surviving spouse. The remaining half goes to the descendants of the decedent pursuant to UPC §2-103(a)(1).

[36] UPC §2-102(3). The surviving spouse receives 'up front' money of $225,000 (more than if it were the decedent who had brought the children into the new marriage) plus half. The comments note that this assures that the decedent's descendants will receive some assets when the estate exceeds $225,000. The descendants then receive the other one-half under UPC §2-103(1)(a).

[37] UPC §2-103(2). The surviving spouse receives the first $300,000 and then three-quarters of the balance of the estate. The parents or surviving parent receives one-quarter of the estate after the payment has been made. See §2-103(1)(a)(2).

[38] See L Rosenbury, 'Two Ways to End a Marriage: Divorce or Death' (2005) 2005 *Utah Law Review* 1227, 1264 noting that the conduit theory does not seem to apply when the surviving spouse brings in children to the marriage even if the decedent and the survivor also had children. One might contemplate why the UPC wants the descendants or parents to share some of the estate if it exceeds the amount of the 'up front' money but not otherwise. Nonetheless, it is consistent with studies cited in UPC §2-103(2) that modest testate estates often are given to the surviving spouse.

[39] Unlike the UPC and more modern statutes, Kentucky has three separate statutes which must be applied. See n 12.

has abandoned the decedent and has lived in adultery may not inherit.[40] The other half of the property passes first to the descendants of the decedent; then to any surviving parent; and next to the descendants of the parents.[41]

Given today's societal changes, it is likely that there will be stepchildren and the surviving spouse will not receive the entire estate under the UPC scheme if the estate is large enough. The distribution then resembles the Kentucky scheme absent the 'up front' money.

Using the proposal, a court may decrease the surviving spouse's share in a UPC jurisdiction if the spouse receives it all and others, (such as a child or a parent), were dependent on the decedent. The court may want to increase the spouse's share if there is a blended family because the surviving spouse was more dependent than another such as an adult descendant. The court should consider the factors noted as well as the actual needs of the surviving spouse, descendants, parents, and siblings of the decedent to increase or decrease a share.[42]

In Kentucky, a court may want to increase the surviving spouse's share. Again the factors noted in the proposal should be considered as well as the actual needs of the parties. In addition, the court may look to the age and dependency of those who would take the other half of the estate. If the descendants are minors, a costly guardianship might be otherwise required and thus a court might want to give all to the surviving spouse (especially if the surviving spouse is the parent of the descendants).[43] On the other hand, if the surviving spouse had been married for only a limited period of time and the descendants are all adults, no alteration need be made unless the surviving spouse was dependent on the decedent. The share of the surviving spouse might be increased in those cases where the decedent left no descendants and the surviving spouse would be sharing the estate with the siblings of the decedent.[44]

In addition, an individual could petition the court for relief based on justice or morality. One who has been in a long-time relationship with the decedent, but was not married to the decedent (either because such a marriage was prohibited or

---

[40] KRS §392.090(2). The statute was modelled on the English statute enacted in 1285 and commonly known as the Statute of Westminster Second (13 Edw 1 c 34). Kentucky initially adopted the statute in 1796 and it was codified in 1942. In a recent Kentucky case, *Griffin v Rice* 381 SW 3d 198 (2012), the court held that the wife was entitled to inherit because, although she had abandoned her husband, she had engaged in only a single act of adultery. Four other states are similar to Kentucky and include Indiana, Missouri, North Carolina, and Ohio. Other states which note abandonment (without the addition of adultery) are discussed in AM Rhode, 'Consequences of Heirs Misconduct: Moving from Rules to Discretion' (2007) 33 *Ohio Northern University Law Review* 975, 982.

[41] KRS §391.010(2) and (3). If there are no descendants, then the other half passes to blood relatives prior to being given to the surviving spouse. It is often a surprise to a surviving spouse that he or she must share the estate with the decedent's sibling or even children of siblings. This is beyond the approach taken by the UPC which may require the spouse to share with descendants or parents but not with descendants of parents.

[42] Thus, if the surviving spouse were wealthy in his or her own right, the court might want to increase the shares received by the children or the parents. On the other hand, if the descendants or parents were wealthy in their own right, it might be proper to increase the share to the spouse either because of dependency or because the marriage was of a significant duration.

[43] See n 52.

[44] If the surviving spouse was sharing the estate with an adult nephew of the decedent, the court might find it more appropriate to give the spouse a greater share either because of dependency or because the parties had been married for a long time and the decedent had had little contact with the nephew. See n 41.

by choice) should have a claim for relief even if such an individual was not dependent on the decedent. Again the factors noted above could be used.[45] Descendants (or others) could petition the court for relief, not only because of dependency, but because the marriage was short; the surviving spouse abandoned the decedent; or there was evidence of abuse either financial or physical, etc.[46]

C. Descendants

After providing for the surviving spouse, descendants of the decedent are protected.[47] As noted, descendants take nothing if all descendants are the descendants of the decedent and the surviving spouse under the UPC.[48] The surviving spouse may or may not serve as a conduit for the descendants.[49] If the decedent or the surviving spouse had descendants by a prior relationship, the surviving spouse receives 'up front' money and one-half of the estate. The other one-half goes to the descendants of the decedent.[50]

In Kentucky, such descendants either share with the surviving spouse, or, if there is no surviving spouse, take to the exclusion of all other relatives.[51] In this way, descendants are protected from the surviving spouse who does not serve as a conduit. On the other hand, if the children are minors or otherwise handicapped, an expensive guardianship may need to be instituted.[52]

Stepchildren of the decedent do not inherit under the UPC or Kentucky, absent an adoption, unless the decedent left no blood relatives regardless of how long the stepchildren may have lived with the decedent.[53]

Foster-children or others who were living with the decedent in general will not share in the decedent's estate no matter how long they may have lived with the

[45] Committed partners of the same or opposite sex could seek relief even if not dependent on the decedent. See nn 13 and 32.

[46] A spouse who had abandoned the decedent or is otherwise an unworthy heir (nn 82–89) hereinafter perhaps should have their share decreased.

[47] Descendants take all if there is no surviving spouse even if there is a surviving parent under UPC §2-103(1)(a). In like manner, descendants will take all if there is no surviving spouse in Kentucky. KRS §391.010(1)(a). Descendants include those related by blood or adoption. They include posthumous children and non-marital children. The 2008 amendments to the UPC clarified the rights of descendants especially in the area of artificial reproductive technology. See n 13 for various proposals to help descendants. See also J Oldham, 'What Does the US System Regarding Inheritance Rights of Children Reveal about American Families?' (1999–2000) 33 *Family Law Quarterly* 265.

[48] See n 34.

[49] See the discussion (n 38) that the surviving spouse may consume most of the estate or may not serve as a conduit. See also Batts (n 13) 200 who notes that except in Louisiana a testator may disinherit even needy, minor children regardless of the size of the estate. The minor child, unlike an adult, cannot acquire property or decide how to leave property.

[50] See nn 35 and 36.

[51] See n 41.

[52] KRS §§387.010 to 387.330 deals with guardianships for a minor (although a guardianship is not required if the estate is under $10,000).

[53] UPC §2-103(b). The stepchild would take if there is no surviving spouse, no descendants; no parents or their descendants; no grandparents and their descendants. The property would first go to the other side. Kentucky also provides that a stepchild will take just before escheat to the estate; however, the potential heirs goes out to great-grandparents and their descendants; great-great-grandparents, etc on both sides before the stepchild takes. KRS §391.010(6). See also T Jones, 'Intestate Inheritance and Stepparent adoption: A Re-approval' (2013) 48 *Real Property, Trust and Estate Law Journal* 327.

decedent under the UPC or Kentucky unless they had been equitably adopted.[54] Child support obligations may, or may not terminate on the death of the decedent.[55]

Using the proposal, a descendant might seek additional estate assets based either on dependency or justice. Under the UPC, a child or other descendant may have been dependent on the decedent either financially or because of a handicap. It is not clear under the UPC why descendants take only if there are children from another marriage involved and the estate is above a certain level. The surviving spouse may have sufficient assets by themselves.[56] In Kentucky, a descendant might seek relief if the marriage with the surviving spouse was of a short duration and the spouse has adequate assets by themselves.

In like manner a stepchild who was raised in the family home may seek relief under the proposal.[57] In an appropriate case, a foster-child may seek relief. The latter would be especially true in states such as Kentucky that do not recognise the doctrine of equitable adoption.[58] A child whose support payments were terminated by the death of the decedent might seek relief.[59]

Other relatives might seek relief if a descendant is an unworthy descendant.[60]

D. Parents and Descendants of Parents

After a surviving spouse and descendants, the parents, or the surviving parent, are protected. In a UPC jurisdiction, the parent takes if the decedent is not survived by a spouse or descendants or if no parents survive then the parents' descendants take.[61] In addition, even if there is a surviving spouse, the parent(s) receive one-quarter of the estate with the surviving spouse receiving 'up front' money of $300,000 and the remaining three-quarters of the estate if there are no descendants.[62]

In Kentucky, the parent receives all the estate if there is no surviving spouse nor descendants and half of the estate if there is a surviving spouse but the decedent left no descendants.[63] Furthermore, in Kentucky, if there are no descendants and no

---

[54] See UPC §2-122. Thus, under the theory of equitable adoption, a child may be able to inherit from a parent though usually the parent cannot inherit from the child. Although Kentucky does not recognise the doctrine, if a child is so adopted in another jurisdiction and then the parents move to Kentucky, the child may have some claims in Kentucky. See *Rader v Celebrezze* [E D Ky 1966) 253 F Supp 325 (ED Ky 1966). See also Higdon (n 4) who reviews the equitable adoption theory and suggests a statutory solution.

[55] See York (n 13) 882 noting that death often extinguishes the duty to pay future child support in the absence of an agreement to the contrary. Some will continue the support if equitable considerations are present. Her proposal would continue posthumous support whether there is an order or not.

[56] Unlike the excellent proposal made by Gary (n 14) 821, the share need not be limited to that received by and share with the other children.

[57] As noted, in general a stepchild takes only if there are no other relatives. See n 53. On the other hand, if the stepchild has been raised in the family home from the time of minority, such a child may seek relief. This is provided by statute in California. West's Ann Cal Prob. Code §6454.

[58] In like manner, the proposal might be used if it is the child who died and the elements of equitable adoption are present and allow the 'parent' to inherit.

[59] See n 60.

[60] Eg a grandchild might be a more appropriate heir (based on either dependency or justice) than a parent. See discussion below starting at n 77. See also the discussion of unworthy heirs starting at n 82.

[61] UPC §§2-103(2) and (3).

[62] UPC §§2-102(2) and 2-103(2). In general, the parent(s) is the individual who functioned as a parent. UPC §§2-115-121.

[63] KRS §§391.010(2).

surviving parents, siblings of the decedent (and their descendants) share with the surviving spouse.[64] This is an approach not followed by most jurisdictions.[65]

A parent or a descendant of a parent may, in fact, have been dependent on the decedent. Thus, in a UPC jurisdiction using the proposal, a dependent parent or descendant of a parent may seek additional protection especially if the marriage was short and the surviving spouse has sufficient assets.

In Kentucky, a spouse may seek additional protection especially before the estate is distributed to the decedent's siblings or their descendants.

A parent may be an unworthy parent. The parent's parental rights may have been terminated. Under the UPC and Kentucky the parent may not inherit from or through the child.[66] The child may be able to continue to inherit from the parent, however, at least until adoption.[67] Using the proposal, a child may be able to inherit from the parent even if adopted.[68]

A parent may have abandoned the child or has not supported the child but their parental rights have not been terminated. The child could continue to inherit from the parent but should the parent be able to inherit from the child? The UPC provides that the parent may if the child died before the age of majority.[69] Kentucky allows such a parent to inherit only if the parent resumed the care of the child a year before the death of the child or the parent complied with all court orders even if the parent did not have physical custody.[70] Using the proposal a court may alter the inheritance rights for such a parent.

E. Grandparents and their Descendants

If the decedent left no descendants, surviving spouse, or parents (and their descendants), grandparents are the next protected. Both the UPC and Kentucky provide that one-half of the estate will go to the paternal side and one-half of the estate

---

[64] KRS §§391.010(3). See n 41.

[65] Although the UPC contemplates the possibility of a surviving spouse sharing a part of the estate with a parent, it is not extended to siblings of the decedent and their children. As noted in n 41, a surviving spouse in Kentucky may have to share half of the estate with a sibling of the decedent or with nieces and nephews.

[66] UPC §2-114(a)(1). KRS §625.100(1) provides that if parental rights are terminated involuntarily that this releases the parent from all legal obligations. It says nothing about the inheritance rights of the parent but it would seem that the parent can no longer inherit. See Brown, 'Disinheriting the "Legal Orphan": Inheritance Rights of Children after Termination of Parental Rights' (2005) 70 *Missouri Law Review* 125. See nn 86 and 87.

[67] Brown (n 66) who discusses the various types of statutes. Many states have statutes similar to KRS §625.104 that a child can continue to inherit from the parent until adoption. Some states divest the child of inheritance rights on termination of parental rights and others are unclear.

[68] See P Monopoli, 'Deadbeat Dads: Should Support and Inheritance be Linked' (1994) 490 *University of Miami Law Review* 257 and R Scalise, 'Honor Thy Father and Mother?: How Intestacy Law Goes too Far in Protecting Parents' (2006) 37 *Seton Hall Law Review* 171 who suggests a 'bad parent statute'.

[69] UPC §2-114(a)(1), (2) provides that a parent of a child who dies under the age of majority and there is clear and convincing evidence that immediately before the child's death the parent rights could have been terminated, the parent may not inherit. Using the proposal, such a parent could not inherit even if the child died after reaching majority.

[70] KRS §391.033(1) provides that a parent who has abandoned a child may not inherit unless the parent resumed the care and support of the child at least one year prior to the death of the child and had continued such support until death or substantially complied with all court orders regarding support.

will go to the maternal side.[71] If there are no grandparents, the share will pass to their descendants. If there are no grandparents on one side, the estate will pass to the grandparents and their descendants on the other side in a UPC jurisdiction.[72]

Kentucky continues to distribute the property on each side beyond the level of grandparent. Thus, if there are no maternal grandparents nor their descendants but there is a maternal great-grandparent, the latter individual will take. If there are no relatives on one side, it is distributed to those on the other side.[73]

In both a UPC jurisdiction and in Kentucky, if there are now no takers, but there are descendants of the decedent's deceased spouse (ie stepchildren), such individuals will take.[74] If no such descendants exist the estate then escheats to the state.[75]

It is possible under the UPC approach that a great-grandparent may be alive and was dependent on the decedent. It is possible that stepchildren under either system were dependent on the decedent. It may be more just for a stepchild to take or a great grandparent to take prior to escheat to the state. Under the proposal, such an individual could seek relief.[76]

F. Grandparents and Grandchildren

One of the most significant relationships not covered by intestacy statutes is that of a grandparent raising grandchildren. Often the parents of the grandchild are alive but are not caring for their children. The parents may have abandoned the grandchild, are incarcerated, or for some other reason are not able to care for the children.[77] Often the arrangements are informal; the grandchildren are young and the grandparent is elderly; and the grandchildren have not seen his or her parents for years. The grandparent provides for all the child's needs.

What happens if the grandparent then dies intestate? Today, under the UPC, Kentucky and probably all states the child's parent will inherit to the exclusion of the child.[78] In like manner, if the grandchild died intestate, it is the parent who will inherit (unless there are descendants or a spouse) to the exclusion of the grandparent, unless there has been a formal order of termination.[79]

---

[71] UPC §2-103(4), KRS §391.010(5)(a).

[72] UPC §2-103(5).

[73] KRS §391.010(5)(c)(d). If there are no relatives on one side, Kentucky then distributes the property to the relatives on the other side in KRS §381.010(6).

[74] Stepchildren could then take. See n 53.

[75] Except for possible stepchildren inheritance, escheat basically occurs under the UPC when there are no relatives closer than grandparents or their descendants. UPC §2-105. In Kentucky, the line can stretch out indefinitely before escheat occurs under KRS §393.020.

[76] An elderly grandparent or, in Kentucky great-grandparent, may not have the financial need (eg the government may be caring for him or her). On the other hand the decedent may not even have known of the elderly relative especially in Kentucky where the line can extend beyond that of grandparent. But see Orth, 'The Laughing Heir What's So Funny?' (2013) 48 *Real Property, Trust and Estate Law Journal* 321 who suggests remote heirs may be preferable to escheat.

[77] This issue has been addressed by many commentators. See n 13.

[78] UPC §2-103(2) and KRS §391.010(2). Again, the grandparent would inherit only if the child's parent was deceased and the grandchild left no descendants or a spouse. See discussion in n 66 regarding a formal order of termination.

[79] See n 59 which may allow for an equitable adoption.

Especially, in the former situation, the grandchild was probably dependent on the grandparent. It is also just that the grandchild should inherit to the exclusion of such a parent. The concept of equitable adoption may allow the grandchildren to inherit a portion of the estate if recognised in the jurisdiction and if it can apply. On the other hand, equitable adoption would not allow the grandparent to inherit from the grandchild.[80]

Allowing the grandchild or the grandparent to petition for relief from the intestacy statute would be highly appropriate whether because of dependency or justice.[81]

G. Unworthy Heirs

There is a group of unworthy heirs who will not inherit from a decedent. Thus, an individual who has been convicted of murder generally cannot inherit from his or her victim.[82] On the other hand, perhaps the murderer in fact was dependent on the victim or it would be just given the circumstances of the case to allow inheritance.[83] The use of the proposal might be appropriate.

In Kentucky, and in a few states, a spouse who has abandoned the decedent, is prevented from inheritance.[84] Kentucky also requires adultery. It may be just to deny inheritance rights to a surviving spouse who in fact abandoned the decedent (regardless whether or not there was adultery).[85]

As noted previously, a parent who has had his or her parental rights terminated typically cannot inherit from the child although the child may be able to do so at least until adoption.[86] A parent who has abandoned the child but whose rights have not been terminated may still be able to inherit.[87] Again, the use of the proposal adopted here may be used to assist the child.

Some states have recently addressed the issue of elder abuse which abuse may be either financial or physical.[88] In the absence of such a statute, the proposal could be used to deny inheritance rights to one who has abused an elder.[89]

---

[80] Allowing for deviation from the statutes in this situation is often advocated. See n 54.

[81] The grandparent has been serving as the parent for the child. The parent is no longer in the picture. This proposal would allow the grandparent to inherit to the exclusion of the parent.

[82] Bogert and Yzenbaard (n 30) s 479 for a discussion of 'slayer statutes'. See also L Kisabeth, 'Slayer Statutes and Elder Abuse: Good Intentions, Right Results? Does Michigan's Amended Slayer Statute do Enough to Protect the Elderly' (2013) 26 *Quinnipiac Probate Law Journal* 373; C Spivack, 'Killers Shouldn't Inherit from their Victims—or Should They' (2013 Fall) 48 *Georgia Law Review* 145; C Spivack, 'Let's Get Serious: Spousal Abuse Should Bar Inheritance' (2011) 90 *Oregon Law Review* 247.

[83] See Spivack (n 82) who suggests that often depriving a murderer from inheriting is neither legally justified or sound public policy because the murderer may have been abused or suffered a mental illness.

[84] See n 40.

[85] Abandonment alone could be sufficient. See n 40.

[86] See n 66.

[87] See nn 69 and 70.

[88] Kentucky amended its statute in 2012 to include elder abuse. See KRS §381.280. The UPC to date has not addressed this issue. Kisabeth (n 82), lists the states that have above statutes. See also Note, 'The Underserving Heir: Domestic Elder Abuser's Right to Inherit' (2010) 23 *Quinnipiac Probate Law Journal* 373; R Preble, 'Family Violence and Family Property: A Proposal for Reform' (1995) 13 *Law and Inequality Journal* 401.

[89] Thus, if an heir in fact abused the decedent, the proposal advocated in this paper could prevent such a person from inheriting.

The UPC allows for a so-called negative will.[90] This concept notes that if the will provides that a potential heir is not to inherit, the clause in the will is effective even if some of the estate passes by intestate succession. Even in a state that does not have such a provision, it would be appropriate for such a provision to be given credence in a particular case by use of the proposal advocated.[91]

III. ADDITIONAL CONSIDERATIONS

Unhappiness with intestacy statutes has led to various proposals over the past 20 years especially in the area of committed partners and with the issue of grandparents raising grandchildren.[92] But there are additional issues which arise with intestacy statutes which should also be addressed.

A. Half-bloods

Blended families, as has been noted previously, are common today and the issue of stepchildren has been addressed.[93] A couple may each have had children by a prior marriage as well as children together. What about siblings (or other relatives) who are half-bloods?[94] For example, dad has a daughter with mother number one. Later dad has two sons with mother number two. The younger son dies leaving as his sole potential heirs his full-blooded brother and his half-blooded sister; his parents having predeceased him. How should the estate be distributed?

The UPC adopts the majority view that full and half-blood members share equally.[95] Thus, the sister and the brother would each take half of the estate.

Kentucky follows the minority rule and provides that if, within a class of relatives who are to inherit, there are full and half-blood heirs that those of the full blood should take twice as much as those of the half-blood.[96] In this situation, the brother would take two-thirds of the estate and the sister would take one-third.

Mississippi states that if within the class to inherit there are members of the full blood and of the half-blood that the full blood members take to the exclusion of the half-blood members.[97] In this situation, the brother would take the entire estate.

---

[90] See UPC §2-101(b). See Note, 'The Intestate Claims of Heirs Excluded by Will: Should "Negative Wills" Be Enforced?' (1985) 52 *University of Chicago Law Review* 177.

[91] Thus, if the will specifically stated that an heir were not to take, and decedent died either totally or partially intestate, the proposal could prevent such an individual from taking.

[92] See n 13.

[93] See nn 1 and 53.

[94] The term half-blood arises when two heirs share only a common ancestor rather than two. Thus, there can only be collateral half-bloods such as siblings or aunts and uncles. The term is not used in the context of the popular Harry Potter series where a half-blood is used to identify an individual who has both magical and non-magical heritage.

[95] UPC §2-107.

[96] KRS §391.050. Other states which follow the Kentucky view include Florida, Missouri, Texas, and Virginia. Some states combine the ancestral statute with the half-blood state (Kentucky, however has a separate ancestral statute which is KRS §391.020). Ancestral states with half-blood statutes may be found in Hawaii, Nevada, Oklahoma, and Washington.

[97] Miss Code Ann §91-1-5.

The correct view could well depend on the circumstances of the case. Adoption of this proposal would allow the court to provide for dependency as well as adopt the more just result depending on the facts. Thus, if in the situation noted above, if the children were all raised together in a common household because mother number one might have died or dad had been given complete custody it would be appropriate to treat them equally. The siblings have lived together. In states following the Kentucky or Mississippi view, the daughter could petition the court to be treated the same as her full-blooded brother.

On the other hand if mother number one had primary custody of the daughter and the two sons lived with dad and mom number two and the daughter had only limited contact with the second family additional information may be needed and adjustments made.

On the other hand, dad may have had multiple families in different jurisdictions. The siblings may not even know of each other. The younger brother may not have known of his half-sister. He may deliberately not have made a will thinking all would go to his brother. Heir tracking services are common especially if the estate is large. Here the brother may want to petition the court for relief similar to that of Kentucky or Mississippi.[98]

B. *Per stirpal* Distribution

If an intestate decedent is survived by heirs who take by way of representation (eg a sibling sharing with children of a deceased sibling), an issue often arises regarding the appropriate place to divide the estate into shares.

The traditional rule, followed by Kentucky, is often referred to as the English view or 'strict *per stirpes*'. Each line of descendants is treated equally.[99] Division is made at the first stage where there is either a living member or a deceased member leaving issue. This is the view often taken by estate planners.[100]

---

[98] R Brashier, 'Consanguinity, Sibling Relationships, and the Default Rules of Inheritance Law: Reshaping Half-blood Statutes to Reflect the Evolving Family' (2005) 58 *SMU Law Review* 137. See *Estate of Griswald* 24 P 3d 1191 (Cal 2001) in which case the decedent died intestate leaving a significant amount of separate property. An heir hunter ascertained that the decedent had two half-siblings. The decedent and the half-siblings did not know each other, however, under the intestate statute those half-siblings were entitled to one-half of the estate. Another possible solution for the probate courts to use is a constructive trust theory. If the siblings did not know of each other, the court might hold that the half-bloods hold the property for the benefit of the whole blood. See Bogert and Yzenbaard (n 82) regarding constructive trusts.

[99] KRS §391.040. See *Kentucky Trust Co v Sweeney* [W D Ky 1963] 163 F Supp 45. Those states which follow this view include Connecticut, Delaware, Florida, Georgia, Illinois, Iowa, Kansas, Maryland, Mississippi, Rhode Island, Tennessee, and Wyoming. According to J Schoenblum, *Multi-State Guide to Estate Planning* Table 7 (USA, Wolters Kluwer 2010) 12 other states follow this view.

[100] See J Pennell, 'It's Not Your Father's Buick Anymore: Estate Planning for the Next Generation(s) of Client (June 2009) 43 *University of Miami Institute of Estate Planning* paras 13-1–13-59 in which article the author notes that views of estate planning are changing. He also notes that most estate planners continue to use the strict *per stirpes* model. In fn 50, he notes that the UPC just 'got it wrong'. The author notes that often estate planners do not adequately explain the difference to their clients.

The pre-1990 UPC view is currently the majority view and is often referred to as 'modern *per stirpes*' or 'per capita with representation'. Division is first made at the stage where there is a living member.[101]

The current UPC view expands upon the pre-1990 UPC view and is known as a 'per capita at each generation' (or more commonly as 'equally near, equally dear' at each generation). The thought is that the decedent would want to treat relatives of the same degree equally. Thus, division is first made at the stage where there is a living member. The shares of any deceased member who left issue are then combined and redivided.[102]

Again, depending on the circumstances, one view may be more preferable than the other either because of dependency or justice. A decedent may have had three children all of whom predeceased him leaving issue. The share of a grandchild may be one-third (if strict *per stirpes* is used) or less if modern *per stirpes* is used. The larger share may be appropriate (or even a larger one) if the grandchild had been dependent on the decedent or had been the sole care-giver of the decedent or perhaps it should be less because of the dependency of cousins or that another was the sole care-giver. This proposal would allow for modifications to be made.

C. Advancements

The doctrine of advancements promoted the concept of equality among the heirs of an intestate. It provided that if a gift was made to an heir during lifetime that the gift may be considered when distribution is made of the decedent's estate.[103]

As an example, a father died intestate survived by two children: a son and a daughter. As we have seen, all jurisdictions would divide the estate equally between them. If, however, the father had made a lifetime gift to the son, and if it is viewed as an advancement, the son's share would be adjusted to reflect the lifetime gift. This is what would occur in Kentucky. If the gift was made to a child by a parent or grandchild, it is an advancement unless it were for the maintenance or education of the child. Intent is irrelevant.[104]

---

[101] UPC §2-106 (pre-1990 version) read as follows: 'If representation is called for by this Code, the estate is divided into as many shares as there are surviving heirs in the nearest degree of kinship and deceased persons in the same degree who left issue who survive the decedent, each surviving heir in the nearest degree receiving one share and the share of each deceased person in the same degree being divided among his issue in the same manner'. According to Schoenblum (n 99) 24, jurisdictions use this approach.

[102] UPC §2-106(b) and (c). According to Schoenblum (n 99) 14, jurisdictions follow this approach.

[103] See Yzenbaard (n 7) para 2:15. The purpose of the advancement statute is to have equality. If a gift is viewed as an advancement, the hotch-pot system method is used to compute the shares. See the comments to UPC §2-109 to explain the hotch-pot system.

[104] KRS §391.140(1). An advancement is when a gift has been made by a parent to a child or a grandparent to a grandchild. The donor cannot avoid the statute by noting that advancement is not intended. The only exception is the expenditure of money for the maintenance and education of a minor child nor is money spent for the care of an adult incompetent child. *Crain v Mallone* 113 SW 67 (1908). Of course, the statute does not apply if the decedent died totally testate.

The UPC, and the majority of jurisdictions, now hold that a gift to the heir is an advancement only if at the time the gift was made the donor declared in a contemporaneous writing, or the heir acknowledges in writing that the gift is an advancement. Many lay persons do not know of the writing requirement.[105]

The use of the proposal would allow intent to be considered in Kentucky to do justice or to provide for a needed dependency. Its use could excuse the requirement for writing in a UPC jurisdiction when appropriate.

IV. CONCLUSION

More than half of decedent people die intestate. Intestate statutes are needed to distribute property owned at the time of death. Intestate statutes today are efficient and easy to administer. The statutes are not, however, necessarily just or fair. In the exceptional case if an individual can prove that they either were dependent on the decedent or that the distribution under the statute is unfair or unjust, adjustments can and should be made. Clear and convincing evidence would be required (or even a higher standard).

---

[105] UPC §2-109(1).

Part IV

Property and Ownership

11

Challenging 'Home' as a Concept in Modern Property Law: Lessons from the Supreme Court Post-Stack and Jones

CHRIS BEVAN[*]

I. INTRODUCTION

MODERN PROPERTY LAWYERS have, for some time now, debated and indeed been divided over the precise conceptualisation of 'home' and its relevance in property law. What is 'home'? Does 'home' provide identity? Or is 'home' merely an asset?[1] What weight, if any, should be attached to 'home'? Does 'home' exhibit any discreet legal meaning at all? Those who call for the recognition of a distinct concept of 'home' suggest that, not just legal academics, but also the courts are now beginning to engage meaningfully with these questions.[2] This chapter will evaluate how far assertions of judicial engagement with the concept of 'home' can be substantiated and what lessons can be learned from the Supreme Court in cases in which the fact of property as 'home' formed a material consideration.

The starting point for this chapter is the important yet somewhat well-trammelled case law of *Stack v Dowden*[3] and *Jones v Kernott*.[4] The court in both *Stack* and *Jones* underscored that in response to changing social and economic conditions the law had 'moved on' and consequently the courts should give legal effect to the context of 'home'.[5] Both welcomed[6] and bemoaned,[7] these two crucial decisions reflect a clear policy shift towards treating domestic property disputes differently from those arising in commercial circumstances. As is well-rehearsed, the court in

---

[*] Assistant Professor in Property Law, University of Nottingham; Barrister (Middle Temple).

[1] See A Hudson, 'Rapporteur's Overview: Differentiation in Property Law' in A Hudson, *New Perspectives on Property Law, Human Rights and the Home* (London, Routledge Cavendish, 2003) 324 noted in N Hopkins, 'Regulating Trusts of the Home: Private Law and Social Policy' (2009) 125 *LQR* 310, 311

[2] See L Fox, *Conceptualising Home: Theories, Laws and Policies* (Oxford, Hart Publishing, 2007); L Fox, 'The Meaning of Home: A Chimerical Concept or a Legal Challenge?' (2002) 29(4) *Journal of Law and Society* 580 and A Buyse, 'Strings Attached: The Concept of "Home" in the Case Law of the European Court of Human Rights' (2006) 3 *European Human Rights Law Review* 294.

[3] *Stack v Dowden* [2007] UKHL 17, [2007] 2 AC 432.

[4] *Jones v Kernott* [2011] UKSC 53, [2012] 1 AC 776.

[5] See Hopkins (n 1).

[6] M Harding, 'Defending *Stack v Dowden*' (2009) 4 *Conveyancer and Property Lawyer* 309.

[7] M Dixon, 'The Never-ending Story: Co-ownership after *Stack v Dowden*' (2012) 71 *Conveyancer and Property Lawyer* 456.

these cases placed particular emphasis on the fact of property as 'home'.[8] This is perhaps best captured by Baroness Hale's oft-cited observation that 'in law "context is everything"'.[9] Moreover, as Lord Hope observed, 'cohabiting couples are in a different kind of relationship. The place where they live together is their home'.[10] For the majority in *Stack* and *Jones* this was the foundation upon which the application of different rules for the family home was premised. These decisions represent a significant step towards the recognition of a concept of 'home' in modern property law. It is stimulating, therefore, to consider how far *Stack* and *Jones* can be seen as initiating a process of greater engagement by the Supreme Court with notions of 'home'? *Stack* and *Jones* will not be considered in detail here[11] but rather are adopted as a point of departure from which will be examined the three cases which will form the focus of this piece: *Manchester City Council v Pinnock*;[12] *Hounslow LBC v Powell*[13] and *Sharif (FC) v London Borough of Camden*.[14]

The chapter argues that, taken together, the three decisions reflect an important legal moment for the emergence of such a concept of 'home'. This chapter will critically analyse the reasoning of the court in *Pinnock*, *Powell* and *Sharif* before pausing to evaluate the broader ramifications of these judgments for the development and viability of a concept of 'home' in English and Welsh property law. It will be argued that following *Pinnock*, *Powell* and *Sharif* a more nuanced picture is required of the traction being gained by the concept of 'home' in this jurisdiction's highest court than exponents of the concept would suggest. In this way, the concept of 'home' is subjected to important challenge and this chapter sends a warning shot across the bows to those who argue in favour of the concept.

This chapter will begin with a discussion of the legal significance of the concept of 'home' by drawing on the theoretical literature in this area. The subsequent section analyses the judgments and reasoning of the Supreme Court in the *Pinnock*, *Powell* and *Sharif* decisions before moving to proffer several observations that can be distilled from these important cases; insights which will be of use and resonance to policymakers as well as academics researching in this field. A concluding section seeks to weigh up the consequences of these Supreme Court decisions for the future of the concept of 'home' and to cast new light on this most 'chimerical' of concepts.[15]

II. WHAT IS THE CONCEPT OF HOME?

The concept of home appears to be in need of legal counsel ... we know that there is 'no place like home' that 'home is where the heart is'. Yet the legal conception of home cannot be summed up so neatly.[16]

---

[8] See, amongst others, S Gardner, 'Family Property Today' (2008) 124 *LQR* 422.

[9] *Stack* (n 3) 459 (Baroness Hale).

[10] Ibid, 439 (Lord Hope).

[11] For eloquent consideration of these cases, see S Gardner and K Davidson, 'The Future of *Stack v Dowden*' (2011) 127 *LQR* 13; Dixon (n 7); M Yip, 'The Rules Applying to Unmarried Cohabitants' Family Home: *Jones v Kernott*' (2012) 2 *Conveyancer and Property Lawyer* 159.

[12] *Manchester City Council v Pinnock* [2010] UKSC 45, [2010] 3 WLR 1441.

[13] *Hounslow LBC v Powell* [2011] UKSC 8, [2011] 2 WLR 287.

[14] *Sharif (FC) v London Borough of Camden* [2013] UKSC 10; see generally C Bevan, 'Living "Together" Apart: s 176 of the Housing Act 1996' (2013) 4 *Conveyancer and Property Lawyer* 334.

[15] See S Merrett, *Owner-Occupation in Britain* (London, Routledge & Kegan Paul, 1982) 65.

[16] Fox, 'The Meaning of Home' (n 2).

Whilst most academics and indeed members of the public would readily accept that 'home' is something altogether different from the bricks-and-mortar connotations of 'house' precisely how to quantify and define the distinction remains largely a contested question. This struggle to make sense of the meaning of 'home' in the legal sphere has found its clearest expression in what has become known as the 'concept of home'.[17] Along with studies from the United States,[18] the work by Fox O'Mahony in this area provides the key foundation for a consideration of this concept of 'home'. It must not however be assumed that such a concept is in any way uncontroversial in academic study and particularly in the legal sphere. Indeed, for some there remains considerable debate as to the value, utility and even the existence of such a concept.[19] As a starting point, it is important to note that the concept of 'home' as an area of research has its origins not in legal jurisprudence nor legal academia but rather has grown out of a large body of literature primarily of non-legal social science disciplines, such as environmental sciences, through the study of 'place' and most crucially from psychology.[20] This may go some way to explain an anticipated reluctance on the part of some doctrinal property lawyers to engage more fully and in a more meaningful manner with the concept. There will be those[21] who would doubt its place in modern property law and question its very significance and the extent to which it adds anything to property law reasoning. From a traditionalist perspective, the concept may create an unhelpful, nebulous subdivision of property law. Fox herself concedes that the concept is not without its challenges, for example, by identifying the 'mutualist' problem; namely that the concept of 'home' subsumes within one single unit what may be a number of individuals' rights rather than recognising individual entitlement to property; thus masking individual rights to property.[22]

How is one therefore to assess the significance of 'home' from a distinctly property law perspective and within the specific context of property law? The central problem here for the development of a concept of 'home' is the tension that exists between, on the one hand, a key focus of modern property law being free alienability of land, of land as asset or investment[23] and the claims of creditors, and on the other, occupiers' innately intangible and almost exclusively, immeasurable personal attachment to their home. As a reaction to the more subjective flavour of 'home' there are those who argue against the development of such a concept at all.[24] Merrett

[17] See generally work by L Fox O'Mahony (nee Fox).

[18] See, eg DB Barros, 'Home as a Legal Concept' 46 *Santa Clara Law Review* 255.

[19] See, amongst others, Merrett (n 15).

[20] See, eg DN Benjamin (ed), *The Home: Words, Interpretations, Meanings and Environments* (Aldershot, Avebury Publishing Ltd, 1995).

[21] See N Hopkins, 'The Relevance of Context in Property Law: A Case for Judicial Restraint?' 31(2) *Legal Studies* 175 who calls for restraint in context-specific judicial decision-making; see comments by J Dewar, 'Land, Law and the Family Home' in S Bright and J Dewar (eds), *Land Law: Themes and Perspectives* (Oxford, Oxford University Press, 1998), as to the problem of the piecemeal nature of considerations of 'home'. See also Merrett (n 15); K Dovey, 'Home and Homelessness' in I Altman and CM Werner (eds), *Home Environments* (New York, Plenum, 1985) who identifies profound challenges with the development of a concept of 'home'.

[22] See Fox (n 2) above.

[23] See N Hopkins, '*City of London Building Society v Flegg* (1987): *Homes as Wealth*' in N Gravells (ed), *Landmark Cases in Land Law* (Oxford, Hart Publishing, 2013).

[24] Merrett (n 10) above; also Dovey (n 21); J Moore, 'Placing Home in Context' (2000) 20 *Journal of Environmental Psychology* 207.

has argued that attempts to ascribe a special, particular legal meaning to home are 'purely phantasmal'[25] noting that, in the search for a specific meaning for 'home', 'the hunter always circles back to his starting point and finds no more, yet no less than a dwelling, located in space beyond which individual human beings grouped in households engage in a complex set of activities'.[26] Likewise, a further barrier to the development of a distinct concept of 'home' is the contention that the notion of 'home' does not reflect a concrete concept at all and rather, as Moore argues, 'home' is better explained as an 'imposed ideal', forming part of a larger ideology of home[27] rather than a tangible 'reality'. Into the debate which encircles the recognition of a concept of 'home' must also feed a wider but related and thorny issue which pervades property law more broadly; namely the extent to which weight should attach, if at all, to matters of 'context' in property law disputes.[28] A discussion of this issue is beyond the scope of this chapter.

For Fox O'Mahony however, though an occupier's interest in property *as a home* is indeed intangible, this is 'certainly not an insurmountable hurdle to the recognition of legally defensible rights'.[29] Fox O'Mahony's research is buttressed by Gray and Symes[30] who have noted the essential primacy of home: that all individuals (including the homeless) live somewhere and, consequently, all have a relationship with the land whether that be as proprietor, tenant or squatter.[31] It is in this way that property law reaches most directly into all aspects of society and from which the significance of 'home' emerges. Equally, nor are the pages of statute books free from references to 'home'. From the law surrounding capital gains tax,[32] to regulation of the matrimonial home,[33] to measures designed to address domestic violence,[34] the home is routinely provided with a special significance that extends beyond the mere physical structure of a house.[35] Thus, for Fox O'Mahony, the need for recognition of a distinct legal concept of 'home' to assist policymakers and judges when called upon to balance the interests of occupiers in the home is made out; particularly in the creditor context where it is argued consideration of issues of 'home' would be most useful. She identifies a four-part categorisation or 'four main clusters of value-types'[36] associated with 'home': home as physical structure; home as territory; home as identity; home as social and cultural unit. These value-types are used to better explain the psychology of 'home' and to assist in developing a clearer understanding of the meaning of 'home'.

---

[25] Merrett (n 15) above.

[26] Ibid.

[27] Moore (n 24) above.

[28] See, eg N Hopkins (n 21); also A Hayward, 'The "Context" of Home: Cohabitation and Ownership Disputes in England and Wales' in M Diamond and T Turnipseed (eds), *Community, Home and Identity* (Farnham, Ashgate, 2012) 179.

[29] Fox (n 2) 609.

[30] KJ Gray and PD Symes, *Real Property and Real People* (London, Butterworths, 1981).

[31] See generally Benjamin (n 20) above.

[32] Taxation of Chargeable Gains Act 1992, s 222.

[33] Family Law Act 1996; Matrimonial Causes Act 1973.

[34] Family Law Act 1996, Pt IV.

[35] See, eg DG Hayward, 'Home as an Environmental and Psychological Concept' (1975) 20 *Landscape* 2; H Dittmar, *The Social Psychology of Material Possessions* (Hemel Hempstead, Harvester Wheatsheaf, 1992) 113; M Csikszentmihalyi and E Rochberg-Halton, 'Home as Symbolic Environment' in M Csikszentmihalyi and E Rochberg-Halton (eds), *The Meaning of Things—Domestic Symbols and the Self* (Cambridge, Cambridge University Press, 1981) 123.

[36] Fox (n 2) 590.

It must be underlined that these categories are not static and a particular factual scenario may give rise to a combination of all or none of these values.[37] As noted briefly above, the concept is however not without its serious defectors and Fox O'Mahony herself acknowledges the ambiguities and difficulties in searching for a legal framework of 'home' here conceding that, 'obviously home is a difficult concept to pin down ... a complex and multi-dimensional amalgam of financial, practical, social, psychological, cultural, politico-economic and emotional interests'.[38] This remains so despite some definitional assistance offered from various legal sources such as the Inheritance (Provision for Family and Dependants) Act 1975, the Administration of Justice Act 1970, and article 8 of the ECHR case law amongst others.

Certainly, if a concept of 'home' does exist it appears to rest on less than concrete foundations. One reason for this is that the term 'home' is itself one that is extremely emotionally-charged; one imbued with diffuse meanings and associative of a whole range of idiosyncratic characteristics. Moreover, in any discussion surrounding its meaning, old adages and aphorisms abound: home, as they say, being where the heart is and an Englishman's home being his castle. Others point to the importance of 'home' as being observed as far back in literature as Homer's classical poem 'The Odyssey'.[39] Whatever the starting point, however, there is an immediate, universal and societal appreciation for and familiarity with the idea of 'home'; with every person bringing their own particular background and sensibilities to bear on the issue. However, this does little to inform how the law should regard such a concept; how it should be defined, construed by the courts or whether the law should pay heed to the particularities of 'home' whatsoever. Repeated references to adages and truisms present a very real risk of sentimentalising and trivialising our understanding of 'home' and thus preventing its development into a recognisable and coherent concept; minimising its potential to play a meaningful role in legal jurisprudence. Moreover, for lawyers, and property lawyers most specifically, the concept incites particular difficulties. As has been noted 'home is a subjective phenomenon'[40] and any distinct legal concept of 'home' is very much at the 'pre-scientific, speculative stage'.[41] Further complications arise from the inherently 'socio-emotional' considerations that all too often attach to individuals' relationship with 'home'.[42] Ideas of 'home' may prove difficult to communicate and consequently scrutinise.[43] Moreover, as Dovey explains, 'understanding in this area is plagued by a lack of verifiability that many will find frustrating'.[44] Yet, as Benjamin has argued, the phenomenon of

---

[37] Fox builds on the work of Despres, 'The Meaning of Home' (n 2). See also Csikszentmihalyi and Rochberg-Halton (n 35) above; J Hayward, 'Psychological Concepts of Home' (1977) *Challenge* 10; R Sebba and A Churchman, 'The Uniqueness of Home' (1986) 3 *Architecture and Behaviour* 7; SG Smith, 'The Essential Qualities of Home' (1994) 14 *Journal of Environmental Psychology* 31.

[38] Fox (n 2) 607.

[39] See Buyse (n 2) above.

[40] Fox (n 2) 581.

[41] Ibid, 588.

[42] See MJ Radin, *Reinterpreting Property* (Chicago, University of Chicago Press, 1993); MJ Radin, 'Property and Personhood' (1982) 34 *Stanford Law Review* 957; DB Barros, 'Symposium: A Psychological Perspective on Property Law: Legal Questions for the Psychology of Home' (2009) 83 *Tulane Law Review* 645; Buyse (n 2) above.

[43] Hayward (n 35).

[44] Dovey (n 21).

'home', however perplexing, is too significant to be 'deemed inappropriate and then forgotten'.[45] This search for home leads Fox to identify the so-termed 'enigmatic x factor' under 'which *'home* = house + x';[46] with x being that intangible quality which forms the sum of personal experiences that take place within a home. The true challenge is to be found in a determination of how the law (and here, property law) should define that 'x factor', how the concept can be of use, when the courts should engage with the concept and the weight that ought to attach to it. These questions remain the central source of debate as to the development of a distinct legal concept of 'home'.

A further hurdle in recognising a distinct concept of 'home' is that both research into and critique of the concept have almost exclusively been confined to theoretical analyses with very little if any material academic engagement with the role played by the courts in the development of this concept or of how decided cases inform the debate here. As Fox O'Mahony acknowledges, the values of 'home', 'have not been recognised by policy makers, nor yet translated into a coherent legal concept which could inform the task of balancing interests'[47] in property law disputes. Moreover, she highlights the 'challenge … to find ways to articulate "home" meaning; to place this type of claim on the policy agenda'.[48] This may be due to the inherent ambiguity embedded within the concept and the concept being very much in its infancy. Nevertheless, it is suggested that the justificatory underpinning of the concept would be strengthened by an enquiry as to the relationship between the concept of 'home' and the courts. It is in this way that this chapter through analysis of *Pinnock*, *Powell* and *Sharif*, three important and, in the case of *Sharif*, much-overlooked Supreme Court decisions, seeks to make a contribution to the research around 'home'.

Much ink has been spilled identifying and discussing the particular values that encompass 'home' both within and without legal academia and the suggestion has now been made that the courts are beginning to take account of the concept of 'home'. Moreover, there has been a flurry of Supreme Court decisions which, on their face, appear to engage with arguments around the family home, communality and interconnectedness of family life, which provide scope for the assertion that the concept of 'home' as a distinct concept is gaining traction. As such, proponents of the concept would argue that a judicial as opposed to a merely theoretical concept of 'home' is emerging. The following section will therefore probe the extent to which this assertion withstands scrutiny. Thus, having outlined and introduced the concept this chapter now turns to consider the Supreme Court decisions in *Pinnock*, *Powell* and *Sharif* and what they have to tell us as to the debate that surrounds the concept of 'home', its status, its relevance and its application in our highest court.

---

[45] DN Benjamin, 'Afterword' in Benjamin, *The Home* (n 20) 294.
[46] See Fox (n 2) 590.
[47] Ibid, 607.
[48] L Fox O'Mahony, 'The Meaning of Home: From Theory to Practice' (2013) 5(2) *International Journal of Law in Built Environment* 156, 167.

III. THE DECISIONS IN *PINNOCK* AND *POWELL*[49]

Described as having 'the potential to be the most significant judgment in housing law since *Street v Mountford*',[50] the case of *Pinnock*[51] introduced and *Powell*[52] refined the proportionality defence in mandatory possession proceedings.[53] Thus, where a local authority brings possession proceedings relying on a mandatory ground for possession, the occupier is entitled to have the proportionality of his eviction assessed by a court under the Human Rights Act 1998, Schedule 1, article 8. Domestically, this was a significant step and affirmed the long-held stance in the European Court of Human Rights (ECtHR) where there had been repeated assertions by the court that a proportionality defence should be open to any person facing interference with his or her home.[54]

Pre-*Pinnock*, the domestic courts had, for some time, been struggling with the relationship between the protection and respect for property rights and the effect of article 8.[55] In *Harrow LBC v Qazi*,[56] for example, widely regarded as 'the high watermark of the judicial preference for property rights',[57] the English courts resisted the notion that article 8 'could disturb the established order of property rights'.[58] The Supreme Court in *Pinnock*, faced with the 'unambiguous and consistent approach of the European Court of Human Rights'[59] overturned the earlier decisions in the House of Lords, holding that:

> [I]f our law is to be compatible with Article 8, where a court is asked to make an order for possession of a person's home at the suit of a local authority, the court must have the power to assess the proportionality of making the order, and, in making that assessment, to resolve any relevant dispute of fact.[60]

Pinnock thus pulled the domestic courts in line with the Strasbourg jurisprudence and as such the 'absoluteness of the right to recovery of possession'[61] as seen in the pre-*Pinnock* case law was modified. The rights paradigm, previously in place, that meant ownership of land would always be grounds for the grant of a possession

---

[49] See generally, S Bright, '*Manchester City Council v Pinnock*: Shifting Ideas of Ownership of Land' in Gravells (ed), *Landmark Cases in Land Law* (n 23) 272; D Cowan, C Hunter, '"Yeah but, no but"— *Pinnock* and *Powell* in the Supreme Court' (2012) 75(1) *MLR* 78; S Nield, N Hopkins, 'Human Rights and Mortgage Repossession: Beyond Property Law Using Article 8' (2013) 33 (3) *Legal Studies* 431.

[50] Cowan and Hunter (n 49) 78.

[51] *Pinnock* (n 12).

[52] *Powell* (n 13).

[53] See D Astin, *Housing Law* (Legal Action Group, 2011); D Cowan, *Housing Law and Practice* (Cambridge, Cambridge University Press, 2011) 378–405.

[54] See *McCann v United Kingdom* (2008) 47 EHRR 40 [50].

[55] See S Nield, 'Article 8 Again—the Continuing Dialogue!' (2010) 6 *Conveyancer and Property Lawyer* 498.

[56] *Harrow LBC v Qazi* [2003] UKHL 43.

[57] Cowan and Hunter (n 49) 78.

[58] Bright (n 49) 253.

[59] *Pinnock* (n 12) [50].

[60] Ibid, [49] (Lord Neuberger).

[61] Bright (n 49) 257.

order against an occupier with no proprietary, contractual or statutory right to be in occupation, was recast in *Pinnock*. Thus,

> [a]ny person at risk of being dispossessed of his home at the suit of a local authority should in principle have the right to raise the question of the proportionality of the measure, and to have it determined by an independent tribunal in the light of Article 8 ... Traditional judicial review (that does not permit the court to make its own assessment of the facts) is inadequate for this purpose as it is not appropriate for resolving sensitive factual disputes.[62]

The Supreme Court in *Powell* made two central qualifications to the application of the article 8 proportionality question as introduced in *Pinnock*, that the 'Court will only have to consider whether the making of a possession order is proportionate if the issue has been raised by the occupier *and* if it has crossed the high threshold of being seriously arguable' (emphasis added).[63]

As Cowan and Hunter note, 'despite being ostensibly concerned with the practical application of the proportionality defence, [*Powell*] is singularly unhelpful in providing any guidance as to what might make a decision to seek possession disproportionate'.[64] While the court suggested that 'exceptionality' was not the appropriate test,[65] little clarification was given of the factors that might go to indicate possession as disproportionate. Crucially, considerations of 'home' are suffused and taken into account within this proportionality exercise.

IV. THE DECISION IN *SHARIF V CAMDEN LBC*[66]

Sharif, another Supreme Court decision, on this occasion in a non-possession proceedings context, provides further insights into how the judiciary engage with the concept of 'home'. In *Sharif*, the principal issue before the court was the extent to which the statutory language 'available for occupation' and 'together with' in section 176 of the Housing Act 1996 (hereafter 'the 1996 Act') implied a requirement that a homeless person be accommodated by a local authority not only with his family but under the same roof within a single unit of accommodation. Reversing the decision of the Court of Appeal, the Supreme Court adopted a highly pragmatic (and arguably controversial)[67] definition of the concept of living 'together' in section 176; holding that the local authority had indeed adequately discharged its duty under the 1996 Act by the provision to Ms Sharif and her family of two separate units of accommodation; with the family split across two flats. Despite, the Council's conceding that the two split units were not an 'ideal living arrangement' for Ms Sharif and her unwell father (who had previously lived together within a single unit), it argued that the accommodation was, nevertheless, suitable and that, as such, the Council had adequately discharged its housing duty under section 193 of the 1996 Act.

---

[62] *Pinnock* (n 12) [45] (Lord Neuberger).
[63] Ibid.
[64] Cowan and Hunter (n 49) 84.
[65] *Pinnock* (n 12) [51] (Lady Hale), 'exceptionality is an outcome and not a guide'.
[66] For a discussion of this judgement see Bevan (n 14); also, 'Accommodating Homeless Families in Separate Units—Resurrecting the Spirit of *Puhlhofer*? (April 2013) *Housing Law Monitor* 1.
[67] Ibid.

The Court of Appeal[68] reversing the decision at first instance was persuaded on the 'ordinary use of the legislative language'[69] that two units meant that Ms Sharif and her father 'would be living close by each other, but separate from one another'.[70] Etherton LJ took the view that 'it cannot be said, on any ordinary use of language, that persons living in separate self-contained flats, however close, and not sharing any communal area, are residing together'.[71]

Etherton LJ expressed sympathy for the difficulties encountered by local housing authorities but underscored the policies underlying the homelessness provisions of the 1996 Act. It was 'common ground', said Etherton LJ that the policy objective at the heart of section 176 of the 1996 Act was to keep families together.

In the Supreme Court, Lord Carnwath, delivering the leading judgment, emphasised by reference to the somewhat infamous House of Lords case of *Puhlhofer*,[72] that Parliament had set down no statutory standard or qualification as to the nature of 'accommodation' under the 1996 Act.[73] Subsequent amendments to the legislation such as the inclusion of the 'suitability' requirement,[74] whilst mitigating the harshness of the *Puhlhofer* test, did not change the definition of 'accommodation' or diminish the authority of the House of Lords' authority in *Puhlofer*.

For Lord Carnwath, the 'ordinary meaning' to be ascribed to the statutory language of section 176 did not lend support to the interpretation engaged by Etherton LJ in the Court of Appeal. Following *Puhlofer*, the term 'accommodation' was a neutral one and it would not be an abuse to talk of a family being 'accommodated' in two adjoining flats.[75] His Lordship was clear that:

> The statutory test [in section 176] will be satisfied by a single unit of accommodation in which a family can live together. But it may also be satisfied by two units of accommodation if they are so located that they enable the family to live 'together' in practical terms.[76]

This reference to family life 'in practical terms' is extremely interesting from the 'home' perspective and warrants further consideration which will follow in the subsequent section of this chapter. In essence, the Supreme Court held that it was a matter of fact for the authority as to whether accommodation satisfied this statutory test and, short of irrationality, such decisions would rarely raise points of law necessitating the court's determination.

A. Lord Kerr's Dissent

Lord Kerr argued there was nothing in the legislation to suggest that the statutory duty could be satisfied by providing accommodation 'in conjunction with other

---

[68] *Sharif* (n 68).
[69] Ibid, [17].
[70] Ibid.
[71] Ibid.
[72] *R v Hillingdon London Borough Council, Ex p Puhlhofer* [1986] AC 484; see MA Jones, 'Recent cases' (Sept 1986) *Journal of Social Welfare Law* 305.
[73] *Sharif* (n 14) [5].
[74] See s 206 (1) of the 1996 Act. For a full consideration of the issue of suitability in provision of social housing, see J Luba and L Davies, *Housing Allocation and Homelessness: Law and Practice*, 3rd edn (Bristol, Jordan Publishing, 2013) 867–921.
[75] *Sharif* (n 14)[17].
[76] Ibid.

accommodation' such as in the present case. Lord Kerr emphasised that 'sufficient proximity' as advanced in argument by the Council was not the same as 'living together'. The section 176 duty was essentially one 'to provide accommodation, the physical dimensions of which are sufficient to allow it to be occupied by the person to whom it is made available together with the members of his or her family'.[77]

Lord Kerr drew attention to the latest Code of Guidance: 'Homelessness Code of Guidance for Local Authorities' (2006)[78] noting that there was nothing to recommend a separatist or split accommodation policy. Finally, Lord Kerr expressed concern that, given the pressures faced by housing authorities, were split accommodation to be a very real option, they would likely seek to exploit it most severely. If this was to happen, a 'principal purpose of the legislation (that of bringing and keeping families together) will be, if not undermined, at least put under considerable strain'.[79]

The Supreme Court decisions in *Pinnock*, *Powell* and *Sharif* raise interesting and important questions as to the concept of 'home': to what extent do these judgments evidence the court engaging with the discourse of 'home'? Is the proportionality defence shown in *Pinnock* and *Powell* offering a conduit for judicial consideration of 'home'? What can this judicial attention or lack thereof tell us as to the traction gained by the concept of 'home' in this jurisdiction's highest court? Is regard being had to the psychological, intangible values of 'home' or is the court eschewing such a consideration? Finally, what might these three important decisionssignal for the future development of the emerging concept of 'home'? It is to these questions that we now turn.

V. THE SUPREME COURT AND THE CONCEPT OF 'HOME': LESSONS AND OBSERVATIONS

A. Engagement of the Supreme Court with the Concept of 'Home'

Pinnock is widely regarded as a significant case in modern property law so far as it resolved a difficult tension that existed between the ECtHR and the domestic courts concerning the absoluteness of property rights and an article 8 proportionality defence. In so doing, it arguably also evidences a burgeoning engagement on the part of the Supreme Court with the concept of 'home'. As Bright notes, the proportionality defence heralded in *Pinnock* necessarily 'involves a more personal dimension: whether the measure as applied to *this* occupier *in these circumstances* and in *this manner* is proportionate'.[80] Thus, *Pinnock* can be seen as signalling a wider shift towards a more contextualised approach by the courts under which account will be taken of the personal circumstances of occupiers and the impact of the granting of a possession order on them and their wider family. For Bright, *Pinnock* can be interpreted as a new way of thinking about ownership that 'courts must not only "take ownership seriously" but also must "take home seriously"'.[81] If this

---

[77] Ibid, [35].
[78] Department for Communities and Local Government, 'Homelessness Code of Guidance for Local Authorities' (2006).
[79] *Sharif* (n 14) [38].
[80] Bright (n 49) 263.
[81] Ibid, 274, modifying Dworkin's phraseology.

is correct, *Pinnock* reflects a very important legal development indeed and one in which the previously, largely-irrelevant considerations of vulnerability and attachment to 'home' (irrelevant particularly in mandatory possession proceedings) are to assume a new significance. On this view, precisely the 'value-types' elucidated by Fox O'Mahony and others as part of their research into 'home' may factor heavily in any proportionality argument advanced with a consequential surge in the profile of the concept of 'home' in the domestic court system. In assessing the proportionality question, matters going to 'home' such as identity, security and cultural signifier on one view could become important issues. It is therefore possible to point to *Pinnock* as evidence of the increasing attention being paid by the Supreme Court to matters of 'home' as part of the proportionality balancing act exercise.

However, caution is very much required so as not to overstate the significance of *Pinnock* for the concept of 'home'. It is at this point that the decisions in *Powell* and in *Sharif* offer an important brake on any potential exaggeration of the development of the concept of 'home' in the Supreme Court. As Cowan and Hunter rightly have argued, in fact, the implications of the decision in *Pinnock* 'are probably extremely limited'.[82] In this way, care must also be taken when extrapolating conclusions from *Pinnock* as to the emerging concept of 'home'. Thus, while an argument may be mounted that *Pinnock* might messenger a novel engagement with considerations of 'home', communality, interconnectedness, *Powell* acts as an anchor on the true scope of *Pinnock's* significance. Indeed in view of the strict authority in *Powell*, *Pinnock* may not require consideration of 'home' at all.

First, as noted in *Powell*, the proportionality defence is only likely to apply in exceptional cases[83] meaning that the effect of the judgment for the concept of 'home' is itself limited at best. Secondly, as explored above, the 'twin aims' of the vindication of local authority property rights and management of housing stock will, it appears, always be regarded as constituting the pursuit of a legitimate aim thus defeating most proportionality arguments founded on an occupier's personal circumstances. Thirdly, the requirement for occupiers themselves to raise the article 8 defence coupled with the 'high threshold' of a seriously arguable case, as set out by the Supreme Court in *Powell*, underlines the restrictions placed on the proportionality defence; a restriction which in turn will mean that personal circumstances and considerations of 'home' will rarely be considered by the court at all. Given that such a proportionality defence is likely be considered summarily by a District Judge in a busy possessions list in over-stretched county courts,[84] any perceived increase in engagement of the courts with the concept of 'home' must also be cast in considerable doubt. As Lord Hope noted in *Powell*'there will be no need, in the overwhelming majority of cases, for the local authority to explain or justify its reasons for seeking a possession order'.[85]

The natural corollary of this is that there will in the overwhelming majority of cases be no need for the courts to undertake a 'home' analysis either. Similarly, there

---

[82] Cowan and Hunter (n 49) 84; see also I Loveland, 'The Holy Grail as an Empty Chalice? Proportionality Review in Possession Proceedings after *Pinnock* and *Powell*' (2013) 6 *Journal of Public Law* 622.
[83] *Pinnock* (n 12) [50].
[84] As explored by the court in *Pinnock* (n 12) [57].
[85] *Powell* (n 13) [37] (Lord Hope).

is little clarification, following *Pinnock* and *Powell*, as to which personal factors, in any event, might be relevant in determining proportionality and as to just how context will be used by the courts. A rather troubling remark by Lord Neuberger in the Supreme Court in *Pinnock* only lends further support for this concern namely that, 'the wide implications [of a proportionality defence] will have to be worked out'.[86] As such, much doubt surrounds the real impact of the *Pinnock* decision. As Lord Phillips concluded in *Powell*, it is only in 'highly exceptional cases, that it will be appropriate for the court to consider a proportionality argument'.[87] Thus, whilst Bright posits that *Pinnock* requires academics and policymakers to re-evaluate the very idea of ownership and what it means to possess property,[88] equally the argument can be made that, in light of *Powell*, *Pinnock* marks a far more illusory, than symbolic practical change both for the proportionality defence and the concept of 'home' more generally.

An altogether different perspective is offered by *Sharif*. Whilst neither the Court of Appeal nor the Supreme Court judgments make explicit reference to the language of the concept of 'home', each court evinces a different approach as regards the more intangible, socio-emotional qualities of communality, interconnectedness and living together as a family which are said to form part of the wider concept of 'home'.[89] In this way, the decision in *Sharif* does indeed have something to say about the Supreme Court's treatment of the concept of 'home' albeit in a more tacit sense.

In the Court of Appeal, any evidence of such an engagement with 'home' stems from Etherton LJ's more sympathetic attitude to the desire of Ms Sharif to be housed 'together with' her father and sister under the same roof as opposed to across split accommodation. Etherton LJ places particular emphasis on the ordinary meaning of 'living together' as axiomatically requiring a proximate residence.[90] On one view this approach demonstrates a willingness to take account of the values Fox O'Mahony associates with 'home' such as home as security and shelter. In addition, Etherton LJ's repeated references to the policy underlying the 1996 Act are important too. He makes much of the policy objectives of Part VII of the Housing Act 1996 and the statute's forerunner the Housing (Homeless Persons) Act 1977; citing dicta of Lord Wilberforce in *Din v Wandsworth*[91] that, 'it is designed for the expressed purpose of bringing families together'.[92] It could be argued that this is a recognition of the significance of proximate habitation for families and can (albeit indirectly) be seen as lending support to the considerations aligned to the concept of 'home'. Whilst this falls short of expressly referencing the concept per se, it goes some way to recognising the intentions of Parliament that families have a meaningful and, by implication, psychological attachment to living together and their shared space. This mirrors several of the value-types Fox O'Mahony identifies in her research and in particular engages: home as identity; home as territory and security; and home as cultural signifier.[93] Thus, 'home' is 'a place of self-expression [which] through its familiarity

---

[86] *Pinnock* (n 12) [57] (Lord Neuberger).
[87] *Powell* (n 13) [92].
[88] Bright (n 49) 274.
[89] See Fox O'Mahony (n 48) above.
[90] *Sharif* (n 68) [17].
[91] *Din v Wandsworth* [1983] 1 AC 657.
[92] Ibid, [663] per Lord Wilberforce.
[93] See Fox (n 2) above.

can foster a sense of belonging, "rootedness" and continuity'.[94] This notion of 'root-edness' is perhaps best described by Smith who notes that 'home' provides 'a place to return to … [and] also engenders feelings of continuity, stability and permanence'.[95] Further, empirical studies show that 'home' is frequently associated with a sense of security and with a perception of protection and that this is particularly heightened where there are vulnerability factors such as illness of a family member as in *Sharif* itself.[96] Etherton LJ further cites the words of Lord Fraser in *Din*[97] in noting that the 1977 Act was intended to end the practice of housing parents and children apart and the splitting up of families that a separatist accommodation policy imports. This could also be regarded as evidence of weight being attached to the subjective, intan-gible, socio-emotional qualities of family and 'home' in which 'home' is the sphere where the personal and the cultural coalesce and crucially 'a special setting in which one makes commitments to those [familial] relationships'.[98] Finally, in rejecting the argument put forward by the Council founded on dicta of Scott Baker J in *Ex parte Surdonja*,[99] Etherton LJ emphasised that Scott Baker J's statements in that case were merely obiter and couched in equivocal terms. Accommodation in separate rooms in the same hotel was 'quite different from occupation of separate self-contained residential units with no sharing of any living areas'.[100] Thus, once more there is an acknowledgment and appreciation here on the part of the court of precisely what constitutes a 'home' and of living arrangements that would negative 'home' and give rise to very separate lives.

Caution is, however, again required. One must be prudent not to overstate any apparent engagement with the concept of 'home' here. It could be said that the Court of Appeal is merely conducting an exercise in statutory interpretation by reference to the legislative history of the provisions. That said, an argument can be made that nevertheless this interpretation is itself one which involves a consid-eration and recognition of the importance of 'home', of living together as a family and of sharing communal space and facilities in this way lending support to Fox O'Mahony's contention[101] that the courts are beginning to grapple with the special significance and meaning of 'home' and with the concept of 'home' more manifestly. If Fox O'Mahony is correct about this, then *Sharif* sits alongside cases such as *Qazi* and *Pinnock* as potentially providing further evidence of judicial engagement with the concept of 'home'. When one considers the judgment of the Supreme Court, however, an altogether more complex picture emerges.

In stark contrast, the approach of the Supreme Court offers overall a far less home-centric, home-sympathetic judicial analysis than undertaken in the Court of Appeal. It is noteworthy that the Supreme Court did not engage so directly with

---

[94] Ibid, 593.

[95] Smith (n 37) 43.

[96] See J Fichten, 'When Toxic Chemicals Pollute Residential Environments: The Cultural Meanings of Home and Home Ownership' (1989) 48 *Human Organisation* 313, 316; see also Fox (n 2) 592–98.

[97] *Din v Wandsworth* (n 91) [668D-F].

[98] J Hayward, 'Psychological Concepts of Home' (1977) *Challenge* 10, 12.

[99] *R v Ealing LBC, Ex p Surdonja* [1999] 31 HLR 686 where Scott Baker J suggested accommodation in separate rooms in the same hotel might be sufficient for the purposes of the HA 1996, Pt VII.

[100] *Sharif* (n 68) [36].

[101] Fox O'Mahony (n 48) 159.

the legislative history of the 1996 Act and its 1977 predecessor. Thus, while Lord Fraser's words were indeed cited by Lord Carnwath, the court neglected to consider the full citation from Lord Fraser when he stressed the 1977 Act's 'emphasis on treating the family as a unit'.[102] In this way, it can be said that the Supreme Court gave far less regard to considerations of the benefits of keeping families together or for the legislative objective of preventing family separation. The failure of the Supreme Court in other decisions to explore fully the statutory purpose of legislation is something which lies outside this chapter but which is nevertheless of note.[103] As to this failure to engage fully with the legislative purpose of the 1996 Act, it feeds into a larger point namely that the Supreme Court in fact, pay little attention to matters which could be said to touch upon the concept of 'home' preferring to underscore the continued application of the (arguably harsh)[104] *Puhlofer* judgment which emphasised the lack of any specific standard of accommodation laid down by Parliament. This can perhaps be seen as judicial focus on *housing* as opposed to *home*. Striking in the submissions advanced by counsel for the local authority was that 'living together' should not be read as containing any implication as to the nature of the facilities to be provided. Counsel for Ms Sharif had argued otherwise that the layout of the accommodation should at least be such that normal and 'shared' family life be facilitated. Thus, one could interpret the submissions of Ms Sharif's counsel as arguing in favour of a greater engagement with issues of 'home', family life and 'home' encompassing shared living and shared experiences. Ultimately however, the majority of the Supreme Court took a bricks and mortar approach to the issue of 'home' and based its reasoning on *Puhlofer*; resisting this invitation from counsel for Ms Sharif to embark on a more subjective, home-centric analysis.

What evidence, if any, is there then in the Supreme Court of engagement with the concept of 'home'? The closest the Supreme Court comes to such an analysis in *Sharif* is in the dissenting judgment of Lord Kerr. Lord Kerr emphasises 'sharing', that the family unit with shared lives and shared experiences occupies 'a central place in the homelessness legislation of the last century',[105] and that the shared family home is the heart and foundation of the family unit.[106] Togetherness, he argues, connotes 'a combination of people into a condition of unity'[107] and that if living together is to mean anything this must be in a single unit of accommodation.[108] Thus, one can discern Lord Kerr approaching the issue at hand with a focus more closely aligned to that of the concept of 'home'. Lord Kerr goes further in discussing the provision of 'communal space where family activities could be enjoyed'.[109] This is particularly interesting as it is suggestive of a new value-type to be ascribed to the concept of 'home'; a new strand, a new prism through which the concept of 'home' could be

---

[102] *Din v Wandsworth* (n 91) [668D-F] (Lord Fraser).

[103] This criticism has recently been made of the Supreme Court in the important case of *Yemshaw v Hounslow LBC* [2011] UKSC 3, [2011] 1 WLR 433 on which see C Bevan, 'Interpreting Statutory Purpose—Lessons from *Yemshaw v Hounslow London Borough Council*' (2013) 76(4) *MLR* 742.

[104] Lord Carnwath in the Supreme Court himself conceded, 'the apparent harshness of the test laid down by the House of Lords in *Puhlofer*' [6].

[105] *Sharif* (n 14) [31].

[106] Ibid.

[107] Ibid, [34].

[108] Ibid.

[109] Ibid, [36].

viewed. This new value of 'home' as 'shared time' or 'shared living' would supplement those pre-existing value-types already identified by Fox O'Mahony and would embrace notions of 'home' as shared activities such as cooking and eating together as a family. Of course, as the lone dissentient voice, Lord Kerr's words must be treated with restraint and are coloured with a degree of emotive flourish not seen in the judgments of the other members of the Supreme Court. However, although in the minority, Lord Kerr's judgment demonstrates a discussion of 'home' and family life considerations which very much go to the values and qualities associated with the concept of 'home'.

B. What Do *Pinnock, Powell* and *Sharif* Tell Us of the Traction Gained by the Concept of 'Home' in the Supreme Court?

In light of Fox O'Mahony's assertion that the concept of 'home' is beginning to capture the attention of the English and Welsh judiciary and with academics such as Buyse arguing that the European Court of Human Rights is increasingly concerning itself with the context of 'home',[110] this chapter, through analysis of the *Pinnock, Powell* and *Sharif* judgments, has demonstrated that these assertions (as far as they relate to this jurisdiction) require significant qualification. Rather, an analysis of these three Supreme Court decisions signals the need for a more nuanced understanding as to the influence of the concept of 'home' in the Supreme Court. As has been shown, whilst *Pinnock* comes closest to an engagement with considerations of 'home' this has been significantly curtailed by the subsequent restrictions placed on the *Pinnock* decision in *Powell* which introduced practical limitations as to when the concept will ever be engaged. Equally, whilst an argument can be made that Etherton LJ in the Court of Appeal in *Sharif* appeared willing to consider the more subjective qualities associated with 'home' and the statutory purpose of keeping families together, this was overturned by the Supreme Court who offered scant discussion of home-orientated considerations.[111] With many statutory provisions containing references to families and, moreover, the fast-growing body and influence of article 8 ECHR jurisprudence, it is worth probing precisely why 'home' as a distinct legal concept is making such little impact at the highest levels of our legal system particularly in cases such as *Sharif* where the facts provided a fitting opportunity to embark upon an analysis founded on a distinct concept of 'home'. It is suggested that four propositions can be made here.

First, the concept of 'home' as a distinct legal entity very much remains in its infancy and at the 'pre-scientific, speculative stage'.[112] One could go further in suggesting it currently exists only as an academic concern. Much of the research around the concept of 'home' can largely be seen as a 'call to arms' to other legal academics to *begin* the discussion around the development of a distinct concept. Moreover, no process of clarification or refinement of how this concept might function has yet

---

[110] See Buyse (n 2) 294–307.
[111] Arguably on the basis that this would put an unjustifiable burden on local authorities: *Sharif* (n 14) [30] (Lady Hale).
[112] Fox (n 2) 588.

been undertaken. As Fox O'Mahony herself acknowledges, 'questions remain as to how a concept of home should be constructed … [this] would require considerable careful thought'.[113] Based on the findings of this chapter, that careful thought is yet to take place.

Secondly, and as a corollary of the first proposition, in no sense is the concept in a form that is easily adopted by the courts as a framework for determination of legal disputes; rather, it currently resembles a series of values, '"clusters" of meaning',[114] which fall far short of a recognisable and functional legal concept capable of application by the courts. It is at this point, that the challenges and criticisms that the concept of 'home' faces as outlined earlier, are recalled to mind. There still remains considerable doubt as to the utility of the concept[115] and should it not become crystallised into a meaningful and readily-applicable model, it risks falling into obscurity given the barriers to its use including ambiguity and intangibility. To some extent, it is just assumed that the courts already concern themselves with 'home' *sub silentio* and that as such no distinct concept of 'home' is required. Of course, by the very nature of a common law legal system, a concept of 'home' will develop incrementally and this process is very much at the early stages of development but consideration needs to be had as to when such a concept would apply and how precisely it would assist litigants.

A third proposition as to why the concept can be seen as not gaining significant traction is discernible from the fact that no single court in this jurisdiction has ever explicitly adopted the language of the concept of 'home' when reaching a determination. Whilst arguably *Stack* and *Jones* provide the clearest exposition of a 'home' or 'domestic' property law analysis, even these decisions fall far short of a discussion of 'home' as a distinct legal concept. Equally, as many legal academics are aware, few practitioners routinely peruse the pages of legal theoretical research and so the concept has yet to be raised in argument before the court. This poses real difficulties for those seeking to evaluate the prominence of this concept in legal jurisprudence and particularly so when analysing decided cases. In light of this, the task of assessing the progression of the concept is more concerned with the identification of considerations within judgments which *suggest* or as discussed in relation to *Shariflend* support, to the concept. This introduces yet further obscurity into the study in this area. That said, given the embryonic emergence of the concept of 'home', the importance of a detailed case law analysis focussing on the particular reasoning of the judiciary to supplement the largely, hitherto theoretical work undertaken in this field, is reinforced. In exploring why the concept is not more firmly rooted in the jurisprudence, it is interesting to consider how hypothetically the concept might have been raised in argument before the Supreme Court for example in the case of *Sharif*. Although it is impossible to know the true impact this would have had, the outcome of the case may have been different had such arguments been advanced by counsel for Ms Sharif. A fully-operative concept of 'home' could have been relied upon by Ms Sharif to assert both the vulnerability of her father's position and the attachment to and interconnectedness of the 'family unit' as a means of bolstering the case for

---

[113] Ibid, 608.
[114] Fox O'Mahony (n 48) 158.
[115] Merrett (n 15) above; Dewar (n 21) above.

reading the statutory language of the 1996 Act as requiring the provision of a single unit of accommodation. At the very least, the Supreme Court would then have been called upon to reach a determination on the concept of 'home' submissions directly, or as a minimum, to have addressed their minds to them. In such a case, the concept of 'home' would be a means of introducing an occupier's personal circumstances and the cultural qualities associated with 'home' as factors to be weighed up in the court's determination of the issues. In *Sharif* most specifically, the concept of 'home' could be used to inform the court's exercise in statutory interpretation to further the argument that the provisions of the 1996 Act were targeted at keeping families together and 'treating the family as a unit'.[116] It is precisely by addressing this type of hypothetical question as to how the concept might be employed that the concept will begin to take shape and form and ultimately realise its application.

Fourthly is the vexed issue of deference to public authority decision-making.[117] Whilst examination of this issue is somewhat beyond the scope of this chapter, it is nevertheless a key factor in the decisions in *Pinnock*, *Powell* and *Sharif*. In all three judgments in the Supreme Court, heed was paid to the difficulty of the task undertaken by local authorities and to the 'practical considerations'[118] of housing stock management. Equally, dicta in *Pinnock* support the view that local authorities are, as a starting point, presumed to be 'acting according to their duties'.[119] So long as this cycle of assumed public authority deference is maintained, arguments based on the personal circumstances, attachment to and meaning of 'home' will be in large part excluded. As Professor Allan has argued this 'pernicious'[120] deference doctrine is one which permits 'the abdication of judicial responsibility in favour of reliance on the good faith or good sense or special expertise of public officials, whose judgments about the implications of rights in specific cases may well be wrong'[121] and which leads the courts to 'forsake fundamental values in favour of capitulation to legislative or executive fiat'.[122]

The foregoing discussion begs the question of what lessons we can draw from the *Pinnock*, *Powell* and *Sharif* decisions. This chapter will conclude by considering this.

VI. CONCLUDING REMARKS: LESSONS
FROM THE SUPREME COURT

The concept of 'home' in modern property law is susceptible to challenge. Serving to illustrate the status currently afforded to the concept, *Pinnock*, *Powell* and *Sharif* lay the foundations for a debate as to the standing and potential future evolution of a concept of 'home'. In analysing these three Supreme Court decisions, three central lessons emerge.

---

[116] *Din v Wandsworth* (n 91) [668D-F] (Lord Fraser).

[117] See A Young, 'In Defence of Due Deference' (2009) 72 *MLR* 554; A Kavanagh, 'Defending Deference in Public Law and Constitutional Theory' (2010) 126 *LQR* 22; TRS Allan, 'Human Rights and Judicial Review: A Critique of "Due Deference"' (2006) *CLJ* 671.

[118] *Powell* (n 13) [35] (Lord Hope).

[119] *Pinnock* (n 12) [53] (Lord Neuberger).

[120] Allan (n 117) 675.

[121] Ibid.

[122] Ibid, at 674.

First, *Pinnock, Powell* and *Sharif*, taken together indicate that there is little evidence of the Supreme Court engaging expressly and in any manifest sense with the concept of 'home'. It is not yet a concept with any consistent or agreed legal content. That said, Kerr's dissent in *Sharif* does introduce a possible new prism through which 'home' can be observed in addition to the already-identified clusters of value-types; namely shared time and shared experience. This novel development could have significant consequences for article 8 jurisprudence going forward under which the courts may be more willing to conceive of home as not simply symbolising 'same roof' but 'same table' in as far as sharing meals and leisure time forms an integral part of 'family life'. As with much here, the precise interrelationship between article 8 and the concept of 'home' remains one of the issues still requiring careful thought. That said, whilst there is no reason to see these two principles as being in conflict neither is there reason to suggest that article 8 obviates the need for development of a distinct concept of 'home' which could apply in domestic law and in disputes not necessarily involving a public authority. A clarification of the meaning of 'home' therefore has obvious ramifications and utility for the article 8 jurisprudence. The case law around article 8 is fast-paced and ever-evolving. The concept of 'home' could very well contribute to the interpretation of 'home' in such cases.

Secondly, and strongly allied to the first, *Pinnock, Powell* and *Sharif* act as a warning shot across the bows of those who advocate for the development of a distinct concept of 'home' signposting the need for clarification and refinement of the concept if it is to have any real value. The concept of 'home' is couched in uncertainty and subjectivity and moreover cast in significant doubt by those that reject it.[123] If the concept is to possess any utility beyond merely an identification or taxonomy of the values associated with 'home' it must become better defined and more tightly demarcated. In particular, this chapter has shown that the central tension between housing as physical shelter and 'home' as emotional, subjective attachment still requires resolution in the legal context. Arguably, the case law analysed here[124] evidences an engagement with housing only and not with 'home'.

Thirdly, for those proponents of the concept of 'home',[125] *Pinnock, Powell* and *Sharif* should be seized as an important moment in its development and as an opportunity to think again as to how such a concept should be constructed and applied judicially. A case such as *Sharif* is precisely of the type in which such a concept might be thought valuable to play a role. For those such as Fox O'Mahony and Buyse, an analysis of these three Supreme Court decisions raises fundamental questions as to the future and survival of the concept and should be viewed as the catalyst for a push for greater research and work in the area.

Post *Stack* and *Jones*, the concept of 'home' currently carries little or no 'profile'. As a consequence, this chapterevidences the grave challenge that the concept faces if it is to become a recognised concept in modern property law. Searching questions must be addressed: why do we need a concept of 'home' at all? How should the concept alter the judicial role and what should be its defining characteristics? Moreover, a far greater exposure and dissemination of the concept to the judiciary is required

---

[123] Merrett (n 15) above; Dewar (n 21) above; Dovey (n 21) above.
[124] In particular, *Sharif* (n 14) above.
[125] Most prominently Fox O'Mahony (nn 2, 16 and 48) above; Buyse (n 2) above; Barros (n 18) above.

and a rigorous examination of its place in legal jurisprudence and in property law specifically must be undertaken. Put simply, the concept of 'home' must develop beyond the pages of legal theoretical research and metamorphose into a practical concept capable of judicial application if it is to endure. This will in turn require further exposition of the exact role that context and 'home' should play in modern property law and wider examination of the housing/home debate. Fitchen[126] wrote 'home is an affective anchor with sacred connotation'. This chapter exposes that the true challenge for the concept of 'home' now is whether this affective anchor can become an effective tool in legal jurisprudence.

---

[126] J Fitchen, 'When Toxic Chemicals Pollute Residential Environments: The Cultural Meanings of Home and Home Ownership' (1989) 48 *Human Organisation* 313, 317.

12

Land Titling and Communal Property

ALISON CLARKE*

I. INTRODUCTION

THERE ARE GOOD reasons why modern societies are prepared to put money and effort into land titling systems.[1] An accurate record of who has what interests in any given piece of land, and in its products and natural resources, benefits everyone—the rights holders themselves, those who want to deal with them or with the resources they use or control, and local, national and international bodies concerned with the regulation, preservation and development of land and natural resources. The difficulty lies in working out how to put together and maintain that accurate record in the real world. Traditional land registration systems are good at recording private ownership of discrete tracts of two dimensional space, where ownership can be expected to carry with it exclusive rights to everything within that space and where the primary purpose of the register is to facilitate trading of ownership in an open market. They are ill-equipped to deal with complex land rights systems where simple private ownership has to coexist with disaggregated land and resource use rights, where rights might be held publicly, institutionally or collectively rather than by individuals, where rights might arise informally and/or out of custom or long use as well as by express grant or assignment, and where tradability may not be the first concern. There are formidable theoretical and practical difficulties in designing and operating land titling systems to suit this complex property world. This chapter focuses on just one aspect of the problem: how should communal land and resource use rights be accommodated within such systems?

This is a problem of current pressing interest because land titling is enjoying a renaissance at present in different parts of the world. In some post-socialist states in Africa, Asia and Eastern and Central Europe land titling is being introduced or

---

* Emeritus Professor in Law, University of Surrey.

[1] 'Land titling' is used in this paper as a general term to describe all systems which record land rights on a register. It is adopted here because it is the term generally used across different disciplines to refer to the new land registration systems discussed in this paper, including those that also operate as cadastres. It is unfortunate that the term is more apt to describe systems where private ownership is the central organising feature (as it is in civil law registers and under Torrens and England and Wales title registration) than it is to describe the kind of registration system advocated in this paper, which would record all property rights even-handedly, not just private property titles.

reintroduced as part of overall land privatisation programmes.[2] In other states land titling, whether in the form of introduction of new systems or reform of old ones, is on the agenda as part of broader land reform programmes. These programmes may be driven by aims as diverse as recognition of indigenous land rights, restitution and/or redistribution of land rights, and formal recognition of the 'informal' use the poorest people in the world make of the rural and urban land they inhabit.[3]

A number of states in post-colonial sub-Saharan Africa are going through this process and a remarkable feature of their experience so far has been the lack of success of most of the programmes they have initiated. This is not to say that failed land titling initiatives are confined to Africa, nor that Africa may not have its own success stories,[4] but in general the experience in Africa has been particularly discouraging. All too often their land titling programmes have failed to achieve their stated objectives and have worsened the position of women and vulnerable or minority groups without producing anticipated increases in prosperity and economic growth.[5] David Atwood, writing in 1990 about land titling in Africa, was one of the first of many to comment on the phenomenon:

> Land titling or registration is widely believed to increase efficient land use and agricultural production by easing land transfers, providing collateral for agricultural loans, and increasing incentives to adopt new technology, on-farm investment, and soil conservation practices. This very simple model abstracts from a number of important variables, including: the differences in transaction costs; credit sources; productivity; security; and access to formal or informal institutions faced by different groups of people. There are many African situations that do not fit the model, and where land titling or registration would not have the intended impact, would not be economically justifiable, or would even be counterproductive.

> The conventional and largely erroneous view of land registration's impact on agricultural efficiency and productivity in Africa stems from a failure to take adequate account of the

[2] China is in a similar position, embarking on a nationwide land titling programme as part of the process of marketising its socialist system: Y Zhao, 'China Rural Land Registration and Certification Piloting Project' available at www.fig.net/pub/fig_wb_2009/papers/sys/sys_3_zhao.pdf.

[3] O de Schutter, 'The Green Rush: The Global Race for Farmland and the Rights of Land Users' (2011) 52 *Harvard International Law Journal* 503, 525–33 provides a good overview, highlighting the influence in particular of World Bank policies in the 1980s and the work of Hernando de Soto who argued, most notably in *The Mystery of Capital: Why Capitalism Triumphs in the West and Fails Everywhere Else* (New York, Basic Books, 2000), that land and other resources used by the poor represented 'dead capital' which could be realised for the benefit of its users if they were given formal legal title to it through land titling programmes.

[4] Compare, eg Cambodia (see Human Rights Watch criticism of what was once a highly regarded land titling programme in Cambodia, from which the World Bank withdrew support in 2012: www.hrw.org/news/2013/06/12/cambodia-land-titling-campaign-open-abuse) and Ethiopia, whose rural land certification programme has attracted favourable, if not wholly uncritical, attention: see, eg A Hoekema, 'If Not Private Property, then What? Legalizing Extra-legal Rural Land Tenure via a Third Road' in Ubink et al (eds), *Legalising Land Rights; Local Practices, State Responses and Tenure Security in Africa, Asia and Latin America* (Leiden, Leiden University Press, 2009) 59; K Deininger, D Ayalew, S Holden and J Zevenbergen, 'Rural Land Certification in Ethiopia: Process, Initial Impact, and Implications for other African Countries' (2008) 36 *World Development* 1786 and World Bank Report No 6163, *Federal Democratic Republic of Ethiopia—Options for Strengthening Land Administration* (Washington, World Bank, 2012).

[5] See, eg S Lastarria-Cornhiel, 'Impact of Privatisation on Gender and Property Rights in Africa' (1997) 25 *World Development* 1317 and A Kapur, '"Catch-22": The Role of Development Institutions in Promoting Gender Equality in Land Law—Lessons Learned in Post-Conflict Pluralist Africa' (2011) 17 *Buffalo Human Rights Law Review* 75.

extra-legal, informal, local institutional environment through which most rural Africans continue to acquire and maintain their claims to land. Establishing a land registry or land titling system often does not lead to a wholesale change from a traditional, informal set of property rights and rules to a modern, legal one. It is more likely, as has occurred in Kenya (the best-documented case), to simply create one more source of opportunities and uncertainties, among several others already existing in many areas, for establishing and maintaining one's land claim. It is not at all certain that the net effect on either productivity or equity is positive.[6]

Atwood and others have ascribed these land registration disasters to a failure to appreciate the extra-legal environment, and to the effects of other non-legal factors such as path dependence.[7] This chapter focusses on an additional factor, which is a legal one. It is now acknowledged that, until very recently, those advocating, designing and implementing land titling programmes in many African states have not fully appreciated or taken into account the legal complexity of the land tenure systems under which most of the intended beneficiaries of the programmes live. Land titlers of this generation have modelled their land titling programmes on traditional western-style land registration systems which were designed primarily to facilitate commercial transactions between private owners, and they have attempted to utilise this model in land tenure systems where private ownership is either not the norm, or is but one of several different norms. A key element which is integral to complex land tenure systems in many sub-Saharan African states but not taken into account in traditional land registration systems is communal property. In sub-Saharan African states (as in most other jurisdictions in the world) people sometimes utilise land and other natural resources individually for their own private benefit, but at other times they organise themselves into communities to utilise them collectively, either for their collective benefit or for the better realisation of benefit for their members. The patterns of resource use of most communities in sub-Saharan states involves a mix of individual and collective use, as noted below. For present purposes the collective use can be regarded as giving rise to communal property whenever the collective use is exclusive of outsiders, in the sense that each member of the community regards the resource as 'ours' rather than as 'mine' but also regards herself and the community as entitled to exclude anyone who is not a member of the community.[8] In this chapter it is argued that if collective use of this kind is integral to a community's pattern of resource use, the absence of a mechanism for recording it on a land register

---

[6] DA Atwood, 'Land Registration in Africa: The Impact on Agricultural Production' (1990) 18 *World Development* 659. For similar conclusions, if not identical diagnoses, see also M Trebilcock, PE Veel, P Ho and M Spoor, 'Whose Land? The Political Economy of Land Titling in Transitional Economies' (2006) *Land Use Policy* 580; J Quan, 'Land Tenure, Economic Growth and Poverty in Sub-Saharan Africa' in C Toulmin and JF Quan (eds), *Evolving Land Rights, Policy and Tenure in Africa* (DFID, IIED and NRI, London, 2000) 31–49; D Bromley, 'Formalising Property Relations in the Developing World: The Wrong Prescription for the Wrong Malady' (2009) 26 *Land Use Policy* 20.

[7] See, in particular, M Trebilcock and PE Veel, 'Property Rights and Development: The Contingent Case for Formalisation' (2008–09) 30 *University of Pennsylvania Journal of International Law* 397 on path dependence.

[8] This exclusivity is important here because it distinguishes communal resource rights from public resource rights such as public rights of way or rights of access over private land recognised in the UK and in much of Europe and Scandinavia. There are strong arguments for also incorporating public resource rights into land registers, but they are not considered here.

which does record private property rights will severely disadvantage the community. New land titling initiatives therefore must find some way of bringing communal land and resources use rights on to an integrated register with individually held rights, as part of the process of providing a full picture of complex land and natural resource holdings.

The chapter sketches out first how modern land titling works and how technological advances now make it feasible to record on land registers complex rights systems such as those described below. It then considers how England and Wales are tackling their (relatively) straightforward task of registering communal land rights in England and Wales. Communal land rights in England and Wales provide an interesting comparator because the ways in which they interact with private and public land rights is very much simpler than in complex rights systems in other parts of the world. In particular, communal land rights holders in England and Wales are not ethnically, socially or culturally different or separate from their neighbours or from the inhabitants of other parts of Great Britain. This means that problems and failings in registration of their interests cannot be obscured by or mis-attributed to larger issues arising out of ethnic or cultural difference, as can happen in other parts of the world. For this reason it is easier to identify what, if anything, the England and Wales experience can tell us about registration of communal rights in more complex systems.

II. LAND TITLING SYSTEMS

It is useful to start with a closer examination of what, in principle, a land titling system does and how it works.[9] For these purposes a land titling system can be taken to be a system designed to provide a formal public record of property rights in land. If starting with a clean slate—an unlikely scenario in any jurisdiction—how would you now design such a system?

When we undertook that process in England and Wales in 1925, building on earlier abortive attempts,[10] we used an ingeniously cheap and simple method, designed by lawyers[11] and intended to achieve the single objective of increasing the marketability of land at the least cost to the state. To put it in (very) generalised terms, we started with a blank ordnance survey map of the whole of England and Wales.[12] Whenever

---

[9] This chapter focuses on title registration systems (recording who holds what property rights in specified land) rather than deeds registration systems (recording transactions dealing with property rights). Deeds registration may nevertheless still be a viable option: see D Fitzpatrick, '"Best Practice" Options for the Legal Recognition of Customary Tenure' (2005) 36 *Development and Change* 449, 469.

[10] Our present system originated in the Land Transfer Act 1875 although there had been an earlier unsuccessful voluntary system introduced by the Land Registry Act 1862. For the full history of land registration up to 1925 see J Stuart Anderson, *Lawyers and the Making of English Land Law* 1832–1940 (Oxford, Clarendon Press, 1992); Cavill et al (eds), *Ruoff & Roper: Registered Conveyancing* (London, Sweet & Maxwell, Looseleaf) (*Ruoff & Roper*) ch 1 provides a short history up to the present.

[11] For an account of the involvement of lawyers, see Anderson (n 10).

[12] Initially there was not even a master map. The Ordnance Survey was founded in 1791 and although there have been links between the Ordnance Survey and land registration since the late 19th century, the first titles were registered (under the Land Registry Act 1862) without the benefit of any national master plan: there was nothing against which plans submitted by purchasers could be plotted and checked. It was only when land registration was made compulsory by the Land Transfer Act 1879 that the Ordnance

a piece of land was transferred thereafter, we required the transferee—the purchaser, or if the transfer followed the death of the landowner, the person who had inherited the land—to send a map of that piece of land to the Land Registrar, together with a list of all the private third party property interests affecting the land and the names of all the current holders of those interests. The purchaser's map was then pinned to what the Registrar took to be the appropriate place on the master map—but no guarantees were given[13]—and every person who held a fee simple or long leasehold interest in the land was given a unique reference number and was registered as the titleholder of that interest. All the other third party property interests were noted in the register against the registered fee simple and leasehold interests they affected, and the registered titles were all cross-referenced between themselves and with the map. 'Third party' interests did not include interests under a trust, and therefore did not include any rights that family members who were not legal title holders might have had. Anyone searching the register might be able to discover from the register whether a title holder held the title on trust, but would not be able to discover what the trust interests were or who held them. The only protection offered to those who had trust interests in the land was entry of a restriction on the register. This was not even intended to safeguard the trust interest in land itself: its primary purpose was to trigger off a process whereby the trust interest in land automatically shifted to an interest in its proceeds of sale should the registered owner ever chose to sell the land.[14] Most importantly for present purposes, 'third party' interests did not include communal or public property interests—only private property interests were registered or recorded on the register.

Modern land titling systems introduced over the last few decades in sub-Saharan African countries (and probably everywhere else where they have recently been introduced) are typically very different. They usually involve systematic proactive registration. They often have broader objectives, and those responsible for their design and implementation are trained not in law but in disciplines relating to land administration. They are technology driven: modern technology enables land titling systems to do very effectively and relatively easily and cheaply what was once impossible or prohibitively expensive. It is the people who are trained in this technology—geographers, scientists, agronomists and engineers specialising in computerised data collection, storage and analysis, in satellite technology, GIS technology and visual imaging, etc—who design and implement land titling programmes. Other social scientists also have an input in implementation: the development of participatory mapping techniques makes it feasible to settle boundaries definitively with the consent

---

Survey map was made the official basis for all descriptions of registered land: see further, CJ Sweeney and JA Simson, 'The Ordnance Survey and Land Registration' (1967) 133 *Geographical Journal* 10, 12–13, and R Oliver, 'A Short History of the Ordnance Survey of Great Britain' available at www.charlescloseso-ciety.org/files/HistoryOSGB.pdf.

[13] Under the Land Registration Act 2002 and its predecessors boundaries are not guaranteed: s 60 of the 2002 Act. For the problems this causes see JT Farrand and A Clarke, *Emmet & Farrand on Title* (London, Sweet & Maxwell, Looseleaf) (*Emmet & Farrand*) para 17.035.

[14] Ie through the operation of overreaching: see now s 44 Land Registration Act 2002 and *Emmet & Farrand* (n 13) paras 5.141 and 10.007.

of everyone concerned on the ground, minimising the risk of igniting or re-igniting boundary disputes.[15] Land lawyers, however, do not appear to be involved.[16]

With the benefit of this technology, modern land titling would typically involve the following five steps:[17]

— Surveying what is physically there—the surface of the land and everything in, on, under and above the surface, including features such as trees, vegetation, water resources, mineral deposits, rock formations and soil conditions, as well as buildings, walls, bridges, roads, etc.
— Drawing up a digitalised map and database recording the physical information found.
— Investigating who has what rights in respect of those physical things.
— Recording that information, and all subsequent changes in it, in a centralised register by reference to that digitalised map and database.
— Giving rights-holders formal paper or electronic documentation authenticating or evidencing their rights (certificates, title deeds, paper or electronic copies of register entries).

The England and Wales registration of title system does hardly any of this. It does the first only in exceptional circumstances (and then only in relation to land and buildings) and so its interest in doing the second is limited. It does the third and fourth processes, but crucially for present purposes, it does so only in a very limited way. Specifically, it is reactive rather than proactive in that usually it only investigates the entitlements of those who claim them, and as noted above, as a matter of deliberate policy it does not record all interests, only a selected few.

In modern land titling systems the focus is quite different. Technology makes it possible for modern systems to do the first and the second of these (and the fourth, in so far as it relates to the first and the second) to a very high level, and indeed it is these processes that now drive the whole programme. Progress in the development of the technology allows a huge amount and variety of data to be collected, processed, analysed and accessed quickly, cheaply and accurately. This includes data such as exact location and nature of physical features (rivers, roads, wells, trees, forests, crops, buildings, boundaries) as well as land attributes such as soil type and condition. The implications of this are enormous. Because modern systems can collect, hold and analyse multi-layered and multi-dimensional data, it is possible to record graphically, for example, the places different groups of pastoralists travel through, the times when they do so, the resources they use at each point, and the livestock that travels with them. This would have been virtually impossible in traditional land registration systems. Similarly, there is now no technical impediment to recording graphically and in words complex shared resource use. So, for example, a modern titling system can record graphically sharecropping arrangements,

---

[15] J Bryan, 'Walking the Line: Participatory Mapping, Indigenous Rights, and Neoliberalism' (2011) 42 *Geoforum* 40.
[16] See, eg the website of commercial land administration consultants Airbus Defence and Space, formerly Astrium www.astrium-geo.com/en/89-land-administration.
[17] For a more sophisticated analysis, see I Williamson, S Enemark, J Wallace and A Rajabifard, *Land Administration for Sustainable Development* (California, ESRI Press Academic, 2009) in particular chs 12–15.

or gendered use of forest trees (eg women from the community collect wood for firewood whereas men collect fallen timber for building and repairing), or arrangements by which pastoralists walk their herd over agricultural land after the harvest, fertilising the land as they go.[18] However, observing these activities is one thing; appreciating that they might be attributable to property rights, and recording them as such on a register is another. Modern technology is not much help here. Until very recently, modern titling systems could see the cadastral significance of this level of detail—in other words, could see the value of recording it for resource management purposes, or taxation or policy implementation—but they did not have the legal sophistication to see that it might be a manifestation of a property rights system which ought to be recorded on the register.

In other words, there is a real problem in modern titling systems, and it lies in the third step outlined above: exactly what are the rights that the system wants to record? In many earlier initiatives it was assumed that they must be the same rights that traditional land registration systems record—private ownership and the short *numerus clausus* of real rights that cluster around private ownership. However, to record only these rights has disastrous consequences in countries where some sectors of the population have quite different relationships with the land and natural resources they utilise and on which they depend. Their relationships with their resources do not approximate to private ownership nor to traditional real rights. They live by a different property rights system, involving a complex mix of communal property rights and private property rights not commensurate with the western *numerus clausus*.

III. COMMUNAL PROPERTY IN SUB-SAHARAN AFRICA

There is of course no standard pattern of land rights in sub-Saharan Africa, but in most post-colonial states the land tenure system will encompass rights in land derived from a variety of sources.[19] There may be a western-style private ownership and private property rights system introduced in colonial times, which still covers some areas and/or some peoples in the land. This kind of tenure will quite often now be held by elites. It will be based on the land law system(s) of the colonial power(s), and it may include vestiges of colonial era registration systems, all probably in a rather bad state physically (eg records not up-to-date, difficult to read and physically disintegrating).[20] There may also be multiple systems of customary law tenure covering different and/or overlapping areas, which may or not be formally

---

[18] All examples of what Hoekema describes as 'secondary rights': Hoekema, 'If Not Private Property, then What' (n 4) 5–6.

[19] For detailed analyses see the works cited in nn 5, 6 and 7 and R Home, 'Culturally Unsuited to Property Rights?: Colonial Land Laws and African Societies' (2013) 40 *Journal of Law and Society* 403; B Chigara, *Land Reform Policy* (Aldershot, Ashgate Publishing, 2004); F Obeng-Odoom, 'Land Reforms in Africa: Theory, Practice and Outcome' (2012) 36 *Habitat International* 161; HWO Okoth-Ogendo, 'Some Issues of Theory in the Study of Tenure Relations in African Agriculture' (1989) 59 *Africa* 6; P MacAuslan, *Land Law Reform in Eastern Africa: Traditional or Transformative?* (Abingdon, Routledge, 2013).

[20] An equally apt description of the contents of the English and Welsh registers of common land and town and village greens described below: Report of the Stakeholder Group Working Group, *Agricultural Use and Management of Common Land* (2003) Pt 7.

recognised by legislation. There is very likely to be recent or fairly recent legislation setting up a new statutory land tenure system, certainly post-colonial and probably influenced by international development agencies such as the World Bank. The place of pre-existing customary law may be left ambiguous in this kind of legislation. Alternatively some customary law systems may be recognised and others not, or all may be recognised. In any event, recognition may be made subject to human rights provisions embedded in the constitution prohibiting tenure and succession provisions which discriminate against women or on the basis of ethnicity. Provision may also be made for conversion of customary rights into private property rights. There are likely to be different land tenure regimes for rural and for urban land. Finally, underlying ownership of all or some land and natural resources may be vested in the state or formally declared to be vested in the people. This kind of underlying state/people's ownership may be as vestigial as Crown ownership of land in England and Wales, leaving the immediate grantees with property rights as extensive as fee simple ownership in England and Wales. Alternatively state ownership may have more substance, so that grantees have little more than long term use rights.

The question of where communal property rights are to be found in this mix is complicated by two factors. The first is that in many systems land rights, whether held under customary law or conferred by legislation, are held by households rather than by individuals, making it difficult to draw clear lines between private and communal rights. The second is that in some of the literature there is a tendency to equate customary land rights with communal land rights. That is an unfortunate confusion. The legal and factual reality is that most systems of customary law contain a mix of private and communal rights, with the community consisting of anything from a household to a lineage, a tribe, an ethnic group, or a common interest group. Some of these communities may be communities of equals whereas others will be strictly hierarchical; some may be self-governing, whilst others will be subject to some degree of external control or otherwise nested within a horizontal or hierarchical framework of interests held by private individuals, other communal groups and/or the state. So, for example, a tribe consisting of several different lineages may be essentially a community of equal-ranking households, but governed by a chief or elders who have powers of adjudication and in some cases also powers to allocate and re-allocate resources between households. Each household within the tribe might also be hierarchical, with the head of the household being the rights holder for external purposes, but also having duties and responsibilities in relation to the resources as against other household members, past and future as well as present. Finally, when viewed from the outside, overall ownership of the territory may be viewed as held by the tribe, either directly as a form of community ownership or mediated through a kind of stewardship ownership held by an elder. Within the territory, however, individuals and households may have rights to use some resources for their own individual/household purposes but use others in common with other individuals or households or subgroups.[21]

---

[21] For analysis of how this applies in South Africa, eg see J Bennett, A Ainslie and J Davis, 'Contested Institutions? Traditional Leaders and Land Access and Control in Communal Areas of East Cape Province, South Africa' (2013) 32 *Land Use Policy* 27; HWO Okoth-Ogendo, 'The Nature of Land Rights under Indigenous Law in Africa' in Claasens and Cousins (eds), *Land Power and Custom: Controversies Generated by South Africa's Communal LandRights Act* (Athens OH, Ohio University Press, 2008) 95.

If comprehensive land titling is introduced into this mixed system and it allows registration only of western style private property rights, there is a real risk that these other types of rights and interests will be overridden.[22] It may still be argued by some that the answer is to convert these rights into private property rights so that everyone can enjoy the advantages of traditional western-style land titles. However, even those who believe that this is politically, economically and socially desirable have come to admit now that in most countries it is at best a long-term aim.[23] An alternative approach is to side-step the registration problem by recognising traditional communities as legal entities and conferring on them full 'ownership' of their territories. This allows them to participate in the private property world: the community becomes a self that can hold a traditional western-style land title. The formidable objection to this approach is that it can distort the reality of the land holdings within the group, strengthening the hold of traditional hierarchies and increasing the vulnerability of those within the group who do not have traditional western-style property rights.[24] In other words, it is just another way of keeping complex land holdings off the register: the problem is indeed side-stepped, but it is not solved. The only realistic long-term solution is to accept the complexity and design comprehensive land titling systems which accurately reflect the plural property rights worlds in which they operate.

IV. REGISTERING COMMUNAL PROPERTY RIGHTS IN ENGLAND AND WALES

In England and Wales the property rights world is not particularly complex. We do recognise a limited range of communal land rights although they do not have the same importance as communal property has in sub-Saharan Africa. The ones considered here are town and village green rights and rights of common. Both are of ancient common law origin. They are interesting for present purposes for two reasons. The first is that they represent two different types of communal property right, each found in most legal systems including most of the sub-Saharan African systems described above. The second is that in 1965 it was decided that they should be registered. This was achieved by the Commons Registration Act 1965, currently due to be replaced by the Commons Act 2006 which has itself been significantly amended by the Growth and Infrastructure Act 2013.

---

[22] Government initiated 'land grab' by commercial and/or foreign state investors is just an example of a more widespread and long-standing problem: Schutter, 'The Green Rush' (n 3).

[23] K Deininger et al (eds), *Land Policies for Growth and Poverty Reduction*, World Bank Policy Research Report (Washington DC, World Bank and Oxford University Press, 2003).

[24] For revealing accounts of the many problems arising out of incorporation of land holding communities in Australia and Papua New Guinea, see in particular JF Weiner and K Glaskin (eds), *Customary Land Tenure and Registration in Australia and Papua New Guinea: Anthropological Perspectives* (Canberra, Australian National University E Press, 2007).

Town and village green rights are recreational rights which local inhabitants can acquire by long use over land—any land[25]—owned by someone else.[26] The land can be owned by the Crown, or by a local or public authority or by any private individual. Rights of common are rights that defined individuals have to take specified natural resources from land owned by someone else, in common with other private individuals having a like right. Rights of common are usually, but not necessarily, appurtenant to other land held by the rights-holders. The rights of common most frequently encountered today are rights of local farmers to graze animals on a common pasture,[27] a communal property right of a type recognisable over most of the world.

The Commons Registration Act 1965 made these rights registrable for the first time. However, they are not registrable in the national Land Register. The 1965 Act designated local government authorities[28] as Commons Registration Authorities and these Authorities were required to set up and maintain two separate registers, the Commons Register and the Town or Village Greens Register. The registration authorities were, and are, required to register in the Commons Register all common land in their area and all rights of common exercisable over it, and to register in the Town or Village Greens Register all town and village greens in their area.

The underlying principle of the 1965 Act was that these were ancient rural rights in decline and in danger of disappearing altogether, which ought to be preserved for heritage and environmental reasons.[29] So, the motivation and the objectives of the legislation were initially very different from those that formed the stimulus of our registration of title system, and different again from those stimulating land titling in sub-Saharan Africa.

The preservation method chosen for rights of common and town and village green rights was the one-off registration of all pre-existing rights, which were made void if not registered before a cut-off date in 1970. In this sense registration was proactive and comprehensive, unlike the reactive piecemeal process adopted earlier for central land registration. Broadly, the system adopted by the 1965 Act was that those who considered themselves entitled at common law to town or village green rights or rights of common were invited to apply for registration of their rights. If no one objected, the registration went ahead. If the landowner or someone else objected, the Registration Authority would appoint an adjudicator and if appropriate the matter would be settled by public inquiry.

---

[25] After a long struggle in the courts the House of Lords confirmed (by a majority) in *Oxfordshire County Council v Oxford City Council* [2006] UKHL 25 that it need not be in a town or village, it need not be green or grassy, nor need it resemble in any other respect what is traditionally thought of as a village green. Applying this in *Newhaven Port and Properties Ltd v East Sussex County Council* [2013] EWCA Civ 2013 it was held that a tidal beach, under water for part of each day, was eligible for registration as a town or village green, although registration was refused for other reasons.

[26] The rights can also arise by express grant: a landowner can apply for its own land to be registered as a town or village green under what is now s 15(8) of the Commons Act 2006.

[27] The natural resource taken is grass and other grazing crops grown on the land; the taking is via the mouth of the animal.

[28] In England, county councils and, in areas without county councils, district councils and London borough councils; in Wales, county or county borough councils.

[29] See further, A Clarke, 'Re-establishing Diversity' in M Freeman (ed), *Law and Opinion at the End of the Twentieth Century*, Current Legal Problems vol 50 (Oxford, Oxford University Press, 1997) 119, 123–37.

It is fairly clear that no-one gave much thought to the question of how these registers should be kept up-to-date once pre-existing rights were registered by the cut-off date. Registers of marketable private property rights can be kept up-to-date by putting the onus on purchasers, grantees and inheritors of the rights. Generally they can be relied upon to take the initiative to get the register up-dated in their favour: proactive up-dating by registration authorities is not usually thought to be necessary. However, this does not appear to work with communal property rights, especially if they are not transmissible and/or if they arise or change in nature over time through changes in customary use. In these circumstances machinery has to be put in place for the registrar to be systematically proactive in up-dating the register. This was not done in the 1965 Act. In particular, not much thought was given to what would happen when new town and village green rights and rights of common were created after the cut-off date for registering all the pre-existing ones. Again, the 1965 Act says almost nothing about this, presumably assuming these would be rare occurrences. However, as it happened the 1965 Act re-awakened interest in these rights and stimulated their regeneration. Over the next few decades applications for registration of newly created town and village greens in particular were made in increasing numbers. The attendant publicity persuaded the Government that these applications for new registrations posed a threat to development and as a result substantial curbs on new registrations were introduced by the Growth and Infrastructure Act 2013.[30] Meanwhile the Commons Act 2006 has amended both the Commons and the Town or Village Greens Registers so that they can be brought up-to-date and cope with those new registrations that manage to surmount the new procedural hurdles. However, even after the enactment of the 2006 Act and the curtailing of new registrations, progress towards complete, accurate and up-to-date registers has been painfully slow. At the time of writing, there are still key provisions of the 2006 Act which are in force in a few pilot areas only, with no timetable for rolling them out to cover the rest of England and Wales.[31]

These problems are exacerbated by the fact that registration occurs at local government level rather than by a national dedicated land registration administration. It is not clear why it was decided that they should be registered in separate local registers rather than in the national Land Register. Before 1965 communal rights such as these were (and to some extent still are) governed by common law and by specialised, often local or private, acts of parliament, and they had never been registrable under the central land registration system. It may therefore never have occurred to anyone to consider whether, if they were to become registrable, they should be registered on the national Land Register. However, whatever the reason was for devolving registration to local government level, it has had consequences that will sound familiar to other jurisdictions which have attempted to do the same with land administration—lack of resources, lack of local expertise,[32] difficulties in

---

[30] Growth and Infrastructure Act 2013, ss 14–17, outlined in *Emmet & Farrand* (n 13) paras 1.126, 1.132 132.01 and 1.133.01.

[31] For precise details see *Emmet & Farrand* (n 13) para 1.126.

[32] Common land and town and village greens are not evenly distributed over England and Wales, and some Commons Registration Authorities have relatively few within their areas.

ensuring implementation of national policy,[33] and lack of uniformity in what was recorded and in what kind of a system.

Other problems arise out of the nature of the rights. Town and village green rights and rights of common are both communal land rights, and they are both particular use rights—*jurae in re aliena*—rather than ownership-type rights. So, this is not communal *ownership*:[34] the rights are necessarily exercisable over private or state-owned land. This makes their absence from the national Land Register of land ownership even more problematic.

The precise problems that arise are not the same for town and village green rights and for rights of common. Although both rights are communal in nature in that both are held by a community which is defined by reference to a shared characteristic, there are significant analytic differences between them, and the registration requirements applicable to them are significantly different.

In the case of town and village green rights, the registration machinery introduced by the 1965 Act provided for the registration of *land* as a town or village green. As already noted, the Act provides that land must be registered as a town or village green if local inhabitants can prove they have used it for 'lawful sports or pastimes' for at least 20 years. However, the Act says nothing at all about the rights the inhabitants (or anyone else) actually have over land once the land is registered as a town or village green. Nothing is said about what the rights are or who holds them, and there is no provision for those rights to go on the register. The question of who holds these rights, and what the rights are, had to be resolved by the House of Lords in 2006 in *Oxfordshire County Council v Oxford City Council*.[35] The effect of the *Oxfordshire* decision appears to be that town and village green rights are held by a community of fluctuating membership defined by reference to the place the members 'inhabit'. This is a familiar type of communal property right in many jurisdictions, but in our jurisdiction ascertainment of exactly who qualifies as a member at any given point is extremely difficult. Specifically, under the 1965 Act land can become registered as a town or village green in the first place only if 'a significant number of the inhabitants of a locality, or of any one or more neighbourhoods within a locality'[36] have used it for 'lawful sports and pastimes as of right' for at least 20 years since 1970. Once the land is registered as a green, the class of people entitled to use it for those purposes appears to become *all* inhabitants of that locality, or of that or those neighbourhoods.[37] That is not the end of the difficulties in

[33] For an indication of the range of difficulties, see DEFRA's 2010, *Review of the Pilot Implementation of Part I of the Commons Act 2006*, explaining the problems central government has had in making Commons Registration Authorities in the pilot areas aware of the action they need to take to up-date the registers within the time frame already imposed by the legislation.

[34] Compare the communal ownership communities can acquire under Pts 2 and 3 of the Land Reform (Scotland) Act 2003: see Land Reform Review Group, *Interim Report* (May 2013).

[35] *Oxfordshire County Council v Oxford City Council* [2006] UKHL 25.

[36] Derived from s 22 of the Commons Registration Act 1965 as amended by s 98 of the Countryside and Rights of Way Act, and now appearing in s of the Commons Act 2006.

[37] The majority of the House of Lords in *Oxfordshire County Council* (n 35) took the considered (though strictly *per incuriam*) view that the effect of registration of land as a town and village green under the 1965 Act is to give local inhabitants the *right* to use it for lawful sports and pastimes (this is nowhere stated in the 1965 Act): Lord Hoffmann ([45]–[53]). It seems to follow from what Lord Hoffmann says ([53]) that the right to use for these purposes extends to all inhabitants of the relevant locality/neighbourhood, even if it is not clear precisely what the relevant locality/neighbourhood is.

identifying the geographic catchment area. After considerable uncertainty the courts have confirmed that whereas 'locality' means any area of land 'within legally significant boundaries',[38] 'neighbourhood' has no technical meaning: Lord Hoffmann in *Oxfordshire County Council v Oxford City Council* described it as 'obviously drafted with a deliberate imprecision'.[39] The only way of finding out *which* locality/ neighbourhood is the relevant one is to look at the application for registration made by the applicant users, modified (if at all) by what is said in the decision to register made by the Registration Authority. Understandably, since the Act makes no provision for registration of the community's rights, it contains no requirement for that information to be recorded on the register.[40] It also says nothing at all about the nature and scope of the community's rights, and this again has had to be settled by the courts. In the *Oxfordshire* case the House of Lords came to the conclusion that the rights the inhabitants acquire by virtue of the land becoming registered as a town or village green are *not* confined to rights to continue to do on the land whatever it was they were doing over the last 20 years (perhaps holding an annual Guy Fawkes bonfire and party, or dancing around maypoles in May, or more prosaically playing football or going for walks). Instead, the House of Lords concluded, the inhabitants acquire the right to use the land for *any* 'lawful sports or pastimes'.[41] This simplified the position for potential purchasers, Lord Hoffmann suggested, because registration of land as a green would have identical consequences whatever the nature of the land.[42] However, the unfortunate effect is that registration of the right distorts the nature of the right and, by authorising use that may go beyond the established customary use, disrupts the pattern of shared resource use evolved over time by the landowner and the local inhabitants.

As in all communities defined by reference to residence or habitation, membership of the community is automatic not voluntary and there is no right of exit; individual members have no right to dispose of their interest and the community has no inherent right to sell, rent or mortgage the communal right. The community has no legal identity, and because of the loose definition of 'neighbourhood' the community of inhabitants will not necessarily have any links to any pre-existing governance institution or structure. In most cases, therefore, there will be no pre-existing management structure and no-one with whom outsiders can deal or negotiate. Since the rights nearly always arise by customary use rather than by agreement with or grant by the landowner, there will undoubtedly be locally accepted norms about sharing the resource between members and between the community and the landowner, and these are very likely to be unwritten and evolving rather than static. In other words,

---

[38] *Adamson v Paddico* (267) Ltd [2012] EWCA Civ 262.

[39] *Oxfordshire County Council* (n 35) [27]. To add to the imprecision, it now seems that the combined effect of the cases is that if the inhabitants are inhabitants of a 'locality', it must be one locality only, whereas if they are inhabitants of 'neighbourhoods within a locality', there may be one or more neighbourhoods, and they may straddle one or more localities. This makes more sense when one appreciates that local people who live on opposite sides of a large open space which they use for recreation may well live in different neighbourhoods, whatever 'neighbourhood' is taken to mean.

[40] Although this appears to be envisaged, for some cases at least, in Model Entry 18 set out in Pt 1 of Sch 3 to the Commons Registration (England) Regulations 2008 (SI 2008/1961).

[41] *Oxfordshire County Council* (n 35) [50]–[51], [69], [114] and [124]. For the opposing minority view, see Lord Scott, ibid [104]–[106].

[42] Ibid, [53].

the nature and extent of the community's resource use is virtually undiscoverable by outsiders. In practice, therefore, it tends to be assumed by outsiders that land registered as a town or village green can never again be used by anyone else for any other purpose. The failure to articulate the rights on the register, together with the House of Lords' enlargement of the rights to cover all lawful sports and pastimes, therefore sterilises the land, probably to a greater extent than is necessary to protect the customary usage. This can only be described as a missed opportunity. Particularisation of a communal property right on a register is seen as valuable in other jurisdictions because it enables the communal right to be part of a mixed economy where the same piece of land supports not only the traditional usages and activities but also other activities such as exploration for or extraction of minerals,[43] or tourism or nature conservation.[44] This kind of shared resource use is ruled out in the case of town and village greens because of the failure of the registration machinery to allow particularisation of the right.

Rights of common are quite different from town and village green rights. Rights of common which are appurtenant[45] demonstrate the mix of private property and communal property found in many customary law systems: each rights-holder has private ownership or leasehold rights in her own appurtenant land together with a communal resource use right over the common land. Unlike town or village green rights, rights of common are freely marketable. This is self-evidently true of non-appurtenant rights of common but also true of those which are appurtenant, within the bounds of appurtenance. In other words the appurtenant land is freely alienable, and the right of common automatically passes with the appurtenant land to the assignee of the land. So, whether the rights of common are appurtenant or non-appurtenant, the members of the right-holders' community each have clear exit rights.

The registration machinery for rights of common is also different from the town or village green registration machinery. Under the 1965 Act the Commons Registration Authority must register in the Commons Register both the rights (the rights of common) and the land over which they are exercisable (the common). The names of the rights-holders are recorded on the register, so the number and identity of the members of the community are easily ascertainable. Rights of common can be acquired by long use by the users or by express grant by the landowner, and because the rights-holders are all sharing a limited resource they are very likely to have agreed or evolved norms for sharing which will govern their relationship with the owner of the common as well as their relationships between themselves. For the same reason they are likely to develop a governance structure. In any event, the Commons Act 2006 provides a default governance structure which can be adopted by commons which do not yet have one, or where the users are dissatisfied with the one they have.[46]

---

[43] Discussed in relation to Australia and Papua New Guinea in Weiner and Glaskin (eds), *Contemporary Land Tenure and Registration in Australia and Papua New Guinea* (n 24).

[44] See H van Gils, G Siegl and RM Bennett, 'The Living Commons of West Tyrol, Austria: Lessons for Land Policy and Land Administration' (2014) 38 *Land Use Policy* 16.

[45] The Commons Act 2006, s 9 requires all grazing rights to be appurtenant to neighbouring land, restoring the common law position upset by the decision of the House of Lords in *Bettison v Langton* [2001] 2 AC 27: see further *Emmet & Farrand* (n 13) para 1.127.04.

[46] Pt 2 of the Commons Act 2006.

Again unlike the town and village green rights registration system, the commons registers must record the specific nature of the right. For example, in the case of grazing rights the type of animal and the number that can be grazed by each right-holder on each piece of common land must be specified in the register. On the face of it this may appear undesirably inflexible, inhibiting fluctuations in grazing dictated by changes in environmental and demographic pressures on the common land. However, the courts (with some support from the legislation) have introduced some flexibility by holding that the specified level of grazing is a maximum only: the actual extent of the right is subject to customary constraints, regardless of what is said in the register. In *Dance v Savery*,[47] for example, it was held that the rights-holder might be bound by an agreed reduction in the number of animals prescribed on the register. Similarly, in *Hall v Moore*[48] it was accepted that registered grazing rights were exercisable only one year in three, in accordance with an accepted change in custom which did not appear anywhere on the register. This sensitivity to the fluidity of custom and community governance was however rather spoiled by the Court of Appeal's finding in the same case that the applicant rights-holder was not in fact bound by temporary constraints on grazing rights agreed between the informal association of commoners and the landowner. Faced with an agency problem typical of those arising when considering the effects of dealings between an informal community and outsiders, the Court of Appeal retreated into contract law, sidestepping the difficult but necessary task of assessing how far the informal association was able to speak for the community of rights-holders as a whole. Adopting instead a purely contractual analysis it found that the applicant was not bound by the actions of the association.

The experience of registering rights of common in England and Wales is therefore in many ways more encouraging than the experience of registering town and village green rights. Both, however, reveal significant problems that have to be tackled if centralised registration of communal land rights is to be effective.

V. CONCLUSION

There is now a growing recognition amongst those advocating land titling in sub-Saharan Africa and other parts of the world that these problems in registering communal property rights have to be tackled, as part of an overall project of registration of all property rights within complex land tenure systems, not just private property rights.[49] The World Bank and the International Federation of Surveyors (FIG), once foremost amongst those who advocated 'formalisation' of land rights in developing countries by moving towards private ownership titles, are now adopting a more

---

47 *Dance v Savery* [2011] EWCA Civ 1250.
48 *Hall v Moore* [2009] EWCA Civ 201.
49 See, eg C Toulmin and J Quan, 'Registering Customary Rights' in C Toulmin and J Quan (eds), *Evolving Land Rights, Policy and Tenure in Africa* (London, DfID/IIED/NRI, 2000) and P Van Der Molen, 'Future Cadastres' in JM Otto and A Hoekema (eds), *Fair Land Governance: How to Legalise Land Rights for Rural Development* (Chicago, University of Chicago Press, 2012); compare JF Weiner and K Glaskin in Weiner and Glaskin (eds), *Customary Land Tenure and Registration in Australia and Papua New Guinea* (n 24) para 1-15.

nuanced approach. In their joint report, *Fit-For-Purpose Land Administration* published in 2014[50] they say, in the context of discussing what makes land administration systems 'fit for purpose':

> The fit-for-purpose concept directly supports what is called 'Continuum of Continuums' ... This term occurred in response to the view that the traditional cadastral systems, as known in most developed countries and which often operate with fixed (high level) technical standards and a legal perspective, predominantly support freehold as the sought after form of tenure. The concept 'Continuum of Continuums' has many continuum dimensions [including that] ... It recognizes that a continuum of tenure exists in terms of social tenure relationships, such as occupancy, usufruct, informal rights, customary rights, indigenous right and nomadic rights. In the same way, parties holding the rights may not only be natural or legal persons, but could be a family, tribe, community, village, or a farmers' cooperative.

Meanwhile FIG has put forward a Land Administration Domain Model as a design standard for land administration systems, particularly for use in developing countries where land rights do not match the western private ownership model. It was formally recognised as an International Standard by the International Standardisation Organisation in December 2012 as ISO 19152.[51] Lemmen et al report that it has already 'gained recognition and support' not only from FIG but also from the Food and Agriculture Organisation of the United Nations, UN Habitat and the European Commission's INSPIRE.[52] For present purposes the significant point is that it too recognises that rights holders may be groups as well as individuals, that land rights to be represented on a register may not be confined to traditional real rights, and that representing rights on a register does not always require or involve drawing a line on the ground enclosing an area from which the owner is entitled to exclude all others.

Registration of town and village green rights and rights of common in England and Wales provides some indications of how this might be done, even though the communal rights regulated, and the social, economic and political dimensions of the problem, are so very much less complex in England and Wales than they are elsewhere.

The Commons Register demonstrates that mixed private/communal rights can be recorded on a register, and that it is possible to particularise communal rights falling short of ownership without sacrificing the flexibility necessary to accommodate the shifts in patterns of usage which occur in customary communal usage of resources. It does however still have some way to go in recognising and dealing with agency problems, in particular in recognising that it may be necessary to look beyond contract rules to decide when community members are bound by community decisions. On the other hand, the registration system adopted for town and village greens—to register the land as a green but not record on the register the nature and extent of the rights exercisable over it—has been less successful. This is significant because

---

[50] FIG/World Bank, Fig Publication No 60, *Fit-For-Purpose Land Administration* (2014).

[51] See also, FIG/UN Habitat, FIG Publication No 52, *The Social Tenure Domain Mode: A Pro-Poor Land Tool* (2010).

[52] C Lemmen, P van Oosterom and P van der Molen, 'Standards for New Approaches' (June 2013) *Geospatial World* 53.

it is a model often advocated for registering customary land tenures incorporating communal rights in sub-Saharan African states and elsewhere. The experience in England and Wales has been that it merely displaces problems of definition leaving them to be resolved elsewhere, and cuts off the possibility of communally used resources becoming part of a mixed economy, supporting both communal and individual resource uses.

Finally, the experience in England and Wales demonstrates no advantages in registering communal property rights in a separate register, certainly not enough to compensate for the considerable disadvantages. If private landowners are to be made subject to communal property rights they are in no better position if the rights are recorded in a separate register than they would be if they are recorded in the central register of titles. Our experience has been that separate registers of communal property rights still have to be kept up-to-date, and that there are significant practical difficulties in administering them at a local level. These difficulties can be expected to be greater and more intractable in countries with less developed local government administration, particularly since the rights that local administrations would be expected to register are considerably more complex than the rights we register in the town or village greens registers and commons registers.

Once that is conceded, it is difficult to see what justification there is for not having a single central register on which all property rights are registered, private and communal. Any other registration regime marginalises communal property rights and carries real risks of leaving them inadequately protected, whatever the nature of the property rights system.

13

Subsurface Ownership: English or American Rules, Ok?

JILL MORGAN[*]

I. INTRODUCTION

IN RECENT decades, the issue of subsurface ownership has become the subject of renewed academic debate, primarily within the context of carbon capture and storage (CCS). Geological storage (GS) (which is currently considered to be the most promising form of CCS) enables CO_2 emitted from fossil fuel power plants or other industrial installations to be captured at source (ie before it is emitted into the atmosphere), converted into a high pressure liquid-like form and transported (usually by pipeline) to a storage site where it is injected directly into porous sedimentary rock, thereby displacing salt water, oil or gas already present in microscopic pores within the rock. After injection, the CO_2 moves up through the storage site until it reaches the impermeable layer of rock (the 'caprock' or 'seal') that lies over the storage site.

Potential GS storage sites (which are at depths generally exceeding 700m)[1] include depleted oil and gas reservoirs, saline aquifers (saline water-filled basalt volcanic rocks), and unworkable coal seams.[2] A storage site may lie under thousands of square kilometres of surface land owned by scores of different individuals or companies. There may be others who do not own the surface of the overlying land but have rights underneath it. In such circumstances, the issue of who owns the pore space, that is the voids within the rock where the CO_2 can be stored, is critical,[3] determining, first, who may grant storage rights and, secondly, who may be entitled to compensation in the event of expropriation.[4]

---

[*] Reader, College of Law, Swansea University.

[1] International Energy Agency, *Energy Technology Perspectives* (OECD/IEA, 2008) 268.

[2] www3.imperial.ac.uk/carboncaptureandstorage/whatisccs.

[3] So far as hydraulic fracturing is concerned, the focus has been on whether hydraulic fracturing which crosses property lines constitutes a subsurface trespass. With the aim of promoting the UK Government's commitment to developing shale gas and oil exploration and deep geothermal industries, the Department of Energy and Climate Change has recently issued a *Consultation on Proposal for Underground Access for the Extraction of Gas, Oil or Geothermal Energy* (May 2014). It proposes that underground access rights are granted by statute to companies extracting petroleum (as defined under the Petroleum Act 1998—including gas or oil) or geothermal energy in land at least 300m below the surface.

[4] BN Grave, 'Carbon Capture and Storage in South Dakota: The Need for a Clear Designation of Pore Space Ownership' (2010) 55 *South Dakota Law Review* 72, 88.

It has been claimed that in the United States 'pore space designation has the potential to be the most contentious and problematic of the regulatory hurdles facing CCS'.[5] A particular difficulty there is that commonly title to strata containing minerals (the 'mineral estate') has been severed from the surface title. Subsurface property rights are subject to state rather than federal law with states applying either the so-called 'American' or 'English' rules. According to the American rule, the surface owner who transfers the mineral estate to a third party retains the right to use for storage the space which remains after the removal of underground minerals, oil, or gas while the English rule (which is said also to be practised in much of Canada)[6] holds that the mineral owner owns the subsurface space even after the minerals have been removed. The English rule is said to derive from a series of cases decided in the nineteenth and early-twentieth centuries and the aim of this chapter is to discover whether those cases have been correctly applied to justify the finding of a specific rule.

The first part of what follows outlines the extent of subsurface rights while the second part considers severance of surface and mineral estates. The discussion then turns to a selection of nineteenth-century cases concerning mineral rights in freehold land and land which was formerly copyhold. The penultimate section touches upon application of the 'English rule' in Canada and the United States. The chapter concludes that the cases which are said to form the basis of the English Rule were decided in the context of a factual matrix which is distinguishable from pore space ownership for CCS purposes and that Anglo–Welsh law has already moved towards the American rule.

II. RIGHTS IN SUBSURFACE LAND

The oft-made assertion that in most jurisdictions outside of the United States the 'subsurface geology' is 'owned by the government'[7] is misleading. A landowner's rights in the subsurface vary from country to country but, as Prosterman and Hanstad point out, three main models may be identified.[8] Examples of the first can be found in the United States and many Western European countries, where private ownership of land carries with it the right to use 'the entire subsurface' (unless rights have been granted to a third party or reserved and excepted by a former owner). The second

---

[5] EL Aldrich and C Koerner, 'Analysis of Carbon Capture and Sequestration Pore Space Legislation: A Review of Existing and Possible Regimes' (2011) 24(3) *The Electricity Journal* 22.

[6] E Wilson and M de Figueiredo, 'Geologic Carbon Dioxide Sequestration: An Analysis of Subsurface Property Law' (2006) 36 *Eastern Law Reporter* 10114, 10123.

[7] Global CCS Institute, *The Global Status of CCS: 2010* (2011) 107 cdn.globalccsinstitute.com/sites/default/files/publications/12776/global-status-ccs-2010. Similar statements appear in other policy and guidance documents, eg International Risk Governance Council, *Regulation of Carbon Capture and Storage* (2008) 13 www.irgc.org/IMG/pdf/Policy_Brief_CCS; International Energy Agency, *Carbon Capture and Storage Model Regulatory Framework* (OECD/IEA, 2010) 3.2.3 www.iea.org/publications/freepublications/publication/model_framework; EL Aldrich, C Koerner and D Solan, *Analysis of Existing and Possible Regimes for Carbon Capture and Sequestration: A Review for Policymakers* (Energy Policy Institute/Centre for Energy Studies, 2011) 16 epi.boisestate.edu/media/9042/epi%20liability%20regimes%20for%20ccs_review%20for%20policymakers.

[8] RL Prosterman and T Hanstad, *Legal Impediments to Effective Rural Land Relations in Eastern Europe and Central Asia* (The World Bank, 1999) 32.

is discernible in those countries in which, even where land is privately owned, the state has expressly asserted ownership over all subsurface minerals, and either established national mineral extraction companies, or granted licences to third parties to explore for and extract minerals. Where the third model applies, the state retains ownership of only valuable subsurface resources, leaving private landowners with ownership of 'commonly found subsurface resources'.[9] Under the law of England and Wales (which comes within the third category) the Crown is entitled to all mines of gold and silver (whether situated on public or private land).[10] Further, as a result of statutory provision, coal vests in the Coal Authority,[11] and all rights in petroleum (including mineral oil and natural gas) vest in the Crown.[12] The Crown also has the right to store gas (including captured CO_2) in offshore sites.[13] Otherwise, however, 'the grant of the land includes the surface and all that is supra—houses, trees and the like ... and everything that is infra—mines, earth and clay, etc'.[14]

In the law of England and Wales, the largest estate in land, the fee simple absolute in possession has come increasingly to resemble absolute ownership. In the words of Challis:

> It confers, and since the beginning of legal history has always conferred, the lawful right to exercise over, upon, and in respect to the land, every act of ownership which can enter into the imagination, including the right to commit unlimited waste; and, for all practical purposes of ownership, it differs from the absolute dominium of a chattel, in nothing except the physical indestructibility of its subject.[15]

However, although proprietors of land are commonly referred to as its owners,[16] Anglo–Welsh land law still retains its original basis in that, albeit in a 'spectral sense',[17] all land in England and Wales is owned by the Crown. A small part of that land is in the Crown's own occupation but the remainder is occupied by 'tenants' holding either directly or indirectly from the Crown.[18] The fee simple estate consists therefore of a series of rights to use and control the land. Clearly, from the viewpoint of GS, the extent of an estate owner's rights extend under his or her land is critical, as it determines who is entitled to grant access to the proposed storage site. Lord Hope took the view in *Bocardo SA v Star Energy Onshore Ltd*,[19] that the maxim *cuius est solum, eius est usque ad coelum et ad inferos* (he who owns the soil owns also up to the heavens and down to the centre of the earth) still serves as a useful

---

[9] Ibid.

[10] *The Queen v Earl of Northumberland* (1567) 1 Plowden 310, 336, 75 ER 472.

[11] s 7(3) of the Coal Industry Act 1994.

[12] ss 1 and 2 of the Petroleum Act 1998.

[13] Energy Act 2008, s 1.

[14] *Mitchell v Mosley* [1914] 1 Ch 438, 450 (Cozens-Hardy MR). According to Bradbrook, the Crown's entitlement to certain minerals does not necessarily mean that all other mines and minerals which lie under the surface belong absolutely to the surface owner: AJ Bradbrook, 'The Relevance of the *cujus est solum* Doctrine to the Surface Landowner's Claims to Natural Resources Located Above and Beneath the Land' (1989) 11 *Adelaide Law Review* 462, 463–64.

[15] C Sweet, *Challis's Law of Real Property* (London, Butterworths, 1911) 218.

[16] C Harpum, S Bridge and M Dixon, *Megarry and Wade: The Law of Real Property* (London, 2008) para 2-006.

[17] P Birks, 'Five Keys to Land Law' in S Bright and J Dewar (eds), *Land Law: Themes and Perspectives* (Oxford, Oxford University Press, 1998) 480.

[18] Harpum et al (n 16) para 2-001.

[19] *Bocardo SA v Star Energy Onshore Ltd* [2010] UKSC 35, [2010] 3 WLR 654.

starting point (even though it has been the subject of considerable criticism as being out of place in the modern world).[20] His Lordship felt, however, that there must be a stopping point, 'a greater understanding of geology [having] taught us that most of the earth's interior, due to extremes of pressure and temperature, is a complex and inhospitable structure that is beyond man's capacity to enter or make use of'.[21] The Supreme Court concluded in *Bocardo* that an estate owner's rights extend to the depth at which pressure and temperature made the concept of ownership so absurd as to be not worth arguing about, and that the owner of the surface will also be the owner of the strata beneath it, including any minerals to be found there, unless the whole or a particular part of the strata has been transferred by conveyance, at common law or by statute to someone else.[22]

In the United States, the *cuius est solum* maxim still holds sway, thus 'allocating private ownership interests in coal and other stationary subsurface mineral deposits to the owners of surface land immediately above those resources'.[23] Some commentators maintain that the current law based on the *cuius est solum* rule seems to do a 'decent job of apportioning property interests among landowners and thereby limiting neighbor disputes, facilitating efficient exchanges of mineral rights, and encouraging investment in these valuable assets'.[24] Others, however, propose that a distinction should be made as regards the stratum immediately beneath the surface (which is necessary for the surface owner's reasonable enjoyment of his land) and a deeper one, over which he has no greater rights than anybody else.[25] Following on from this is an emerging train of thought that pore space should be seen as 'a public resource, similar to the navigable airspace',[26] while another suggestion is that a landowner's private interests in the subsurface should cease at 1,000ft below the ground.[27]

III. SURFACE ESTATES AND MINERAL ESTATES

Acquisition by the CCS operator of 'the entire and undivided fee simple estate' in the land in which the storage site is situated is clearly the most straightforward means by which a CCS operator can secure all the property rights it needs to sequester captured CO_2.[28] Then, in line with the *cuius est solum* principle—although subject

---

[20] It was said in *Commissioner for Railways v Valuer-General* [1974] AC 328, 351–52 that 'so sweeping, unscientific and unpractical a doctrine is unlikely to appeal to the common law mind'.

[21] *Bocardo* (n 19) [19].

[22] In *Bocardo*—in which an oil company had, without Bocardo's knowledge or consent, drilled a well diagonally from its own land to access an oil deposit under Bocardo's land, the wells extended from about 800ft to 2, 800ft below the surface. The fact that the strata could be worked upon at those depths indicated that they were far from being so deep as to reach the point of absurdity.

[23] TA Rule, 'Property Rights and Modern Energy' (2012–13) 20 *George Mason Law Review* 803, 806.

[24] Ibid.

[25] This would mirror the treatment of rights in airspace. See J Morgan, 'Digging Deep: Property Rights in Subterranean Space and the Challenge of Carbon Capture and Storage' (2013) 62 *ICLQ* 813.

[26] JR Zadick, 'The Public Pore Space: Enabling Carbon Capture and Sequestration by Reconceptualising Subsurface Property Rights' (2011) 36 *William and Mary Environmental Law and Policy Review* 257, 269.

[27] JG Sprankling, 'Owning the Center of the Earth' (2008) 55 *University of California at Los Angeles Law Review* 979–92, 986.

[28] A Stamm, 'Legal Problems in the Underground Storage of Natural Gas' (1957) 36 *Texas Law Review* 161, 164.

to obtaining any necessary permits or licences and consents—it will be free to store the captured CO_2 in the strata lying under the surface of the land. However, this is unlikely to be a practical option, given that thousands of square kilometres of surface land may overlie a storage site and the operator will not necessarily need to own the surface in order to access the site. Moreover, as has already been noted, it is commonly the case in the US that title to strata in which minerals are to be found (the 'mineral estate') has been severed from the surface title (the 'surface estate').[29] Severance may occur—via grant or reservation and exception—when either the mineral estate or the surface estate is sold or leased.[30] A complex network of arrangements can develop where the land in question is rich in minerals. As Wenzel explains, the owner of a fee simple may create—by way of exception, reservation, grant, or lease—'as many separate estates as there are different minerals or strata of minerals under his or her land'.[31] Thus, for example, 'the owner of the entire interest [in land] may sell the surface to A, the stratum of iron to B, the stratum of coal to C, the stratum of oil to D, and a stratum of the air space above'.[32] A CCS operator would have to obtain permission from all affected parties before it could lawfully use the land for storage.

To complicate matters further, while severed mines and minerals may be held in the form of corporeal interests (estates in fee or terms of years absolute) there may (additionally or alternatively) be 'lesser interests' which allow for their use.[33] Thus, a licence may exist to enter land and to search and dig for a hard mineral such as coal and to remove it for the licensee's own use,[34] or a *profit à prendre* may be granted conferring a right to enter the land and sever the mineral therefrom, acquiring by severance title to the substance removed.[35]

Usually in the past, 'the valuable component of a mineral interest was the minerals themselves, and ownership of the minerals and the right to extract them were clearly a part of the mineral interest'.[36] Exercise by the lessee under a mining lease

---

[29] Traditionally, the mineral estate is regarded as the dominant estate so that the mineral owner 'has the right to the use and possession of so much of the surface as is reasonably required in the operation of his [or her estate]': *Getty Oil Co v Royal* 422 S W 2d 59, 593 (Tex Civ App 1967). See ME Mansfield, 'On the Cusp of Property Rights: Lessons from Public Land Law' (1991) 18 *Ecology Law Quarterly* 43, 67.

[30] It appears that 'title to [a mineral estate] may be lost or acquired by adverse possession, but such possession must be actual and not merely constructive. Before severance, the person in possession of the surface is constructively in possession of the minerals beneath, but not so after severance': 'Interests created by grants of coal apart from the surface' (1921–22) 31 *Yale Law Journal* 747, 748.

[31] MA Wenzel, 'Comment: The Model Surface Use and Mineral Development Accommodation Act: Easy Easements for Mining Interests' (1993) 42 *American University Law Review* 607, 618.

[32] *Davison v Reynolds* 103 S E 248, 249 (Ga 1920).

[33] B Barton, 'Surface Rights under the Mineral Act of British Columbia' (Ph D thesis, University of British Columbia, 1984) 10.

[34] *Chetham v Williamson* (1804) 4 East 469, 102 ER 910; *Doe d Hanley v Wood* (1819) 2 B & Ald 724, 106 ER 529.

[35] *Duke of Sutherland v Heathcote* [1892] 1 Ch 475. Here, Lindley LJ explained that a *profit à prendre*—which gives a right to take something off another person's land—'does not prevent the owner from taking the same sort of thing from ... his own land; the first right may limit, but does not exclude, the second'. While it might be possible to grant an exclusive right to all the profit of a particular kind, 'such a right cannot be inferred from language which is not clear and explicit' (484–85).

[36] PS Glaser, DA Henderson, M McGuffey and BW Kirkpatrick, 'Global Warming Solutions: Regulatory Challenges and Common Law Liabilities Associated with the Geologic Sequestration of Carbon Dioxide' (2008) 6 *Georgetown Journal of Law and Public Policy* 429, 438. Whether a particular substance is a mineral or not is a question which may depend upon its use and value for the time being, and a 'mineral one year may not be a mineral the next'.

of his right to work and remove the mineral meant that 'the land in its wider sense [was] permanently impoverished'.[37] To that extent, a mining lease (which effectively was 'a sale of a portion of the earth's crust, the purchase money being paid in instalments as rent and royalties') was 'essentially different from an agricultural or an occupation lease'.[38] As regards GS, however, instead of permanently impoverishing the land, the removal of minerals means that 'the value is in the geologic formation's capacity for long-term, stable storage' and the focus therefore is on 'the ownership of the formation, not the minerals'.[39] The question thus arises as to who owns the space left behind when the minerals have been extracted, that is the space in which other materials (including CO_2) may be stored. It may be that 'the landowner's intent[ion] regarding underground storage rights' has been 'expressly articulated in the conveyance instrument'.[40] If, however, the conveyance or lease is silent as to storage rights,[41] resort may be had to either the so-called 'American' or 'English' rules to settle the issue. As indicated in the introduction, according to the American rule, the surface owner who transfers the mineral estate to a third party retains the right to use for storage the space which remains after the removal of underground minerals, oil, or gas while the English rule holds that the mineral owner has the exclusive right to use the subsurface space even after the minerals have been removed.[42] The question is unresolved in many American states, and authorities appear to be divided on whether the rights to pore space are held by the surface owner or the owner of the mineral estate.[43]

Severance of the surface and mineral estates occurs in two main ways. The first is on a sale or lease of the mines and minerals, or their exception and reservation where the surface land is sold or leased to a third party. The second—which applies only in England and Wales—is where the land was formerly copyhold.

IV. FREEHOLD LAND

The English rule is said to derive from a series of cases decided in the nineteenth and early-twentieth centuries—a period when the question of whether a grant of mineral rights included a right to the chamber or open spaces left after the minerals had been extracted was a 'live issue' in England and Scotland.[44] All of these cases involved

---

[37] J Sinclair, *Coal Mining Law* (London, Pitman, 1958) 349.

[38] Ibid.

[39] Glaser et al (n 36) 438.

[40] A Mojdehi, 'Ownership Rights in Subsurface Natural Gas Storage Areas' (1981) 16 *Tulsa Law Journal* 470, 473.

[41] Alternatively, there may be no evidence of how the occupation of the superior and inferior strata came into different hands and no deeds therefore to regulate their respective rights (*Humphries v Brogden* (1850) 12 QB 739, 116 ER 1048).

[42] E Wilson and M de Figueiredo, 'Geologic Carbon Dioxide Sequestration: An Analysis of Subsurface Property Law' (2006) 36 *Eastern Law Reporter* 10114, 10123. See too J Lyndon, 'The Legal Aspects of Underground Storage of Natural Gas—Should Legislation be Considered before the Problem Arises?' (1961) 1 *Alberta Law Review* 543, 545.

[43] For a list of authorities, see D Hayano, 'Guarding the Viability of Coal and Coal-fired Power Plants: A Road Map for Wyoming's Cradle to Grave Regulation of Geologic CO_2 Sequestration' (2009) 9 *Wyoming Law Review* 139, fn 16.

[44] B Barton, 'Carbon Capture and Storage Law for New Zealand: A Comparative Study' (2009) *New Zealand Journal of Environmental Law* 1, 18.

coal and the right of 'outstroke',[45] that is a mineral owner's right to convey to the surface coal mined from adjoining lands ('foreign' coal) through the mine which had been leased or sold, no express provision having been made for such conveyance.[46] The right of outstroke appears also to have involved 'the right to excavate so much of the surrounding rock as may be necessary to build adequate passageways for the transportation of the mineral to the surface'.[47] There existed in addition the right of 'instroke' which entailed 'the right of conveying minerals from a demised mine to the surface through a pit or shaft in an adjoining mine'.[48] The right of instroke was implied unless the lease expressly excluded it,[49] but because in outstroke a working mineral owner would be making use of the mine for a secondary purpose, the right of outstroke depended on the extent of the grant (or exception and reservation). Given the expense involved in sinking a pit or shaft, such rights were clearly important. The two cases which are generally cited as the source of the English rule are *Batten Pooll v Kennedy*[50] and *Bowser v Maclean*,[51] but reference will be made in what follows to other cases which may help to shed light on the matter.

In *Batten Pooll v Kennedy*, the defendants' predecessors in title (owners in fee simple of the surface of the land and the mines underneath it) had conveyed the surface to the plaintiff predecessors in title but had reserved to themselves 'all mines and veins of coal'. The defendants, who carried on a mining and colliery business, had constructed an underground road running through the coal seams lying under the surface. The road was higher than the coal seams, and was cut partly through the adjacent strata. The plaintiff complained that the road had been unduly enlarged, arguing that the defendants had no right to use it for the carriage of coal dug from other mines beyond the limits of the property.

The defendants insisted that the road was constructed entirely in their own property reserved to them by the conveyance and that they were therefore entitled to carry foreign coal along it. They argued that an exception, or grant, of 'mines' of coal included not only the bed or seam of the mineral itself, but also as much of the adjacent strata as was necessarily or reasonably removed to get out and carry the mineral. This included the space left after removal of such adjacent strata. Because it was, and remained, the defendants' property, they could use it for any purpose they pleased, including the right of outstroke, regardless of whether or not all the coal had been worked out. Warrington J found in favour of the defendants on the basis that the exception and reservation of the 'mines and veins of coal' was an exception in the true sense and 'never passed out of their hands'. Because the road had been constructed entirely in the property reserved to them by the conveyance, they had a right to carry foreign coal along it. He concluded that 'inasmuch as "mines" unquestionably include not merely the bed of coal, but the workings of the coal, and

---

[45] NJ Stewart, 'The Reservation or Exception of Mines and Minerals' (1962) 40 *Canadian Bar Review* 229, 333.

[46] JW Simonton and SC Morris, 'The Nature of Property Rights in a Separately Owned Mineral Vein' (1920–21) 27 *West Virginia Law Quarterly and the Bar* 332, 333.

[47] J Bishop Ballem, *The Oil and Gas Lease in Canada* (Toronto, University of Toronto Press, 2008).

[48] RF MacSwinney, *The Law of Mines, Quarries and Minerals* (W Maxwell & Son, 1884) 230.

[49] *Whalley v Ramage* (1862) 10 WR 315.

[50] *Batten Pooll v Kennedy* [1907] 1 Ch 256.

[51] *Bowser v Maclean* 45 ER 682, (1860) 2 De G F & J 415.

the cavity after the coal has been removed', the road in question was part of the mine and, therefore, was comprised in the reservation.[52]

Batten Pooll v Kennedy serves as an illustration that the wording of the relevant deeds should play a key role in establishing the extent of mineral owner's rights. What is included in a grant of 'mines and minerals' is a question of fact depending on what these words meant 'in the vernacular of the mining world and commercial world and landowners' at the time when the grant took place.[53] The decision appears to establish that 'mines' is a wider, more comprehensive term than minerals, because 'it relates not only to the minerals but also to the passages in the mine'.[54] According to MacSwinney, it is generally wide enough therefore to include the space or chamber which is created as the minerals are being removed, and 'the vacuum which is left after they have been worked out'.[55] Because a 'mine' is, by definition, prima facie a void, the [mineral owner] enjoys—'from the moment of completion'—title to a void, the void subsequently expanding as minerals are extracted.[56] The mineral owner's interest 'is precisely the same when [the chamber] is in its natural state and filled with minerals; or when its natural state is altered by workings, and it consists partly or wholly of empty space'.[57] Since the mineral owner also owns the airspace created by the extraction of the minerals, 'his rights ... would extend to any lawful use, including building and any form of commercial exploitation, including purposes which might seem wholly remote from the original purposes of the exception and reservation'.[58] MacSwinney suggests that there is no reason why the words 'vein' or 'seam' should not be as extensive as that of 'mine' for this purpose.[59]

However, as demonstrated in *Duke of Hamilton v Graham*,[60] the wording employed in the 'instrument of severance' may produce surprising results. In that case, the House of Lords held that a reservation of 'coal and limestone' together with a right 'to set down coal-pits, shanks, and sinks, and win coal and limestone within the bounds of the lands' nonetheless encapsulated a reservation of the mines rather than simply the minerals together with a servitude or easement to extract the coal. Consequently, as 'absolute proprietor of the reserved coal and limestone', the Duke could tunnel through the strata which he had reserved to himself to convey foreign minerals from adjacent lands.[61] Even though the reservation was simply of 'coal and limestone', Lord Westbury referred to 'the undiminished, undeteriorated, absolute

---

[52] *Batten Pooll* (n 50) 267.
[53] *Hext v Gill* (1871–72) LR 7 Ch App 699 (James LJ).
[54] C Harpum, S Bridge and M Dixon, *Megarry and Wade: The Law of Real Property* (London, 2008) para 2-029.
[55] MacSwinney (n 48) 7.
[56] M West, 'The Ownership of Surface Voids Left by Mineral Extraction' [2011] *Conveyancer and Property Lawyer* 30, 36.
[57] MacSwinney (n 48) 7.
[58] West (n 56) 43. Such 'lawful use' could of course include storage of CO_2 in appropriate circumstances.
[59] MacSwinney (n 48) 8.
[60] *Duke of Hamilton v Graham* (1871) 9 M (HL) 98.
[61] Ibid. Lord Hatherley, the Lord Chancellor, observed (101) that 'there appears really to be no distinction whatever between the law of *Scotland* and the law of *England*, with regard to this question'.

estate in the mines' which could be 'enjoyed in every way in which it was competent or fit to enjoy it' prior to the grant and reservation. He explained:

> You may approach it laterally, from another estate, for the purpose of winning the minerals. You may use the strata which you have reserved to yourself, or rather declare to remain in yourself ... in any matter consistent with ownership. You may traverse it from any adjoining land you have. You may create a road or tunnel through it. And you may through that road or tunnel carry either the minerals or any other proceeds of an adjoining estate. You, therefore, have ... the same universal right and unlimited power of enjoyment of the estate that remains in you, as you had antecedently to the grant of the dominium utile, the enjoyment of which that grant of the dominium utile in no respect impairs or affects.[62]

Already therefore we can see a flaw in the so-called English rule. Although it would ostensibly be dependent upon a grant or exception or reservation of a 'mine' (or 'vein' or 'seam'), in *Duke of Hamilton v Graham* the court was prepared to reach the same conclusion in a reservation of a 'mineral'. Another challenge to the English rule can be found in the final case considered in this section, *Mitchell v Mosley*,[63] which was recently approved by the UK Supreme Court in *Bocardo SA v Star Energy UK Onshore Ltd*. *Mitchell v Mosley* did not concern the right of outstroke and none of the cases discussed in the preceding part of this section was cited. The facts of the case were as follows. In 1740 a lease for a term of 200 years of 'all and every the mines, veins, seams and beds of coal, and cannel' under a large part of Manchester was granted. In 1791 and 1828, the Mosleys (the successors of the lessors) executed conveyances of the land to the Mitchells (the predecessors in title of the plaintiff) severing the reversion. Only the conveyance of 1828 was made subject to the 1740 lease. The plaintiff claimed to be entitled to all mines and minerals in the lands comprised in the conveyances of 1791 and 1828—subject only to the mines, etc demised in 1740. However, the Court of Appeal agreed with the defendants' argument that in 1791 and 1828 it was 'extremely improbable' that the Mosleys intended to convey 'any interest in the mines' or indeed 'anything but the surface' and the grant should be construed therefore 'as if the minerals were excepted'. Cozens-Hardy MR was clear that the court would be going 'contrary to perfectly well settled principles of law' if it were to allow any doubt to arise on the construction of the conveyances. Significantly, because 'the grant of the land includes the surface and all that is supra ... and all that is infra' then subject to the lessees' right to get the coal and cannel, it was 'not merely the surface rights but the whole substratum to the centre of the earth, *even including the vacant spaces from which during the term the coal may have been worked out by the lessees*' which passed by the conveyances to the Mitchells. While the reference to 'vacant spaces' was made obiter, Cozens-Hardy MR appears to have been in no doubt that 'the rights under the mining lease did not provide consequent rights to control the use of the vacant spaces left' and that these were held 'in default by the owner of the land' (ie the surface owner).[64]

---

[62] Ibid, 112.
[63] *Mitchell v Mosley* [1914] 1 Ch 438.
[64] B Barton, 'The Common Law of Subsurface Activity: General Principle and Current Problems' in DN Zillman et al (eds), *The Law of Energy Underground: Understanding New Developments in Subsurface Production, Transmission and Storage* (Oxford, Oxford University Press, 2014) 34.

Barton suggests that although *Mitchell v Mosley* may not be easy to reconcile with the old authorities, the fact that it was referred to in *Bocardo v Star Energy* may mean that it is 'more compatible with a modern approach to subsurface ownership'.[65] The conflation of the English rule and American rule—if indeed separate rules can be said ever to have existed—would appear to be a result and it would therefore be the surface owner with whom a CCS operator would have to negotiate to secure rights of access and agree payment therefor.

Discussions of cases underpinning the so-called English rule have pointed to authorities involving not only freehold but also copyhold land.[66] However, they seem not to have appreciated that the rules regarding severance of the surface and mineral estates in copyhold land do not support the so-called English Rule but can in fact be distilled into the American Rule. Before discussing the relevant cases, however, it is helpful to remind ourselves of what copyhold entails.

V. COPYHOLD

The origins of copyhold lie in the open field system, a communal system of agriculture in which all the members of a small village community formed a largely self-sufficient economic unit, occupying arable land—in which the villagers had individual holdings and which they cultivated in accordance with local custom—and waste land over which they had rights in common to graze their cattle, dig turf and gather wood, etc. After the Conquest by William of Normandy in 1066, these communities were gradually absorbed into the feudal system and became part of the manorial organisation. Those who were 'villein' tenants held a certain amount of land of their lord in return for which they were obliged to produce enough food to sustain him for a given period such as a night, a week or a fortnight. By the middle of the fifteenth century, most villein tenants no longer provided personal services to their lords but paid them rent instead. The consequent enhancement of their social status was accompanied by the relabelling of villein tenure as copyhold tenure.[67] Theoretically, a copyholder held at the will of the lord and might therefore be dispossessed whenever the lord wanted but in most cases the lord's will was controlled by the customary law of the manor. Simpson notes that with the passage of time, 'the courts worked out a compromise between the old view, under which the lord was treated as "owner" of the lands of his unfree tenants, and the new view, under which the unfree tenant was to be regarded as "owner"'.[68] Although the lordship of a manor lost many of the benefits of seisin of a freehold estate, it carried with it a bundle of rights over land within the manor, including the right to mines and minerals.

---

[65] Ibid.

[66] See, eg Lyndon (n 42).

[67] The title 'copyhold' reflected the increased recognition in the customary courts of the rights of villein tenants. The process of alienating villein lands—by surrender and re-grant—was recorded in the court rolls ('to save the inconvenience of looking them up if there was a dispute over the land') as a result of which 'the villein tenant was said to hold "by copy of the court roll", the copy being his title deed ... since all transactions were recorded upon the roll, it provided conclusive evidence of a copyholder's rights': AWB Simpson, *A History of the Land Law* (Oxford, Clarendon Press, 1986) 151.

[68] Ibid, 158.

However, the lord of the manor could only enter the land to work them with the copyholder's permission.[69] By the nineteenth century copyhold was 'an anachronism which served no social or economic purpose'.[70] Before 1841 enfranchisement could only be effected at common law by the lord of the manor granting to the copyholder a freehold estate in his land. From 1841 onwards, a series of statutes made it possible for copyholders to enfranchise, the effect of which was that the land became of freehold tenure.[71] However, the right of the lord in or to mines, minerals and other substances was unaffected. By the Law of Property Act 1922 all land of copyhold tenure was enfranchised as from 1 January 1926.[72] Again, the situation regarding minerals tended to stay the same, with the result that in former copyhold land, the minerals commonly remain in the ownership of the lord of the manor.[73]

Turning to the cases, *Bowser v Maclean* concerned a dispute between the plaintiff copyholders and a lessee to whom the lord of the manor had granted 'all the coal mines' within the manor of Bondgate.[74] Having discovered that the lessee was conveying coal from outside the manor via an underground railway running through their land, the plaintiffs then sought an injunction. The Court of Chancery held that the lord of the manor had a right to drive carriages along an underground tramway for the purpose of working mines within the manor, but not of working mines beyond its limits. Those rights—and the same limitation upon them—transferred to the defendant when the mines were leased to him. Lord Campbell explained that when the original freeholder of the land granted the surface to another party, excepting the mines 'his intent was to reserve not just the mineral but rather the entire strata'.[75] He observed that a distinction could be drawn between a copyhold tenement with minerals under it, and freehold land subject to separate surface and mineral estates. In the latter case, the owner of the surface could not have complained of the construction or use of a tramway through the subsoil. Here, however, the plaintiffs, (after letting the surface to a farmer for a fixed term), were in possession of the subsoil ('from the surface to the centre of the earth'),[76] subject only to the

---

[69] Ibid, 168. See too, *Bourne v Taylor* (1808) 10 East 189, 103 ER 747.

[70] See WS Holdsworth, *An Historical Introduction to the Land Law* (Oxford, Clarendon Press, 1927) 46–47 for a summary of the defects of copyhold as found by the Royal Property Commissioners in 1832.

[71] Copyhold Acts of 1841, s 82; 1852, s 48; and 1894, s 23.

[72] Law of Property Act 1922, ss 128–37.

[73] Manorial rights became 'overriding interests' under s 70(1)(j) of the Land Registration Act 1925 so that registered dispositions took effect subject to them even though they were not entered on the register (and, in practice, could be almost impossible to discover). Section 117 of the Land Registration Act 2002 (which aims to reduce the number of such automatically protected unregistered interests) provides that manorial rights shall retain their overriding status for a period of 10 years from the date the Act came into force (12 October 2003). During that period, anyone entitled to such rights could protect them by lodging a caution if the subject land was unregistered or a notice on the register if it was registered. By 15 January 2014 the Land Registry had received more than 73,000 claims to manorial rights in England and Wales and approximately 6,000 properties had been voluntarily released from notices (HC Deb 15 January 2014, cols 334WH, 335WH). Manorial rights can continue to be registered after 12 October 2013 until such time as the land is sold.

[74] *Bowser v Maclean* 45 ER 682, (1860) 2 De G F & J 415.

[75] According to Duncan et al, this means that 'rather than being a decision that holds that surface owners do not own spaces left after the extraction of minerals, *Bowser* is simply a decision finding that a particular mineral reservation was worded in a way that reserved more than just the minerals': I Duncan, S Anderson and J-P Nichot, 'Pore Space Ownership Issues for CO_2 Sequestration in the US' (2009) 1 *Energy Procedia* 4427. This overlooks the fact, however, that the land in question was copyhold.

[76] *Bowser* (n 74) 419.

rights of the lord (or his lessee) in getting the minerals according to the custom of the manor. Because the copyholder had 'the whole right in him', the lord could not use an underground way for the purpose of passing through any portion of the copyhold premises.

Bowser v Maclean was applied in *Proud v Bates,*[77] in which Proud, the plaintiff, was the lessee of a farm granted by the then lord of the manor. The lessor had reserved to himself, his heirs or assigns

> the mines and quarries lying and being within and under the same, with full power and free liberty and power to sink for, win, and work the same, with pit room and heap room for the same, and with all liberties, privileges, and conveniences necessary and convenient for the winning, working, and management thereof.

Bates, the defendant, to whom benefit the reservation passed, worked certain mines adjoining the tract in question, and by means of 'outstroke' made use of the passageway under Proud's farm to evacuate the coal from adjoining mines. So that the passageway was sufficiently high to be used by carriages and horses, about 18in was cut out of the stone above the roof of the mine. Wood VC found in favour of Bates, explaining that whether the word 'mines' was used in the sense of 'minerals' (ie 'the thing dug out of the mine'), or 'that which contains the minerals', the latter could not be less than the thing it contained. There was no doubt therefore that 'the mine' denoted 'the whole containing chamber which has the minerals'. This meant that the mines were excluded from the demise so that the representatives of the lessor could use them 'for any purpose whatsoever, and at any period'.

In *Eardley v Granville,*[78] Jessell MR shed some helpful light on the matter, distinguishing between freehold land and copyhold. The plaintiffs were copyholders of part of the manor of Newcastle-under-Lyne and the Crown, in right of the Duchy of Lancaster, was seised in fee of the manor. The defendant, Earl Granville, was the lessee under the crown of the collieries, mines and minerals within the manor. By the custom of the manor, the crown and its lessees were entitled to enter upon the land for the purpose of working the mines and minerals. Lord Granville was also the lessee of the mines under an adjoining tract of freehold land belonging to one Sneyd, and he claimed a right to use an underground passageway beneath the plaintiff's land for the purpose of conveying minerals from Sneyd's mine to the deep pit by which the manorial mines were worked, and thence by a branch railway constructed by the defendant over part of the same copyhold to the main line. It was held that this user was a trespass, and that the plaintiffs were entitled to an injunction to restrain the defendant from carrying the Sneyd minerals over or under their copyhold land.

Jessell MR pointed out that

> where a freeholder grants lands excepting the mines, he intends, first of all, as a matter of construction, to except not merely minerals, but the portion of the subsoil containing minerals; in other words, to retain a stratum of the property. And if he does that … the lessee or grantee has no title whatever to the portion of the stratum reserved.[79]

---

[77] *Proud v Bates* (1865) 34 LJ Ch 406.
[78] *Eardley v Granville* (1876) LR 3 Ch D 826, quoted in *Batten Pooll v Kennedy.*
[79] Ibid, 835.

By excepting the mines, 'he grants out his estate in parallel horizontal layers' and 'the grantee [of the surface] only gets the parallel layer granted to him'. The grantor retains any underlying mineral layer or stratum as part of his ownership and 'whether or not he takes the minerals or subsoil out of the stratum, the stratum still belongs to him as part of the vertical section of the land'.[80]

As for copyhold, Jessell MR explained that the estate of the copyholder is 'in the soil throughout' except as regards trees, mines, and minerals, the property in which remains in the lord. The possession is in the copyholder; the property is in the lord. If a tree were to be cut down, the lord could not compel the copyholder to plant another:

> The copyholder has a right to the soil of the copyhold where the tree stood, including the stratum of air which is now left vacant by reason of the removal of the tree. So, if the lord takes away the minerals, the copyholder becomes entitled to the possession of the space where the minerals formerly were, and he is entitled to use it at his will and pleasure. If you have a shaft made for working the mines, the copyholder may descend in the shaft.[81]

In contrast to a vendor of freehold land who has reserved mines, and remains the owner of the vacant space from which minerals have been removed, the former copyholder's 'possession throughout' (including possession of the space) he—and only he—is entitled to occupy the space from 'the moment that the minerals are taken away'.[82] It is this approach that seems to comprise the 'American' rule.

Although there was no equivalent to copyhold tenure in the United States (nor indeed in Scotland where so many of the cases involving the right of outstroke in freehold land took place),[83] the copyhold position is reflected in the American Rule. The reasons for this however are probably coincidental. One possible explanation lies in the principle observable in the United States that 'ownership of the surface, coal, oil, gas, water, limestone, sand … and all other parts of the lands are capable of being severed and owned as separate estates'.[84] This intimates that once the coal, oil or gas, etc is exhausted, then the mineral owner's estate in it must necessarily end as well.

VI. THE 'ENGLISH RULE' IN CANADA AND THE UNITED STATES

Batten-Pooll v Kennedy was referred to in a judgment by the Appellate Court of the Supreme Court of Alberta in *Little v Western Transfer and Storage Co*,[85] in which Little, the registered owner of 'the coal and surface rights' of a 26-acre piece of land leased 'all the said coal together with the right to work the same and together with such portion of the surface rights as may necessarily be interfered with in the working of the mine'. If the lessee owned the property in the stratum containing the coal,

[80] Ibid, 834.
[81] Ibid, 832.
[82] Ibid, 834.
[83] E Nugee, 'The Feudal System and the Land Registration Acts' (2008) 124 *LQR* 586.
[84] JT Lane, 'Oil and Gas' (2000) 7. Available at www.wvyounglawyers.com/wp-content/uploads/2013/10/chapter26.pdf.
[85] *Little v Western Transfer and Storage Co* 18 Alta LR 407, [1922] 3 WWR 356, 69 DLR 364.

it also had the right to work its adjoining mining properties from a tunnel made from the mine and to carry 'foreign' coal obtained from adjoining properties over its surface. If, by contrast, it had a mere easement to carry away the minerals mined upon the leased property, such easement would not include the right to transport foreign materials. The court concluded that 'all the said coal' meant that there was a lease of the stratum or strata in which the coal was embedded and not merely an easement to take away the coal. The lessee was therefore entitled to the whole of the depleted stratum and was able to use the shaft through which it transported coal from adjoining property. Beck JA pointed out that even though the cases discussed in *Batten-Pooll v Kennedy* dealt with cases of 'grants, exceptions and reservations', it was clear that the distinction between a grant which was effective as a grant of mineral strata and a grant of a mere right to take the mineral depends solely on whether 'what was granted, excepted or reserved was or was not in such terms as to constitute on the one hand the grant of a stratum or on the other the grant of a mere right'. He also quoted from *Campbell's Ruling Cases*, viz:

> Where the owner of the freehold of inheritance grants *the mines* (opened as well as unopened) under his land to one, and the land excepting the mines to another, the effect is to carve out the land in superimposed layers; the grantee has the property and exclusive right to possession [of] the whole space occupied by the minerals; and, after the minerals are taken out, is entitled to the entire and exclusive use of that space for all purposes.

Lyndon describes the court in *Little v Western Approach and Storage Co* as having 'expressly adopted' the English rule yet it can be seen that the court's decision does not endorse a principle of general application but merely highlights the fact that the nature and extent of rights to minerals and the strata in which they are embedded will depend upon the wording of the document which purports to grant or except and reserve them.

Turning to the United States, it has been suggested that one of the first applications of the 'English Rule' in in which 'ownership of the geological formation' was first addressed was *Central Kentucky Natural Gas v Smallwood*.[86] Here, approximately 500 acres of land was conveyed to Smallwood, the grantors expressly reserving to themselves one-half of the minerals. Six years later, Smallwood (the surface owner) executed an oil and gas production and storage lease in favour of the Central Kentucky Natural Gas Company. The lease conferred on the lessee

> the right of drilling and operating for and marketing oil and gas, and of storing gas of any kind regardless of the source thereof, including the right of injecting gas in the oil and gas strata and removing the same therefrom.

It provided for a minimum annual rental of $1 per acre. No oil was produced and no gas was extracted from wells located on the leased premises and the only use to which the Gas Company put the property was the storage of gas from wells located on adjoining lands. Smallwood sought a declaration that he was entitled to payment of all of the gas storage rentals (rather than just half), arguing that such rentals were payable to the surface rather than the mineral owner.

In a much criticised decision, the Kentucky Court of Appeals held that rentals from a storage space must be paid to the mineral owner. It reasoned that, unless

---

[86] *Central Kentucky Natural Gas v Smallwood* 252 SW2d 866, 868 (Ky Ct App 1952).

the lease provided otherwise, the mineral owner would have the exclusive right to explore for and produce gas released for storage as well as native gas. Were a gas storage lease to be granted, the mineral owner would relinquish that right and it would be conferred instead upon the lessee. Duncan J concluded:

> Mere ownership of the surface does not confer on the owner the right to explore for and produce native gas merely because it is located beneath the surface which he owns. There being no distinction as to ownership, [the surface owner] has no greater rights with respect to the gas released for underground storage. A lease from a mere surface owner confers no rights on the lessee in connection with the production of gas, native or stored, because he has no rights to confer.

Citing *Bowser v Maclean* and *Batten Pooll v Kennedy*,[87] he explained that 'the rule in England' was that in the case of a grant of the minerals under land 'the grantee has the exclusive right of possession of the whole space occupied by the layer containing the minerals, and after the minerals are taken out, is entitled to the entire and exclusive use of that space for all purposes'.[88] However, the court added that in arriving at its conclusion, it did not need to determine whether the cavern or strata from which a mineral has been removed becomes the property of the mineral or surface owner. Therefore, as Duncan et al point out, 'the case contains no precedent for application of an English rule for pore space ownership'.[89]

VII. HARD MINERALS AND FUGACIOUS MINERALS

As indicated in the introduction, although unworkable coal fields may be used for GS, old oil and gas fields are most likely to be used for the storage of captured CO_2. Given the different characteristics of fugacious minerals and of solid or hard minerals, it is debatable therefore as to how much reliance should be placed on the old cases involving coal and the right of outstroke. Fugacious minerals such as gas and oil 'do not necessarily remain under the same surface area' but can flow from one place to another. In addition, even where there has been no severance of the surface and mineral estates, 'the owner of the solid minerals' in a piece of land will not necessarily be the owner of the oil and gas it contains because they can migrate elsewhere.[90] Thus, while laws based upon the *ad coelum* principle may have been effective in 'allotting interests in coal and other immobile subsurface minerals', they are less obviously appropriate in the context 'fugitive energy sources that can migrate across subsurface property boundaries during extraction activities'.[91]

---

[87] It is strange that *Bowser v Maclean* (a copyhold case) was cited as a source of the English rule, given that in relation to copyhold land, the American Rule applies: a former copyholder (ie the surface owner) owns the vacant space from which minerals have been removed. See too JR Patterson, 'Ownership of a Depleted Gas Formation—*Humble Oil and Refining Company v West*: The Underground Storage of Natural Gas Causes Confusion' (1975) 27 *Baylor Law Review* 806, 809 in which *Bowser v Maclean* is cited incorrectly as authority for the common law rule that 'the coal owner was entitled to the entire and exclusive use of the space occupied by the coal even after all the coal had been extracted'.

[88] *Central Kentucky Natural Gas* (n 86) 868.

[89] Duncan et al (n 74) 4429.

[90] NJ Stewart, 'The Reservation or Exception of Mines and Minerals' (1962) 40 *Canadian Bar Review* 229, 372, referring to WL Summers, *The Law of Oil and Gas*, vol IA (St Paul MN, Thomsn West, 1938–55) 290–303.

[91] Rule (n 23) 806.

In *Central Kentucky Natural Gas v Smallwood*, the court took that view that although the mineral owner's 'ownership' involved 'merely the right to explore and reduce the minerals to possession', the fugacious nature of oil and gas meant that the geological formations or strata in which they are found might be 'exhausted a thousand times' and yet the mineral owner would still retain the exclusive right to take all the minerals which found their way into the formation 'whether through injection or in any other way'. It felt that to regard the mineral owner as being entitled to rent the spaces once occupied by the gas in the limestone formation would in effect be saying that the deed which vested title to the minerals in him also conferred upon him 'title to the air spaces in that formation'. The court pointed out that to date the word 'mineral' had not been expanded to include air or a vacuum, as well as coal, iron, oil and gas, etc. The fundamental purpose of any grant of minerals or mineral rights, it said, was that subsurface minerals should be released and brought to the surface where they could be 'utilized by man'. Thus, any construction of such grants which would permit the mineral owner to inject gas to be stored in the shell of the emptied substrata would seem to be repugnant.

Because 'oil and gas-bearing strata are never entirely depleted ... a worked out stratum ... of porous rock can [still be] of ... benefit to the mineral owner'.[92] By contrast, 'solid minerals remain in one place until removed' and in the past the 'cavern remaining' after their removal was of no benefit to the mineral owner.[93] The American Rule (that the 'cavern remaining' reverts to the surface owner) is commensurate with this lack of utility—but of course it emerged before technologies developed to allow for storage of natural gas or captured CO_2—hence the revived interest in the United States as to the question of pore space ownership.[94]

VIII. CONCLUSION

Whether the English and Scottish cases discussed in this chapter justify the finding of an English rule as distinct from an American rule is questionable. All of those cases—except for *Mitchell v Mosley*—centred on the right of outstroke. As such, they were decided in the context of a particular factual matrix which has little bearing on issues involving CCS. They also concerned the right to mine coal—a hard mineral—and it is doubtful too whether cases relating to coal and other hard minerals are apposite in situations involving the storage of oil and gas, given the very different natures of hard minerals and fugacious minerals.

Because it has been decided not to allow onshore storage in the UK at present, questions of pore space ownership in England and Wales are merely academic. The

---

[92] OA Merrill, 'Oil and Gas: Substratum Storage Problems' (1954) 7 *Oklahoma Law Review* 225, 227.
[93] Ibid.
[94] In the UK, ownership of subsurface land has become important in the context of shale gas and hydraulic fracturing. See DECC, *Underground Drilling Access: Consultation on Proposal for Underground Access for the Extraction of Gas, Oil or Geothermal Energy*, URN 14D/099 (London, DECC, 2014); DECC, *Underground Drilling Access: Government Response to the Consultation on Proposal for Underground Access for the Extraction of Gas, Oil or Geothermal Energy* (London, DECC, 2014).

right to store gas (including CO_2) is vested in the Crown,[95] and if onshore were to be permitted in the UK in the future, doubtless that right would be extended accordingly. Once a potential storage site had been identified, the CCS operator would have to obtain a carbon storage licence but this would not authorise entry onto another person's land and the licence holder would have to obtain permission from the owner of the land in which storage was proposed (or a court order) in order to access, or operate under, it. In situations where the surface and mineral estates had been severed, and questions arose as to pore space ownership (and whether therefore permission was required from both surface *and* mineral owners), courts in England and Wales would probably be disposed to depart from the outstroke cases and to adhere instead to the pronouncement of Cozen-Hardy MR in *Mitchell v Mosley* that a surface owner's rights extends through 'the whole substratum to the centre of the earth, even including the vacant spaces from which ... coal may have been worked out'. As the reader will appreciate, this pronouncement encapsulates the American Rule.

Most US commentators appear to agree that 'ownership rights in underground storage areas should belong to the surface estate owner' and that 'severance of minerals or an oil or gas lease should not be construed to give the mineral estate or interest owner subsurface gas storage rights in the absence of language expressly granting such rights'.[96] There are sound practical reasons for adopting such an approach, given the scale on which CCS may take place and the added problem of private mineral rights, the division and subdivision of which may make it very difficult 'to assemble land for exploration' and storage of CO_2.[97]

---

[95] Energy Act 2008, s 1.
[96] Mojdehi (n 40) 472.
[97] Barton (n 64) 35.

14

Temporal Pluralism: Voluntary Sector Property Partnerships

CHRIS WILLMORE*

T HIS CHAPTER EXPLORES some of the property law obstacles in the path of voluntary sector bodies seeking to pursue a partnership approach to the use of property, and in particular the complexity of establishing a mechanism to provide for temporal sharing of property, where the same space is used by different organisations at different times, within a property law framework. Three approaches are explored, in particular limited use and discontinuous leases. Both suffer from unclear scope/status, and a lack of guidance or precedent. The chapter concludes that there are suitable options available, but their complexity, transaction costs, and risk aversion in the voluntary sector mean further guidance is needed to support voluntary sector access to the solutions.

I. INTRODUCTION: DEFINING THE CHALLENGE

Collaboration and partnership is a 'hot topic' for the third sector. The Coalition Government continued previous governmental initiatives to articulate a greater role for third sector organisations in the provision of public services.[1] However the pace of change has accelerated in the changed context of public sector spending, divestment programmes and fresh government incentives.[2] The prospects of that divestment leading to a proliferation of new relationships and structures in the third sector has led to a number of policy and guidance documents. The management and distribution of assets and access to their use is evolving as part of this process, but against a backdrop of reduced total assets and increased risk aversion leading funders to tighten funding criteria.

---

* Reader in Sustainability and Law, University of Bristol Law School.
[1] See HM Treasury/Cabinet Office, *The Future Role of the Third Sector in Social and Economic Regeneration* (London, 2007); Department for Communities and Local Government, *Strong and Prosperous Communities* (Local Government White Paper, 2006).
[2] Eg some local authorities have divested all direct youth provision.

The proliferation of guidance[3] is not matched by coverage of the property law issues. Attention is drawn to the complexities of staffing issues, particularly when undertakings are transferred from one body to another,[4] but property issues are not. Staffing issues can be complex, but there is clear and extensive on line guidance available. Whilst the variety of permutations associated with property issues and the lack of any extensive online guidance makes it harder for the Commission to produce succinct guidance, this should not preclude the Commission from drawing attention to the potential minefields in the area. In both CC34[5] and the associated CC37[6] the focus is upon alerting people to public regulatory obligations as opposed to private law pitfalls, other than the general duties of trusteeship. One might argue that the focus of the guidance is more upon the conceptual issues associated with partnership working: in particular the importance of organisations defining their objectives and the nature of the relationship—but if it is in scope to warn of the staffing pitfalls, a mention of property complexities might be merited.

Of particular significance is CC34, the Charity Commission guidance on collaborative working and mergers. One might expect the Charity Commission to be precise in its guidance about property issues. It notes the option of colocating and sharing accommodation and premises,[7] using a case study of a joint venture to provide a new purpose built complex. There is no mention of the potential complexity of such an arrangement. It may involve the land being conveyed into joint ownership, or the site being rented to the two providers as joint tenants of the site; with a joint venture agreement specifying liability, maintenance, occupation and aftercare provision for the life of the building. There may be a single ownership with everything else managed contractually. The risk of these lacuna in guidance is first that people are not alerted to the potential complexities and the need for appropriate advice and second, may not realise that establishing such arrangements can be so resource intensive that only large projects can afford the legal advice associated with a joint venture agreement, and specified investment/usage arrangements.

Beyond that example, the focus of the Charity Commission guidance is joint activity, not joint use of property, except insofar as it is a risk issue. In looking at joint

---

[3] NCVO, *Quick Guide to Building Great Partnerships* (2010); Charity Commission, *Collaborative Working and Mergers: An Introduction* (CC34) (2009). NCVO knowhownonprofit.org is a key resource for the voluntary sector and does not mention the issues and see www.asauk.org.uk/wp-content/uploads/2013/.../Joint-Working-Agreements.doc.

[4] TUPE Transfer of Undertakings (Protection of Employment) Regulations 2006 (SI 2006/246) as amended by the Collective Redundancies and Transfer of Undertakings (Protection of Employment) (Amendment) Regulations 2014 (SI 2014/16).

[5] Charity Commission (CC34) (n 3) and see also Charity Commission, *Choosing to Collaborate: How to Succeed* (2009).

[6] Charity Commission, *Charities and Public Service Delivery: An Introduction and Overview* (CC37) (2012).

[7] Eg British Association of Settlement and Social Action Centres, *Sharing without Merging: A Review of Collaborative Working and Sharing Back Office Support in the Voluntary and Community Sector* (London, 2005).

activities, the Charity Commission highlights three particular formats for collaboration arrangements:

— Contracts.
— Service level agreements.[8]
— Memoranda of understanding.[9]

The Commission also highlights the importance of adopting formal arrangements:

> Formal arrangements enable charity trustees to better identify and manage risks. Formal contracts may mitigate some risks, mainly legal, and if they are drawn up carefully they may also protect charities from risks to their assets and reputation. Depending upon their trustee and staff skills and experience, charity trustees may need to seek specialist professional advice when entering into a formal collaborative working arrangement. Collaboration may take the form of a joint venture which is operated through the vehicle of a separate company, set up to separate the collaborative working element from the continuing activities of each charity in the arrangement.[10]

Whilst contracts, service level agreements and memoranda of understanding are now common place in public sector commissioning, the formal arrangements associated with property rights are well beyond the resources or expertise of most voluntary sector organisations, whose focus and expertise is upon their core business, and for whom the transaction costs of such negotiating such complex arrangements are excessive. The silence, in terms of guidance upon property matters or the provision of models, other than contractual joint use agreements, leaves the voluntary sector in a difficult position. There is a body of guidance online from the Charity Commission about property issues for the charity, but none of those documents addresses the relationship between property rights and collaborative working.[11]

Increasingly, when third sector organisations are seeking funding particularly for works to the building, for example in relation to accessibility, funders require evidence that the voluntary sector's occupation is secure.

In parallel, reductions in available funding have led to increased pressure on groups to colocate and to intensify use of space to generate income in the case of the estate owner and to reduce costs in the case of the user. The study looked at how organisations are managing these problems.

The range of arrangements varies from simple licences, to the creation of complex trusts and joint associated joint venture agreements running to many pages. This chapter takes one example, to illustrate the sort of arrangement voluntary sector organisations may want to enter, the difficulties that can arise in mapping these arrangements onto recognised property law categories, and the lack of appropriate guidance.

One example will illustrate the sort of situation that can arise.

---

[8] Service level agreements are effectively commissioning contracts in which the level of service is specified in a measurable form.

[9] MoUs set out a shared understanding between parties of the way a relationship is to operate, but do not give rise to legally binding obligations.

[10] Charity Commission (CC34) (n 3) 15.

[11] www.charitycommission.gov.uk/detailed-guidance/land-and-property/ (accessed April 2014).

Table 1: Case Study Example

A, a charity, owns property, which A uses on Sundays. A wants to generate income.
B, a voluntary sector organisation, wishes to use it, Monday—Friday 8am—6pm, such that they would be the main user, but their use would fit around A's use.
A will find it beneficial to have a regular user rather than a series of casual bookings. But as B is going to have most of the use, A wants B to bear the running costs, and to carry out repairs.
A is happy for B to carry out adaptations to the property to meet their needs, as long as they are consistent with A's use, and A's agreement is sought.
B needs to secure external funding for adaptations to the property. To securing that funding B needs to be able to demonstrate to the funder that they have a legal right to remain in the property for what the funder considers a sufficiently long period to justify the investment (assuming A is not also a group the funder would be willing to support).
In general funders will not accept contractual arrangements as providing sufficient security of occupation, so B wants a lease.
A is worried about granting a lease. Whilst happy with giving B long-term certainty, they do not want the rights to be transmissible. A also want to continue to use the building and does not feel they want to grant B exclusive possession under a lease, meaning B would need to sublease the property back to A for A's use.
A understands that their transmissibility concerns can be addressed by excluding the right to assign—but that will not address their own security of tenure concern.
Historically, A and B used a document called a 'lease' and thought they had created a durable shared use lease.

Here the parties have a practical and workable understanding about a way of sharing use that will be mutually beneficial. Their entire problem is focused upon how to frame that understanding within legal agreements that offer both parties, and their funders, the sort of assurance they require. Their aim is simply to attempt to manage use to provide for temporal pluralism through:

— Shared use.
— Multiple coterminous durability, sufficient to satisfy funders.

In collaboration contexts it is common for organisations to seek models of diverse temporal title. Often, in essence, they are seeking to create a flexible space agreement but are precluded because their intentions are overridden by legal doctrinal requirements of certainty.

This chapter explores how such temporal needs can be addressed within the current law. It concludes that licences coupled with estoppel, could offer sufficient security but are not likely to be understood by financiers, and that the discontinuous or limited use lease, despite their uncertainties offer a potential solution, but that the voluntary sector deserve greater guidance about all three routes.

II. TYPOLOGY OF OCCUPATION MODELS

As far back as 2005 the British Association of Settlement and Social Action Centres (BASSAC)[12] was arguing for the merits of shared space. At the time, it focused upon the concept of clustering, a modern variant of the settlement movement, in which voluntary sector organisations cluster around a building or location, often deliberately seeded in an area of social need to act as a physical focal point for social action. More broadly, the Institute for Voluntary Action Research (IVAR)[13] analysed the collaboration spectrum into three: interaction, sharing and merger. The sharing spectrum ranged from consortium tendering, through joint venture covering service delivery and campaigning, through sharing back office function to colocation. Critically, the report did not consider colocation, although it does identify risk aversion as an important factor in the collaboration agenda. It saw colocation as something that would occur once there were well-established joint venture relationships, rather than as something that occurs as a first step in a relationship, and possibly the only step. This chapter crucially focuses upon the latter: where colocation is either the first or only step in a relationship and is not an incident of partnership working as such.

Remembering the Charity Commission exhortation 'A key overall message is that it is important to set the ground rules but not to over complicate the arrangements',[14] organisations are encouraged by all the key national advisory organisations to focus upon identifying and articulating the relationship between the organisations, so as to leave minimal scope for confusion, whilst not of course overcomplicating things. Such a practical focus, does not necessarily map well onto the legal packages into which such agreements have to be shoehorned: and in particular does not assist organisations where the relationship exists solely because of property use.

Whilst contract law may offer an apparently infinite flexibility for partners to articulate relationships, there are some relationships the law will simply not permit, or at least not permit without very careful scaffolding—the most obvious being a durable right to possession binding third parties: *durable shared possession*.

What options are currently available? Do they deliver shared use and durability without adversely impacting the current legal estate owner's title?

With so many options, it is not necessarily the case that solutions cannot be molded out of a careful use of legal tools, but rather that what may seem to the parties a straightforward practical arrangement can engage complex and little documented areas of property law. The lack of current guidance leaves the voluntary sector navigating these complex waters largely unaided, without guidance about the relative merits of these models, generating risk, uncertainty and inadvertently importing unexpected obligations.

This chapter considers two principle routes through which bodies could articulate durable shared possession, in non-partnership contexts: through limited purpose leases and discontinuous leases. These were chosen for exploration because they

---

[12] See above (n 7).
[13] Institute for Voluntary Action Research, *Getting Ready for Collaboration: Learning from Experience* (London, 2010).
[14] Charity Commisioners CC34 (n 3).

Table 2: Potential vehicles for shared use agreements

Table	Impact on title	Durability	Shared use	Advantages	Disadvantages
Trust	✓			— co-ownership of estate in land — can provide for temporal and spatial security as long as purpose survives — works within established property law concepts — suits acquisition — can regulate shared use, as long as the joint tenants between them have exclusive possession — can be leasehold or freehold	— significant expertise required to adapt appropriately — importance of parties understanding the default consequences under TOLATA and making provision for cessation, and maintenance — requires willingness to give up existing rights if between an existing estate owner and a proposed partner
Contract		✓	✓	— flexible — can confer actual possession — can protect actual possession vs strangers — durability between original parties — can handle common parts — highly nuanced arrangements possible — no impact upon current title—not 'giving up' anything	— no durability beyond current parties — so funders consider uncertain — damages remedy may not be adequate — risks of inadvertent creation of equitable estate
Lease and sublease			✓	— Community Action Network clustering model works on the basis of one management organisation taking the lease and then renting specific spaces within the building to others or through incubator schemes. Not dissimilar to commercial incubator organisations — primarily focused upon office space, with shared servicing mirroring private sector leases	— shared use needs to be sufficiently defined — significant impact on title holder if needs to lease and sublease back — need to be established from the outset as the basis upon which lead tenant undertakes that responsibility and needs to be underpinned by clear agreements about shared services — requires advice re law around the leasehold covenants — hierarchic premise

	✓	✓	✓		
Co-operative				— needs management organisation — similar to lease and sublease but with less hierarchic premise	— shared use needs to be sufficiently defined — significant impact on title holder if needs to lease and sublease back — needs to be established from the outset as the basis upon which lead tenant undertakes that responsibility — needs clear agreements about shared services, etc — requires advice re leasehold covenants
Lease	✓	✓		— where one partner has long held freehold or leasehold, but is now seeking to intensify use — leasehold covenants could limit B's use to specific times and purposes, the problem therefore is not in restricting B's use but rather to the ability to preserve A's occupation without a lease and lease back — discontinuous lease possible	— exclusive possession — affects title — requires advice re leasehold covenants — little case law or guidance around discontinuous leases or restricted use leases
Estoppel	✓			— contractual agreement + assurance that will honour any funding agreements /support for application and consequential expenditure — assurance to funders — protects investment	— not likely to result in title/trust as remedy so not durable against third parties — funders unlikely to understand estoppel as an assurance

offer what may seem an attractive solution—voluntary sector bodies are used to leases. They may inadvertently create invalid leases through not understanding the severity of the doctrine of exclusive possession—and as a result may produce apparent 'leases' which either restrict use for the 'tenant' and permit continued but consistent freeholder use, or create a discontinuous lease.

III. LEASES AND THE 'EXCLUSIVE POSSESSION' REQUIREMENT

The problem of accidentally falling outside of the criteria for a valid lease in this situation derives from the role and meaning afforded to the concept of 'exclusive possession'. The 'lease' appears to third sector organisations to be the natural solution through which parties would seek to articulate a property relationship and confer durability. Whether the law of leases is capable of offering an appropriate partnership relationship will ultimately depend in England upon the scope of the discontinuous lease and purpose lease, but a first step is to consider the centrality of the concept of 'exclusive possession' in the English law on leases which gives rise to the problem.

The concept of possession is imperfectly defined with courts moving between a range of words: possession, occupation and exclusive possession. The latter is said to be an essential characteristic of a lease, although in fact courts often use 'exclusive possession' to mean the presence of that bundle of rights that includes the ability to protect the right against the world including the grantor's successor in title, that is a lease, making the definition circular.

Hill stresses the importance of a single legal entity as having possession and equates property interests with exclusivity: 'possession as a property interest which the law recognises and protects, involves, by its very nature, a relationship of exclusivity between the possessor and the thing possessed',[15] relying inter alia upon Pollock and Wright: 'Possession is single and exclusive … Physical possession is exclusive or it is nothing'.[16] Hill argues that the word 'exclusive' is redundant in that it is a particular form of possession which gives rise to the ability to vindicate a right and that form of possession is called 'exclusive possession'.

Modern judicial comment upon on exclusive possession comes primarily from discussion in the context of residential leases. In *Street v Mountford*,[17] Lord Templeman attributed the status of 'exclusive possession' within the definition of a lease to the final ending of the feudal position of leases in the 1925 legislation. It is interesting to note that the Scottish law on leases, which is not entirely post-feudal, does not afford the same status to 'exclusivity' and at least appears to confer more flexibility.[18] There is very little in that case about what is *meant* by exclusive possession, and use of the phrase within the judgments is inconsistent. Hill demonstrated that the phrase

---

[15] Ibid, 27.

[16] Pollock and Wright, *An Essay on Possession in the Common Law* (London, Clarendon Press, 1888) 3.

[17] *Street v Mountford* [1985] AC 809.

[18] McAllister A, *Scottish Law of Leases*, 4th edn (Edinburgh, Bloomsbury, 2013); *Brador Property v British Telecom* [1992] SC 12; *Jackson v Simons* [1923] 1 Ch 373; *South Lanarkshire v Taylor* [2005] 1 SC 182; *Miller v Wilson* [1919] 1 SLT 233; *Scottish Residential Estates Development Co Ltd v Henderson* [1991] SLT 490.

'exclusive possession' is used to mean at least three distinct things just in Lord Templeman's judgment: (i) the right to exclusive possession as the description of the rights enjoyed by holders of freehold and leasehold estates; (ii) actual possession in the sense of a squatter; and (iii) the use or enjoyment of a lodger.[19]

It is not just in Lord Templeman's judgment that 'exclusive possession' is used inconsistently. A group of subsequent statutory housing cases[20] accepted that a local authority landowner may be able to grant exclusive possession under a license, because otherwise they would be limited in the ability to discharge their statutory duties. Courts in these cases argued that the interpretation of the agreement depended upon whether the framing as a license was a genuine response to the circumstances rather than an attempt to avoid the consequences of granting a lease per se. The courts accepted that 'exclusive possession' does not automatically connote vindication via a lease. If it does not, and only refers to physical possession or use, then it is being used in Hill's third category, and is a descriptive phrase not one that is by definition tied to vindication.

These cases suggest exclusive possession can be a physical description distinct from a definitional one. The problem, however in this chapter is the opposite one: can a lease exist without 'exclusive possession' or at least in the context of limited use and discontinuous leases are two people validly in a possession that counts as sufficient for a legal lease to exist?

IV. LIMITED USE LEASES

Case law prior to *Street v Mountford*, but largely overlooked subsequently, suggests that the legal consequences of a lease do not necessarily require complete 'exclusivity' in the physical sense, but can embrace possession for a limited purpose or intermittent time period. In its current manifestation this is reflected in two areas of discussion:

— Limited use leases.
— Discontinuous leases.

The genesis of both the discontinuous lease and limited use lease in modern discussion is *Lavery v Pursell*.[21] There the plaintiff purchased a right to demolish a property and salvage the materials. The auction papers stated that 'possession of the premises to be then given to the purchaser for the purpose only of taking down and removing the materials'. A date for completing the removal was specified, after which remaining materials were to be deemed a trespass. The question was whether this was a contract for the sale of an 'interest in or concerning land' or a contract for the removal of demolition material as chattels.

---

[19] Hill, 'The Proprietary Character of Possession' in E Cooke (ed), *Modern Studies in Property Law*, vol 1 (Oxford, Hart Publishing, 2000) 21.
[20] *Westminster City Council v Clarke* [1992] 2 AC 288; *Westminster City Council v Basson* (19910 62 P & CR 57); *Ogwr Borough Council v Dykes* [1989] 1 WLR 295; *Bruton v London and Quadrant Housing Trust* [1999] 3 WLR 150; *Kay v London Borough of Lambeth* [2006] 2 AC 465; *London Borough of Islington v Green* [2005] EWCA Civ 56.
[21] *Lavery v Pursell* (1888) LR 39 Ch D 508.

Chitty J concluded it conferred an interest in land, for a limited purpose, saying it:

> [D]oes give him either a complete or a qualified possession; but still a possession of the soil itself—of the land, tenements and hereditaments; certainly of the whole of the house … Of course I am not forgetting the mode in which the property is sold. It is sold as building materials, and if the intention of the parties prevailed, it might mean that it is sold as a chattel, but the point still is that it is not a chattel at the time of the sale; and the Statute of Frauds, so far as I can see, does not enable parties to say, 'We will agree to treat this thing as a chattel', when in point of law it is a hereditament.[22]

The court in *Lavery* distinguished *Marshall v Green*,[23] a contract for standing trees to be cut as timber, on the basis that in *Marshall* there was no stipulation about possession, the contract specified he should cut the trees, although it was 'of course part of the terms of the contract that he should enter for that purpose'. In *Marshall* the question was whether he was a trespasser. Chitty J and the Lord Chief Justice in *Lavery* relied upon the:

> [W]ell-known passage in *Williams Saunders* … where it was said that where the parties agree that the thing sold shall be immediately withdrawn from the land, the land is to be considered as a mere warehouse of the thing sold, the contract is for goods.[24]

Chitty J recognises the problem this creates of line drawing. If possession for the purpose of tree felling is a licence, how can that be distinguished from, for example, coal mining?

> It is evident that if that view is right, which I will assume it to be, a line must be drawn somewhere, because, if this principle were carried to the full extent, there being no distinction between the timber on the land in point of law and the mines, then it would have to be said, following out what the Plaintiff says was the principle of this decision, that a contract for all the coal or minerals under a man's land, with a licence to enter and get it, is not within sect. 4. Some explanation why that should be was attempted to be given by Plaintiff's counsel, but without success. The answer perhaps is, that Courts of Justice ought not to be puzzled by such old scholastic questions as to where a horse's tail begins and where it ceases. You are obliged to say, 'This is a horse's tail,' at some time. What I say is that I must draw the line at this case, because on the facts it is quite different, or materially different, from *Marshall v. Green*, and I leave that case as it stands on its own footing, and must hold that this case comes within the 4th section.[25]

Lord Templeman in *Street v Mountford* explored this, at least in part, but used as his starting point the later case of *Glenwood Lumber Co Ltd v Phillips*,[26] and failed to consider the earlier authority, which had not been cited in *Glenwood*. Lord Templeman said:

> My Lords, there is no doubt that the traditional distinction between a tenancy and a licence of land lay in the grant of land for a term at a rent with exclusive possession. In some cases it was not clear at first sight whether exclusive possession was in fact granted. For example, an owner of land could grant a licence to cut and remove standing timber. Alternatively the owner could grant a tenancy of the land with the right to cut and remove standing timber

---

[22] Ibid, 515.
[23] *Marshall v Green* 1 C P D 35.
[24] *Lavery v Pursell* (n 20) 516.
[25] Ibid, 517.
[26] *Glenwood Lumber Co Ltd v Phillips* [1904] AC 405.

during the term of the tenancy. The grant of rights to standing timber therefore required careful consideration in order to decide whether the grant conferred exclusive possession of the land for a term at a rent and was therefore a tenancy or whether it merely conferred a bare licence to remove the timber.[27]

Glenwood was 'licensed' to hold land for the purpose of cutting and removing timber for a 'term' of 21 years at 'an annual rent'. The 'license' was of 'all that tract, piece or parcel of land particularly described to hold for the purpose aforesaid for the term of twenty one years from the date of the licence at an annual rental'. The right was limited to cutting and removing timber, and did not grant exclusivity as the landowner reserved the right to enter and cut timber as well. Yet Lord Davey, on behalf of the Privy Council, said:

> [I]f the effect of the instrument is to give the holder an exclusive right of occupation of the land, though subject to certain reservations or to a restriction of the purposes for which it may be used, it is in law a demise of the land itself. By [the Act] it is enacted that the lease shall vest in the lessee the right to take and keep exclusive possession of the lands described therein subject to the conditions in the Act provided or referred to.[28]

So there a grant with an extensive reservation or limitation of use could amount to a lease. This would suggest coterminus but differentiated occupation is at least conceptually possible. A body owning a building could use it, but also grant a lease to someone else to use it, in a complimentary or possibly identical manner, but limited in duration or extent. That would enable the parties in the example in Table 1 to draft a limited use lease.

However, the status of that approach is in doubt. The House of Lords in *Street v Mountford* cited *Taylor v Caldwell*[29] as reaching an opposite conclusion, although it did not consider *Smallwood v Sheppards*[30] or reconcile *Taylor* with *Glenwood*. *Taylor v Caldwell* dealt with a contract to let the Surrey Gardens and Music Hall, for four separate nights in 1861. Before the first event the Music Hall was destroyed by fire. The contract used the normal formulation for a demise. The court drew a distinction between possession and use, Blackburn J summarily dismissing this as a lease:

> The parties inaccurately call this a 'letting,' and the money to be paid a 'rent;' but the whole agreement is such as to shew that the defendants were to retain the possession of the Hall and Gardens so that there was to be no demise of them, and that the contract was merely to give the plaintiffs the use of them on those days.

It is not possible on the information in the report to identify how the intention of the parties could be distinguished from their written word, save for an implicit view in the court that these intermittent arrangements are inherently likely to be licenses. Lord Templeman in *Street* concluded:

> That was a case where the court after considering the purpose of the grant, the terms of the grant and the surrounding circumstances came to the conclusion that the grantee was not entitled to exclusive possession but only to use the land for limited purposes and was therefore a licensee.

---

[27] *Street v Mountford* (n 17) 816F–G.
[28] *Glenwood Lumber Co Ltd v Phillips* (n 25) 408.
[29] *Taylor v Caldwell* (1863) 3 B & S 826.
[30] *Smallwood v Sheppards* [1895] 2 QB 627.

But he did not explain how that differs from *Glenwood*, by implication leaving the cases as distinct on their facts.

That leaves the role and nature of limited use leases in an uncertain position. These limited purpose agreements are not uncommon in the rural context: grazing rights, for example, sometimes take this form. However, the majority of limited purpose uses, where use is shared, have come to be seen as *profits a prendre* or can be accommodated via contractual provisions. Voluntary sector bodies seeking to share the use of property can accommodate such activity via contractual provisions, but where there is a need for a more durable solution to satisfy funders, the *profit a prendre* option is not available, so only the *Glenwood* and *Lavall* approach to limited use leases is available. It would be a brave, and singularly knowledgeable voluntary sector body that consciously constructed such an agreement.

V. DISCONTINUOUS LEASE SOLUTIONS

The discontinuous lease derives from the same foundation, but offers a slightly firmer footing for voluntary sector bodies. Whilst the concept does clearly exist, and a number exist in practice, its conceptual basis is unclear and as a result there are practical unanswered questions about its status and effect. Until recently it has been used as an occasional basis for timeshare agreements, in areas such as market stalls, as an alternative to a licence.

The logic of the discontinuous lease is that someone can have a lease for a week, a year, or Monday to Friday, or every Bank Holiday. One might question whether this affords 'exclusive possession' but, albeit not expressly, the courts have apparently been willing to consider the nature of the possession on the days when the agreement grants possession as the basis for considering whether there is exclusive possession.

Although little considered judicially or academically,[31] the concept is in general use, and a number of discontinuous leases are registered with the Land Registry. Despite its occasional use as the bases for timeshare agreements, few timeshare cases dwell upon the nature of the interest conferred[32] with most timeshare questions couched in terms of the right to use immovable property under European law.[33]

There seem to be two questions:

a. The term of the lease.
b. The duration and nature of the agreement.

In relation to the first question, the term of such leases could be interpreted as:

a. A single lease for distinct days.
b. A lease for a term spanning from the first to the last date, with occupation only on specific dates.

---

[31] A noted exception being R Duddridge and J Brown, 'Continuing the Discontinuous' (1998) 18(2) *Rent Review and Lease Renewal* 130.

[32] Focusing in general upon the circumstances of the sale. Cf *Jarrett v Barclays Bank plc* [1999] QB 1; *Rosler v Rottwinkel* (241/33) [1986] QB 33 on rights of immoveable property: art 16 Brussels Convention.

[33] European Directive 2008/122/EC.

   c.   An agreement for the whole period, but with the term specified as days.

   d.   A contract binding for the whole period to provide separate leases, one for each day.[34]

The Law Commission[35] sourced justification for the concept of the discontinuous lease to *Cottage Holiday Associates Ltd v Customs and Excise Commissioners*.[36] Although a VAT case, the tax exception sought required Woolf J to determine whether an agreement giving a right to occupy for one week a year for 80 years amounted to a 'major interest in land'. In that case the agreement included the payment of 'a yearly rent of a peppercorn'.

   Woolf J did not explore the rationale for discontinuous leases, accepting:

> That such leases could be lawfully granted was decided in *Smallwood v Sheppards* [1895]. In that case Wright J. described a lease granting the right of occupation for three successive Bank Holidays as 'an agreement for a single letting (although the period of the agreed letting was not continuous)'.[37]

Woolf J concluded that 'Wright J in *Smallwood v Sheppards* [1895], in the passage which I have cited from his judgment, appears to be regarding the term created by leases of this sort as being discontinuous'.[38]

   Smallwood v Sheppards[39] concerned an oral agreement to let the plaintiff use a piece of waste ground on three successive Bank Holidays. On those days the plaintiff had exclusive possession and planned to run a funfair. On the first day he did so, but then declined to pay for the two remaining days. In the subsequent litigation the questions were whether the oral agreement could have created a lease, and, on the basis that it could not, whether the entry and use on the first day created a lease that covered all three days. Wright J concluded, in a brief 10 line judgment, that it was 'an agreement for a single letting (although the period of the agreed letting was not continuous)', but did not make clear which conceptualisations underpinned the decision. More recently the Supreme Court of Victoria classified as a lease, an agreement for the appellants to use a theatre on specified nights each week for three years, relying on *Smallwood*,[40] again without determining the underlying rationale.

   Woolf J in the *Cottage Holidays* case, whilst not required to determine the precise nature of the property interest, opined that the agreement creating the interest and the interest itself were distinct, adopting an analysis reflected in the third or fourth of the possible interpretations. He ruled out the second, in that he concluded the property interest was not major and did not amount to a lease of over 21 years. Woolf J referred to 'the right to occupy for "80 holiday periods"', which might suggest the fourth option, a contract for three separate leases. But, Customs and Excise, he said, 'conceded the lease was granted for 'a single discontinuous term', the only issue

---

[34] Duddridge and Brown (n 30); M Palowski, 'Questions and Answers' (2006) 10(5) *Landlord and Tenant Review* 10(5) 153; (1999) 3(2) *Landlord and Tenant Review* 48 setting out the second, third and fourth options.

[35] *Land Registration for the Twenty-first Century* (LC271) (2001).

[36] *Cottage Holiday Associates Ltd v Customs and Excise Commissioners* [1983] QB 735.

[37] Ibid, 739.

[38] Ibid, 740.

[39] *Smallwood v Sheppards* [1895] 2 QB 627.

[40] *Radio Theatres Pty v City of Coburg* [1948] VLR 84.

being its duration, ruling out the fourth option. It was a term totalling 80 weeks, not a lease for 80 years, and it was unnecessary then to decide whether it was 80 leases each of a week or one term of 80 weeks for the purposes of the case.

The wording of the judgments in *Cottage Holidays* and *Smallwood* might suggest there is an incompatibility in the conceptualisations of the process, although that is to overstrain the limited conceptual analysis in the cases and it is perhaps better to conclude that there is not a clear conceptualisation that emerges.

Woolf J accepted the argument put by Customs and Excise, that

> the key to the problem was to be found by recognising that there was a distinction between the lease which created the interest and the interest itself, and ... although the lease could be regarded as continuing for more than 21 years, the interest, because it was discontinuous did not do so.

That distinction is important.

Woodfall takes the view that 'it would seem that in the case of an 80-year agreement the right to a holiday week is void in each year after the 21st year' by reason of section 149(3) of the Law of Property Act 1925.[41] This must be based on a conceptualisation in which each week of occupation is seen as a distinct lease that is the fourth option.

Duddridge and Brown,[42] in contrast, opt for the third of these interpretations, distinguishing the agreement period from the lease term, and regarding it as a single lease, just on discontinuous dates. However, they note that a strict interpretation of that conceptualisation would lead to some absurd consequences when calculating notice periods under the Landlord and Tenant Act 1954, Part II.

The third option makes the agreement binding as granting an estate, where possession is to happen at the date of the first occupation, with the protections associated with a lease in possession taking effect. In the gap between that physical occupation and the next period, there is no occupation, and those dates do not form part of the term. Pawlowski,[43] at least in the case of a student accommodation agreement under which the student pays rent termly, but is permitted to leave his materials in the accommodation during the vacations, has suggested a licence covers those interim periods.

The duration of the lease is then calculated by adding up the days specified as being the term, as distinct from the length of the agreement. This enables a court to conclude that the tenant has exclusive possession for all the dates upon which the lease term exists, and the intermediate dates on which the superior titleholder resumes possession do not detract from that possession. The focus then lies upon the nature of the rights granted on the dates specified.

This may be of purely academic interest, except that it has consequences in terms of determining the duration of the lease, formalities requirements and resolving disputes during the intervening periods.

---

[41] Lord Justice Lewison et al (eds), *Woodfall, Landlord and Tenant* (London, Sweet and Maxwell, 2014) para 5.086.

[42] Duddridge and Brown (n 30).

[43] M Pawlowski, 'Questions and Answers: Tenancy of Student Accommodation until the Cessation of Studies—Certainty of Term—Contractual Licence' (2013) 17(4) *Landlord and Tenant Review* 148.

The Land Registration Act 2002 sidesteps the conceptual problem by making express provision under section 27 of the Act, requiring dispositions where 'the right to possession is discontinuous' to be completed by registration in order to be valid in law. That phrase in itself suggests interpretation as a single term, with a discontinuous right to possession. However, Harpum, with his central role in designing the 2002 Act, has adopted the third approach that is a term as the aggregate of the discontinuous periods. Whilst section 27 required all discontinuous leases to be registered, first registration under section 4 only applies where the actual periods of use exceed seven years.[44]

Land Registry Guidance describes discontinuous leases thus:

> The lease may be of a property, e.g. a flat, apartment or market stall, that is for either: a specified number of days in a week, e.g. every Monday to Friday (inclusive), or a specific week(s) in a calendar year.

The guidance avoids the conceptual question, but indicates the calculation of the term is to multiply the number of complete weeks each year the property is demised by the number of years granted.[45]

In contrast, the 2013 Draft Universal Torrens Act in Australia, picking upon state Torrens legislation[46] defines the term of a lease as

> the period beginning when the lessee is first entitled to possession of a lot or part of a lot under the lease and ending when the lessee is last entitled to possession, even if the lease consists of 2 or more discontinuous periods.[47]

Here, therefore, the lease term is conceptualised as including the entire duration of the instrument, not just the periods of exclusive possession—that is the second option in the original list. So, whilst the majority of English sources adopt the third option, the Australian position seems to adopt the second.

The Australian approach gives rise to problems in relation to exclusive possession, as for the bulk of the term, the tenant will not be entitled to possession at all, and therefore it is difficult to describe this as exclusive possession. The third approach, of confining the term to the period for which exclusive possession actually exists seems to preserve exclusive possession doctrines more effectively. However that then gives rise to the question of whether there is one or several leases, with the section 149(3) problem. The best view, therefore, is to argue that the lease is for a single period, for a number of discontinuous days—the third way.

Whilst English courts have interpreted the agreement as running for the entire period, from the start to the expiry of the last period of occupation, they have not specified the nature of that agreement. It manifestly exists and can be enforced as a contract throughout the time. However does it give rise to any property law interest/ estate? Registration requirements under the 2002 Act mean that the lease term, will be protected as a registered estate, and will bind successors. The terms of the contract in relation to that occupation will bind as part of that lease. Provisions in the contract that do not relate to the lease itself will not bind successors, but will bind

---

[44] C Harpum, 'Leases under the Land Registration Act 2002' (2002) *Landlord and Tenant Review* 51.
[45] Land Registry Practice Guide 25 (2014) para 3.9
[46] Eg Queensland Land Title Act 1994, Sch 2.
[47] www.plra.com.au/DraftUTTA.pdf.

the original parties. In this way the dual nature of the instrument and the duration of the term can be preserved.

Putting aside the conceptual difficulties with discontinuous leases, there are also questions about the limits of the discontinuous lease. If a lease can cover, for example, three disconnected days, or weekly arrangements Monday to Friday, could it cover an arrangement where the landowner entered to clear and change the sheets on a regular basis, say every morning between 10 and 11? At present this would be a classic example of a lack of exclusive possession and not a lease. But could it be framed as a discontinuous set of daily leases between 11am and 10am the following day?

The shades of grey offered by the discontinuous lease can be used in many situations to provide the necessary shared occupation and durability for tax and other regimes—recently for example in relation to car parking.[48] As the case law stands, the capacity to use and adapt the discontinuous lease is not circumscribed, and it would offer a solution to the problem posed in this chapter. However its foundations and limitations are at present too ill-defined as a basis upon which anyone could advise a voluntary sector group to make significant decisions. With guidance, however, this might offer the basis for a solution.

VI. RECONSIDERING LICENCES AND ESTOPPEL

An alternative approach to the problem would be through clarifying to the voluntary and funding sector the extent to which licences can give rise to durability in the sense of vindication against third parties and the original licensor, although not against successors in title to the licensor.

The licence cases seem to have developed in isolation from the discontinuous lease cases, at least post 1895.[49] A number of theatre cases illustrate the difficulty of distinguishing leases for intermittent purposes/occupation for a purpose from a contractual arrangement where possession is incidental. In *Frank Warr & Co v London County Council*[50] an agreement to supply refreshments at a theatre and to make 'necessary use' of the bar areas to do so, was considered not to confer a lease. Indeed, Romer LJ concluded that even if the agreement had said 'exclusive use' it would not have amounted to a lease:

> I think 'necessary use' only means use so far as is necessary to enable the plaintiffs to supply refreshments in the theatre at the proper times when it is being used as a theatre, and certainly does not involve an absolute parting with the possession of those parts of the theatre by the lessees to the plaintiffs.

The Court of Appeal considered *Edwardes v Barrington*[51] as closer to the line, but still only a licence. The key appears to be the retention of legal possession,[52] but the

---

[48] *Pointon York Group plc v Poulton* [2006] EWCA Civ 1001, relying expressly on *Smallwood v Sheppards*.

[49] In earlier cases there is some overlap of cases that would now be considered licences, estoppel and discontinuous leases.

[50] *Frank Warr & Co v London County Council* [1904] 1 KB 713.

[51] *Edwardes v Barrington* (1901) 85 LT 650.

[52] *Peebles v Crosthwaite* 13 *Times Law Report* 37; affirmed ibid 198.

court did not define the distinction between legal and factual possession, taking matters back to Hill's analysis of the meaning of possession.

In *Winter Garden Theatre v Millennium Productions*[53] an agreement to use a theatre for entertainment events for six months with an option to renew had to be treated as a licence not a lease, because of the Theatres Act 1843. The case turned on the revocability of the licence, and makes clear that where third-party investment is made on the basis of a licence drafted on terms that severely limit revocability, prohibiting it until the occurrence or completion of an event, the court is likely to protect that limitation upon termination through specific performance or possession actions.[54] Put in those terms, the *Winter Gardens* case perhaps offers a different solution for shared use—through a licence with strict limits on termination, and external grants explicitly linked to its durability.

This suggests that there might be scope for articulating a clearer rationale for not for profit organisations seeking to develop appropriate contractual arrangements binding all except a successor in title to the grantor. Appropriate terms could provide for any resultant financial indemnity, and the current judicial approach to estoppel may perceive expenditure incurred by a licensee under grant terms, repayable if occupation is ended within a specific time as giving rise to a proprietary estoppel: with probably a case remedy. Explaining that to a potential funder as the basis for funding would be an interesting challenge!

VII. CONCLUSION

A primary rationale in the law of leases is to give effect to the intention of the parties, so that law supports rather than frustrates the wishes of the parties, however there are a number of barriers, which hinder the ability of voluntary sector bodies and others to create leases with the flexibility of occupation they require.

The question driving this work is whether there can be more effective means to enable voluntary sector partnership arrangements affecting the use of property to provide sufficient durability against third parties within shared use models? The focus of various agencies upon colocation as something emerging from a longer-term relationship, as opposed to something which may arise outside of a wider relational context has meant little attention has been paid to the question.

Whilst the issue is not problematic in Scotland, three options have been explored for use in England—the limited use lease, discontinuous lease and a licence coupled with an estoppel giving rise to a lease or compensation as a remedy.

Leases for limited purposes, whilst conceptually possible, depend on historic cases whose status is, at best, uncertain, in the wake of the strong doctrinal statements of Lord Templeman in *Street v Mountford*.

Discontinuous leases offer a partial solution. They require registration and the nature of such arrangements is conceptually uncertain, hardly mentioned in reference works, and, it is argued here, mis-analysed in *Woodfall* which hardly makes it a sensible approach for the voluntary sector.

[53] *Winter Garden Theatre v Millennium Productions* [1948] AC 173.
[54] *Hounslow London Borough Council v Twickenham Garden Developments Ltd* [1971] Ch 233; *Verrall v Great Yarmouth BC* [1980] 1 All ER 839.

Alternatively, the *Winter Gardens* case suggests funders should not be unwilling to accept occupation licences as affording sufficient security, particularly given developments in estoppel. However, with funders having a surfeit of applications there is no incentive for them to explore beyond the confines of the basic lease/licence, secure/insecure analysis.

The pressure to develop partnerships working in the voluntary sector and the necessary need to articulate more flexible forms of property arrangements is not going to go away. There is no reason to suggest a specific model of 'voluntary sector' property partnerships. The realistic solution will lie in the hands of the voluntary sector to develop documents that use these legal solutions to deliver acceptable relationships. If that is to be achieved, given the complexity of the options available, and the risk aversion of the sector identified by IVAR,[55] there is a need for clear and consistent guidance to the voluntary sector about the legal vehicles available, supported by model agreements, similar to the currently available contractual 'Joint Use Agreement'. This would reduce the temptation to 'knit your own'.

Desires for certainty, for a clear distinction between property and contract, and the ability to alienate estates in land with minimum transaction costs/risk, militate in favour of a strict definitional approach to property rights. Yet the only mentions of the property issues in current documenting of voluntary sector partnerships conceptualises cohabitation as something that is likely to arise a long way into the development of a relationship. However, shared use can occur as the first and possibly only part of a relationship. As such, it deserves more attention in the guidance to the voluntary sector.

The fact that the voluntary sector needs such guidance to navigate the minefields of sharing their property is a criticism of the current property law regime, and does not enable the voluntary sector to act on the Charity Commission exhortation 'not to over-complicate the arrangements'.[56] At the very least, the voluntary sector deserves a clear way in which to articulate the temporal relationships they have developed, without substantial transaction costs, available only for large or significant schemes. That cannot be a satisfactory position.

[55] See above n 13.
[56] CC34 (n 3).

15

Reflections on Formalities

GRAHAM FERRIS*

ORMALITIES IN PROPERTY law are usually examined in the context of non-compliance. Obviously, the problem of failed formalities is not a simple problem. The possible requirements of the formality failed, and the ways that any formality might fail, are various. The law will sometimes correct or fix a failure of formalities, and sometimes it will not. A very important factor is whether the disposition not achieved was attempted in the course of carrying out a legal obligation. Where there is an ascertainable obligation then the content of the obligation can be taken to be the intention that the disposition was meant to give effect to. A failure to comply with formalities can be remedied in order to meet the obligation.[1] Therefore, two situations are particularly problematic: a disposition pursuant to an obligation that is undefined,[2] or a voluntary disposition.[3]

Where any obligation is unclear, so that it is not apparent what the intention should be taken to be, there is a risk of imposing the wrong disposition upon the parties. Where there is no obligation then intention cannot be ascertained by reference to obligation. In the absence of very clear evidence of actual intention there is a temptation to construct an intention, and in the absence of a legal obligation the only source is the sense of justice of the court.[4]

---

* Reader in Law, College of Business Law and Social Sciences, Nottingham Law School, Nottingham Trent University.

[1] Equity looks on that as done which ought to be done.

[2] This should not arise, because an undefined obligation is not an obligation that can be enforced: 'To be a good contract there must be a concluded bargain, and a concluded contract is one which settles everything that is necessary to be settled and leaves nothing to be settled by agreement between the parties'. *May and Butcher v R* (1929) [1934] 2 KB 17n per Viscount Dunedin. However, the situation is hardly unheard of in practice. The obligations imposed by the constructive trust that arises under the doctrine of mutual wills would be one example. See: *Re Dale* [1994] Ch 31; *Birmingham v Renfrew* (1937) 57 CLR 666, 689 per Dixon J: 'But when he dies he is to bequeath what is left in the manner agreed upon. It is only by the special doctrines of equity that such a floating obligation, suspended, so to speak, during the lifetime of the survivor can descend upon the assets at his death and crystallize into a trust. No doubt gifts and settlements, *inter vivos*, if calculated to defeat the intention of the compact, could not be made by the survivor and his right of disposition, *inter vivos*, is, therefore, not unqualified. But, substantially, the purpose of the arrangement will often be to allow full enjoyment for the survivor's own benefit and advantage upon condition that at his death the residue shall pass as arranged'.

[3] There is no equity to perfect an imperfect gift.

[4] *Stack v Dowden* [2007] UKHL 17; *Jones v Kernott* [2010] UKSC 2. See: W Swadling, 'The Common Intention Constructive Trust in the House of Lords: An Opportunity Missed' (2007) 123 *LQR* 511, 515: 'Chadwick L.J. reached his result on the basis of what the court, i.e. Chadwick L.J., considered "fair". The problem with this approach is that ... it seems little different from that of Lord Denning M.R. in the 1960s, where he asserted a jurisdiction in the court to create trusts, not on the basis of any bargain or

It is hoped that a speech act analysis will help clarity of analysis. This chapter argues that a speech act is constitutive of all dispositions of property.[5] It introduces the philosophical analysis of the speech act, and argues that this analysis enables us to distinguish more clearly between different types of failures that dispositions are prone to. When the speech act is fully realised in a failed disposition then there is no problem of intention to resolve. When the speech act fails then the nature of the failure should be taken into account in considering whether a remedy is possible or required at all.

Our jurisprudence has tried to resolve all of the issues that arise from failed dispositions through two routes, either by using the presence of absence of a determinable obligation as the sole relevant criterion, or through an unstable and unclear concept of intention. The reliance upon obligation has led to tensions where the result seems unjust to judge or jurist. The use of an unstable variant on the concept of intention has permitted a mystifying language of intention to develop, and to obscure the principles and policies actually driving legal development.[6]

It is suggested that some legal problems, usually analysed as problems concerned with formalities, are illuminated by a speech act analysis. Obviously, a clearer analysis alone cannot resolve issues of justice that are concerned with conflicting values protected by our legal system. However, clarity of thought can help make any necessary value conflicts apparent. Sometimes, solving a problem is equivalent to restating the problem in a manner that makes the solution obvious.[7]

I. AN OUTLINE OF KEY CONCEPTS

It is necessary to try and set out some concepts for this chapter. The definitions below are required to make distinctions necessary for the articulation of the argument. The nature and analysis of the speech act is dealt with more fully under the heading 'What Are Speech Acts?'.

— A disposition is a legally effective act that alters the rights held in relation to some item of property. Thus, it refers to the words or actions that dispose.
— A formality is a legally specified required element of a disposition.

Thus, a disposition may not have any specific formal requirement at law: one may transfer legal title to a tin of beans by passing possession, or by acknowledgment

---

expressed intention, but because it was "reasonable and fair in the circumstances"'. M Dixon, 'Editor's Notebook: The Still Not Ended, Never-ending Story' [2012] *Conveyencer and Property Lawyer* 83, 86: 'is it that the Supreme Court has recognised what commentators have not: that what we need, and what we now have, is a reasonably structured judicial discretion to vary the property rights of cohabitants and other property sharers that is not based on property law at all. It is something else: call it family law, call it an exercise of the court's inherent equitable jurisdiction, but, maybe, do not call it property law'. Judicial discussion has been in terms of types of intention. The problem is that absent a speech act all forms of intention are at best speculative.

[5] As defined below—by act of the party and not by act of law.
[6] See n 4.
[7] Herbert A Simon, *The Sciences of the Artificial* (Cambridge, MIT Press, 1981) 153: 'solving a problem simply means representing it so as to make the solution transparent'.

of the new owner, or by allowing the new owner to take possession.[8] There is no required form of words, indeed, no words may be said or written when a tin of beans is scanned, and payment is tendered and accepted at a supermarket till.

Obviously, there are formalities that are observed at the supermarket till, but they are socially required rather than legally required. People will generate social regularities when the law does not impose formality requirements upon them. One reason for this social generative impulse is the need for clarity and predictability. Legal formalities are fairly clearly authoritative elaborations of a socially expressed desire for definitive acts that bind.[9]

It is submitted that every formality (as defined above, being a legal formality rather than a merely social formality) is either associated with, or is itself, a speech act.

Therefore, when deciding whether a disposition of property has been validly made, there are two analytical issues that will be present: whether the necessary speech act is present; and whether any necessary formality is present.

A speech act does not have to involve spoken words. One may effect a speech act by the use of written words.

Sometimes, there will be no formality requirement, as illustrated by an oral or written declaration of trust of personal property. Sometimes the speech act and the formality will be realised in the same set of physical acts or objects, as illustrated by the written contract, duly signed, for a contract for the sale of land. Sometimes the speech act and the formality will require separate acts, or the production of separate objects, as illustrated by the completion of a share transfer form, and the subsequent presentation of the form at the company office, and the alteration of the company register.

Therefore, this analysis asserts that a speech act is always necessary, sometimes identical with a formality, and sometimes one element in a complete disposition. If correct, that means there will always be a speech act present in a disposition, and that there might also be some other requirement, as to the form of the speech act, or as to some extra requirement for a disposition to be complete.

The speech act is pre-legal. The law has adopted the speech act rather than invented it. Speech acts are ubiquitous in society, and some of them are legally significant, and some of the legally significant ones are dispositions of property.

The issue of whether a speech act has been successful in a disposition is sometimes treated as a question of intention, and sometimes treated as a question of compliance with a formality, and sometimes not recognised. If the concepts of disposition, formality, and speech act outlined above are correct then difficulty in this area of law

---

[8] When a transfer is voluntary (a gift) then a legally recognised transfer of possession may be required: *Cochrane v Moore* (1890) 25 QBD 57; *Re Cole* [1964] Ch 175. However, there is no need for the transfer to involve an act by the owner of the chattel: *Thomas v Times Book Co Ltd* [1966] 1 WLR 911. The acquisition or retention of possession with consent seems to be the step required, rather than the passing of possession or delivery, see: *Kilpin v Ratley* [1892] 1 QB 582. On a sale of goods title will pass when the parties intend it to pass.

[9] JM Perillo, 'The Statue of Frauds in the Light of the Functions and Dysfunctions of Form' (1974) 43 *Fordham Law Review* 39, 43–44 for spontaneous formalities amongst children. The marking off of speech acts as binding through imposition of a form such as writing or a deed, ceremony such as witnessing, often called the cautionary aspect of formalities, is widely recognised as important, see: Perillo, above; L Fuller, 'Consideration and Form' (1941) 41 *Columbia Law Review* 799; TG Youdan, 'Formalities for Trusts of Land, and the Doctrine in *Rochefoucauld v Boustead*' (1984) 43 *CLJ* 306.

may be due in part to a failure to clearly identify the analytically pertinent elements of the disposition. Specifically, a lack of clarity in regard to the speech act element may have been productive of confusion in legal analysis.

II. DISCUSSIONS OF FORMALITY IN LEGAL DISCOURSE

Discussion of formality in property law is most often encountered in discussions of failure to comply with formal requirements for dispositions, or situations in which compliance is dubious for some reason. For obvious reasons, judicial considera-tion of formality tends to occur when there is some dispute over what formality was required, or whether a required formality was complied with. Successful use of formality generates a level of certainty that renders recourse to law otiose. Avoiding legal disputes is one reason the law supports formalities: a regular use of formalities means that investigation of intention is unnecessary.

This function, of generating certainty in the future as to events concerning property that happened in the past is fundamental to property law. It is sometimes referred to as formality serving an evidential function. However, that usage implies there is something other than the successful disposition that is being evidenced. Presumably the extra thing would be intention. The argument here is that a formal disposition is normally not evidence of some extraneous intention; rather, the disposition will include a speech act, and that speech act coupled with the correct formality, is the enactment of the legal event. The disposition evidences itself alone.

When disposition and intention are separate then the disposition has misfired. Our jurisprudence is focussed upon cases of attempted dispositions not doing what they should do; thus our paradigm tends to be not the regular use of formality but the disputed or not-use of formality. This paradigm assumes a separation of form and intention that should not exist in the ordinary case. This can be understood if we consider the 'channelling' function of form. The classic modern statement of this channelling effect was given by Lon Fuller:[10]

> The thing which characterizes the law of contracts and conveyances is that in this field forms are deliberately used, and are intended to be so used, by the parties whose acts are to be judged by the law. To the business man who wishes to make his own or another's promise binding, the seal was at common law available as a device for the accomplishment of his objective. In this aspect form offers a legal framework into which the party may fit his actions, or, to change the figure, it offers channels for the legally effective expression of intention. It is with this aspect of form in mind that I have described the third function of legal formalities as 'the channelling function'.

The channel described here is constitutive of the intention. The channel determines both where the metaphorical fluid it constrains can flow to, and the shape of the vessel the fluid can fill at the end of the channel. If there is no form then there can be no legally effective event.[11] One might dream of a disposition of a right in one's

---

[10] Fuller (n 9).

[11] Bentham proposed an abundance of specific forms that would be required for different types of transaction: J Bentham, *Rationale of Judicial Evidence: Specially Applied to English Practice: In Five Volumes*, vol 2 (first published 1827) (Nabu Press, 2011) bk 4, ch 3, para 2. This was not adopted by the

house that will grant rights to use that will endure *in specie* for one's descendants for all eternity. Such a legal estate is impossible to create, and such an equitable estate would be terminable upon sale by two trustees. An intention can only be given effect if a form is legally recognised that makes it effective. Institutionally or substantively this is the 'principle of *numerus clausus*' in terms of dealings or disposition it is the law of formalities.

The aspect of form that Fuller draws to our attention is form as intermediary. The law of formalities determines what representations are legally effective intermediaries. One cannot intelligibly be said to transfer land by means of attaching a photograph to an email and writing: 'here is the land, it is yours now'. The law might view this as a promise, or as a declaration of trust, or let it give rise to an estoppel. The law might view it as a nullity. It is clearly not a transfer of the land. The electronic image does not represent the 'title' to the land, that used to be something a deed could do, but now it is something only an entry in the Land Registry can do. We do deal with images or representation, but must work within the framework of what is understood to be a legally effective mode of representation.

When an effective disposition is plainly made then the intention is to do what is done, and what is done is 'the disposition'. One is not taken to have wanted or 'intended' to do something other than what the disposition achieves. There is something wrong with trying to separate the intention from the expression of the intention. The speech act element does not need any intention behind it. If I declare a trust then the words that I say or write are the declaration of trust. My intention is to be construed by reading those words. There is no further 'intention' that the words can be compared with to check if the declaration fitted. Only a mistake gives rise to a gap. This is because a declaration is a speech act. What one declares, if the declaration is successful, is the declaration. Only some problem with the declaration generates the possibility of divergence between the declaration and some intention. A failure to declare raises the question of what was attempted. A declaration is what was intended and what was done.

law, wisely, as a multiplicity of forms generates a multiplicity of boundaries between forms. Even with the three generally recognised modes for gratuitous disposition the classification of a disposition can pose problems because it has aspects of more than one permitted mode of disposition, and this throws up problems over which formality or formalities it must comply with: *T Choithram International SA and others v Pagarani and others* [2001] 1 WLR 1, 11–12: 'Though it is understandable that the courts below should have reached this conclusion since the case does not fall squarely within either of the methods normally stated as being the only possible ways of making a gift, their Lordships do not agree with that conclusion. The facts of this case are novel and raise a new point. It is necessary to make an analysis of the rules of equity as to complete gifts. Although equity will not aid a volunteer, it will not strive officiously to defeat a gift. This case falls between the two common form situations mentioned above. Although the words used by TCP are those normally appropriate to an outright gift—"I give to X"—in the present context there is no breach of the principle in *Milroy v Lord* if the words of TCP's gift (ie to the foundation) are given their only possible meaning in this context. The foundation has no legal existence apart from the trust declared by the foundation trust deed. Therefore the words "I give to the foundation" can only mean "I give to the trustees of the foundation trust deed to be held by them on the trusts of foundation trust deed". Although the words are apparently words of outright gift they are essentially words of gift on trust'. In *Choithram* the court resolved the problem by imposing the requirements for declaration of trust upon a transaction that involved both declaration of self as trustee, and transfer to other trustees, on the facts before the court. The transaction had to fall into one of the available channels or modes of gratuitous disposition and declaration was given primacy, there had to be some legal event capable of marking the irrevocability of the disposition.

III. WHAT ARE SPEECH ACTS?

The first third of the twentieth century saw theories of language such as positivism ascendant. Statements were understood as being expressions of propositions that were true or false according to principles of verification that were ultimately cashed out in sense experiences.[12] Language was objective and it referred to things in the world in some way, just how it did this was disputed. This general approach to language suffered fatal attack by analyses that made language use central. Language did not do things, people did things with language. The speaker or writer became visible. One way this happened was through the identification of speech acts. Language was not only used to make statements that expressed propositions that were true or false. Language was used to promise, and warn, and threaten, and dispose. This performative use of language was termed the speech act and it was first clearly described by John Austin.[13]

The idea of the speech act was developed by Austin. He started from things done with words, or 'performatives', but he broadened his account to all language use. When he applied the theory of speech acts to the making of statements he undermined the positivist understanding of the world.[14] Austin's work has been influential,[15] however, it is difficult to know how to deploy Austin's conceptual analysis. Although Austin's style of writing is a model of clarity it is not well integrated into the philosophical literature of his era,[16] and he made little effort to highlight or elaborate upon the consequences of his work. Also, he was not a systematic thinker.

---

[12] AJ Ayer, *Language, Truth and Logic* (London, Penguin Books, 2001) first published in 1936 is the classic exposition.

[13] JL Austin, *How to Do Things with Words* (JO Urmson and M Sbisa eds, 2nd edn, Cambridge, Harvard University Press, 1975).

[14] Austin also attacked the idea of a special primacy or validity to sense perception in lectures that were later edited for publication: JL Austin, *Sense and Sensibilia* (GJ Warnock ed, Oxford, Oxford University Press, 1962). The concept of speech acts shares conceptual features with the concept of the language game as developed by Wittgenstein: L Wittgenstein, *Philosophical Investigations*, revd 4th edn (GEM Anscombe, PMS Hacker and J Schulte trs, Chichester, Wiley-Blackwell, 2009).

[15] Austin's concept of the speech act has been incorporated into the work of significant contemporary thinkers: JR Searle, *The Construction of Social Reality* (London, Penguin Books, 1995); J Habermas, *On the Pragmatics of Communication* (Maeve Cooke ed, Cambridge, Polity Press, 1999). In jurisprudence Austin must have influenced the thinking of HLA Hart, who JL Austin unusually expressly acknowledged as the source of some of his examples (Austin rarely referred to contemporaries in his published lectures or scholarly writing). Austin was a towering intellectual presence in Oxford, and played an important role in Hart's career: N Lacey, *A Life of HLA Hart: The Nightmare and the Noble Dream* (Oxford, Oxford University Press, 2004). Hart's account of the facilitative rules of law seems obviously influenced by the theory of the speech act. Yet there are very few express acknowledgements in Hart's published work of JL Austin's influence, so the links remain subterranean. In HLA Hart, *The Concept of Law*, 2nd edn (Oxford, Oxford University Press, 1994) the sole reference to JL Austin is to the essay 'A Plea for Excuses', although he quotes Austin in the Preface. Lacey (above) 226, suggests that Austin's direct influence on the *Concept of Law* was in the development of the contrast between internal and external viewpoints and the sense of obligation he tried to develop from it. She does not take note of the fact that power conferring rules operate through speech acts, and that formal primary rules are also established through speech acts, and that Austin may have importance in this regard. This may reflect Hart's struggle to articulate the concept of legal obligation, contrasted with his easy familiarity with speech acts, a field in which he tended to provide useful legal examples for Austin.

[16] He wrote very little and there is virtually no scholarly apparatus in either of the two books derived from his lectures or his few published articles: JL Austin, *Philosophical Papers*, 3rd edn (Oxford, Oxford University Press, 1979).

Hence, his work is sometimes neglected because it is difficult to know where it fits within broader accounts.[17]

Austin did not distinguish analytically between oral speech acts and written speech acts. His examples of speech acts included public notices.[18] However, his focus was on the spoken speech act, which he clearly regarded as the paradigm. He did distinguish performative and constative speech acts. Performative ones being speech acts that had an effect in the social world and constative being statements that could be described as true or false.[19] In this chapter 'speech acts' is a reference to a performative speech act.

The key aspect of Austin's work for dispositions is the speech act: the idea that words spoken, or words written, can, merely by being said or written, have effects in the world. Austin often used legal examples of speech acts: such as giving, or promising, or marrying.[20] His theory brings into focus the creative or generative aspect of law. When the law works and dispositions are made then property owners have the power to make their plans effective with greater certainty than merely personal relations of trust would allow. However, this central aspect of the law of property is often obscured by two circumstances: the fact that some speech acts can be used to generate useful evidence; and the systematic focus in litigation upon failures to execute dispositions correctly.

Austin analysed the speech act into three aspects:[21] the locution; the illocution; and the perlocution. It is convenient to briefly examine the locutionary and perlocutionary aspects of speech acts before undertaking a more detailed analysis of illocution.

Locution is complex.[22] Speech involves making a sound if spoken; or gestures if using sign language, or marks on paper if writing. However, mere production of a noise does not constitute speech. The noise must be recognisable as words of the language being used and the words have to be used as language. They must be grammatically ordered, and most vitally the grammatically ordered words must make sense.

Perlocution is the effects of the speech act on other people.[23] The perlocutionary effect may be the natural result of a successful illocution.[24] An order is given and

---

[17] A good example of this is the way Kenny uses Austin merely as a foil for Derrida: A Kenny, *Philosophy in the Modern World: A New History of Western Philosophy*, vol 4 (Oxford, Oxford University Press, 2007) 91–92.

[18] Austin (n 13) 57–58, 60–62, 65, 75.

[19] The distinction was more of degree than of the quality of the speech acts: JL Austin, 'Performative-Constative' in JR Searle (ed), *The Philosophy of Language*, Oxford Readings in Philosophy (Oxford, Oxford University Press, 1971).

[20] Sadly his law was usually not very reliable. His treatment of gift seems ignorant of the role played by delivery in the law of property, Austin, *How to Do Things with Words* (n 13) 37, fn 1; he took little interest in the difference between reciprocal and unilateral promises; and he also continued to use an inaccurate account of the marriage ceremony ibid, 5, fn 2.

[21] Austin (n 13) 100–08.

[22] Ibid, 94–100.

[23] Ibid, 109–20.

[24] J Habermas, 'Social Action, Purposive Activity, and Communication' (first published 1981) presented a different account, however he seemed to accept this proposition in 'Communicative Rationality and the Theories of Meaning and Action' (first published 1986) both republished in Cooke (ed), *On the Pragmatics of Communication* (n 15).

obeyed. Things may not be so straightforward. A speaker might have an intention other than the patent illocutionary one. One might speak in confidence confident that the hearer will repeat the words to a person who the speaker wishes to reach, and who will react to the information.

By separating out speaking and consequences of speaking we have isolated the aspect most characteristic of the speech act. The illocutionary force of a speech act is conventional.[25] Indeed, one may perform a speech act without utilising language if the conventions are well enough established.[26] Speech acts can be accomplished without speech; however, the speech act can only have illocutionary force in the context of social conventions. An attempt at a speech act may fail, as any act may fail. Or it may be carried out under duress or mistaken belief. These types of failure are not particularly interesting from the point of view of the analysis of speech acts, but they may be very important in practice.

Illocutionary acts have peculiar ways of failing, what John Austin termed 'infelicities'. Austin classified these infelicities into two broad categories: misfires and abuses. By misfires he wanted to identify situations where the attempted speech act was of no effect, or void. Austin subclassified misfires into four types: first, is the absence of a convention;[27] second, is the inappropriateness of the person speaking or the act attempted given the nature of the convention that exists;[28] third, is faulty execution;[29] and fourth, is unfinished execution.[30] Abuses are concerned with insincerity.[31] Austin subclassified into two categories: first, the correct speech act is carried out but without the necessary belief or intention for a sincere performance; and second, the commitment required to deliver the sequela of the speech act is not present.

IV. WHERE DO WE FIND SPEECH ACTS IN PROPERTY LAW?

Speech acts are usually subsumed in written instruments in property law. The required formality is made a subject of analysis, and the words used are taken to be important as indications of intention. The speech act is dismembered into a formality and an intention.

Legal formalities are generally linked to fear of fraud and the generation of evidence. Hence, writing that is in some way authenticated is common: signing a document, or signing before witnesses are the usual means of authentication. This obscures an aspect of the law of dispositions that has been in retreat for very many years.[32] It seems likely that the original acts of disposition of property were oral

---

[25] JR Searle, 'Introduction' 8; and PF Strawson, 'Intention and Convention in Speech Acts' in Searle (ed), *The Philosophy of Language* (n 19).

[26] Austin (n 13) 119: 'Strictly speaking, there cannot be an illocutionary act unless the means employed are conventional, and so the means of achieving it non-verbally must be conventional'.

[27] Ibid, 26–34.

[28] Ibid, 34–35.

[29] Ibid, 36: this is the type of error typified by *Milroy v Lord* (1862) 4 DeGF & J 264, 45 ER 1185.

[30] Ibid, 36–37: this is the type of error typified by *Choithram v Pagarani* [2001] 1 WLR 1.

[31] Ibid, 39–52.

[32] MT Clanchy, *From Memory to Written Record: England from 1066–1307*, 3rd edn (Chichester, Wiley-Blackwell, 2013).

speech acts combined with symbolic actions. When reduced to writing the speech act is likely to be identifiable as an operative clause, a written speech act that effects the disposition. Formally required spoken words are still present in law: in the oaths of witnesses, or jurors, and in the marriage ceremony for example.

The formality, much neglected in practice, for the declaration of a trust in land enacted by section 53(1)(b) Law of Property Act 1925 keeps the primacy of the spoken word. It is still possible to declare a trust of land orally, however, the declaration, or evidence of it, must subsequently be committed to writing if it is to be enforceable against the property owner.

The link between speech act and disposition is not merely of historical interest because it challenges the traditional analysis of and criticism of formality law. The law of formalities is usually given attention when there is some problem with compliance. Although, as Hart quite correctly emphasised, the essential quality of the law governing dispositions is facilitative.[33] Ironically, however, the law of formalities is generally regarded as being obstructive to the property owner's intention. It is not the productive use of formality to give authority to the action of the property owner that is the focus of attention, it is the failure of an intention to be realised due to a failure to comply with a formality requirement. Such was the case in *Milroy v Lord* where an inappropriate formality was deployed (a deed rather than share transfer).[34] The combination of formality with judicial formalism, the combination of arbitrary demands with punctilious regard to form, is particularly prone to excite critical comment:[35]

> The law of wills is notorious for its harsh and relentless formalism. The Wills Act prescribes a particular set of formalities for executing one's testament. The most minute defect in formal compliance is held to void the will, no matter how abundant the evidence that the defect was inconsequential ... This article contends that the insistent formalism of the law of wills is mistaken and needless ... the finding of a formal defect should not lead to automatic invalidity, but to a further inquiry: does the non-complying document express the decedent's testamentary intent, and does its form sufficiently approximate Wills Act formality to enable the court to conclude that it serves the purposes of the Wills Act?'

The accusation is that the property owner's intention is defeated by regard to inessential and superfluous form. This accusation is coherent where a statement exists, oral or written, that is evidentially safe and sufficiently complete. However, the analytical separation of words (form) and intent (substance) is only coherent when the locutionary element of the attempted speech act is substantially completed. The concept of intention is actually parasitical upon speech acts being partially or fully performed: it is the saying that generates the intention. The channelling and clarifying functions of formalities are constitutive of the disposition and the intention. It is the need to make express in words that forces the choices required for the generation of a clear and particular intention to take shape. An analytical focus upon the speech

---

[33] It is a vital aspect of power conferring rules which: 'provide individuals with facilities for realizing their wishes' Hart (n 15) 27.

[34] *Milroy v Lord* (1862) 4 De GF & J 264, 45 ER 1185.

[35] JH Langbein, 'Substantial Compliance with the Wills Act' (1975) 88 *Harvard Law Review* 489, 489.

act thus displaces over-simplistic accounts of an intention that exists outside of its expression. It enables a description that is as simple as is possible but no simpler.[36]

The practical feature of the speech act that is of interest here is that it is an action that has an effect. The action is the use of words, oral or written. The effect may be instant or delayed, as in a will or when a deed is delivered in escrow. The analytically important quality of the speech act is that the words are what constitute the action—there is no separation between the intent and the words. The account is of a successful speech act, the use of a facilitative rule of law to enable an actor to bring about an alteration of legal relations and thereby enhance the ability to plan, and rely upon the predictability of the actions of others. In this account of the law governing dispositions; a law that demands a speech act that is formally performed, or less typically that demands a speech act and separate formality; is not destructive of intent. It is constitutive of intent, and this is the normal situation. The law gives institutional support to the acts of property owners, and provides one mechanism for doing so in its rules that facilitate dispositions, and formality provisions are one part of that law.

Requiring writing rather than spoken words has facilitative effects independent of the certainty acquired through formality. Making the speech act in writing enables greater elaboration than would be convenient for spoken speech acts. The use of language, a symbolic system, can be combined with the distributive intelligence achievable through writing.[37] Furthermore, writing enables the use of forms and precedents to standardise and elaborate the disposition. The formality of writing is facilitative because it supports more complex dispositions. Indeed, it is possible, and common, to adopt writing without legal compulsion. However, many unsophisticated property owners are likely to resist writing because it imposes transaction costs that are obvious and immediate, for gains that are obscure and deferred. Although justified primarily through the benefits brought to third parties by producing reliable evidence, the imposition of writing as a formality is also good policy for facilitating the legal ordering of naïve legal users. Habituation to writing in turn will encourage its adoption even when it is not required.

V. DOES A SPEECH ACT ANALYSIS OF CONTENTIOUS CASES MAKE ANYTHING MORE OBVIOUS?

A. Share Transfers and the Identification of an Illocutionary Intent

The seminal case on formalities is *Milroy v Lord*. The reason for the fame and influence of the case lies in its identification of the illocutionary choice of property owners who seek to make a voluntary disposition. It is for the analysis of the three modes of gratuitous disposition in the judgment of Turner LJ that the case earned its place of honour in legal doctrine:[38]

---

[36] An expression attributed to Albert Einstein.
[37] E Hutchins, *Cognition in the Wild* (Cambridge, Massachusetts Institute of Technology Press, 1995).
[38] *Milroy v Lord* (n 34) 274–75 and 1189–90.

In order to render a voluntary settlement valid and effectual, the settler must have done everything which, according to the nature of the property comprised in the settlement, was necessary to be done in order to transfer the property and render the settlement binding upon him. He may of course do this by actually transferring the property to the persons for whom he intends to provide, and the provision will then be effectual, and it will be equally effectual if he transfers the property to a trustee for the purposes of the settlement, or declares that he himself holds it in trust for those purposes; and if the property be personal, the trust may, as I apprehend, be declared either in writing or by parol; but, in order to render the settlement binding, one or other of these modes must, as I understand the law of this Court, be resorted to, for there is no equity in this Court to perfect an imperfect gift. The cases I think go further to this extent, that if the settlement is intended to be effectuated by one of the modes to which I have referred, the Court will not give effect to it by applying another of those modes. If it is intended to take effect by transfer, the Court will not hold the intended transfer to operate as a declaration of trust, for then every imperfect instrument would be made effectual by being converted into a perfect trust.

The three modes channel the disposition, the settler must decide to perform one of them, and comply with the speech act and formality requirements of the mode chosen. The rule in *Milroy v Lord* not only states the law clearly, but specifies a reason behind the rule: because declaration requires merely a speech act and no formality (for personal property) the risk is that unless the courts police the boundaries then failed gifts will be transformed into successful declarations. This would be to perfect an imperfect gift, and equity has no such jurisdiction.

The locution was complete in *Milroy v Lord*, the intention to create a trust was clear, the subject matter of the intended trust was clear, the identity and beneficial interest of the object was clear. The illocutionary intention or mode of disposition chosen, third-party trustee, was clear. The trust was perfectly workable, and the beneficiary had already received benefits under the trust that were held not recoverable by the settler's estate, as these were held upon a valid trust for the beneficiary.[39] In all respects the speech act was complete and the intention of the settler was clear.

On its facts *Milroy v Lord* is at best a punctilious decision against the justice of the case. There is no doubt that the intention of the settler would have been better honoured by holding him to be a trustee of the shares that he had intended to transfer to Lord on trust for the beneficiary.[40] Equally, there is no doubt that his intention was not to declare himself a trustee of the shares but to make Lord his trustee.

Of course, the three modes of gratuitous disposition are not exclusive in the sense that to intend one necessarily implies that one rejects the use of the others. One might declare a trust, decide to transfer the trust property to a third-party trustee in due course, and the trust might provide that the beneficiary becomes entitled to the transfer of the legal title to the trust property upon reaching majority. As has

---

[39] Ibid, 273, 1189 and 277–78, 1190–91.

[40] A transfer to the beneficiary outright in the future was contemplated in the trust deed in *Milroy v Lord*. The decision in *Milroy v Lord* is the type of result Langbein was so critical of in the context of wills in the quotation above (n 35). Holding Medley subject to the trust of the shares that he had tried to establish, and thought he was honouring when he paid dividends to his niece, would have better respected his dispositive intent than the invalidation of the trust. The decision cannot be defended in terms of the need for formality as evidence of genuine intention, nor on the grounds of the need for a cautionary formality—as Medley had used a formal instrument to establish his trust. The decision is quite a pure example of the channelling effects of the law governing dispositions of property.

been noted above it is also possible that one might decide to become one of several trustees, and then either transfer the property to one's self and the other trustees, or declare oneself trustee, and come under an obligation to transfer the trust property to oneself and the other trustees in due course.[41] What one cannot do coherently is to intend any two of the dispositions at the same time. They may be sequentially intended, but not simultaneously intended. Indeed, if one wishes to act immediately, whether for practical or emotional reasons, then it makes sense to first declare and then transfer property that requires a delay prior to title being transferred. A good example of this is *Shah v Shah*:[42]

> Here there is no doubt that Mr Dinesh Shah manifested an intention that the letter should take effect forthwith: see the words 'as from today'. To give effect in law to those words, there has to be a disposition only of a beneficial interest, since, for the reasons given above, legal title did not pass until registration. The parties clearly intended registration to take place in due course because otherwise Mr Dinesh Shah would not have simultaneously executed and delivered a stock transfer form. Judged objectively, did the words used convey an intention to give a beneficial interest there and then or an intention to hold that interest for Mr Mahendra Shah until registration? Mr Dinesh Shah used the words 'I am ... holding', not, for example, the words 'I am assigning' or 'I am giving' and the concept that he holds the shares for Mr Mahendra Shah until he loses that status on registration can only be given effect in law by the imposition of a trust. Accordingly Mr Dinesh Shah must be taken in law to have intended a trust and not a gift. Added to that, as Norris J points out, he calls the document 'a declaration' in his letter, which is more consistent with its being a declaration of trust than a gift.

Illocutionary intention is an important aspect of the speech act necessary for a disposition. *Milroy v Lord* did identify this aspect of the law, and for this reason deserves the respect it has enjoyed. However, it confounded illocution with formality, and produced a statement that implied an exclusive set of alternatives where the facts and the law would have been better served by a statement of the law that recognised that modes could be combined or used exclusively. The channelling function exists to enhance security of transactions into the future. *Milroy v Lord* in its result laid a trap that undermined security in what was thought by all relevant parties to the disposition to be an established and perfect settlement.

B. Wills and their Execution—Can We Find a Speech Act

In *Barrett v Bem* the Court of Appeal overruled the judgment at first instance.[43] Certainly it did not use an analysis based upon speech acts. However, the decision of the Court of Appeal is clearly correct on such grounds, and a speech act analysis articulates the real issues more clearly than the references to dictionary definitions of 'direction'.[44] The 'something more' that section 9(a) Wills act 1837 demands by the reference to 'direction' is a speech act. Such act requires locution, and it must have

---

[41] See: *T Choithram International SA and others v Pagarani and others* (n 11).
[42] *Shah v Shah* [2010] EWCA 1408 [13] per Arden LJ.
[43] *Barrett v Bem* [2011] EWHC 1247 (Ch), [2012] EWCA Civ 52, [2012] Ch 573.
[44] Ibid, [124]–[126].

the illocutory force of a direction (in this context a species of imperative). It may be given in writing, or without words, possibilities commonly recognised in speech act analysis. However, the paradigm is the speech act, and any non-oral speech act must meet the same requirements of sense, reference, and happiness as an oral speech act. The trial judge held:[45]

> There is no evidence that he said anything at that stage, but the act of attempting to sign personally and failing to do so, having expressly said he wanted to make a will and expressly approved its contents, together with allowing Anne [the beneficiary] to sign on his behalf, can and should be taken as a direction by conduct to Anne to sign the will in those terms of his behalf. He had tried and failed to do so himself. He wanted the 2004 will signed. Moreover, if as I suspect may have happened, Martin [the testator] made an attempt to sign with Anne's help but that attempt failed, it can be taken as further evidence of a wish to direct Anne to sign for him following his failed attempt or attempts.

There is no locution and no illocutionary force. A speech act is an act. It is not something that arises from an interpretation or as an implication of other acts. Trying to sign a document is obviously not directing someone else to do so: indeed the two acts are contradictory—in the same way that attempts to use conflicting modes of disposition simultaneously are contradictory.

The execution of the will is a speech act performed by signing the document in the presence of two witnesses and with the requisite intention. Directing someone else to sign is another different speech act. The confusion in the judgment is due to an analysis in terms of overall intention. If the speech act is 'executing the will in some manner' then how this is achieved is mere technique. But the speech act is either signing the will or directing someone else to sign it. It is not possible to 'execute in some manner' because that is not a perfomative speech act, it is the perlocutionary aim of the speech act that is being identified: to make the will effective. Furthermore, the 'intention' is really not very well-established without a speech act that gives it voice, by execution or by some species of declaratory speech act. One important aspect of speech acts is that they articulate 'intention' and often force the formation of some specific intention.

This absence of a speech act of direction is at the centre of the judgment by the Court of Appeal which was delivered by Lewison LJ:[46]

> The judge's crucial finding of fact was that after Martin tried and failed to sign the will Anne 'stepped in, took the pen, and signed the ... will on Martin's behalf.' There is no finding here (nor would there have been any evidence to support such a finding) that Martin asked Anne to step in and sign the will; or that Anne asked Martin whether she should sign the will before she 'stepped in'.

The trial judge, by resting upon an 'intention' he found to exist, held that the testator must be taken to have silently (silent in word or deed—beyond not raising himself from his death bed to struggle with the beneficiary) 'directed' what he wanted to happen, and the beneficiary must be taken to have acted on the understanding that that was what the testator wanted. However, there is no explanation of why the

---

[45] Ibid, [86].
[46] *Barrett v Bem* [2012] EWCA Civ 52, [2012] Ch 573 [142] Hughes and Maurice Kay LJJ concurred.

testator did not, if he so intended, say what he wanted to happen—he was capable of speech at this time but could not physically sign.

One suspects the 'intention' is not real in the necessary sense until it is articulated. The judge supplanted the testator by finding a series of intentions that together would generate a narrative that satisfied the judge.[47] The judge made sense of the evidence before him, and once the narrative had been established it dominated his analysis. The law of dispositions insists upon speech acts to prevent this type of well-intentioned discovery of unexpressed and unformulated intentions, a performative must be performed. The failure in *Barrett v Bem* was not *merely* to sign, as the act of signing would have been the sole clear expression of the testator's intention. There was no clear locution: the idea for the will was his according to the beneficiary and her daughter; but the words were not his, as it was drafted by the beneficiary's daughter on instructions that probably came from the beneficiary; and the execution was not his.[48] Upon being told he was a man soon to be dead he said something no one remembers to his sister, who told her daughter to write a will on his behalf. The women stood around the dying man's bed and convinced themselves they were doing what he wanted them to do. However, he did nothing. He may have tried to sign; or he may have held the pen and not signed. The sister signed for him and the women agreed everything was in order. The person present in the room who was least involved in the whole transaction was the second nurse witness. We are told she felt:[49]

> [Q]uite shaken and suddenly felt that, in witnessing the will, I had done something wrong professionally. I then began to regard my witnessing of that will as a bad experience and did not want to think about it any further.

She had been disturbed by whatever she witnessed. She remembered that the testator had not been able to sign, as his hand shook too much. She remembered the beneficiary helped by guiding his hand, although this memory was inconsistent with the handwriting expert evidence. It is hard not to conclude that several competing narratives are supportable on the evidence and the demand of the legislature that a formally recorded speech act, in written form, be produced is sound. Absent that, conjectures about intention seem largely speculative and unsatisfactory.

A speech act and formality requirement analysis is superior to traditional accounts because a rhetorical false dichotomy, between true intent and mere formality, generates an illusion of a free-floating intention. There is more narrative form, and

---

[47] *Barrett v Bem* (n 43) [38] and [43] seem to be the origins of the 'findings of fact', findings that were never actually supported by any positive evidence even at the second trial. Vos (QC) clearly felt that the general account given by the beneficiary's daughter was accurate, although she was not telling the truth about the actual events around the execution of the will. [44]–[45] illustrate how Vos approached the issue.

[48] Ibid, [32]–[37] are the key paragraphs: the testator was told he was terminal by his sister and her daughter; he responded (the daughter testified) by saying he wanted to make a will leaving all of his property to his sister; the daughter wrote a will to that effect, and he appeared to read it, and she checked he understood the will she had drafted; one nurse witness also asked him if he understood what he was doing; the daughter and nurse also testified (incorrectly) that he signed. Reconstructed rather than remembered was the judge's view of the evidence. It was also the sole independent (outside the document) evidence of the intentions of the testator. Memory of this evidence convinced the judge that he knew what the dead man had wanted, see: Ibid, [85] and [100].

[49] Ibid, [87].

confirmation bias of established hypotheses, than evidential certainty about the intention in this and many cases.[50] Speech acts identify tractable evidential issues because they generate the evidence required to resolve them. In doing this they generate certainty and secure expectations. However, as *Barrett v Bem* demonstrated the generation of the evidence can occur in the absence of the requisite speech act.

We can contrast this with *Marley v Rawlings*.[51] *Marley v Rawlings* concerned a mistaken execution of two wills. The testator and his wife had given instructions to their solicitor to draw up two wills in complementary form. The husband left everything to the wife if she survived him; and if not the entire estate to Marley. The wife left everything to the husband if he survived her; and if not the entire estate to Marley. Each executed the document drawn up for the other. The solicitor presented the wrong document for signature to each of the couple, and witnessed the signatures, together with a secretary from the firm. The mistake was not noticed when the wife died. The document executed by the husband was challenged by those entitled in his intestacy. Marley sought rectification of the will under section 20(1)(a) Administration of Justice Act 1982.

Here it seems a speech act was performed by the signing of the document. Thus, the case is not the same as *Barrett v Bem*. The question, in speech act terms, seems to be whether the speech act was merely badly articulated or was it ineffective because it was the wrong speech act. The Court of Appeal took the view that it was the performance of the wrong speech act:[52]

> Undoubtedly he intended to give effect to a will when he signed the document placed in front of him but not to the will that was in fact in front of him and which he signed. It is also beyond doubt that he intended to give effect to testamentary provisions.

The printed document took on an independent force: the words it contained embodied an identity, and determined the effects of its execution. Thus:[53] 'if asked whether he intended to give effect to the will which he signed, he would have said "no, of course not, that is my wife's will"'.

The Supreme Court took the view it was a badly articulated attempt at the right speech act:[54]

> It is unchallengeable that Mr Rawlings signed it, and that he did so, both on the face of the document, and as a matter of fact, with the intention of it being his last will and testament … it was indeed his will.

This reasoning denies agency to the document and places agency in the testator. It is the person who performs the speech act whose act it is:[55]

> It is true that the will purports in its opening words to be the will of Mrs Rawlings, but there is no doubt that it cannot be hers, as she did not sign it; as it was Mr Rawlings who signed it, it can only have been his will.

---

[50] J Frank, 'Are Judges Human?' (1931) 80 *University of Pennsylvania Law Review* 17.
[51] *Marley v Rawlings* [2012] EWCA Civ 61, [2013] Ch 271; [2014] UKSC 2, [2014] 2 WLR 213.
[52] Ibid, [52].
[53] Ibid, [55].
[54] [2014] UKSC 2, [2014] 2 WLR 213 (SC) [57].
[55] Ibid, [59].

This is true to the spirit of the philosophical analysis of the speech act: it is people that mean things, or do things, not words. In *Marley v Rawlings* there was a locution failure, the words of the speech act were wrong, the husband and wife each performed the wrong words. However, the illocutionary aspect of the speech act was intact, each was giving effect to their will, and in the circumstances the error of expression was easy to understand and correct. The Supreme Court correctly decided that the slip of the pen did not prevent the clear illocutionary force being given effect.

C. Intention at Large—Disposition without Speech Act?

Given a speech act, oral or in writing, then it makes one sort of sense to seek to establish the intention of the speaker or writer:[56]

> In interpreting a document, the court should not have regard to the subjective intention of its maker but to the intentions of the maker as manifested by the words he has used in the context of all the relevant facts.

This is the common law tradition of objective construction. It allows non-verbal aspects of the speech act to be incorporated into the interpretation. However, where there is no speech act then ascertaining intention is not a comparable exercise:[57]

> In this case, there is no need to impute an intention that the parties' beneficial interests would change, because the judge made a finding that the intentions of the parties did in fact change. At the outset, their intention was to provide a home for themselves and their progeny. But thereafter their intentions did change significantly. He did not go into detail, but the inferences are not difficult to draw. They separated in October 1993 … The logical inference is that they intended that his interest in Badger Hall Avenue should crystallise then. Just as he would have the sole benefit of any capital gain in his own home, Ms Jones would have the sole benefit of any capital gain in Badger Hall Avenue. In so far as the judge did not in so many words infer that this was their intention, it is clearly the intention which reasonable people would have had had they thought about it at the time. But in our view it is an intention which he both could and should have inferred from their conduct.

The nature of this exercise is very different. A speech act is an event in which meaning is inherent, it is communicative in nature. It is an attempt to mean something and to have some conventionally recognised effect or illocutionary force. The passage from *Jones v Kernott* above is the narrative of a life. It recites a few events taken from a possible set of innumerable events, and the selection of relevant events reflects more the purpose of the person constructing the narrative than any inherent rationale. It is an attempt to derive intention from a narrative, it is akin to the first instance judgment in *Barrett v Bem*.

The breadth of the concepts denoted by 'intention' enables us to speak about intention when reviewing the events of two or more people's lives as well as when we are reading a document. They intended to live together, to seek new partners, to do their best for the children. The common intention constructive trust has always

---

[56] *Shah v Shah* [2010] EWCA 1408 [13].
[57] *Jones v Kernott* [2011] UKSC 53, [2012] 1 AC 776 [48] per Walker and Hale.

been a pantomime horse: half an express trust that needs to be constructive because it does not respect section 53(1)(b) Law of Property Act 1925; half judicial remedy to alleviate unjust outcomes upon the break-up of non-matrimonial relationships. A speech act analysis drives us to drop the pretence that there is one animal on stage, by removing the costume stitched together from different types of intention.

Where there is a speech act then there can be a disposition of the equitable interest. The effects of the speech act can be construed from the words expressed and other actions taken in the context in which they took place. The intention sought would be that of the co-owners. Where there is no speech act then the law might impose a distribution upon the parties. In so doing the judges will try to respect what they feel the parties would think fair. The necessity for a speech act marks the difference between disposition and distribution. In so doing it gives a more useful distinction than a distinction between an inferred and an imputed intention.

16

Constitutional Land Law: Mexfield and the 40-Shilling Freehold

JUANITA ROCHE*

I. INTRODUCTION

I N *MEXFIELD HOUSING* Cooperative Ltd v Berrisford,[1] the UK Supreme Court accepted the submission that there was an ancient rule of common law that had been forgotten for nearly a century yet remained binding. The alleged rule was that tenancies stated to determine only on the occurrence of an uncertain event must be deemed, 'automatically', to be tenancies for life, subject to earlier determination on that event; the rule applied no matter what, on construing the relevant agreement, the parties could reasonably be held to have intended.[2] This rule was said to have been stated in Bracton in the thirteenth century but most clearly by Littleton in the fifteenth and Coke's commentary on Littleton in the seventeenth century, and to have remained good law down to 1925; the court relied particularly on one nineteenth-century textbook, one textbook from 1920, and two nineteenth-century cases.[3]

Against the existence of such a rule, the Supreme Court had before it *Zimbler v Abrahams*.[4] In *Zimbler*, the Court of Appeal held, in 1903, that a particular tenancy agreement expressed to be terminable only on the occurrence of an uncertain event was an agreement for a determinable life tenancy, on ordinary principles of interpretation of that agreement. The Supreme Court in *Mexfield* said that *Zimbler*'s ratio was 'wrong', solely because *Zimbler* did not apply (nor mention) the alleged ancient rule.[5]

---

* Lecturer in Property Law, University of Manchester. I am grateful to Martin Dixon, Stuart Jones, John Mee, and Matthew Harding for comments on earlier drafts, and to the anonymous referees; all faults remain my own.

[1] *Mexfield Housing Cooperative Ltd v Berrisford* [2011] UKSC 52, [2012] 1 AC 955. *Mexfield* is generally viewed as being about the alleged rule that a lease must have a fixed maximum term. This paper will not deal with that aspect, for which see, eg J Roche, 'The Madwoman in the Attic: Freeing Landlord-Tenant Law' [2011] *Conveyancer and Property Lawyer* 444, KFK Low, 'Certainty of Terms and Leases: Curiouser and Curiouser' [2012] *MLR* 401.

[2] *Mexfield* (n 1) eg 958F, [44], [93], [117].

[3] Ibid [39]–[41]; the judgments were *Doe d Warner v Brown* (1807) 8 East 165 and *Re Carne's Settled Estates* [1899] 1 Ch 324.

[4] *Zimbler v Abrahams* [1903] 1 KB 577.

[5] *Mexfield* (n 1) [44].

However, neither the textbooks nor the judgments relied on by the Supreme Court actually support the alleged rule, which I will call 'the *Mexfield* rule'. In particular, in neither of the two judgments relied on was the *Mexfield* rule part of the ratio, nor in either case was there a record of any submissions putting forward such a rule. This raises an obvious question: had the *Mexfield* rule ever been relied on as ratio, or even asserted in submissions, in any case?

The answer appears to be no—except that something similar to the *Mexfield* rule emerges in disputes about qualification for the vote between 1832 and 1884. Further, this proposal of something like the *Mexfield* rule, and its popularisation as an argument, were associated particularly with one individual; and, as soon as the court had the chance to consider the proposed rule, the court rejected it, consistently, and adopted as ratio the same approach as in *Zimbler*.

Analysing this incident leads us into a largely unexplored part of the history of land law.[6] It is widely known that, down to the twentieth century, there were property qualifications for the vote in England. There were actually also property qualifications for many other forms of participation in the state, from jury service to being a tax commissioner; and these were overwhelmingly qualifications in terms of interests in land. The relationship between possession of particular sorts of interests in land and the constitution of the state ended, in historical terms, only recently—its last vestige, the property requirement for jury service, was not swept away until 1972.[7] As late as 1888, Maitland, in his lectures on the constitutional history of England, said that 'we [must] begin our survey of public law by examining' land law, as 'even now it is impossible for us fully to understand our modern public law unless we know something of our law of property'.[8] However, even by 1888, this constitutional role of land law 'seem[ed] strange',[9] and Maitland's focus on the medieval and early-modern periods foreshadowed a modern assumption that any relationship between land law and the state, other than the one-way traffic of statute affecting land law, was confined to a very distant past. In fact, as will be seen, land law and the state had their most direct and reciprocal engagement in the nineteenth century.

I use the term 'constitutional land law' primarily in a very simple sense: to refer to those aspects of land law which for centuries were literally part of the constitution—part of how the state was constituted—in that they determined who could formally participate in the state. However, the persistence of this simple practical relationship over centuries seems likely to have generated a more complex relationship between ideas of the constitution and doctrinal land law.[10] This chapter is primarily concerned with solving one aspect of the puzzle of *Mexfield*, but the solution reveals clear resonances between the nineteenth-century legal argument over the *Mexfield* rule's precursor and contemporaneous ideas of the constitution.

---

[6] *Cf* the dearth of research on the law on electoral process: C Morris, *Parliamentary Elections, Representation and the Law* (Oxford, Hart Publishing, 2012) 2.

[7] Criminal Justice Act 1972, s 25; *cf* JH Baker, *The Oxford History of the Laws of England*, vol VI: 1483–1558(Oxford, Oxford University Press, 2003) 353.

[8] FW Maitland, *The Constitutional History of England* (Cambridge, Cambridge University Press, 1908) 23.

[9] Ibid.

[10] *Cf* on the genuine and subtle interaction between legal and political ideas, M Lobban, 'The Politics of English Law in the Nineteenth Century' in P Brand and J Getzler (eds), *Judges and Judging in the History of the Common Law and Civil Law* (Cambridge, Cambridge University Press, 2012) 102–37.

Section II outlines the system of property qualifications for the vote from 1430 to 1884, two views of the justification for property qualifications, and the procedure by which disputes concerning these qualifications were decided. In section III, the 'Littleton rule'—the rule the Supreme Court in *Mexfield* thought it was applying—is explained, as is a particular problem for that rule in relation to property qualifications for the vote. Section IV introduces James Manning and places him in the legal and political world of the time; and section V describes his proposed variation of the Littleton rule in the context of property qualifications, and how he promoted his argument. The sixth section describes the court's response, in a series of cases from 1844 to 1879, against the backdrop of controversy over franchise reform and two different views of the nature of the constitution. Finally, I propose one answer and two questions.

II. PROPERTY QUALIFICATIONS AND PROCEDURE TO 1884

The history of qualifications for the parliamentary franchise in the UK is far more complex than most people realise: it was only the Representation of the People Act 1948 which finally produced a relatively simple system of adult suffrage, by ending plural votes for university graduates and occupiers of business premises.[11]

But, in crude terms, and considering only England and Wales and, for the moment, the period before 1832, there were three different types of parliamentary franchise. From 1603, the universities of Cambridge and Oxford each elected their own members of parliament, and all MAs of each university could vote.[12] Then there were the boroughs, towns and cities which had been made parliamentary constituencies in past centuries; the borough franchise was enormously varied. Finally, there were the counties. The county franchise had been formally uniform since 1430: due to concerns about corruption and disorder in county elections, the vote was restricted by statute to those with a freehold interest in land of a yearly value of 40 shillings or more.[13] This was even in 1430 a modest value threshold[14] and became ever lower in real terms as it was never revised: at least by the seventeenth century 'those at the bottom end of the scale would be cottagers or labourers'.[15]

The petition on which the statute of 1430 was based described those to be excluded from the franchise as '*de null valu*'—translated as 'without property', but literally 'of no value';[16] this points toward one tradition of thinking about property qualifications, described as late as 1885 as being 'the modern theory, that Property as such …

---

[11] C Turpin and A Tomkins, *British Government and the Constitution*, 7th edn (Cambridge, Cambridge University Press, 2011) 51; T Oppermann, 'Universitätsvertretung im britischen Unterhaus 1603–1950' (1957) 113 *Zeitschrift für die gesamte Staatswissenschaft* 314.

[12] A Thrush, 'Cambridge University' in A Thrush and JP Ferris (eds), *The History of Parliament: The House of Commons 1604–29*, vol 2 (Cambridge, Cambridge University Press, 2010).

[13] See generally, SJ Payling, 'County Parliamentary Elections in Fifteenth-Century England' (1999) 18 *Parliamentary History* 237.

[14] Ibid, 244.

[15] D Hirst, 'The Seventeenth-Century Freeholder and the Statistician: A Case of Terminological Confusion' (1976) 29 *Economic History Review* 306, 310.

[16] Payling (n 13) 244.

is entitled to representation.'[17] But there was another strand of thought, as far back as the fourteenth century, which emphasised the elector's duty to vote for a member of the House of Commons on behalf of the community as a whole, as opposed to the Lords, each of whom, in the words of a fourteenth-century source, 'comes for his own individual self to parliament'.[18] In this tradition, as Blackstone influentially put it, 'The true reason of requiring any qualification, with regard to property, in voters, is to exclude' those whose situation was such that they could 'have no will of their own', who would be unable to resist pressure from the 'great' and the 'wealthy' to vote in those individuals' interests. At least in the existing state of society, it was necessary that those who 'are under the immediate dominion of others ... are excluded from voting, in order to set other individuals, whose wills may be supposed independent, more thoroughly upon a level with each other.'[19]

It was always clear that a freehold interest in land could mean many more things than a fee simple; a huge range of interests were capable of being freeholds.[20] Saliently, life tenancies were always understood to be freeholds. On the other hand, studies of actual constituencies show a 'widespread lack of clarity' as to what exactly constituted a freehold; in practice, the question of whether or not someone had a freehold interest in land, such as to qualify him for the vote, seems to have been primarily a matter of local understandings.[21]

The main reason for this lack of clarity was that, down to 1832, disputes as to a voter's qualification could only be decided after a contested election and could not be decided in the ordinary courts.[22] For much of English history and large parts of the country, uncontested elections were the norm.[23] It was widely believed that there ought to be informal assessment and agreement as to who should represent the constituency, such that a contested election represented a failure—even, in an early nineteenth-century opinion, a manifestation of 'Original Sin'.[24]

If there were a contested election, people who believed themselves entitled to vote just turned up at the polls. If some were turned away, or some who were believed not to be qualified actually voted, this could only be challenged by a petition to Parliament challenging the result of the election, and the petition would be decided by a committee of the House of Commons.[25] These committees did not consider

---

[17] WR Anson, 'The Reform Bill' (1885) 1 *LQR* 25, 27.

[18] Payling (n 13) 238–40.

[19] W Blackstone, *Commentaries on the Laws of England*, Bk 1 (Oxford, Clarendon Press, 1765) 165; cf W Treanor, 'The Original Understanding of the Takings Clause and the Political Process' (1995) 95 *Columbia Law Review* 782, 818–55.

[20] FSP Wolferstan, *Rogers on Elections, Election Committees, and Registration*, 10th edn (London, Stevens & Sons, 1865) 21–27.

[21] D Hirst, *The Representative of the People? Voters and Voting in England under the Early Stuarts* (Cambridge, Cambridge University Press, 1975) 7, 34–42.

[22] See generally, C Morris, 'From "Arms, Malice, and Menacing" to the Courts: Disputed Elections and the Reform of the Election Petitions System' [2012] *Legal Studies* 226.

[23] D Beales, 'The Electorate before and after 1832: The Right to Vote, and the Opportunity' (1992) 11 *Parliamentary History* 139; P Salmon, *Electoral Reform at Work: Local Politics and National Parties, 1832–41* (Woodbridge, Boydell Press, 2002) 124, fn 28.

[24] Quoted in F O'Gorman, *Voters, Patrons, and Parties* (Oxford, Clarendon Press, 1989) 113.

[25] For details of the election–petition system down to 1868, see Morris, 'From "Arms, Malice, and Menacing"' (n 22) 232–40.

themselves bound by precedent and often lacked legal expertise; put more bluntly, by an early nineteenth-century commentator, 'nine-tenths of the House of Commons are hopelessly and incurably incompetent to the decisions of legal questions, and ... more than the suspicion of wilful partiality attaches to their judicial eccentricities.'[26] So the decisions on petitions as to whether a particular interest in land was a freehold were difficult to reconcile.

The First Reform Act, the Representation of the People Act 1832, famously expanded the franchise; in the counties, the main effect was that, for the first time, some tenants other than for life and some copyholders got the vote.[27] But the Act also introduced voter registration. Roughly, the process in the counties was that, every year, unless they were already registered and their qualification was unchanged, would-be voters had to submit a claim to be registered, including a brief description of the property and the interest in it by which they claimed to be qualified.[28] The draft lists would then be made public, and anyone could submit an objection to any name on the list. The burden of proof was then on the claimant to prove his qualification, before a new sort of judicial officer created by the Act, a 'revising barrister', who would hold hearings in the constituency.

Under the 1832 Act, appeals from revising barristers' decisions went to Parliament,[29] but the Parliamentary Voters Registration Act 1843 redirected these appeals to the Court of Common Pleas. Thus by 1844 there was a straightforward means to have disputes as to an individual's qualification, a mechanism to ensure that such disputes were decided by lawyers, and a route by which such disputes could enter the ordinary legal system—creating, for the first time, an opportunity to build up a consistent body of law.

Despite the fact that after 1832 a broader range of interests in land gave a qualification to vote in the counties, disputes about the nature of a freehold remained important due to the difference in qualifying values for different interests. Remember that 40 shillings equals £2. After 1832, in the counties, holders of leases other than for life got the vote only, depending on the length of the term, where the land had an annual value of £10 or more or the annual rent was £50 or more; the Second Reform Act, in 1867, made the value threshold for leases of 60 years or more £5 a year and introduced a qualification for occupiers of property with a rateable value of £12 or more.[30] By comparison, it has been estimated that a family on median income, in 1860, would if renting be paying a rent of around £8 per year.[31] Thus, at least down to the Third Reform Act, in 1884, there remained for many people an incentive to claim that their interests in land were freehold.[32] Further, there was a

---

[26] C Neate, 'A Few Parting Words to the Election Committee of 1838' quoted in (1838) 77(2) *The Jurist* 1 (anonymous and untitled review).

[27] See Salmon (n 23) 253–54; Anson (n 17).

[28] For this and what follows on the registration process under the 1832 Act, see Salmon (n 23) 20–21, 31–32.

[29] By s 60 of the Act: ibid 30, fn 84.

[30] Anson (n 17) 27–29.

[31] S Berlinski and T Dewan, 'Did the Extension of the Franchise Increase the Liberal Vote in Victorian Britain?' (2010) *LSE Political Science and Political Economy Working Paper No 16* and Table 2 www.lse.ac.uk/government/research/resgroups/PSPE/pdf/PSPE_WP1_10.pdf (accessed 9 March 2014).

[32] *Cf* Wolferstan (n 20) 9.

long-established rule that receipt of alms within a particular period before an election would disqualify one from voting—except for freeholders; and this rule was incorporated in the 1832 Act.[33]

III. THE LITTLETON RULE TO 1832

How does all of this relate to the *Mexfield* rule? In the judgments in *Mexfield*, the alleged rule is said to be stated in Littleton, above all Coke's commentary on Littleton at paragraph 42a ('Co Litt 42a').[34] But, as Low pointed out, the rule as stated in *Mexfield* omits a crucial part of the rule as stated in Littleton and Coke ('the Littleton rule'): a tenancy expressed to determine only on the occurrence of an uncertain event was deemed to be a determinable life tenancy, and therefore a freehold, only if livery of seisin or a deed had been used.[35]

Livery of seisin is mentioned only once by the Supreme Court in *Mexfield* and is treated as insignificant, a formalities requirement which was not part of the core Littleton rule.[36] On the contrary, the requirement was a necessary part of the rule, because livery of seisin demonstrated the intention to create a freehold.[37] To understand that intention, we must return to the fact that, before 1925, it could include the intention to create a lease for life (or lives). For us, an intention to create a freehold necessarily excludes any intention to create a lease, because, for us, the conceptual divide between freehold and leasehold is absolute; in the past, it was perfectly possible to speak of a 'freehold lease'.[38] Life tenancies pre-dated both the fee simple and the term of years, and the law's treatment of them was rooted in 'memory of a time when all the military fiefs had been little more than life tenancies'.[39]

The consequence of this history was that the opposite of a freehold was a tenancy at will. Maitland describes the concept of freehold as arising from the contrast with unfree, or villein, tenure: a tenant whose obligations were not clearly specified was unfree, because he was subject to the will of his lord.[40] This fundamental distinction was incorporated in the Littleton rule: if a tenancy or other interest was expressed to terminate only on the occurrence of an uncertain event and there was no livery of seisin nor deed, there was merely a tenancy or interest at will.[41] This is, again, a feature of the Littleton rule which the Supreme Court in *Mexfield* mentions only once and in passing;[42] yet it is this 'flip side' of the Littleton rule which turns out to determine the course of the rule's evolution.

---

[33] Ibid, 47, 179–80.
[34] *Mexfield* (n 1) 958E, [25], [39]–[40], [44], [48].
[35] Low (n 1) 406.
[36] *Mexfield* (n 1) [25], [41], [93].
[37] Cf Low (n 1) 406–07.
[38] eg *Philpotts v James* (1784) 3 Doug 425. This is, with respect, where Low falls into error, eg ibid.
[39] AWB Simpson, *A History of the Land Law*, 2nd edn (Oxford, Clarendon Press, 1986) 73, cf 49–51, 70–71.
[40] Maitland (n 8) 35–36.
[41] eg *The Bishop of Bath's Case* (1605) 6 Co Rep 34b, 35b.
[42] *Mexfield* (n 1) [25].

Littleton's *Tenures* was first published in 1481.[43] At that time livery of seisin was required in order to grant or convey a corporeal freehold and, conversely, had no other use or meaning. It was an 'overt ceremony' consisting of acts and words done and said in a particular place.[44] If this ceremony was used, demonstrating the intention to create a freehold, but the grantor did not make clear whether his intention was to grant a fee simple, a fee tail, or a life tenancy—the three types of freehold—it was reasonable to assume an intention to grant the smallest freehold, a tenancy for the life of the grantee. So, if there was livery of seisin but the grantor said only that the grant would end on the occurrence of an uncertain event, the law assumed the intention to grant a tenancy for life, determinable on the event.

This sounds like a simple, 'certain' rule, and it would have been, if there had been a fixed form of livery of seisin; but there was not. The matter was simple enough if one party said to the other, 'Here I deliver you seisin and possession of this house'; but what if the words said were 'Enter into this house, and God give you joy of it'?[45] These and other ambiguous words and acts were in particular cases held to constitute livery of seisin. This was a jury question, and in such cases the jury will have had to decide, by interpretation in all the circumstances, whether there had been an intention to grant a freehold, in order to decide whether there had been livery of seisin;[46] scratch the surface, and livery of seisin turns out to be less a formalities requirement in the modern sense than shorthand for a finding of 'objective intention'.

As for incorporeal freeholds, it had always been possible to grant or convey these by deed, and the law eventually evolved to allow the same for corporeal freeholds.[47] Use of a deed made it easy to apply the Littleton rule, given the rule's flip side: one can just about imagine saying 'Enter into this house, and God give you joy of it' even to an intended tenant at will, but no one would use a deed to create a tenancy at will.

However, a difficulty for the Littleton rule arose when an 'equitable freehold' became a qualification for the vote. By the Parliamentary Elections Act 1695, trustees and mortgagees were disqualified from voting unless they were 'in actual possession or receipt of the rents and profits', and, conversely, 'the mortgagor or cestui que trust in possession ... may vote ... notwithstanding such mortgage or trust'; this wording was essentially repeated as section 23 of the 1832 Act.[48]

This was unproblematic where, for example, the terms of a trust expressly gave a beneficiary a life tenancy, even if determinable: that was plainly the equitable equivalent of a legal freehold. But, if the terms of the trust created an interest expressed only to terminate on an uncertain event, it was unclear whether one could apply the Littleton rule at all or, if so, how—given that, on the face of it, the rule appeared to require the formalities necessary to create a legal freehold. There were two obvious possibilities. One was to convert the Littleton rule into the *Mexfield* rule, at least for trusts: where the interest was expressed to terminate only on an uncertain event, it

---

[43] JH Baker, 'Littleton, Sir Thomas (d 1481)' *Oxford Dictionary of National Biography* (2007) www.oxforddnb.com/view/article/16787 (accessed 22 February 2014).

[44] W Sheppard, *The Touchstone of Common Assurances*, vol 1, 8th edn (London, Samuel Brooke, 1826) 209.

[45] Ibid, 214.

[46] Ibid, 209.

[47] Co Litt 42a; Sheppard (n 44) 213; Low (n 1) 406.

[48] Wolferstan (n 20) 31.

could be deemed to be a determinable life interest, with no further requirement—in particular, no matter what the parties could reasonably be held to have intended. Alternatively, one could expose and use the underlying principle of the Littleton rule, interpreting the documents creating the interest to decide the intention; and one could do that in a more or a less restrictive way, either insisting on a clear intention to create a determinable life interest or merely requiring that there be no clear intention that the interest be terminable at the grantor's will.

The question was eventually resolved in favour of the second option, and in its less restrictive version—but only through a debate started by James Manning, who proposed and promoted an extreme version of the first option, purportedly backed by a formidable array of ancient sources.

IV. JAMES MANNING

In order to understand why Manning proposed the sort of rule he did, and how he came to be in a position to promote it so effectively, we need to consider his background, and what it meant in terms of his place in legal society and political culture.

Manning was born in 1781, the son of a Unitarian minister in Exeter; he was called to the Bar at Lincoln's Inn in 1817, but had already 'acquired an early familiarity with history, antiquities, and European languages.'[49] Pollock described Manning as the 'one man' who more than any other 'revived the study of' the Year Books, the closest thing we have to case reports before the mid-sixteenth century.[50] By 1821, Manning's historical expertise was sufficiently well known for the Inner Temple to commission him, and pay him handsomely, to translate a number of their manuscript Year Books from medieval 'law French' into English.[51]

At the same time, he rapidly established himself as a barrister: by 1820, he was assisting Henry Brougham in the defence of Queen Caroline, arguably the most high-profile political event of the early nineteenth century.[52] He then became a serjeant[53] and sat as a Recorder for many years.[54] He also became a member of two influential organisations set up by Brougham, the Society for the Diffusion of Useful Knowledge[55] and the Law Amendment Society.[56] Finally, from 1828 to 1857,

---

[49] GC Boase, rev E Metcalfe, 'Manning, James (1781–1866)'*Oxford Dictionary of National Biography* (2004) www.oxforddnb.com/view/article/17971(accessed 22 February 2014).

[50] F Pollock, 'Introduction' in WC Bolland, *The Year Books* (Cambridge, Cambridge University Press, 1921) ix.

[51] Bolland (n 50) 47.

[52] Boase rev Metcalfe (n 49); B Hilton, *A Mad, Bad, and Dangerous People? England 1783–1846* (Oxford, Clarendon Press, 2006) 269.

[53] See W Cornish et al, *The Oxford History of the Laws of England*, vol XI, 1820–1914 (Oxford, Oxford University Press, 2010) 1055–57.

[54] Boase rev Metcalfe (n 49).

[55] R Ashton, 'Society for the Diffusion of Useful Knowledge (Act 1826–46)' *Oxford Dictionary of National Biography* (2013) www.oxforddnb.com/view/theme/59807 (accessed 22 February 2014). For a list of members of the Society's committee, see an anonymous publication of the Society, *The Rights of Industry: Addressed to the Working-Men of the United Kingdom* (London, Charles Knight, 1831) 2.

[56] G Sutherland, 'Manning, (Elizabeth) Adelaide (1828–1905)' *Oxford Dictionary of National Biography* (2007) www.oxforddnb.com/view/article/48451(accessed 22 February 2014);L Goldman, *Science, Reform, and Politics in Victorian Britain: The Social Science Association, 1857–86* (Cambridge, Cambridge University Press, 2002) 33–58.

Manning was the editor of three series of case reports in succession;[57] as was not uncommon in this period, his reports often have footnotes containing commentary.

So, by 1832, Manning was well regarded as a legal historian and barrister, and was publishing his own views on the law. Further, although he does not appear to have engaged in directly party-political activity, his individual and social connections are characteristic of the history of Liberalism.[58] Then, in 1832, he became one of the first revising barristers.[59]

V. THE MANNING RULE

It seems that Manning became interested in the Littleton rule sometime between 1832 and 1838, and that his proposed variation of it first appeared in print in 1838, in a law journal called *The Jurist*.

A. *The Jurist* (1838)

By way of introduction, the journal said only, 'The following is a Decision by Mr Manning at the last Revision for South Hants.'[60] The decision regarded an objection to the registration of George Silly (*sic*), whose qualification was described as 'minister for life of the freehold independent chapel.'[61] Manning begins by saying that Mr Silly was appointed by 'the ordinary mode':

> [B]y a letter of invitation ... [which was,] as usual, wholly silent as to the period during which this gentleman's ministry was to be exercised ... In these cases I have been in the habit of inquiring whether, at the time of the invitation, the parties ... understood the engagement to be for life ... Upon further consideration, however, I think that such an inquiry is as unnecessary as it is commonly found to be unsatisfactory; and I am of opinion, that wherever ... property is held upon trust to pay over the rents and profits to the minister, the latter is entitled to be registered as a voter.[62]

It is thus obvious that Manning had dealt with a number of similar cases before as a revising barrister, and had been asking his own questions on the basis of his own legal analysis, and that his initial reflex had been an analysis focused on intention, albeit subjective intention.

It was 'necessary to examine the claim upon general legal principles' because 'the decisions of committees of the House of Commons which bear upon this point

---

[57] GC Boase, 'Manning, James' in S Lee (ed), *Dictionary of National Biography*, vol 36 (London, Smith Elder & Co, 1893) 69.

[58] See nn 55 and 56 above; and Hilton (n 52) eg index entries for Unitarianism, Brougham, Caroline and the SDUK.

[59] Anon, 'Review: *Notes of Proceedings in Courts of Revision held in October and November 1832, before James Manning, Esquire, Revising Barrister. And the Reform Act, with Explanatory Remarks. By William M Manning*' (1833) 5 *The Legal Observer* 217.

[60] Anon, 'Elective Franchise of Dissenting Ministers' (1838) 2 *The Jurist* 459, 459 col 1.

[61] Ibid.

[62] Ibid.

are not uniform, nor are the grounds of those decisions always very intelligible.'[63] Manning notes that, by statute, both legal and equitable freehold interests in land can confer the vote. He then asserts that, if a minister had an interest in land conveyed to him for so long as he remained minister, he would have an estate for life and therefore a legal freehold 'even if it had been expressly stipulated that the minister should be removable—at the will of … the church'.[64] To support this last, rather startling, assertion, Manning puts together, on the one hand, Co Litt 42a and a number of similar sources[65]—including some cited in *Mexfield* 173 years later, but not the one judgment relied on in *Mexfield* which would have been available to him[66]— and, on the other hand, a statement by Brudnell CJ in the Year Books saying that a lease 'at the will of the lessor … is a lease for life.'[67]

As Manning must have known from translating them, the Year Books do not contain reports of judgments; they consist of notes of discussion during hearings. JH Baker emphasised that we cannot 'confidently tell which of the jotted remarks were intended or thought to lay down the law, which merely to provoke a response, or even, perhaps, calculated to make things sufficiently unclear to alarm the parties into a compromise'.[68] During a hearing, judges might even advance an argument for intellectual entertainment, or at least be suspected of it—in a hearing in 1522, Broke J is recorded as saying to Brudenell (Manning's 'Brudnell') CJ, 'truly you have made a good case out of this, but I think you have been arguing mainly for your pleasure'.[69] Further, individual copies of the Year Books are notoriously unreliable: Baker quotes Maitland lamenting 'the hopeless mass of corruption that passes as a text of the year books'.[70] Nonetheless, Manning presents statements from the Year Books as though they were said as ratio and in a reliable transcript of judgment.

Manning mentions that the Littleton rule turns a tenancy expressed to determine solely on the occurrence of an uncertain event into a tenancy for life only 'if livery be made' or a deed is used, and that otherwise the estate or interest is only 'at will'; but he asserts that the trustee's legal seisin of the trust property is per se 'the equitable seisin' of the beneficiary in his interest under the trust.[71] He then repeats his proposed rule:

> [A] dissenting minister has an equitable freehold … in all those cases in which the legal freehold is held in trust, to pay the rents to the minister, such equitable freehold being— defeasible, if the appointment be held subject to a power of dismissal—absolute, if it be not so subject; the interest being, in either case, sufficient to support the elective franchise.[72]

Manning accepts that his rule might be 'considered by some persons' to be 'negatived' by two comparatively recent judgments, *Doe d Jones v Jones*[73] and *Doe d*

---

[63] Ibid.
[64] Ibid.
[65] Ibid.
[66] *Doe d Warner v Browne* (1807) 8 East 165; see *Mexfield* (n 1) [29]–[30] and [41].
[67] Anon, 'Elective Franchise of Dissenting Ministers' (n 60) 459, col 2.
[68] JH Baker, 'Why the History of English Law Has Not Been Finished' [2000] *CLJ* 62, 67.
[69] *Gervys v Cooke* (1522), in JH Baker (ed), *Year Books of Henry VIII, 12–14 Henry VIII 1520–23* (119 Selden Society, 2002) 122. Some barristers may feel that little has changed.
[70] Quoted in Baker, 'Why the History of English Law Has Not Been Finished' (n 68) 64.
[71] Anon, 'Elective Franchise of Dissenting Ministers' (n 60) 459, cols 1–2.
[72] Ibid, 460, col 1.
[73] *Doe d Jones v Jones* (1830) 10 Barn & Cress 718.

Nicholl v M'Kaeg.[74] These held that 'the trustees of ... lands of which they are seised in trust for the support of the minister' could evict the minister 'upon a simple demand of possession, without any notice to quit'.[75] Manning's response is that even if, in law, there is a tenancy at will, there is still an equitable freehold for electoral purposes.[76]

This first version of Manning's proposed rule is therefore much narrower than the *Mexfield* rule in applying only where there is an express trust. But it seems in another sense much broader: the Supreme Court in *Mexfield* did not go so far as to say that its rule would convert into a determinable life tenancy even a tenancy expressly terminable at the mere will of the landlord. Then again, in modern English law, it is hard to imagine any practical difference between a tenancy at will and a tenancy for life subject to determination at the landlord's will. A difference could however arise in the context of nineteenth-century property qualifications.

Finally, Manning's decision in the case before him is illuminating:

> [T]he building appears to be the private property of fourteen persons, who hold it subject to no trust, and who allow it to be used as a place of worship, merely because, and so long as, they think it proper to do so ... [T]herefore, the respondent ... has no estate or interest, legal or equitable, in the chapel or building in respect of which he has claimed. His name must, therefore, be expunged.[77]

Manning's lengthy reasoning and scholarship were therefore unnecessary to his decision; he plainly wanted to get his proposed rule into the public domain for its own sake.

B. *Hayes on Conveyancing* (1840)

Two years later, Manning's proposed rule was published in a popular land-law textbook, 'Hayes on Conveyancing'. In the fifth edition, Hayes inserted nearly the whole of Manning's 1838 judgment as a footnote running to nearly five pages.[78] Hayes introduces it by saying, 'The following extract from a decision by Mr Manning (Recorder of Oxford, and Revising Barrister for South Hants) ... will throw some light upon the legal character and nature of *freehold* interests.'[79]

What follows has not, however, simply been extracted from *The Jurist*. There are more cases cited; in particular, a second statement in the Year Books, from Brian CJ, is quoted as supporting the statement by Brudnell CJ.[80] There is the same assertion as in the *Jurist* version, that '[i]n the case of equitable interests, the legal seisin of the trustee, whether acquired by livery or otherwise, is the equitable seisin of the *cestui que trust*', but the Hayes version inserts a reference, 'Co Litt 42, note 10.'[81]

---

[74] *Doe d Nicholl v M'Kaeg* (1830) 10 Barn & Cress 724; Anon, 'Elective Franchise of Dissenting Ministers' (n 60) 460, col 1.
[75] Anon, 'Elective Franchise of Dissenting Ministers' (n 60) 460, col 1.
[76] Ibid.
[77] Ibid, 460, col 2.
[78] W Hayes, *An Introduction to Conveyancing*, vol 2, 5th edn (London, S Sweet, 1840) 38–43.
[79] Ibid, 38.
[80] Ibid, 40.
[81] Ibid, 39–40.

The Hayes version then puts the proposed rule in capitals for emphasis.[82] Finally, the Hayes version both starts and ends by citing Littleton and Coke on Littleton;[83] and, as already noted, Hayes tells his general land-law readers that this decision illuminates the nature of freehold interests generally, not only for electoral purposes.

C. *Wynne v Wynne* (1840)

Later the same year, Manning published this argument in his own series of case reports, albeit in much shorter form, in his report of *Wynne v Wynne*.[84] This was not a registration case but rather involved married women's property. As with the 1838 judgment, it was not necessary to have any discussion of the Littleton rule or Manning's variation: the dispute concerned Sarah Wynne's rent-charge, which under the terms of the relevant trust was expressly for life unless a particular event happened (which was not the mere will of the trustees).[85] Manning nonetheless makes the argument in the case report in a footnote.

As already noted, in the usual practical sense of resisting eviction, there would be no point in a rule converting a tenancy at will to a tenancy for life determinable at the grantor's will. In Manning's time, though, there would be a point, for a man, in terms of his ability to vote and, for a married woman, in terms of her control over property. Down to the late nineteenth century, a married woman's personal property became, in law, her husband's absolutely, whereas her real property vested in her and her husband jointly during the marriage. A life interest, even if determinable, was a freehold, and freeholds were classically real property, whereas leaseholds, let alone tenancies at will, were and technically still are personal property.[86]

For current purposes, what is salient is that, in his footnote to *Wynne*, Manning appears to assert the *Mexfield* rule per se: 'any interest in land of uncertain duration (though not expressed to be for life), determinable by matter subsequent ... constitutes a freehold for life',[87] with no mention of any difference between legal and equitable interests. He then gives references to 12 textbooks—including Co Litt 42a, and the volume and page in Hayes containing Manning's own judgment—and 25 cases, largely from the Year Books.

VI. THE COURT'S RESPONSE

When, after the 1843 Act, disputes concerning property qualifications for the vote finally came to court, Manning's argument was picked up and used by other barristers. Understanding the court's response requires some further historical context.

---

[82] Ibid, 42.

[83] Ibid 43, citing Littleton, sect 350, and Co Litt 214b, 218a.

[84] *Wynne v Wynne* (1840) 2 M&G 8.

[85] Ibid, 9.

[86] JH Baker, *An Introduction to English Legal History*, 4th edn (Butterworths, 2002) 485; S Bridge, M Dixon, and C Harpum, *Megarry & Wade: The Law of Real Property*, 8th edn (London, Sweet & Maxwell, 2012) para 1-011.

[87] *Wynne* (n 84) 19.

First, registration disputes had become fiercely party-political. After 1832, local party organisations were rapidly established to get party supporters or potential supporters to register—and to lodge objections to actual or suspected opponents;[88] in due course, the political 'parties themselves took on responsibility for defending the votes of their own supporters' against objections.[89] Every judge hearing registration appeals must have been aware of this background. Moreover, from the 1840s down to 1867, there was constant controversy over further extension of the franchise—but controversy which was obsessed with details. Most MPs agreed that there should be further reform, but there was ever-increasing awareness that the details of how the franchise was extended could have consequences which were not immediately obvious and might be enormous.[90] Again, judges must have been aware of the risks involved in destabilising the fundamental land-law terms of this party-political debate and of the existing franchise.

At the same time, judges were, consciously or unconsciously, working within a framework of ideas in which there were not only, as described earlier, two views of the purpose of property qualifications but also more broadly two different views of the constitution. Crudely summarising one aspect of a complex and extensive literature: in one view, what made the British constitution 'the "most perfect" ever devised'[91] was that it was 'organic' and had always evolved; in another, there was an ancient 'true' constitution which had been suppressed. To the extent that these views mapped onto party politics at all, it was radicals who were most likely to appeal to the idea of reviving an ancient constitution.[92]

On 21 November 1844, the Court of Common Pleas handed down two decisions which would go on to be commonly cited in later registration appeals. The same judges—Tindal CJ and Coltman, Maule, and Erle JJ—heard both appeals, and both concerned similar facts. Yet, in *Davis v Waddington*,[93] the would-be voters lost, whereas in *Simpson v Wilkinson*[94] the would-be voters won.

A. *Davis v Waddington* (1844)

In *Davis*, the 25 appellants were inhabitants of Jesus Hospital—what we would call an almshouse—founded in 1597 to provide for 'poor and infirm men'.[95] Its charter, in Latin, gave its governors the power 'to elect' but also to 'expel' its principal or

---

[88] Salmon (n 23) 11, 27–29, 34, 40.

[89] Ibid, 34.

[90] R Saunders, *Democracy and the Vote in British Politics, 1848–67* (Farnham, Ashgate, 2011) eg 7–9, 118–30.

[91] Ibid, 3.

[92] See, eg ibid 3–6; B Weinstein, '"Local Self-Government is True Socialism": Joshua Toulmin Smith, the State and Character Formation' [2008] *English Historical Review* 1193; DR Kelley, 'Historians and Lawyers' in G Stedman Jones and G Claeys (eds), *The Cambridge History of Nineteenth-Century Political Thought* (Cambridge, Cambridge University Press, 2011); J Greenberg and M Sechler, 'Constitutionalism Ancient and Early Modern: The Contributions of Roman Law, Canon Law, and English Common Law' [2013] *Cardozo Law Review* 1021; and, generally, J Vernon (ed), *Re-reading the Constitution* (Cambridge, Cambridge University Press, 1996).

[93] *Davis v Waddington* (1844) 7 M&G 37.

[94] *Simpson v Wilkinson* (1844) 7 M&G 50.

[95] *Davis* (n 93) 38.

any of its 24 inmates, who were to hold their positions in the hospital 'for the time being … as it shall seem to be convenient [*conveniens*] to' the governors.[96]

Despite these provisions, '[n]o instance is recorded of any principal or inmate having been expelled from the hospital'; new inmates were only appointed when an existing inmate died.[97] 'The principal has a house and garden within the hospital, and each inmate, on his appointment, is provided with a room and piece of ground, for his own separate use, of the value of more than 40s. per annum'.[98] All of them claimed the vote as freeholders; Mr Waddington had objected, on the grounds that 'the power of amotion by the governors … prevented [the principal and inmates] from acquiring any estate of freehold'; and the revising barrister had upheld the objection.[99]

Counsel for the appellants relied first on the construction of the charter, submitting that, in the Elizabethan period, the meaning of '*conveniens*' was such that the principal and inmates could only be evicted for misconduct. Therefore, counsel argued, this was 'an estate during good behaviour, [and thus] … equivalent to an estate for life … since it must be by [the grantee's] own act … that his estate can determine.'[100] Counsel for the respondent submitted simply that '[t]he inmates have not an estate for life' because '[t]hey may be removed by the governors whenever it shall seem convenient to them'. He added, significantly, 'They hold their situations upon the same tenure as the king's judges did before the Revolution, who were appointed *durante bene placito nostro* [during his Majesty's pleasure].'[101] In reply, counsel for the appellants fell back on Manning:

> At any rate, this is an interest of uncertain duration, and consequently it constitutes a tenancy for life. This rule is laid down as collected from the ancient authorities, in a note to *Wynne v. Wynne*; and is also to be found in Co. Litt. 42 a.[102]

The court dismissed the appeal, in short judgments. They relied solely on the construction of the charter, which made the principal and inmates 'subject to removal at the arbitrary discretion' of the governors. They dismissed the idea that such an interest could be deemed to be a tenancy for life without even mentioning, let alone discussing, Manning's note to *Wynne* or any of his sources, including Co Litt 42a.[103]

Manning's response was to insert a 2,400-word footnote to his report of *Davis*, drawing on material from his 1838 judgment and his note to *Wynne*. He asserted that the judgments in *Davis* contradicted a 'long and unbroken series of decisions' that even 'an absolute power … [of a grantor] to remove [a grantee] at pleasure' was not 'inconsistent with the existence of a freehold interest';[104] if an office or appointment under a trust carried with it an interest in land, that interest was a life interest even 'if the office or appointment was determinable … at the mere will of … the

---

[96] Ibid, 39.
[97] Ibid, 38.
[98] Ibid, 38.
[99] Ibid, 40–41.
[100] Ibid, 41–42.
[101] Ibid, 42–43.
[102] Ibid, 43.
[103] Ibid, 45.
[104] Ibid, 45, n 5.

trustee.'[105] The key steps and sources for the argument remained the same: first Co Litt 42a,[106] then the statements by Brudnell CJ[107] and Brian CJ,[108] and finally the assertion that livery or a deed is not necessary for an equitable freehold.[109]

B. *Simpson v Wilkinson* (1844)

In *Simpson*, an objection had been made to the registration of the inmates of Lord Burghley's Hospital, founded to provide for 'thirteen poor men' who had 'by sickness or any other impediment' become 'unable to get their livings'.[110] 'Each bedesman keeps the key of his room', and each room had an annual value of £4.[111] There was 'no trace of … any charter [or] deed' founding the hospital,[112] but there was a copy of what were thought to be its original rules, stated to be made by Lord Burghley. Reprinted apparently in full in the report, there was a long list of rules, some of them very odd, and a statement that inmates could be removed for breach, but no express statement either that the 'bedesmen' were appointed for life, or for a particular term, or that they were removable at anyone's will.[113] As in *Davis*, '[n]o person appointed … as a bedesman, has ever been known to be removed during his life.'[114] Lord Burghley's heirs, by this time Lord Exeter, appeared to remain the 'owner' of the hospital.[115]

The objection had been on a number of grounds, including '[t]hat if the claimants had any freehold estate,' it was 'only as members of a corporation aggregate'—it was settled law that, if a corporation aggregate held a qualifying interest, that did not confer a vote on the corporation's members.[116] The revising barrister had rejected all of these arguments, holding 'that, under the circumstances, a legal foundation might be presumed, not necessarily investing the claimants with a corporate character, and that they were respectively entitled to a separate freehold estate in their respective rooms.'[117]

Counsel for the appellant attempted to argue that either the hospital was a corporation aggregate, such that the bedesmen were unqualified to vote, or 'it is a mere gratuitous act on the part of Lord Exeter to continue the charity; and consequently the bedesmen have no rights conferred upon them.'[118] Counsel then argued that some of the rules for breach of which a bedesman could be removed were so 'very singular' as to be tantamount to a power to remove at will.[119] Finally, he tried to raise an additional objection, that providing these men with accommodation was in

---

[105] Ibid, 49.
[106] Ibid, 45–46.
[107] Ibid, 46.
[108] Ibid, 47.
[109] Ibid, 47–48.
[110] *Simpson* (n 94) 53, 56[10]–57[11].
[111] Ibid, 51.
[112] Ibid, 51–52.
[113] Ibid, 53–61.
[114] Ibid, 51.
[115] Ibid, 52, 53[1].
[116] Ibid, 52; Wolferstan (n 20) 29.
[117] *Simpson* (n 94) 53.
[118] Ibid, 62.
[119] Ibid, 63.

itself a giving of alms, such as to disqualify them from voting; but this submission was ended by Erle J saying, 'Was there ever a case in which an estate for life in lands, was considered to be alms?'[120]

Counsel for the respondents said only that the revising barrister's finding that the hospital was a foundation by royal licence rather than incorporation was 'an inference of fact … in respect of which there can be no appeal. He was then stopped by the court.'[121] The court swiftly and shortly dismissed the appeal. Maule J, whose judgment of seven sentences is the longest of the four, said: 'We may fairly presume that the hospital was endowed by a licence from the Crown … The only question in the case is, whether these bedesmen have an equitable estate. I think they have; as they are not liable to arbitrary amotion.'[122]

Manning's report of *Simpson* follows his report of *Davis* in the same volume, so there is only a short footnote: 'Upon the question, whether the existence of an arbitrary power determining the interest will derogate from the freehold character of such interest as a legal life estate, see [Brudnell CJ, Brian CJ, and] Co Litt. 42 a. As to equitable interests, vide ante [his note to *Davis*].'[123]

C. *Beeson v Burton* (1852)

In the next eight years, a number of judgments followed the pattern established by *Davis* and *Simpson*, with similar results on similar reasoning, taking no account of Manning's argument or his sources.[124] Those sources were finally addressed in *Beeson v Burton*.[125]

Before and after the 1832 Act, men with interests in property within a borough which would qualify them to vote in the surrounding county could vote in the county.[126] In the borough of Leicester, in 1845, a private Act of Parliament (8 & 9 Vict c 6) had made provisions for allotments. Under this Act, the resident freemen of Leicester elected deputies in whom the allotment land was vested on trust for the resident freemen. By section 17, the deputies had a power of sale, which, by section 22, was exercisable only with the consent of the majority of the resident freemen. There was no express provision that the allotments were to be held either for any particular term or for life subject to earlier termination; the Act said only, at section 8, that the allotments were:

> to be held respectively by each resident freeman desiring to become the occupier, and obtaining possession thereof, so long as he shall be willing to hold the same, and shall pay the annual rent, and conform to the orders and regulations to be made from time to time by the said deputies

with the deputies having a power of re-entry for non-payment of rent or other breach.[127]

---

[120]   Ibid, 63–64; *cf Fryer v Bodenham* (1869) LR 4 CP 529.
[121]   *Simpson* (n 94) 64.
[122]   Ibid, 65.
[123]   Ibid, 65, n 7.
[124]   Eg *Ashmore v Lees* (1845) 2 CB 31; *Burton v Brooks* (1851) 11 CB 41.
[125]   *Beeson v Burton* (1852) 12 CB 647.
[126]   Wolferstan (n 20) 45–46.
[127]   *Beeson* (n 125) 648, *cf* 647–49.

Mr Burton and 28 others held allotments with a value above 40s per annum and had registered to vote in Leicestershire as freeholders; Mr Beeson had objected, the revising barrister had dismissed the objections, and Mr Beeson appealed.[128]

Counsel for the appellant pointed out that the revising barrister had relied on *Davis* and *Simpson*, and that the ratio of *Davis* was that the claimants in that case were 'not entitled to be registered as freeholders' because 'the trustees had power to remove the inmates at their pleasure.' He submitted that similarly, in the present case, the deputies' power of sale enabled them to terminate the respondents' interests, so the respondents had only a 'tenancy at will' and could not have a freehold: 'It is of the very essence of a freehold, that it should be held without being subject to the will of anybody.'[129]

Counsel for the respondents first submitted that 'the 11th section [of the Act] obviously contemplates the death of the occupier as the ordinary determination of his estate'; that section is neither quoted nor described in the report, but it was not in the event relied on by the court. His main argument expressly relied on 'Serjeant Manning's ... very learned' notes to *Wynne* and *Davis*—but only for Manning's sources; Manning's interpretation of them was not mentioned.[130] Instead, counsel interpreted the sources (excluding the statements of Brudnell and Brian CJJ, which were also not mentioned), as supporting the court's decisions and reasoning from *Davis* and *Simpson* on:

> The result of the authorities referred to in that note [to *Davis*], is, that, where the interest is determinable at the will of the grantor, it is a mere estate at will; but, where it is made to depend upon the will of the grantee, or the uncertain act of a stranger, the law considers it as an estate for life. That is in conformity with the rule laid down in Co. Litt. 42 a ... Here, there is an uncertain event which may put an end to the estate, viz. a sale of the land; but ... the act expressly provides that that shall only take place with the consent of the majority of the resident freemen,—which practically is, with the consent of the occupier himself.[131]

The court unanimously dismissed the appeal—and, for the first time in this line of authority, considered the ancient sources.

Jervis CJ and Maule and Williams JJ gave separate judgments (Talfourd J merely concurred), but all in the same terms, focused on interpreting the 1845 Act, and all with reference to 'the older cases.'[132] Jervis CJ gave the most detailed judgment, largely repeating the main submission of counsel for the respondents: section 8 meant that the allottee might hold an allotment for life, and sections 17 and 22 meant that this interest could not be terminated by the deputies at will. Therefore, the case 'falls within the definition of an estate for life in Co Litt 42a.'[133] He also emphasised that there should be no separate electoral version of land law:

> If this is not a freehold, what estate is it? It clearly is not an estate for years: nor is it an estate at the absolute and uncontrolled will of the lessors. It is suggested that it is a sort of parliamentary estate, floating between an estate of freehold and an estate at will. It would

---

[128] Ibid, 649, 647.
[129] Ibid, 655.
[130] Ibid, 656–57.
[131] Ibid, 657.
[132] Ibid, 660.
[133] Ibid, 658–59.

manifestly be very inconvenient so to hold; and I do not see how we can consistently with the rules of law hold this to be any other than an estate of freehold.[134]

Maule J spelled the matter out simply:

> It is well established that an estate which may last for a man's life is, ordinarily, a freehold … An estate determinable on a condition, which condition cannot arise at the absolute will of the lord, is a freehold. Here … the estate is capable of being determined upon … an event which is not dependent on the will of the lord … [This] is clearly such an estate as according to the older authorities is an estate of freehold.

He too emphasised that this conformed to 'the general law'.[135]

Williams J said only:

> This is clearly an estate of freehold, inasmuch as it is for an uncertain interest, which may last for the life of the party, and is not confined to the will of the grantors. It comes, therefore, within the examples given in some of the older cases.[136]

Thus, in *Beeson*, the court used the very sources that had been brought back to light by Manning, particularly Co Litt 42a, to support the approach the court had already settled on, focused on construing the relevant documents. Further, the court did not draw any distinction between legal and equitable freeholds. For legal freeholds, this meant substituting, for the Littleton rule per se, interpretation on the basis of the principle underlying that rule.

This development of the law, in a fraught, party-political context, was supported by the framework of constitutional ideas. Manning's approach directly contradicted the Blackstonian justification for property qualifications, while also being reminiscent of appeals to 'the ancient constitution' in purporting to resurrect ancient rules and denounce deviation from them.[137] The court's approach, by contrast, incorporated the Blackstonian principle underlying property qualifications—those with property (even under a charitable trust) should be represented, unless they were subject to their landlord's will; and, being also clearly derivable from the Littleton rule, the court's approach aligned with the widespread belief that the constitution did and should evolve.

D. Epilogue: *Spencer v Harrison* (1879)

From *Beeson* until at least the 1870s, Manning's notes to *Wynne* and *Davis*, and, with them, Co Litt 42a, continued occasionally to be raised in submissions in registration appeals.[138] But the court did not change its approach; it simply saw less and less need to refer to the ancient sources, as they had been considered and a simple principle extracted from them in *Beeson*.[139] It is therefore unsurprising that, by

---

134 Ibid, 658–59.
135 Ibid, 659–60.
136 Ibid, 660.
137 See eg J Vernon, 'Notes Towards an Introduction' in Vernon (n 92).
138 eg *Trenfield v Lowe* (1869) Law Rep 4 CP 454; *Ashworth v Hopper* (1875) 1 CPD 178.
139 eg *Fernie v Scott* (1871) 7 CP 202.

1903, the Court of Appeal in *Zimbler* relied on pure construction; by then, this had been established for half a century as the rightful heir to the Littleton rule.

As for James Manning, he seems to have turned his attention to another issue, foreshadowed by *Wynne*. His first wife died in 1847. Manning subsequently became involved in the movement to reform the law on married women's property. In 1857 he remarried, to a widow in her fifties who had recently published a well-regarded study of ancient India. His daughter and his second wife became good friends with each other and with Emily Davies, the future founder of Girton College, Cambridge; and all three were active in particular on issues relating to women and education, with James's assistance until his death in 1866.[140]

After Manning's death, his proposed rule, already buried, got a stake through its heart. In *Spencer v Harrison*,[141] it appears that counsel did not raise Manning's argument or the related sources. Nonetheless, Lopes and Lindley JJ expressly considered Manning's notes to *Wynne* and *Davis*, and showed that Manning had wrongly interpreted his key Year Book source—the one aspect of Manning's argument which had not previously been dealt with. They then arrived at the same conclusion as in *Beeson*—that the question was one of the proper interpretation of the agreement, in particular whether it was intended to be terminable at the will of the grantor.[142]

VII. CONCLUSION

The story of the Manning rule raises more questions than it answers; but three conclusions may be suggested. First, the Supreme Court in *Mexfield* was, with the greatest respect, wrong in accepting the submission that there had ever been such a thing as the *Mexfield* rule, and wrong in disapproving *Zimbler*. The real ratio of *Mexfield* remains the same: although the court insisted that it preferred to get to the result by the alleged rule, it also held (with the greatest respect, correctly) that the relevant agreement, on ordinary principles of interpretation, was intended to be a determinable life tenancy; and only this reasoning was necessary to reach the result.[143]

Second, in investigating the roots of today's land law, constitutional land law should not be overlooked. Some of the most important debates as to the definition of particular interests in land will have taken place in the context of disputes about property qualifications. If the answer to the puzzle of *Mexfield* can be found in this forgotten realm, there may be answers to other land-law puzzles in there too.

Finally, in the Manning line of cases, the court rejected a crude allegedly ancient rule in favour of an approach which was principled and fact-sensitive, derived from but not arbitrarily constrained by ancient sources, in a way which reflected a particular set of ideas about the constitution. One might ask what it says about the current court's vision of the constitution that the Supreme Court, in *Mexfield*, did precisely the reverse.

---

[140] Sutherland (n 56); A Murphy and D Raftery (eds), *Emily Davies: Collected Letters, 1861–75* (Charlottesville VA, University of Virginia Press, 2004) 103, 183–94, 201–03.
[141] *Spencer v Harrison* (1879) 5 CPD 97.
[142] Ibid, 103–04.
[143] *Mexfield* (n 1) [44]; Roche (n 1) 444–46, 447–49; cf *Secretary of State for Transport v Blake* [2013] EWHC 2945 (Ch) [20]–[21].

Part V

Property and Title

17

Registered Title and the Assurance of Reliability

I. INTRODUCTION

THE DEFINING FEATURE of systems for registration of title is, of course, that the information about title displayed by the register is in some sense reliable. But reliability need not be seen as a quality of the information itself in the abstract. Systems for registration of title have been designed to serve a variety of social goals and so the reliability of the information in the register may need to be assured only to the restricted classes of person necessary to fulfil the particular social goal that motivated the registration law. The English version of registration is noteworthy for the convoluted means by which it indicates who gets the benefit of the assurance of reliability as well as for the opaque motivations underlying the choice of the particular class of persons in whose favour the assurance of reliability is given.

The English land registration system, like many others, famously emerged as a response to the difficulties and uncertainties troubling the investigation of title to land[1] and therefore its key component is a provision which gives a categorical assurance to a purchaser about the state of title that he will receive if the correct steps are followed. Since their first introduction, all of the English registration statutes have afforded at least this minimum protection: in favour of a prospective purchaser who inspects the register, and on the strength of it proceeds with the purchase and becomes proprietor, the system guarantees that the former proprietor had the ability to transfer an unimpeachable title in accordance with the registered entry. By such a strategy, the register deems a good root of title in the person named as proprietor and, subject to interests which override the register, allows the prospective acquirer to rely on the register as an accurate indicator of what he will receive from the seller. That is the minimum necessary for a workable system in which register entries are to take the place of inconclusive deeds and oaths as proof of title.

---

* Reader in Property Law, School of Law, Oxford Brookes University.

[1] *Second Report of the Commissioners Appointed to Inquire into the Law of England respecting Real Property* (1830, HCP xi 1) 18; *Report of the Commissioners Appointed to Consider the Subject of the Registration of Title with Reference to the Sale and Transfer of Land* (1857, c 2215) 8; *Report of the Royal Commissioners Appointed to Inquire into the Operation of the Land Transfer Act* (1870, c 20) para 64.

But it seems that there is much more to the English model of registration than protection for purchasers. Its assurance of reliability appears to be given to a far wider class of persons than is necessary to protect prospective purchasers who rely on the register in anticipation of a dealing. The assurance of reliability also appears to operate in favour of those who had no acquisitive intention. For example, it will be shown below that if a person is wrongly registered as proprietor by an internal registry error, then the law allows him to keep the land or compensation for its loss even if he never expected to acquire the land and even if he was unaware of his new status until he received notification of the proceedings to reverse the error. That provides an assurance of reliability which goes far beyond the level necessary to encourage prospective purchasers to rely on the register. It is significant because the assurance of reliability, however broad or narrow, comes with associated burdens.

Whenever the register content is made reliable, it is accompanied by the possibility that an erroneous entry will be preserved in order to fulfil the commitment to reliability. This causes immediate sources of disadvantages for actors in the registration system: it increases the risk that the former owner will lose his property and it increases the burden on the indemnity fund contributors due to the ensuing compensation claim. The assurance of reliability is therefore suited to a cost-benefit assessment. In respect of its application to prospective purchasers, those disadvantages are suffered for a social benefit that has long been regarded as compelling: it is the foundation of cheap and secure conveyancing, eliminating the ancient source of delay in investigating title, and removing uncertainties in the root of title. Yet even when pursuing these worthy objectives, the assurance of reliability has recently come under scrutiny and experienced a degree of retrenchment in the case law: restricting the statutory vesting provision to a bare legal title,[2] expanding the overriding interests,[3] rectifying the register against a good faith purchaser,[4] qualifying the register by using off-register material as an aid to interpretation,[5] and upholding a restrictive approach towards issuing guaranteed titles.[6] At a time when even the protection of purchasers is reined in, how much more difficult it is to substantiate any assurance of reliability in favour of other persons whose interests were not expressed to be the motivation for introducing registration of title.

This chapter responds to the issue by examining the English land registration system and the privileged class to whom it extends the assurance of reliability. It identifies who is covered by the extended form of the assurance of reliability, it

---

[2] *Fitzwilliam v Richall Holdings Services Ltd* [2013] EWHC 86; A Goymour, 'Mistaken Registrations of Land' [2013] *CLJ* 617, A Nair, 'Forgery and the Land Registration Act 2002' (2013) 24 *King's Law Journal* 403.

[3] Eg *Link Lending Ltd v Bustard* [2010] EWCA Civ 424; B Bogusz, 'The Relevance of "Intentions and Wishes" to Determine Actual Occupation' [2014] *Conveyancer and Property Lawyer* 27; *Chaudhary v Yavuz* [2013] Ch 249; B McFarlane, 'Eastenders, Neighbours, Upstairs Downstairs' [2013] *Conveyancer and Property Lawyer* 74.

[4] *Knights Construction (March) Ltd v Roberto Mac Ltd* [2011] EWLandRA 2009/1459; E Lees, 'Title by Registration: Rectification, Indemnity and Mistake and the Land Registration Act 2002' (2013) 75 *MLR* 62.

[5] *Cherry Tree Investments Ltd v Landmain Ltd* [2013] Ch 305 (Arden LJ, dissenting); P Butt, 'The Interpretation of Easements' in N Gravells, *Landmark Cases in Land Law* (Oxford, Hart Publishing, 2013) 33.

[6] *R (on the application of Diep) v Land Registry* [2010] EWHC 3315; M Dixon, 'Editor's Notebook' [2011] *Conveyancer and Property Lawyer* 1.

explores what potential social policy objective might justify extending the assurance of reliability to them, and how well the policy objective is being implemented. There are sound reasons for pursuing this enquiry. An understanding of the policy behind the extended assurance of reliability is essential as a precursor to any effective evaluation of its merits and the extent to which it justifies the disadvantages noted earlier, and it would better equip legal scientists and reformers to make an appraisal of whether current legislative rules effect a satisfactory means of implementation. An explicit articulation of the policy should assist in a purposive interpretation of the provisions of the legislation concerning the guarantee of title. It is also important for the study of the English registration system in comparative perspective: the approach to the reliability of the register and its underlying policy is vital to its functional classification and the viability of any cross-border transplants.

Those issues will be examined by reference to the rules which provide for the register to be rectified in the event of a mistake. If the register is susceptible to being rectified, its reliability is inevitably put in jeopardy and it is only through the associated rules which provide for individuals to resist rectification and claim state compensation that a degree of reliability can be salvaged. It is these rules that are the focus of this chapter. It regards the assurance of reliability as being provided where either: (a) the individual is immune from rectification; (b) the individual is afforded an opportunity to be heard to resist the proceedings for rectification and the tribunal refuses rectification; or (c) the register is rectified but the individual is eligible for state compensation.

The chapter proceeds as follows. The first step is to identify the statutory provisions and indicative case law which demonstrate the range of persons to whom the assurance of reliability is extended. That will lead to a proposed explanation of the policy underlying the provisions. It is argued that the explanation for the extended scope of reliability lies in the protection of expectations that have been induced by the register. The next section then considers how this seemingly trite conclusion is obscured by its embodiment in rules which constitute a poorly aligned proxy for the underlying policy and thus contribute to the impression that the case law diverges from any coherent policy. Finally, the chapter examines the arguments which justify imposing potential limits to the extended scope of reliability.

II. EXTENDING RELIABILITY BEYOND PROSPECTIVE PURCHASERS

It is beyond question that a registration system which was motivated by facilitating conveyancing and introducing certainty to titles must make the register reliable in favour of prospective purchasers who use the information to influence a decision to purchase. But it is far from self-evident that the system should make the register reliable in other circumstances; for example, where a prospective donee inspects it before deciding whether to accept or reject a gift, or where a registered proprietor examines his own title to confirm the detail of his own holdings before taking action. To address these concerns, this part will investigate the extent to which the English system makes the register reliable beyond the remit of protecting purchasers and why it might do so.

A. The Scope of Protection Against the Reversal of Mistakes

The lack of authoritative instruction on the purpose behind the rectification and indemnity clauses means that normal technique of research into the *travaux prépara-toires* does not yield sufficiently detailed information of the parliamentary intention and it is necessary to adopt the circuitous technique of making inductive inferences from the statutory text as applied in the cases.

Under the English model, register reliability is achieved through a variety of techniques. First, the estate vests in the person who becomes registered proprietor.[7] Second, an unrecorded limitation cannot be the basis for questioning the title of a registered disponee.[8] Third, an unprotected precarious interest cannot be enforced against a registered transferee for value.[9] These three techniques are relatively crude and the introduction of any sophistication or subtlety is left to the fourth technique, which is the focus of this chapter: in the event of a mistake in the register, a later acquirer receives protection in the event of a claim to rectify the mistake.[10] The acquirer's protection is expressed by allowing the acquirer the opportunity to resist any claim for rectification and the losing party is eligible to claim state indemnity. It is not yet settled whether the protection arises from an absolute jurisdictional bar on rectifying against a registered disponee for value,[11] or whether it is manifested merely in the judicial reluctance to exercise the discretionary rectification power in such circumstances,[12] but in the case of an adverse exercise of discretion against a later acquirer, protection would be expected in the form of state indemnity.[13]

Those aspects of the English model are uncontroversial insofar as they make the register reliable in favour of a purchaser who checked the register to confirm title before taking a disposition: they give effect to a policy of easing the land transfer process by simplifying investigation of title, increasing predictability, and reducing transaction costs. But the English model takes a rather more controversial step when it appears to offer the assurance of reliability to others as well. It is far from apparent what interests are being promoted by giving a guarantee to someone who is not a prospective purchaser in need of reassurance that the current proprietor has good title to the estate. To the extent that the assurance of reliability is given to people who look at the register for other purposes, the operation of the system demands confirmation and explanation.

---

[7] Land Registration Act 2002, s 58(1).

[8] LRA 2002, ss 23 and 26.

[9] LRA 2002, ss 29 and 30.

[10] LRA 2002, Sch 4 (discretion in rectification) and Sch 8 (indemnity claim).

[11] See DJ Hayton, *Registered Land*, 3rd edn (London, Sweet & Maxwell, 1981) 180; EJ Cooke, *The New Law of Land Registration* (Oxford, Hart Publishing, 2003) 125–27; E Lees, 'Title by Registration: Rectification, Indemnity and Mistake and the Land Registration Act 2002' (2013) 75 *MLR* 62; A Goymour, 'Mistaken Registrations of Land: Exploding the Myth of Title by Registration' [2013] *CLJ* 617.

[12] 'The factor which should carry most weight in the circumstances of the present case': *Kingsalton Ltd v Thames Water Developments Ltd* [2001] EWCA Civ 20 [52] (Sir Christopher Slade), a decision under the LRA 1925.

[13] Eg E Lees, 'Title by Registration: Rectification, Indemnity and Mistake and the Land Registration Act 2002' (2013) 75 *MLR* 62, 75, describing the pressure exerted by the Human Rights Act 1998, s 3, to interpret the legislation so as to make indemnity available here in order to comply with art 1, Protocol 1 of the Convention.

Two case examples will be noted in order to indicate the way in which the system has been applied. The first is an early case typifying a classic situation. In *Re 139 High Street, Deptford*,[14] Dobkins bought an unregistered shop, neither the contract nor conveyance referring to any plan. The seller and buyer believed the land to include an annexe which was in truth owned by BTC. Dobkins became first registered proprietor of the shop and by mistake the registry included the annexe. The court ordered removal of the annexe in rectification proceedings, but Dobkins was subsequently awarded indemnity.[15] The case prompts a troubling question: on what principle could it be right to open up the possibility of resisting rectification, or awarding indemnity, when Dobkins had caused his own misfortune by not properly investigating the title to the unregistered land? The result enabled to Dobkins to gain from registration when he could not have relied on the register as a source of information at the time of purchase. Even if Dobkins had never expected to acquire the annexe, the outcome would presumably have been the same: indemnity would have been available and the result would have been even more surprising as he would have been compensated not for dashed hopes but for having failed to keep an unanticipated windfall.

The second example comes from *Totton and Eling Town Council v Caunter*.[16] The defendants successfully claimed adverse possession before the adjudicator and they were entered as new proprietors. On appeal, the decision was reversed and the court ordered that they be removed as proprietors. It was decided that this order for removal amounted to rectification of the register. But on what principle could it be right to open up the possibility of declining to rectify against the Caunters, or to award them indemnity, when they were perfectly well aware that the decision of the adjudicator was liable to appeal and that their entry was accordingly susceptible to reversal pending the appeal outcome?

To confer protection on Dobkins and the Caunters in such circumstances appears to lack any sound justification. In neither case is it possible to point to the promotion of any market interest, such as maintaining confidence in security of receipt or facilitating transaction behaviour. At first glance it seems preposterous that a former owner might be denied recovery of the land because of an error on which nobody had ever relied; on the other hand, if the error were rectified (as indeed happened in both cases) it is doubtful that the defendants' subsequent indemnity claim could be ruled out by any contribution to the mistake and yet an indemnity award appears to be an unwarranted burden on the indemnity fund contributors. The decisions in these cases give registered land participants a measure of protection which appears inexplicable. It seems to confer an unmerited and unexpected windfall at the expense of the former owner or the indemnity contributors. This approach of either upholding the error or compensating for it would be unthinkable in many other jurisdictions. In Scotland, for example, recent legislation ensures that these mistaken entries

[14] *Re 139 High Street, Deptford* [1951] Ch 884.
[15] TBF Ruoff, *An Englishman Looks at the Torrens System* (Sydney, Law Book Co, 1957) 91, decided under the LRA 1925.
[16] *Totton and Eling Town Council v Caunter* [2008] EWHC 3630. Compare *Chief Land Registrar v Franks* [2011] EWCA Civ 772 which implies that alteration could be achieved by a restoration order under the Civil Procedure Rules 1998 SI 1998/3132, r 52 without being troubled by the constraints of rectification. For correcting, setting aside and appealing tribunal decisions, see Tribunal Procedure (First Tier Tribunal) (Property Chamber) Rules 2013, SI 2013/1169, rr 51–55.

will be removed administratively without any prospect of declining rectification or offering compensation.[17] Clearly there is a need to identify what policy drives the opposing view that is found in the English cases.

B. Towards an Explanatory Proposition

Two superficially attractive explanations for the provisions must be rejected before passing on to one that appears to fit the case. The first false effort at explanation is that the reliability of the register (in the sense of protection stemming from the ability to resist rectification or claim indemnity) in these cases is simply part and parcel of the principle that underlies the principle of statutory vesting of title and thus pursues the same purposes. The vesting principle, which confers title merely by entry as proprietor,[18] whether or not mistakenly, serves the special purpose of identifying the locus of the legal estate to the benefit of those who might need to know for the application of legal doctrines which hinge on it, such as merger.[19] That special purpose is pursued regardless of whether an entry is liable to be rectified. It therefore operates independently of rectification and indemnity, and consequently cannot explain why anyone should be able to resist the prospective reallocation of title through rectification or claim indemnity.

A second inadequate effort to account for extending protection to those who did not rely on the register to inform a decision to acquire could be based on its effect in facilitating the conveyancing process.[20] This can be demonstrated through the illustration of a purchaser who fears that the seller might have stolen the identity of the registered proprietor. A registration system could be designed so that the rectification and indemnity clauses provide the means of sustaining the reliability of the register when the victim whose identity was stolen seeks to reverse the entry. The English model appears at first glance to adopt this technique: reliability is not generally promised to all prospective purchasers from the moment of inspection, but instead is deferred until the moment of registration, when the purchaser *qua* proprietor may then invoke the guarantee of reliability in respect of any disturbance to his status—whether stemming from a defect in the former proprietor's root of title or a defect in the immediate disposition to himself. This design could tend to discourage conveyancers from indulging in excessive measures to verify the seller's identity which are costly, delaying, ultimately inconclusive and might jeopardise the deal. The rectification and indemnity clauses which create the assurance of reliability could therefore be attributed to the policy of facilitating conveyancing. However, that policy basis is rejected for two reasons. First, it cannot be sustained in the face

---

[17] Land Registration, etc (Scotland) Act 2012, ss 80 and 85.

[18] LRA 2002, s 58.

[19] *Royal Commission on the Land Transfer Acts: Second and Final Report of the Commissioners* (1911, Cd 5483) para 30, responding to *Capital & Counties Bank Ltd v Rhodes* [1903] 1 Ch 631.

[20] R Sackville, 'The Torrens System—Some Thoughts on Indefeasibility and Priorities' (1973) *Australian Law Journal* 526, 531; M Neave, 'Indefeasibility of Title in the Canadian Context' (1976) 23 *University of Toronto Law Journal* 173, 192. Contrast the view that it would reward carelessness: W Taylor, 'Scotching *Frazer v Walker*' (1970) 44 *Australian Law Journal* 248, 254.

of opposing influences elsewhere in the conveyancing system which demand investigation of identity, including the conveyancer's duties of care and loyalty to the purchasing client, registry standards,[21] professional guidance,[22] as well as imperilling the entitlement to rectification and indemnity for 'lack of proper care'.[23] This reflects a pattern of contemporary anti-fraud measures internationally, for apart from a passing recommendation in Canadian reform policy[24] there has been a strong recent trend of intensifying the duty of verification borne by the purchaser's lawyers.[25]

The second reason for rejecting that account of the rectification and indemnity rules as a source of reliability is that it is under-inclusive: it lacks the capacity to explain the full range of circumstances in which reliability is assured. The supposed rationale of facilitating conveyancing transactions can function only in a very limited range of circumstances, namely those involving a prospective acquirer who might have otherwise undertaken conveyancing investigations or precautions (beyond investigating whether title vested in the named proprietor). The English system does not separate out those circumstances for bespoke protection; instead it treats them only as an undifferentiated subset of the circumstances in which the assurance of reliability is currently available under the English statute.[26] Consequently, there remain many other instances where a beneficiary of a mistake in the register is able to invoke the assurance of reliability where doing so would have no impact on conveyancing. It occurs wherever a new proprietor is mistakenly entered on the register without having consciously engaged in any acquisitive behaviour, such as a neighbouring landowner's disposition which the registry wrongly took to affect the proprietor's land, or an internal error when the registry changes its mapping system.[27] No conveyancing precautions could be dispensed with here because no conveyancing activity is undertaken. To confirm the assurance of reliability in such cases, as the English statute does, therefore far exceeds the circumstances which could be explained by a policy of facilitating conveyancing.

Having rejected those two possible accounts of protection under the statute, a better explanation for the cases might be inferred from the role of the register in transmitting, creating and suppressing information. The register transmits pre-existing information that could be acquired less easily from other sources; insofar as it contains mistakes, it creates new information; and in relation to unprotected, precarious interests, it has the capacity to suppress information and deprive it of legal effect in favour of a transferee for value. The communication of this information may have a causative effect on the thoughts and actions of the audience who encounters it. The information could induce expectations about ownership. This is the one and only

---

[21] Land Registry Practice Guide 67, 'Evidence of Identity' (2010).

[22] Eg Law Society Practice Notes, 'Property and Registration Fraud' (2010) and 'Mortgage Fraud' (2014); SRA, 'Warning Notice on Bogus Law Firms and Identity Theft' (2012).

[23] LRA, Sch 4, para 3(2)(a); LRA Sch 8, para 5(1)(b).

[24] Joint Land Titles Committee of Canada, *Renovating the Foundation: Proposals for a Model Land Recording and Registration Act for the Provinces and Territories of Canada* (Edmonton, 1990) para II G (6)(f)(iii), following the principle of cost-efficiency in conveyancing laid out by TW Mapp, *Torrens' Elusive Title* (Edmonton, AILRR, 1978) 132.

[25] Eg Land Transfer Bill 2010, cll 11 and 12 (New Zealand); Real Property Act 1900, s 56C (New South Wales); Land Titles Act (RSA 2000, c L-4), s 170 (Alberta).

[26] Eg *Ajibade v Bank of Scotland* [2008] EWLandRA 2006/0163 and *Swift 1st Ltd v Chief Land Registrar* [2014] All ER (D) 12 (indemnity for duped mortgagee following de-registration).

[27] Eg *Safeway Stores plc v Tesco Stores Ltd* [2004] SC 29.

effect that could always ensue from every type of mistake about title in the register. If a particular regime gives protection against the rectification of mistaken entries regardless of whether they have been relied on by a prospective acquirer to inform the decision to acquire, as the English model does, the only explanation for that protection which is dependent upon the unique institutions of registered land could be one which follows from the register's effect of inducing expectations.

For example, long after his acquisition, the proprietor might inspect his own register to confirm the boundaries or the absence of covenants against building before developing the land. The protective rules which allow him to resist rectification or claim indemnity in the event of discovering a mistake are explained by the expectations induced in his mind by seeing the register's mistaken content, even if those expectations were induced only after initial purchase (as would be the case, for example, when buying from an imposter[28] or buying unregistered land and becoming first registered proprietor, when there can have been no reliance on the land register at the time of acquisition).[29] It is the protection of those expectations that justifies extending the assurance of reliability beyond prospective purchasers. Not only does that logic accommodate the utilitarian ideal of pursuing the result which inflicts the least anxiety on all concerned, it also advances the constitutional ideal of an opportunity to review state involvement in non-consensual transfer of property rights between citizens.

The proposed explanation of the protection against register mistakes through the rectification discretion and indemnity would also find normative support in the ideal of safeguarding investment in land. Before making expenditure in development works, the prudent proprietor may turn to the register to confirm the details of his title. If it cannot be relied upon to give an accurate picture of the state of title, the prospective development would be discouraged because of the possibility of wasting efforts on land that may have to be restored to another. To guarantee the reliability of the register here would serve to protect and encourage investment. It sits comfortably within the tradition of understanding property as an artificial social convention to promote social utility, which has dominated modern thought since the rejection of divinely-instituted natural law as the origin of individual rights. It was famously expounded by David Hume[30] who derived the virtue of property from its fulfilment of the future expectations that arise from current usage and explained from it the individual property law rules which connect the fact of possession to legal right, such as prescription, first occupation, and accession.[31] His concentration on possession is perhaps unhelpful in justifying entitlements by force of a register entry, but he recognised that possession was not the exclusive basis for property and could be controlled by the broader principle of fulfilling expectations, as when he refers to

---

[28] The classic observation comes from *Gibbs v Messer* [1891] AC 248, 255 (Lord Watson): 'Those who deal, not with the registered proprietor, but with a forger who uses his name, do not transact on the faith of the register'. Once registered, however, they may well do subsequent acts on the faith of a register entry which confirms their status as proprietor.

[29] RJ Smith, 'Land Registration: Reform at Last?' ch 8 in P Jackson and D Wilde, *The Reform of Property Law* (Aldershot, Ashgate Dartmouth, 1997) 143; *Royal Commission on the Land Transfer Acts: Second and Final Report of the Commissioners* (1911, Cd 5483) para 57.

[30] D Hume, *A Treatise on Human Nature* (London, Noon, 1738) paras 3.2.2.9 and 3.2.2.12.

[31] Ibid, para 3.2.3.5.

property rights stemming from 'the sight of a thing',[32] referring to the rule that even a whole continent belongs to the nation which first discovered it.[33]

The strictly utilitarian account of property to serve economic ends—protecting investment backed expectations—was developed by Bentham who was prepared to extend Hume's lead by tying expectations not only to physical possession but also to the knowledge of abstract title:

> Everything which I possess, or to which I have a title, I consider in my own mind as destined always to belong to me. I make it the basis of my expectations, and of the hopes of those dependent upon me; and I form my plan of life accordingly.[34]

The standard teleological account of property, which holds that legal security encourages investment and discourages imprudent management by allowing the holder to reap what he has sown, is easily applied to the context of register reliability. That it was consciously perceived as one of the driving objectives of land registration is evident from the writing of Robert Torrens, champion of land reform in the Australian colonies:

> A very considerable extent of land which, but for doubts, for the most part upon mere technical points, affecting the title, would possess peculiar value as building sites, lie waste, receptacles of the offensive refuse of towns. If, by the operation of law, these defects could be cured, or the capitalist be assured against deprivation of the wealth expended upon the land, the vacant blocks which now disfigure the rising streets would immediately become available as building sites, and the wealth of the community be increased by the value restored to them as such.[35]

This policy statement relies on a justification for the assurance of register reliability which is not restricted to prospective purchasers. It is equally relevant where the proposed form of reliance lies not in the payment of the price to a seller, but rather in the labour or expenditure on improvement of land already in the ownership of the developer. It therefore lends support to the explanatory proposition put forward to account for the wide remit of reliability under the English rectification and indemnity scheme.

C. Inferences from the Explanatory Proposition

The previous section proposed that the English approach to the reliability of the register is explained by protecting expectations that have been induced by the register's content. That proposition is put forward in order to explain the rectification and indemnity provisions outside of circumstances of reliance by a prospective purchaser. If the proposition is to be accepted as an accurate description of the motivation behind the rectification and indemnity scheme, it can be used as the source for deductions about the due scope of protection. In particular, there are logical limits to

---

[32] Ibid, para 3.2.3.7, fn 73.

[33] Ibid.

[34] J Bentham, *Theory of Legislation* (Hildreth tr, London, Stevens, 1876) 115. Beyond settled possession, he includes property from first discovery of new islands (159) and finding chattels (154).

[35] RR Torrens, *The South Australia System of Conveyancing by Registration of Title* (Adelaide, Register/Observer, 1859) 26.

the occasions when expectations ought to be protected, revealing that it is not necessary to go as far as the extravagant proposition that the information in the register should be guaranteed reliable in favour of all persons for all purposes.

First, because the protection of expectations is attributed to the practical effects on peoples' minds stemming from the register entry, the explanatory proposition is restricted to those whose expectations are induced by seeing or otherwise learning of the content of the register. There is no scope for protecting the person whose expectations about future enjoyment of property are generated by, for example, current factual enjoyment of the land. Even if expectations arising from such sources happened to coincide with the mistaken content of the register, they should not be protected if the person had never learned of the register content. Equally, the need for expectations induced by the register indicates that where a person has seen the mistaken register yet put no faith in its content, as when knowing of its mistaken nature, there is no scope for protection according to the explanatory proposition.

Secondly, the protection justified by the presence of expectations induced by the register is relevant only to persons who would suffer by those expectations being thwarted upon rectification of the mistaken entry. There is no scope for protecting those who, on the contrary, would benefit from having a particular entry rectified. This leads to the further proposition that the protection of expectations is restricted to those persons whose induced expectations from the register relate to their unwarranted holding of property rights. Protection of expectations explains why reliability is given only in favour of a privileged class of rightholders who have standing to resist an attack on the validity of the mistaken entry and not to others such as inquisitive neighbours.[36]

Those two limitations can be combined explicitly with the original formulation of the explanatory theory in order to create a general proposition about the approach of a coherent legislative scheme which incorporates the English model of rectification and indemnity provisions: when a rightholder learns of a register entry which actually induces him to believe he has greater rights than those which would have existed in the absence of the mistake, the apparent state of his title should be made good by either declining rectification of the mistake or awarding indemnity. The difficulty with this proposition, however, is that it is not entirely borne out by the operation of the system in practice. In particular, neither statute nor case law requires actual reliance on or knowledge of the register content as a precondition to resisting rectification or seeking indemnity. The empirical data, illustrated by the decisions in *Deptford* and *Totton* among many others, demonstrates that the presence of actual reliance on the register, or the expectations induced by it, cannot be the sole explanation for having mistaken register entries upheld or indemnified. Further examination is required into how the explanatory proposition integrates with the seemingly discordant content of the statutory rules.

---

[36] There may, however, remain concerns that this restriction would exclude people seeking to avoid infringement of the proprietor's rights from obtaining easy access to reliable information on ownership, thus inefficiently increasing their information costs: see TW Merrill and HE Smith, 'Optimal Standardization in the Law of Property' (2000) 110 *Yale Law Journal* 1, 26.

III. HARMONISING THE EXPLANATORY PROPOSITION WITH
THE OBSERVED RULES

A. Implementation by Proxy

English registration law is capable of protecting proprietors against the reversal of entries even when there has been no actual sight of the register, and presumably even if they are entirely unaware of the entry.[37] But it is submitted that this departure from the explanatory proposition does not indicate that induced expectations ought to be rejected as the foundation for protecting proprietors from mistaken entries. Instead, it is submitted that expectations induced by the register constitute the reason for conferring protection, but that the deviation between the ideal of protecting expectations and the effect of the legal rules is due to practical reasons of efficiency. It is submitted that it is out of convenience that the legislature has chosen to implement the policy of protecting induced expectations by using rough and ready proxy rules to stand in for induced expectations. The use of the proxies may obscure the policy underlying the protection afforded by rectification and indemnity, but does not displace it. Protection of induced expectations remains a convincing explanation for the scheme so long as it is understood that the rules effectuating it represent a compromise between perfectly targetting the policy objective and practical convenience in their implementation.

The rules for introducing the discretion to refuse rectification and award indemnity are contingent on this criterion: a mistake[38] (one which can be corrected by alteration of the register,[39] implying that it must be a mistake in compiling the register) whose correction would prejudicially affect the title of a registered proprietor.[40] That is all that is necessary for a proprietor to prove in order to be eligible to resist rectification proceedings or claim indemnity. It deviates from the pure ideal of protection in that it does not require knowledge of the mistaken entry to reach the proprietor and induce an expectation that he will retain the benefit of the entry. But to fulfil the ideal in a perfectly targetted fashion by insisting on proof of induced expectations would involve extraordinarily costly processes, including proof of a range of difficult facts: that the proprietor or his agent had sight of the mistaken register, or the content of the register had come to his attention via an intermediary or via hearsay reports through however many hands; that any hearsay report of the mistaken entry was narrated accurately and comprehensively; that the proprietor had appreciated the import of the mistaken entry; that the proprietor had formed an expectation that he would retain the property which the register mistakenly represented as his; that the expectation was sufficiently developed and convincing in his mind; that the proprietor's expectations were causatively connected to the content of the register; that the proprietor did not disbelieve the register entry or doubt the

---

[37] No reported judgment has been uncovered in which this has occurred, although it would be compatible with the cases summarised in Ruoff (n 15) 96, decided under the LRA 1925. It may be anticipated that most mistakes occur in processing a disposition, and nowadays the practice of automatically returning a printout to the new proprietor is likely to reduce the incidence of cases in which the proprietor did not have the register information at his disposal: Land Registry Public Guide No 3 (Nov 2012) para 3.

[38] LRA 2002, Sch 4, para 2(1)(a).

[39] LRA 2002, Sch 4, para 2(1).

[40] LRA 2002, Sch 4, para 1(b).

veracity of the media by which the information was indirectly conveyed. In addition there might be costs associated with argument over legal issues such as the burden of proof and the existence of minimum legal thresholds such as the reasonableness of a proprietor's alleged subjective expectations.

Such enquiries as these are eliminated at a stroke by tying the availability of protection to the crude factual question of whether the register bears a mistaken entry.[41] The only remaining issues for enquiry are compact legal questions over interpretation of 'mistake' and 'prejudice to title', for which there is limited scope to propose competing interpretative theories. By adopting this approach to rule-making, the rectification and indemnity scheme effectively concerns itself not with the question whether induced expectations actually exist in the mind of the mistakenly entered proprietor, but instead focusses merely on whether there was an opportunity to induce expectations. Although the statutory rules may ultimately over-protect, as where rectification is declined or indemnity awarded to a proprietor who never relied on the mistaken entry but heard of it for the first time when the registry forwarded the notification of the rectification claim, this over-protection must be understood as the lesser evil conceded by the legislature in order to employ cost-efficient short cuts that occasionally miss the target.

B. Actual Reliance and the Discretion to Decline Rectification

Although the proof of induced expectations may be perceived as too costly an exercise to insist on as a strict precondition to protection, there is nothing to preclude parties from raising actual expectations as a factor in rectification proceedings. Once the rectification power is engaged by the existence of a mistake whose correction would prejudice title, the decision whether or not to rectify will rest on discretionary standards—in particular, whether there are exceptional circumstances to warrant upholding the mistaken entry or whether it would be unjust not to rectify it.[42] The rectification proceedings can therefore be used as the forum to look into wide-ranging issues of fairness between the parties. Either litigant in the rectification proceedings is free to make the case that there was or was not inspection of and reliance on the erroneous register. The mere opportunity for reliance outlined above is therefore far from determinative of whether rectification will be declined, and the rectification scheme's connection to actual induced expectations is reinforced by evidence that in rectification proceedings the courts have consistently allowed an enquiry into actual reliance.

The courts have demonstrated a willingness to explore factual material relating to the defendant's knowledge of and reliance on the mistaken entry. For example, the court has accepted that in exercising the rectification discretion it would be a 'critical matter' to assess whether the defendant believed that the entry on the register

---

[41] D Baird and T Jackson, 'Information, Uncertainty and the Transfer of Property' (1984) 13 *Journal of Legal Studies* 299, 319–20 (recognising the costs associated with proof of reliance in filing systems).
[42] LRA 2002, Sch 4, para 2(1)(a). Land Registration Rules 2003 SI 2003/1417, r 126 applies a similar test for correction in cases of mistake which does not amount to rectification.

conferred good title on him.[43] Cases have also disapproved of proprietors resisting rectification where it would give an 'undeserved and unbargained for windfall'[44] or confer land

> which it never intended to acquire and which is of no use to it save as a means of extracting a ransom payment from [the former owner], a stance which however legitimate commercially does not commend itself to this court as in any way meritorious.[45]

These indicate a desire to correlate the rectification outcome to the actual expectations of the proprietor who benefitted from the mistaken entry.[46]

Where the defendant from the outset was aware of the mistake in the entry, then reliance is likely to be negated by that knowledge and the courts correspondingly less willing to protect the proprietor. For example, a factor pointing in favour of rectification in one case was that the defendant:

> [K]new there was a dispute which he did not disclose to the Land Registry. All of the acts of possession and expenditure relied on by Mr Moore were carried out in the teeth of objections by Mr Saxon and in the full knowledge of the dispute.[47]

In another case, emphasis was placed on the defendant's actual knowledge of the mistaken omission of an entry in reaching the court's decision to rectify against him.[48] In yet another case, one of the factors in favour of granting rectification was that 'The claimant knew, or ought to have known, that she had no paper title to the axe-head [the disputed land]. A glance at her own conveyancing documents would have told her that'.[49] Collectively they signify that knowledge of the mistaken nature of an entry is a factor which tends to negate expectations and reliance so that the mistaken entry should not be upheld.

On the other hand, there has been some recognition that induced expectations are not necessarily incompatible with knowledge or suspicion that the status of the entry might be controverted. It comes from a judgment in rectification proceedings brought under the Land Registration Act 1925 against joint purchasers who bought after having inspected the register, but the comments are expressed sufficiently broadly to cover non-purchaser cases. It was said that one of the 'crucial factors'[50] was that the purchasers were:

> [E]ntitled to assume that their title would be afforded the protection normally afforded to the title of registered proprietors in possession—and no less so because they knew that before the title of their predecessors, the Mayhews, was registered, there had been doubts as to the true boundaries of the disputed land. The very purpose of registration was to resolve such doubts.[51]

---

[43] *Paton v Todd* [2012] EWHC 1248 [90] (Morgan J).

[44] *Horrill v Cooper* (1999) 78 P & CR 336 (HHJ Colyer at first instance).

[45] *James Hay Pension Trustees Ltd v Cooper Estates Ltd* [2005] EWHC 36 [41] (Hart J).

[46] Followed in *Sainsbury's Supermarkets Ltd v Olympia Homes Ltd* [2006] 1 P & CR 17 [94] (Mann J).

[47] *Saxon v Moore* [2005] EWHC 27 [94] (HHJ Behrens).

[48] *Rees v Peters* [2011] EWCA Civ 836 [24] (Morritt C).

[49] *Johnson v Shaw* [2003] EWCA Civ 894 [48(3)] (Peter Gibson LJ).

[50] *Kingsalton Ltd v Thames Water Developments Ltd* [2001] EWCA Civ 20 [57] (Sir Christopher Slade), a decision under the LRA 1925.

[51] Ibid.

The extract suggests that in rectification proceedings the court is willing to entertain submissions that explore the subjective expectations and state of mind of a proprietor who had inspected the register with a view to confirming the presence of actual induced expectations.

C. Actual Reliance and the Award of Indemnity

As with protection through the exercise of the rectification discretion, the award of indemnity is not dependent on proof of any form of reliance on the register: indemnity is available, without reference to induced expectations, to any defendant proprietor against whom rectification proceedings are successfully brought. Again, this can be explained as accepting proof of the mere opportunity to have seen a mistaken entry as a handy proxy standing in for the complexities of actual reliance on a mistaken entry. The result is that indemnity is payable even in cases where the proprietor did not rely on the register or know of the entry in question.

In many typical cases, indemnity will be withheld or reduced in these circumstances due to the loss being suffered by the claimant wholly or partly 'as a result of his own lack of proper care'.[52] The loss of indemnity on grounds of carelessness does not, however, precisely equate to absence of reliance on the register. A good test scenario is that of rectifying an unexpected windfall. According to Ruoff, former Chief Land Registrar, indemnity has been awarded in a number of instances where:

> [T]he benefit of an easement has been unwarrantably or mistakenly entered as appurtenant to an owner's registered land. This has usually occurred on the occasion of the transfer of part of the land in a title. When, later, it has been found that the vendor did not grant, or did not have the power to grant the easement in question, the benefit of it was removed from the registered title.[53]

If indemnity is to be awarded in those cases, then it would be difficult to see how the award of indemnity could be any different in the event that the entry of the unwarranted rights occurred after the acquisition rather than contemporaneously with it; and if the proprietor never expected to acquire them; and if indeed the proprietor was entirely unaware of their entry. There is even authority implying that proof of the absence of any reliance does not take away indemnity. In *Dougbar Properties Ltd v Keeper of the Registers of Scotland*,[54] the register mistakenly conferred car parking rights on the proprietor of plot A. Dougbar, knowing of the mistaken inclusion, bought plot A and, when the register was corrected, claimed on the state guarantee. The court upheld the full indemnity award, finding that Dougbar knew of the mistaken nature of the entry but would not be barred from indemnity on the ground that it had contributed to the loss by its lack of care.

---

[52] LRA 2002, Sch 8, para 5.

[53] Ruoff (n 15) 96 (Case 4) decided under the LRA 1925.

[54] *Dougbar Properties Ltd v Keeper of the Registers of Scotland* [1999] SCLR 458 (decided under the Land Registration (Scotland) Act 1979 resembling the provisions of the English LRA 1925). It involved a prospective purchaser, but the point raised in it would be equally relevant to any other persons to whom the assurance of reliability was given.

In Ruoff's cases and *Dougbar*, the claims to indemnity are strikingly unmeritorious: they compensate a proprietor for failing to retain an adventitious bonus from the registry's oversight which was never due to him, which he never sought or expected to acquire, and which he had no expectation of retaining. But results such as those are inevitable if the indemnity clause is to be explained as protecting reliance through an imperfect but convenient proxy which sidesteps the need for proof of actual induced expectations.

The explanatory account of the striking results coming out of rectification and indemnity cases has been premised on the use of proxies which are justified by cost efficiency. If that correctly represents the legislature's thinking, it merits an empirical enquiry into the supposed cost effectiveness of the trade-off. Every time indemnity is paid out to a proprietor who did not rely on the erroneous register entry, it devotes resources to unnecessary payments that advance no policy objective. The payment of market-value indemnity to proprietors who, as prospective purchasers, relied on the register, is always justified in order to facilitate conveyancing and preserve market confidence in registered land, whereas the same compelling policy objective does not apply to any other class of persons who might claim indemnity following rectification. For the latter class, there should be an assessment of whether subsidising them through indemnity in the absence of reliance truly represents good value for money in the form of the social cost-saving that results from the convenience of administering indemnity claims by a legal rule which depends on registration as a proxy for expectations. If not, other options are open to the legislature: indemnity could be withheld unless the claimant could demonstrate an actual induced expectation of retaining the property or perhaps actual knowledge of the entry in dispute.[55] Alternatively, an even more restrictive regime, stopping short of deferred indefeasibility, could depend on the claimant demonstrating the same condition of reliance, but then restricting the indemnity award to a sum equal to the detriment, if any, that had been suffered by having relied on the mistaken entry. The latter measure of indemnity would effectively uproot the role of indemnity in securing the fulfilment of expectations and replace it with the limited role of reimbursing reliance expenditure.

IV. THE LIMITS OF EXPECTATIONS

This part considers how the proposed explanation of the rectification and indemnity scheme, resting on the fulfilment of induced expectations by proxy rules, might interact with other moral and legal factors affecting land registration.

A. Moral Principles

It was proposed that the mere opportunity for inducing expectations stands as a proxy for actual induced expectations in the legislative scheme and that it advances a policy of convenience and efficiency in rule administration. It was not empirically substantiated,

---

[55] The approach taken by the Scottish Law Commission, *Discussion Paper on Land Registration: Void and Voidable Titles* (Discussion Paper No 125, Edinburgh, 2004) paras 3.15–3.41. See Land Registration, etc (Scotland) Act 2012, s 85.

but merely put forward as a plausible justification for the statutory scheme. While the use of this proxy might imbue the system with a greater degree of efficiency, it hinders the system from responding to the influence of external moral forces. There may be occasions when the proprietor who benefits from a mistaken entry ought not to be able to take advantage of it. In particular, a moral duty may arise on that proprietor to protect others by taking precautions to minimise the loss caused by the mistaken entry. Such a moral duty might be attributed to the prevention of anti-social conduct, whether on grounds of selfishly exploiting the mistake in a way that exacerbates the losses inflicted on others, or on grounds of economic efficiency in wastefully passing up the cheapest way to avoid embroiling other parties in a priority dispute.

No such duty should be recognised where the proprietor has no actual subjective doubt over the validity of the register entry, as the imposition of the duty would then encourage investigations into the validity of the title information that would conflict with the very motive for introducing the registration system. But this potential moral duty is implicated where the proprietor is aware of facts from which he forms the view that the register entry ought not to be relied on. Some jurisdictions have explicitly denied protection in these circumstances. They insist on proof that the proprietor believed the entry to be authorised and had no knowledge of the facts that rendered it unauthorised.[56] There is little material in the English model of registration from which to mount any argument that the proprietor in these circumstances could not claim protection through resisting rectification and thereby casting the loss on the former landowner, or could not claim indemnity and thereby pass the burden to the indemnity fund contributors. The moral objection to upholding the register content in these conditions might be factored into the discretion available in rectification proceedings, but there is no equivalent mechanism for indemnity. So long as indemnity is barred only by contribution to the error, and not to exacerbating its effects, then the proprietor stands to gain from reprehensible conduct.

Moral objections to the unmitigated effects of the proxy are already reflected in certain other legal doctrines. Wherever the supposed policy of fulfilling a proprietor's expectation of retaining the registered rights appears to transgress such an external legal rule, it becomes necessary to identify which must give way to the other. Two potentially conflicting legal rules demand consideration: the rule of chronological priority for unprotected, precarious interests,[57] and the rule permitting rescission of voidable dispositions.

B. Precarious Interests

The proposed explanation for the rectification and indemnity scheme is founded on the protection of the expectations of those who have inspected or who had the

---

[56] Eg Land Registration Act 2001 (c 6), s 35(7) (Nova Scotia) and Métis Settlements Land Registry Regulation (Reg 36/1991), r 34(1) (Alberta). The Foreign and Commonwealth Office's model statute for title registration in the colonies was intended to restrict indemnity to entries pursuant to an intended disposition: SR Simpson, *Land Law and Registration* (Cambridge, Cambridge University Press, 1976) 596 (making an all too subtle distinction between 'damage' and 'loss').

[57] That is, those interests which, if unregistered, are liable to cede priority to a registered transferee under LRA 2002, ss 29 or 30.

opportunity to inspect the mistaken entry in the register. It is possible to imagine circumstances in which this protective function could collide with the basic rule that the priority of precarious interests vis-à-vis other interests is to be determined by their chronological order.[58] For example, if the proprietor were to grant an option to purchase, which the optionee protected by entry but the registry later deleted without authorisation, then the proprietor might long afterwards review the register to confirm his title before investing in development of the land, having forgotten the existence of the option.[59] In these circumstances, the proposed policy of protecting the expectations of a proprietor who relies on the register otherwise than for informing a decision to buy would require that the proprietor be able to resist the optionee's rectification proceedings or claim indemnity. To protect the proprietor in that fashion would deny the enforcement of the option. No doubt an appropriate response could be achieved by enforcement through contract law, thereby sidelining any question of rectifying the register, but that solution would not assist if the example were altered from the grant of an option to the grant of an easement to a donee with no overlying contractual relation. Short of some remedial equitable intervention to create an obligation out of the omitted easement, the supposed policy of protecting the proprietor's expectations induced from the clear register would remain intact, despite its intuitively repugnant consequences of allowing the grantor to resile from his own grant. This is a case in which the policy of upholding expectations would be in tension with the policy of upholding the grantee's security of receipt.

The solution through *in personam* obligations such as contract would be equally unavailing if the land had passed to a new proprietor otherwise than for valuable consideration, such as the heir of the original grantor. The policy of preserving the priority of precarious interests according to chronological order would apply here, but in these circumstances there is a rather stronger justification for protecting the proprietor's expectations. The heir might have few leads to follow in seeking off-register information on title, yet might require perfectly sound title before committing expenditure to investment in the land. Without an assurance of reliability of the register, the heir would be discouraged from improvements without wide-ranging and inconclusive enquiries into potential outstanding precarious interests. Offering protection to the heir's reliance on the register in these circumstances would at least serve the purpose of removing the incentive to incur title investigation costs,[60] but it nevertheless remains in tension with the policy of preserving the priority of precarious interests against all but a transferee for value.

One field in which these opposing arguments will be tested is likely to be found in the statutory definition of rectification, which requires that it 'prejudicially affects the title of a registered proprietor'.[61] This neglected phrase has not been the subject

---

[58] LRA 2002, s 28.

[59] There is little coherent jurisprudence on the failure of a right holder to forestall priority disputes due to his forgetfulness or failure of corporate memory: see *Sinclair Investments (UK) Ltd v Versailles Trade Finance Ltd* [2011] EWCA Civ 347 and *William Sindall plc v Cambridgeshire County Council* [1993] EWCA Civ 14.

[60] TW Mapp, *Torrens' Elusive Title* (Edmonton, AILRR, 1978) 125; P O'Connor, 'Registration of Title in England and Australia: A Theoretical and Comparative Perspective' in E Cooke, *Modern Studies in Property Law*, vol II (Oxford, Hart Publishing, 2003) 91.

[61] LRA 2002, Sch 4, para 1(b). The first modern case to raise it has just appeared: *Swift 1st Ltd v Chief Land Registrar* [2014] All ER (D) 12.

of significant analysis. There are alternative interpretative options. First, it might refer to derogating from the state of a proprietor's title as appearing from the register entries. Taking this approach, the proposed insertion of an unprotected precarious interest would constitute rectification, enabling the proprietor to mount a discretionary resistance to the alteration or claim indemnity, even though the interest was binding on the proprietor according to the priority rules. The proprietor would claim that the relevant form of prejudice was depriving him of the opportunity to represent a clear title to others, such as prospective purchasers, and to negotiate a price based on unencumbered ownership, even though he himself was bound and the unprotected interest would be defeated by the sale. That line of argument was rejected in *Attorney-General v Odell*[62] under a forerunner of the modern legislative provision.[63] It is submitted that the argument should be similarly rejected under the current legislation.[64] It would not only have preserved the informational asymmetry between the proprietor and buyer which he had hoped to exploit, but it would more generally impede the mission to increase the comprehensiveness of the register as a record of rights.[65]

The second interpretative option would be that proprietor's plea of 'prejudice to title' must refer to a proposed change to the register which derogates from the priority rules established elsewhere in the Act (particularly the basic and special rules).[66] The insertion of a precarious interest which was already binding on the proprietor according to the priority rules would not amount to rectification under this interpretation. It would therefore avoid the rectification jurisdiction altogether and consequently deny eligibility for indemnity. Presumably the insertion of the precarious interest could be achieved through the separate head of alteration that is available to 'bring the register up to date' and for which no indemnity is available.[67] This route would avoid the criticisms aimed at the interpretation proposed in *Odell* and would have the advantage of reflecting the actual allocation of entitlements in the land rather than the incomplete information about title that is revealed from the register which excludes unprotected precarious interests and overriding interests. This second interpretation of 'prejudice to title' would therefore provide a satisfactory means to resolve the tension between the protection of the proprietor's induced expectations and the preservation of precarious interests in favour of the latter.

C. Voidable Transactions

The supposed policy of protecting the expectations of those who have inspected, or who had the opportunity to inspect the mistaken entry in the register, could also run into competition with the rule permitting rescission of voidable dispositions. For

---

[62] *Attorney-General v Odell* [1906] 2 Ch 47, 75 (Vaughan-Williams LJ).
[63] Land Transfer Act 1897, s 7(4) referring to the claimant 'suffering loss' by the alteration.
[64] It has observed that this theory might, however, explain the decision in *Rees v Peters* [2011] EWCA Civ 836: A Goymour, 'Mistaken Registrations of Land: Exploding the Myth of Title by Registration' [2013] *CLJ* 617, fn 112.
[65] Law Commission and HM Land Registry, *Land Registration for the Twenty-First Century* (Law Com 271, 2001) para 1.5.
[66] LRA 2002, ss 28 and 29.
[67] LRA 2002, Sch 4, para 2(1)(b).

example, if a purchaser were to become registered pursuant to a disposition tainted by his undue influence, he might afterwards review the register to confirm his title before investing in development of the land, unmindful of the circumstances that rendered the disposition voidable. This scenario requires examination of whether such genuine reliance on a clear register should affect the status of the grantor's undisclosed right to rescind.

The mainstream approach is to regard the voidable character of a transaction as inappropriate for handling through rectification or indemnity, even once the victim has rescinded.[68] Instead, it would see the voidable disposition as initially effective to transfer ownership, and the subsequent rescission would be categorised as a supervening event which changed entitlements. That analysis treats the event of rescission as the foundation for an application to bring the register up to date[69] which is all but mandatory. It has the effect of detracting from the reliability of the register, since the proprietor's expectations induced by inspection are unprotected: he has no opportunity to resist rectification or recover indemnity. This effect has been perceived as unsatisfactory and is the origin of a minority critical approach that would insist on running the reversal of voidable grants through the discretionary power of rectification by classifying the entry of the defective disposition as a statutory mistake from the start.[70] Despite the authority of the joint report of the Land Registry and Law Commission,[71] the courts have so far been cautious to avoid choosing between the mainstream and critical positions.[72]

The central issue over voidable dispositions of registered land is whether the policy of protecting the grantee's reliance on the register should ever be able to trump the policies which justify the grantor's rescission. If so, the grantor's claim to rescind must be governed by rectification and the grantee must be given the opportunity to raise his induced expectations as a discretionary factor in the rectification proceedings. Had the recipient himself been implicated in creating the circumstances leading to the defect in the grant, no doubt this would be a powerful factor in the exercise of discretion and should also block indemnity due to the contribution to the error since even the amoral register should not tolerate the outrage of an oppressor gaining by his oppression. But where the vitiating factors arise from another source, a policy decision must be taken. On the one hand, the goal of protecting the vulnerable, which lies at the heart of voidable dispositions, suggests that there is, at the least, a conceivable policy in favour of limiting the extent to which register-based expectations should be upheld. On the other, there is the moral force of the grantee's honest

---

[68] *Norwich & Peterborough Building Society v Steed* [1993] Ch 116, decided under the LRA 1925; Law Commission and HM Land Registry, *Land Registration for the Twenty-First Century* (Law Com 271, 2001) para 10.7(1), fn 23. This is also the approach taken explicitly in Land Registration, etc (Scotland) Act 2012, s 65(4).

[69] LRA 2002, Sch 4, para 2(1)(b).

[70] PJ Clarke, 'Registered Land' [1993] *All England Law Reports Annual Review* 242, 246; C Davis, 'A Restrictive Approach to Rectification' [1992] *Conveyancer and Property Lawyer* 293, 297.

[71] Law Commission and HM Land Registry, *Land Registration for the Twenty-First Century* (Law Com 271, 2001) para 10.7(1), fn 23.

[72] *Baxter v Mannion* [2011] EWCA Civ 120 [31] (Jacob LJ), 'I would reserve my position'; *Garwood v Bank of Scotland plc* [2012] EWHC 415 [70]–[72] (Norris J), 'I do not have to decide this issue'. Under the New Zealand reforms, the reversal of voidable dispositions will be governed by discretionary rectification: New Zealand Land Transfer Bill 2010, cl 13.

forgetfulness and good faith reliance on the register, although these are matters that must be evaluated with an eye to the obvious moral hazard of the proprietor misrepresenting his mental state. These are the considerations which must ultimately influence the decision whether the grantor's claim is allocated to discretionary rectification or administrative updating of the register.

V. CONCLUSION

This chapter has attempted to dispel the air of puzzlement over a registration system which, in the event of a mistaken registered entitlement, appears to confer the right to claim compensation, or resist its reversal, on a person who was not expecting it, never relied on it, did not plan his affairs around it, and perhaps never even knew of it. The answer lies in a defensible policy of fulfilling expectations induced by the register, coupled with a practical concession to convenience by employing proxy rules for the implementation of this policy. Proxy rules have an important place in property law. Their ability to provide a simple route to a predictable result strikes a chord with the aspirations of land law in providing *ex ante* certainty of entitlement which enables people to plan investment in land with confidence. But there are important caveats: the use of proxy rules must not conceal the policy objectives which underlie them so as to risk leading the interpreter astray, and in simplifying the implementation they must not deviate too far from their underlying policy objectives with a counterproductive result. This chapter has shown that there is reason to object on both counts to the English provisions for rectification and indemnity.

First, it was argued that those provisions were explicable only by the policy objective of fulfilling the expectations that had been induced by knowledge of the register content. The obliqueness of the statutory text from which this was inferred can be demonstrated by contrasting it with the elegant form of assurance in Scotland, which overtly recognises that register entries are guaranteed in favour of particular persons for particular purposes and that it is a fallacy to think of register information as reliable in the abstract: 'The Keeper, in accepting an application for registration, warrants to the applicant that, as at the time of registration, the title sheet is accurate'.[73] Secondly, it was argued that the rectification and indemnity provisions deviate significantly from the underlying policy objective due to their embodiment as ill-fitting proxy rules. This is particularly dangerous for property as it might uphold the rights of a mistakenly-entered new proprietor who falls within the proxy rules but outside the policy objective underpinning them, and might therefore expropriate the former proprietor without any justification other than the convenience of having rules that are easy to administer. This is of questionable compatibility with the constitutional principle that deprivation of possessions must not only be compensated but also strictly justified by public interest.[74]

This chapter has dwelt on the issue of the operation of and justification for the rectification and indemnity provisions in relation to persons other than prospective purchasers seeking a good root of title, showing that it is quite inadequate to

---

[73] Land Registration, etc (Scotland) Act 2012, s 73.
[74] *Ying v Governor in Council* [1997] 3 LRC 101 (PC); *Kelo v City of London* (2005) 545 US 469 (US Supreme Court).

describe English land registration as merely a purchaser's system. This naturally invites a review of the wider impact of protecting the register-induced expectations of all registered proprietors even though they could not or should not have relied on the entry. The current policy of protecting such a wide constituency of actors weighs heavily on the indemnity fund contributors and has the capacity to destroy conflicting property rights where the justification for doing is distinctly weak. To excise the most egregious examples, the legislation should at least adopt a pared down version of the assurance of reliability which would decline protection on proof of the absence of induced expectations. The chapter has also suggested compensating only the expenditure incurred in reliance on the register rather than the value of the property lost, and refusing relief in the cases of oppression as embodied in the law of voidable transactions. Given the contemporary sensitivity to the pressures on the compensation fund and to the constitutional propriety of expropriating private owners, an even more robust response would rebalance social priorities so as to focus protection exclusively on purchasers. Reform need not halt there: far from the past reform ambitions of easing purchaser's conveyancing investigations in the interests of efficient market allocation of land, future reform should recognise the strength of the compensation and constitutional arguments of the current environment in justifying the costs of higher standards of diligence on purchasers—such as more onerous steps for identity verification—as a precondition to their benefitting from the assurance of reliability.

18

Commonhold Developments in Practice

LU XU*

I. INTRODUCTION

COMMONHOLD AS A new form of land ownership in England and Wales was introduced by statute in 2002 and commenced in 2004.[1] Although it is a system designed mainly for newly built apartment buildings, it can facilitate developments of structurally independent houses, mixed commercial and residential buildings, and conversion from long leasehold. The owner of a commonhold unit, for example an apartment, owns the freehold estate of the unit.[2] The common parts of the apartment building, such as stairs and the surrounding grounds, are owned by the commonhold association,[3] a company limited by guarantee.[4] Each unit owner is automatically a member of the commonhold association,[5] hence enjoying a sense of ownership and certain level of collective control over the parts that he does not individually own. The freehold status of commonhold makes it immediately distinguishable from the system of long leasehold, which governs the vast majority of existing apartment buildings in England and Wales. The 'owner' of a leasehold apartment holds only a lease, often for an artificially long period such as 100 years so that it resembles ownership in some regards. But the leaseholder is bound by covenants in the lease, such as the obligations to pay for maintenance and repairs. Such arrangements sidestep the difficulty of imposing positive obligations on freehold land under English law, but at the costs of sacrificing ownership and creating its own problems such as the conflicting interests of landlords and tenants. For many years, commonhold has been envisaged as the modern replacement of leasehold that would solve such problems.

* Senior Lecturer in Property Law, Lancaster University; formerly Lecturer in Property Law at University of East Anglia. I am grateful to the British Academy for providing the funding that made this research possible. I would like to thank UEA colleagues from the Law School and the Research Office who helped at various stages of this project. I am indebted to my two successive assistants, Mavis Amonoo-Acquah and Simone Schroffe. Their commitment and perseverance in being sent on often thankless tasks have been an integral part of this research. I would like to thank the editor and the anonymous referee for their valuable comments. All mistakes and omissions remain my own.

[1] Commonhold and Leasehold Reform Act 2002, hereinafter CLRA 2002; Commonhold and Leasehold Reform Act 2002 (Commencement No 4) Order (SI 2004/1832).
[2] CLRA 2002, ss 11–13.
[3] CLRA 2002, s 7.
[4] CLRA 2002, s 34.
[5] CLRA 2002, Sch 3, para 7.

Many jurisdictions have systems similar to commonhold, though under different names such as condominium or strata titles, governing hundreds of thousands of flats, houses and complexes.[6] What makes the English commonhold stand out is its failure to take root despite a lengthy legislative process that stretched back more than 20 years. Fewer than 20 developments have been registered as commonhold in the 10 years since its commencement. Such unpopularity puzzled long-time supporters and commentators for a few years, who offered explanations and even suggestions that things might change for the better. They did not. Nobody has really talked about commonhold anymore in the last few years.

Yet it would seem inappropriate to simply forget about such a long-awaited innovation in land ownership for its lack of success. This project, Commonhold Developments in Practice, kindly funded by the British Academy, embarked in 2012 to look closer at the neglected commonhold system from practical and empirical perspectives. The project examined registration documents of all existing commonhold developments. It then contacted many individuals in various capacities who had dealt with commonhold including unit owners, directors, conveyancers, estate agents and financial advisors. The goal was to understand how well the limited number of existing commonhold developments function in practice, the problems that they encounter, their understanding and perception of commonhold, as well as their reasons for choosing commonhold in the first place.

The findings of this research will not be heartening for anyone who still hopes that commonhold could survive the initial cold reception and grow on its theoretical merits when its time comes. Commonhold is a dying idea and is becoming less and less attractive and feasible. It can function reasonably well in some rare cases thanks to the knowledge and dedication of individuals involved. But there are also a number of unit owners who feel trapped in a failed system with no obvious way out. There are difficulties in getting people involved in the property market to understand, let alone to accept, the concept. There are major factors such as the availability of mortgage finance that actively hinders the continued normal operation of existing schemes. Without coordinated efforts and commitment from all the major stakeholders including the government, banks, property developers and conveyancers, commonhold had no chance and will continue to have no chance of taking root in England and Wales. The question, it seems, is not whether there is any obvious cure for the system of commonhold, but whether it should be cured at all. It is submitted on the basis of the findings that it is now time for policymakers to make a decision, as doing nothing will only lead to a protracted and painful extinction of the idea of commonhold.

II. BACKGROUND

It is possible to identify two related but distinguishable origins for the idea of commonhold. The first is the inability to impose positive covenants on freehold land in English law. This aspect of the law was well documented and criticised by

---

[6] Eg New South Wales, which was one of the first jurisdictions to establish such a system, now has over 700,000 strata titles lots. Canada reported 1.6 million households living in condominiums in 2011.

the Wilberforce Committee in 1965,[7] which is often seen as planting the seed of commonhold.[8] The 1960s was incidentally the decade when the idea of a statutory structure for apartment ownership was being adopted for the first time in many other English-speaking jurisdictions such as the US, Australia and Singapore.[9] The Law Commission made a couple of notable efforts to follow up on the main findings of the Wilberforce Committee in the shape of a working paper and a report.[10] Their 1984 report contained the idea of a 'development scheme' which could be seen as the earliest incarnation of commonhold that we know today.[11]

Meanwhile, the name 'commonhold' was coined by Sir Brandon Rhys Williams MP in 1978 in a Ten Minute Rule Bill,[12] in the context of leasehold reform, which would be the second stream of initiatives that led to the eventual commonhold system. The term was 'adopted' by the Aldridge Committee,[13] an interdepartmental government working group set up in 1986 to formalise a proposal of condominium style legislation. The Committee produced a landmark report in 1987.[14] This was followed by a Draft Bill prepared by the Law Commission and a Consultation Paper in 1990,[15] another Consultation Paper and Draft Bill in 1996, before the third Draft Bill with a Consultation Paper in 2000[16] eventually made to the statute book in 2002. Henceforth 'commonhold' meant to lawyers something very different from what it was first composed by politicians to denote, which would be a form of leasehold enfranchisement or management entity. However, such differences or fundamental change in content was not always appreciated by the political parties who promoted the idea. Commonhold legislation was explained as giving residential leaseholders the right to acquire freehold of their flats at market rate in the 1992 Conservative Party general election manifesto. The Labour Party's 2001 election manifesto pledged to promote housing choices 'with reforms to leasehold and commonhold law', despite the fact that there was no commonhold law in existence to be reformed at that time.

What could be discerned from the lack of precision in understanding in political propaganda was that commonhold had always been some kind of add-on or accessory to other, more substantial initiatives.[17] At first it was a specialised area

---

[7] *Report of the Committee on Positive Covenants Affecting Land* (Cmnd 2719, 1965).

[8] G Fetherstonhaugh, M Sefton and E Peters, *Commonhold* (Oxford, Oxford University Press, 2004) para 1.4.2.

[9] Model Statute for the Creation of Apartment Ownership (1961); Conveyancing (Strata Titles) Act 1961 (New South Wales); Land Titles (Strata) Act 1967; CG van der Merwe, *Apartment Ownership* in Drobnig and Zweigert (eds), *International Encyclopaedia of Comparative Law*, vol VI, ch V (Dordrecht, Martinus Nijihoff Publishers, 1994) paras 10–14.

[10] Law Commission, *Transfer of Land: Appurtenant Rights* (Law Com Working Paper No 36, 1971); Law Commission, *Transfer of Land: The Law of Positive and Restrictive Covenants* (Law Com No 127, 1984).

[11] Law Com No 127, Pt VII.

[12] N Roberts, 'Commonhold: A New Property Term—but no Property in a Term!' [2002] *Conveyancer and Property Lawyer* 341.

[13] *Commonhold—Freehold Flats and Freehold Ownership of Other Independent Buildings* (Cm 179, 1987) Preface, v.

[14] Ibid.

[15] Lord Chancellor's Department, *Commonhold: A Consultation Paper* (Cm 1345, 1990).

[16] Lord Chancellor's Department, *Commonhold and Leasehold Reform: Draft Bill and Consultation Paper* (Cm 4843, 2000).

[17] Such dual characteristics of commonhold were touched upon before, see N Roberts, 'The "Widows and Orphans" of Leasehold Reform' in E Cooke (ed), *Modern Studies in Property Law*, vol 2 (Oxford, Hart Publishing, 2003) 281.

under the general objective to introduce positive obligations on freehold estates. That reform has yet to materialise nearly 50 years after the Wilberforce Committee, with the added volume of another Law Commission report on land obligations in 2011 yet to be acted upon by the legislature.[18] In this regard, commonhold was perhaps fortunate to become more closely associated with leasehold reform, taking on the name which was first meant for leasehold, and finally cementing its place on the statute book at least a decade ahead of any sign of positive land obligations. Nevertheless by explicitly joining the company of leasehold reform in various election manifestos as well as the Commonhold and Leasehold Reform Act 2002 (CLRA) itself, commonhold perhaps always had to strive for its 'market share' from scratch, alongside the familiar and well-established leasehold system already governing millions of flats. There were views in the 1990s that the protracted process of introducing the commonhold could mean that it would be 'otiose' by the time it was introduced because leasehold reform could come into effect quicker.[19] In some sense only if the leasehold reform turns out to be a disaster would commonhold get its chance of becoming a major success.

Still, as far as background and preparations went, there was no reason to believe that commonhold would not enjoy some success even without challenging the domination of leasehold. It featured in four manifestos of the two frontrunners in three general elections, hence having the support of three successive governments.[20] In the four decades leading to the legislation, there were at least five governmental or Law Commission papers, three Draft Bills, a number of publications from other organisations,[21] hundreds of articles and commentaries from academics and practitioners, numerous consultations and discussions dealing with principles, details, perceived problems and suggestions for improvement. It seems reasonable to suggest that the failure of the commonhold was not down to lack of understanding and preparation, or any untimely change of government and shift in public opinion and perception. Of course there would have been people sceptical about a new idea. But perhaps even the most audacious of them would not have foreseen the scale of the failure awaiting commonhold.

III. HOW MANY?

Hard numbers are perhaps the most obvious indication of any problem of scale. One rather blunt estimate by the Lord Chancellor's Department following the enactment of the CLRA 2002 was that there could be as many as 6,500 new commonhold units every year once the Act commenced.[22] That was an optimistic estimate. The first thing the project set out to establish was how many commonhold schemes were in

---

[18] The Law Commission, *Making Land Work: Easements, Covenants and Profits à Prendre* (Law Com No 327, 2011).

[19] 'Commonhold Again' (Conveyancer's Notebook) [1996] *Conveyancer and Property Lawyer* 321, 322.

[20] The Conservative Party in 1992 and 1997, Labour Party in 1997 and 2001.

[21] Most notably College of Estate Management Research Paper 90/03, *Commonhold: Is the Cure Worse than the Complaint?* (Reading, 1990).

[22] Lord Chancellor's Department Consultation Paper, *Commonhold Proposals for Commonhold Regulations* (Oct 2002) Annex F, para 9.

operation, by correlating information from the Companies House to registered titles at the Land Registry. In short, there were 16 commonhold schemes in operation as of 1 January 2014.

That figure could be explained a bit further. There have been more than 40 companies registered with the Companies House since the 1990s with the word 'commonhold' in their names. Many of these predate the commencement of the CLRA 2002 in September 2004 so such names are probably by-products of the confusion over the commonhold concept mentioned earlier. A commonhold association in the context of CLRA 2002 must have 'Commonhold Association Limited' at the end of its registered name.[23] But that did not prevent one particular commonhold association changing its name into a 'Commonhold Association' without 'Limited' in 2008. On the other hand, a leasehold management company incorporated in 2006 decided to change its name into a 'Commonhold Limited' in 2007. Leaving aside these minor anomalies, there have been 33 'true' commonhold associations incorporated as intended by the CLRA 2002. Eleven of those 33 had been dissolved or struck off since incorporation by 2012, to be discussed further below in relation to timing. The remaining 22 were operational as companies on 1 January 2014.

But not every commonhold association in operation as a company is necessarily an active commonhold development or community. To borrow a term from Professor Clarke, a commonhold will need to be 'activated' by having freehold land registered to its name.[24] Five of those 22 had had no landholding by the end of 2013, and thus not activated. Another commonhold association incorporated in 2007 received a parcel of land but went into administration in 2010 without completing the development. This scheme would seem to be the reason why the Land Registry previously reported a total of 17 commonhold schemes.[25]

In any case, we arrive at the final number count of 16 commonhold developments in practice. There is hardly any word to describe the insignificance of such a number amongst thousands of new leasehold schemes being created every year, or the amasing shortfall from the governmental estimate of 6,500 new units per year.

IV. WHEN?

Aside from the number of schemes, another equally interesting question is when they were created. The chart below illustrates the time when all 33 commonhold associations were incorporated, as well as the time when those 11 commonhold associations were dissolved or struck off.

It could be seen that there was an early rush, relative to the total number of commonhold developments, within two years of the commencement of CLRA 2002 in September 2004. But it seems that some people soon started to realise that there was a problem and promptly withdrew from commonhold before 'activation'. Few came

---

[23] Or its Welsh equivalent Cymdeithas Cydradd-Ddaliad, Commonhold Regulations 2004 (SI 2004/1829) reg 12. No company has been registered in the latter form in Welsh.

[24] DN Clarke, *Commonhold: The New Law* (Bristol, Jordan Publishing, 2002) xxxiv.

[25] C Harpum, S Bridge and M Dixon, *Megarry & Wade's The Law of Real Property*, 8th edn (London, Sweet & Maxwell, 2012) para 33-001.

after 2006. In fact no commonhold association was incorporated for nearly four years between September 2008 and July 2012. There have been three incorporated since July 2012, but none has been 'activated' with land ownership.

Table 1: Commonhold companies date of incorporation and dissolution

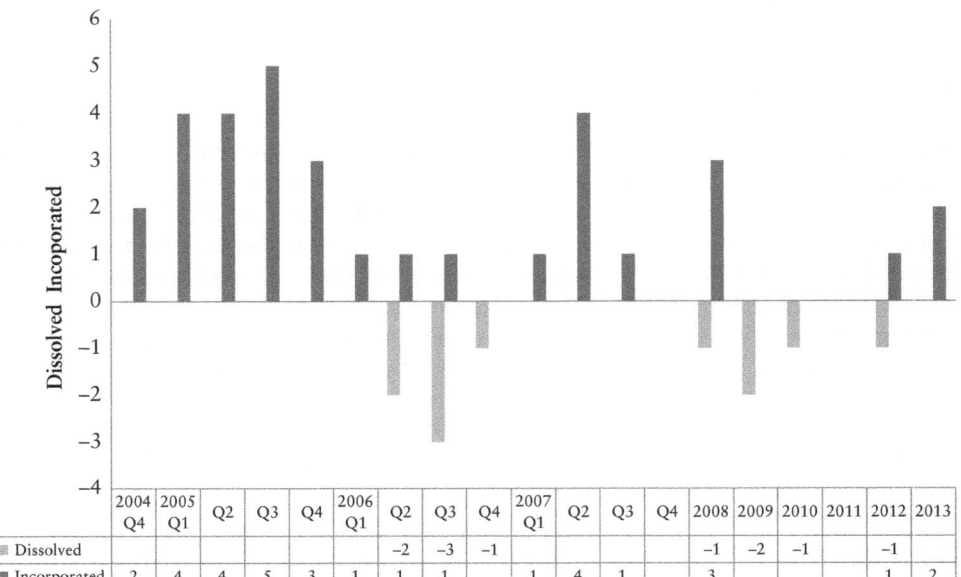

	2004 Q4	2005 Q1	Q2	Q3	Q4	2006 Q1	Q2	Q3	Q4	2007 Q1	Q2	Q3	Q4	2008	2009	2010	2011	2012	2013
Dissolved							−2	−3	−1					−1	−2	−1		−1	
Incorporated	2	4	4	5	3	1	1	1		1	4	1		3				1	2

Looking at the data in more detail, it could be said that the turning point in the fate of commonhold was sometime in 2006. Thirteen of the 21 commonhold associations registered before August 2006 were eventually 'activated' with land holding and have since survived into the current 16. At the same time, between May and December 2006, six other companies registered at roughly the same time as those 13 dissolved and abandoned the idea of commonhold. It would seem that some people must have realised or sensed something wrong with commonhold during those eight months. Commonhold did not recover from that setback. Of the 12 companies to be incorporated since 2007, only three have been activated. By the time the unpopularity of commonhold became public knowledge in print, it was perhaps already too late to hope for a different ending. With hindsight, some suggestions by commentators during those years that commonhold could perhaps become popular on its own were overly optimistic.[26] Then there was of course the complication of the global financial crisis which certainly had profound impact on the construction industry. Nevertheless, the findings of this research indicate that the crisis for commonhold

---

[26] Eg S Rowe, 'Uncommon Title' (2007) 0704 *Estates Gazette* 136; J Driscoll, 'Whatever Happened to Commonhold' (2008) 158 *New Law Journal* 1137.

arrived at least one year or 18 months before the economic storm. Thus it would seem unwarranted to blame such untimely turns of world events for the failure of the commonhold. Nor would it be realistic to hope that once the general economy and housing market recovers, as we are now led to believe, commonhold would perhaps get its share of the growth.

V. SIZE, VARIETY AND LOCATION

The system of commonhold sets a minimum number of two units for any scheme with no maximum limit.[27] In practice, a large proportion of the 16 developments in operation are very small. There are 141 units in total across all 16, averaging just below nine units per scheme. However, only three schemes have more than 10 units, and together they account for almost half of all commonhold units. The average number of units for the other 13 schemes is below six units per scheme. This is somewhat surprising as the previous expectation was that smaller developments might not want the 'complication' of running a commonhold association.[28]

Bearing in mind the small number of schemes and units, there is certainly a good variety of commonhold, including newly built and conversions, residential and mixed-use, flats and detached houses, even a scheme with no substantial 'building'. A commonhold in Bristol with seven units has ground floor offices and six residential flats over three upper storeys. The largest commonhold development by number of units is a caravan park in Kent with 30 units. The smaller developments with

Table 2: Number of commonhold schemes by size

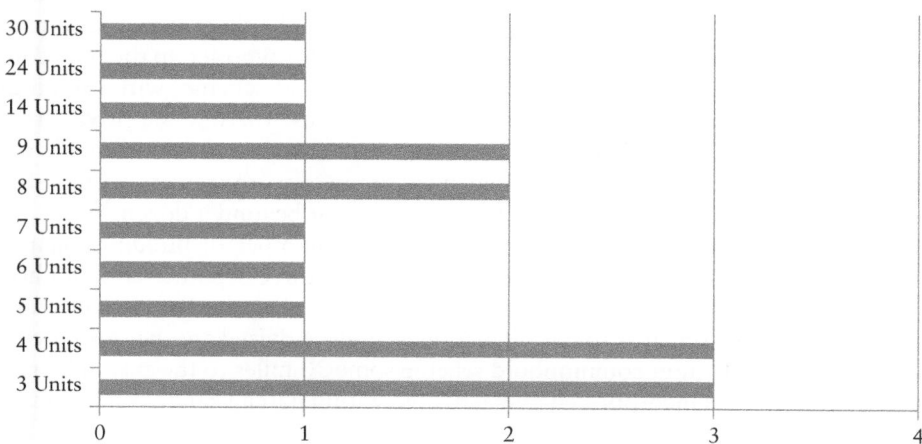

27 CLRA 2002, s 11(2)(a).
28 N Roberts, 'Two Cheers for Commonhold?" (2002) 152 *New Law Journal* 338.

three or four units, on the other hand, were converted from existing semi-detached or terrace houses in well-established residential areas. One would not realise that these are commonhold buildings without examining their registered titles.

With so few commonholds scattered around the country, it is unsurprising that there is no meaningful pattern as to their location. With the exception of one instance of three commonhold schemes clustered in the same place, to be discussed below, no scheme is within 10 miles of another. Even major cities such as London or Manchester only have one scheme each.

VI. WHY (OR WHY NOT) COMMONHOLD?

The great diversity of these schemes and the lack of any obvious trend make the question of 'why commonhold' even more fascinating. The answers from those involved in commonhold provided helpful insight into the components of status quo.

For the smaller commonhold consisting of three or four units, several were set up by owners who converted existing buildings into flats for their own use by different family members or other parties already known. They often heard about the idea by chance (Radio 4 was mentioned by two individuals from different schemes) and were attracted to it by some of the advertised advantages, such as the notion of a freehold as different from the 'wasting asset' of a lease, and the avoidance of the complications in leases and a landlord (especially amongst family members and friends). Often the person who made the decision had some related experience in property matters, such as having been a builder, an independent financial advisor, or a retired solicitor. But these were not decisions made in the course of business or profession. And in order to deal with the conveyancing aspects of creating a commonhold, they often asked for favours from solicitors who were friends or ex-colleagues.

The larger schemes were mostly built or converted by locally based property developers in the course of their business. The decision to go for commonhold often came from the solicitor advising them, who at the time thought there were advantages under the specific circumstances. For example, the solicitor who set up the only commonhold in Wales, which is also the largest commonhold scheme 'with buildings' comprising 24 newly built detached houses, did it because there was a private road serving the estate which could require long-term maintenance and attention. He was concerned that the traditional style management company arrangement would often encounter difficulty once the number of properties went beyond a dozen.[29]

Another developer based in Somerset renovated a number of buildings sharing a courtyard. The solicitor it instructed recommended three separate commonhold schemes with five, eight and nine units respectively, creating the largest concentration of commonhold schemes to date. This solicitor also advised another local developer to establish a 14-unit commonhold scheme some 30 miles to the east in Dorset. With all four schemes incorporated and activated within half a year, they account for a quarter of all existing commonhold schemes in England and Wales.

---

[29] This particular scheme would seem to fit the description of 'gated communities' as discussed by urban planners, eg C Webster and R le Goix, 'Planning by Commonhold' (2005) *Economic Affairs* 19.

Another individual effort that made a huge numerical difference was behind the 30-unit caravan park, the largest commonhold scheme by number of units to date. A Canadian businessman who bought the site was understandably excited to hear that something similar to a condominium was being introduced into English law, avoiding the need to create the artificial structure of leases while retaining some collective control over individually owned caravan spaces. In his words he had to 'educate' not just buyers into the caravan park, but also their solicitors and even the Land Registry office he was dealing with. This owner has since stepped down from being a director of the commonhold but stayed on in an advisory role, to allow the unit-owners to run the scheme. It has been rather successful apparently as according to him there has been near full attendance at every general meeting with everyone feeling involved in the management of their properties.

Meanwhile, some of the ideas that did not eventually lead to operational commonhold schemes are nevertheless interesting as to what the limit of the current structure of commonhold should be. A group of house owners near Holyhead, Wales had been using a parcel of vacant land near their houses for parking for a number of years. The land concerned was apparently unregistered and ownerless. One of owners, who had family members in the building industry, suggested using commonhold as a vehicle for collectively taking over the ownerless land through adverse possession. They instructed a solicitor, incorporated the company, collected all the evidences of their usage and submitted application to the Land Registry. However, their application was rejected twice by the Land Registry on the grounds that their usage was seen as insufficient for possession and any usage was exercised by a number of individuals rather than a single entity. After a few years the owners on the advice of the solicitor decided to suspend the efforts and dissolved the commonhold association. The doctrinal questions that could be asked on the basis of such a scenario are fascinating to those who study the subject of statutory apartment ownership regimes. The popular theory is that such a statutory structure is based on a threefold unity of individual ownership of units, joint or common ownership of common parts by the company, and membership of the company for individual unit-holders.[30] However, it seems difficult to think of any reason why a commonhold association with no land holding cannot acquire land through adverse possession and then achieve such threefold unity. If that is indeed permissible, then there may be some ingenuity in the suspended efforts of these owners, especially given the fact that the legal title to any land under English law can only be held by up to four joint tenants, which would not be ideal for a group of more than four neighbours.

Adverse possession is not the only audacious usage people have come up with for commonhold: a property owner in Bristol incorporated two commonhold associations, yet to be activated with land holding. The plan contemplated was to ultimately convert two properties into one commonhold, despite the fact that the two sites are more than 10 miles apart from each other. The reasoning behind this was that the owner wanted to leave these two properties to his three minor children when they grew up, but also to keep them together as much as possible. And under

---

[30] CG van der Merwe (n 9) 47.

a commonhold, it would be very difficult for any one of them to sell one-third of both properties without the cooperation of the other two siblings. Such 'multiple site commonhold' is specifically provided for under CLRA 2002 to include 'two or more parcels of land, whether or not contiguous'.[31] However, commentators have always seen this as facilitating a single commonhold on both sides of a public road.[32] It has certainly never been envisaged to accommodate two properties on opposite ends of a city. Apparently no solicitor that the owner approached was prepared to help setting up any commonhold. But the owner suggested that he might go ahead in future with the plan anyway.

VII. FACTORS AND OBSTACLES IN CREATING COMMONHOLD SCHEMES

From the varied life stories of these commonhold schemes a couple of notable commonalities emerge. A considerable number of commonhold schemes were created by people not acting in any professional capacity such as conveyancers or property developers. Their source of information for making such decision was often coincidental such as a conversation with a friend or a radio programme. Some of them had relevant experience or knowledge of related matters from their employment or association, but still they were not in the best position to judge the exact trajectory of the idea of commonhold around the time of 2005 and 2006. They certainly could not have foreseen many of the problems to be encountered by commonhold in later years, to be discussed further below.

A very small number of professionals certainly did take on board the advantages and attractions of commonhold. They made a huge difference to the number of commonhold units, relatively speaking. In fact, three individuals who liked commonhold were behind the creation of 36, 30 and 24 commonhold units respectively. The three of them accounted for more than 60 per cent of all commonhold units in England and Wales, which in turn illustrated how unpopular commonholds have been with the rest of the tens of thousands of conveyancers and property developers.

It is perhaps fair to say that the attitude shown by most of the solicitors and firms towards commonhold ranged from professionally uninterested to downright ignorant. Quite a few solicitors did the incorporation and conveyancing work as a favour for a friend. One solicitor even convinced her firm to do this free of charge as staff training and a good public relation initiative. On the other hand, when there is no such helpful friend, a couple of people have found it difficult to get the advice or help they need from their local solicitors without being given some drastically higher price quotes than the run-of-the-mill leasehold matters.

Worse still, a considerable number of people contacted during this research felt they were not properly informed by their solicitors when buying into a commonhold. More than one person said that they were told by the solicitors that 'commonhold is not much different from a freehold' or that 'commonhold company is

---

[31] CLRA 2002, s 57(1).
[32] Clarke (n 24) para 2.11; Fetherstonhaugh (n 8) para 2.2.2.

just like a freehold or leasehold management company' and so on. One owner, who is a school teacher, bought a commonhold flat without any idea as to how recent or how unusual the whole system was, having heard the word 'commonhold' on only one occasion from her conveyancer. Beyond her expectation to say the least, she has since taken on company secretary and directorship because nobody else in this small scheme of three flats would do it. She is very upbeat and reckons that dealing with the Companies House and other matters is quite manageable once one learns after a few years of experience. A number of others are notably more displeased with the service provided by their conveyancers when they failed to explain the full implications of buying into a commonhold. One owner claimed to have taken serious consideration in bringing formal complaints against his conveyancer, because in his words had he known everything about commonhold he would never have bought the flat.

And if that is the level of familiarity with commonhold that some conveyancers are displaying, with all their rigorous continued professional development commitments, it perhaps should come as no great surprise that other people involved in the property market, such as estate agents or mortgage advisors, are now largely unable to come to terms with the concept at all. Many estate agents and financial advisors would have heard of commonhold back in the time when it was heralded as being a new revolutionary form of flat ownership.[33] Yet 10 to 12 years down the line, this knowledge without being reinforced has certainly faded. One estate agent, who is currently paid to be the director and manager of a commonhold, mentioned that she remembered learning about commonhold back in her university years, but had never encountered any in work until recently. So far as the marketing of properties is concerned, at the moment there is far more disinformation regarding commonhold than meaningful information. For example, a leading property marketing website advertised more than 40 listings for property described as 'commonhold' between 2010 and 2013. On close inspection, not a single one of these was a true commonhold as under the framework of CLRA 2002. Meanwhile, genuine commonhold units would frequently encounter difficulty fitting into the existing marketing structure. One estate agent told a commonhold unit owner that the system of his company could only deal with properties in either leasehold or freehold. And given the fact that a freehold flat might raise suspicion, it would perhaps be better to categorise a commonhold flat as leasehold and to explain things to potential purchasers later when they make enquiries.

Although individual tales could hardly present a rigorous analysis of the situation, they nevertheless vividly depict some of the difficulty faced by commonhold schemes and their current and future owners in asking for help from the professionals. Those who know enough about commonhold have mostly decided to stay out of it. Those who do not know enough are being vague about it and hope the trouble of having to learn about something new could be avoided through ignorance, which in many cases could not. In turn those who stayed out would perhaps congratulate

[33] There was suspicion even then that the industry was unprepared, see 'Industry Unprepared for the Arrival of Commonhold' *Financial Advisor*, 30 September 2004.

themselves on not getting involved in the first place. The downward spiral of having even less and less knowledge of the subject is complete within the conveyancing and property trade.

VIII. RUNNING AND DISPUTE RESOLUTION

Leaving aside the prevalent ignorance of commonhold from the outside, once a commonhold scheme is established it tends to function rather well internally. Among the 10 currently operational commonhold schemes that responded to the research, there has been no significant problem or dispute amongst the owners regarding the daily running of commonhold properties or the commonhold association. People living in close proximity and rather small communities adapt, with or without legal basis. Many of them never had a general meeting or a vote as prescribed by the grandeur of CLRA 2002 or Companies Act 2006. If the carpet in the hall needs replacing, someone goes around the block speaking to everyone. There have been some concerns when, for example, an owner is rather late in paying for maintenance bills or has had a few loud parties. But again these were sorted out in good neighbourly manners without anyone trying to invoke any 'law' within such small developments.

Such a finding could potentially mean that some of the discussion and criticism of commonhold in the last decade has been premature, or even misdirected. For instance, the lack of clarity in the dispute resolution mechanism of the commonhold legislation, without the ability to go to a clearly defined body such as the Lands Tribunal under Scots law, has been questioned by this author.[34] The fact that commonhold associations lacked 'teeth' in terms of enforcing financial obligations through property law means, such as a charge over the unit, was also widely criticised by many when commonhold was being ushered in.[35] In practice it would seem that such theoretical worries might not have been necessary. As against the background of the limited number and small size of those schemes in existence, none of them encountered any incident of serious financial dispute or default.

With hindsight, not having any 'teeth' was a sensible move for the initial introduction of commonhold.[36] The threat of a charge or lien could have confused or further alienated solicitors when advising their clients about potential purchase into a commonhold. It is reasonable to conclude from the evidence gathered in this research that the current statutory structure works, and works reasonably well for existing schemes, without the need to introduce new ground-breaking provisions or paradigm-shifting powers. Any ambition to emulate the intricate structures of foreign condominium law is likely to be counter-productive in the foreseeable future without substantial improvement in the general understanding of commonhold ideology by solicitors and the general public.

---

[34] L Xu, 'Managing and Maintaining Flatted Buildings: Some Anglo-Scottish Comparisons' [2010] *Edinburgh Law Review* 236, 256–57.

[35] Clarke (n 24) paras 11.18–11.24; Fetherstonhaugh (n 8) para 6.3.9; PF Smith, 'An Initial Assessment of English Commonholds' [2005] *Stellenbosch Law Review* 514, 529–30.

[36] It was certainly not a fatal flaw as suggested by some, eg A Jack, 'Commonhold: The Fatal Flaw' (2003) 153 *New Law Journal* 1907.

IX. THE DIFFICULTY OF MORTGAGE FINANCE

Despite the generally smooth internal operation, there is one significant difficulty outside of the confinement of the concrete and mortar of these schemes that is singled out by many owners. Mortgage finance on commonhold property is frowned upon by a number of major lenders, and is outright declined by several others.

The *Lenders' Handbook* on the Council of Mortgage Lenders website contained the question whether a lender will lend on commonhold property.[37] Of the 98 lenders who provided an answer, 39 said 'yes' outright, representing just below 40 per cent of the group. Fifteen said 'yes' with added qualification, such as acceptance for existing mortgage only, or the need to refer on a case-by-case basis. Amongst them were notable institutions such as Halifax/Bank of Scotland and Virgin Money. Forty-four more said 'no' outright, including lenders such as Royal Bank of Scotland/ Natwest and Santander.

For many years commonhold was said to be welcomed by financial institutions.[38] Such prevalent rejection of the idea in practice would firmly contradict such observation. Having not been able to get any sort of explanation from individual lenders, it would be difficult to know the exact reasoning behind a 'no' answer. In theory commonhold offers standardised terms without the need for lenders to examine individual leases and carry no risk such as forfeiture or restriction on assignment. It has been suggested that lenders may have concerns over the possibility of an 80 per cent majority decision to sell the development without the need to obtain unanimous consent.[39] Whether that is an important reason remains unclear. What is clear is that such concerns were never published in the public domain before or after the enactment of CLRA 2002. Meanwhile it could be observed that some of the rejection by individual lenders would seem irrational in the context of their own policies. For example, Royal Bank of Scotland and Natwest would lend on flying freehold and freehold flats with only one qualification that the loan is for less than 90 per cent of property valuation. Surely a commonhold flat with all the statutory structure and mechanisms in place is a more stable and secure asset than freehold flats maintained on the basis of private agreement between neighbours, if at all. On the other hand, the obvious commercial factor would be that with 98 lenders contending for 141 commonhold units in total in the whole country, even the largest banks would be lucky to get a handful of applications in a decade. Hardly any mortgagee would feel poorer for not having a slice of the commonhold cake.[40]

Whatever the reasons lie behind the lenders' decision, the fact remains that a potential buyer has roughly a 50/50 chance of running into a problem simply because the flat or house is a commonhold unit. That lenders will not lend on commonhold

---

[37] CML, *Lenders' Handbook*, Pt 5.9, www.cml.org.uk/cml/handbook/englandandwales#C5053 (accessed 31 March 2014).

[38] 'Commonhold Again' (Conveyancer's Notebook) [1996] *Conveyancer and Property Lawyer* 321, 322; Council of Mortgage Lenders, 'CML News and Views' No 16/2004 (31 August 2004).

[39] M Dowden, 'Very Little Appetite for a Change in Tenure' (2009) 0917 *Estates Gazette* 98.

[40] Such 'commercial reasons' were suggested before as explanation for the lack of enthusiasm from lenders. Eg N Martin, 'Commonhold Case Completed' *Mortgage Strategy*, 15 Aug 2005, 6; 'CML Considers Commonhold Mess' *Financial Advisor*, 17 Nov 2005.

is not 'a false assumption' as it was previously dismissed.[41] Instead this has been the most daunting of all problems in practice for commonhold owners, outweighing virtually all other practical or doctrinal advantages they care to notice. The viral effect of this was experienced by different owners in several schemes. As soon as one buyer got turned down by a high street name, he was always more likely to pull out of any attempt to buy the commonhold unit, rather than turn to another bank. It did not really matter that there were other major financial institutions offering loans on commonhold. Word got out in the block that there would be a problem in selling their units because some banks would not lend on commonhold. Everyone started to worry, including those with no intention to sell in the immediate future, because they felt unsure whether the situation would get better or worse in five or 10 years' time. Bad news travels fast and stays on people's mind for many years. Lawyers and estate agents will tell their future clients. When it came to real life experience, the suspicion and discontent created by one mortgage rejection from a major bank could not be repaired by any amount of governmental or scholarly publications promoting the soundness of the concept.

On knowing that a significant group of major lenders would not offer mortgage finance, why would any individual buy a commonhold flat instead of a leasehold flat? Even if the imminent purchase does not involve any loan, this will still over-shadow any future prospect of resale value. And if that is the logical assessment of individuals, why should any major property developer commit to building hundreds of commonhold units as was optimistically wished for by many people? But of course if no major project goes ahead, the number or market share of commonhold will not increase by any meaningful scale to prompt those lenders to rethink their seemingly irrational rejection of commonhold in the first place. Hence another unbreakable downward spiral leading to the practical non-acceptance of commonhold is in place. It is submitted on the basis of the finding of this research that this chain reaction started by the lending policy of some major financial institutions is the main and, as things stand, insurmountable stumbling block preventing the commonhold idea of having any chance to take root in England and Wales.

X. COMPANY LAW PERSPECTIVES

There were concerns over the potential impact of regulating commonhold associations within the framework of mainstream company law as companies limited by guarantee.[42] This author argued that the requirement of two directors,[43] in line with company law, would be a disadvantage in smaller developments.[44] Such inconvenience has certainly been noticed by some schemes where they would need to put forward two persons able and willing to deal with Companies House, annual returns and accounts from a rather limited choice of three or four ordinary people who had no previous experience of such things. Quite often one director ended up doing

---

[41] Driscoll (n 26) 1138.
[42] Reid and Gretton saw this as part of the reason why commonhold was unpopular in England, KGC Reid and GL Gretton, *Conveyancing 2009* (Edinburgh, Avizandum Publishing, 2010) 147.
[43] Commonhold Regulations 2004, Sch 2 para 38.
[44] L Xu (n 34) 255.

everything anyway. If this person then somehow lapsed into inaction after a number of years, there could be rather serious consequences later for the owners, to be discussed below. In one commonhold scheme where all but one unit were let out to tenants, they simply struggled to find two names to fill the directorship. In the end, the owners had to pay an estate management company to act as the directors of the commonhold association limited.

As mentioned above, the reality in many smaller commonhold schemes is that no annual general meeting is held, despite this being the regulation requirement of the standard articles of association for commonhold.[45] Other than dealing with matters arising as they do, the main part of the directors' duties seems to be compliance with regulatory formalities under the Companies Act, more specifically filing annual returns and accounts in time.

It has been questioned whether these very small, non-trading companies comprising of people not accustomed to company law routines would comply with such formalities.[46] In practice virtually all the operating commonhold schemes, having been in place for at least five years by now, do comply with such requirements. Sometimes the returns could be overdue for a few months but in general things seem to be reasonably up-to-date. Expectedly, it is not a task met with any enthusiasm and a couple of directors commented on the modest cost and rather pointless nature of such operation in the context of commonhold.

Many of these 'annual reports' from commonhold associations are indeed pointless. For example, in the latest annual accounts for all 16 operating commonhold schemes available by the end of 2013, nine of them produced a figure of 'nil' or simply left blank for asset balance, notwithstanding the fact that each company must at least own the common parts of the scheme. Among the other seven that supplied some information, at least two used rather obvious figures that would not take an accountant to realise its artificial nature. Equally interestingly, a number of commonhold associations in their accounts declared a share capital (at £1 each ordinary share), while being a company limited by guarantee with no share capital. Hence if anyone is serious about these accounts lodged with the Companies House, two-thirds of all commonhold associations would perhaps need to redo their homework. But of course nobody is at any loss because of this and it is difficult to see the merit in forcing these companies which hardly ever deals with the outside world to incur the extra costs and efforts for meticulously reporting. The false corporate veil of the commonhold association in terms of limited liability has been exposed before.[47] There is really no risk for creditors or any other party dealing with commonhold schemes or unit owners based on unreliable accounts, as the company can always impose additional levy on its member owners should it struggle to meet its liabilities. That is perhaps the main reason why everyone turns a blind eye to the majority of commonhold accounts reporting no income, no liability and no asset.

---

[45] Commonhold Regulations 2004, Sch 2 para 5.

[46] L Crabb, 'The Commonhold and Leasehold Reform Act 2002: A Company Law Perspective' [2004] *Company Lawyer* 213, 215.

[47] Ibid. See also SMJ Wong, 'Potential Pitfalls in the Commonhold Community Statement and the Corporate Mechanisms of the Commonhold Association' [2006] *Conveyancer and Property Lawyer* 16, 33–34.

Nevertheless not engaging in this box ticking exercise could have disastrous implications for commonhold associations. In one commonhold scheme, the director who was supposed to carry out such duties failed to take any note for a few years. The company was subsequently struck off for non-compliance without the knowledge of the other owners for a while. The situation only came to light when one owner tried to sell his flat to a friend and no company was in the position to issue any commonhold unit information certificate.[48] Eventually the owners had to go through the court to have the company reinstated, incurring at least £3,000 in costs.

Hard cases such as this could certainly lead to questions as to why commonhold associations must be treated as normal trading companies despite all its apparent differences in many aspects. It has to be said that such a serious incident of non-compliance is an unusual occurrence rather than a prevalent threat. Most commonhold directors see the company law side as a niggling inconvenience and not a necessary aspect in calling for the law to be reformed.

XI. LACK OF ATTENTION

There are other minor frustrations for commonhold owners. The lack of reliable information, for example, is getting worse the longer commonhold stays unpopular. The Lord Chancellor's Department, which was in charge of the commonhold legislative project, was first transformed into the Department for Constitutional Affairs and then into the current Ministry of Justice. With each transformation, existing webpages and documents on commonhold seemed to go missing from the government website. Many other webpages on commonhold elsewhere are considerably out of date, often talking about its great potential and advantages over leasehold with no mention of the serious problems such as those highlighted by this chapter. The decline of interest is also evident in publications. A journal keyword search of 'commonhold' on Westlaw produced 103 pieces between 2000 and 2004, 42 pieces between 2005 and 2009, two in 2010, one each in 2011 and 2012 (by the same author under the same title in different publications), and two in 2013. Commonhold is of negligible importance so it is being forgotten as much as possible.

And the unimportance of commonhold is a self-fulfilling prophecy. When questions were asked in Parliament about commonhold, most noticeably by Baroness Gardner, the governmental response tended to be that commonhold was rare so it would not be considered by new policies, such as the £10 billion debt guarantee offered by the state for building new homes.[49] Hence commonhold as a newcomer, which never received any preferential treatment by policies to help it take root, is now apparently being left out of future plans for growth because it did not win the contest against the mammoth of leasehold. Even the lip service once paid to its theoretical merits has now disappeared.

---

[48] Commonhold Regulations 2004, Sch 3, para 4.7.2.
[49] *Hansard*, HL Deb 19 Nov 2012, cols 1620–21.

XII. A WAY OUT OF COMMONHOLD?

Without some dramatic change of fortune, the trend of commonhold as a whole is unlikely to take a turn for the better in the foreseeable future. That would offer very little comfort to those commonhold unit owners in the existing schemes. Many of them have encountered difficulties, especially the problem of mortgage finance as discussed above. Several of them have looked for a way out for their own scheme. And here lies another rather unpleasant surprise for those pioneers into a new legal concept: there is no obvious way out.

CLRA 2002 contains two methods of termination for a commonhold scheme, either voluntary winding-up or winding-up by court.[50] However, neither method was designed to allow the owners to simply give up on commonhold but continue to be owners of the existing building.

The winding-up by court procedure governs insolvent commonhold in line with related insolvency procedures.[51] The unique feature of this procedure is the power for the court to grant a succession order, effectively transferring the land forming the common parts from the insolvent commonhold to another newly created, debt-free commonhold.[52] This 'phoenix' company, in the words of Professor Clarke,[53] would then ensure the continuation of the commonhold scheme and all its normal functionality despite the major overhaul on the company law front. But another commonhold association is exactly what those owners looking for a way out of commonhold do not want. Without a succession order, on the other hand, the owners may have major problems hanging on to their common parts such as stairs and pathways, which clearly would not be feasible for any development carrying on beyond the winding-up.

The voluntary winding-up procedure requires 100 per cent or 80 per cent consent and a solvent commonhold association, which would not cause any problem given the small size of most existing schemes. However, the purpose and effect of such procedure is to wipe the land clean of the threefold unity, mentioned earlier, of collective and individual ownership as well as membership of the company. The commonhold association will take away the title of every individual owner and instead becomes the freehold proprietor of every flat and house within the development.[54] The most likely use of such a procedure is where there is an offer to purchase the whole commonhold, such as for redevelopment.[55] For those commonhold schemes without a whole-site buyer down the line and who merely want the development to carry on a new life without commonhold, this is another near impossible route to follow. On top of the trouble and unease of having to lose all individual titles, what structure would be in place after the commonhold is gone? Would it be a flying freehold without the ability to impose positive obligations on successors?[56] Would it

---

[50] ss 43–49 and 50–54 respectively.
[51] Insolvency Act 1986, s 124.
[52] CLRA 2002, s 51.
[53] Clarke (n 24) para 12.28.
[54] CLRA 2002, s 49.
[55] Clarke (n 24) para 12.10.
[56] This was a notable reason for promoting commonhold in the first place, see DN Clarke, 'The Enactment of Commonhold—Problems, Principles and Perspectives' [2002] *Conveyancer and Property Lawyer* 349, 362–63.

be leasehold? And who or what entity should be the landlord? What about the common parts previously owned by the commonhold association? There is a long list of questions without answers. At least two schemes approached solicitors for advice. Both were quoted in excess of £10,000 to even look at the case. They did not pursue the option any further.

The truth is that, in the 20-year efforts that eventually led to the establishment of commonhold, many contemplated the feasibility and requirement of converting leasehold into commonhold.[57] But the solution for a systemic failure of the commonhold structure in practice was never a relevant concern. Commonhold was seen as such a theoretically superior modern concept. How could it possibly fail? Why would any commonhold ever want to join the 'fundamentally flawed'[58] system of leasehold? Consequently nobody ever asked whether and how a commonhold scheme could be converted into leasehold. That leaves many current commonhold owners with little help in their efforts to find a way out of a system that they do not like.

XIII. ANALYSIS AND CONCLUSIONS

The system of commonhold has failed by any measure one can think of—even as its most enthusiastic and optimistic supporters. It is nowhere near as popular as Bob Dylan as it was once compared to.[59] More leasehold units are being created in a day than the sum of all commonhold units since 2004. Indeed as pointed out above, had three ordinary individuals somehow changed their mind about commonhold, more than half of the existing units in England and Wales would not be commonhold.

There were multiple factors which contributed to the failure of commonhold and they tended to self-aggravate as time went on. The legal profession as a whole never truly embraced this idea. After the initial hype about commonhold quietened down, the level of understanding only deteriorated due to non-use. Major property developers never accepted commonhold.[60] After a few years of seeing very little impact made by commonhold, there was absolutely no reason to change. Estate agents hardly ever got their heads around the legislative innovations and doctrinal differences. The general public in turn was not well informed by anyone. The slide from curiosity to indifference, then to ignorance and suspicion came in only a few years.

Rather than monitoring the situation, coordinating with different stakeholders, and providing support and incentives for commonhold, the government at the time seemed to have viewed this as job done soon after the regulations were made and the new system commenced in 2004. As it turned out, seven schemes comprising 97 units were in place before the end of 2005, which, though far short of spectacular,

---

[57] Eg ibid, 354–61; PF Smith, 'The Purity of Commonholds' [2004] *Conveyancer and Property Lawyer* 194.

[58] Words from *Commonhold and Leasehold Reform: Draft Bill and Consultation Paper* (Cm 4843, 2000) Pt II, s 1, para 1.

[59] PH Kenny, 'Commonhold: Can't Sing Can't Play the Mouth Organ but Nevertheless a Star?' [2002] *Conveyancer and Property Lawyer* 206.

[60] D Danskin and S Jackman, 'Lenders Have Fear' (2005) 0524 *Estates Gazette* 170. Major developer Crest Nicholson did announce the intention to build a large project near Milton Keynes as commonhold in early 2006, to the excitement of many, yet no progress or further information has been forthcoming since then.

would not be a complete disaster to start an innovation. There is no evidence to suggest that any government official looked at commonhold six, 12 or 18 months into operation to see if it was progressing anywhere near the estimate of thousands of new units every year. Nobody asked what could be done if things were not going so well at an early stage. It could be argued that had the government been seen to insist on promoting and supporting the idea two or three years further down the line, with anything that resembled a 'sustained press campaign extolling the virtues of the new system',[61] over crucial periods in 2005 and 2006 which preceded a sharp downturn in interest level, the fate of commonhold could have been quite different. Yet in doing nothing during those couple of crucial years, by the time anyone raised this as a problem, the problem was already too difficult to deal with.

Another major factor, one that still haunts existing commonhold today, is the lending policy of a large number of financial institutions, counting for about half of the Council of Mortgage Lenders members including major high street names. Again this was something the government or other bodies could have looked into before it simply became an accepted fact due to inaction over time.

The only thing that seems to work well in practice is the statutory structure for the 'internal functions' of commonhold schemes, which is no doubt a credit to all those efforts of discussion and deliberation in the lengthy legislative process. Most schemes operate smoothly, especially where there is enough enthusiasm from individuals. The absence of drastic enforcement measures or intricate dispute resolution mechanism suits the smaller schemes reasonably well. In general the statutory structure is accessible to laypersons and is not much different from what owners would do by common sense. As a piece of legislation intended for the idea to take root in this country first, the legislators largely got things right before 2002 or 2004. It was the follow up efforts to the introduction of a good idea that failed commonhold.

It is now very clear that commonhold will not take root on its own in England and Wales. With all the problems such as the unavailability of mortgage finance from many lenders, the refusal by government to extend at least equal benefits under new policies and the reduced level of understanding of commonhold across different sectors, it will take a miracle for there to be another batch of commonhold schemes in the future. If nothing is done, the number of schemes is perhaps as likely to go down as it would go up, despite the great difficulty in current legislation for any commonhold to pull out. Commonhold will be a lesson of warning, if not laughing stock, for decades to come as one of the worst examples of carefully considered legislation having done more harm than good, due to the lack of follow-up efforts and support from crucial stakeholders. That would of course not be of any comfort to those individual owners who happen to be stuck in a commonhold.

It is submitted that an important decision now needs to be made by policy makers. Either something is done to promote and revive commonhold, or something is done to close the book on commonhold and to help existing schemes if they choose to find an alternative. Neither option is easy. But perhaps either is better than doing nothing by ignoring the problem.

---

[61] G Fetherstonhaugh, 'Developers Need a Nudge in the Right Direction' (2007) 0742 *Estates Gazette* 292.

The closing option will limit the damage of commonhold on those small number of individuals entangled in this practically difficult concept. There are commonhold owners worried about their units' short-term prospect for sale or long-term value. They seem to deserve some help in finding an option out of commonhold which does not involve any £10,000 legal bill. At the other end, three commonhold associations were incorporated in the 18 months before 1 January 2014. With none of them having responded to any enquiry in this research, it was difficult to assess their exact rationale or knowledge of the larger picture. They may of course never get activated with actual land holding and dissolve in a few years' time, like many before them. Still the current situation is that if one searches online today, the problem facing commonhold is not always apparent due to the existence of many out-of-date documents, still boasting about the theoretical advantages of commonhold. There is no official acknowledgement of any problem with commonhold. Commonhold has failed completely to take root and this fact should be recognised openly. It would not seem unreasonable to suspend new incorporation promptly, should closing be the option that policymakers prefer. And if by shutting down commonhold, all relevant efforts would again be focused on leasehold reform without the occasional half-hearted excuse to give commonhold a try when the leasehold system encounters problems, then the detour into commonhold may still be of some value to English law after all.[62]

The reviving option is certainly more challenging; the failure of the commonhold so far is perhaps the best lesson to be learnt in any efforts to create its success. The government would need to coordinate with and to convince key stakeholders, including conveyancers, property developers, financial institutions, and estate agents, to support such an initiative with more than a few welcoming words. If a major bank decides to lend on flying freeholds but not commonholds, it would seem reasonable to demand some sensible explanation. Other incentives, such as preferential policies in planning procedure, taxation or funding directed at building affordable homes would also be extremely valuable, for the message it can send out to the professions and the general public. The underlying statutory framework for commonhold was well thought and it works in practice. If there is the will to create again the level of understanding and marginal curiosity about commonhold that was in existance back in 2004 or 2005, with lessons learned and a more realistic expectation as to the extent of its potential for success at an early stage, there may be a real chance for commonhold to finally take root.

Commonhold is dying as a concept in England and Wales. It is time for the policymakers to have a plan to do something, rather than merely hoping for things to improve as they did in the last decade.

---

[62] It certainly seems to be the case that when leasehold law runs into difficulty, commonhold may get mentioned as a notional alternative, eg P Rainey, 'Alternatives to Frustration' (2013) 1323 *Estates Gazette* 74.

Practical Approaches to the Numerus Clausus of Land Rights: How Legal Professionals in South Africa and the Netherlands Deal with Certainty and Flexibility in Property Law

HANRI MOSTERT* AND LEON VERSTAPPEN**

I. INTRODUCTION

MOST CIVIL LAW jurisdictions acknowledge that legal certainty is achieved by a 'regimentation' of the rights, remedies and processes comprising property law.[1] This is the *numerus clausus* principle. It dictates that only real rights, means of delivery of movables and modes of original acquisition of ownership that fall into one of a limited number of recognised categories will be countenanced by the law. This restrictive approach is meant to achieve certainty regarding the kinds of rights that may be held in respect of things, and to prevent owners from hampering the tradeability of property by unnecessarily burdening it.[2] The *numerus clausus* principle thus constitutes a limitation on party autonomy.[3]

* Professor, Faculty of Law, University of Cape Town, South Africa; Visiting Professor, Groningen Centre for Law and Governance, Department of Private and Notary Law, University of Groningen, the Netherlands. Hanri.Mostert@uct.ac.za.

** Professor, Department of Private Law and Notary Law and Academic Director, Centre for Law and Governance, University of Groningen, the Netherlands; Legal advisor, Hekkelman Lawyers and Notaries. L.C.A.Verstappen@rug.nl.

This research was funded by the South African National Research Foundation, the Groningen Centre for Law and Governance of the University of Groningen, and the University of Cape Town. Sincere thanks to Richard Cramer who rendered valuable research assistance, the anonymous peer reviewers, and to the members of the Department of Private Law at UCT, the participants at the 2012 Property Law Teachers' Colloquium and the Progressive Property Law Group who commented on earlier versions of the work. Opinions and errors are our own and should not be attributed to the people or institutions mentioned.

[1] A Di Robilant, 'Property and Democratic Deliberation: The Numerus Clausus Principle and Democratic Experimentalism in Property Law' (2014) 62(2) *American Journal of Comparative Law* 301, 302–06.

[2] CG Van der Merwe and MJ De Waal, *The Law of Things and Servitudes* (Durban, Butterworths, 1993) para 8.

[3] THD Struycken, *De Numerus Clausus in het Goederenrecht* (Deventer, Kluwer, 2007) 1.

In unregimented systems, users can customise arrangements to suit their specific needs, but they may not have the force of property law behind them. The law is 'inherently more flexible, but the options are inherently less certain'.[4] Property law thus contrasts with contract law, where the same dichotomy between certainty and flexibility that haunts property law manifests itself in the converse. Contractual freedom underpins the ability to tailor arrangements to the needs of the parties involved and hence is as fundamental to contract law as the *numerus clausus* principle is to property law. Yet recent trends towards standardisation of positions[5] demonstrate how contractual freedom is compromised for the sake of achieving more certainty.

This chapter examines the application of the *numerus clausus* in respect of types and content of rights in two jurisdictions strongly subscribing to the civil law tradition of property, the Netherlands and South Africa. In categorising real rights according to content and type, these two systems start at opposite ends of the spectrum: the Dutch system from a strict *numerus clausus* approach, and the South African system from an open system of registration of rights in land. The analysis below shows, however, that these two systems seem to be converging in their approaches. The specific problems of both systems—rigidity and uncertainty, respectively—drive each jurisdiction to gravitate towards qualities from the opposite spectrum. This chapter is about how this process is brought about. Investigating these jurisdictions, we touch on the role of functionaries—the Dutch notary (notaris), the South African Registrar of Deeds, and the judge in both jurisdictions—who deal with the practical problems of distinguishing between real and contractual rights. This enables some surprising insights about the *numerus clausus* and its attribution as a fundamental principle of property law.

One caveat at the outset: several of the mechanisms discussed here have equivalents in the Anglo–American legal context.[6] Scope restriction does not allow engagement with the law beyond the two jurisdictions focused on here, and our terminology is chosen such that it represents the jurisdictions investigated.

II. SHARED ROOTS, DIFFERENT APPROACHES

Dutch and South African property law are rooted in the same set of Roman law based legal principles. South African property law is strongly civil law oriented,[7] being based on Roman law as it was practiced in the area of its first coloniser: seventeenth-century Holland. The difference between real and contractual rights,

---

[4] H Mostert and A Pope (eds), *The Principles of the Law of Property in South Africa* (Southern Africa, Cape Town, Oxford University Press, 2010) 341. HW Heyman, 'Contents of the Real Right: Dogmatic Rigidity and Pragmatic Flexibility of Dutch Property Law' in SE Bartels and JM Milo (eds), *Contents of Real Rights* (Nijmegen, Wolf Legal Publishers 2004).

[5] See, eg the cooling-off period protection for the home buyer (art 7:2(2) of the Dutch Civil Code (DCC)), or the special provisions with regard to agreements over a distance, regulating the use of the internet in consumer contracts (art 7:46aff DCC). See generally: Struycken, *Numerus Clausus* (n 3) and B Akkermans, *The Principle of Numerus Clausus in European Property Law* (Antwerpen, Intersentia, 2008).

[6] Eg the restriction on positive burdens. See M Thompson, *Modern Land Law*, 5th edn (Oxford, Oxford University Press, 2012) 542–43; EH Burns and J Cartwright, *Cheshire and Burn's Modern Law of Real Property*, 18th edn (Oxford, Oxford University Press, 2011) 641–42.

[7] R Zimmerman and D Visser, 'Southern Cross' in R Zimmerman (ed), *Southern Cross* (Kenwyn, Juta, 1996) 28.

for example, is described similarly in both systems: real rights establish legal relationships to goods; contractual rights establish legal relationships between people.[8] The differences in consequences, ways of acquisition, exercise and protection that distinguish real rights from contractual rights are also similar.[9] Registrability is an easy example: real rights to land are registrable in these jurisdictions; personal rights (generally) not.[10]

Adherence to the *numerus clausus* principle, however, is not one of the similarities. Admittedly, the *numerus clausus* principle is a post-medieval creation,[11] with Von Savigny being one of its main proponents. Dutch law saw the *numerus clausus* principle taking root in the Dutch Code in the early half of the nineteenth century.[12] The principle became firmly entrenched, reinforced by the Dutch courts,[13] and the codification process of the twentieth century.[14] It remained largely uncontested until about 1996. Contemporary scholars[15] now question its continued relevance. At the centre of the contestation is that aspect of the *numerus clausus* that concerns the types of rights that may be regarded as real (*in rem*).

Even though Von Savigny's writings are generally deemed authoritative also in South African law, there strangely does not seem to be as strict an adherence to the *numerus clausus* principle in relation to types of rights as there is in its parent jurisdiction, the Netherlands. South African law acknowledges[16] the *numerus clausus* in respect of constructive methods of derivative acquisition, and also as regards original modes of acquisition.[17] But unlike Dutch law, it does not acknowledge a *numerus clausus* of real rights in property.[18] Our comparison focuses on this ostensible divergence as regards the types of rights that qualify as real, and their content.

In the Netherlands, a restricted number of right types are acknowledged, the main object being to bring clarity and simplicity to private relations. The idea is that limiting the options available results in more legal clarity overall. German Pandectism originally provided the descriptive terminology.[19] It promoted the limitation of the

---

[8] See, eg EB Rank-Berenschot, *Over de scheidslijn tussen goederen- en verbintenissenrecht* (dissertation, Universiteit Leiden 1992; Deventer, Kluwer 1992) 13ff; CG Van der Merwe and A Pope, 'Part III: Property' in F Du Bois (ed), *Wille's Principles of South African Law* (Cape Town, Juta, 2007) 429.

[9] Rank-Berenschot, *Scheidslijn* (n 8); PJ Badenhorst, JM Pienaar and H Mostert, *Silberberg and Schoeman's The Law of Property*, 5th edn (Durban, LexisNexis Butterworths, 2006) 47–70, 137–272.

[10] arts 3:10, 3:89 and 3:98 DCC; Mostert and Pope (eds), *Principles* (n 4) 45.

[11] Struycken (n 3) 124.

[12] Ibid, 127ff, 205.

[13] HR 8 Jan 1895, W 6916 (1897): HR 3 March 1905, W8191, WPNR 1844 and HR 28 Nov 1913, NJ 1913, 1313, further Struycken (n 3) 42ff.

[14] The revisions culminated in the property law part of the new Dutch Civil Code (new DCC) coming into force in 1992.

[15] PL Nève, 'Uit de Bonte Berm van de Juridische Begrippenflora: Ons "Gesloten Stelsel" van Beperkte Rechten' in SCJJ Kortman (ed), *Op recht* (Zwolle, WEJ Tjeenk Willink, 1996) 41–64, 223–32; S Van Erp, 'A Numerus Quasi-Clausus of Property Rights as a Constitutive Element of a Future European Property Law?' in K Boelewoelki et al (eds), *Het Plezier van de Rechtsvergelijking. Opstellen over Unificatie en Harmonisatie van het Recht in Europa aangeboden aan prof Mr EH Hondius* (Deventer, Kluwer, 2003) 39–52; V Sagaert, 'Het Goederenrecht als Open Systeem van Verbintenissen? Poging tot een Nieuwe Kwalificatie van de Vermogensrechten' [2005] *Tijdschrift voor Privaatrecht* 983.

[16] For the time being. See commentary on the dilution of the *numerus clausus* principle in relation to modes of acquisition and delivery in Mostert and Pope (eds), *Principles* (n 4) 341–43.

[17] Van der Merwe and Pope, 'Property' (n 8) 410.

[18] CG Van der Merwe, *Sakereg*, 2nd edn (Durban, Butterworths, 1989) 11–12.

[19] Akkermans, *Numerus Clausus* (n 5) 6–7.

number of burdens on property. This is referred to as *Typenzwang*. Pandectism also supported circumscribing of the content of such burdens. This is referred to as *Typenfixierung*: by attaching certain legal consequences to a certain kind of real right, the mere identification of the type of right invokes an understanding of the legal instrument at stake.

The practical implications of *Typenzwang* and *Typenfixierung* are apparent in the *Blauboer/Berlips* decision[20] of the Dutch Supreme Court, considered a landmark because it stated the basic rule for the principle of *numerus clausus* and emphasised the dichotomy of property law and contract law. The matter concerned a subdivision of A's land, of which a part was then sold to B. Their agreement obliged A to construct a road on B's land. But A sold his remainder to C, who refused to construct the road. The court ruled that the obligation was on A personally, and not on the land. Not C but A had to pay damages, because the obligation arose from the contract, not the property. To hold differently, the court argued, would blur the distinction between real and contractual rights. Accordingly, parties to a contract cannot create new types of real rights.

The new Dutch Civil Code (DCC) demonstrates how entrenched the *numerus clausus* principle has become. Article 3:81(1) DCC provides that limited rights may be created only within acknowledged categories. There is no longer a catalogue of real rights as under article 584 of the Old Civil Code, but new categories of real rights can only be created by the legislature. Private parties cannot create new types of real rights. The law moreover prescribes the exact scope and content of such rights types that do exist.[21] Adherence to the *numerus clausus* principle in Dutch property law thus gives credence to the Dutch understanding of legality.[22] As only the legislature can introduce new right types and adjust content, the legislature is responsible for adjusting the system when changes in modern-day practice so demand.[23]

South African law rejects the *numerus clausus* principle in relation to real rights: a small number of real rights (taken from Roman law)[24] are accepted as trite, while extension of rights types and content occurs subject to strict requirements.[25] Within each of the acknowledged categories there is much room for manoeuvre. This is best illustrated with reference to servitudes. In respect of praedial servitudes, some 'typically South African' rights have been developed, for example *trekpad* and *uitspan*. Moreover, the closed list of personal servitudes prevalent in Roman law (*ususfructus, fructus, usus, habitatio*) have been opened with the acknowledgement of so-called 'irregular' servitudes, meaning those that resemble praedial servitudes, but are vested in a particular person. This complicates the categorisation of real rights significantly.

The *numerus clausus* principle is regarded as useful to distinguish between property and contract. Scholars in Germany,[26] and the Netherlands[27] acknowledge the

---

[20] HR 3 March 1905, W8191, WPNR 1844.

[21] Struycken (n 3) 14.

[22] Ibid, 762–65.

[23] TW Merrill and HE Smith, 'Optimal Standardisation in the Law of Property: The *Numerus Clausus* Principle' (2000) 110 *Yale Law Journal* 1, 58.

[24] Servitudes; real security rights; *emphyteusis* and *superficies*.

[25] Van der Merwe, *Sakereg* (n 18) 65–69.

[26] JT Füller, *Eigenständiges Sachenrecht? Ius Privatum: Beiträge zum Privatrecht* (Tübingen, Mohr Siebeck, 2006).

[27] Rank-Berenschot, *Scheidslijn* (n 8) 13ff; Akkermans, *Numerus Clausus* (n 5) 1–7.

clear distinction between property and contract as an historic fact. But in Europe the purpose of upholding the idea that property rights can be reduced to a short list of types, each with a set content, has been questioned recently under the 'pressure of changes in economic organization, information technology, social practices of production and new environmental challenges'.[28] Given this ongoing debate, the treatment of right types and content in South Africa, where there is no acknowledged *numerus clausus* of real rights, becomes an interesting point of comparison. The consequences of customisation frequently pose interesting challenges to the South African Deeds Registry. The sections below consider the practical implications of the presence/absence of the *numerus clausus* of real rights in each of the jurisdictions investigated.

III. THE (LACK OF A) *NUMERUS CLAUSUS* IN THEORY AND PRACTICE

There may be interesting historical reasons for the practical divergences between the Dutch and South African positions. But the more captivating question is whether these divergences have any impact on the types of rights nowadays acknowledged as real. A practically relevant context is the land register.

A. Functionaries and Officials

Several mechanisms maintain the balance between stability and flexibility in property law. Publicity is one: the special relationship towards goods—especially land—must be made known to others. Establishing and transferring real rights to land are bound to formalities. Professionals and functionaries such as the South African Registrar of Deeds and the Dutch *notaris* work with the question which types of land rights are registrable. The question arises because not all types of land rights are real, and hence they cannot all enjoy the publicity offered by the register. To understand the manner in which these officials influence approaches to certainty and flexibility of the law, it is necessary to examine their functions in the respective jurisdictions. This is the purpose of the following paragraphs. Thereafter, the limitations upon this 'organic' development of the law through notarial or registration practices are considered in a section dealing with the practical encounters with the *numerus clausus*, and how they are eventually approached.

A state-supported Cadastre or Registry operates through the officials involved in the registration process: the functionaries who must translate the theory and principles of property law into practically implementable mechanisms. We focus here on the Dutch notary and the South African Registrar of Deeds, because these two offices encounter daily the problems that challenge the parameters of property law; especially those relating to the (lack of a) *numerus clausus*.

---

[28] Di Robilant, *Property and Deliberation* (n 1) 8; Akkermans (n 5) 397ff.

B. The Dutch Process and Functionaries

Dutch law[29] requires limited real rights to land to be established by notarial deed, publicly registered and recorded subsequently in the Basisregistratie Kadaster, a database of all proprietors, rights and land parcels.[30] Notarial deeds must meet the requirements of the law, notably the Kadasterwet (Cadastre Law),[31] which deals with the registration of land.

The Dutch Registrar controls compliance with the legal requirements for registration of rights, but this role remains rather formal. The Registrar may not, for example, refuse the registration when in his opinion the content of the right created does not fit the particular type of real right identified by the creators of the right in question.[32] It is the Dutch notary (notaris) who must ascertain whether the arrangements parties want to formalise can be accommodated by the available legal instruments, and so must identify the real right appropriately.[33] The notaris is, generally speaking, fully liable for damages when the deed creating the real right (the 'deed of establishment') does not fit the categories prescribed by law. Consequently, the notaris will generally be reluctant to draft real rights with dubious content.

It is through the office of the notaris that standard provisions for real rights are developed *outside of* the legislative process. In the hands of the notaris, the task of ensuring that the rights and obligations of servitude/real security right holders and the owners are balanced fairly becomes one of seeking consensus between the legal practitioners representing these parties. A good example is apartment ownership: standard general provisions, developed by the Royal Organisation of Dutch Notaries, are applicable to almost every apartment building. These provisions are updated regularly. Legal practitioners publish their standard contracts for general use as precedents.[34] Municipalities that issue leasehold contracts for real estate also have their own standard contracts, established after extensive consultation and adapted by the local municipal council.[35] All these standard contracts are registered in the public records and incorporated by reference where applicable real rights are established.

C. The South African Process and Functionaries

The office of Notary Public in South Africa is also a specialised one, through which practicing attorneys, who have passed a specialised notarial examination[36] are allowed to execute notarial documents provided for in the Deeds Registries Act (DRA).[37] The notary takes responsibility for the correctness of the contents of

---

[29] art 3:16 DCC read with the Kadasterwet. See further arts 3:17–3:31 DCC, which deal specifically with third-party protection.

[30] See: www.ruimtelijkeplannen.nl.

[31] Unabbreviated title: the 'Law containing rules with regard to the public registers for registered goods, as well as with regard to the cadastre'.

[32] Raad van State 1 Dec 2010, ECLI:NL:RVS:2010:BO5723; Further: LCA Verstappen and WD Kolkman (eds), *Handboek Registergoederenrecht* (Zutphen, Walburg Pers, 2013–14).

[33] art 24:2:b, Kadasterwet.

[34] Eg in the series 'Modellen voor de Rechtspraktijk' (Deventer, Kluwer).

[35] See, eg for the city of Amsterdam: www.amsterdam.nl/wonen-leefomgeving/erfpacht/professionals/algemene-bepalingen/.

[36] s 18, Attorneys Act 53 of 1979.

[37] s 102, DRA definition of 'notary public'.

notarial deeds or documents. These duties supplement and are enhanced by the role of the conveyancer, another specialised office, very often fulfilled by those who are also notaries. The conveyancer, typically authorised by a power of attorney,[38] acts for an owner by performing registration acts such as preparing and executing deeds and registration documents.[39] Conveyancers are by law responsible for the accuracy of certain facts.[40] The South African Registrar of Deeds controls the work of conveyancers and notaries: the conveyancer might be the one preparing the documentation for creating rights to land, but the Registrar determines whether registration can proceed,[41] by interpreting and applying the DRA.[42]

Deeds Registry practice is significant in decisions about whether to register particular kinds of arrangements. So, for instance, past practice to register mineral rights as separate from the title of the land originated from practice in the Transvaal and Orange Free State registries, and gave rise to the idea of juridical severance of mineral rights from land title.[43] It was only recently, after more than a century of dispute about the nature of mineral rights, that our Constitutional Court gave direction: severance created mineral title—ownership of the mineral rights—separately from the landownership.[43a]

The Registrar's office being descendant from that of a judge,[44] the Registrar's duties are described as 'semi-judicial'.[45] The Registrar must weigh evidence submitted and determine whether to allow registration (of rights) or to compel the parties to apply for a court order permitting a specific registration act.[46] All the duties and functions of the South African Registrar of Deeds contribute to establishing security of title with regard to land.[47] Non-adherence to the *numerus clausus* principle in South Africa really is an exercise in self-restraint by Deeds Registry officials, on behalf of the Registrar, and by the courts, who must deal with the ultimate difficult cases.

IV. FLEXIBILITY THROUGH SIDESTEPPING THE *NUMERUS CLAUSUS*: THE DUTCH EXAMPLE

Despite scholarly arguments against perpetuating the *numerus clausus* as a governing principle,[48] the new DCC relies on it extensively.[49] New categories of real rights

---

[38]   DRA, reg 44(1).
[39]   s 15, DRA; also reg 16. RJM Jones and HS Nel, *Conveyancing in South Africa* (Cape Town, Juta, 1991) 16.
[40]   ss 15A and 50A, DRA and regs 43 and 44A.
[41]   See, eg *Reeskens v Registrar of Deeds* 1964 (4) SA 369 (N) 371A–C; *Barclays Bank DCO v Minister of Lands* 1964 (4) SA 284 (T) 289Hff.
[42]   s 3 DRA defines the scope of the registrar's capacities and responsibilities.
[43]   See further, Mostert, *Mineral Law Principles and Policies in Perspective* (Cape Town, Juta, 2012) 8–11, 26–28, 37. See ch 3 in general for an historical overview of the regulation of minerals.
[43a]   *Agri South Africa v Minister for Minerals and Energy* [2013] ZACC 9 para 38.
[44]   *Rosenberg v Dry's Executor's and Others* 1911 (AD) 679.
[45]   *Transvaal Land Company v Registrar of Companies* 1910 (TPD) 1247.
[46]   See further, RJM Jones and HS Nel, *Conveyancing in South Africa* (Cape Town, Juta, 1991) 14–15.
[47]   s 3(1)(b) DRA gives the Registrar broad powers to determine whether a deed or document has legal force, but these powers are tempered by duties imposed to ensure that deeds and documents are in order. See, eg *Denel (Pty) Ltd v Cape Explosive Works Ltd* 1999 (2) SA 419 (T) 437G–438B; *Cape Explosive Works and Another v Denel (Pty) Ltd and Others* 2001 (3) SA 569 (SCA).
[48]   Struycken (n 3) 205.
[49]   Ibid, 11–39.

can only be created by the Dutch legislature;[50] never by private parties or judges. The law moreover prescribes the exact scope and content of such rights types.[51]

Admittedly, such strict adherence to the *numerus clausus* principle brings its own difficulties. It restricts individual autonomy, a main tenet of civil law.[52] A recent study of the Dutch context[53] demonstrates that situations are particularly problematic where a notarial deed is meant to produce the real right of leasehold, but contains elements that are outside the statutory definition or the field of application of this real right. So, for instance, prescriptions may be added to a right of leasehold that pertain to the employment contracts relating to those working on the land; or a developer that is granted a leasehold for a social housing development can be obliged to rent only to tenants from certain income levels.

Uncertainty reigns as to the extent to which the content and boundaries of the real right of leasehold are static. One of the questions to be answered is whether such unconventional elements in the established real right will indeed bind successors in title. The limitations of the *numerus clausus* system become clear especially where certain types of legal instruments are explicitly forbidden by law; for example transfer of ownership of goods as collateral for the repayment of debts in the Netherlands.[54]

The following paragraphs demonstrate how existing categories of real rights do not fully meet needs or notarial practice in the Netherlands.[55] Also, they show that a rigidly regimented system with static content attributed to predetermined right types is not conducive to natural development of the law, especially when new types of property appear. Notaries are challenged, for example, by questions around the proprietary nature of internet domain names,[56] transferable licences,[57] carbon credits[58] or financial security agreements.[59] In the strictly regimented Dutch system, the inevitable question is how rights in respect of such new types of goods align with existing categories of right types and content. It hence is necessary to look at how the strict Dutch system of real rights is dealt with in practice and in law, when it comes to new types of property.

---

[50] art 3:81:1 DCC.

[51] Struycken (n 3) 14.

[52] J Merryman, *The Civil Law Tradition* (Stanford, Stanford University Press, 1985) 92.

[53] See FJ Vonck, 'De Flexibiliteit van het Recht van Erfpacht' (PhD thesis, University of Groningen, 2013).

[54] art 3:84(3) DCC.

[55] See AA van Velten, *Privaatrechtelijke Aspecten van Onroerend Goed* (Deventer, Kluwer, 2012) 705ff.

[56] *Rechtbank Leeuwarden* 18 May 2009, ECLI:NL:RBLEE:2009:BI3871. See domjur.nl for more case law.

[57] CL Knijff, 'Rechtsopvolging bij Vergunningen' (PhD thesis, University of Utrecht, 2003). See also HR 16 mei 1997, ECLI:NL:HR:1997:AG7234, NJ 1998, 238 (Dirc/cs c.s./Dircks).

[58] Ie Certified Emission Reduction. J Button, 'Carbon: Commodity or Currency—The Case for an International Carbon Market Based on the Currency Model' (2008) 32 *Harvard Environmental Law Review* 571.

[59] Council Directive 2002/47/EC of 6 June 2002 on financial collateral arrangements OJ L 168, 27 June 2002, 43–50. See also TRMP Keijser and JAMP Keijser, *Financiëlezekerheidsovereenkomst* (Deventer, Kluwer, 2008).

A. New Needs, Greater Variety in Notarial Practice and in Law

Changes to the ways people use land, the creation of new types of goods, collectivisation of property relations, new financial instruments and new ways of circulating property in the market all contribute to the need for a more flexible approach with regard to land rights in the currently rigid Dutch system. Land use has changed in modern times, and with it conceptions of land rights.[60] Population growth and urbanisation foreground the problem that land is a finite resource and raise the need for more efficient land use practices.[61] New building techniques allowing new kinds of buildings[62] and land usage[63] highlight the need for new legal concepts, frameworks and mechanisms. The law's current catering for two-dimensional property rights is outdated. New types of land use cannot fit easily into classical descriptions of real rights. The law pertaining to the cadastre needs to start taking account of at least a third dimension (ie height); perhaps even a fourth (ie time).[64] This adds complexity to property law and adds to the need to develop new legal instruments to accommodate land and buildings owned collectively or by specific user-type groups and to manage the multiple interests involved.[65]

Moreover, all manner of new property types appear in practice. Technical, environmental and economic factors contribute to bring about new kinds of goods that must be accommodated by the legal system in terms of denomination, legal content and modes of transfer. Examples include: emission or production rights and other permits, financial collateral agreements, and intellectual property.[66]

In addition, there is an increasing need for financial instruments to accommodate investments in multi-use and multi-storey buildings.[67] Public and private sources usually finance these investments. Interests in these projects must be marketable and fit to be used as collateral. The legal instruments that support such interests must be efficient and provide transparency, accountability, and fair and balanced decision-making processes.

Furthermore, not only the acknowledgement of these new mechanisms is important, but also the legal instruments which facilitate how new goods types circulate in the economy. Whereas existing legal instruments may be used for such circulation, new instruments may also be developed. For example, the proposal for a new legal

---

[60] See, eg on three-dimensional ownership: J Paulsson, '3D Property Rights: An Analysis of Key Factors Based on International Experience' (PhD thesis, Stockholm, Royal Institute of Technology, 2007); JE Stoter, '3D Cadastre' (PhD thesis, Delft University of Technology, 2004).

[61] See further, eg DA Groetelaers and HD Ploeger, 'Juritecture of the Built Environment: A Different View on Legal Design for Multiple Use of Land' (2007) 25 *Structural Survey* 293–305.

[62] Eg HD Ploeger, 'De Flexibiliteit van een Schip, zo vast als een Huis' (2004) 6590 *Weekblad voor Privaatrecht, Notariaat en Registratie* 717–20.

[63] Eg the increasing infrastructure for transportation of people, supply of goods, resources (water, gas, electricity), etc in a rapidly urbanising world; use of land as basins for overflow of water in river areas; and use of the deep underground for carbon capture and storage.

[64] See sources in n 62 above.

[65] A Mes, 'Juridische Aspecten van de Invoering van een Driedimensionaal Kadaster in Nederland' (2012) 6951 *Weekblad voor Privaatrecht, Notariaat en Registratie* 812ff.

[66] See, eg Akkermans (n 5) 489–564.

[67] Van Velten, *Aspecten* (n 55) 637ff on park management in airports (Schiphol) or transportation hubs (Hooge Catharijne in Utrecht), etc.

tool to transfer company assets and liabilities *'uno acto'* and the establishment of collateral rights serve as examples.[68]

Though strict adherence to the *numerus clausus* would require the legislator to respond to new social developments by allowing for parallel development of the law, legislators are rarely at the vanguard of developments to create more flexibility. Mostly a legislator reacts to, rather than drives, societal changes. Creating new legislative instruments usually takes time and much parliamentary debate, and in the interim outcomes remains uncertain. More often, practitioners—especially notaries—must find ways to stretch the available legal instruments to align them with practical needs, frequently by compromising legal certainty. This is the focus of the next two sections.

B. The Dutch Legislative Response

A legislative milestone in the gradual progress towards more flexibility in the Dutch setting is the introduction of the new DCC property law and contract law books[69] in 1992. Comparing the old and the new DCC, two developments with regard to the dichotomy of contractual and real rights become apparent: first, the list of real rights is now shorter than was the case under the old DCC,[70] but there is more freedom to shape them and thus they are already more flexible. Secondly, although the principle of freedom of contract is still upheld, more contractual rights are becoming standardised through legislative interventions that limit party autonomy in one way or another. Some of these are even afforded the characteristics of real rights.[71] These developments have imported more flexibility into the Dutch system, but also have blurred the clear distinction between real and contractual rights. The following examples are illustrative.

First, the obligation conventionally accompanying the right to usufruct, to maintain the goods subject to the right, was omitted when Books 3–7 DCC came into force. The new DCC permits transfer of the goods under usufruct with the consent of the owner.[72] The goods that the usufructurary gets in return become subject to the usufruct automatically.[73] The usufructuary may be permitted to consume the goods. These changes certainly introduced more flexibility in relation to the right of usufruct.[74]

---

[68] Further: LCA Verstappen, 'Overdracht onder Algemene Titel' in MGJC Raaijmakers (ed), *Preadvies van de Vereeniging 'Handelsrecht': Onderneming en Overdracht onder Algemene Titel* (Deventer, Tjeenk Willink, 2002) 41ff.

[69] Books 3–7.

[70] Eg they skipped the so called *'grondrente'* or neighbour roads.

[71] Like the the so-called collective labour agreement ('collectieve arbeidsovereenkomst' or 'cao'), agreements between one or more companies and labour organisations applicable on every employment contract issued by those employers. Another example is the standards on rent of dwellings that have been developed in practice. Examples of contracts that have been given characteristics of a real right are: the rent of dwellings (arts 7:201ff DCC) of agrarian land (arts 7:311ff DCC).

[72] Or based on the powers conferred to the usufructuary by the establisher (art 3:215 DCC).

[73] By the way, this provoked the discussion whether this ('real substitution') is also the case with goods registered in the name of a person like real estate.

[74] Parlementaire Geschiedenis Boek 3 BW 642 and 664.

Secondly, leasehold is an instrument by which the Dutch Government can grant land-use rights to citizens, without transferring land ownership. Some cities (notably Amsterdam) even rely on this mechanism to extend the availability of urban land to the housing market and businesses.[75] Reclaimed sea bed has been leased in this way to farmers. The new Dutch Civil Code defines the right of leasehold broadly, as the right to hold and use a land parcel.[76] Leasehold may even have perpetual duration, and a single payment can reimburse all land rent. This type of leasehold comes very close to resembling ownership, which confirms the flexibility of this instrument. This has rendered leasehold a widely used tool in notarial practice, even to finance land investments.[77]

Another example bears testimony to the Dutch legislature's attempt to introduce more flexibility into property law. The new definition of servitude is much broader than under the old DCC.[78] Departing from the list of typical servitudes under the old DCC, the new DCC simply provides a very broad description,[79] leaving the determination of the content up to the dominant and servient estate owners. A similar drive towards flexibility is seen in the new Code's regulation of certain types of co-ownership,[80] apartment ownership,[81] and joint ownership of buildings and plants on the boundary between two estates.[82] These are all new tools for notaries and other legal practitioners. These examples induce a conclusion that despite the preservation of the *numerus clausus* principle, the legislature is introducing more party autonomy, and thus flexibility. This allows parties increasingly to tailor the content of real rights to suit their needs.[83]

Conversely, a greater trend towards standardisation is visible in contract law. Some types of contracts have even been afforded characteristics usually associated with real rights. For one, article 3:298 DCC extends the '*prior tempore*' rule to purchase rights out of contract.[84] Further, article 6:252 DCC introduces an obligation into contracts pertaining to land, ensuring that certain personal obligations to tolerate or refrain from certain actions are devolved upon persons who subsequently acquire the land or a personal or residual right to it.[85] Personal obligations relating to land are given real effect. They are then similar to servitudes, but ones without dominant estates.

---

[75] See Vonck, *Erfpacht* (n 53) 19ff.

[76] Parlementaire Geschiedenis Boek 5 BW 297.

[77] A bank buys the land and issues a leasehold contract to the lessee, who pays an annual reimbursement that closely resembles the interest payable by the home owner towards the bank. See Vonck, *Erfpacht* (n 53) 39ff.

[78] Parlementaire Geschiedenis Boek 5 BW 15.

[79] '[A]n obligation to suffer or not to do something on, above or under either of the properties'. Art 5:71(1) DCC.

[80] arts 3:166ff DCC.

[81] Earlier dealt with in Book 5 of the Dutch Civil Code (arts 5:106ff DCC).

[82] Book 5, arts 5:60ff (DCC).

[83] See, eg the debate that took place in the Dutch Parliament, Parlementaire geschiedenis Boek 5 BW (Deventer, Kluwer, 1981) 14.

[84] See Rank-Berenschot, *Scheidslijn* (n 8) 205ff. A related example concerns the priority notice in art 7:3 DCC.

[85] art 6:252(1) DCC.

Beyond the new DCC, the legislature has introduced other novel mechanisms, such as production rights, like those for the production of milk and other agricultural products,[86] and, most recently, carbon emission rights. A capped number of emissions permits allow the permit holders the discharge or production of a specific volume of a waste or by-product. When a company needs to increase its emissions beyond what its permit allows, it must buy emission permits from someone else who does not need them. Generally, because these permits are transferable, they can serve also as collateral.

The same can be said for rights to underground networks for transporting signals, energy or other resources (pipelines, cables, wires etc).[87] Such underground networks are now largely privatised, their management being in the hands of private organisations who had to pay for the acquisition of these structures, their maintenance and renewal. These rights can be used as collateral to investors because they are registerable and thus transferable.[88]

C. How Notarial Practice Addresses Modern Needs

Dutch legal practice clearly struggles with upholding the *numerus clausus* principle in property law. The inflexibility of the law, which prohibits some useful constructions, has induced practitioners to be inventive. This is where the role of the Dutch notary becomes apparent:

First, contractual 'binding'-clauses[89] are used to enforce performance where a contractual obligation with regard to, say, land, which does not fall into any categories of real rights: if one does not fulfil the obligation, one must pay a fine. The core obligation is supplemented by an additional obligation: the contracting party undertakes to bind a potential successor-in-title of the land right to the additional contractual obligation, again at the risk of being fined. The payment of such a fine can be secured by a hypothec on the land. In the chain of succession the binding effect of these clauses is as strong as the weakest link. Where the proprietor burdened by such an obligation becomes insolvent, the liquidator is not bound. Insolvency poses a threat to the enforceability; hence the binding-clause construction does not serve practical needs fully. Since the obligation to pay the fine in case of default can be secured by a hypothec on the land, the claimant could sell the property on a public auction to recover the fine.[90] However, establishing a hypothec is not always a practicable solution, especially where a hypothec already burdens the land, which might render full recovery of the fine less likely, especially if the debt secured by the first hypothec is high.[91]

---

[86] Council Regulation (EC) No 1234/2007 of 22 Oct 2007 establishing a common organisation of agricultural markets and on specific provisions for certain agricultural products (Single CMO Regulation) OJ L 299, 16 November 2007, 1–149.

[87] art 5:20(2) DCC.

[88] art 5:17(1)(k) DCC.

[89] Van Velten, *Aspecten* (n 55) 590ff.

[90] See AA Van Velten, *Kopers en Economische Eigenaars van Onroerend Goed* (Deventer, Kluwer, 1982); WG Huijgen, *Economische Eigendom* (Zwolle, Tjeenk Willink, 1995).

[91] Collecting the fine is not the desired outcome, rather upholding the obligation as such.

The way this binding clause works is illustrated by the so-called 'economic' transfer of land. 'Economic ownership' is a surrogate for actual ownership: the landowner sells to a purchaser, the price is paid, but the agreement is—upon the wish of the buyer—not executed by a notarial deed of transfer and public registration. The obligation to deliver is secured by a binding clause which gives the buyer the proxy to transfer the land on behalf of the owner. But he also can resell this economic ownership to another person, giving him the same position as the former. The fine is enforced by a hypothec on the land.[92] In practice, the right of the 'economic' owner is relatively strong: it is enforceable like a real right, in insolvency for example. The hypothec takes preference, even where the seller becomes insolvent, and if the agreed-upon fine is at least equivalent to the value of the estate, the buyer-not-yet-owner (ie the 'economic owner') is in a very strong position.

The binding clause is also useful when statutory law bars certain provision parties want to agree upon as part of the real right, when those provisions transgress the limitations set by the law. For example, for the purpose of 'park management' in leisure developments.[93] Apartment ownership constructions are of limited use. The Dutch law provision that all holiday home owners must have a share in all the properties renders it only useful for single-building developments. The alternative, leasehold, affords the right to hold, use and enjoy another's land. The deed establishing the leasehold and setting out the relation between the leaseholder and the landowner, can prescribe, for example, that the land may only be used for housing purposes. But it is questionable whether the deed can bind the leaseholder to contribute to the park management. A binding clause may bridge the gap, ensuring that successors-in-title are bound.[94] This would solve the problem, except where insolvency occurs.

The inflexibility of the *numerus clausus* of real rights types in Dutch law is further illustrated by the *fiducia cum creditore*, that is, the transfer of property to secure loan repayment, a form of security abolished in 1992. The new legislative alternative is the non-possessory ('silent') pledge, which can include, for example, claims a company may have against its customers or buyers. Article 3:239(1) DCC allows such claims to be used as collateral. Since following up these claims individually is burdensome and unnecessary, a bank typically will use a proxy mechanism to establish rights of pledge periodically (even daily) on all the claims of a debtor. Although there is no statutory basis for establishment of a pledge over indefinite numbers of claims *uno acto*, a notary can[95] establish a non-possessory ('silent') pledge on all claims by

---

[92] Until the law changed (Law of 18 Dec 1995, Stb 1995, 659), the economic owner could avoid payment of 6% transfer tax, due upon delivery. The professional investor avoids transfer tax by using this instrument when reselling the estate. Nowadays, transfer taxes have to be paid upon these kinds of agreements. Also, the economic owner would avoid being visible in the public records.

[93] Holiday homes are often situated in parks with lots of joint property for common use, like swimming pools, roads, gardens, fences, signposting, etc. This only works if all the holiday home owners and their successors in title are all bound as owners to contribute financially to the park management.

[94] See case law on the problem of binding successors in title within the context of park management mentioned by AA van Velten, 'Een vereniging van eigenaren is geen vereniging van eigenaars!' (2011) 6889 *Weekblad voor Privaatrecht, Notariaat en Registratie* 464–71 and (2013) *Weekblad voor Privaatrecht, Notariaat en registratie* 6981.

[95] HR 3 Feb 2012, ECLI:NL:HR:2012:BT6947, NJ 2012/261 (Dix q.q./ING) and HR 1 Feb 2013, ECLI:NL:HR:2013:BY4134, NJ 2013/156.

registering a simple, straightforward deed to this effect at the tax administration. Such deeds are registered daily, allowing new claims automatically to become collateral, without their having been individually described in that deed.

The examples of how binding clauses and other mechanisms are used, in practice, by Dutch notaries to sidestep the inflexible system of the *numerus clausus* illustrate the practice of 'stacking' rights: by combining several rights in this way, more flexibility is possible, but the disadvantage is that a proprietor's position becomes complicated (especially where real rights are combined with binding clauses). An example would be subdivision of a building, on land held under leasehold, for use in an apartment scheme. An apartment right as such can be the object of a subdivision in sub-apartments and two of the owners of these apartment rights in the subdivision can decide to establish a right of servitude between their apartments. These kinds of legal constructions imply different levels of real rights; different levels of joint interests in the land and the building on it; as well as different levels of interconnected decision-making.

D. Scholarly Responses

Scholars have responded variedly to innovations—both legislative and practical—that suggest a move towards a more flexible system of property rights in the Netherlands.

Akkermans, who writes specifically to support the drive towards harmonisation of property systems within the European Union, acknowledges that 'a system without a rule of *numerus clausus*' in respect of property rights 'can be fully functional' despite lowered standards of legal certainty. He stresses that even within the civil law family there are differences in the types of rights, and the content of those rights that form part of the national lists.[96] Upholding these differences has become difficult in the integrated, twenty-first century Europe. This makes for a new dynamism in property law in continental Europe.[97] Akkermans nevertheless finds that the *numerus clausus* principle may remain relevant as a filter between property and contract.[98]

Bringing these views back to the Dutch context, one encounters opposing responses. Van Velten proposes the introduction of 'regulated' ownership into Dutch law.[99] He argues that introducing three types of property (namely conventional ownership, regulated ownership, and real rights to property) would allow rights and obligations to be shaped to suit the needs at stake, while landowners, their successors-in-title and their contracting parties would be bound in law. This proposal clearly undermines the *numerus clausus* principle, calling for an open system of ownership rights. Van Velten proposes, for instance, that the 'park management' problem be resolved by statutorily obliging membership of home-owners' associations to contribute financially to the park management. This would ensure joint responsibility for joint management of common areas and facilities.

---

[96] Akkermans (n 5) 485–86.
[97] Ibid, 487, 569 (and see 489–564).
[98] Ibid, 569.
[99] Van Velten, *Aspecten* (n 55) 711ff.

Struycken, also commenting specifically on the Dutch context, cautiously supports the continued distinction between property and contract. He argues that, absent a *numerus clausus* as a filter between property and contract, problems will arise in the context of registrability, destruction and execution, as well as seizure of property.[100] He reminds us of the rationale behind the *numerus clausus*: first, it serves to protect basic freedoms, by extending the protection of ownership to a limited number of real rights. The list of acknowledged rights reflects the lawmaker's choices about the economic and social orders it is willing to support. Second, the list serves to increase tradeability of property through the standardisation of property rights. Hence, the *numerus clausus* principle provides clear rules on the content of each type and the rights and obligations flowing from it. Finally, the *numerus clausus* increases legal certainty. That the content and types of rights are set, means that there is less need to develop generalised rules or definitions as matters arise.

V. CERTAINTY AND ITS LIMITS IN THE ABSENCE OF A *NUMERUS CLAUSUS*: SOUTH AFRICAN LAW

Struycken's motivations (above) in favour of a *numerus clausus* also apply to the South African context, where the law is not completely devoid of support for the *numerus clausus* principle.[101] Yet, South African law does not recognise the *numerus clausus* principle in relation to the creation of real rights.[102] As mentioned, it builds upon historically recognised categories of real rights, but supplements through statutorily created rights as and when the need arises.[103]

The DRA[104] provides that real rights to land must be registered to be enforceable against the world, hence adhering to the principle of publicity.[105] The provision in the DRA is general, not limiting registrations only to those types of rights which are obviously falling into one of the historical categories.[106] Consequently, a testator or a party to a contract *can* in principle establish new, hitherto unrecognised, land rights[107] to suit her purposes. She need not rely, as must her Dutch counterpart, on the legislator to anticipate her needs.

The South African system seems to afford far more autonomy as concerns creation of real rights than its European counterparts. As a result, however, unorthodox rights can be created. In a recent example, the Supreme Court of Appeal found[108] that the right to name a soccer stadium built for the World Cup of 2010 was 'carved

---

[100] Struycken, *Numerus Clausus* (n 3) 759, relying on E Meijers, *Algemene Leer van het Burgerlijk Recht* (Universitaire Pers Leiden, 1948) 269–70.

[101] Van der Merwe, *Sakereg* (n 18) 11–13 discusses the *numerus clausus* as the very first in a collection of basic principles of property law.

[102] Badenhorst et al, *Property* (n 8) 48.

[103] Eg reciprocal servitudes of support and conduit in the Sectional Titles Act 95 of 1986, s 28.

[104] ss 63, 16, 50–62, 65–69 *bis*, 75–76, DRA.

[105] Van der Merwe, *Sakereg* (n 18) 300–01.

[106] s 63(1) and (2) DRA.

[107] It is especially in relation to land that the creation of new types of rights have been developed. Van der Merwe, *Sakereg* (n 18) 70ff.

[108] *National Stadium South Africa (Pty) Ltd and Others v Firstrand Bank Ltd* 2011 (2) SA 157 (SCA) paras 33–34.

out of the [stadium] owner's full ownership right', and hence was registrable as a personal servitude. Still, it would be erroneous to assume that, because the system has no *numerus clausus*, rights created by a testator or contracting party in respect of land are always and automatically real and that there is no divide between property and contract. We elaborate below.

A. Distinguishing Between Real and Contractual Rights

The South African legal system, in contending with the uncertainty created by the lack of a *numerus clausus* of real rights, and in recognising the risk of hampering the tradeability of land by allowing excessive burdens, devised a system to continue distinguishing between real and contractual rights, especially in the context of land.

In practice these criteria have been developed judicially, because the DRA renders it necessary to continue distinguishing between real and contractual rights for purposes of including such rights in the land register. Hence, the land register and its officials often find themselves embroiled in disputes about the nature of rights. This enables the courts to give guidance. Accordingly, the development of the law in this respect is almost as attributable to the judiciary as it is to the quasi-judicial office of the Registrar. The role of the Registrar is foremost, however. The majority of disputes about the nature of rights to land involve the Deeds Registry, either as a party represented by the Registrar of Deeds, or in other capacity. Our account here of what the Registrar contributes is gathered from the difficult cases—the ones of which there is a record because they have been litigated.

Someone may wish, for example, to attach a monetary obligation to the award of a land right created in an agreement or a will.[109] The nature of the right to receive monies needs to be determined, to know whether it would be registrable against the title deed of the land under the DRA. The absence of a *numerus clausus* of real right types means that what is regarded as a real right in one context and a personal right in another, can be functionally similar, although the consequences of the rights will be different. Because of such overlaps in content of real and personal rights, it may be difficult to distinguish between these types of rights. There are various theories explaining the distinction,[110] but even so, the lack of a *numerus clausus* renders the distinction itself difficult to make. Over time, the South African courts developed a coping mechanism, primarily to deal with disputes emanating from the Deeds Registry's engagement with the distinction between real and personal rights for purposes of registration.[111] A registrability dispute may arise because the Registrar refuses to

---

[109] As in the cases of *Ex p Geldenhuys* 1926 (OPD) 155, *Pearly Beach Trust v Registrar of Deeds* 1990 (4) SA 614 (C) and *Lorentz v Melle* 1978 (3) SA 1044 (T). But see, eg *Nel NO v Commissioner for Inland Revenue* 1960 (1) SA 227 (A) where the question about the nature of the right arose in the context of taxability.

[110] The two popular theories are the classical theory and the personalist theory. See Badenhorst et al, *Property* (n 8) 50–54.

[111] *Geldenhuys* (n 109); *Schwedhelm v Hauman* 1947 (1) SA 127 (E); *Lorentz* (n 109); *Pearly Beach* (n 109); *Cape Explosive Works* (SCA) (n 47).

register a specific condition,[112] or because a particular condition was registered and the parties later contest the validity of its registration.[113]

The courts apply a twofold test: they examine the creator's intention to bind successors-in-title and ask whether the correlative obligation to the purported right amounts to a *subtraction from the dominium*. These two aspects operate in tandem and are equally significant. However, it is the *subtraction from dominium* criterion, eloquently formulated[114] in *Ex p Geldenhuys* that deserves closer scrutiny here.

To determine registrability, the court will look at the correlative obligation created by the right. If it is an obligation upon the landowner *as landowner*, that is, if it burdens the land, then the right is real and registrable. If the obligation rests upon the landowner in a personal capacity (ie does not burden the landowner *because of the fact of landownership*) then the right is personal and not registrable.[115]

The peculiarity of *Geldenhuys* was that the court ordered registration of two rights. The one was obviously real: a testator, in bequeathing his land to his children, had restricted how and when they could divide their inheritance. The court did not find it difficult to class the rights contained in this bequest as real and registrable.[116] But it also ordered the registration of another right, typically regarded as contractual, because it involves a performance: as part of the bequest, the testator wanted the child receiving the land parcel with the homestead to pay the others a sum of money. Monetary payments typically stem from contractual obligations to perform. Without denying the contractual nature of the correlative right, the court allowed its registration, because it was 'intimately connected' to the restriction on division of the land, so obviously real and registrable. The *Geldenhuys* court made it clear that a registered contractual right, remains contractual by nature.[117] The approach in this case, which confirmed older Deeds Registry practices,[118] were subsequently incorporated in section 63(1) DRA, which allows contractual rights to be registered against the title deeds alongside other, registrable real rights to which they are 'closely connected'.

Another variation on the theme of registering contractual rights is the Supreme Court of Appeal's approach in *Cape Explosive Works v Denel*,[119] which concerned a use limitation: the land was sold subject to the provision that it could only be used for manufacturing armament. Impossibility of performance gave the seller the right of repurchase. The provision was registered, but mistakenly omitted from subsequent transfers. In considering whether the omitted rights bound successors-in-title, the court had to determine whether the rights were real or contractual. The two aspects of the condition, the use limitation and the right of repurchase, were treated as a single burden. By treating the right of repurchase (typically contractual) as an

---

[112] See, eg *Geldenhuys* (n 109).

[113] See, eg *Lorentz* (n 109), *Schwedhelm* (n 111), *Van der Merwe v Wiese* 1948 (4) SA 8 (C).

[114] Earlier formulations, eg in *Consistory of Steytlerville v Bosman* 1893 (10) 67; *Registrar of Deeds (Transvaal) v The Ferreira Deep Ltd* 1930 169 (AD) relied on existing registration practices sanctioned by usage in the Transvaal.

[115] *Geldenhuys* (n 109) 164.

[116] Ibid, 164–65.

[117] Ibid, 165–66.

[118] *Hollins v Registrar of Deeds* 1904 (TS) 603; *Van Vuren and Others v Registrar of Deeds* 1907 289; *Kotze v Civil Commissioner of Namaqualand* 1900 (17) 37.

[119] *Cape Explosive Works* (SCA) (n 47).

element of the use limitation (typically real), the court avoided the difficulty of having to explain why the right of repurchase was registered initially.

Looking only at *Geldenhuys* and *Denel*, it seems that allowing a legal system the flexibility that would support individual autonomy can work. But there is a caveat: since the *subtraction of the dominium* test was formulated by the court in *Ex p Geldenhuys*, courts have applied it often, but with different interpretations and varying results. This complicates an understanding of the applicable rules. *Lorentz v Melle*[120] and *Pearly Beach v Registrar of Deeds*[121] present two examples.

B. Subtraction Complicated

Lorentz v Melle[122] concerned a condition already registered against a title deed. When the land was subdivided some 30 years earlier, the co-owners included a condition of division which allowed them mutually to retain the right to benefit from possible future township development, by sharing the profits. A successor-in-title later disputed this obligation, refusing to share the proceeds when the land was finally developed, and requesting the court to cancel what was regarded as an erroneous registration of a contractual right. On the question of erroneous registration, the court found that the particular condition, being contingent, did not burden the land 'in a physical sense',[123] and hence was not a subtraction from dominium.

Though lauded widely for its outcome,[124] scholars regard *Lorentz* as a restrictive interpretation of the *subtraction from dominium* test.[125] Some have used this case to point to the 'essential unreliability of the "subtraction from the dominium" test in properly identifying a right as real'.[126] Even the *Lorentz* court itself was mindful that an uncritical application of the test would have yielded a different result. It acknowledged that the profits clause actually amounted to a *subtraction from the dominium*, but this was not enough: the user's enjoyment of the land is curtailed 'in a physical sense'.[127]

At the opposite pole is *Pearly Beach*.[128] The dispute was with the Registrar of Deeds, who refused to register a condition of sale that obliged the purchaser of the land 'and/or its successors in title' to pay a third party a percentage of consideration for the potential future expropriation of the property, or for any option or right to prospect for minerals on it. Upon a *Geldenhuys*-type test the question would be whether the correlative obligation (to be divested of potential future consideration)

---

[120] *Lorentz* (n 109).
[121] *Pearly Beach* (n 109).
[122] *Lorentz* (n 109).
[123] At 1052E.
[124] See, eg Van der Merwe, *Sakereg* (n 18) 76ff.
[125] Eg AJ Van der Walt, 'Personal Rights and Limited Real Rights: An Historical Overview and Analysis of Contemporary Problems Related to the Registrability of Rights' (1992) 55 *Tydskrif vir Hedendaagse Romeins-Hollandse Reg* 170, 200.
[126] MJ De Waal, *Numerus Clausus and the Development of New Real Rights in South African Law* (1999) www.ejcl.org/33/art33-1.html#N_1_, 3.
[127] At 1052D–E.
[128] Above (n 109).

rests on the landowner in that capacity. A *Lorentz*-type interpretation would result in the answer that no real right was created: it was not certain that the ownership would ever be influenced by an expropriation or the sale of mineral options. But in *Pearly Beach*, rejecting the Registrar's objections, the court found that the condition was registrable, because it impaired the owner's right to dispose of the property (*ius disponendi*). This is a less restrictive interpretation than *Lorentz*. However, the decision was criticised for various reasons,[129] but most notably for applying property law reasoning to a dispute which clearly needed a resolution on the basis of contract law principles.[130]

Apart from further revealing the uncertainty inhabiting even the South African judiciary's best attempts to address the lack of a *numerus clausus* of real rights, the problem demonstrated by *Pearly Beach* is how virtually limitless autonomy may hamper the negotiability of land, and diminish its value. The indeterminacy in this part of the law continues to engage South African lawyers. It complicates matters at the Deeds Registry, where the Registrar must continue to implement the arrangements fashioned in wills and contracts relating to land, and must do so without the benefit of being able to rely on strictly regimented categories of real right types.

C. Addressing Indeterminacy through Passivity?

The problems of indeterminacy could perhaps be addressed by reassessing the role of the passivity rule,[131] applicable to the creation of praedial servitudes, in identifying burdens running with the land. According to the passivity rule, no positive obligation may burden the servient owner.[132] The landowner can be expected to tolerate the inroads upon her property; but not to do anything actively to help the servitude holder benefit from the right.

In *Schwedhelm v Haumann* the court had to consider a scenario very similar to that of the Dutch *Blauboer/Berlips* case[133] of whether a disputed condition in a title deed obliging one landowner to maintain certain equipment on the neighbouring land, and to lead water to it, was binding on successors-in-title. The court confirmed that a servitude cannot oblige the owner of the servient tenement actively to do something.[134] It then found that where a condition involves rights and obligations, but is 'inconsistent with the fundamental character of a servitude', it does not create a servitude.

---

[129] JC Sonnekus, 'Saaklike Regte of Vorderingsregte?—Tradisionele Toetse en "n Petitio Principii"' (1991) *Tydskrif vir die Suid-Afrikaanse Reg* 173; CG Van der Merwe, 'Law of Property (Including Mortgage and Pledge)' 1990 *Annual Survey of South African Law* 205; PJ Badenhorst and PJJ Coetzer, '*Pearly Beach Trust v Registrar of Deeds* 1990 (4) SA 614 (C)' [1991] *De Jure* 388ff.

[130] Sonnekus, 'Saaklike Regte of Vorderingsregte?' (n 129) 173ff.

[131] *Van der Merwe* (n 113) came to a contradictory conclusion than *Schwedhelm* on similar facts. *Van der Merwe* is regarded as erroneously decided and is criticised as having disregarded the 'basic difference in the nature of real and personal rights'. Badenhorst et al, *Property* (n 8) 324–25.

[132] *Servitus in faciendo consistere non potest.* See Badenhorst et al, *Property* (n 8) 324–25.

[133] HR 3 March 1905, W8191, WPNR 1844.

[134] *Schwedhelm* (n 111) 133.

That *Schwedhelm*'s facts resemble *Blauboer/Berlips* is significant, considering the absence of the *numerus clausus* of real right types in South Africa. It shows that the known categories of real rights are still relevant to determine the applicable rules. For real rights in respect of land—specifically those that would be classed as praedial servitudes—an obligation to do something more than tolerate an inroad on the bearer's autonomy will preclude it from constituting a real right. Since South African law allows for greater degrees of flexibility, extending the application of the passivity rule to new categories of rights should be possible, even desirable.

D. The Future of Autonomy

The challenge of the open South African system lies therein that it is more difficult to predict whether a customised arrangement will be found to constitute a burden on land. The lack of a *numerus clausus* renders vague the scope and content of real rights. The development in case law of a priori criteria to identify real rights, attests to the need for more transparency and clarity with regard to the burdens on land, and has brought about case law in which criteria are developed for a clearer demarcation of real rights compared to personal rights. Here, the flexibility afforded the creators of rights, identified as problematic, is palliated by the application of existing rules of servitude. This may temper the autonomy that the law allows and the blurring of the boundaries between property and contract which results from it.

VI. INSIGHTS GAINED

In analysing the continued relevance of the *numerus clausus* principle, the central conflict is one between stability and flexibility. Closed categories or systems supposedly ensure high levels of certainty in dealings with property.[135] Open systems supposedly achieve more flexibility, but sacrifice certainty. The inherent tension between certainty and flexibility renders it difficult to adapt the law to modern conditions,[136] and places in question some of the very foundational principles of property law. This is clearly illustrated with reference to the jurisdictional ideosyncracies of real rights recognition.

Comparing the Dutch and South African systems of ensuring certainty in relation to classes of real rights show that legal mechanisms, ostensibly there to ensure flexibility, or doing the opposite, may be manipulated by various role players to achieve consequences very different from what is intended. The South African system, for all the flexibility its denial of the *numerus clausus* of real rights promises, turns out to be conservative in its acknowledgment of unorthodox real rights. This is largely due to the role played by the Registrar. By contrast, the Dutch system, for all its rigidity when it comes to classes and content of real rights, has made giant steps towards incorporating flexibility. This was achieved through legislative intervention, and also

---

[135] CG Van der Merwe, 'Things' in Joubert WA (ed), *Law of South Africa*, vol 27 (Durban, LexisNexis Butterworths, 2001) para 198.
[136] Mostert and Pope (eds), *Principles* (n 4) 341.

by the creative solutions carved out of existing law by notaries when they stack various real and personal rights to meet the needs of their clients whilst staying on the right side of the law.

This leads to another insight about the role of the *numerus clausus*, which seems to be a largely misunderstood mechanism. Labelled a 'principle' of property law, it is used to distinguish the way in which property law and contract law deal with the practicality of user-friendly arrangements. Even in civil law, its old stronghold, the *numerus clausus* is, in fact, no more than a guideline in how to ensure certainty in law without compromising flexibility of personal arrangements. The dichotomy between property and contract is not all as stark as it is always made out to be. In studying the mechanisms to achieve more flexibility around property arrangements, one cannot help but notice that the converse is happening in contract law: that increasingly, contractual arrangements are standardised through legislative intervention, especially in the consumer context. This opens up new trajectories for the study of the boundaries between property and contract—a task for further research.

Looking at the role players who must negotiate the space between stability and flexibility, the differences between the Dutch and South African systems provide interesting insight into the importance of some basic property law principles. Whereas the two systems have their points of departure at opposite sides of the *numerus clausus* spectrum, there is a mutual attraction to the positive elements in each other's systems. The work of the Registrar and the courts in South Africa shows the yearning for greater determinacy. This was sought through establishing registry practices in earlier years, and through law-making more recently.[137] The Dutch system craves greater autonomy. Notaries pursue it through creative interpretations of the existing law, while waiting for the lawmaker to respond to social change.

There is not really so much divergence between the two systems as first meets the eye. This shows that dogmatic approaches at best serve to clarify legal systems and give structure to our knowledge of legal systems; and, at worst, give rise to misdirected arguments in property law, causing unnecessary polemics. The law must adapt to society's needs; not vice versa.

---

[137] Eg Sectional Titles Act, Mineral and Petroleum Resources Development Act 28 of 2002, Restitution of Land Rights Act 22 of 1994; Extension of Security of Tenure Act 62 of 1997.

Index

All legislation and cases refer to England and Wales unless otherwise indicated.
Page references in **bold** indicate information in tables.